The New Humanities Reader

The New Humanities Reader

SIXTH EDITION

RICHARD E. MILLER
Rutgers University

KURT SPELLMEYER
Rutgers University

CENGAGE
Learning

Australia • Brazil • Mexico • Singapore • United Kingdom • United States

The New Humanities Reader,
Sixth Edition
Richard E. Miller and
Kurt Spellmeyer

For product information and
technology assistance, contact us at **Cengage Learning
Customer & Sales Support, 1-800-354-9706.**

For permission to use material from this text or product,
submit all requests online at **www.cengage.com/permissions**.
Further permissions questions can be e-mailed to
permissionrequest@cengage.com.

Student Edition:

ISBN-13: 978-0-357-04364-6

ISBN-10: 0-357-04364-2

Cengage Learning
200 First Stamford Place, 4th Floor
Stamford, CT 06902
USA

Cengage Learning is a leading provider of customized learning
solutions with office locations around the globe, including
Singapore, the United Kingdom, Australia, Mexico, Brazil, and
Japan. Locate your local office at **www.cengage.com/global**.

Cengage Learning products are represented in Canada by
Nelson Education, Ltd.

To learn more about Cengage Learning Solutions, visit
www.cengage.com.

Purchase any of our products at your local college store or at our
preferred online store **www.cengagebrain.com**.

Printed at CLDPC, USA, 11-19

Contents

Is God a father? Is heaven a place? Do we have immortal souls? None of these questions, Armstrong maintains, were important to religion in the past. Instead, for tens of thousands of years, religion was seen as an art of consciousness designed to restore our natural sense of connection to the world.

Supporters and detractors alike regard Donald Trump as unprecedented: combative, independent, indifferent to customs and rules. But for journalist Ta-Nehisi Coates, these qualities are beside the point. What matters about Trump is the explicitly racialized appeal that carried him from reality TV to the White House. And his racism, Coates insists, is really nothing new. Trump has broken with precedent only by displaying so openly attitudes that his predecessors kept behind closed doors.

The Internet has transformed publishing, the music industry and other forms of entertainment, but what about education? Combining responsiveness to personal needs with a capacity for collaboration, Web-based education might be poised to produce a renaissance of learning. Or is it?

If we learned nothing else from our biology class, we came away convinced that evolution means "natural selection," a term coined by the great Charles Darwin. We might also remember that environments "select" for the traits that benefit the animals that live to reproduce. But as ornithologist Richard O. Prum argues, natural selection is only half the story. Later in his life, Darwin identified a second mechanism—mate choice—that depends on an animal's ability to attract members of the opposite sex. And how do animals attract future mates? By becoming beautiful.

The phenomenon known as Human-Elephant Conflict—as measured by events where elephants destroy villages and crops, attacking and killing humans—is on the rise. Elephants, who travel in herds and mourn their dead, are profoundly social creatures. The collapse of elephant culture, brought on by predation, stress, and trauma, may point to what lies ahead for human culture.

Once couples decide to have children of their own, they expect their offspring to become the adults they imagine. But the development of identity is unpredictable, and children's relations to parents are always complicated. Part of who we are is an accident of birth; another part we create for ourselves by discovering new possibilities.

In America today, economic inequality has never been more extreme. The latest figures show the top 1% controls almost half of the nation's wealth. Nobel Prize-winner Joseph Stiglitz blames the widening gap on rent seeking—forms of investment that do not produce good jobs but only increase paper wealth.

The term *divided consciousness* refers to those times when we withdraw mentally from the world around us. Daydreams and other forms of subjective escape often help us to keep our mental balance by shutting out events when they threaten to overwhelm us. But when does our power to shut things out begin to close the door on sanity itself?

Losing one's sense of self or having an empty self is typically imagined to be a fate worse than death. But Robert Thurman, an expert on the Buddhism of Tibet, argues that we have misjudged the experience of "no self," which is not a dark corridor to oblivion, but the road to what he calls "infinite life."

As technology increasingly blurs the line between machines and organic life, are we humanizing our inventions, or have we allowed those inventions to make us more like machines? Will our naivety about technology—which is never simply a tool—train us to look in the wrong places for friendship and intimacy?

What it means to have a self has changed over the course of the past thirty years. While Baby Boomers set out to transform the world, Generation Me seeks out fun as the highest value and promotes self-esteem as the greatest good. Drawing on data taken from 1.3 million young people, Twenge argues that this obsessive focus on the self is not just bad for society, it's also bad for the individual.

Everybody likes to get a good deal. And Walmart offers the best deals of all—with prices that nobody can rival. Yet Walmart drives down wages by forcing manufacturers to move overseas in order to reduce their costs. Journalist Rick Wartzman makes the case that higher wages, not lower prices, hold the key to a healthy economy. And he insists that unions are indispensable if we want to halt our race to the bottom.

As the American way of life spreads across the world, so do our ideas about mental health. Even though we think of mental illness as a scientific fact, the big pharmaceutical companies know that selling antidepressants in Japan starts with the effort to export our model of the mind. Has pharmacology become a form a cultural imperialism?

Thematic Contents

Religion and Secularity

The Mind

Politics and Culture

Reading and Writing About the New Humanities

This book probably differs from many you have encountered, at least those that you have encountered in school. Generally, the books taught in school tell students how or what to think, but ours has a different purpose. We wanted to put in your hands a book that would let you think for yourself, and do so while you read and write about some of the most important issues of our time. Environmental breakdown, rapid cultural change, the effects of electronic media on our ways of interacting—these are just a few of the issues we address.

The articles and essays collected here touch on subjects as diverse as the psychology of elephants and the practice of Tibetan meditation, but these subjects in and of themselves aren't the real point of the book. The real point is thinking, and we believe that thinking in our time needs to assume a new and more appropriate form. In the last 100 years our world has seen change more rapid and profound than it witnessed in the previous thousand. From the media, we get daily reports on subjects our great-grandparents might have found absolutely incomprehensible: breakthroughs in nanotechnology; mergers of U.S. firms with partners overseas; the covert spread of weapons that could destroy humanity many times over; a new account of the universe in the first few seconds after the Big Bang; melting polar icecaps and rising seas; and a growing gap between the poor and mega-rich, while the middle class slowly withers away. Such events are truly without precedent.

We need a new kind of thinking because we live in a world defined by possibilities, and possibilities go hand in hand with risk and unintended consequences. The globalized economy could lead to a future where poverty will become a distant memory, or the whole planet could be transformed into a sweatshop run by a One Percent indifferent to the suffering of ordinary people. The Web could produce a Renaissance of learning, or it could degrade all forms of communication, ushering in a new Dark Age of vulgarity and mass ignorance. Cultures long divided by geography might greet one another with open arms, or we could see a clash of civilizations that would unleash the worst instincts of everyone. Unlike the problems from your textbooks in school, the questions arising from events in our time don't have answers hidden in the teacher's edition. The best educated, most experienced people still can't predict with certainty how the next century will turn out. And even expertise is not good enough because the questions we face now are more complex than people anywhere have ever faced before. Globalization, to take one good example, is not just the concern of economists, or historians, or anthropologists. Instead, it is an issue for all of them together—and for everybody else as well. The degradation of the biosphere is not exclusively the concern of environmental science, but also a matter for political theory, sociology, and economics. The complexity and open-endedness of the big problems of our time require us to work hard to devise new understandings of ourselves and of the world. One purpose of this book is to provide a forum for these understandings to emerge.

Perhaps it may seem strange that we would entertain such lofty goals in a course designed for undergraduates. Surely the experts are better equipped than students just beginning their careers at college or the university. But this assumption might be unjustified. While the forms of expertise available today clearly have enormous value, most of the current academic disciplines were created more than a century ago, and the divisions of knowledge on which they are based reflect the needs of a very different day. In 1900, gas-powered cars were a new technology, while airplanes and radios had yet to be invented. Scientists still wrestled with the structure of the atom. The British Empire dominated three-fourths of the globe, and "culture" meant the traditions of Western Europe's elite, never more than one-tenth of one percent of the population of that region. In a certain sense, the current generation of college students and teachers needs to reinvent the university itself, not by replacing one department with another, but by forging broad connections across areas of knowledge that still remain in relative isolation. Forging these connections is the "new way of thinking" that we had in mind when we created this book.

NEW HUMANITIES FOR NEW TIMES: THE SEARCH FOR COHERENCE

Probably some readers will be surprised by the absence of material from the traditional humanities: poems and plays, photographs of paintings and statues, excerpts from great works of philosophy such as Plato's *Republic* and Descartes's *Discourse on Method*. Clearly, no one should leave Aristotle, Shakespeare, or Toni Morrison unread. And anyone unfamiliar with Leonardo da Vinci, Frida Kahlo, Thelonious Monk, and Georgia O'Keeffe has missed a priceless opportunity. Yet this book grows out of our belief that the humanities today must reach further than in centuries past. Without consciously intending to, humanists might have contributed to the decline of their own influence. One could even argue their devotion to the past led them to neglect the future. Humanists have often been quite willing to leave real-world concerns to other fields, devoting themselves primarily to passive contemplation, aesthetic pleasure, and the production of criticism few people ever read. Consequently, outside the university many people see the humanities as entertainment or pretentiousness while putting business and technology on a pedestal as the only real truth.

If the humanities are going to survive, they must be understood in a new way: not as a particular area of knowledge but as the human dimension of *all* knowledge. Robotics and artificial intelligence may lie outside the boundaries of the old humanities, but they enter the purview of the New Humanities when we stop to ponder, as Sherry Turkle does, the cultural consequences of technologies that seemed tremendously exciting at first but now appear to make us more like our machines. Once we define the humanities this way—as the human dimension of all knowledge—it may come as a surprise to observe that some of today's foremost humanists work in disciplines quite far removed from English, History, and Philosophy. Richard O. Prum, one of the writers in this collection, is a world-renowned ornithologist who has revived Darwin's neglected ideas about the way animals choose their mates. And Prum has prodded fellow scientists to recognize the central evolutionary role played by aesthetics—beauty—which some would call the most important concern of the arts and humanities.

The New Humanities, as represented by this book, enlarge the arena of human inquiry in other ways as well. They invite us to take academic knowledge beyond the confines of the university. In a certain sense, this operation requires that we all become our own teachers: we have to find in our own lives—our problems, values, dreams, goals, and commitments—an organizing principle that cannot be found in the curriculum. The great, unspoken secret of higher education is that the curriculum has no center: specialization makes sure of that. Historians write primarily for historians; literary critics for other critics. As we shuttle back and forth between these specialized disciplines, the only coherence we will ever find is the coherence we construct for ourselves. Under these conditions, the New Humanities can teach us a different way of using knowledge, a way of thinking that connects many different fields of study.

Specialized learning in the disciplines typically deals with the "how," but it often leaves unanswered the "why." There has never been a course called "Life 101," and given the persistence of specialization, such a course will probably never exist. But something important will be missing if we leave the "why" questions unexplored. Should we continue to pursue a technological utopia? Does modern science mean the end of religion? Is social inequality an acceptable price to pay for economic growth? Any attempt to answer these questions requires specialized knowledge, yet knowledge alone is not enough. Because a cogent, well-informed case can be made on either side of almost every issue, the source of our ultimate commitments has to be found in our own lives. The "why" questions shape these commitments because they address our most basic relations to other people and the world. In different ways, these questions ask us how we ourselves will choose to think and act. No expert can choose on our behalf, because no expert can live our lives for us or define what our experience should mean.

The coherence missing from the curriculum is not a quality of knowledge in itself. When it emerges, that coherence comes instead from our own creative activity. Again and again, we need to make connections that bridge the gaps between areas of knowledge, linking the formal learning we acquire to our personal experience. But even after we have created this coherence, it will still be incomplete because there is always something more to learn that remains unconnected. We might think of coherence, then, not as a goal we can finally reach but as an ideal worth pursuing throughout the course of our lives. Needless to say, cynicism and fragmentation are always options, too, and they require no special effort. One could easily live as though nothing and no one mattered, but in such a case, learning and living become exercises in futility. The New Humanities offer a better path.

KNOWLEDGE IN DEPTH AND KNOWLEDGE OF THE WORLD

As everybody understands, formal education has been carefully designed to keep the disciplines separate. In economics classes, we typically read economics; in history classes, we read history. This approach allows information to be conveyed in small, efficiently managed packages. We can divide, say, biology from chemistry, and then we can divide biology into vertebrate and invertebrate, and chemistry into organic and inorganic. We start with the general and move to the particular. Ideally, we learn in depth, with increasing mastery of details that become more and more refined. At the end of the semester, if everything goes well, we can distinguish between an ecosystem and a niche, a polymer and a plastic, a neo-Kantian and a neo-Hegelian. We can contrast Hawthorne's treatment of the outsider with Salinger's, or we can explain the debate about whether slavery or states' rights actually caused the Civil War.

Knowledge in depth is indispensable. But it can also produce a sense of disconnection, the impression that education is an empty ritual without real-world consequences beyond getting a grade or fulfilling a requirement. In the classroom, we learn to calculate sine and cosine without ever discovering how these calculations might be used and why they were invented. Searching for symbols in a poem or a short story becomes a mental exercise on par with doing a crossword puzzle. Instead of reflecting on why events have happened and how they get remembered and recorded, we refine our ability to recapitulate strings of dates and names. At its worst, learning in depth can produce a strange disconnect: the purpose of learning becomes learning itself, while activity in the real world seems increasingly remote. As students reach the final years of high school, they may grasp vaguely that they should have read *Hamlet,* be able to identify *The Declaration of Independence*, and explain how photosynthesis has influenced the shape of leaves, but in response to an actual tragedy—an environmental disaster or a war—they might feel unqualified to speak and completely at a loss about what to do.

College-level learning can offer an escape from this predicament by giving students greater freedom to choose what they will study, and in many cases the subjects they choose are closely related to their real-world goals. But even with this newfound freedom, the problem of disconnection crops up in other ways. After years of hard work, a student who has mastered electrical engineering may still leave college poorly informed about the global economy in which most engineers now do their work. Students well versed in Renaissance drama or the history of World War I could understand the past quite well but find the events of their own time impossible to explain. For some people, this problem of disconnection may arise long before they graduate. The student who sets out to memorize facts from, say, a social psychology text might find that these facts grow increasingly stale. Easily memorized one day, they are quickly forgotten the next. The risk of knowledge in depth is that we lose our sense of the larger world and we forget that a field like psychology, for all its current sophistication, began with tentative and somewhat clumsy questions about how the mind might work. Ironically, the more we treat an area of knowledge as a reality in itself, the less we may be able to understand and use what we have supposedly learned.

There is another kind of knowledge we create when we ask ourselves how our learning applies to the world outside the classroom. This line of questioning is more complex than it might seem initially because the larger world is never simply waiting there for us. All knowledge starts with parts and fragments, even our knowledge of the private lives we know in most detail. To each of us, our private life may seem complete, just as a field like psychology can seem to explain everything once we are immersed in its methods and facts. But this sense of completeness is an illusion produced by the limits of our perspective. Beyond the reach of what we know here and now, nothing seems to matter. We begin to get a glimpse of the larger world only when we shift our focus from one reality to another: only then can we become aware of the holes in our prior certainties, and only then are we able to think in new and revealing ways. This movement from the known to the unknown is the essence of all learning; indeed, the most successful learners are generally those who have developed the highest tolerance for not knowing—those who continue to question and explore issues beyond their own areas of specialization, entertaining alternatives that others might find unimaginable.

Knowledge itself can be defined in many ways: as a quantity of information, as technical expertise, as cultivated taste, as a special kind of self-awareness. Various as these definitions might appear, they share an underlying commonality.

Whatever form knowledge eventually takes, it always emerges from a process we might describe as **connecting**. The eighteenth-century English scientist Sir Isaac Newton, who first understood the relations between force, mass, and acceleration, might have been inspired in his scientific work by his deeply held religious convictions about the rational perfection of God and His Creation. Many other notable thinkers have also found inspiration through connection. Roughly 200 years after Newton's discoveries sparked a scientific revolution, a young lawyer born in India, Mohandas K. Gandhi, drew on Henry David Thoreau's *Civil Disobedience*, written in support of abolitionists just before the Civil War, to launch a campaign of passive resistance against the racist government of South Africa. Two years before Gandhi spent his first term in jail as a political prisoner, a French artist and intellectual, Marcel Duchamp, shocked the art world with a painting— *Nude Descending a Staircase*—inspired by scientific photographs of athletes in motion. Whether we are talking about physics or political systems, epidemiology or art, knowledge by its very nature brings together disparate worlds of thought and action.

Creative Reading I: The Prospective View

The selections in this book are intended for creative reading. Our assumption is that the humanities should do more than preserve the past or let professors flaunt their brilliance. After all, studies have consistently shown that people retain little of what they are taught unless they put that knowledge to use. At its best, higher learning can offer beginners the chance to practice the same activities that more accomplished thinkers engage in: beyond receiving knowledge, beginners too should have a hand in its creation. The articles and book chapters collected here offer many occasions of that kind. It's true that the selections pose challenges—sometimes because they are long and complex, sometimes because they draw on specialized fields, and sometimes because they open up unusual perspectives. But those challenges are also opportunities: they ask the reader to become an active co-creator with the writer.

The phrase "creative reading" might sound strange. Almost every college and university has a program in creative writing, but creative reading programs don't exist. It's not hard to understand why: many people think of reading as nothing more than passively internalizing words on a page. Yet reading is always more complex than the common sense view would suggest. Like a conversation or dialogue, reading requires us to engage in an active back-and-forth that calls on our attentiveness, imagination, patience, and receptivity. Just as the participants in a conversation have to imagine what the other people think, what they expect to hear, and what they might say next, so readers need to see themselves as involved in a kind of dialogue, moving back and forth from textual details to a sense of the larger whole. And just as we can't know where a conversation is going until it's actually over, so reading transports us to a place we can never entirely predict.

When we try to understand a difficult text like the ones collected here, we won't get far by following along, word by word and detail by detail. As we read we also need to ask ourselves what the writer's larger point might be and how each small step contributes to the unfolding of the entire argument. When Karen Armstrong starts "Homo religiosus" with a description of the way it feels to descend into the caverns of Lascaux, few of us might be able to foresee the direction her ideas will take. But we can begin with a **prospective view**, a guess at the argument that might lie ahead. Reading further we could be surprised to find that the cave paintings of Lascaux get left behind as we move from Stone Age shamanism to the rise of the world religions we are familiar with today. Actually, a dramatic shift like this—from cave paintings to theology—is quite typical of complex thought, and skillful readers are the ones who know how to keep revising their prospective views as they move ahead. Working with a complex text means continuing the dialogue until we reach an understanding that seems to include everything we've learned.

One way to test your understanding of a text after you have finished reading is to look for key words or ideas and ask how they fit with everything else. Here for example is a question we ask in the "Questions for Making Connections within the Reading" that follow the Armstrong selection:

> Re-read the chapter and carefully note the many differences between religion then and religion now. Next go back and look for the continuities. In spite of the differences, would you say that much of the Paleolithic legacy survives to this day? Can we conclude that religion has become more mature and sophisticated, or is it possible that we have lost touch with what religion actually represents?

A question like this is designed to find out how well you have managed to create a comprehensive understanding of the text. Unless you test your understanding in this way, you might assume that simply having read the words automatically confers a working knowledge when in reality what you really know might be quite limited. Each time you extend your prospective view by looking carefully at a text's details, you draw closer to the kind of mastery that accomplished readers can achieve.

Creative Reading II: Interpretation and the Retrospective View

The fact that reading goes on all the time should not lead us to overlook just how complicated it can get. The act of reading starts with nothing more than ink marks on a page, and those marks cannot tell us anything in and of themselves. But when you read with a prospective view, you are actually creating a text that exists only after you have done the work. The reader's job, however, does not end there. Even after reading with a prospective view has created a coherent text, the **meaning** of that text still remains unclear because what we call "meaning" actually depends on the connections we make within the text or

between one text and another. Meaning is a product of interpretation, and interpretation demands from us another form of creative reading: the search for a
retrospective view. If "prospective" means "looking forward," "retrospective"
means "looking back." The most basic form of interpretation starts when we
isolate one part of the text—even if it's only a sentence—and use it as a frame
or window through which we can take a second, retrospective look at the entire
document.

Consider, for example, the first sentence of Jonathan Lethem's controversial
essay, "The Ecstasy of Influence: A Plagiarism." That first sentence is not
Lethem's at all. Instead, he identifies it as the work of the poet and Anglican
preacher John Donne, writing in the seventeenth century: "All mankind is of
one author, and is one volume." Everything that follows in Lethem's argument
can be interpreted in the light of Donne's claim that mankind is indeed "one
volume," not many isolated individuals whose creations belong exclusively to
them. Bob Dylan's "thefts" from popular movies, Shakespeare, and F. Scott
Fitzgerald; episodes of *The Simpsons* that draw on *The Flintstones* and *The Honeymooners*; Walt Disney's earliest Mickey Mouse cartoon, which borrows from actor/
director Buster Keaton's classic silent film *Steamboat Bill*—all of these examples can
be used to support the truth of Donne's observation.

If we try to explain what Lethem meant by writing "The Ecstasy of
Influence," we could simply say that he wanted to show that creative people
often borrow from each other. But his examples push that insight much farther.
Not only do creative people borrow, but they also appear to steal in ways that
often seem to violate conventional morality. And yet, what if Donne is right and
all of us are ultimately "one volume"? Wouldn't that mean that we are free to
use everybody's work as our own? If we reread Lethem's essay in the light of the
Donne quotation, we might see the stories Lethem tells in a more positive
fashion: less as examples of stealing and more as evidence of a generosity implicit
in all human relations. If we really are all one, then the work of every individual
becomes a kind of gift to everybody else. Using Donne for our retrospective
view, we might conclude that creativity always involves what universities condemn as plagiarism. Far from trying to stamp out intellectual dishonesty, we
could see the persistence of "theft" as proof we are interconnected in a way
that makes private property impossible when it comes to the life of the mind.
Explicitly, Lethem ventures no such claim, but we could use the passage from
Donne to maintain that plagiarism is a creative act when we use the words of
others to say something new.

Creative Reading III: Connective Thinking and the Search
for a Shared Horizon

The simplest form of interpretation links one part of the text to other parts—
linking the Donne passage, for example, to Bob Dylan's lyrics. But what about
connections to other texts? These connections are especially important because

no one's world is entirely defined by the perspective or "horizon" of any single text alone. Indeed, there is far more to creativity than Lethem's essay can fully express, however complex and many-layered it might be. Because no one lives in a one-text world, the truths we learn from "The Ecstasy of Influence" cannot be confined to the pages of that essay. As soon as we read something in another class, or we engage in conversations with our friends, all sorts of new connections will begin to compete for our attention. The different texts we encounter might come from worlds of experience far removed from ours, but once they have entered into our own lives, we need to bring them together in a way that creates a shared horizon, a greater, more inclusive coherence.

One great tragedy of formal education is that it often works against this shared horizon by promoting imitative thinking: we learn to reproduce information made and organized by someone else. Imitative thinking presupposes the sufficiency of knowledge in its present state, and it preserves the separateness of different texts and differing realities. But this separateness cannot be maintained except at the cost of a greater incoherence. Maybe the lecture in English today contradicted a point made yesterday in anthropology class. Or perhaps an article you are asked to read describes an aspect of the social world in a way that you consider incomplete, biased, or flatly incorrect. On occasions like these, when we come face-to-face with the limitations of knowledge, imitative thinking cannot help us. Instead we are obliged to think connectively—to think *across texts* rather than thinking only from inside them.

Connective thinking calls for another kind of interpretation. Instead of starting with one part of a text and using it as a window to review the rest, we can use it as a window to begin a retrospective reading of another writer's work. We might start again with the Donne passage Lethem quotes: "All mankind is of one author, and is one volume." Then, with this sentence, we could take a second look at Joseph Stiglitz's argument in "Rent Seeking and the Making of an Unequal Society." At first glance these two texts might appear as completely unrelated as any two could be. The first deals with uses that creative people make of work done by others, the second with the growth of inequality in the United States. And yet when we start to read retrospectively, a shared horizon can emerge. The easiest way to search for that horizon would be to find a passage from Stiglitz that makes a point central to his argument. One passage describes the failure of our current political system to redistribute the nation's wealth to benefit the whole society:

> We have a political system that gives inordinate power to those at the top, and they have used that power not only to limit the extent of redistribution but also to shape the rules of the game in their favor and to extract from the public large "gifts." Economists have a word for these activities: they call them rent seeking, getting income not as a reward [for] creating wealth but by grabbing a larger share of the wealth that would otherwise have been produced without their effort....
> Those at the top have learned how to suck out money from the rest in ways the rest are hardly aware of.

Clearly, this passage has nothing to do with Bob Dylan's lyrics or *The Simpsons*. But it still says something important about our obligations to other human beings. Although Stiglitz never suggests, as Donne does, that everything we do belongs to everyone else, he still seems to argue that the good of each person depends in some manner on the good of all. Lethem's argument for the "cultural commons" has no explicit parallel in Stiglitz's argument, yet Stiglitz's argument still implies that wealth belongs to the whole society, and that inequality is basically unjust because it overlooks this fact. Lethem never uses the word "redistribution," a key term in Stiglitz's analysis, yet "The Ecstasy of Influence" might be read as a call for the continuous redistribution of words, images, and ideas. If Stiglitz wants both a free market and a strong government to save working Americans from ruin, Lethem also argues for a "market" as well as a "gift economy."

These connections between Lethem and Stiglitz certainly do not exhaust the possibilities, and we will find many more connections by rereading other passages. Eventually, as we work through these new connections, we might begin to discover that a larger point has begun to emerge—such as the conclusion that free markets depend on high levels of equality. An overarching point like this one seldom arises right away. For a nerve-wracking interval, the individual connections might appear disjointed, even contradictory, but then, suddenly, a larger view may present itself—like the pattern in a Persian carpet we unroll a few inches at a time.

Of course some passages in Stiglitz might not connect in a fruitful way to Lethem. Initially, a connection might look promising, but then we could discover that it leads to a dead end. It's possible to spend many frustrating hours following connections that go nowhere. But this is precisely what thinking involves: forging new connections where none exist now. Imitation means letting others do that work and sitting back to admire the results; creativity means taking risks. Some of the risks we take will truly surprise us with their spectacular results, while others may prove quite disappointing. Both risk and failure, on occasion, are the price of creative reading—the price of discovery.

Some people are convinced that creativity cannot be taught at all, but we believe that it can be taught and learned by asking readers to make connections between texts that might appear unrelated at first glance. Many of the questions you will find in this book seem to push hard in that direction. One question, for example, asks you to work out the connections between Charles Siebert's report on the fate of elephants in Africa and Barbara Fredrickson's discussion of the complex biology that underlies our experience of love. Attempts by preservationists to rescue a species may seem worlds away from the science behind our intimate lives, but we are asking you to undertake what all creativity involves—venturing beyond the familiar.

Prospective Writing

Imitative thinking goes hand in hand with writing to tell—writing for the purpose of demonstrating a command of existing knowledge. In American schools, the classic example of writing to tell is the venerable book report. Like imitative thinking, writing to tell has its appropriate place. Connective thinking calls, however, for a different approach that might be described as prospective writing. Just as you can read prospectively, looking for a larger coherence behind all the individual details, so you can write without knowing from the start where your ideas will lead. A good example of this kind of writing is Maggie Nelson's essay "Great to Watch." Unlike authors who adopt a pose of absolute certainty, Nelson takes many conceptual risks as she struggles to make sense of our collective attachment to violence. She begins with the admission that knowledge alone is unlikely to improve the situation—since we already know that violence is "bad" but still behave the same way. So Nelson adopts a different approach by exploring our consumption of violence when we feel anxious, isolated or bored, or when we want to become more aware, more creative and more free. And these explorations take Nelson in directions no one could foresee—from Stephen King's novel *The Running Man* to the reality TV show "To Catch a Predator" to the Texas Virtual Borderwatch Program (http://blueservo.com/), which asks its viewers to help patrol that state's border with Mexico. From the Borderwatch Program, Nelson turns to the Hub's Witness Project (https://witness.org/), where activists can post videos of atrocities that might go unnoticed by the world. And this example leads her in turn to filmmaker Errol Morris's documentary "Standard Operating Procedure," an exposé of the prisoners tortured by American soldiers—who took photos of themselves in the act—during our invasion of Iraq.

As these examples pile up, the task of making sense of them becomes so difficult that Nelson looks to thinkers who have wrestled with similar dilemmas in the past—philosophers like Hannah Arendt, Susan Sontag and Jacques Rancière, as well as the musician John Cage and the essayist Annie Dillard. Using their insights to support and complicate her own investigation, Nelson finally gets to a place where she recognizes that no single approach can account for the violence in our society. Rather than keep looking for a single cause, or a single solution, she realizes that the more perspectives she takes in, the more complete will be her grasp of the problem. And she suggests that the more we know, the more alternatives we have—if we trust the process of questioning.

In order for an author like Nelson to become a resource for our writing, we should start with a question her work leaves unresolved. Why, for example, does she conclude that after we have viewed Ryan Trecartin's video *I-Be Area*, we will feel less overwhelmed and can start to "swim" freely in the "sea of multiplicity"? Nelson makes this claim, but she never explains how or why the change will happen. And what does it mean to "swim" in this "sea"? In order to fill the spaces she leaves blank, we will need to do exactly what Nelson does, starting with one tentative answer but then following ideas wherever they might lead. Like Nelson herself, we may not know where exactly we are headed, but our multiple perspectives will finally bring us to a fuller understanding. And in order to extend that understanding even more, we might draw on an essay like Jonathan Lethem's "Ecstasy of Influence," which argues that creative people always borrow from the achievements of others. If Lethem is correct, then swimming in the sea of multiplicity might mean using Trecartin's video to support an argument of our own.

Developing a Thesis: From Prospective to Retrospective Writing

A thesis is not exactly an argument in the ordinary sense of the word. In everyday speech, the term *argument* suggests an adversarial stance: with great vehemence we might argue for, or against, online education of the kind that Cathy Davidson describes. "Making an argument" tends to mean deciding ahead of time what you think and then looking for "support" to back up your points. There is, however, another way. Instead of simply taking sides in an existing controversy, each of us can move beyond such debates, which are often hackneyed and overly simplistic, in order to say something genuinely new. To do so is to imagine ourselves in a different light, not as combatants but as engaged participants in a conversation. Even if we read a writer with distaste, what matters most are the questions raised, not the answers given. Precisely because the search for a thesis starts with some degree of uncertainty, it demands a willingness on our part to suspend judgment and pursue ideas wherever they might lead. Remember, however, that this pursuit does not require our complete assent or unwavering commitment. We can always entertain and explore ideas we will eventually reject.

The writing process closely parallels the process of reading. Once readers create an understanding of the text through prospective reading, they can go on to view it retrospectively in the search for meaning. Much the same holds true for writing in its different stages. We might consider the first few drafts to be essentially prospective. As we explore possible connections and see how they unfold, we will notice that the process has carried us in unforeseen directions, some highly productive and some cul-de-sacs. But a later stage in the process requires that we move from a preliminary draft, replete with loose ends and promising connections, to become the interpreter of the work we've done. Retrospective writing is interpretive because it tries to tease out the implicit meaning, which it develops further and refines. If the first drafts are exploratory, the final draft is meant to present the writer's discoveries in a way that will conform to the reader's expectations. A thesis statement, logical organization, transitions, and well-structured paragraphs are all tools at our disposal for an effective public presentation.

Let's suppose we start writing with the idea that Fredrickson's "positivity resonance," the sense of rapport two people sometimes feel in each other's company, is an experience we can always trust. But when we turn to Michael Moss's account of the way the food industry has used psychological research to manipulate our behavior, our initial trust in resonance might begin to seem less persuasive than it did. And then we face a question we may not have foreseen, one that Fredrickson never entertains: when does resonance cross the line into something like addiction? Instead of treating this change in our position as a failure or a lapse, we should appreciate its value as a genuine discovery, which we could achieve only after a great deal of hard work. When revising we should not try to conceal the evidence of such a redirection in our thinking. By trying to erase the steps that led us to confusion, we can fail to show our audience the great discovery we have actually made. The strongest writing doesn't simply argue a point but also leads the reader through a thinking process.

The genre most familiar to students starting college is the "five paragraph essay" they learn to compose throughout their high school years. The first paragraph should present the main idea. Three body paragraphs should elaborate, and the final paragraph should sum up the main idea yet again. This format was designed to give beginners some control over a process that can become overwhelming with its sheer complexity. But this virtue is also the greatest defect of the five paragraph model. None of the selections in *The New Humanities Reader* look remotely like the kind of essay students write while they are in high school. Not only do most of the selections connect with many areas of knowledge at once, but they also offer thinking far more layered and nuanced than the high school format could allow. Instead of pounding home a single idea, they guide the reader through a journey of the mind that typically has many twists and turns, that takes two steps forward and one step back, that entertains alternative possibilities and, at times, answers criticisms. Instead of suppressing complexity, the writers here embrace it as the source of a deeper understanding. In your own writing you can learn to do the same.

THE SPIRIT OF THE NEW HUMANITIES

Because we can learn from everything, no one should fear making mistakes. We should never forget that the greatest thinkers of every age have often been refuted later, whereas ordinary people have sometimes lived more wisely than they were given credit for. Not so long ago, the best-educated Europeans believed that all celestial bodies beyond the moon were eternal and changeless. Scholars taught that matter in every form could be reduced to the basic elements of earth, air, fire, and water. Medical experts sternly warned against the perils of regular bathing and eating whole grains. In sexual reproduction, men were supposed to contribute the blueprint, while women provided the raw material. One could spend a lifetime enumerating the follies that have passed for knowledge. And when we pause to consider such a checkered history, we might decide that education is itself a folly.

But maybe not. Instead of expecting knowledge to be true once and for all, we might try to see it as pragmatic and provisional, always subject to revision given further evidence or new circumstances. In our society today, the sciences may offer the best example of this experimentalist attitude, but some philosophers and artists of every generation have also refused the twin consolations of dogmatism and disillusionment. In the years ahead, our society will face many challenges—environmental, social, cultural, economic and political—that are sure to seem overwhelming. Given the high level of uncertainty that has become a constant feature of our lives, people may be drawn to ideologies that promise truths exempt from all revision and insulated from the challenges of diversity. If this book does nothing else, we hope that it will offer an alternative more compatible with the values espoused by the readings we have chosen: trust in the world and trust in ourselves.

QUESTIONS FOR READING

1. "Reading and Writing About the New Humanities" makes this claim on the very first page: "We need a new kind of thinking because we live in a world defined by possibilities, and possibilities go hand in hand with risk and unintended consequences." How do "possibilities" define the life of our times, and what role does "possibility" play in these detailed accounts of reading and writing? As you reread each section, ask yourself about the place of possibility in teaching and learning. How does an approach that stresses possibility differ from one that privileges strict rules, fixed methods, and pre-ordained answers?

2. Reading and writing are often taught as highly predictable activities. Supposedly, when we read, we follow word by word until we have transferred the writer's thoughts from his or her mind to ours. When we write, we should have a clear argument that we ought to outline before we compose. But "Reading and Writing About the New Humanities" takes a different view. It represents reading and writing as complex activities. Readers are not passive receivers, after all, but actively help to create what they read. And writing is a process of discovery that can lead to insights we seldom have when we first sit down to write. Not only are reading and writing more complex than many people assume but both involve moments of real uncertainty. Using this introduction as your guide, consider the role that uncertainty plays in the acts of reading and writing. Should we try to avoid uncertainty, or is the experience somehow liberating? What is the relation between uncertainty and the learning process?

3. When people write, they often have in mind what is called an "implied reader." The implied reader for the Harry Potter books might be someone who likes fantasy, mystery, and adventure. The implied reader for the *Financial Times* is probably an investor. Using specific evidence from "Reading and Writing About the New Humanities," create a detailed portrait of the implied reader of this book. Does this implied reader coincide with the normal image of "the student"? Does it coincide with what we ordinarily think of as a "consumer," "an informed citizen," an "individualist"? Feel free to choose the term that best describes the implied reader of this book, and then explain how you have reached that conclusion.

QUESTIONS FOR WRITING

1. The term *creative writing* seldom gets applied to the prose that students are required to grind out for their high school essays on *Great Expectations* or for term papers about the Civil War. *Creative writing* is usually reserved for the poems, plays, and fiction students read and sometimes write outside of class, far from the judgments of teachers and the pressure to get good grades. This

way of thinking is not inaccurate. It reflects a cultural commonplace: the humanities supposedly provide a time-out for the freedom of imagination, while the other disciplines deal with difficult real-world concerns. The problem with this way of thinking is that it implicitly assumes creative writing cannot be factual or conceptually dense. And it assumes that writing about the real world has to be a boring, empty routine. In what ways does "Reading and Writing About the New Humanities" reject the conventional division between the creative and the real world? In what ways does it challenge the idea that creativity is spontaneous, subjective, and disconnected from reality?

2. We invite you to use this introduction to frame the first essay you read in the course. Whichever selection your instructor assigns, write an essay that explores moments where you see the essay's author engaged in creative reading and/or connective thinking. Are there other kinds of reading and thinking evident in the selected essay, kinds deserving of other adjectives? How do you know when creative reading has occurred? Is the evidence there on the page or is it in the eye of the beholder?

3. We make much of the limits of the five-paragraph essay in our introduction. It's a pretty easy target, actually, and none of the essays collected here fit that mold. Consider the organization of the first essay you've been assigned. How is its organization connected to the meaning of the piece? Which organizational decision would you say is the most important one made by the author?

◆◆◆

KAREN ARMSTRONG

IN 1981, KAREN ARMSTRONG published *Through the Narrow Gate,* a controversial account of her experience as a Sister of the Society of the Holy Child Jesus, a Roman Catholic order. Armstrong left the convent and the Church in 1972, "wearied by religion" and "worn out by years of struggle," and then spent the intervening years pursuing a doctorate in literature and teaching at an English girls' school. Although her first book was a milestone, Armstrong has described her life's real turning point as a series of trips she made to Jerusalem beginning in 1982. Shocked by Israel's invasion of Lebanon and also by the Palestinians' intifada, Armstrong found herself questioning just how accurately most Westerners—herself included—understood the lives and beliefs of Muslims in the Middle East.

Convinced that the West was "posing as a tolerant and compassionate society and yet passing judgments from a position of extreme ignorance and irrationality," Armstrong set out to help rectify cross-cultural misperceptions and religious misunderstandings. She has written a number of books that explore relations among Judaism, Christianity, and Islam, including *Holy War: The Crusades and Their Impact on Today's World* (1991); *Mohammed: A Biography of the Prophet* (1992); and *Islam: A Short History* (2000). She has also written a biography, *Buddha* (2001), and *The Battle for God* (2000), an account of the rise of fundamentalism in modern societies.

The selection that follows comes from *The Case for God* (2009), in which Armstrong, a self-described "freelance monotheist," responds to the writings of New Atheists Richard Dawkins, Daniel C. Dennett, Sam Harris, Victor J. Stenger, and Christopher Hitchens. Armstrong makes the case that their view of religion has been shaped by the very fundamentalism they reject. Dawkins, for example, assumes that religion rests on faith in "a superhuman, supernatural intelligence who deliberately designed and created the universe and everything in it." Today this view of God is accepted by hundreds of millions of believers, yet Armstrong argues that in earlier times, religion was understood quite differently—as *mythos,* a

Biographical information and opening quotations are taken from http://www.islamfortoday.com/karenarmstrong.htm; the middle quotation is from www.washington-report.org/backissues/0293/9302038.htm. The quotation from Richard Dawkins appears on p. 304 of *The Case for God.* The final quotation is drawn from http://speakingoffaith.publicradio.org/programs/armstrong/transcript.shtml.

1

symbolic language meant to transform our consciousness and our ways of being. As she told an interviewer in 2008, she sees religion as "poetry":

> Now a poet spends a great deal of time listening to his unconscious, and slowly calling up a poem word by word, phrase by phrase, until something beautiful is brought forth, we hope, into the world that changes people's perceptions. And we respond to a poem emotionally. And I think we should take as great a care when we write our theology as we would if we were writing such a poem ... because I do see religion as a kind of art form.

Homo religiosus

When the guide switches off his flashlight in the underground caverns of Lascaux in the Dordogne, the effect is overwhelming. "The senses suddenly are wiped out," one visitor recalled, "the millennia drop away ... You were never in darker darkness in your life. It was—I don't know, just a complete knockout. You don't know whether you are looking north, south, east, or west. All orientation is gone, and you are in a darkness that never saw the sun." Normal daylight consciousness extinguished, you feel a "timeless dissociation from every concern and requirement of the upper world that you have left behind."[1] Before reaching the first of the caves decorated by our Palaeolithic ancestors in the Stone Age, seventeen thousand years ago, visitors have to stumble for some eighty feet down a sloping tunnel, sixty-five feet below ground level, penetrating ever more deeply into the bowels of the earth. Then the guide suddenly turns the beam of his flashlight onto the ceiling, and the painted animals seem to emerge from the depths of the rock. A strange beast with gravid belly and long pointed horns walks behind a line of wild cattle, horses, deer, and bulls that seem simultaneously in motion and at rest.

In all there are about six hundred frescoes and fifteen hundred engravings in the Lascaux labyrinth. There is a powerful bellowing black stag, a leaping cow, and a procession of horses moving in the opposite direction. At the entrance to another long passage known as the Nave, a frieze of elegant deer has been painted above a rocky ledge so that they appear to be swimming. We see these images far more clearly than the Palaeolithic artists did, since they had to work by the light of small flickering lamps, perched precariously on scaffolding that has left holes in the surface of the wall. They often painted new pictures over old images, even though there was ample space nearby. It seems that location was crucial and that, for reasons we cannot fathom, some places were deemed more suitable than others. The subject matter was also governed by rules that we can never hope to understand. The artists selected only a few of the species known to them, and there are no pictures of the reindeer on which they relied for food.[2] Animals are consistently paired—oxen and bison with horses, bison with mammoths—in combinations that would not occur in real life.[3] Lascaux is not unique. There are about three hundred decorated caves in this region of southern France and northern Spain. In some the artwork is more elementary, but in all these caverns the imagery and layout are basically the same. The earliest site, at Grotte Chauvet, dates from about 30,000 BCE, a time when *Homo sapiens* seems to have undergone an abrupt evolutionary change in this locality. There was a dramatic rise in population, which may have resulted in social tension. Some historians believe that the cave art records a "corpus of socially constructed rituals ... for conflict control ... pictorially encoded for storage and transmission through generations."[4] But the paintings also express an intensely aesthetic appreciation of the natural world. Here we have the earliest known evidence of an ideological system, which remained in place for some twenty thousand years, after which the caves fell into disuse in about 9000 BCE.[5]

It is now generally agreed that these labyrinths were sacred places for the performance of some kind of ritual. Some historians have argued that their purpose was purely pragmatic, but their upkeep alone would have required an immense amount of unproductive labor. Some of these sites were so deep that it took hours to reach their innermost core. Visiting the caves was dangerous, exhausting, uneconomical, and time-consuming. The general consensus is that the caves were sanctuaries and that, as in any temple, their iconography reflected a vision that was radically different from that of the outside world.[6] We do not build temples like this in the modern West. Our worldview is predominantly rational, and we think more easily in concepts than images. We find it hard enough to decode the symbolism of a medieval cathedral such as the one in Chartres, so these Palaeolithic shrines offer an almost insurmountable challenge.

But there are a few clues to aid our understanding. A remarkable picture, dated to about 12,000 BCE, in a cave at Lascaux known as the Crypt because it is even deeper than the other caverns, depicts a large bison that has been eviscerated by a spear thrust through its hindquarters. Lying in front of the wounded beast is a man, drawn in a far more rudimentary style than the animals, with arms outstretched, phallus erect, and wearing what seems to be a bird mask; his staff, which lies on the ground nearby, is also topped by a bird's head. This seems to be an illustration of a well-known legend and could have been the founding myth of the sanctuary. The same scene appears on an engraved reindeer horn at nearby Villars and on a sculpted block in a cliff shelter at Roc de Sers near Limoges, which is five thousand years older than the Lascaux painting.[7] Fifty-five similar images in the other caves and three more Palaeolithic rock drawings in Africa have been found, all showing men confronting animals in a state of trance with upraised arms.[8] They are probably shamans.

We know that shamanism developed in Africa and Europe during the Palaeolithic period and that it spread to Siberia and thence to America and Australia, where the shaman is still the chief religious practitioner among the indigenous hunting peoples. Even though they have inevitably been influenced by neighboring civilizations, many of the original structures of these societies, which were arrested at a stage similar to that of the Palaeolithic, remained intact until the late nineteenth century.[9] Today there is a remarkable continuity in the descriptions of the shaman's ecstatic flight all the way from Siberia, through the Americas to Tierra del Fuego:[10] he swoons during a public stance and believes that he flies through the air to consult the gods about the location of game. In these traditional societies, hunters do not feel that the species are distinct or permanent categories: men can become animals and animals human. Shamans have bird and animal guardians and can converse with the beasts that are revered as messengers of higher powers.[11] The shaman's vision gives meaning to the hunting and killing of animals on which these societies depend.

The hunters feel profoundly uneasy about slaughtering the beasts, who are their friends and patrons, and to assuage this anxiety, they surround the hunt with taboos and prohibitions. They say that long ago the animals made a covenant with humankind and now a god known as the Animal Master regularly sends flocks from the lower world to be killed on the hunting plains, because the hunters promised to perform the rites that will give them posthumous life. Hunters often abstain from sex before an expedition, hunt in a state of ritual purity, and feel a deep empathy with their prey. In the Kalahari Desert, where wood is scarce, the Bushmen have to rely on light weapons that can only graze the skin, so they anoint their arrows with a lethal poison that kills the animal very slowly. A tribesman has to remain with his victim, crying when it cries and participating symbolically in its death throes. Other tribes identify with their prey by donning animal costumes. After stripping the meat from the bones, some reconstruct their kill by laying out its skeleton and pelt; others bury these inedible remains, symbolically restoring the beast to the netherworld from which it came.[12]

The hunters of the Palaeolithic age may have had a similar worldview. Some of the myths and rites they devised appear to have survived in the traditions of later, literate cultures. Animal sacrifice, for example, the central rite of nearly every religious system in antiquity, preserved prehistoric hunting ceremonies and continued to honor a beast that gave its life for the sake of humankind.[13] One of the functions of ritual is to evoke an anxiety in such a way that the community is forced to confront and control it. From the very beginning, it seems, religious life was rooted in acknowledgment of the tragic fact that life depends upon the destruction of other creatures.

The Palaeolithic caves may have been the scene of similar rites. Some of the paintings include dancing men dressed as animals. The Bushmen say that their own rock paintings depict "the world behind this one that we see with our eyes," which the shamans visit during their mystical flights.[14] They smear the walls of the caves with the blood, excrement, and fat of their kill in order to restore it, symbolically, to the earth; animal blood and fat were ingredients of the Palaeolithic paints, and the act of painting itself could have been a ritual of restoration.[15] The images may depict the eternal, archetypal animals that take temporary physical form in the upper world.[16] All ancient religion was based on what has been called the perennial philosophy, because it was present in some form in of the transcendent may be *the* defining human characteristic. In about 9000 BCE, when human beings developed agriculture and were no longer dependent on animal meat, the old hunting rites lost some of their appeal and people ceased to visit the caves. But they did not discard religion altogether. Instead they developed a new set of myths and rituals based on the fecundity of the soil that filled the men and women of the Neolithic age with religious awe.[26] Tilling the fields became a ritual that replaced the hunt, and the nurturing Earth took the place of the Animal Master. Before the modern period, most men and women were naturally inclined to religion and they were prepared to work at it. Today many of us are no longer willing to make this effort, so the old myths seem arbitrary, remote, and incredible.

Like art, the truths of religion require the disciplined cultivation of a different mode of consciousness. The cave experience always began with the disorientation of utter darkness, which annihilated normal habits of mind. Human beings are so constituted that periodically they seek out *ekstasis,* a "stepping outside" the norm. Today people who no longer find it in a religious setting resort to other outlets: music, dance, art, sex, drugs, or sport. We make a point of seeking out these experiences that touch us deeply within and lift us momentarily beyond ourselves. At such times, we feel that we inhabit our humanity more fully than usual and experience an enhancement of being.

Lascaux may seem impossibly distant from modern religious practice, but we cannot understand either the nature of the religious quest or our current religious predicament unless we appreciate the spirituality that emerged quite early in the history of *Homo religiosus* and continued to animate the major confessional traditions until the early modern period, when an entirely different kind of religiosity emerged in the West during the seventeenth century. To do that we must examine a number of core principles that will be of fundamental importance to our story.

The first concerns the nature of the ultimate reality—later called God, Nirvana, Brahman, or Dao. In a rocky overhang at Laussel, near Lascaux, there is a small stone relief that is seventeen thousand years old and was created at about the same time as the earliest of the nearby cave paintings. It depicts a woman holding a curved bison's horn above her head so that it immediately suggests the rising, crescent moon; her right hand lies on her pregnancy. By this time, people had begun to observe the phases of the moon for practical purposes, but their religion had little or nothing to do with this protoscientific observation of the physical cosmos.[27] Instead, material reality was symbolic of an unseen dimension of existence. The little Venus of Laussel already suggests an association between the moon, the female cycle, and human reproduction. In many parts of the world, the moon was linked symbolically with a number of apparently unrelated phenomena: women, water, vegetation, serpents, and fertility. What they all have in common is the regenerative power of life that is continually able to renew itself. Everything could so easily lapse into nothingness, yet each year after the death of winter, trees sprout new leaves, the moon wanes but always waxes brilliantly once more, and the serpent, a universal symbol of initiation, sloughs off its old withered skin and comes forth gleaming and fresh.[28] The female also manifested this inexhaustible power. Ancient hunters revered a goddess known as the Great Mother. In large stone reliefs at Çatalhüyük in Turkey, she is shown giving birth, flanked by boars' skulls and bulls' horns— relics of a successful hunt. While hunters and animals died in the grim struggle for survival, the female was endlessly productive of new life.[29]

Perhaps these ancient societies were trying to express their sense of what the German philosopher Martin Heidegger (1899–1976) called "Being," a fundamental energy that supports and animates everything that exists. Being is transcendent. You could not see, touch, or hear it but could only watch it at work in the people, objects, and natural forces around you. From the documents of later Neolithic and pastoral societies, we know that Being rather than *a* being was revered as the ultimate sacred power. It was impossible to define or describe because Being is all-encompassing and our minds are only equipped to deal with particular beings, which can merely participate in it in a restricted manner. But certain objects became eloquent symbols of the power of Being, which sustained and shone through them with particular clarity. A stone or a rock (frequent symbols of the sacred) expressed the stability and durability of Being; the moon, its power of end-less renewal; the sky, its towering transcendence, ubiquity, and universality.[30] None of these symbols was worshipped for and in itself. People did not bow down and worship a rock *tout court;* the rock was simply a focus that directed their attention to the mysterious essence of life. Being bound all things together; humans, animals, plants, insects, stars, and birds all shared the divine life that sustained the entire cos-mos. We know, for example, that the ancient Aryan tribes, who had lived on the Caucasian steppes since about 4500 BCE, revered an invisible, impersonal force within themselves and all other natural phenomena. Everything was a manifestation of this all-pervading "Spirit" (Sanskrit: *manya*).[31]

There was, therefore, no belief in a single supreme being in the ancient world. Any such creature could only be *a* being—bigger and better than any-thing else, perhaps, but still a finite, incomplete reality. People felt it natural to imagine a race of spiritual beings of a higher nature than themselves that they called "gods." There were, after all, many unseen forces at work in the world—wind, heat, emotion, and air—that were often identified with the vari-ous deities. The Aryan god Agni, for example, *was* the fire that had transformed human life, and as a personalized god symbolized the deep affinity people felt with these sacred forces. The Aryans called their gods "the shining ones" *(devas)* because Spirit shone through them more brightly than through mortal creatures, but these gods had no control over the world: they were not omniscient and were obliged, like everything else, to submit to the transcendent order that kept everything in existence, set the stars on their courses, made the seasons fol-low each other, and compelled the seas to remain within bounds.[32]

By the tenth century BCE, when some of the Aryans had settled in the Indian subcontinent, they gave a new name to the ultimate reality. Brahman was the unseen principle that enabled all things to grow and flourish. It was a power that was higher, deeper, and more fundamental than the gods. Because it transcended the limitations of personality, it would be entirely inappropriate to pray to Brahman or expect it to answer your prayers. Brahman was the sacred energy that held all the disparate elements of the world together and prevented it from falling apart. Brahman had an infinitely greater degree of reality than mortal creatures, whose lives were limited by ignorance, sickness, pain, and death.[33] You could never define Brahman because language refers only to individual beings and Brahman was "the All"; it was everything that existed, as well as the inner meaning of all existence.

Even though human beings could not think about the Brahman, they had intimations of it in the hymns of the Rig Veda, the most important of the Aryan scriptures. Unlike the hunters of Lascaux, the Aryans do not seem to have thought readily in images. One of their chief symbols of the divine was sound, whose power and intangible quality seemed a particularly apt embodiment of the all-pervasive Brahman. When the priest chanted the Vedic hymns, the music filled the air and entered the consciousness of the congregation so that they felt surrounded by and infused with divinity. These hymns, revealed to ancient "seers" (*rishis*), did not speak of doctrines that the faithful were obliged to believe, but referred to the old myths in an allusive, riddling fashion because the truth they were trying to convey could not be contained in a neatly logical presentation. Their beauty shocked the audience into a state of awe, wonder, fear, and delight. They had to puzzle out the underlying significance of these paradoxical poems that yoked together apparently unrelated things, just as the hidden Brahman pulled the disparate elements of the universe into a coherent whole.[34]

During the tenth century, the Brahmin priests developed the Brahmodya competition, which would become a model of authentic religious discourse.[35] The contestants began by going on a retreat in the forest, where they performed spiritual exercises, such as fasting and breath control, that concentrated their minds and induced a different type of consciousness. Then the contest could begin. Its goal was to find a verbal formula to define the Brahman, in the process pushing language as far as it could go, until it finally broke down and people became vividly aware of the ineffable, the other. The challenger asked an enigmatic question, and his opponent had to reply in a way that was apt but equally inscrutable. The winner was the contestant who reduced his opponents to silence—and in that moment of silence, when language revealed its inadequacy, the Brahman was present; it became manifest only in the stunning realization of the impotence of speech.

The ultimate reality was not a personalized god, therefore, but a transcendent mystery that could never be plumbed. The Chinese called it the Dao, the fundamental "Way" of the cosmos. Because it comprised the whole of reality, the Dao had no qualities, no form; it could be experienced but never seen; it was not a god; it predated heaven and earth and was beyond divinity. You could not say anything about the Dao, because it transcended ordinary categories: it was more ancient than antiquity and yet it was not old; because it went far beyond any form of "existence" known to humans, it was neither being nor nonbeing.[36] It contained all the myriad patterns, forms, and potential that made the world the way it was and guided the endless flux of change and becoming that we see all around us. It existed at a point where all the distinctions that characterize our normal modes of thought became irrelevant.

In the Middle East, the region in which the Western monotheisms would develop, there was a similar notion of the ultimate. In Mesopotamia, the Akkadian word for "divinity" was *ilam,* a radiant power that transcended any particular deity. The gods were not the source of *ilam* but, like everything else, could only reflect it. The chief characteristic of this "divinity" was *ellu* ("holiness"), a word that had connotations of "brightness," "purity," and "luminosity." The gods were called the "holy ones" because their symbolic stories, effigies, and cults evoked the radiance of *ellu* within their worshippers. The people of Israel called their patronal deity, the "holy one" of Israel, Elohim, a Hebrew variant on *ellu* that summed up everything that the divine could mean for human beings. But holiness was not confined to the gods. Anything that came into contact with divinity could become holy too: a priest, a king, or a temple—even the sacred utensils of the cult. In the Middle East, people would have found it far too constricting to limit *ilam* to a single god; instead, they imagined a Divine Assembly, a council of gods of many different ranks, who worked together to sustain the cosmos and expressed the multifaceted complexity of the sacred.[37]

People felt a yearning for the absolute, intuited its presence all around them, and went to great lengths to cultivate their sense of this transcendence in creative rituals. But they also felt estranged from it. Almost every culture has developed a myth of a lost paradise from which men and women were ejected at the beginning of time. It expressed an inchoate conviction that life was not *meant* to be so fragmented, hard, and full of pain. There *must* have been a time when people had enjoyed a greater share in the fullness of being and had not been subject to sorrow, disease, bereavement, loneliness, old age, and death. This nostalgia informed the cult of "sacred geography," one of the oldest and most universal religious ideas. Certain places that stood out in some way from the norm—like the labyrinthine caverns of the Dordogne—seemed to speak of "something else."[38] The sacred place was one of the earliest and most ubiquitous symbols of the divine. It was a sacred "center" that brought heaven and earth together and where the divine potency seemed particularly effective.

A popular image, found in many cultures, imagined this fructifying, sacred energy welling up like a spring from these focal places and flowing, in four sacred rivers, to the four quarters of the earth. People would settle only in sites where the sacred had once become manifest because they wanted to live as closely as possible to the wellsprings of being and become as whole and complete as they had been before they were ejected from paradise.

This brings us to the second principle of premodern religion. Religious discourse was not intended to be understood literally because it was only possible to speak about a reality that transcended language in symbolic terms. The story of the lost paradise was a myth, not a factual account of a historical event. People were not expected to "believe" it in the abstract; like any *mythos,* it depended upon the rituals associated with the cult of a particular holy place to make what it signified a reality in the lives of participants.

The same applies to the creation myth that was central to ancient religion and has now become controversial in the Western world because the Genesis story seems to clash with modern science. But until the early modern period, nobody read a cosmology as a literal account of the origins of life. In the ancient world, it was inspired by an acute sense of the contingency and frailty of existence. Why had anything come into being at all, when there could so easily have been nothing? There has never been a simple or even a possible answer to this question, but people continue to ask it, pushing their minds to the limit of what we can know. One of the earliest and most universal of the ancient cosmologies is particularly instructive to us today. It was thought that one of the gods, known as the "High God" or "Sky God" because he dwelt in the farthest reaches of the heavens, had single-handedly created heaven and earth.[39] The Aryans called him Dyaeus Pitr, the Chinese Tian ("Heaven"), the Arabians Allah ("*the* God"), and the Syrians El Elyon ("Most High God"). But the High God proved to be an unviable deity, and his myth was jettisoned.

It suffered from an internal contradiction. How could a mere being—even such a lofty one—be responsible for being itself? As if in response to this objection, people tried to elevate the High God to a special plane. He was considered too exalted for an ordinary cult: no sacrifices were performed in his honor; he had no priests, no temples, and virtually no mythology of his own. People called on him in an emergency, but otherwise he scarcely ever impinged on their daily lives. Reduced to a mere explanation—to what would later be called First Cause or Prime Mover—he became *Deus otiosus,* a "useless" or "superfluous" deity, and gradually faded from the consciousness of his people. In most mythologies, the High God is often depicted as a passive, helpless figure; unable to control events, he retreats to the periphery of the pantheon and finally fades away. Today some of the indigenous peoples—Pygmies, Aboriginal Australians, and Fuegians—also speak of a High God who created heaven and earth, but, they tell anthropologists, he has died or disappeared; he "no longer cares" and "has gone far away from us."[40]

No god can survive unless he or she is actualized by the practical activity of ritual, and people often turn against gods who fail to deliver. The High God is often mythologically deposed, sometimes violently, by a younger generation of more dynamic deities—gods of storm, grain, or war—who symbolized relevant, important realities. In Greek *mythos,* the High God Uranus ("Heaven") was brutally castrated by his son Kronos. Later Kronos himself was overthrown by his own son Zeus, head of the younger gods, who lived more accessibly on Mount Olympus. In our own day, the God of the monotheistic tradition has often degenerated into a High God. The rites and practices that once made him a persuasive symbol of the sacred are no longer effective, and people have stopped participating in them. He has therefore become *otiosus,* an etiolated reality who for all intents and purposes has indeed died or "gone away."

In the ancient world, the High God myth was replaced by more relevant creation stories that were never regarded as factual. As one of the later hymns of the Rig Veda insists, nobody—not even the highest *deva*—could explain how something had issued from nothing.[41] A good creation myth did not describe an event in the distant past but told people something essential about the present. It reminded them that things often had to get worse before they got better, that creativity demanded self-sacrifice and heroic struggle, and that everybody had to work hard to preserve the energies of the cosmos and establish society on a sound foundation. A creation story was primarily therapeutic. People wanted to tap into the massive implosion of energy that had—somehow—brought the world we know into being, so they would recite a creation myth when they were in need of an infusion of sacred potency: during a political crisis, at a sickbed, or when they were building a new house. The creation myth was often re-enacted during the New Year ceremonies, when the old year was ebbing away. Nobody felt obliged to "believe" in a particular cosmology; indeed, each culture usually had several creation stories, each of which had its own lesson to impart, and people thought nothing of making up a new one if their circumstances changed.

Once people had abandoned the myth of the High God, there was no concept of creation "out of nothing" (*ex nihilo*) in the ancient world. A god could only assist a creative process that was already well under way. In the tenth century, another Indian *rishi* suggested that the world had been set in motion by a primordial sacrifice—something that made sense in India, where new vegetation was often seen to sprout from a rotting tree so that it was not unnatural to think of death resulting in new life. The *rishi* imagined the Purusha ("Person"), the first, archetypal human being, striding of his own free will to the place of sacrifice and allowing the gods to put him to death; thence everything—animals, horses, cattle, heaven, earth, sun, moon, and even some of the gods—emerged from his corpse.[42] This *mythos* encapsulated an important truth: we are at our most creative when we do not cling to our selfhood but are prepared to give ourselves away.

The cosmology was not influenced by current scientific speculation because it was exploring the interior rather than the external world. The priests of Mesopotamia undertook the first successful astronomical observations, noting that the seven celestial bodies they sighted—later known as Sun, Moon, Mercury, Venus, Mars, Jupiter, and Saturn—moved in an apparently circular path through the constellations. But the chief inspiration behind their creation myth was their pioneering town planning.[43] The first cities had been established in Sumer in the Fertile Crescent in about 3500 BCE; it was an enterprise that required enormous courage and perseverance, as time and time again, the mud-brick buildings were swept away by the flooding of the Tigris and the Euphrates. Constantly it seemed that the Sumerians' fragile urban civilization would sink back into the old rural barbarism, so the city needed a regular infusion of sacred energy. And yet it seemed such an extraordinary achievement that the city was extolled as a holy place. Babylon was the "Gate of the gods" (*Babi-lani*), where heaven and earth could meet; it re-created the lost paradise, and the ziggurat, or temple tower, of Esagila replicated the cosmic mountain or the sacred tree, which the first men and women had climbed to meet their gods.[44]

It is difficult to understand the creation story in Genesis without reference to the Mesopotamian creation hymn known from its opening words as the *Enuma Elish*. This poem begins by describing the evolution of the gods from primordial sacred matter and their subsequent creation of heaven and earth, but it is also a meditation on contemporary Mesopotamia. The raw material of the universe, from which the gods emerge, is a sloppy, undefined substance—very like the silty soil of the region. The first gods—Tiamat, the primal Ocean; Apsu, the "Abyss"; and Mummu, "Womb" of chaos—were inseparable from the elements and shared the inertia of aboriginal barbarism and the formlessness of chaos: "When sweet and bitter mingled together, no reed was plaited, no rushes muddied the water, the gods were nameless, natureless, futureless."[45] But new gods emerged, each pair more distinct than the last, culminating in the splendid Marduk, the Sun God and the most developed specimen of the divine species. But Marduk could not establish the cosmos until he had overcome the sluggish torpor of Tiamat in a tremendous battle. Finally he stood astride Tiamat's massive carcass, split her in two to make heaven and earth, and created the first man by mixing the blood of one of the defeated gods with a handful of dust. After this triumph, the gods could build the city of Babylon and establish the ritual "from which the universe receives its structure, the hidden world is made plain, and the gods assigned their places."[46]

There was no ontological gulf separating these gods from the rest of the cosmos; everything had emerged from the same sacred stuff. All beings shared the same predicament and had to participate in a ceaseless battle against the destructive lethargy of chaos. There were similar tales in neighboring Syria, where Baal, god of storm and life-giving rain, had to fight the sea dragon Lotan, symbol of chaos, Yam, the primal sea, and Mot, god of sterility, in order to establish civilized life.[47] The Israelites also told stories of their god Yahweh slaying sea monsters to order the cosmos.[48] In Babylon, the *Enuma Elish* was chanted on the fourth day of the New Year festival in Esagila, a re-enactment that symbolically continued the process Marduk had begun and that activated this sacred energy. There was a ritualized mock battle and a saturnalia that re-created the lawlessness of chaos. In archaic spirituality, a symbolic return to the formless "nothingness" of the beginning was indispensable to any new creation.[49] It was possible to move forward only if you had the courage to let go of the present, unsatisfactory state of affairs, sink back into the potent confusion of the beginning, and begin again.

As life became more settled, people had the leisure to develop a more interior spirituality. The Indian Aryans, always in the vanguard of religious change, pioneered this trend, achieving the groundbreaking discovery that the Brahman, being itself, was also the ground of the human psyche. The transcendent was neither external nor alien to humanity, but the two were inextricably connected. This insight would become central to the religious quest in all the major traditions. In the early Upanishads, composed in the seventh century BCE, the search for this sacred Self (*atman*) became central to Vedic spirituality. The Upanishadic sages did not ask their disciples to "believe" this but put them through an initiation whereby they discovered it for themselves in a series of spiritual exercises that made them look at the world differently. This practically acquired knowledge brought with it a joyous liberation from fear and anxiety.

We have a precious glimpse of the way this initiation was carried out in the Chandogya Upanishad. Here the great sage Uddalaka Aruni slowly and patiently brings this saving insight to birth within his son Shvetaketu and has him perform a series of tasks. In the most famous of these experiments, Shvetaketu had to leave a lump of salt in a beaker of water overnight and found, of course, that even though the salt had dissolved, the water still tasted salty. "You, of course, did not see it there, son," Uddalaka pointed out, "yet it was always right there." So too was the invisible Brahman, essence and inner self of the entire world. "And you are *that,* Shvetaketu."[50] Like the salt, the Brahman could not be seen but was manifest in every single living thing. It was the subtle essence in the tiny banyan seed, from which a giant tree would grow, yet when Shvetaketu dissected the seed, he could not see anything at all. The Brahman was also the sap in every part of the tree that gave it life, and yet it could never be pinned down or analyzed.[51] All things shared the same essence, but most people did not realize this. They imagined they were unique and special and clung to these particularities—often with extreme anxiety and expenditure of effort. But in reality these qualities were no more durable than rivers that flowed into the same sea. Once they had merged, they became "just the ocean," and no longer asserted their individuality by insisting "I am that river," "I am this river." "In exactly the same way, son," Uddalaka persisted, "when all these creatures reach the Existent, they are not aware that: 'We are reaching the Existent.'" Whether they were tigers, wolves, or gnats, they all merged into Brahman. To hold on to the mundane self, therefore, was a delusion that led inescapably to pain, frustration, and confusion, which one could escape only by acquiring the deep, liberating knowledge that the Brahman was their atman, the truest thing about them.[52]

The Upanishadic sages were among the first to articulate another of the universal principles of religion—one that had already been touched upon in the Purusha myth. The truths of religion are accessible only when you are prepared to get rid of the selfishness, greed, and self-preoccupation that, perhaps inevitably, are ingrained in our thoughts and behavior but are also the source of so much of our pain. The Greeks would call this process *kenosis,* "emptying." Once you gave up the nervous craving to promote yourself, denigrate others, draw attention to your unique and special qualities, and ensure that you were first in the pecking order, you experienced an immense peace. The first Upanishads were written at a time when the Aryan communities were in the early stages of urbanization; *logos* had enabled them to master their environment. But the sages reminded them that there were some things—old age, sickness, and death—that they could not control; things—such as their essential self—that lay beyond their intellectual grasp. When, as a result of carefully crafted spiritual exercises, people learned not only to accept but to embrace this unknowing, they found that they experienced a sense of release.

The sages began to explore the complexities of the human psyche with remarkable sophistication; they had discovered the unconscious long before Freud. But the atman, the deepest core of their personality, eluded them. Precisely *because* it was identical with the Brahman, it was indefinable. The atman had nothing to do with our normal psycho-mental states and bore no resemblance to anything in our ordinary experience, so you could speak of it only in negative terms. As the seventh-century sage Yajnavalkya explained: "About this Self [atman] one can only say 'not ... not' [neti ... neti]."[53]

> You can't see the Seer who does the seeing. You can't hear the Hearer who does the hearing; you can't think with the Thinker who does the thinking; and you can't perceive the Perceiver who does the perceiving. This Self within the All [Brahman] is this *atman* of yours.[54]

Like the Brahmodya, any discussion of the atman in the Upanishads always ended in silence, the numinous acknowledgment that the ultimate reality was beyond the competence of language.

Authentic religious discourse could not lead to clear, distinct, and empirically verified truth. Like the Brahman, the atman was "ungraspable." You could define something only when you saw it as separate from yourself. But "when the Whole [Brahman] has become a person's very self, then who is there for him to see and by what means? Who is there for me to think of and by what means?"[55] But if you learned to "realize" the truth that your most authentic "Self was identical with Brahman, you understood that it too was "beyond hunger and thirst, sorrow and delusion, old age and death."[56] You could not achieve this insight by rational logic. You had to acquire the knack of thinking outside the ordinary "lowercase" self, and like any craft or skill, this required long, hard, dedicated practice.

One of the principal technologies that enabled people to achieve this self-forgetfulness was yoga.[57] Unlike the yoga practiced in Western gyms today, it was not an aerobic exercise but a systematic breakdown of instinctive behavior and normal thought patterns. It was mentally demanding and, initially, physically painful. The yogin had to do the opposite of what came naturally. He sat so still that he seemed more like a plant or a statue than a human being; he controlled his respiration, one of the most automatic and essential of our physical functions, until he acquired the ability to exist for long periods without breathing at all. He learned to silence the thoughts that coursed through his mind and concentrate "on one point" for hours at a time. If he persevered, he found that he achieved a dissolution of ordinary consciousness that extracted the "I" from his thinking.

To this day, yogins find that these disciplines, which have measurable physical and neurological effects, evoke a sense of calm, harmony, and equanimity that is comparable to the effect of music. There is a feeling of expansiveness and bliss, which yogins regard as entirely natural, possible for anybody who has the talent and application. As the "I" disappears, the most humdrum objects reveal wholly unexpected qualities since they are no longer viewed through the distorting filter of one's own egotistic needs and desires. When she meditated on the teachings of her guru, a yogin did not simply accept them notionally but experienced them so vividly that her knowledge was, as the texts say, "direct"; bypassing the logical processes like any practically acquired skill, it had become part of her inner world.[58]

But yoga also had an ethical dimension. A beginner was not allowed to perform a single yogic exercise until he had completed an intensive moral program. Top of the list of its requirements was *ahimsa,* "nonviolence." A yogin must not swat a mosquito, make an irritable gesture, or speak unkindly to others but should maintain constant affability to all, even the most annoying monk in the community. Until his guru was satisfied that this had become second nature, a yogin could not even sit in the yogic position. A great deal of the aggression, frustration, hostility, and rage that mars our peace of mind is the result of thwarted egotism, but when the aspiring yogin became proficient in this selfless equanimity, the texts tell us that he would experience "indescribable joy."[59] Their experience of yoga led the sages to devise a new creation myth. In the beginning, there was only a single Person, who looked around him and discovered that he was alone. In this way, he became aware of himself and cried: "Here I am!" Thus the "I," the ego principle, was born. Immediately the Person became afraid, because we instinctively feel that we must protect the fragile ego from anything that threatens it, but when the Person remembered that because he was alone, there was no such threat, his fear left him. But he was lonely, so he split his body in two to create a man and a woman, who together gave birth to every single being in the cosmos "down to the very ants." And the Person realized that even though he was no longer alone, there was still nothing to fear. Was he not identical with Brahman, the All? He was one with all the things that he had made; indeed, he was himself his own creation.[60] He had even created the gods, who were essentially a part of himself.[61]

Even now, if a man knows "I am *brahman*" in this way, he becomes this whole world. Not even the gods are able to prevent it, for he becomes their very self [atman]. So when a man venerates another deity, thinking, "He is one, and I am another," he does not understand.[62] This insight, Yajnavalkya explained, brought with it a joy comparable to that of sexual intercourse, when one loses all sense of duality and is "oblivious to everything within or without."[63] But you would not have this experience unless you had performed the yogic exercises. Other traditions would also find that these fundamental principles were indispensable: Buddhism, Jainism, Confucianism, and Daoism, as well as the three monotheistic faiths of Judaism, Christianity, and Islam. Each had its own unique genius and distinctive vision, each its peculiar flaws. But on these central principles they would all agree. Religion was not a notional matter. The Buddha, for example, had little time for theological speculation. One of his monks was a philosopher manqué and, instead of getting on with his yoga, constantly pestered the Buddha about metaphysical questions: Was there a god? Had the world been created in time or had it always existed? The Buddha told him that he was like a man who had been shot with a poisoned arrow and refused medical treatment until he had discovered the name of his assailant and what village he came from. He would die before he got this perfectly useless information. What difference would it make to discover that a god had created the world? Pain, hatred, grief, and sorrow would still exist. These issues were fascinating, but the Buddha refused to discuss them because they were irrelevant: "My disciples, they will not help you, they are not useful in the quest for holiness; they do not lead to peace and to the direct knowledge of Nirvana."[64]

The Buddha always refused to define Nirvana, because it could not be understood notionally and would be inexplicable to anybody who did not undertake his practical regimen of meditation and compassion. But anybody who did commit him- or herself to the Buddhist way of life could attain Nirvana, which was an entirely natural state.[65] Sometimes, however, Buddhists would speak of Nirvana using the same kind of imagery as monotheists use for God: it was the "Truth," the "Other Shore," "Peace," the "Everlasting," and "the Beyond." Nirvana was a still center that gave meaning to life, an oasis of calm, and a source of strength that you discovered in the depths of your own being. In purely mundane terms, it was "nothing," because it corresponded to no reality that we could recognize in our ego-dominated existence. But those who had managed to find this sacred peace discovered that they lived an immeasurably richer life.[66] There was no question of "believing" in the existence of Nirvana or taking it "on faith." The Buddha had no time for abstract doctrinal formulations divorced from action. Indeed, to accept a dogma on somebody else's authority was what he called "unskillful" or "unhelpful" (*akusala*). It could not lead to enlightenment because it amounted to an abdication of personal responsibility. Faith meant trust that Nirvana existed and a determination to realize it by every practical means in one's power.

Nirvana was the natural result of a life lived according to the Buddha's doctrine *of anatta* ("no self"), which was not simply a metaphysical principle but, like all his teachings, a program of action. *Anatta* required Buddhists to *behave* day by day, hour by hour, as though the self did not exist. Thoughts of "self" not only led to "unhelpful" (*akusala*) preoccupation with "me" and "mine," but also to envy, hatred of rivals, conceit, pride, cruelty, and—when the self felt under threat—violence. As a monk became expert in cultivating this dispassion, he no longer interjected his ego into passing mental states but learned to regard his fears and desires as transient and remote phenomena. He was then ripe for enlightenment: "His greed fades away, and once his cravings disappear, he experiences the release of the mind."[67] The texts indicate that when the Buddha's first disciples heard about *anatta*, their hearts were filled with joy and they immediately experienced Nirvana. To live beyond the reach of hatred, greed, and anxieties about our status proved to be a profound relief.

By far the best way of achieving *anatta* was compassion, the ability to *feel with* the other, which required that one dethrone the self from the center of one's world and put another there. Compassion would become the central practice of the religious quest. One of the first people to make it crystal clear that holiness was inseparable from altruism was the Chinese sage Confucius (551–479 BCE). He preferred not to speak about the divine because it lay beyond the competence of language, and theological chatter was a distraction from the real business of religion.[68] He used to say: "My Way has one thread that runs right through it." There were no abstruse metaphysics; everything always came back to the importance of treating others with absolute respect.[69] It was epitomized in the Golden Rule, which, he said, his disciples should practice "all day and every day":[70] "Never do to others what you would not like them to do to you."[71] They should look into their own hearts, discover what gave them pain, and then refuse under any circumstance whatsoever to inflict that pain on anybody else.

Religion was a matter of doing rather than thinking. The traditional rituals of China enabled an individual to burnish and refine his humanity so that he became a *junzi,* a "mature person." A *junzi* was not born but crafted; he had to work on himself as a sculptor shaped a rough stone and made it a thing of beauty. "How can I achieve this?" asked Yan Hui, Confucius's most talented disciple. It was simple, Confucius replied: "Curb your ego and surrender to ritual (*li*)."[72] A *junzi* must submit every detail of his life to the ancient rites of consideration and respect for others. This was the answer to China's political problems: "If a ruler could curb his ego and submit to *li* for a single day, everyone under Heaven would respond to his goodness."[73]

The practice of the Golden Rule "all day and every day" would bring human beings into the state that Confucius called *ren,* a word that would later be described as "benevolence" but that Confucius himself refused to define because it could be understood only by somebody who had acquired it. He preferred to remain silent about what lay at the end of the religious journey. The practice of *ren* was an end in itself; it was itself the transcendence you sought. Yan Hui expressed this beautifully when he spoke of the endless struggle to achieve *ren* "with a deep sigh."

> The more I strain my gaze towards it, the higher it soars. The deeper I bore down into it, the harder it becomes. I see it in front, but suddenly it is behind. Step by step, the Master skil[l]fully lures one on. He has broadened me with culture, restrained me with ritual. Even if I wanted to stop, I could not. Just when I feel that I have exhausted every resource, something seems to rise up, standing over me sharp and clear. Yet though I long to pursue it, I can find no way of getting to it at all.[74]

Living a compassionate, empathetic life took Yan Hui beyond himself, giving him momentary glimpses of a sacred reality that was not unlike the "God" worshipped by monotheists. It was both immanent and transcendent: it welled up from within but was also experienced as an external presence "standing over me sharp and clear."

Religion as defined by the great sages of India, China, and the Middle East was not a notional activity but a practical one; it did not require belief in a set of doctrines but rather hard, disciplined work, without which any religious teaching remained opaque and incredible. The ultimate reality was not a Supreme Being—an idea that was quite alien to the religious sensibility of antiquity; it was an all-encompassing, wholly transcendent reality that lay beyond neat doctrinal formulations. So religious discourse should not attempt to impart clear information about the divine but should lead to an appreciation of the limits of language and understanding. The ultimate was not alien to human beings but inseparable from our humanity. It could not be accessed by rational, discursive thought but required a carefully cultivated state of mind and the abnegation of selfishness.

NOTES

1. Joseph Campbell, *Primitive Mythology: The Masks of God,* rev. ed. (New York, 1988), p. 305; Joseph Campbell with Bill Moyers, *The Power of Myth* (New York, 1988), p. 79.

2. André Leroi-Gourhan, *Treasures of Prehistoric Art* (New York, n.d.), p. 112. This rules out the suggestion that the paintings were simply a form of hunting magic.

3. Ibid., p. 118.

4. John E. Pfeiffer, *The Creative Explosion* (New York, 1982), p. viii.

5. André Leroi-Gourhan, *Les religions préhistorique: Paléolithique* (Paris, 1964), pp. 83–84; Mircea Eliade, *A History of Religious Ideas,* 3 vols., trans. Willard R. Trask (Chicago and London, 1978, 1982, 1985), 1:16.

6. Joseph Campbell, *Historical Atlas of World Mythologies*, 2 vols. (New York, 1988), 1,1:58.

7. Ibid., 1,1:65.

8. Leo Frobenius, *Kulturgeschichte Africas* (Zurich, 1933), pp. 131–32; Campbell, *Primitive Mythology*, p. 300.

9. Mircea Eliade, *History of Religious Ideas*, 1:24.

10. Joseph Campbell with Bill Moyers, *Power of Myth*, pp. 85–87.

11. Ibid., pp. 72–79; *Historical Atlas*, 1,1:48–49; Mircea Eliade, *History of Religious Ideas*, 1:7–8.

12. Walter Burkert, *Homo Necans: The Anthropology of Ancient Greek Sacrificial Ritual and Myth*, trans. Peter Bing (Berkeley, Los Angeles, and London, 1983), pp. 16–22.

13. Walter Burkert, *Structure and History in Greek Mythology and Ritual* (Berkeley, Los Angeles, and London, 1980), pp. 54–56; Walter Burkert, *Homo Necans*, pp. 42–45.

14. Joseph Campbell, *Historical Atlas*, 1, 2:xiii.

15. Ibid., 1,1:93.

16. Joseph Campbell, *Primitive Mythology*, p. 66.

17. Mircea Eliade, *The Myth of the Eternal Return, or Cosmos and History*, trans. Willard R. Trask (Princeton, N.J., 1954), pp. 1–34.

18. Huston Smith, *The World's Religions*, rev. ed. (New York, 1991), p. 367.

19. Mircea Eliade, *History of Religious Ideas*, 1:17.

20. Mircea Eliade, *Birth and Rebirth: The Religious Meanings of Initiation in Human Cultures* (New York, 1958); Mircea Eliade, *Myths, Dreams and Mysteries: The Encounter between Contemporary Faiths and Archaic Realities*, trans. Philip Mairet (London, 1960), pp. 194–226; Joseph Campbell with Bill Moyers, *Power of Myth*, pp. 81–85.

21. Mircea Eliade, *Myths, Dreams*, p. 225.

22. Herbert Kuhn, *Auf den Spuren des Eiszeitmenscken* (Wiesbaden, 1953), pp. 88–89; Joseph Campbell, *Primitive Mythology*, pp. 307–8.

23. Abbé Henri Breuil, *Four Hundred Centuries of Cave Art* (Montignac, France, 1952), pp. 170–71.

24. Joseph Campbell, *Primitive Mythology*, p. 311.

25. Walter Burkert, *Homo Necans*, pp. 27–34.

26. Mircea Eliade, *Patterns in Comparative Religion*, trans. Rosemary Sheed (London, 1958), pp. 331–43.

27. Alexander Marshack, "Lunar Notations on Upper Palaeolithic Remains," *Scientia* 146 (1964).

28. Mircea Eliade, *Patterns in Comparative Religion*, pp. 146–85.

29. Walter Burkert, *Homo Necans*, pp. 78–82.

30. Mircea Eliade, *Patterns in Comparative Religion*, pp. 1–124, 216–39.

31. Mary Boyce, *Zoroastrians: Their Religious Beliefs and Practices*, 2nd ed. (London and New York, 2001), p. 2; Peter Clark, *Zoroastrians: An Introduction to an Ancient Faith* (Brighton and Portland, Ore., 1998), p. 18.

32. Mary Boyce, *Zoroastrians*, pp. 9–11.

33. Jan Gonda, *Change and Continuity in Indian Religion* (The Hague, 1965), p. 200; Louis Renou, "Sur la notion de *brahman*," *Journal Asiatique* 237 (1949).

34. Louis Renou, *Religions of Ancient India* (London, 1953), pp. 10, 16–18; Michael Witzel, "Vedas and Upanishads" in Gavin Flood, ed., *The Blackwell Companion to Hinduism* (Oxford, 2003), pp. 70–71.

35. J. C. Heesterman, *The Inner Conflict of Tradition: Essays in Indian Ritual, Kingship and Society* (Chicago and London, 1985), pp. 70–72, 126.

36. Zhuangzi, *The Book of Zhuangzi*, 6:29–31.

37. Mark S. Smith, *The Origins of Biblical Monotheism: Israel's Polytheistic Background and the Ugaritic Texts* (New York and London, 2001), pp. 41–79.

38. Mircea Eliade, *Patterns in Comparative Religion*, pp. 367–88; Mircea Eliade, *The Sacred and the Profane: The Nature of Religion*, trans. Willard R. Trask (New York, 1959), pp. 50–54, 64; Mircea Eliade, *Images and Symbols: Studies in Religious Symbolism*, trans. Philip Mairet (Princeton, N.J., 1991), pp. 37–56.

39. Mircea Eliade, *Patterns in Comparative Religion*, pp. 38–63; Mircea Eliade, *Myths, Dreams*, pp. 172–78; Wilhelm Schmidt, *The Origin of the Idea of God* (New York, 1912), passim.

40. Mircea Eliade, *The Sacred and the Profane*, pp. 120–25.

41. Rig Veda 10.129.

42. Rig Veda 10.90.

43. Gwendolyn Leick, *Mesopotamia: The Invention of the City* (London, 2001), p. 268.

44. Thorkild Jacobsen, "The Cosmos as State," In H. and H. A. Frankfort, eds., *The Intellectual Adventure of Ancient Man: An Essay on the Speculative Thought in the Ancient Near East* (Chicago, 1946), pp. 186–97.

45. "The Babylonian Creation" 1.1 in N. K. Sanders, trans. and ed., *Poems of Heaven and Hell from Ancient Mesopotamia* (London, 1971).

46. *Enuma Elish* 6.19, In Sanders, *Poems of Heaven and Hell*.

47. E. O. James, *The Ancient Gods* (London, 1960), pp. 87–90.

48. Psalms 89:10–13; 93:1–4; Isaiah 27:1; Job 7:12; 9:8; 26:12; 38:7.

49. Mircea Eliade, *Myths, Dreams*, pp. 80–81.

50. Chandogya Upanishad (CU) 6.13; my italics. All quotations from the Upanishads are from Patrick Olivelle, trans. and ed., *Upanisads* (Oxford and New York, 1996).

51. CU 6.11–12.

52. CU 6.10.

53. Brhadaranyaka Upanishad (BU) 4.5.15.

54. BU 3.4.

55. BU 4.5.13–15.

56. BU 3.5.1.

57. Mircea Eliade, *Yoga, Immortality and Freedom*, trans. Willard R. Trask (New York, 1958).

58. Women participated in Upanishadic spirituality and, later, in Buddhist practice.

59. Patanjali, Yoga Sutra 2.42, in Eliade, *Yoga*, p. 52.

60. BU 1.4.1–5.

61. BU 1.4.6.

62. BU 1.4.10.

63. BU 4.3.21.

64. Samyutta Nikaya 53:31. The quotations from the Pali Canon of Buddhist scriptures are my own version of the texts cited.

65. Sutta-Nipata 43:1–44.

66. Majjima Nikaya 29.

67. *Vinaya:* Mahavagga 1.6.

68. Confucius, Analects 17.19. Unless otherwise stated, quotations from the Analects are taken from Arthur Waley, trans. and ed., *The Analects of Confucius* (New York, 1992).

69. Analects 4.15.

70. Analects 15.23.

71. Ibid.

72. Analects 12.1. Translation suggested by Benjamin I. Schwartz, *The World of Thought in Ancient China* (Cambridge, Mass., and London, 1985), p. 77.

73. Ibid.

74. Analects 9.10.

QUESTIONS FOR MAKING CONNECTIONS
WITHIN THE READING

1. In "Homo religiosus," Armstrong takes us back to the roots of religion in the Paleolithic era. The portrait she paints might surprise many readers. "In archaic thinking," she argues, "there [was] no concept of the supernatural, no huge gulf separating human and divine." There was "no belief in a single supreme being," and indeed belief itself was beside the point because religion was openly understood as a myth, not a literal truth. Reread the chapter and carefully note the many differences between religion then and religion now. Next, go back and look for the continuities. In spite of the differences, would you say that much of the Paleolithic legacy survives to this day? Can we conclude that religion has become more mature and sophisticated, or is it possible that we have lost touch with what religion actually represents? Where does Armstrong herself seem to stand on this final question?

2. Whether we are looking at the Middle East, ancient China, or the culture of Aryan peoples who came off the steppes and settled in India, Armstrong insists that religion was "a matter of doing rather than thinking." But what exactly does she mean by "doing"? What kinds of activities might religion have entailed in ancient times? Start with the ancient shamans whose activities are hinted at by the frescoes at Chauvet, and then follow the historical thread until you reach Heidegger. Clearly, religious activities are meant to enhance ordinary life, but at the same time they appear to involve forms of behavior that are quite distinct from everyday existence. How do the mundane and the sacred interact in the history of religious "doing"?

3. One central concern of "Homo religiosus" is the self in its connections to the universe as a whole. Even though religion in our time is quite commonly understood in terms of a personal relationship with God, Armstrong emphasizes the importance of what the ancient Greeks called *ekstasis,* a "stepping outside the norm," and *kenosis,* the "emptying" of the self. In what way does self-emptying connect the individual with the "sacred energy" of the universe? How might the experience of "nothingness" make people more alive and creative? What gets lost, in Armstrong's view, when we imagine the "ultimate reality" as a "Supreme Being"?

QUESTIONS FOR WRITING

1. According to Armstrong, "All ancient religion was based on what has been called the perennial philosophy, because it was present in some form in so many premodern cultures." To support this claim she looks at religion among such disparate groups as the Australian Aborigines, the ancient Aryans and Chinese, the peoples of the Middle East, and the ancient Greeks. While their belief systems can appear quite dissimilar today, Armstrong points to underlying commonalities. For example, just as the Aryans thought of their gods as *devas* or shining ones, so the forerunners of the Abrahamic faiths—Judaism, Christianity, and Islam—used the world *ilam,* meaning "radiant power," to describe their own deities. What are the implications of these parallels? Have we put so great an emphasis on the differences that we have lost touch with the greater unity? What factors might explain the emphasis on such differences?

2. One theme of Armstrong's recent work has been the distinction between two forms of knowing that she calls *logos* and *mythos. Logos* describes a kind of truth that strives for objectivity through the use of critical reason, while *mythos* describes a truth whose purpose is to overcome our subjective sense of separateness from the world and other living beings. Though past societies understood the distinction between the two, Armstrong contends that in our time both skeptics and religious people treat *mythos* as a set of objective claims. After reading "Homo religiosus," would you say that *mythos* should have a place in our lives today? Is it really possible for us to keep *mythos* separate from *logos*? How might the two become confused, and what dangers might arise from confusing them?

QUESTIONS FOR MAKING CONNECTIONS
BETWEEN READINGS

1. What might Armstrong have to say about our relationship with technology as it is described by Sherry Turkle in Selections from *Alone Together: Why We Expect More from Technology and Less from Each Other?* One place

to start in developing your response might be this passage from "Homo religiosus":

> Human beings are so constituted that periodically they seek out *ekstasis,* a "stepping outside" the norm. Today people who no longer find [*ekstasis*] in a religious setting resort to other outlets: music, dance, art, sex, drugs, or sport. We make a point of seeking out these experiences that touch us deeply within and lift us momentarily beyond ourselves. At such times, we feel that we inhabit our humanity more fully than usual and experience an enhancement of being.

Can our attitude toward technology be defined as *religious* in Armstrong's sense of the word? Think about the popular notion of the *singularity*—does that qualify as religious? Does our current technology "lift us ... beyond ourselves" and allow us to "inhabit our humanity more fully"? Or, by contrast, does our reliance on technology amount to an inversion of *ekstasis,* a contraction rather than an opening? Have machines taken the place of the animals that once figured in our rituals and mysteries? If we are no longer connecting to nature, what are we connecting to?

2. Armstrong sees religion as "matter of doing" rather than a matter of allegiance to unchanging beliefs. Reread her chapter and carefully note the many different forms of "doing" she explores, from ritual sacrifice to yoga. In what sense might we understand premodern religion as a form of psychotherapy of the kind practiced today by Martha Stout, author of "When I Woke Up Tuesday Morning, It Was Friday"? Were religious practices possibly designed to overcome dissociated states and the pathologies that they cause? Or does religion actually encourage dissociation? If the answer to this last question is yes, what might be the purpose of turning away from the here and now, at least temporarily?

TA-NEHISI COATES

IN 2017, JOURNALIST, BLOGGER, and fiction writer Ta-Nehisi Coates won a MacArthur Foundation "genius" award. The MacArthur committee cited his ability to bring "personal reflection and historical scholarship to bear on America's most contested issues." The citation singles out the qualities that make Coates's work so powerful: his ability to combine personal stories with historical, economic, and sociological research (often based on statistics and graphs) in a way that grabs at the hearts and minds of readers.

He learned this skill in his first paid gig at *The Washington City Paper*, whose freewheeling style was more to his taste than school. But he learned his love for research in the library. As he writes in his bestselling book of essays *Between the World and Me*, "The classroom was a jail of other people's interests. The library was open, unending, free":

> I needed more books. At Howard University, one of the greatest collections of books could be found in the Moorland-Spingarn Research Center.... Moorland held archives, papers, collections, and virtually any book ever written by or about black people. For the most significant portion of my time at The Mecca, I followed a simple ritual. I would walk into the Moorland reading room and fill out three call slips for three different works. I would take a seat at one of these long tables. I would draw out my pen and one of my black-and-white composition books. I would open the books and read, while filling my composition books with notes on my reading, new vocabulary words, and sentences of my own invention. I would arrive in the morning and request, three call slips at a time, the works of every writer I had heard spoken of in classrooms or out on the Yard.

This diligent research is a habit that Coates maintains and one he explicitly hopes to inspire in others. His longer articles are often followed up by a slew of posts or articles about the scholarship he read in preparation; his blog is, as often as not, an annotated exhortation to readers to look up and read his sources. Coates equates "hard" scholarship with the ability to deal with "hard" truths. "I have," he writes, "great respect and love for people who dig through the archives, who do the calculations, who do the case-studies, and perform the field research."

The reading reprinted here, "The First White President," first appeared in *The Atlantic* in October 2017, eleven months after Donald Trump's election. In it, Coates argues that the victory should be seen as a retreat from the historic achievement of Barack Obama, the United States's first black president. But Coates also insists that Trump and his supporters are far from unique or unprecedented. Instead, they represent a tradition of "political whiteness" reaching back to our Republic's earliest moments. Crude, bullying, and impetuous, Trump is quite capable of branding all Mexicans as "rapists" or denigrating Third World countries as "shit holes." But Coates warns that we should not allow Trump's Twitter feeds to distract us from the deeply entrenched system that has enabled his rise.

Not everyone admires "The First White President." The liberal journalist George Packer acknowledges the power of the article but expresses reservations:

> There's a lot to admire in Ta-Nehisi Coates's new essay. It's one of those pieces that grabs you with its first paragraph and never lets go.... At its heart is the undeniable truth that racism remains fundamental in American politics.

To Packer's way of thinking, Coates oversimplifies a more complicated reality:

> At the heart of American politics there is racism. But it's not alone— there's also greed, and broken communities, and partisan hatred, and ignorance. Any writer who wants to understand American politics has to find a way into the minds of Trump voters. Any progressive politician who wants to gain power has to find common interests with some of them, without waiting for the day of reckoning first to scourge white Americans of their original sin. This effort is one of the essential tasks of politics.

The "original sin" Packer references here is slavery, legally abolished in 1865 by the Thirteenth Amendment. But laws are one thing; culture quite another. Coates argues that we have to change the culture first. Packer counters that this task will take too long. But both agree about one thing: the shadow of this "sin" hangs over us all.

REFERENCES

"Macarthur Fellows/Meet the Class of 2015." Ta-Nehisi Coates. 28 September 2015 http://rwinonajohnson.weebly.com/uploads/4/5/3/2/45322833/ta-nahesis-

Ta-Nahasi Coates. *Between the World and Me*. New York: Spiegel & Grau, 2015. 46.

George Packer, "George Packer Responds to Ta-Nahasi Coates." *The Atlantic: Notes, First Drafts, Conversations, Stories in Progress*. 15 September 2017.

The First White President

It is insufficient to state the obvious of Donald Trump: that he is a white man who would not be president were it not for this fact. With one immediate exception, Trump's predecessors made their way to high office through the passive power of whiteness—that bloody heirloom which cannot ensure mastery of all events but can conjure a tailwind for most of them. Land theft and human plunder cleared the grounds for Trump's forefathers and barred others from it. Once upon the field, these men became soldiers, statesmen, and scholars; held court in Paris; presided at Princeton; advanced into the Wilderness and then into the White House. Their individual triumphs made this exclusive party seem above America's founding sins, and it was forgotten that the former was in fact bound to the latter, that all their victories had transpired on cleared grounds. No such elegant detachment can be attributed to Donald Trump—a president who, more than any other, has made the awful inheritance explicit.

His political career began in advocacy of birtherism, that modern recasting of the old American precept that black people are not fit to be citizens of the country they built. But long before birtherism, Trump had made his worldview clear. He fought to keep blacks out of his buildings, according to the U.S. government; called for the death penalty for the eventually exonerated Central Park Five; and railed against "lazy" black employees. "Black guys counting my money! I hate it," Trump was once quoted as saying. "The only kind of people I want counting my money are short guys that wear yarmulkes every day." After his cabal of conspiracy theorists forced Barack Obama to present his birth certificate, Trump demanded the president's college grades (offering $5 million in exchange for them), insisting that Obama was not intelligent enough to have gone to an Ivy League school, and that his acclaimed memoir, *Dreams From My Father*, had been ghostwritten by a white man, Bill Ayers.

It is often said that Trump has no real ideology, which is not true—his ideology is white supremacy, in all its truculent and sanctimonious power. Trump inaugurated his campaign by casting himself as the defender of white maidenhood against Mexican "rapists," only to be later alleged by multiple accusers, and by his own proud words, to be a sexual violator himself. White supremacy has always had a perverse sexual tint. Trump's rise was shepherded by Steve Bannon, a man who mocks his white male critics as "cucks." The word, derived from *cuckold*, is specifically meant to debase by fear and fantasy—the target is so weak that he would submit to the humiliation of having his white wife lie with black men. That the slur *cuck* casts white men as victims aligns with the dicta of whiteness, which seek to alchemize one's profligate sins into virtue. So it was with Virginia slaveholders claiming that Britain sought to make slaves of them. So it was with marauding Klansmen organized against alleged rapes and other outrages. So it was with a candidate who called for a foreign power to hack his opponent's email and who now, as president, is claiming to be the victim of "the single greatest witch hunt of a politician in American history."

In Trump, white supremacists see one of their own. Only grudgingly did Trump denounce the Ku Klux Klan and David Duke, one of its former grand wizards—and after the clashes between white supremacists and counterprotesters in Charlottesville, Virginia, in August, Duke in turn praised Trump's contentious claim that "both sides" were responsible for the violence.

To Trump, whiteness is neither notional nor symbolic but is the very core of his power. In this, Trump is not singular. But whereas his forebears carried whiteness like an ancestral talisman, Trump cracked the glowing amulet open, releasing its eldritch energies. The repercussions are striking: Trump is the first president to have served in no public capacity before ascending to his perch. But more telling, Trump is also the first president to have publicly affirmed that his daughter is a "piece of ass." The mind seizes trying to imagine a black man extolling the virtues of sexual assault on tape ("When you're a star, they let you do it"), fending off multiple accusations of such assaults, immersed in multiple lawsuits for allegedly fraudulent business dealings, exhorting his followers to violence, and then strolling into the White House. But that is the point of white supremacy—to ensure that that which all others achieve with maximal effort, white people (particularly white men) achieve with minimal qualification. Barack Obama delivered to black people the hoary message that if they work twice as hard as white people, anything is possible. But Trump's counter is persuasive: Work half as hard as black people, and even more is possible.

For Trump, it almost seems that the fact of Obama, the fact of a black president, insulted him personally. The insult intensified when Obama and Seth Meyers publicly humiliated him at the White House Correspondents' Dinner in 2011. But the bloody heirloom ensures the last laugh. Replacing Obama is not enough—Trump has made the negation of Obama's legacy the foundation of his own. And this too is whiteness. "Race is an idea, not a fact," the historian Nell Irvin Painter has written, and essential to the construct of a "white race" is the idea of not being a nigger. Before Barack Obama, niggers could be manufactured out of Sister Souljahs, Willie Hortons, and Dusky Sallys. But Donald Trump arrived in the wake of something more potent—an entire nigger presidency with nigger health care, nigger climate accords, and nigger justice reform, all of which could be targeted for destruction or redemption, thus reifying the idea of being white. Trump truly is something new—the first president whose entire political existence hinges on the fact of a black president. And so it will not suffice to say that Trump is a white man like all the others who rose to become president. He must be called by his rightful honorific—America's first white president.

The scope of Trump's commitment to whiteness is matched only by the depth of popular disbelief in the power of whiteness. We are now being told that support for Trump's "Muslim ban," his scapegoating of immigrants, his defenses of police brutality are somehow the natural outgrowth of the cultural and economic gap between Lena Dunham's America and Jeff Foxworthy's. The collective verdict holds that the Democratic Party lost its way when it abandoned everyday economic issues like job creation for the softer fare of social justice. The indictment continues: To their neoliberal economics, Democrats and liberals have married a condescending elitist affect that sneers at blue-collar culture and mocks the white man as history's greatest monster and prime-time television's biggest doofus. In this rendition, Donald Trump is not the product of white supremacy so much as the product of a backlash against contempt for white working-class people.

"We so obviously despise them, we so obviously condescend to them," the conservative social scientist Charles Murray, who co-wrote *The Bell Curve*, recently told *The New Yorker*, speaking of the white working class. "The only slur you can use at a dinner party and get away with is to call somebody a redneck—that won't give you any problems in Manhattan."

"The utter contempt with which privileged Eastern liberals such as myself discuss red-state, gun-country, working-class America as ridiculous and morons and rubes," charged the celebrity chef Anthony Bourdain, "is largely responsible for the upswell of rage and contempt and desire to pull down the temple that we're seeing now."

That black people, who have lived for centuries under such derision and condescension, have not yet been driven into the arms of Trump does not trouble these theoreticians. After all, in this analysis, Trump's racism and the racism of his supporters are incidental to his rise. Indeed, the alleged glee with which liberals call out Trump's bigotry is assigned even more power than the bigotry itself. Ostensibly assaulted by campus protests, battered by arguments about intersectionality, and oppressed by new bathroom rights, a blameless white working class did the only thing any reasonable polity might: elect an orcish reality-television star who insists on taking his intelligence briefings in picture-book form.

Asserting that Trump's rise was primarily powered by cultural resentment and economic reversal has become de rigueur among white pundits and thought leaders. But evidence for this is, at best, mixed. In a study of preelection polling data, the Gallup researchers Jonathan Rothwell and Pablo Diego-Rosell found that "people living in areas with diminished economic opportunity" were "somewhat more likely to support Trump." But the researchers also found that voters in their study who supported Trump generally had a higher mean household income ($81,898) than those who did not ($77,046). Those who approved of Trump were "less likely to be unemployed and less likely to be employed part-time" than those who did not. They also tended to be from areas that were very white: "The racial and ethnic isolation of whites at the zip code level is one of the strongest predictors of Trump support."

An analysis of exit polls conducted during the presidential primaries estimated the median household income of Trump supporters to be about $72,000. But even this lower number is almost double the median household income of African Americans, and $15,000 above the American median. Trump's white support was not determined by income. According to Edison Research, Trump won whites making less than $50,000 by 20 points, whites making $50,000 to $99,999 by 28 points, and whites making $100,000 or more by 14 points. This shows that Trump assembled a broad white coalition that ran the gamut from Joe the Dishwasher to Joe the Plumber to Joe the Banker. So when white pundits cast the elevation of Trump as the handiwork of an inscrutable white working class, they are being too modest, declining to claim credit for their own economic class. Trump's dominance among whites across class lines is of a piece with his larger dominance across nearly every white demographic. Trump won white women (+9) and white men (+31). He won white people with college degrees (+3) and white people without them (+37). He won whites ages 18–29 (+4), 30–44 (+17), 45–64 (+28), and 65 and older (+19). Trump won whites in midwestern Illinois (+11), whites in mid-Atlantic New Jersey (+12), and whites in the Sun Belt's New Mexico (+5). In no state that Edison polled did Trump's white support dip below 40 percent. Hillary Clinton's did, in states as disparate as Florida, Utah, Indiana, and Kentucky. From the beer track to the wine track, from soccer moms to NASCAR dads, Trump's performance among whites was dominant. According to *Mother Jones*, based on preelection polling data, if you tallied the popular vote of only white America to derive 2016 electoral votes, Trump would have defeated Clinton 389 to 81, with the remaining 68 votes either a toss-up or unknown.

Part of Trump's dominance among whites resulted from his running as a Republican, the party that has long cultivated white voters. Trump's share of the white vote was similar to Mitt Romney's in 2012. But unlike Romney, Trump secured this support by running against his party's leadership, against accepted campaign orthodoxy, and against all notions of decency. By his sixth month in office, embroiled in scandal after scandal, a Pew Research Center poll found Trump's approval rating underwater with every single demographic group. Every demographic group, that is, except one: people who identified as white.

The focus on one subsector of Trump voters—the white working class—is puzzling, given the breadth of his white coalition. Indeed, there is a kind of theater at work in which Trump's presidency is pawned off as a product of the white working class as opposed to a product of an entire whiteness that includes the very authors doing the pawning. The motive is clear: escapism. To accept that the bloody heirloom remains potent even now, some five decades after Martin Luther King Jr. was gunned down on a Memphis balcony—even after a black president; indeed, strengthened by the fact of that black president—is to accept that racism remains, as it has since 1776, at the heart of this country's political life. The idea of acceptance frustrates the left. The left would much rather have a discussion about class struggles, which might entice the white working masses, instead of about the racist struggles that those same masses have historically been the agents and beneficiaries of. Moreover, to accept that whiteness brought us Donald Trump is to accept whiteness as an existential danger to the country and the world. But if the broad and remarkable white support for Donald Trump can be reduced to the righteous anger of a noble class of smallville firefighters and evangelicals, mocked by Brooklyn hipsters and womanist professors into voting against their interests, then the threat of racism and whiteness, the threat of the heirloom, can be dismissed. Consciences can be eased; no deeper existential reckoning is required.

This transfiguration is not novel. It is a return to form. The tightly intertwined stories of the white working class and black Americans go back to the prehistory of the United States—and the use of one as a cudgel to silence the claims of the other goes back nearly as far. Like the black working class, the white working class originated in bondage—the former in the lifelong bondage of slavery, the latter in the temporary bondage of indenture. In the early 17th century, these two classes were remarkably, though not totally, free of racist enmity. But by the 18th century, the country's master class had begun etching race into law while phasing out indentured servitude in favor of a more enduring labor solution. From these and other changes of law and economy, a bargain emerged: The descendants of indenture would enjoy the full benefits of whiteness, the most definitional benefit being that they would never sink to the level of the slave. But if the bargain protected white workers from slavery, it did not protect them from near-slave wages or backbreaking labor to attain them, and always there lurked a fear of having their benefits revoked. This early white working class "expressed soaring desires to be rid of the age-old inequalities of Europe and of any hint of slavery," according to David R. Roediger, a professor of American studies at the University of Kansas. "They also expressed the rather more pedestrian goal of simply not being mistaken for slaves, or 'negers' or 'negurs.'"

Roediger relates the experience, around 1807, of a British investor who made the mistake of asking a white maid in New England whether her "master" was home. The maid admonished the investor, not merely for implying that she had a "master" and thus was a "sarvant" but for his basic ignorance of American hierarchy. "None but negers are sarvants," the maid is reported to have said. In law and economics and then in custom, a racist distinction not limited to the household emerged between the "help" (or the "freemen," or the white workers) and the "servants" (the "negers," the slaves). The former were virtuous and just, worthy of citizenship, progeny of Jefferson and, later, Jackson. The latter were servile and parasitic, dim-witted and lazy, the children of African savagery. But the dignity accorded to white labor was situational, dependent on the scorn heaped upon black labor—much as the honor accorded a "virtuous lady" was dependent on the derision directed at a "loose woman." And like chivalrous gentlemen who claim to honor the lady while raping the "whore," planters and their apologists could claim to honor white labor while driving the enslaved.

And so George Fitzhugh, a prominent 19th-century Southern pro-slavery intellectual, could in a single stroke deplore the exploitation of free whites' labor while defending the exploitation of enslaved blacks' labor. Fitzhugh attacked white capitalists as "cannibals," feeding off the labor of their fellow whites. The white workers were " 'slaves without masters;' the little fish, who were food for all the larger." Fitzhugh inveighed against a "professional man" who'd "amassed a fortune" by exploiting his fellow whites. But whereas Fitzhugh imagined white workers as devoured by capital, he imagined black workers as elevated by enslavement. The slaveholder "provided for them, with almost parental affection"—even when the loafing slave "feigned to be unfit for labor." Fitzhugh proved too explicit—going so far as to argue that white laborers might be better off if enslaved. ("If white slavery be morally wrong," he wrote, "the Bible cannot be true.") Nevertheless, the argument that America's original sin was not deep-seated white supremacy but rather the exploitation of white labor by white capitalists—"white slavery"—proved durable. Indeed, the panic of white slavery lives on in our politics today. Black workers suffer because it was and is our lot. But when white workers suffer, something in nature has gone awry. And so an opioid epidemic among mostly white people is greeted with calls for compassion and treatment, as all epidemics should be, while a crack epidemic among mostly black people is greeted with scorn and mandatory minimums. Sympathetic op-ed columns and articles are devoted to the plight of working-class whites when their life expectancy plummets to levels that, for blacks, society has simply accepted as normal. White slavery is sin. Nigger slavery is natural. This dynamic serves a very real purpose: the consistent awarding of grievance and moral high ground to that class of workers which, by the bonds of whiteness, stands closest to America's aristocratic class.

This is by design. Speaking in 1848, Senator John C. Calhoun saw slavery as the explicit foundation for a democratic union among whites, working and not:

> With us the two great divisions of society are not the rich and poor, but white and black; and all the former, the poor as well as the rich, belong to the upper class, and are respected and treated as equals.

On the eve of secession, Jefferson Davis, the eventual president of the Confederacy, pushed the idea further, arguing that such equality between the white working class and white oligarchs could not exist at all without black slavery:

> I say that the lower race of human beings that constitute the substratum of what is termed the slave population of the South, elevates every white man in our community ... It is the presence of a lower caste, those lower by their mental and physical organization, controlled by the higher intellect of the white man, that gives this superiority to the white laborer. Menial services are not there performed by the white man. We have none of our brethren sunk to the degradation of being menials. That belongs to the lower race—the descendants of Ham.

Southern intellectuals found a shade of agreement with Northern white reformers who, while not agreeing on slavery, agreed on the nature of the most tragic victim of emerging capitalism. "I was formerly like yourself, sir, a very warm advocate of the abolition of slavery," the labor reformer George Henry Evans argued in a letter to the abolitionist Gerrit Smith. "This was before I saw that there was *white* slavery." Evans was a putative ally of Smith and his fellow abolitionists. But still he asserted that "the landless white" was worse off than the enslaved black, who at least enjoyed "surety of support in sickness and old age."

Invokers of "white slavery" held that there was nothing unique in the enslavement of blacks when measured against the enslavement of all workers. What evil there was in enslavement resulted from its status as a subsidiary of the broader exploitation better seen among the country's noble laboring whites. Once the larger problem of white exploitation was solved, the dependent problem of black exploitation could be confronted or perhaps would fade away. Abolitionists focused on slavery were dismissed as "substitutionists" who wished to trade one form of slavery for another. "If I am less troubled concerning the Slavery prevalent in Charleston or New-Orleans," wrote the reformer Horace Greeley, "it is because I see so much Slavery in New-York, which appears to claim my first efforts."

Firsthand reports by white Union soldiers who witnessed actual slavery during the Civil War rendered the "white slavery" argument ridiculous. But its operating premises—white labor as noble archetype, and black labor as something else—lived on. This was a matter of rhetoric, not fact. The noble-white-labor archetype did not give white workers immunity from capitalism. It could not, in itself, break monopolies, alleviate white poverty in Appalachia or the South, or bring a decent wage to immigrant ghettos in the North. But the model for America's original identity politics was set. Black lives literally did not matter and could be cast aside altogether as the price of even incremental gains for the white masses. It was this juxtaposition that allowed Theodore Bilbo to campaign for the Senate in the 1930s as someone who would "raise the same kind of hell as President Roosevelt" and later endorse lynching black people to keep them from voting.

The juxtaposition between the valid and even virtuous interests of the "working class" and the invalid and pathological interests of black Americans was not the province merely of blatant white supremacists like Bilbo. The acclaimed scholar, liberal hero, and future senator Daniel Patrick Moynihan, in his time working for President Richard Nixon, approvingly quoted Nixon's formulation of the white working class: "A new voice" was beginning to make itself felt in the country, "it is a voice that has been silent too long," Nixon claimed, alluding to working-class whites. "It is a voice of people who have not taken to the streets before, who have not indulged in violence, who have not broken the law."

It had been only 18 years since the Cicero riots; eight years since Daisy and Bill Myers had been run out of Levittown, Pennsylvania; three years since Martin Luther King Jr. had been stoned while walking through Chicago's Marquette Park. But as the myth of the virtuous white working class was made central to American identity, its sins needed to be rendered invisible. The fact was, working-class whites had been agents of racist terrorism since at least the draft riots of 1863; terrorism could not be neatly separated from the racist animus found in every class of whites. Indeed, in the era of lynching, the daily newspapers often whipped up the fury of the white masses by invoking the last species of property that all white men held in common—white women. But to conceal the breadth of white racism, these racist outbursts were often disregarded or treated not as racism but as the unfortunate side effect of legitimate grievances against capital. By focusing on that sympathetic laboring class, the sins of whiteness itself were, and are still being, evaded.

When David Duke, the former grand wizard of the Ku Klux Klan, shocked the country in 1990 by almost winning one of Louisiana's seats in the U.S. Senate, the apologists came out once again. They elided the obvious—that Duke had appealed to the racist instincts of a state whose schools are, at this very moment, still desegregating—and instead decided that something else was afoot. "There is a tremendous amount of anger and frustration among working-class whites, particularly where there is an economic downturn," a researcher told the *Los Angeles Times.* "These people feel left out; they feel government is not responsive to them." By this logic, postwar America—with its booming economy and low unemployment—should have been an egalitarian utopia and not the violently segregated country it actually was.

But this was the past made present. It was not important to the apologists that a large swath of Louisiana's white population thought it was a good idea to send a white supremacist who once fronted a terrorist organization to the nation's capital. Nor was it important that blacks in Louisiana had long felt left out. What was important was the fraying of an ancient bargain, and the potential degradation of white workers to the level of "negers." "A viable left must find a way to differentiate itself strongly from such analysis," David Roediger, the University of Kansas professor, has written.

That challenge of differentiation has largely been ignored. Instead, an imagined white working class remains central to our politics and to our cultural understanding of those politics, not simply when it comes to addressing broad economic issues but also when it comes to addressing racism. At its most sympathetic, this belief holds that most Americans—regardless of race—are exploited by an unfettered capitalist economy. The key, then, is to address those broader patterns that afflict the masses of all races; the people who suffer from those patterns more than others (blacks, for instance) will benefit disproportionately from that which benefits everyone. "These days, what ails working-class and middle-class blacks and Latinos is not fundamentally different from what ails their white counterparts," Senator Barack Obama wrote in 2006:

> Downsizing, outsourcing, automation, wage stagnation, the dismantling
> of employer-based health-care and pension plans, and schools that fail to
> teach young people the skills they need to compete in a global economy.

Obama allowed that "blacks in particular have been vulnerable to these trends"—but less because of racism than for reasons of geography and job-sector distribution. This notion—raceless antiracism—marks the modern left, from the New Democrat Bill Clinton to the socialist Bernie Sanders. Few national liberal politicians have shown any recognition that there is something systemic and particular in the relationship between black people and their country that might require specific policy solutions.

In 2016, Hillary Clinton acknowledged the existence of systemic racism more explicitly than any of her modern Democratic predecessors. She had to—black voters remembered too well the previous Clinton administration, as well as her previous campaign. While her husband's administration had touted the rising-tide theory of economic growth, it did so while slashing welfare and getting "tough on crime," a phrase that stood for specific policies but also served as rhetorical bait for white voters. One is tempted to excuse Hillary Clinton from having to answer for the sins of her husband. But in her 2008 campaign, she evoked the old dichotomy between white workers and loafing blacks, claiming to be the representative of "hardworking Americans, white Americans." By the end of the 2008 primary campaign against Barack Obama, her advisers were hoping someone would uncover an apocryphal "whitey tape," in which an angry Michelle Obama was alleged to have used the slur. During Bill Clinton's presidential-reelection campaign in the mid-1990s, Hillary Clinton herself had endorsed the "super-predator" theory of William J. Bennett, John P. Walters, and John J. DiIulio Jr. This theory cast "inner-city" children of that era as "almost completely unmoralized" and the font of "a new generation of street criminals ... the youngest, biggest and baddest generation any society has ever known." The "baddest generation" did not become super-predators. But by 2016, they were young adults, many of whom judged Hillary Clinton's newfound consciousness to be lacking.

It's worth asking why the country has not been treated to a raft of sympathetic portraits of this "forgotten" young black electorate, forsaken by a Washington bought off by Davos elites and special interests. The unemployment rate for young blacks (20.6 percent) in July 2016 was double that of young whites (9.9 percent). And since the late 1970s, William Julius Wilson and other social scientists following in his wake have noted the disproportionate effect that the decline in manufacturing jobs has had on African American communities. If anyone should be angered by the devastation wreaked by the financial sector and a government that declined to prosecute the perpetrators, it is African Americans—the housing crisis was one of the primary drivers in the past 20 years of the wealth gap between black families and the rest of the country. But the cultural condescension toward and economic anxiety of black people is not news. Toiling blacks are in their proper state; toiling whites raise the specter of white slavery.

Moreover, a narrative of long-neglected working-class black voters, injured by globalization and the financial crisis, forsaken by out-of-touch politicians, and rightfully suspicious of a return of Clintonism, does not serve to cleanse the conscience of white people for having elected Donald Trump. Only the idea of a long-suffering white working class can do that. And though much has been written about the distance between elites and "Real America," the existence of a class-transcending, mutually dependent tribe of white people is evident.

Joe Biden, then the vice president, last year:

> "They're all the people I grew up with ... And they're not racist. They're not sexist."

Bernie Sanders, senator and former candidate for president, last year:

> "I come from the white working class, and I am deeply humiliated that the Democratic Party cannot talk to the people where I came from."

Nicholas Kristof, the *New York Times* columnist, in February of this year:

> My hometown, Yamhill, Ore., a farming community, is Trump country, and I have many friends who voted for Trump. I think they're profoundly wrong, but please don't dismiss them as hateful bigots.

These claims of origin and fidelity are not merely elite defenses of an aggrieved class but also a sweeping dismissal of the concerns of those who don't share kinship with white men. "You can't eat equality," asserts Joe Biden—a statement worthy of someone unthreatened by the loss of wages brought on by an unwanted pregnancy, a background-check box at the bottom of a job application, or the deportation of a breadwinner. Within a week of Sanders lambasting Democrats for not speaking to "the people" where he "came from," he was making an example of a woman who dreamed of representing the people where she came from. Confronted with a young woman who hoped to become the second Latina senator in American history, Sanders responded with a parody of the Clinton campaign: "It is not good enough for someone to say, 'I'm a woman! Vote for me!' No, that's not good enough ... One of the struggles that you're going to be seeing in the Democratic Party is whether we go beyond identity politics." The upshot—attacking one specimen of identity politics after having invoked another—was unfortunate.

Other Sanders appearances proved even more alarming. On MSNBC, he attributed Trump's success, in part, to his willingness to "not be politically correct." Sanders admitted that Trump had "said some outrageous and painful things, but I think people are tired of the same old, same old political rhetoric." Pressed on the definition of political correctness, Sanders gave an answer Trump surely would have approved of. "What it means is you have a set of talking points which have been poll-tested and focus-group-tested," Sanders explained. "And that's what you say rather than what's really going on. And often, what you are not allowed to say are things which offend very, very powerful people."

This definition of political correctness was shocking coming from a politician of the left. But it matched a broader defense of Trump voters. "Some people think that the people who voted for Trump are racists and sexists and homophobes and just deplorable folks," Sanders said later. "I don't agree." This is not exculpatory. Certainly not every Trump voter is a white supremacist, just as not every white person in the Jim Crow South was a white supremacist. But every Trump voter felt it acceptable to hand the fate of the country over to one.

One can, to some extent, understand politicians' embracing a self-serving identity politics. Candidates for high office, such as Sanders, have to cobble together a coalition. The white working class is seen, understandably, as a large cache of potential votes, and capturing these votes requires eliding uncomfortable truths. But journalists have no such excuse. Again and again in the past year, Nicholas Kristof could be found pleading with his fellow liberals not to dismiss his old comrades in the white working class as bigots—even when their bigotry was evidenced in his own reporting. A visit to Tulsa, Oklahoma, finds Kristof wondering why Trump voters support a president who threatens to cut the programs they depend on. But the problem, according to Kristof's interviewees, isn't Trump's attack on benefits so much as an attack on *their* benefits. "There's a lot of wasteful spending, so cut other places," one man tells Kristof. When Kristof pushes his subjects to identify that wasteful spending, a fascinating target is revealed: "Obama phones," the products of a fevered conspiracy theory that turned a long-standing government program into a scheme through which the then-president gave away free cellphones to undeserving blacks. Kristof doesn't shift his analysis based on this comment and, aside from a one-sentence fact-check tucked between parentheses, continues on as though it were never said.

Observing a Trump supporter in the act of deploying racism does not much perturb Kristof. That is because his defenses of the innate goodness of Trump voters and of the innate goodness of the white working class are in fact defenses of neither. On the contrary, the white working class functions rhetorically not as a real community of people so much as a tool to quiet the demands of those who want a more inclusive America.

Mark Lilla's *New York Times* essay "The End of Identity Liberalism," published not long after last year's election, is perhaps the most profound example of this genre. Lilla denounces the perversion of liberalism into "a kind of moral panic about racial, gender and sexual identity," which distorted liberalism's message "and prevented it from becoming a unifying force capable of governing." Liberals have turned away from their working-class base, he says, and must look to the "pre-identity liberalism" of Bill Clinton and Franklin D. Roosevelt. You would never know from this essay that Bill Clinton was one of the most skillful identity politicians of his era—flying home to Arkansas to see a black man, the lobotomized Ricky Ray Rector, executed; upstaging Jesse Jackson at his own conference; signing the Defense of Marriage Act. Nor would you know that the "pre-identity" liberal champion Roosevelt depended on the literally lethal identity politics of the white-supremacist "solid South." The name Barack Obama does not appear in Lilla's essay, and he never attempts to grapple, one way or another, with the fact that it was identity politics—the possibility of the first black president—that brought a record number of black voters to the polls, winning the election for the Democratic Party, and thus enabling the deliverance of the ancient liberal goal of national health care, "identity politics ... is largely expressive, not persuasive," Lilla claims. "Which is why it never wins elections—but can lose them." That Trump ran and won on identity politics is beyond Lilla's powers of conception. What appeals to the white working class is ennobled. What appeals to black workers, and all others outside the tribe, is dastardly identitarianism. All politics are identity politics—except the politics of white people, the politics of the bloody heirloom.

White tribalism haunts even more-nuanced writers. George Packer's *New Yorker* essay "The Unconnected" is a lengthy plea for liberals to focus more on the white working class, a population that "has succumbed to the ills that used to be associated with the black urban 'underclass.'" Packer believes that these ills, and the Democratic Party's failure to respond to them, explain much of Trump's rise. Packer offers no opinion polls to weigh white workers' views on "elites," much less their views on racism. He offers no sense of how their views and their relationship to Trump differ from other workers' and other whites'.

That is likely because any empirical evaluation of the relationship between Trump and the white working class would reveal that one adjective in that phrase is doing more work than the other. In 2016, Trump enjoyed majority or plurality support among every economic branch of whites. It is true that his strongest support among whites came from those making $50,000 to $99,999. This would be something more than working-class in many nonwhite neighborhoods, but even if one accepts that branch as the working class, the difference between how various groups in this income bracket voted is revealing. Sixty-one percent of whites in this "working class" supported Trump. Only 24 percent of Hispanics and 11 percent of blacks did. Indeed, the plurality of all voters making less than

$100,000 and the majority making less than $50,000 voted for the Democratic candidate. So when Packer laments the fact that "Democrats can no longer really claim to be the party of working people—not white ones, anyway," he commits a kind of category error. The real problem is that Democrats aren't the party of white people—working or otherwise. White workers are not divided by the fact of labor from other white demographics; they are divided from all other laborers by the fact of their whiteness.

Packer's essay was published before the election, and so the vote tally was not available. But it should not be surprising that a Republican candidate making a direct appeal to racism would drive up the numbers among white voters, given that racism has been a dividing line for the national parties since the civil-rights era. Packer finds inspiration for his thesis in West Virginia—a state that remained Democratic through the 1990s before turning decisively Republican, at least at the level of presidential politics. This relatively recent rightward movement evinces, to Packer, a shift "that couldn't be attributed just to the politics of race." This is likely true—the politics of race are, themselves, never attributable "just to the politics of race." The history of slavery is also about the growth of international capitalism; the history of lynching must be seen in light of anxiety over the growing independence of women; the civil-rights movement can't be disentangled from the Cold War. Thus, to say that the rise of Donald Trump is about more than race is to make an empty statement, one that is small comfort to the people—black, Muslim, immigrant—who live under racism's boot.

The dent of racism is not hard to detect in West Virginia. In the 2008 Democratic primary there, 95 percent of the voters were white. Twenty percent of those—one in five—openly admitted that race was influencing their vote, and more than 80 percent voted for Hillary Clinton over Barack Obama. Four years later, the incumbent Obama lost the primary in 10 counties to Keith Judd, a white felon incarcerated in a federal prison; Judd racked up more than 40 percent of the Democratic-primary vote in the state. A simple thought experiment: Can one imagine a black felon in a federal prison running in a primary against an incumbent white president doing so well?

But racism occupies a mostly passive place in Packer's essay. There's no attempt to understand why black and brown workers, victimized by the same new economy and cosmopolitan elite that Packer lambastes, did not join the Trump revolution. Like Kristof, Packer is gentle with his subjects. When a woman "exploded" and told Packer, "I want to eat what I want to eat, and for them to tell me I can't eat French fries or Coca-Cola—no way," he sees this as a rebellion against "the moral superiority of elites." In fact, this elite conspiracy dates back to 1894, when the government first began advising Americans on their diets. As recently as 2002, President George W. Bush launched the HealthierUS initiative, urging Americans to exercise and eat healthy food. But Packer never allows himself to wonder whether the explosion he witnessed had anything to do with the fact that similar advice now came from the country's first black first lady. Packer concludes that Obama was leaving the country "more divided and angrier than most Americans can remember," a statement that is likely true only because most Americans identify as white. Certainly the men and women forced to live in the wake of the beating of John Lewis, the lynching of Emmett Till, the firebombing of Percy Julian's home, and the assassinations of Martin Luther King Jr. and Medgar Evers would disagree.

The triumph of Trump's campaign of bigotry presented the problematic spectacle of an American president succeeding at best in spite of his racism and possibly because of it. Trump moved racism from the euphemistic and plausibly deniable to the overt and freely claimed. This presented the country's thinking class with a dilemma. Hillary Clinton simply could not be correct when she asserted that a large group of Americans was endorsing a candidate because of bigotry. The implications —that systemic bigotry is still central to our politics; that the country is susceptible to such bigotry; that the salt-of-the-earth Americans whom we lionize in our culture and politics are not so different from those same Americans who grin back at us in lynching photos; that Calhoun's aim of a pan-Caucasian embrace between workers and capitalists still endures—were just too dark. Leftists would have to cope with the failure, yet again, of class unity in the face of racism. Incorporating all of this into an analysis of America and the path forward proved too much to ask. Instead, the response has largely been an argument aimed at emotion—the summoning of the white working class, emblem of America's hardscrabble roots, inheritor of its pioneer spirit, as a shield against the horrific and empirical evidence of trenchant bigotry.

Packer dismisses the Democratic Party as a coalition of "rising professionals and diversity." The dismissal is derived from, of all people, Lawrence Summers, the former Harvard president and White House economist, who last year labeled the Democratic Party "a coalition of the cosmopolitan élite and diversity." The inference is that the party has forgotten how to speak on hard economic issues and prefers discussing presumably softer cultural issues such as "diversity." It's worth unpacking what, precisely, falls under this rubric of "diversity"—resistance to the monstrous incarceration of legions of black men, resistance to the destruction of health providers for poor women, resistance to the effort to deport parents, resistance to a policing whose sole legitimacy is rooted in brute force, resistance to a theory of education that preaches "no excuses" to black and brown children, even as excuses are proffered for mendacious corporate executives "too big to jail." That this suite of concerns, taken together, can be dismissed by both an elite economist like Summers and a brilliant journalist like Packer as "diversity" simply reveals the safe space they enjoy. Because of their identity.

When Barack Obama came into office, in 2009, he believed that he could work with "sensible" conservatives by embracing aspects of their policy as his own. Instead he found that his very imprimatur made that impossible. Senate Minority Leader Mitch McConnell announced that the GOP's primary goal was not to find common ground but to make Obama a "one-term president." A health-care plan inspired by Romneycare was, when proposed by Obama, suddenly considered socialist and, not coincidentally, a form of reparations. The first black president found that he was personally toxic to the GOP base. An entire political party was organized around the explicit aim of negating one man. It was thought by Obama and some of his allies that this toxicity was the result of a relentless assault waged by Fox News and right-wing talk radio. Trump's genius was to see that it was something more, that it was a hunger for revanche so strong that a political novice and accused rapist could topple the leadership of one major party and throttle the heavily favored nominee of the other.

"I could stand in the middle of Fifth Avenue and shoot somebody and I wouldn't lose any voters," Trump bragged in January 2016. This statement should be met with only a modicum of skepticism. Trump has mocked the disabled, withstood multiple accusations of sexual violence (all of which he has denied), fired an FBI director, sent his minions to mislead the public about his motives, personally exposed those lies by boldly stating his aim to scuttle an investigation into his possible collusion with a foreign power, then bragged about that same obstruction to representatives of that same foreign power. It is utterly impossible to conjure a black facsimile of Donald Trump—to imagine Obama, say, implicating an opponent's father in the assassination of an American president or comparing his physical endowment with that of another candidate and then successfully capturing the presidency. Trump, more than any other politician, understood the valence of the bloody heirloom and the great power in not being a nigger.

But the power is ultimately suicidal. Trump evinces this, too. In a recent *New Yorker* article, a former Russian military officer pointed out that interference in an election could succeed only where "necessary conditions" and an "existing background" were present. In America, that "existing background" was a persistent racism, and the "necessary condition" was a black president. The two related factors hobbled America's ability to safeguard its electoral system. As late as July 2016, a majority of Republican voters doubted that Barack Obama had been born in the United States, which is to say they did not view him as a legitimate president. Republican politicians acted accordingly, infamously denying his final Supreme Court nominee a hearing and then, fatefully, refusing to work with the administration to defend the country against the Russian attack. Before the election, Obama found no takers among Republicans for a bipartisan response, and Obama himself, underestimating Trump and thus underestimating the power of whiteness, believed the Republican nominee too objectionable to actually win. In this Obama was, tragically, wrong. And so the most powerful country in the world has handed over all its affairs—the prosperity of its entire economy; the security of its 300 million citizens; the purity of its water, the viability of its air, the safety of its food; the future of its vast system of education; the soundness of its national highways, airways, and railways; the apocalyptic potential of its nuclear arsenal—to a carnival barker who introduced the phrase *grab 'em by the pussy* into the national lexicon. It is as if the white tribe united in demonstration to say, "If a black man can be president, then any white man—no matter how fallen—can be president." And in that perverse way, the democratic dreams of Jefferson and Jackson were fulfilled.

The American tragedy now being wrought is larger than most imagine and will not end with Trump. In recent times, whiteness as an overt political tactic has been restrained by a kind of cordiality that held that its overt invocation would scare off "moderate" whites. This has proved to be only half true at best. Trump's legacy will be exposing the patina of decency for what it is and revealing just how much a demagogue can get away with. It does not take much to imagine another politician, wiser in the ways of Washington and better schooled in the methodology of governance—and now liberated from the pretense of antiracist civility—doing a much more effective job than Trump.

It has long been an axiom among certain black writers and thinkers that while whiteness endangers the bodies of black people in the immediate sense, the larger threat is to white people themselves, the shared country, and even the whole world.

There is an impulse to blanch at this sort of grandiosity. When W. E. B. Du Bois claims that slavery was "singularly disastrous for modern civilization" or James Baldwin claims that whites "have brought humanity to the edge of oblivion: because they think they are white," the instinct is to cry exaggeration. But there really is no other way to read the presidency of Donald Trump. The first white president in American history is also the most dangerous president—and he is made more dangerous still by the fact that those charged with analyzing him cannot name his essential nature, because they too are implicated in it.

QUESTIONS FOR MAKING CONNECTIONS
WITHIN THE READING

1. Coates writes about a contemporary event—the election of Donald Trump—but he does it in a way many readers might not appreciate. Responding to the barrage of the President's lies (more than five a day, according to the *New York Times*), many journalists have chosen to put their energies into countering the lies with facts—objective evidence. But in "The First White President," Coates takes a strikingly different approach by *historicizing* the present. "Historicizing" means that he provides an historical or "diachronic" context missing from responses that focus on the contemporary moment exclusively. Fighting lies with facts is essential work that journalists should never abandon, but facts by themselves cannot explain why some facts escape attention while others crowd out everything else. Reread Coates's essay, looking at the moments when he injects history into the discussion. What effect do these moments have on your experience as a reader? How do they change the way you understand contemporary events?

2. The most important term in Coates's essay is, of course, "whiteness." Underline or highlight all the places where the word appears. What is "whiteness," according to Coates? Does he view it as a biological category or does he see as a cultural and historical construct? What does it mean to say that whiteness is a "cultural construct"? In other words, how did it get constructed, by whom and

for what purposes? Be sure to consider the relationship between race and class. In what ways, according to Coates, did the invention of "whiteness" distract working people of European descent from making common cause with other working people? How did whiteness help to bolster the distinction between a "worker" and a "slave"? What are the differences?

3.   On the basis of your reading of the essay, would you define Coates as a liberal or a Democrat? Would you define him as a conservative or a Republican? To what degree does he fit within any of these categories? What specifically does Coates have to say about liberals and their attitudes towards black Americans? Describe the nature of his reservations about Bill and Hillary Clinton. What seems to be his attitude towards liberal reformers like Senator Bernie Sanders, the political scientist Mark Lilla or the journalists Nicholas Kristof and George Packer? Do you think that Coates sees both parties as complicit in the perpetuation of whiteness? Would he see them as *equally* complicit or complicit in the same ways? Why does whiteness play such an important role in American political life?

QUESTIONS FOR WRITING

1.   Drawing from the information that Coates provides, explain the meaning of "whiteness." As you develop your explanation, be sure to consider its social and cultural roles. What kinds of distinctions and divisions does "whiteness" create, and how do those distinctions and divisions function in our society today? Who benefits from the persistence of whiteness and who is disadvantaged? Why have so many observers, progressive as well as conservative, attributed Trump's victory to working-class resentment instead of a racism that can be found among all classes, including the wealthiest and best educated? To what degree is the system as a whole dependent on the existence of a racialized "other"?

2.   Starting in 2015, the United States ceased to be classified as a "full democracy" by the *Economist* magazine's respected Intelligence Unit (EIU). At the top of the top of the EIU's list of full democracies were Norway, Iceland, Sweden, New Zealand and Denmark, with Ireland and Canada tied for sixth place.

    The writers of the report explicitly say that Donald Trump is not to blame because he was a symptom, rather than the cause, of the country's decline. The cause, they conclude, was a loss of trust in government:

> By tapping a deep strain of political disaffection with the functioning of democracy, Mr. Trump became a beneficiary of the low esteem in which US voters hold their government, elected representatives, and political parties, but he was not responsible for a problem that has had a long gestation.

What role might whiteness play in discrediting our political institutions? To what degree is whiteness at odds with democracy itself? To what degree is it an expression of democracy? Does the problem of whiteness force us to choose between different definitions of democracy: democracy as equality and democracy as majority rule?

QUESTIONS FOR MAKING CONNECTIONS BETWEEN READINGS

1. In "Biographies of Hegemony," anthropologist Karen Ho describes the process of socialization that naturalizes inequality—that makes it seem "natural" and normal. People learn to accept that special privileges rightfully belong to those endowed with "smartness":

    > The "culture of smartness" is central to understanding Wall Street's financial agency, how investment bankers are personally and institutionally empowered to enact their worldviews, export their practices, and serve as models for far-reaching socioeconomic change. On Wall Street, "smartness" means much more than individual intelligence; it conveys a naturalized and generic sense of "impressiveness," of elite, pinnacle status and expertise which is used to signify, even prove, investment bankers' worthiness.

    To what degree does the whiteness described by Coates also support a form of "hegemony"? Explore the parallels between smartness and whiteness, but also the ways they might differ. Is smartness also racialized? Does whiteness rely on competition and merit to justify the advantages it conveys? Does smartness do the same—or does it only appear to?

2. In his chapter, "Son," Andrew Solomon introduces readers to two different kinds of identity:

    > Because of the transmission of identity from one generation to the next, most children share at least some traits with their parents. These are vertical identities. Attributes and values are passed down from parent to child across the generations not only through strands of DNA but also through shared cultural norms. Ethnicity, for example, is a *vertical* identity.... Often, however, someone has an inherent or acquired trait that is foreign to his or her parents and must therefore acquire identity from a peer group. This is a *horizontal* identity.... Being gay is a horizontal identity.

To what degree does whiteness qualify as a horizontal identity, and to what degree is it vertical? To what extent do whiteness and its correlate, blackness, complicate Solomon's account of identity? Generally, people inherit a vertical identity whereas they chose a horizontal identity. Is this true of whiteness? Is it true of blackness?

◆◆◆

CATHY DAVIDSON

REMARKABLY, CATHY N. DAVIDSON occupies two distinguished faculty chairs at Duke University, but reputation never stands in her way when it comes to taking controversial positions. Over the last decade she has become one of the most impassioned advocates of the electronic media—which, she argues, have the potential to transform our ways of thinking more radically than any invention since the printing press. At a time when many observers mourn the demise of the book, Davidson argues that we need to embrace the possibilities of the Web: an explosive growth of new knowledge, nearly immediate access, and an unprecedented freedom in the shaping of information itself. She urges that this spirit of creativity should extend beyond the screen to the schools, which she sees as backward looking at a time when educators finally have the tools to end a spirit-crushing uniformity. Far from pushing the arts and humanities into obsolescence, the new technologies could provide the means for all of us to participate in the making of culture.

Not everyone agrees, however, with Davidson about the new media. In a review for the online journal *Slate*, Annie Paul Murphy accuses her of capitulating to the hype about the wonders of the Web:

> [Davidson] is easily moved to rapture and to dismay, propelled by an enthusiasm for anything new and digital and by an almost allergic aversion to any practices or artifacts from the pre–Internet era. Nor does she have much use for people born before 1980. The inhabitants and the knowledge of the past are merely obstacles to be trampled in the headlong rush toward an interactive, connected, collaborative future. This future, as Davidson imagines it, is one in which games replace books, online collaboration replaces individual effort, and "crowdsourced" verdicts replace expertise.

Other critics of the Web, if not of Davidson herself, argue that it has undermined our ability to read carefully by teaching us to "skim" instead of pausing to reflect. Whatever readers might ultimately decide about these criticisms, Davidson has had the integrity to put her ideas into practice. From 1998 to 2006 she served as Vice

Provost for Interdisciplinary Studies at Duke University and helped to create ISIS, Duke's highly successful program in Information Science and Information Studies. While a vice provost at Duke she created quite a stir when her university, in partnership with Apple, Inc., distributed free iPods to all incoming students. In spite of the scandal, or perhaps because of it, President Obama nominated Davidson to a six-year term on the National Council on the Humanities. The following selection comes from Davidson's book *Now You See It: How Technology and Brain Science Will Transform Schools and Business for the 21st Century* (2011).

Project Classroom Makeover

The *Newsweek* cover story proclaimed, "iPod, Therefore I Am."

On MTV News, it was "Dude, I just got a free iPod!"

Peter Jennings smirked at the ABC-TV news audience, "Shakespeare on the iPod? Calculus on the iPod!"

The online academic publication *Inside Higher Ed* worried for our reputation. How would Duke University "deal with the perception that one of the country's finest institutions—with selective admissions, a robust enrollment, and a plush endowment—would stoop to a publicity ploy"?

And *The Duke Chronicle* was apoplectic: "The University seems intent on transforming the iPod into an academic device, when the simple fact of the matter is that iPods are made to listen to music. It is an unnecessarily expensive toy that does not become an academic tool simply because it is thrown into a classroom."[1]

What had these pundits so riled up? In 2003, we at Duke were approached by Apple about becoming one of six "Apple Digital Campuses." Each campus would choose a technology that Apple was then developing and would propose a campus wide use for it. It would be a partnership of business and education, exploratory in all ways. One university selected Apple PowerBooks loaded with iLife digital audio and video production software. Another chose e-portfolios, online workspaces where students could develop multimedia projects together and then archive them. Another selected audio software for creating audio archives and other infrastructure. What landed us in hot water was that, at Duke, instead of any of these, we chose a flashy new music-listening gadget that young people loved but that baffled most adults: iPods.

In 2003, the iPod did not have a single known educational app, nor did it seem to fall into that staid, stolid, overpriced, and top-down category known as IT, or instructional technology. Gigantic billboards had sprung up everywhere showing young people dancing, their silhouettes wild against brilliant bright backgrounds. What could possibly be educational about iPods? No one was thinking about their learning potential because they were so clearly about young users, not about IT administrators. That's why they intrigued us.

Our thinking was that educators had to begin taking seriously the fact that incoming students were born after the information age was in full swing. They were the last entering class who, as a group, would remember the before and after of the Internet. If they were born roughly in 1985 or so, they would have been entering grade school around the time that Tim Berners-Lee was inventing the protocols for the World Wide Web. These kids had grown up searching for information online. They had grown up socializing online, too, playing games with their friends online and, of course, sharing music files online. Categories and distinctions that an earlier generation of students would have observed in school and at home, between knowledge making and play, came bundled in a new way for this first generation of kids who, in their informal learning, were blurring that boundary. Their schools hadn't changed much, but at home, online, they were already information searchers. They had learned by googling. What if instead of telling them what they should know, we asked them? What if we continued the lesson of the Internet itself and let them lead us into a new, exploratory way of learning in order to see if this self-directed way might mean something when it came to education? What if we assumed that their experiences online had already patterned their brains to a different kind of intellectual experimentation—and what if we let them show us where the pedagogical results of such an experiment might lead?

From the way most schools operated in 2003—from preschool to graduate schools—you wouldn't have had much of an idea that the Internet had ever been invented. It was as if young people were still going to the library to look in the *Encyclopedia Britannica* for knowledge, under the watchful eye of the friendly local librarian. Schools of education were still training teachers without regard for the opportunities and potential of a generation of kids who, from preschool on, had been transfixed by digital media.

The opportunity seemed to be staring us in the face. At home, five-year olds were playing Pokémon every chance they could, exchanging the cards at preschool with their pals, and then designing tools online to customize their characters and even writing elementary code to streamline their game play. They were memorizing hundreds of character names and roles and mastering a nine-year-old reading level just to play, but teacher training on every level was still text-based. It was as if schools were based on a kind of "hunt-and-peck" literacy, whereas kids were learning through searching, surfing, and browsing the Web. They were playing games in 3-D multimedia, learning to read and write not through schoolbooks but as they played games online and then traded their Pokémon cards with their friends.

When Duke announced that we would be giving a free iPod to every member of the entering first-year class, there were no conditions. We simply asked students to dream up learning applications for this cool little white device with the adorable earbuds, and we invited them to pitch their ideas to the faculty. If one of their profs decided to use iPods in a course, the prof, too, would receive a free Duke-branded iPod and so would all the students in the class (whether they were first-years or not). We would not control the result. This was an educational experiment without a syllabus. No lesson plan. No assessment matrix rigged to show that our investment had been a wise one.... After all, as we knew from the science of attention, to direct attention in one way precluded all the other ways. So we asked our basic questions in as broad and open-ended a way possible: *Are there interesting learning applications for this device that is taking over young America as a source of entertainment?* And then the most revolutionary question of all: *What do you students have to tell us about learning in a digital age?*

If it were a reality show, you might call it Project Classroom Makeover. It was a little wild, a little wicked, exactly what you have to do to create a calculated exercise in disruption, distraction, and difference: a lesson in institutional unlearning, in breaking our own patterns and trying to understand more of the intellectual habits of a new generation of students and providing a unique space where those new talents might flourish. Instead of teaching, we hoped to learn. We wanted to tap into a wellspring of knowledge young people brought to college from their own informal learning outside of school. We didn't know what would happen, but we had faith that the students would come up with something interesting. Or not. We couldn't deny that failure was also a possibility.

At the time, I was vice provost for interdisciplinary studies at Duke, a position equivalent to what in industry would be the R & D (research and development) person, and I was among those responsible for cooking up the iPod experiment and figuring out how it could work in the most interesting ways.[2] We wanted to stir up some of the assumptions in traditional higher education. We didn't count on causing the uproar that we did. We assumed some of our fellow educators would raise an eyebrow, but we didn't imagine an educational innovation would land us on the cover of *Newsweek*. Usually, if education is on the cover, it's another grim national report on how we are falling behind in the global brain race. Come to think of it, that *is* what the *Newsweek* cover story was about! Like Socrates before us, Duke was leading youth astray, tugging them down the slippery slope to perdition by thin, white vinyl iPod cords.

We were inverting the traditional roles of teacher and learner, the fundamental principle in education: hierarchy based on credentials. The authority principle, based on top-down expertise, is the foundation of formal education, from kindergarten playgroups to advanced graduate courses. At least since the GI Bill that followed World War II, and the rapid expansion at that time of the public university system, a college degree has been the entry card to middle-class, white-collar achievement. Not graduating from high school and lacking a college degree has constituted failure, and education has constructed its objectives backward from that (negative) goal, in some cities all the way down to competition for the right private nursery school.

What this means for young people who come to an elite private university is that they have taken one of a number of specific routes to get there. One way is to test to get into the best preschools so you can go to the best private grammar schools so you can be admitted to the most elite boarding schools so you can be competitive at the Ivies or an elite school outside the Ivies like Stanford or Duke. Another way is through public schools, a lifetime of determined and focused study, getting A's and even A+ grades in every class, always taking the most difficult courses, earning perfect scores on tests, and doing lots of extracurricular work, too. These students have been focused toward educational achievement their entire lives.[3] We wondered what these astonishing young overachievers would do if given the chance not to follow the rules but to make them.

In the world of technology, *crowdsourcing* means inviting a group to collaborate on a solution to a problem, but that term didn't yet exist in 2003 when we conducted the iPod experiment. It was coined by Jeff Howe of *Wired* magazine in 2006 to refer to the widespread Internet practice of posting an open call requesting help in completing some task, ranging from writing code (that's how the open source code that powers the Mozilla browser was written) to creating a winning logo (such as the "Birdie" design of Twitter, which cost a total of six bucks).[4] Crowdsourcing is "outsourcing" to the "crowd," and it works best when you observe three nonhierarchical principles. First, the fundamental principle of all crowdsourcing is that difference and diversity—not expertise and uniformity—solves problems. Second, if you predict the result in any way, if you try to force a solution, you limit the participation and therefore the likelihood of success. And third, the community most served by the solution should be chiefly involved in the process of finding it.

In the iPod experiment, we were crowdsourcing educational innovation for a digital age to our incoming students. We were walking the walk. Crowdsourced thinking is very different from credentialing, or relying on top-down expertise. If anything, crowdsourcing is suspicious of expertise, because the more expert we are, the more likely we are to be limited in what we even conceive to be the problem, let alone the answer. While formal education typically teaches hierarchies of what's worth paying attention to, crowdsourcing works differently, in that it assumes that no one of us individually is smarter than all of us collectively. No matter how expert we are, no matter how brilliant, we can improve, we can learn, by sharing insights and working together collectively.

Once the pieces were in place, we decided to take our educational experiment one step further. By giving the iPods to the first-year students, we ended up with a lot of angry sophomores, juniors, and seniors. They'd paid hefty private-university tuitions too! So we relented and said *any* student could have a free iPod—just so long as she convinced a prof to require one for a course and came up with a learning app in that course.

Does that sound sneaky? Far be it from me to say that we *planned* this, but once the upperclassmen coveted the iPods, once they'd begun to protest enviously and vehemently, those iPods suddenly tripled and quadrupled in perceived value: Everyone wanted one.

If "Shakespeare on the iPod" is the smirking setup, here's the punch line: Within one year, we had distributed more free iPods to students in forty-eight separate "iPod courses" than we had given without strings to the 1,650 entering first-year students.

That was vindicating enough, but it wasn't all. The real treasure trove was to be found in the students' innovations. Working together, and often alongside their profs, they came up with far more learning apps for their iPods than anyone—even at Apple—had dreamed possible. No one has ever accused Steve Jobs of not being cagey, and Apple's Digital Campus strategy was an R & D winner. The company's flagship technology now had an active lab of students creating new apps for it. There was also plenty of publicity for the iPod as a potential learning tool—the teenagers of America should all thank us for making it easier to pitch the purchase to their parents. In the first year of the iPod experiment, Duke students came up with dozens of stunning new ways to learn. Most predictable were uses whereby students downloaded audio archives relevant to their courses—Nobel Prize acceptance speeches by physicists and poets, the McCarthy hearings, famous trials, congressional debates, or readings by T. S. Eliot or Toni Morrison, or Thomas Edison's famous recitation of "Mary Had a Little Lamb"—one of the first sound recordings ever made. Almost instantly students figured out that they could also record lectures on their iPods and listen at their leisure. Classes from Spanish 101 to Introduction to Jazz to organic chemistry could be taped and listened to anywhere. You didn't have to go to the library or the language lab to study. You could listen to assignments on the bus, at the gym, while out on a run—and everyone did. Because everyone had the device, sound suddenly had a new educational role in our text- and visuals-dominated classroom culture.

Some version of this convenient form of listening was possible with that radical eighties technology, the Sony Walkman. But the Walkman connected to radio and to tapes, not to the World Wide Web, with its infinite amount of information ready for downloading.

Interconnection was the part the students grasped before any of us did. Students who had grown up connected digitally gravitated to ways that the iPod could be used for *collective* learning. They turned the iPods into social media and networked their learning in ways we did not anticipate. In the School of the Environment, with the encouragement of Professor Marie Lynn Miranda, one class interviewed families in a North Carolina community concerned with lead paint in their homes and schools. Each student would upload the day's interviews to a course Web site, and any other student could download and comment on the interviews. At the end of the course, they combined their interviews, edited them digitally, and created an audio documentary that aired on local and regional radio stations and all over the Web.[5]

Some med students realized that there was an audio library of all the possible heart arrhythmias, but no way to access it in a real-time health exam. They came up with a way to put a stethoscope in one ear, using very simple signal-tracking technology to match what they were hearing in the patient's chest to the cataloged conditions. The implications of this original use were obvious, and soon students studying to be doctors and nurses were "operationalizing" such techniques for the diagnostic use of doctors in rural North Carolina and Africa. Dr. Martha Adams, a senior administrator at the Duke School of Medicine, grasped how revolutionary it was to be able to make state-of-the-art medical research available to those far outside major research centers, and to also make it possible for doctors elsewhere to report on health problems and patterns they were observing in their own communities, thus advancing medical research in both directions. Soon she was working with the National Institutes of Health and leading a national outreach iPod initiative. Once again, attention was being focused in multiple directions at once, not just on outcomes but on process and on interaction, the mirroring happening (as it must, definitionally) in both directions.

In the music department, composing students uploaded compositions to their iPods so their fellow students could listen and critique. Music performance students inserted their voices or their instruments into duets or choruses or orchestras. You could listen to how you sounded as first chair in the flute section of a famous philharmonic orchestra. Students in Duke's engineering department had a field day mangling and dissecting their iPods to study (hack, some would say) everything from Apple's ultrasecret computer code to the physical properties of the famous white plastic exterior of the original iPods.

And they began exploring apps, developing applications that could be added to the iPod's repertoire of abilities without Apple having to give away its proprietary code. In other words, the iPod could still remain an iPod with its own distinctive characteristics, but it could change and morph as new features were added and new capabilities emerged, including some developed by users. To me, this was a conceptual breakthrough: that a commercial product might also be susceptible to consumer customization, a way of extending the infinitely changeable open-source properties of the Internet itself to a product with a far more fixed, finite identity. It was a hybrid of old and new thinking. If that isn't a metaphor for attention in the digital age, I don't know what is.

By the end of our first experimental year, Duke was part of a new movement to transform the iPod from a listening device into an interactive broadcasting device. We were proud to host the world's first-ever academic "podcasting" conference early in 2005. I recently found one of our announcements for the conference and was amused to see those quotation marks around *podcasting*. No one was quite sure even what to call this new phenomenon, in which you could record a lecture, upload it to a Web site, and then anyone anywhere in the world could download it. Shakespeare on an iPod? Absolutely. And that lecture on Shakespeare delivered in the Allen Building at Duke could later be listened to by a student riding a bus in Bangkok or Brasilia. That may not seem revolutionary now. It is hard to remember way back then, in the distant past of the Internet, before iPhones and netbooks, before MySpace and Facebook, and a full two years before YouTube was invented with its motto to "Broadcast Yourself."

The first podcasting conference drew standing-room-only attendance. It was sponsored by one of the first programs I'd spearheaded at Duke, something (another hybrid) called Information Science + Information Studies, or ISIS for short—artists and computer scientists, social scientists and engineers, and everyone in between in a new configuration. Lots of news media crowded into the auditorium at the Center for Interdisciplinary Engineering, Medicine, and Applied Science to witness the event. In a short span, the message had changed from "How could anyone possibly think this device could be used for learning?" to "This device facilitates sophisticated academic research and has the potential to make that learning instantly available to anyone in the world—for free."

The conceptual breakthrough of podcasting was access. It was expensive buying all those iPods, but the result was a breakthrough in education far beyond Duke, one whose purpose was to make a world of information cheaper to access than it ever had been before. With very little outlay, you had the potential of transmitting anything you heard, anywhere: You could download anything you heard worldwide. Not prerecorded programs made by professionals but content created and uploaded by anyone, ready for downloading—and for remixing and uploading again. When we launched the iPod experiment, no one expected that someday there would be an iTunes U (formed in 2007) with over 350,000 lectures and other educational audio and video files compiled by universities, libraries, and museums all around the world and available for download.

Duke took a lot of heat for being a "rich, privileged institution" that could afford this frivolity, but a revolution in the democratization of knowledge is not frivolous, especially considering that, once customized, an individual mobile device is actually an inexpensive computer. Several years after the Duke experiment, in the fall of 2008, Culbreth Middle School, a public school in nearby Chapel Hill, North Carolina, created its own iPod program for an experimental group of staff and students. They chose the iPod instead of a more traditional laptop because of "the mobility of the device in one's pocket with instant access to information and apps."[6] In January 2010, seventh graders were encouraged to explore the different ways their iPods could be used to keep them informed in the wake of the disastrous earthquake that brought destruction to Haiti. They used iPods to gather measurements of earthquake magnitude and related information, including demographic data, humanitarian assistance updates, local Haitian news podcasts, and historical information on Haitian culture and politics. The device also performed Creole-language translation. Students were even able to maintain up-to-date communication with a local graduate student who was in Haiti at the time and was badly injured in the earthquake. They used their iPods to educate themselves about a terrible disaster far away and produced their own podcasts from the information they gleaned. The experiment left little doubt that in the event of an emergency closer to home, students would be able to contribute their new knowledge to disaster-relief and fund-raising efforts locally.

The iPod experiment was not an investment in technology. It was an investment in a new form of attention, one that didn't require the student to always face forward, learn from on high, memorize what was already a given, or accept knowledge as something predetermined and passively absorbed. It was also an investment in student-led curiosity, whose object was not a hunk of white plastic, but the very nature of interactivity, crowdsourcing, customizing, and inspired inquiry-driven problem solving. At our most ambitious, we hoped to change the one-directional model of attention that has formed the twentieth-century classroom.[7]

THIS IPOD EXPERIMENT WAS A start at finding a new learning paradigm of formal education for the digital era. As we have [learned], an infant's neural pathways are being sheared and shaped along with his values and his behavior in constant interaction with the people around him who exert influence over his life. The iPod experiment was an acknowledgment that the brain is, above all, interactive, that it selects, repeats, and mirrors, always, constantly, in complex interactions with the world. The experiment was also an acknowledgment that the chief mode of informal learning for a new generation of students had been changed by the World Wide Web. It was an attempt to put the new science of attention together with the new digital technology that both demanded and, in some ways, helped produce it.

I'm not going to argue that the *interactive* task of surfing is better or worse than the reception model that dominated mass education in the twentieth century. "Better" and "worse" don't make a lot of sense to me. But there's a difference and, as we have seen, difference is what we pay attention to. Said another way, we concentrate in a different way when we are making the connections, when we are clicking and browsing, than when we are watching (as in a TV show or movie) or listening or even reading a book. Indisputably, the imagination is engaged in making connections in all of those forms, as it is in anything we experience. It is engaged in a different way when we ourselves are making the connections, when we're browsing from one to another link that interests us and draws our attention. We don't need a "better or worse" because we have both, and both are potentially rich and fascinating cognitive activities. But the relative newness of the surfing/searching experience drove our interest in the potential of the iPod experiment; in 2003, educators already knew how to mine traditional media, but we had not yet figured out how to harness the new forms of attention students who had grown up surfing the Web were mastering. The Web does not prescribe a clear, linear pathway through the content. There is no one way to move along a straight-and-narrow road from beginning to end.

The formal education most of us experienced—and which we now often think of when we picture a classroom—is based on giving premium value to expertise, specialization, and hierarchy. It prepared us for success in the twentieth century, when those things mattered above all. Yet what form of education is required in the information age, when what matters has grown very different? What form of education is required in a world of social networking, crowdsourcing, customizing, and user-generated content; a world of searching and browsing, where the largest-ever encyclopedia is created not by experts but by volunteers around the world—as is the world's second most popular Web browser (Mozilla's Firefox), the world's most massive online multiplayer game (World of Warcraft, with over 11 million subscribers a month), and all the social networking and communication sites, from MySpace and Facebook to Twitter?

Another way of asking the question is: How do we make over the twentieth-century classroom to take advantage of all the remarkable digital benefits of the twenty-first century?

The iPod experiment was a start, but to get a sense of just how big a task we face, it's useful to have a sense of how schools came to be the way they are, shaped by the values of a very different world.

Do you remember the classic story by Washington Irving, "The Legend of Sleepy Hollow"? It was written in 1820 and features a parody of the pompous schoolmaster in the form of Ichabod Crane, a homely, gawky, and self-satisfied pedant who is confident in his role as a dispenser of knowledge. He knows what does and does not constitute knowledge worth having and is equally sure that students must be drilled in that knowledge and tested to make sure they measure up. If you blindfolded Ichabod Crane, spun him around, and set him down in a twenty-first-century classroom, he would be baffled by electricity, dumbfounded by moving images, confused by the computers and cell phones, but he'd know exactly where to stand, and he'd know exactly where he stood.

It's shocking to think of how much the world has changed since the horse-and-buggy days of Sleepy Hollow and how little has changed within the traditional classroom in America. On March 10, 2010, the National Governors Association and the Council of Chief State School Officers even called for "sweeping new school standards that could lead to students across the country using the same math and English textbooks and taking the same tests, replacing a patchwork of state and local systems in an attempt to raise student achievement nationwide."[8] Ichabod Crane lives!

What in the world is going on? In the past in America, times of enormous innovation in the rest of society, including in technology and in industry, have also been times of tremendous innovation in education. What has happened to us? Rather than thinking of ways we can be preparing our students for their future, we seem determined to prepare them for our past.

Literally. The current passion for national standards is reminiscent of the conversations on education at our country's beginnings, back in 1787, the year the U.S. Constitution was adopted. Technology was changing the world then, too. At the time of the signing of the Constitution, the new invention of steam-powered presses, coupled with the invention of machine-made ink and paper, made for mass printing of cheap books and newspapers, putting print into the hands of middle-class readers for the first time in human history. The new institution of the circulating library made books available even to the working poor. Books proliferated; newspapers sprang up everywhere. And that's when a cry for standards and public education was born in America, in response to a new democratic government that needed informed citizens and new technologies of print that made books and newspapers widely available.

Thomas Jefferson himself advocated that America had to launch a "crusade against ignorance" if the nation was to survive as an independent representative democracy.[9] By 1791, when the Bill of Rights was added to the U.S. Constitution, seven states were making provisions for public education. There was not yet anything like an "educational system" in the United States, though. Education was attended to unevenly by local, regional, state, and private institutions, some secular, some sectarian, an inheritance that continues to this day in the form of state-controlled educational policy, local and regional school boards, and other decentralized means of oversight.

Horace Mann, whose name can be found over the entrance of many public schools in America, was the first great champion of national educational reform. The son of a farmer of limited means, Mann clawed his way to an education, earning money by braiding straw to pay the local tuitions for the elementary schools he attended for only six weeks at a time, leaving the rest of his time free to help with family farming operations. He enrolled at Brown University at age twenty, graduated in three years as valedictorian of the class of 1819, and dedicated himself to the creation of the "common schools," which after around 1840 became the predecessor of a free, publicly supported education system.

The common schools were scheduled around the agriculture year so farm kids could attend too. The schools were open to both boys and girls, regardless of class, although several states explicitly forbade the attendance of nonwhite children. The schools were locally controlled, with the kind of local politics governing curriculum and textbook assignments then that we see now in the state-by-state regulation of education, even after our "national educational policy" has been adopted.

Mandatory, compulsory public schooling developed over the course of the last half of the nineteenth century and got its full wind at the turn into the twentieth century as part of America's process of industrialization. Public education was seen as the most efficient way to train potential workers for labor in the newly urbanized factories. Teaching them control, socializing them for the mechanized, routinized labor of the factory was all part of the educational imperative of the day. Whether meant to calm the supposedly unruly immigrant populace coming to American shores or to urbanize farmers freshly arriving in the city, education was designed to train unskilled workers to new tasks that required a special, dedicated form of attention. School was thought to be the right training ground for discipline and uniformity. Kids started attending school at the same age, passed through a carefully graduated system, and were tested systematically on a standardized curriculum, with subjects that were taught in time blocks throughout the day. In ways large and small, the process mimicked the forms of specialized labor on the assembly line, as well as the divisions of labor (from the CEO down to the manual laborers) in the factory itself.

Many features now common in twenty-first-century public education began as an accommodation to the new industrial model of the world ushered in during the last part of the nineteenth century. With machines that needed to run on schedule and an assembly line that required human precision and efficiency, schools began to place a great emphasis on time and timeliness. Curriculum, too, was directed toward focusing on a task, including the mastery of a specified syllabus of required learning. "Efficiency" was the byword of the day, in the world of work and in the world of school. Learning to pay attention as directed—through rote memorization and mastery of facts—was important, and schools even developed forms of rapid-fire question-and-answer, such as the spelling bee or the math bee. This was a new skill, different from the elite models of question-and-answer based on the Socratic method; the agrarian model of problem solving, in which one is responsible for spotting a problem and solving it (whether a wilted corn tassel or an injured horse); and the apprenticeship model of the guild wherein one learned a craft by imitating the skills of a master. An assembly line is far more regular and regulated. One person's tardiness, no matter how good the excuse, can destroy everyone else's productivity on the line. Mandatory and compulsory schooling for children was seen as a way of teaching basic knowledge—including the basic knowledge of tasks, obedience, hierarchy, and schedules. The school bell became a symbol of public education in the industrial era.[10]

So did specialization. With the advent of the assembly line, work became segmented. A worker didn't perform a whole job but one discrete task and then passed the job on to the next person and the next and so forth down the assembly line. The ideal of labor efficiency displaced the ideal of artisanship, with increased attention paid to the speed and accuracy of one kind of contribution to a larger industrial process. Focused attention to a task became the ideal form of attention, so different from, for example, the farmer on his horse scanning his land for anything that might look out of place or simply in need of care.

By 1900, state and regional schools were becoming the norm, replacing locally managed ones, and by 1918, every state had passed laws mandating children to attend elementary school or more. A concession was made to Catholics in that they could create a separate, parochial school system that would also meet these state regulations, another legacy that comes down to the present in the form of "faith-based schools."

During the first six decades of the twentieth century, as America ascended to the position of a world power, the rhetoric of education followed suit, with an increasing emphasis on producing leaders. While the nineteenth-century common schools had focused on elementary education, the twentieth-century focus was increasingly on the institution of high school, including improving graduation rates. In 1900, approximately 15 percent of the U.S. population received a high school diploma, a number that increased to around 50 percent by 1950.

After World War II, there was a rapid expansion of both high schools and higher education, invigorated after 1957 when the Russians surprised the world by launching *Sputnik,* the first man-made object ever to orbit the earth. As America competed against Russian science in the Cold War, policy makers placed more and more emphasis on educational attainment. Many economists argue that America's economic growth through the 1960s was fueled by this educational expansion.

Robert Schwartz, dean of the Harvard Graduate School of Education, notes that since the last quarter of the twentieth century, the pattern of educational expansion that has characterized the United States from the Revolutionary War forward has changed.[11] Since 1975, American educational attainment has leveled off or even dropped while there has been a dramatic increase in the number of jobs requiring exploratory, creative problem solving typically encouraged by postsecondary education. We are seeing the first signs that our education system is slipping in comparison to our needs.

The current high school graduation rate is roughly the same as it was in 1975, approximately 75 percent. Our graduation rate from four-year colleges is

28 percent, also roughly the same as it was thirty-five years ago. That this has even remained consistent in the face of all that has changed in the last thirty-five years is remarkable enough, a credit to both the drive and quality of American students and the patchwork, piecemeal reforms we've used to hold the system together. Yet while we've been holding steady, other countries have made rapid gains. Whereas in the 1960s we ranked first in the proportion of adults with high school degrees, we now rank thirteenth on the list of the thirty countries surveyed by the Organisation for Economic Co-operation and Development (OECD), an organization that coordinates statistics from market-based democracies to promote growth. By contrast, South Korea has moved from twenty-seventh place on that list to our old number one spot.

Most troubling is what happened from 1995 to 2005. During this one decade, the United States dropped from second to fifteenth place in college completion rates among OECD nations. For the wealthiest and most powerful nation on earth to rank fifteenth is nothing short of a national disgrace. This is especially the case, given that our system of education *presumes* college preparation is the ideal, even in environments where most kids are not going on to college. By that standard, we are failing.

It's not that we cared about education before 1975 but don't today. Our heart is not the problem. Look at the numbers. The Swiss are the only people on earth who spend more per child on public education than Americans. According to OECD, we spend over $11,000 per year per child on public education. That's more than double the rate of South Korea. Education spending accounts for more than 7 percent of our GDP.[12] However, the OECD statistics show that our graduation rates now are roughly on a par with those of Turkey and Mexico, not nations to which we like to compare ourselves by other indicators of our power or success.[13]

It is little wonder that educators and parents are constantly reacting to the comparative, global numbers with ever more strident calls for standards. The problem, however, is the confusion of "high standards" with "standardization." Our national educational policy depends on standardized tests, but it is not at all clear that preparing students to achieve high test scores is equivalent to setting a high standard for what and how kids should know and learn.

The real issue isn't that our schools are too challenging. It's the opposite. Among the top quartile of high school students, the most frequent complaint and cause of disaffection from schooling is boredom and lack of rigor. That also happens to be true among the lowest group, for whom low expectations lead to low motivation.[14] Kids aren't failing because school is too hard but because it doesn't interest them. It doesn't capture their attention.

Relevance has been proved to be a crucial factor for keeping students in high school, especially mid- and lower-level students. Tie what kids learn in school to what they can use in their homes, their families, and their neighborhood—and vice versa—and not surprisingly, that relevance kicks their likelihood of staying in school up a few notches. Because in the United States (but not in many countries with higher college attendance), going to college requires money for tuition, our emphasis on college as the grail of secondary education only rubs in its inaccessibility (its irrelevance) to lower-income kids—a fact that contributes to high school dropouts. Finally, for all groups, and especially for students in the lowest-achieving group, relationships with teachers and counselors who believe in them and support them (often against peer, familial, or cultural pressure) is a determining factor in remaining in school. These key factors for educational success—rigor, relevance, and relationships—have been dubbed the new three *Rs,* with student-teacher ratio being particularly important. Small class size has been proved to be one of the single most significant factors in kids' staying in and succeeding in school. Twenty seems to be the magic number.[15] Even on a neurological level, brain researchers have shown that kids improve with directed, special attention to their own skills and interests, the opposite of our move toward standardization.[16]

The biggest problem we face now is the increasing mismatch between traditional curricular standards of content-based instruction and the new forms of thinking required by our digital, distributed workplace. At any level—blue collar or white collar—those jobs requiring "routine thinking skills" are increasingly performed by machine or outsourced to nations with a lower standard of living than the United States. Yet virtually all of contemporary American education is still based on the outmoded model of college prep that prepares students for middle management and factory jobs that, because of global rearrangements in labor markets, in large part no longer exist.

We've all seen industrial jobs for manual laborers dwindle in the United States and other First World economies, either taken over by machines or outsourced abroad to workers who are unprotected by unions or fair labor laws. The same is now the case for routinized white-collar office jobs. In exploitative "digital sweatshops" all around the world, workers at minimal wages can do everything from preparing your tax return to playing your online strategy games for you, so your avatar can be staging raids while you are on the trading floor or in your executive office on Wall Street.

To be prepared for jobs that have a real future in the digital economy, one needs an emphasis on creative thinking, at all levels. By this I mean the kind of thinking that cannot be computerized and automated. This creative thinking requires attention to surprise, anomaly, difference, and disruption, and an ability to switch focus, depending on what individual, unpredictable problems might arise. Perhaps surprisingly, these noncomputational jobs, impervious to automation, occur at all levels across the blue-collar and white-collar spectrum. Many of these jobs require highly specialized and dexterous problem-solving abilities or interpersonal skills—but do not require a college degree.

We were criticized for the iPod experiment. Many treated it as if it were an extravagance, superfluous to real learning and real education. But the iPod experiment exemplifies a form of inquiry-based problem solving wherein solutions are not known in advance and cannot be more successfully outsourced to either a computer or to a Third World laborer who performs repetitive tasks over and over in horrific conditions at minimal wages. The new global economics of work (whatever one thinks about it politically) is not likely to change, and so we must. And that change begins with schooling. Learning to think in multiple ways, with multiple partners, with a dexterity that cannot be computerized or outsourced, is no longer a luxury but a necessity. Given the altered shape of global labor, the seemingly daring iPod experiment turns out actually to be, in the long run, a highly pragmatic educational model.

Part of our failure rate in contemporary education can be blamed on the one-size-fits-all model of standards that evolved over the course of the twentieth century; as we narrow the spectrum of skills that we test in schools, more and more kids who have skills outside that spectrum will be labeled as failures. As what counts as learning is increasingly standardized and limited, increasing numbers of students learn in ways that are not measured by those standards. This is the lesson of attention blindness yet again: If you measure narrowly, you see results just as narrowly. In other words, the more standardized our assessment, the more kids fail. Their failure is then diagnosed as a learning disability or a disorder. But they are failing when assessed by a standard that has almost nothing to do with how they learn online or—more important—what skills they need in a digital age.

The mismatch is just wrong. It's as if we're still turning out assembly-line kids on an assembly-line model in an infinitely more varied and variable customizing, remixed, mashable, user-generated, crowdsourced world. As long as we define their success by a unified set of standards, we will continue to miss their gifts, we will not challenge their skills, and, in the end, we will lose them from our schools just as, implicitly, we have lost interest in them.

We need far more inquiry-based opportunities for our kids. It doesn't have to be as expensive or as radical as the iPod experiment. The world is full of problems to solve that cost little except imagination, relevant learning, and careful guidance by a teacher with the wisdom to *not control* every outcome or to think that the best way to measure is by keeping each kid on the same page of the same book at the same time.

I recently visited a middle school where one girl with green- and blue-striped hair, creatively and eccentrically dyed, sat against the wall, remote from the other kids, as drawn into herself as she could possibly be without disappearing, looking for all the world like the kid who will never hear anything. When I, a stranger, came into the classroom, some of the other kids fussed over my unexpected appearance there, and my *difference*: One girl admired my purple leather jacket, another asked if I was an artist, because I was wearing a black turtleneck and skinny black pants. One boy asked about the image of an electric fan on my long, illustrated scarf from South Africa, and a waggish little boy hummed, with perfect pitch, "Who's That Lady?" when he saw me in his classroom. When I asked how in the world a twelve-year-old knew the Isley Brothers, he said snappily, "The Swiffer commercial." There was a lot of buzz in the class about the visitor, in other words. The green-haired girl in the corner slowly shifted her gaze in my direction, gave the smallest upward movement at the corner of her lips before returning to her frown and letting her eyes move back to outer space again, away from the strange visitor, determinedly *not there*.

I thought of a blog post I'd read earlier that week by the prolific business writer Seth Godin, creator of the popular user-generated community Web site

Squidoo. Godin's post was called "What You Can Learn from a Lousy Teacher," and his list of what you can learn from the teacher you cannot please included: "Grades are an illusion, your passion and insight are reality; your work is worth more than mere congruence to an answer key; persistence in the face of a skeptical authority figure is a powerful ability; fitting in is a short-term strategy, standing out pays off in the long run; and if you care enough about work to be criticized, you've learned enough for today."[17] This remote young woman against the wall didn't look defeated by school. There was something *resolute* in her. I could sense that she had, somehow, taken in intuitively the kinds of lessons Godin was preaching, even if it would take her another decade to fully realize what, in her body language, she was already showing she'd absorbed.

She stayed that way, barely making eye contact with the teacher or any other students, until drawings begun during the previous class were handed around to be worked on again. The transformation I witnessed then was so rapid and thorough that I thought of what Pygmalion must have seen the first time his statue came to life. She went from being still, glassy-eyed, self-contained, and entirely not-present to a concentrated, focused, dedicated bundle of intensity. She still didn't interact with the other kids, but all eyes were on her as she began her day's work on a highly detailed line drawing she was executing. Unlike the bustle at the other tables in the room, there was a silence around her, with the kids practically tiptoeing into the circle of her aura to watch, not speaking to her or to one another, then moving away. I was dying to see her drawing but even more interested in the compact energy she'd created around herself and the other kids, generated from the passion of her drawing. Rather than interrupt that magic, I moved away.

Later in the day, I saw her waiting for her ride home, in the homeroom period at the end of the day, and again the sullen remoteness of I-am-not-here returned After all the kids had gone, I asked her teacher to tell me about her. She'd been diagnosed as profoundly learning disabled, with attention deficit disorder. Her parents sent her to this magnet arts school after she had failed elsewhere. At home, the only thing she seemed to enjoy doing was doodling, but her elementary school had laid off its art teachers, sacrificed to educational cutbacks and the fact that, in our standardized forms of testing, there is no EOG (end-of-grade exam) for art. Art is therefore an add-on that many public schools cannot afford. It was only at the new school that her skills as an artist were recognized. She quickly went from the class failure to the class artist. She mastered the editing tools on the class computer and transferred her imagination and creativity there, too, much to the admiration of her classmates.

I think again about what learning disabilities signify for kids today. In the *Diagnostic and Statistical Manual of Mental Disorders* (the infamous DSM), attention deficit disorder is characterized by distractibility, frequent switching from one activity to another, boredom with a task after just a brief time trying to execute it, and difficulty organizing and completing a task or in focusing on a task in which one is not interested. That last phrase is key. ADD almost never applies to *all* activities, only those in which the child is not interested. This isn't a disability (a fixed biological or cognitive condition) but a disposition (susceptible to change depending on the environment). Keep the kids interested and ADD goes away.

The girl with the green hair has special skills that show up nowhere on her compulsory EOG state tests, on which she continues to score poorly. "Your work is worth more than mere congruence to an answer key." This girl's talents don't count on those tests, and yet she has a special and valued ability that cannot be replaced by a computer program. The problem is that her fate is to a large extent controlled by her performance on the EOG tests, and unless the adults in her life—teachers and parents—are resolute in shepherding her along a path where her talents are valued, they may ultimately wind up undeveloped.

I identified with this girl. When I was in school, my talents had been math and writing, and there was a teacher, Miss Schmidt, who saw those gifts, despite my abysmal test scores, despite the fact that we had to memorize the preamble to the Constitution and the Gettysburg Address to graduate from eighth grade and I just couldn't. I tried and failed over and over many times, staying after school, trying to say it out loud and failing again. Miss Schmidt was feeling certain that I wasn't really trying but just being "obstinate." Then, during one of our painful after-class sessions, she had a hunch. She offered me the opportunity to write an essay instead, one essay about each brief text I was failing to memorize. I stayed up all night working on this and returned the next day with my project. My scrawl filled every page in a small spiral binder—*two hundred* pages.

I remember her eyes widening as she took this smudgy, worn binder from my hand. She looked through it in disbelief and bewilderment as she turned over pages and pages of my barely readable handwriting. There were even footnotes. "You still don't have them memorized, do you?" Miss Schmidt asked. I shook my head. After a moment, she got out the special state certification and, beside my name, put the check mark I needed to graduate from middle school. I'd passed.

Sometimes you learn from the good teachers too. It's not easy to be a good teacher all the time. The girl with the green hair was lucky to find one who honored her talent. Before I left his classroom, I told him, if he thought it appropriate, to let the girl know that the visitor, that professor from Duke University, had noticed her beautiful artwork and admired it. I told him, if he thought it appropriate, to let the girl know that, when the visitor was her age, her hair was purple.

As Matthew b. Crawford argues in *Shop Class as Soulcraft*, his eloquent study of the importance of making and fixing things, our national standards for secondary schools miss kids like this young lady. Our schools are geared, implicitly and explicitly, to be college preparatory. They are weighted toward a twentieth-century, white-collar, middle-management economy.[18] Our standardized education not only bores kids but prepares them for jobs that no longer exist as they once did. Attention blindness again. Our one-size-fits-all educational model focuses steadily and intently on the past.

The space age was America's educational glory moment, when we occupied the number one spot. At that moment, there was a splendid flowering of many kinds of educational theory, including progressive theories, free schools, Montessori schools, science and technology schools, new math, old math, and on and on. It was thought that we were facing a brave new world of science for, after all, incomprehensibly, men had walked on the moon. Education took that fervor to its heart, blossoming, experimenting with innovations as bold and expansive as the solar system itself.

Now, in a digital age, we can communicate and learn in ways not even imagined by Neil Armstrong and Buzz Aldrin walking for the first time on the face of the moon: "One small step for man, one giant leap for mankind." Yet our educational vision has shrunk to the tiny bubble of a multiple-choice exam. Our dreams of new standards of knowledge have shrunk to the right or wrong answer, chosen not among infinitely variable possibilities but among A, B, C, D, and, perhaps, none of the above.

I hate this kind of education. I'm prejudiced, I admit it. So don't ask me. Ask any adult. Ask yourself. What was the most formative experience of your life in school? I suspect your answer isn't "I scored in the 94th percentile on my fifth-grade end-of-grade compulsory exam." Whenever I ask this question, invariably I hear a story of a great teacher who had faith, who inspired and challenged someone to do more than she ever thought was possible before.

Ichabod Crane may nod approval at our current national educational policy. It may seem familiar to him and right. For those of us who remember what inspired us, what commanded our attention, there was always something experimental and daring, there was always something more.

Some of the best teaching I ever witnessed did not happen courtesy of the Internet. It was many years ago, in rural Alberta, Canada. Inez Davidson, the mother of my first husband, Ted, began her teaching career at eighteen, teaching in a one-room schoolhouse in Pincher Creek, a coal-mining town in the Canadian Rockies. She rode half-wild horses to school each morning, alone in the dark and the cold through grizzly country, "putting miles on them," as she would say, before they could be sold to local ranchers as well-trained working horses. Inez was maybe five feet tall, but no one messed with her, ever.

Ted's father was a rancher in the town of Mountain View when he married Inez. Mountain View is as pretty as its name, a gorgeous ranching community in the foothills of the Rockies. The Davidson homestead looked out upon Chief Mountain, the sacred mountain of the Blackfoot and Blood Indian tribes. The area was made up mostly of Native peoples and Mormons or adamant ex-Mormons like the Davidsons, plus elk, moose, black bear, grizzlies, mountain lions, and so forth. Two hundred people in two hundred square miles. The area was poor, too. Rural electrification only came to Alberta in the late 1950s. Even in the 1970s and 1980s, when I was there, the kitchen had a stove that also burned wood (for when the electricity went out), and the entire house had only two additional propane heaters. This was *Canada*, in the foothills of the Rocky Mountains. In winter, it was sometimes 20 or 40 degrees below zero. The hallways and bathrooms and bedrooms were unheated. There was an outhouse for when the plumbing was overtaxed. It was a lot for a gal from Chicago to take in.

My mother-in-law taught in the three-room schoolhouse in Mountain View. For many years, there were more former residents of Mountain View with PhDs, MDs, or law degrees than from any other town in Alberta besides the two major cities in the province, Edmonton and Calgary. By the time I came on the scene, graduate students earning their degrees in education departments in the province were coming to Mountain View to find out what was happening there, that such a backwater was sending students not only to college but well beyond.

Mrs. Davidson, as she was called, was a main reason for this educational success story. How did she do it? First, she got in a lot of trouble, every year, with the school superintendent because she refused, ever, to teach to a test. She covered what the province demanded of third, fourth, and fifth graders and far more, but she always did it her way, as a challenge, a game, an interactive and communal learning activity. She made learning fun—and she was tough.

She was very skeptical of the concept of learning disabilities. She taught long after the normal retirement age and began to see kids coming to school who were more hyperactive than she'd seen in her earlier career and was convinced that part of the reason was environmental and part behavioral. She was concerned about both food additives and contaminants in the air and drinking water even in cattle country, where the water supply was tainted by runoff from oil and smelting plants far away. She was also shocked at how parents were driving kids to school instead of having them walk or ride horses in; these were forms of physical exercise she believed were important to kids' health, well-being, and concentration in the classroom. She loathed it when she saw kids medicated as a remedy for their learning disabilities, and was much more interested in all the subtle and obvious ways kids learned—and learned differently.

She insisted that everyone had a unique way of learning and believed that to be true of the smartest students as well as the academically weakest. She took pride in finding challenges that inspired kids who had clear cognitive restrictions or physical ones, and defied anyone to bring her a kid she couldn't teach. Rodney, a close friend to all the Davidson boys, was a brilliant athlete but very poor in school. Reading was hard and math unbearable. He couldn't conceptualize arithmetic on any level and used his fingers to count even the simplest arithmetic. Other teachers wrote him off as "slow." Mrs. Davidson bought him an abacus and had him research all the sophisticated things the ancient Egyptians could calculate on one. She then taught him to use the different parts of each of his ten fingers as if they were beads on an abacus. He could put his hands under the table and, without anyone seeing, do "rapid calculation" instantly. He did so as a kid, acing math tests, and he did so as an adult, gaining a reputation for uncanny speed and accuracy in the brawny, take-no-prisoners arena of the cattle auctions. Rodney was no one's fool.

Two of Inez Davidson's best teaching tricks involved games. One was that, on every Friday, she would divide up the kids, the fifth graders on one side of the room, the little kids—third and fourth graders—on the other. Whatever they had learned that week would be the subject of the Friday contests. The first part of the day would be spent with the previous week's winners figuring out what kind of competition they would make. They would devise the rules and explain them to the other group. The competition would then require one group testing the other on the answers to various problems in all the different areas they had studied that week.

Mrs. Davidson would serve as the referee. The little kids worked hard to beat the older kids, who of course had their honor to defend, and each team tried to ask harder and harder questions to stump the other. Once Mrs. Davidson felt that the week's work had been covered, she would declare a winning team. The winning group could head out to the playground fifteen minutes early while the losers sat there an *interminable* fifteen minutes—nine hundred seconds!—getting a head start on next week's contest. Some weeks, though, they had so much fun scheming on the hard questions they'd ask the following week that Mrs. Davidson would have to point to the clock to remind them that study hall was over and that it was time to go outside to the schoolyard to play with their friends.

Sometimes they had an hour of these competitions on Friday, sometimes two hours. The other teachers grumbled that Mrs. Davidson's kids got away with murder. Ted, who had his mother as a teacher for all three years because there wasn't anyone else in Mountain View, ended up winning a full scholarship to the University of Chicago, where he tested out of virtually all of his first- and second-year college courses. Not bad for a kid from a cow town in the Canadian Rockies.

Mrs. Davidson taught her kids to dream. Every year, there would be some new, ambitious project with a theme that would unfold over the course of the year. One year, the project was for each child to find a pen pal in another town called Mountain View somewhere in the world. There was only one map in the school, so a first step was to take an enormous piece of newsprint, cover the map, and spend days and days tracing out all the countries on their own map. Then, each child went to the library, which held far fewer books for the entire school than my study holds today, and they each started reading about all the countries in the world, looking for other Mountain Views. They would then mark their particular Mountain View on the hand-drawn map tacked up in the schoolroom. They had to think of ways to communicate with kids in these other Mountain Views. Since this was a Mormon area, there were families who had been on missions to other parts of the world, so that was the obvious way to make contacts, but this was a contest, and ingenuity was rewarded.

One kid remembered that Hang Sang, the elderly Chinese man who ran the local general store, the only store in town, had come over to Canada to work on the railroad, as had so many Chinese immigrants. Taciturn, with a thick accent, Mr. Sang was amused and delighted when one child suddenly wanted help writing a letter—in Chinese. The kid had somehow found out about a town called Mountain View in China. That was the child who won the contest, and long after the contest was over, he spent time with Mr. Sang, talking to him in the back of his store.

But of course they all won. The globe became smaller through the connections they made, and their town became larger. They learned geography and anthropology and foreign languages too. The project lasted not just one full year but many years, and some kids visited those other Mountain Views when they grew up. To this day, I don't drive through a town named Mountain View (there are a lot of them in the world, actually) without wondering if one of Mrs. Davidson's kids sent a letter there and, through the connection made, was inspired to go on, later, to become a professor or a doctor or a veterinarian.

None of what happened in Mrs. Davidson's classroom in Mountain View, Alberta, Canada, depended upon an iPod. None of it required the Internet. But the Internet requires this kind of interactive, motivated, inspired, and curious form of learning. The key here is that Mrs. Davidson's classroom was not really divided up into "subjects" so much as it was into problems, puzzles, brain teasers, challenges, games, word problems, and intellectual obstacle courses, many of which require kids working together toward a solution. What counts is the little kids showing, with pride, that they are every bit as smart as the big kids and the big kids showing, with pride, that they are king, and all of them understanding (although they'd fight you rather than admit it) that they need one another to learn and to dream.

Like the iPod experiment, what this classroom story shows is that kids want to learn and can propel themselves to all kinds of learning as long as there is a payoff, not in what is won or achieved in statistical terms, but what is won and achieved inside, in the sense of self-confidence and competence. Learning, in this sense, is skill and will, an earned conviction that, faced with a challenge ahead, this past achievement will get one through. You can count on your ability to learn, and nowhere is that more important than when what you've learned in the past no longer suffices for the future. That is the glistening paradox of great education: It is not about answering test questions. It is about knowing that, when tested by the most grueling challenges ahead, you have the capacity to learn what is required to succeed.

It is in this sense that unlearning is a skill as vital as learning. It is a skill you have to acquire, too. Unlearning requires that you take an inventory of your changed situation, that you take an inventory of your current repertoire of skills, and that you have the confidence to see your shortcomings and repair them. Without confidence in your ability to learn something new, it is almost impossible to see what you have to change in order to succeed against a new challenge. Lacking confidence in your ability to change, it's much easier to blame the changed situation—typically, new technologies—and then dig in your heels, raising a bulwark against the new. Confidence in your ability to learn *is* confidence in your ability to unlearn, to switch assumptions or methods or partnerships in order to do better. This is true not only for you, as an individual, but for whole institutions.

That's what those kids in a tiny town in rural Alberta learned as fourth and fifth graders pitted against the sixth graders (and vice versa). Mrs. Davidson had to fight the school superintendent every year. Her kids all knew that, too. They knew that she'd put herself on the line for their learning; she'd stand up to anybody, including the superintendent, on their behalf. She dared him, year after year, to fire her. In a different era, he might have, but every year, there'd be the ritual dressing down in his office. I was never in the room with them, but I have a feeling that it wasn't Mrs. Davidson who left feeling chastised.

Put those kids in a lecture hall, give them a standardized curriculum with standardized forms of measuring achievement and ability, and they learn a different lesson. They might well master what they are supposed to learn, but that's not education. When you think of learning as something external to yourself, learning becomes a levy—*an assessment, not an asset.* The assessment no longer matters after the schooling stops. The asset is a resource one draws on for a lifetime.

How can the lessons of this woman's extraordinary classroom be put to use? The model of learning in Mrs. Davidson's classes is probably as old as human history. It is the game. As in a game, there are parameters, what you need to know in order to succeed within the game's rules and requirements, subject matter, or methods. There is a specific target or goal, and you compete with others and against others to win. The real winner, always, is you, not because you earned the trophy but because you learned the inestimable skill of responding to a challenge.

NOTES

1. These are all quoted and the experiment is discussed in James Todd, "The iPod Idea: Wired for Scholarship," *Duke Magazine* 91, no. 5, Sept.–Oct. 2005.

2. The iPod experiment would never have happened without approval and funding of this forward-looking initiative, for which credit goes to my colleagues Tracy Futhey, Vice President for Information Technology, and Provost Peter Lange.

3. On values formation and the blind spots it leaves, see Barbara Herrnstein Smith, *Contingencies of Value: Alternate Perspectives for Critical Theory* (Cambridge, MA: Harvard University Press, 1988).

4. Jeff Howe, *Crowdsourcing: Why the Power of the Crowd Is Driving the Future of Business* (New York: Crown, 2008).

5. Professor Marie Lynn Miranda is a pioneer in using new technologies to help shape community activism on environmental policy. Her Web site is: http://fds.duke.edu /db/Nicholas/esp/faculty/mmiranda (accessed May 6, 2010).

6. Maria Magher, "iPod Gets Top Marks: Culbreth Middle School Is the First in the State to Require Device," *Chapel Hill News*, Mar. 14, 2010.

7. I have written about this at length with my HASTAC cofounder, David Theo Goldberg, in a research report that was first put up on the Web for comment from anyone who wished to offer it, then published in a research report based on colloquia we held all over the country, *The Future of Learning Institutions in a Digital Age* (Cambridge, MA: MIT Press, 2009). The expanded book form of this project is Cathy N. Davidson and David Theo Goldberg, *The Future of Thinking: Learning Institutions in a Digital Age* (Cambridge, MA: MIT Press, 2010).

8. "States Push for Nationalized Educational Standard," *US. and World News*, CBS Interactive, Mar. 10, 2010.

9. The classic studies of American education include Lawrence Cremin, *American Education: The National Experience* (New York: HarperCollins, 1980); Carl Kaestle, *Pillars of the Republic: Common Schools and American Society, 1780–1860* (New York: Hill & Wang, 1983); and Michael Katz, *Reconstructing American Education* (Cambridge, MA: Harvard University Press, 1987).

10. See Alvin Toffler and Heidi Toffler, *Revolutionary Wealth: How It Will Be Created and How It Will Change Our Lives* (New York: Knopf, 2006): 357–62.

11. Robert Schwartz "The American High School in Context," paper delivered to Sino-U.S. Seminar on Diversity in High School, Mar. 23, 2009. This is the single most concise survey and set of statistics I have found anywhere, and one remarkably free of the polemics and politics (left or right) that confuse many of the statistics. This debt to him is not just for this wise assessment and sorting of the numbers but for his distinguished career of contribution to national educational policy since the Carter administration.

12. These are official figures from the Organisation for Economic Co-operation and Development (OECD), an international organization of thirty countries "committed to democracy and the market economy."

13. Ibid.

14. Special thanks to tweeter Michael Josefowicz, a retired printer who tweets as ToughLoveforX, for this clarifying distinction between *standards* and *standardization*. Schwartz's essay discusses the surveys of why students drop out of school.

15. On class size and academic performance, see foundational work in, for example, Glen E. Robinson and James H. Wittebols, *Class Size Research: A Related Cluster Analysis for Decision-Making*. (Arlington, VA: Education Research Service, 1986); Jeremy D. Finn, *Class Size and Students at Risk: What Is Known? What is Next?* (Washington, DC: U.S. Department of Education, Office of Educational Research and Improvement, National Institute on the Education of At-Risk Students, 1998); and Gene V. Glass, Leonard S. Cahen, Mary L. Smith, and Nikola N. Filby, *School Class Size: Research and Policy* (Beverly Hills, CA: Sage, 1982).

16. See William R. Dagged and Paul David Nussbaum, "How Brain Research Relates to Rigor, Relevance and Relationships." See also Peter S. Eriksson, Ekaterina Perfilieva, Thomas Bjork-Eriksson, Ann-Marie Alborn, Claes Nordborg, Daniel A. Peterson, and Fred H. Gage, "Neurogenesis in the Adult Human Hippocampus," *Nature Medicine* 4 (1998): 1313–17. There is a prolific body of research and policy statements on the "new three Rs"–including other xRs, such as responsibility, representing, relating, and so forth. See, for example, Clifford Adelman, *Principal Indicators of Student Academic Histories in Postsecondary Education, 1972–2000* (Washington, DC: US Department of Education, Institute of Education Sciences, 2004); and Anthony P. Carnevale and Donna M. Desrochers, *Connecting Education Standards and Employment: Course-Taking Patterns of Young Workers* (Washington, DC: Achieve Inc., 2002).

17. Seth Godin, "What You Can Learn from a Lousy Teacher," http://sethgodin.typepad.com/seths_blog/2010/03/what-you-can-learn-from-a-lousy-teacher.html (accessed Mar. 20, 2010).

18. Matthew B. Crawford, *Shop Class as Soulcraft: An Inquiry into the Value of Work* (New York: Penguin, 2009).

QUESTIONS FOR MAKING CONNECTIONS
WITHIN THE READING

1. Do you recognize yourself in Davidson's portrayal of the "first generation of kids" to grow up with the Internet? Do you regard yourself and other people your age as *information seekers*? Have the schools that you attended prior to college ignored the potential of the Internet, as Davidson suggests? If most students are adept at finding information via the Web, does it make sense for schools and universities to focus on skills they already have? Have you found that in terms of *quality*, however you wish to define it, the information furnished by the Web can hold its own with other sources, such as books and lectures? Have you found Facebook and Twitter to be effective forms of knowledge delivery?

2. Davidson argues that crowdsourcing has advantages over authority as an organizing principle for education. What forms of social interaction does crowdsourcing involve, and what are its potential strengths as well as its potential liabilities? What forms of interaction are implied by the authority principle? In what ways might the growth of standardized testing reflect the basic values of a system premised on authority? In what ways do crowdsourcing and collaboration offer alternatives to the standardization that Davidson inveighs against? Could crowdsourcing, and the Web in general, inadvertently produce standardization of another kind?

3. It is possible to argue that Davidson sees the new technology—like the free iPods gifted to the students at Duke—as a means to an end rather than an end in itself. What end(s) does she want students to pursue? What, in other words, are her political or cultural objectives? Based on the selection, would you say that Davidson wants to nudge us toward a more egalitarian way of life? What assumptions does she appear to make about ordinary people? Does she see creativity as exceptional? How about intelligence? Does she view failure as socially produced—that is, as forced upon learners by the educational system itself?

QUESTIONS FOR WRITING

1. In the widely read essay "Is Google Making Us Stupid," Nicholas Carr blames the Web for shortening our attention spans and training us to race through online information without stopping to reflect carefully on its meaning or its implications. "Once," Carr writes, "I was a scuba diver in the sea of words. Now I zip along the surface like a guy on a Jet Ski." Does the Web indeed promote "shallowness" in our use of information, and how might Davidson respond to the charge that it is making us less thoughtful? Are the activities she describes, such as inventing new apps, conducive to reflection? How does the experience of surfing the Web differ from reading

a novel? How does it differ from watching TV? Is interpreting a novel or poem a more active process than surfing the Web?

2. What is Davidson's philosophy of education? What does she believe should be its most important goals, and which aspects of contemporary schooling does she regard as detrimental? How has Davidson's experience of "difference" influenced her attitudes toward learning, and how were those attitudes shaped by the example of her mother-in-law, Inez Davidson? How might Davidson respond to Annie Paul Murphy's charge that her program for reform disregards past cultural achievements: "the inhabitants and the knowledge of the past are merely obstacles to be trampled in the headlong rush toward an interactive, connected, collaborative future"? What is the value of the past in Davidson's philosophy?

QUESTIONS FOR MAKING CONNECTIONS
BETWEEN READINGS

1. In what ways might the new technology celebrated by Davidson pose a challenge to the ideology of "smartness" that Ho describes? How might the Internet help undermine a prestige-based hierarchy that *smartness* reinforces? If everyone has access to high status knowledge and can use it in creative ways, what impacts might such a change have on higher education—and on social life in general? Conversely, how might Ho's research complicate Davidson's egalitarian plans because, as Ho suggests, hierarchy is deeply entrenched in higher education? If Davidson were teaching at a less prestigious university than Duke, would her iPod program have generated the same degree of controversy? Does her optimism inadvertently reflect her own privileged situation within an elite institution?

2. The Internet-savvy "kids" whom Davidson lauds and wants professors to learn from are roughly the same people Twenge describes in "An Army of One: Me." Will Davidson's call for a nonhierarchical and student-centered education succeed if the students have been socialized into narcissism, as Twenge alleges? Does the Web actually promote the uncritical self-absorption of "generation me," or might it represent an antidote? Do the social media make people more social, or do they actually encourage psychological isolation? Does the Internet itself promote the idea that everyone will be exceptional if they just develop self-esteem? How might Davidson respond to Twenge's argument?

SUSAN FALUDI

<small>◆◆◆</small>

PULITZER PRIZE–WINNING journalist Susan Faludi first became interested in writing about feminism in the fifth grade, when she polled her classmates to determine their feelings about the Vietnam War and legalized abortion. In the furor
that followed Faludi's release of data showing her peers' liberal attitudes, Faludi
came to realize, as she put it in an interview, "the power that you could have as
a feminist writer. Not being the loudest person on the block, not being one who
regularly interrupted in class or caused a scene, I discovered that through writing
I could make my views heard, and I could actually create change."

The daughter of a Hungarian immigrant who survived the Holocaust, Faludi
was raised in Queens and attended Harvard, where she studied literature and
American history. After graduating in 1981, Faludi worked for a number of
newspapers, including the *New York Times* and the *Wall Street Journal*, before
devoting her time to writing *Backlash: The Undeclared War Against American
Women* (1991), a study of the media's assault on feminism. The following year,
Backlash won the National Book Critics Circle Award for general nonfiction and
made Faludi into a household name. She appeared on the cover of *Time* magazine with Gloria Steinem and, almost overnight, became a national spokesperson
on women's rights and the future of feminism.

While doing research for *Backlash*, Faludi began to wonder why the men
who opposed women's progress were so angry. In setting out to understand
this anger, she interviewed men's groups, sex workers in the pornography industry, union members, the unemployed, and other disenfranchised males. As part
of this project "The Naked Citadel" describes an all-male military academy after
it mistakenly admitted one young woman, an account later included in Faludi's
second book, *Stiffed: The Betrayal of the American Man* (1999). Although now
thirty years old, the story told in "The Naked Citadel" might be more relevant
than ever. According to the Pentagon's own figures, 26,000 servicewomen and
men were victims of sexual harassment or assault in 2012. Faludi's most recent
book, *The Terror Dream: Fear and Fantasy in Post-9/11 America* (2007), returns to
the issues of gender and aggression. While "The Naked Citadel" explores anti-
feminist attitudes in a time of peace, *The Terror Dream* charts the difficulties facing
feminism in a time of war. Faludi concludes in this book that the terrorist attacks

Quotations come from Brian Lamb's interview with Susan Faludi on Booknotes, October 25, 1992 <http://www
.booknotes.org/transcripts/10096.htm> and Kate Melloy's interview with Susan Faludi, "Feminist Author Susan Faludi
Preaches Male Inclusion" <http://www.kollegeville.com/kampus/faludi.htm>.

on September 11, 2001 have created further challenges for feminism by ushering in an era of hysterical insistence on traditional roles for men and women: the men are summoned to protect, while the women must be passively defended. In spite of this predicament, Faludi holds out hope for a society where men and women can work together cooperatively and on equal footing. But she also believes that "[t]o revive a genuine feminism, we must disconnect feminism from the individual pursuit of happiness and reconnect it with the individual desire for social responsibility: the basic human need and joy to be part of a larger, meaningful struggle, which engages the entire society."

◆◆◆ ─────────────────────────────────────

The Naked Citadel

Along the edges of the quad, in the gutters, the freshman cadets were squaring their corners. The "knobs," as they are called for their nearly hairless doorknob pates, aren't allowed to step on the lawn of the broad parade ground, which is trimmed close, as if to match their shorn heads. Keeping off the grass is one of many prohibitions that obtain at The Citadel, a public military college on Charleston's Ashley River. Another is the rule that so many of the cadets say brought them to this Moorish-style, gated campus: Girls keep out.

The campus has a dreamy, flattened quality, with its primary colors, checkerboard courtyards, and storybook-castle barracks. It feels more like an architect's rendering of a campus—almost preternaturally clean, orderly, antiseptic—than the messy real thing. I stood at the far end of the quad, at the academic hall's front steps, and watched the cadets make their herky-jerky perpendicular turns as they drew closer for the first day of class. They walked by stiffly, their faces heat-blotched and vulnerable, and as they passed each in turn shifted his eyes downward. I followed one line of boys into a classroom, a Western Civ class—except, of course, they weren't really boys at all. These were college men, manly recruits to an elite military college whose virile exploits were mythicized in best-selling novels by Calder Willingham and Pat Conroy, both Citadel alumni. So why did I expect their voices to crack when they spoke for the first time? Partly, it was the grammar-schoolish taking of attendance, compulsory at The Citadel. Multiple absences can lead to "tours," hours of marching back and forth in the courtyard with a pinless rifle over one shoulder; or to "cons," confinement to one's room.

But mostly it was the young men themselves, with their doughy faces and twitching limbs, who gave me the urge to babysit. Despite their enrollment in a college long considered "the big bad macho school" (as a former R.O.T.C. commander, Major General Robert E. Wagner, once put it), the cadets lacked the swagger and knowingness of big men on campus. They perched tentatively on their chairs, their hands arranged in a dutiful clasp on their desktops, as if they were expecting a ruler slap to the knuckles. A few dared to glance over at the female visitor, but whenever they made eye contact they averted their gaze and color stained their cheeks.

"As many of you probably know," their teacher said, "this was almost the day the first woman joined The Citadel." The cadets continued to study their polished shoes. "How do you, in fact, feel about whether women should be allowed to attend?"

Silence reigned. Maybe the cadets felt the question put them in an awkward spot. Not only was their teacher in favor of admitting women to The Citadel's Corps of Cadets, the teacher *was* a woman. Indeed, Professor Jane Bishop seemed to be in the strange situation of calling in an air strike on her own position. It was the first day of fall classes in the 1993–94 academic year at The Citadel, and she was broaching the question of the hour. But this incongruity wasn't limited to her classroom. From the moment I stepped onto the school's campus, I had been struck by an unexpected circumstance: though an all-male institution—an institution, moreover, whose singular mission was "making men"—The Citadel was by no means free of women. Female teachers were improving cadets' minds, female administrators were keeping their records, and an all-female (and all-black) staff served the meals in the mess hall. There was also the fact that female students made up seventy-seven percent of the enrollment of the evening school, and many other female students attended summer school with the cadets. What about them? Of course, summer school and evening school aren't part of the military college proper. Cadets don't attend the evening school; and as Major Rick Mill, The Citadel's public-relations director, notes, those cadets who attend the summer school "aren't wearing their uniforms."

Today they were, and so was their teacher. All permanent instructors, regardless of their sex (about fifteen percent are women), wear uniforms as part of their required affiliation with a largely ceremonial outfit once known as the South Carolina Unorganized Militia, and still called by the unfortunate acronym SCUM. Bishop wore hers with what seemed like a deliberate air of disarray.

The cadets' uniforms were considerably tidier—testament to the efficacy of the famous cadet shirt tuck, a maneuver akin to hospital-corners bedmaking and so exacting a cadet cannot perform it without assistance. Even so, the gray cadet uniform, with the big black stripe down the side of the pants and the nametag above the left breast, is the sort more often seen on high-school band members than on fighting soldiers.

"Remember," Bishop prodded them, "speech is free in the classroom."

At last, a cadet unclasped and raised a hand. "Well, I'd have no problem with her in the day program, but she can't join the Corps."

"She," as everyone there knew, was Shannon Faulkner, the woman who had challenged the school's hundred-and-fifty-year-old all-male policy by omitting reference to her sex from her application and winning acceptance to the Corps of Cadets earlier that year—acceptance that was rescinded once the administrators discovered their error. Faulkner's attempt to gain entrance then shifted from the admissions office to the courts. She was allowed under court order to attend day classes during the spring semester of 1994, the first woman to do so. On July 22nd, a United States District Court ruled that The Citadel must admit Faulkner into the Corps of Cadets proper; three weeks later, the Fourth United States Circuit Court of Appeals granted The Citadel a stay pending appeal.

Yet why shouldn't she be permitted into the Corps, Bishop pressed. One of her students recited the fitness requirement—forty-five pushups and fifty-five sit-ups in two-minute sets, and a two-mile run in sixteen minutes. But the administration made passing the fitness test a requirement for graduation only *after* Shannon Faulkner filed suit. An alumnus recounted in court that many upperclassmen he knew who had failed the test skipped the punitive morning run and "sat around and ate doughnuts." Another of Bishop's students cited the shaved-head rule. But this, too, seemed a minor point. A woman cadet could conceivably get a buzz cut. Sinéad O'Connor had done it, Bishop pointed out, without undue injury to her career. And, anyway, after freshman year the men no longer get their heads shaved. Other deprivations of freshman year were invoked: having to "brace" on demand—that is, assume a stance in which a knob stands very erect and tucks in his chin until it puckers up like a rooster's wattle—and having to greet every upperclassman's bellowed command and rebuke with "Sir, yes sir!" or "Sir, no sir!" or "Sir, no excuse sir!" But women, obviously, aren't incapable of obeisance; one might even say they have a long history of it.

Weighing heaviest on the cadets' minds, it turned out, was the preservation of the all-male communal bathroom. The sharing of the stall-less showers and stall-less toilets is "at the heart of the Citadel experience," according to more than one cadet. The men bathe as a group; they walk to the shower down the open galleries, in full view of the courtyard below, and do so, one cadet said, in "nothing but our bathrobes" or "even without any clothes." Another cadet said, "I know it sounds trivial, but all of us in one shower, it's like we're all one, we're all the same, and—I don't know—you feel like you're exposed, but you feel safe. You know these guys are going to be your friends for life." His voice trailed off. "I just can't explain it but when they take that away, it's over. This place will be ruined."

"If women come here, they'll have to put up window shades in all the rooms," a cadet said. "Think of all the windows in the barracks. That could be eight thousand, nine thousand dollars. You've got to look at the costs."

At the end of the hour, the cadets filed out and resumed their double-time jog along the gutters—and their place in the "fourth-class system." This "system" is a nine-month regimen of small and large indignities intended to "strip" each young recruit of his original identity and remold him into the "Whole Man," a vaguely defined ideal, half Christian soldier, half Dale Carnegie junior executive. As a knob explained it to me, "We're all suffering together. It's how we bond." Another knob said, "It's a strange analogy, but it's almost like a P.O.W. camp."

One cadet dawdled, glancing nervously around, then sidled up to me. He spoke in a near whisper, and what he had to say had nothing to do with lavatory

Freshmen are in the "fourth-class system," a regimen to "strip" each recruit of his identity and remold him into the "Whole Man." Illustration by Mark Zingarelli, originally published in *The New Yorker.* © Mark Zingarelli/House of Zing etiquette or military tradition. "The great majority of the guys here are very misogynistic," he said. "All they talk about is how girls are pigs and sluts."

I asked him to explain at greater length. He agonized. "I have to keep quiet," he said, but he finally agreed to meet me later, in an out-of-the-way spot on the upper floor of the student-activities center. He rejoined his classmates with that distinctive knob march, "the march of the puppets," as a professor described it to me later. It was a gait caused in some cases, I was told, by the most conscientious cadets' efforts to keep their shirts perfectly straight with the help of garters—one end of the garter clipped to the shirttail, the other end to the socks.

As I waited for my cadet informant, I decided to kill an hour on the vast parade ground, where the Corps of Cadets marches every Friday afternoon in full dress uniforms, and where, according to an old school brochure, "manhood meets mastery." This is a paramilitary display, not a military one. Despite the regalia and officer ranks, and despite its notoriously fierce military discipline ("To discipline is to teach" is the motto emblazoned on one of the school's books of regulations), this is a military academy by self-designation only. Unlike the federal service academies—West Point, Annapolis, the Air Force Academy— The Citadel has no connection with the United States Armed Forces (other than its R.O.T.C. program and its employment of some active and retired officers). Its grounds are adorned with dusty and decommissioned military hardware—a Sherman tank, a submarine's torpedo-loading hatch, a Phantom jet named Annette, two cannons named Betsy and Lizzie. In most cases, the weapons, including the pinless M-14s the cadets carry, are inoperative. The mouths of the various cannons are stuffed with cement—all except those of Betsy and Lizzie, which are fired during parades, but carefully aimed high enough so that their powder does not dust the crenellated barracks. The overall effect is that of a theme park for post–Cold War kids.

The hokeyness and childlike innocence of the scene—the stage-prop artillery, the toy-soldier clip-clop of the cadets as they squared their corners—were endearing, in a Lost Boys sort of way, and I strolled over to the student-activities center for my rendezvous with my cadet informant thinking that The Citadel's version of martial culture was not so menacing after all. The cadet was not in evidence. I spent the next thirty minutes prowling the halls, which were lined with portraits of stern-faced "generals" (I couldn't tell which were United States military and which were SCUM), and examining ads on the student bulletin board for items like "Save the Males" bumper stickers. I tried to reach the cadet's room by phone—women aren't admitted into the barracks—but he was not there. A bit thoughtlessly, I left a message with an upperclassman and headed toward town.

At my hotel, the receptionist handed me a message from my vanished cadet. "Please, don't ever call here again!" it read. The phone clerk peered at me curiously. "Sorry about that exclamation mark, but he seemed quite distraught," she said. "His voice was shaking."

What brought a young man to an all-male preserve in the last decade of the twentieth century, anyway? What was going on outside the academy gates that impelled thousands of boys, Southern and Northern alike (about a fifth of its student body of about two thousand are Yankees), to seek refuge behind a pair of corroding cannons?

"The forces arrayed against us," an attorney named Robert Patterson declared in a February, 1994, court hearing, consider his military academy to be "some big-game animal to be hunted down, tracked, caught, badgered, and killed so that some lawyer or some organization can go back up and hang a trophy on a wall in an office." Patterson was defending not The Citadel but the Virginia Military Institute, which is the only other public military academy in the United States that does not admit women, and which was involved in a similar sex-discrimination suit. (Three months later, Patterson, a V.M.I. alumnus, returned to court to defend The Citadel.) "I will say this, Your Honor," he went on. "This quest by these people constitutes the longest and most expensive publicly financed safari in the annals of big-game hunting."

The Citadel's administration has fought the female hunters with a legal arsenal of nearly a million dollars and with dour, tight-lipped determination, which has only increased with time. The Citadel's president, Claudius Elmer (Bud) Watts III, who is a retired Air Force lieutenant general and a second-generation Citadel alumnus, views Shannon Faulkner's legal efforts as an enemy invasion, placing his young troops "under attack." "The Citadel is in this to the end," he pronounced at a press conference held in the spring of 1994 on the parade ground, his feet planted between Betsy and Lizzie, his uniform decked with ribbons, and his chin tucked in, as is his custom, as if in a permanent brace position.

Later, in his living room, surrounded by coffee-table books on football, Watts told me firmly, "You cannot put a male and a female on that same playing field," though he couldn't say exactly why. Of his own Citadel years he conceded, "I've not the foggiest notion if it would have been different" had women attended. He was just glad there were no female cadets then; otherwise, he said, the cadets would have faced "a different form of intimidation—not wanting to be embarrassed in front of a girl."

Faulkner has been opposed not only by many Citadel staff and alumni but—at least, publicly—by almost all the current cadets. They say that her presence in the Corps would absolutely destroy a basic quality of their experience as Citadel men. She would be what one Citadel defender called in his court deposition "a toxic kind of virus." Tellingly, even before the United States District Court judge enjoined The Citadel to admit Faulkner to the Corps of Cadets for the fall of 1994, and before the injunction was set aside, the administration announced its selection of her living quarters: the infirmary.

Cadets cite a number of reasons that women would have a deleterious effect on the Corps of Cadets, and the reasons are repeated so often as to be easily predictable, though their expression can be novel. "Studies show—I can't cite them, but studies show that males learn better when females aren't there," one cadet explained to me (a curious sentiment at a school where a knob motto about grades is "2.0 and Go"). "If a girl was here, I'd be concerned not to look foolish. If you're a shy student, you won't be as inhibited." Another cadet said, "See, you don't have to impress them here. You're free." From a third: "Where does it end?

Will we have unisex bathrooms?" But among the reasons most frequently heard for repelling Faulkner at the gate is this: "She would be destroying a long and proud tradition."

The masculine traditions of West Point and Annapolis were also closely guarded by their male denizens, but the resistance to women joining their ranks was nowhere near as fierce and filled with doomsday rhetoric as The Citadel's efforts to repel feminine interlopers. At Norwich University, a private military college in Northfield, Vermont, that voluntarily opened its barracks to women in 1974, two years before the federal service academies, the administration actually made an effort to recruit and accommodate women. "There was no storm of protest," said a Norwich spokeswoman, Judy Clauson. But then, "it was a time when there were so many rules that were being loosened." The Air Force veteran Linnea Westberg, who was one of the eight women in Norwich's first coed class, recalled, of her integration into its corps, that "ninety-five percent of the male cadets were fine, especially the freshmen, who didn't know any different." Westberg said she was baffled by the intensity of The Citadel's opposition to women in its corps. "It's hard for me to believe it's still an issue."

"The Citadel is a living museum to the way things used to be," John Drennan, a Citadel graduate and a public defender in Charleston, told me one day during The Citadel's legal proceedings. But how, exactly, did things use to be? The cadets and the alumni of the school, along with those protesting against its exclusionary policies, envision its military tradition above all. And The Citadel once did have a strong military aspect: it was formed as an arsenal in 1822 in response to a slave revolt purportedly planned by the freed Charleston slave Denmark Vesey, which, though it was foiled, aroused widespread alarm in the region. Yet twenty years later the guns and the gold braid became mere adornment as The Citadel turned into an industrial school of domestic and practical skills. Union troops shut down The Citadel at the end of the Civil War, but it was reinvented and reopened in 1882, after the Union's Reconstruction officials had thoroughly stripped the school of all military muscle. Its new mission was to reinvigorate the masculinity of the South by showing its men how to compete with the business and industrial skills of the Yankee carpetbaggers, who were believed to be much better prepared than the sons of Dixie to enter the Darwinian fray of modern commerce. John Peyre Thomas, who ran The Citadel from 1882 to 1885, wrote of the need to teach spoiled plantation boys the rudiments of self-reliance. "It must be admitted that the institution of African slavery, in many respects, affected injuriously the white youth of the South," he wrote. "Reared from infancy to manhood with servants at his command to bring his water, brush his shoes, saddle his horse, and, in fine, to minister to his personal wants, the average Southern boy grew up in some points of character dependent, and lazy, and inefficient. He was found, too, wanting in those habits of order and system that come from the necessity, in man, to economize time and labor."

What makes the school's Reconstruction-era mission important is that in so many ways it remains current; the masculine and industrial culture of our age and that of the conquered South may have more in common than we care to imagine. Again, we are at a psychic and economic crisis point for manhood. And, again, the gun issues hide the butter issues: the bombast masks a deep insecurity about employment and usefulness in a world where gentleman soldiers are an anachronism and a graduate with gentleman's Cs may find himself busing tables at Wendy's.

The uncertain prospects of Citadel graduates are worsened by military downsizing. Only about a third of recent graduates entered the military—a figure that has fallen steeply since the mid-seventies, when half of The Citadel's graduating class routinely took a service commission. News of Shannon Faulkner's court case competed in the Charleston *Post & Courier* with news of the shutting down of the local shipyards and decommissionings from the local military installations.

The night before the closing arguments in Faulkner's suit, I had dinner at the on-campus home of Philippe and Linda Ross, who have both taught at The Citadel. Philippe, the head of the Biology Department, had just completed his first round of moonlighting as a "retraining" instructor at the Charleston Naval Shipyard. He had been prepping laid-off nuclear engineers to enter one of the few growth industries in the area—toxic-waste management. Facing a room filled with desperate men each day had been a dispiriting experience, he said. He recalled the plea of a middle-aged engineer, thrust out of the service after twenty-six years: "All I want to do is work." Linda Ross, who was then teaching psychology at The Citadel, looked across the table with a pained expression. "That whole idea that if a young man went to college he could make a decent living and buy a house, and maybe even a boat, just does not hold anymore," she said softly. "There's a Citadel graduate working as a cashier at the grocery store. And the one thing these young men felt they could count on was that if things got hard they could always go into the military. No more. And they are bitter and angry."

In the fall of 1991, Michael Lake, a freshman, decided to leave The Citadel. He had undergone weeks of bruising encounters with upperclassmen—encounters that included being knocked down with a rifle butt and beaten in the dark by a pack of cadets. Incidents of hazing became so violent that, in a school where publicly criticizing the alma mater is virtually an act of treason, several athletes told their stories to *Sports Illustrated.* Much of the violence was aimed at star freshman athletes: a member of the cycling team was forced to hang by his fingers over a sword poised two inches below his testicles; a place-kicker had his head dunked in water twenty times until he was unconscious; a linebacker was forced to swallow his chewing tobacco and tormented until, he said later, "I was unable even to speak clearly in my classes." It was a time when the Churchill Society, a literary club reportedly containing a white-supremacist faction, was organized on campus. It was a time when the local chapter of the National Association for the Advancement of Colored People urged a federal investigation into a pair of racial incidents on the school's campus: the appearance of a noose over the bed of a black freshman who had earlier refused to sing "Dixie," and the shooting and wounding of a black cadet by a sniper who was never identified. (A few years earlier, upperclassmen wearing Klan-like costumes left a charred paper cross in the room of a black cadet.) And it was a time when a leader of the Junior Sword Drill, a unit of cadet sword-bearers, leaped off a five-foot dresser onto the head of a prostrate cadet, then left him in a pool of blood in a barracks hall. According to one cadet, a lacrosse-team member returning from an away game at three in the morning stumbled upon the victim's unconscious body, his face split open, jaw and nose broken, mouth a jack-o'-lantern of missing teeth.

One night, at about 2 A.M., high-ranking cadets trapped a raccoon in the barracks and began to stab it with a knife. Beau Turner, a student at the school, was awakened by the young men's yelling. "My roommate and I went out there to try and stop it," Turner recalled, "but we were too late." Accounts of the episode vary. In a widely circulated version (which was referred to in a faculty member's testimony), the cadets chanted, "Kill the bitch! Kill the bitch!" as they tortured the raccoon to death.

In October 1993, two upperclassmen burst into the room of two freshmen and reportedly kneed them in the genitals, pulled out some of their chest hair, and beat them up. They were arrested on charges of assault and battery, and agreed to a program of counseling and community service, which would wipe clean their records. They withdrew from The Citadel, in lieu of expulsion, the spokesman Major Rick Mill said.

One of the offending cadets, Adrian Baer, told me that he and the other accused sophomore, Jeremy Leckie, did indeed come back from drinking, burst into the knobs' room after 10 P.M., and "repeatedly struck them in the chest and stomach" and bruised one of them in the face, but he denied having kicked them in the groin and yanked out chest hair. He said that what he did was common procedure—and no different from the "motivational" treatment he had received as a knob at the hands of a senior who came into *his* room. They entered the freshmen's room, Baer explained, because they viewed one of the occupants as "a problem" knob who "needed some extra motivation." Baer elaborated: "His pinkie on his right hand wouldn't completely close when he went to salute. He caught a lot of heat for that, of course, because it's a military school; it's important to salute properly." The strict rule that upperclassmen not fraternize with knobs, he said, meant that they couldn't simply counsel the freshman kindly. "If we just sat down and said, 'Listen, guy, we have a little problem,' that would be fraternization. And more important, knobs would lose respect for upperclassmen. It's a lot of denial on the part of officials at The Citadel about hazing," Baer said. "They don't want to believe it goes on." Leckie's father, Timothy Rinaldi, said that while he believed his son "was definitely in the wrong," he felt The Citadel's fourth-class system bred such behavior. "They help build this monster," he said of The Citadel. "The monster gets up off the table and starts walking through town—and now Dr. Frankenstein wants to shoot it."

Needless to say, not every cadet embraces the climate of cruelty; the nocturnal maulings likely frighten as many cadets as they enthrall. But the group mentality that pervades The Citadel assures that any desire on the part of a cadet to speak out about the mounting violence will usually be squelched by the threat of ostracism and shame. While group rule typifies many institutions, military and civilian, that place a premium on conformity, the power and authoritarianism of the peer group at The Citadel is exceptional because the college gives a handful of older students leave to "govern" the others as they see fit. (A lone officer provided by the military, who sleeps in a wing off one of the dorms, seldom interferes.) This is a situation that, over the years, an occasional school official has challenged, without success. A former assistant commandant for discipline, Army Lieutenant Colonel T. Nugent Courvoisie, recalled that he "begged" the school's president back in the sixties to place more military officers—and ones who were more mature—in the barracks, but his appeals went unheeded. Discipline and punishment in the dorms is in the hands of the student-run regimental command, and ascendancy in this hierarchy is not always predicated on compassion for one's fellow man. In consequence, the tyranny of the few buys the silence of the many.

This unofficial pact of silence could, of course, be challenged by the Citadel officialdom. On a number of occasions over the past three decades—most recently when some particularly brutal incidents found their way into the media—The Citadel has commissioned "studies." But when the administration does go on the offensive, its animus is primarily directed not at miscreant cadets but at the "unfair" media, which are "victimizing" the institution by publicizing the bad behavior of its boys.

In recent years, enough bad news leaked out locally to become a public-relations nightmare, and the school appointed a committee of Citadel loyalists to assess the situation. Even the loyalists concluded, in a January 1992 report, that the practice of physical abuse of freshmen, along with food and sleep deprivation, had gotten out of hand. As a result, Major Mill told me, The Citadel ordered upperclassmen to stop using pushups as a "disciplinary tool" on individual cadets. "That was the most important one" of the reforms prompted by the report, Mill said. Other reforms were adopted: for example, freshmen would no longer be compelled to deliver mail to upperclassmen after their evening study hours, thus reducing opportunities for hazing; freshmen would—at least officially—no longer be compelled to "brace" in the mess hall. At the same time, the report declared that it "wholeheartedly endorses the concept of the fourth-class system," which it called "essential to the attainment of college objectives and the development of the Citadel man."

Institutions that boast of their insularity, whether convents or military academies, are commonly pictured in the public imagination as static, unchanging abstractions, isolated from the ebb and flow of current events. But these edifices are rarely as otherworldly as their guardians might wish; indeed, in the case of The Citadel, its bricked-off culture has functioned more as a barometer of national anxieties than as a garrison against them. The militaristic tendencies within the Corps seem to vary inversely with the esteem in which the American soldier is held in the larger society. In times when the nation has been caught up in a socially acceptable conflict, one in which its soldiers return as heroes greeted by tickertape parades, The Citadel has loosened its militaristic harness, or even removed it altogether. Thus, during perhaps the most acceptable war in American history, the Second World War, the fourth-class system of knob humiliation was all but discontinued. Upperclassmen couldn't even order a knob to brace. The changes began largely in response to the demands of the real military for soldiers they could use in a modern war. "The War Department and the Navy Department were asking R.O.T.C. to do less drilling, more calculus," Jamie Moore, a professor of history at The Citadel and a former member of the United States Army's Historical Advisory Committee, told me. "The Citadel dismantled its fourth-class system because it was getting in the way of their military training." The changes didn't seem to interfere with the school's production of Whole Men; on the contrary, an extraordinary percentage of The Citadel's most distinguished graduates come from these years, among them United States Senator Ernest (Fritz) Hollings; Alvah Chapman, Jr., the former chief executive of Knight-Ridder; and South Carolina's former governor John C. West.

The kinder, gentler culture of the Second World War–era Citadel survived well into the next decade. Although a new fourth-class system was soon established, it remained relatively benign. "We didn't have the yelling we have today," Colonel Harvey Dick, class of '53 and now a member of The Citadel's governing body, recalled. "They didn't even shave the freshmen's heads."

The postwar years also brought the admission of women to the summer program, and without the hand-wringing provoked by Shannon Faulkner's application. "WOMEN INVADE CITADEL CLASSES FIRST TIME IN SCHOOL'S HISTORY," the Charleston daily noted back on page 16 of its June 21, 1949, edition. "Most male students took the advent of the 'amazons' in their stride," the paper reported cheerfully. "Only the younger ones seemed at all uneasy. Professors and instructors were downright glad to see women in their classes."

The Vietnam War, needless to say, did not inspire the same mood of relaxation on campus. "The fourth-class system was very physical," Wallace West, the admissions director who was an undergraduate at The Citadel during the Vietnam War years, said. "When I was there, there was no true emphasis on academics, or on positive leadership. It was who could be worked to physical exhaustion." Alumni from those years recounted being beaten with sticks, coat hangers, and rifle butts. That was, of course, the era that inspired Pat Conroy's novel *The Lords of Discipline,* a tale of horrific hazing, directed with special virulence against the school's first African-American cadet. "They just tortured us," Conroy recalled from his home in Beaufort, South Carolina. "It taught me the exact kind of man I didn't want to be," he added.

In 1968, the administration appointed a committee to investigate the violence. The committee issued a report that, like its 1992 successor, concluded "there have been significant and extensive abuses to the [fourth-class] system." And, with its strong recommendation that hazing result in expulsion, the report seemed to promise a more pacific future on campus.

In the past decade and a half, however, the record of violence and cruelty at The Citadel has attracted increasing notice, even as the armed forces have been racked by downsizing and scandal. The Citadel president during much of this era, Major General James A. Grimsley, Jr., declined to discuss this or any other aspect of campus life during his tenure. "I don't do interviews," he said. "Thank you for calling, young lady." He then hung up. Others have been less reticent.

Thirteen years before Vice-Admiral James B. Stockdale consented to be Ross Perot's running mate, he took on what turned out to be an even more thankless task: fighting brutal forms of hazing at The Citadel. In 1979, Stockdale, who had graduated from Annapolis, was chosen to be The Citadel's president because of his status as a genuine military hero: he had survived eight years as a P.O.W. in Vietnam. This hero failed to see the point of manufactured adversity. In an afterword to the book *In Love and War,* a collaboration between Stockdale and his wife, Sybil, he wrote that there was "something mean and out of control about the regime I had just inherited."

On his first day in the president's office, Stockdale opened a desk drawer and discovered "what turned out to be Pandora's box," he wrote. "From the top down, what was written on the papers I took out of the desk drawers—and conversations with some of their authors—was enough to break anybody's heart." Among them was a letter from an infuriated father who wanted to know what had happened to his son "to change him from a levelheaded, optimistic, aggressive individual to a fatigued, irrational, confused and bitter one." He also found copies of memos from The Citadel's staff physician complaining repeatedly of (as Stockdale recalled) "excessive hospitalization"—such as the case of a knob who had suffered intestinal bleeding and was later brought back to the infirmary, having been exercised to unconsciousness. Stockdale sought to reform the system, but he was stymied at every turn. He clashed with The Citadel's powerful Board of Visitors, an eleven-member committee of alumni that sets school policy. The Board of Visitors overruled his expulsion of a senior cadet who had reportedly been threatening freshmen with a pistol. A year into his presidency, Stockdale submitted his resignation. After he left, the board reinstated an avenging friend of the senior cadet who, according to Stockdale, had attempted to break into his house one evening. (The then chairman of the Board of Visitors maintains that the cadet was drunk and looking for the barracks.)

"They thought they were helping people into manhood," Stockdale recalled, from a more serene post in Palo Alto, California, where he is a scholar at Stanford's Hoover Institution on War, Revolution, and Peace. "But they had no idea what that meant—or who they were."

After Watts became president, in 1989, some faculty members began to observe a creeping militarization imposed by the administration upon the Corps's already drill-heavy regimen. Four special military days were added to the academic year. At the beginning of one semester, President Watts held a faculty meeting in a room above the mess hall. "Watts had these soldiers standing around the room with their hands behind them," Gardel Feurtado, a political-science professor and one of only two African-American professors, recalled. Watts, he said, lectured the faculty for about three hours. "He didn't talk about academics or educational goals. He just talked about cadets' training, and he showed us a film of it," Feurtado told me. According to Feurtado, Watts told the faculty to line up in groups behind the soldiers for a tour of the barracks.

"I said, 'Enough of this,' and I started to walk out. And this soldier stopped me and said, 'Where do you think you're going, sir?' and I said, 'You do realize that I am not in the military?'" Feurtado had to push by him to leave.

When Michael Lake looked back on the abuse he suffered during his abbreviated knob year of '91, he could now see before him, like the emergence of invisible ink on what appeared to be a blank piece of paper, the faint outlines of another struggle. What he saw was a submerged gender battle, a bitter but definitely fixed contest between the sexes, concealed from view by the fact that men played both parts. The beaten knobs were the women, "stripped" and humiliated, and the predatory upperclassmen were the men, who bullied and pillaged. If they couldn't re-create a male-dominant society in the real world, they could restage the drama by casting male knobs in all the subservient feminine roles.

Illustration by Mark Zingarelli, originally published in *The New Yorker.* © Mark Zingarelli/House of Zing

"They called you a 'pussy' all the time," Lake recalled. "Or a 'fucking little girl.'" It started the very first day they had their heads shaved, when the upperclassmen stood around and taunted. "Oh, you going to get your little girlie locks cut off?" When they learned that Lake would be playing soccer that fall, their first response was "What is that, a girl's sport?" Another former cadet said that he had withstood "continual abuse," until he found himself thinking about jumping out the fourth-story window of the barracks—and quit. He reported an experience similar to Lake's. Virtually every taunt equated him with a woman: whenever he showed fear, they would say, "You look like you're having an abortion," or "Are you menstruating?" The knobs even experienced a version of domestic violence. The upperclassmen, this cadet recalled, "would go out and get drunk and they would come home and haze, and you just hoped they didn't come into your room."

"According to the Citadel creed of the cadet," Lake said, "women are objects, they're things that you can do with whatever you want to." In order to maintain this world-view, the campus has to be free of women whose status might challenge it—a policy that, of course, is rarely enunciated. The acknowledged policy is that women are to be kept at a distance so they can be "respected" as ladies. Several months before Faulkner's lawsuit came to trial, I was sitting in the less than Spartan air-conditioned quarters of the senior regimental commander, Norman Doucet, the highest-ranking cadet, who commanded the barracks. Doucet, who was to be The Citadel's star witness at the Faulkner trial, was explaining to me how excluding women had enhanced his gentlemanly perception of the opposite sex. "The absence of women makes us understand them better," Doucet said. "In an aesthetic kind of way, we appreciate them more—because they are not there."

Women at less of a remove fare less well. In The Citadel's great chain of being, the "waitees"—as many students call that all-black, all-female mess-hall staff—rate as the bottom link. Some upperclassmen have patted them on their rear ends, tried to trip them as they pass the tables, or hurled food at their retreating backs. Cadets have summoned them with "Come here, bitch," or addressed one who dropped a plate or forgot an order as "you stupid whore." The pages of the *Brigadier,* the school's newspaper, bear witness to the cadets' contempt for these women. Gary Brown, now the editor-in-chief of the *Brigadier,* once advised fellow-cadets to beware of "waitee" food contamination—"the germ-filled hands, the hair follicles, and other unknown horrors." Not only was he dismayed by "wavy little follicles in my food" but he found the women insufficiently obedient. "Duty is certainly not the sublimest word in the Waitee language," he wrote. In a letter to the editor, Jason S. Pausman, class of '94, urged fellow-cadets to demand "waitees without chronic diseases that involve sneezing, coughing or wiping of body parts ... The reality is simple, we CANNOT sit by and let the waitees of this school control us."

Some women faculty members report similarly resentful responses to their presence, despite—or because of—their positions of authority. Angry messages on a professor's door are one tactic. When Jane Bishop recently posted on her office door a photocopy of a *New York Times* editorial supporting women's admission to the Corps of Cadets, she found it annotated with heated rejoinders in a matter of days. "Dr. Bishop, you are a prime example of why women should not be allowed here," one scribble read. Another comment: "Women will destroy the world."

The Citadel men's approach to women seems to toggle between extremes of gentility and fury. "First, they will be charming to the women to get their way," Linda Ross said. "But if that doesn't work they don't know any other way. So then they will get angry." It's a pattern that is particularly evident in some cadets' reaction to younger faculty women.

December Green joined The Citadel's Political Science Department in 1988, the first woman that the department had ever hired for a tenure-track position. She was twenty-six and attractive—"someone the cadets might fantasize about," a colleague recalled. They were less enchanted, however, by her left-leaning politics. She soon found herself getting obscene phone calls in the middle of the night. Then obscenities began appearing on her office door. "Pussy" is the one that sticks in her mind.

Though Green's work at The Citadel was highly praised—she received an award for teaching, research, and service—she said that no one in the administration tried to stop her when she left in 1992 in despair over her inability to contain the cadets' fury. Nor, apparently, had anyone responded to her appeals to correct the situation. "A lot of terrible things happened to me there," Green, who is now teaching in Ohio, said, reluctant to revisit them. The hostility ranged from glowering group stares in the hallway to death threats—some of which appeared on the cadets' teacher-evaluation forms. The male faculty offered little support. Green recalls the department chairman instructing her to "be more maternal toward the students" when a cadet lodged a complaint about her (she had challenged his essay in which he praised apartheid). And a professor who stood by one day while his students harassed her and another woman informed her, "You get what you provoke."

Green said she eventually had to get an unlisted number to stop the obscene calls, and also moved, in part out of fear of the cadets' vengeance. The last straw,

The legendary Citadel elder known as the Boo, who oversaw racial integration at The Citadel in the sixties, says, "With women, there's going to be sexual harassment." His wife, Margaret, counters, "Oh, honey, those cadets are harassing each other right now." "That's different," he says. "That's standard operating procedure." Illustration by Mark Zingarelli, originally published in *The New Yorker*. © Mark Zingarelli/House of Zing

however, came when she submitted the written threats she had received to her chairman, who passed them on to the dean of undergraduate studies, in hopes of remedial action. The dean, she said, did nothing for some months, and then, after she inquired, said he had "misplaced" the offending documents.

The dean, Colonel Isaac (Spike) Metts, Jr., told me he didn't recall saying he misplaced the documents but "I might have said it's not on my desk at that time and I don't know where it is." He added that Green was a "very valuable" professor. "I don't know what else we could've done," Metts said. In any event, soon after submitting the threatening notes to the dean, Green gave up. At her exit interview, she recalled, President Watts told her he didn't understand why she had been upset by the cadet harassment. "It's just a bunch of kid stuff," another male colleague said. (Lewis Spearman, the assistant to the president, said that, because of federal privacy law, Watts would have no response to Green's version of events.)

The remaining category of women that cadets have to deal with is "the dates," as the young women they socialize with are generally called. (There are no wives; Citadel policy forbids cadets to marry, and violators are expelled.) In some respects, these young women are the greatest challenge to the cadet's sense of gender hierarchy. While the "waitees" can be cast as household servants and the female teachers as surrogate mothers, the dates are more difficult to place. Young women their age are often college students, with the same aspirations as the cadets, or even greater ones. The cadets deal with young women's rising ambitions in a number of ways. One is simply to date high-school girls, an option selected by a number of cadets. Another strategy, facilitated by The Citadel, is to cast the young women who are invited on campus into the homecoming-queen mold. The college holds a Miss Citadel contest each year, and Anne Poole, whose husband, Roger, is the vice-president of academic affairs and the dean of the college, has sat on the judging panel. Each cadet company elects a young woman mascot from a photograph competition, and their faces appear in the yearbook.

The school also sends its young men to an in-house etiquette-training seminar, in which the Citadel "hostess," a pleasant woman in her forties named Susan Bowers, gives them a lecture on how "to act gentlemanly with the girls." She arms cadets with *The Art of Good Taste,* a do's-and-don'ts manual with a chapter entitled "Helping the Ladies." The guidebook outlines the "correct way of offering an arm to a lady ... to help her down the steps," and the best method for assisting "a lady in distress." (The example of distress provided involves an elderly woman trying to open a door when her arms are full of shopping bags.) Such pointers are illustrated with pictures of fifties-style coeds sporting Barbie-doll hair flips and clinging to the arms of their cadets, who are escorting them to "the Hop." The manual's preface states emphatically, "At all times [ladies] must be sheltered and protected not only from the elements and physical harm but also from embarrassment, crudity, or coarseness of any sort."

Susan Bowers explained the duties of her office: "At the beginning of the year, we do 'situation cards' for the freshmen. And we'll bring in cheerleaders and use them as props.... We show cadets how to go through the receiving line, how to introduce your date, and what to say to them. In the past, we didn't have the cheerleaders to use, so they dressed up some of the guys as girls." Bowers said she felt bad for the cadets, who often come to her seeking maternal consolation. "They are very timid—afraid, almost," she said. "They are so lost, and they need a shoulder."

The Art of Good Taste is silent on the subject of proper etiquette toward women who require neither deference nor rescue. And, as Linda Ross observed, when the gentlemanly approach fails them, cadets seem to have only one fallback—aggression. Numerous cadets spoke to me of classmates who claimed to have "knocked around" uncompliant girlfriends. Some of those classmates, no doubt, were embellishing to impress a male audience, but not always. "I know lots of stories where cadets are violent toward women," a 1991 Citadel graduate named Ron Vergnolle said. He had witnessed cadets hitting their girlfriends at a number of Citadel parties—and observed one party incident in which two cadets held down a young woman while a third drunken cadet leaned over and vomited on her. Vergnolle, a magna cum laude graduate of the Citadel class of '91, recounted several such stories to me, and added that bragging about humiliating an ex-girlfriend is a common practice—and the more outrageous the humiliation, the better the story, as far as many cadets are concerned. Two such cadet storytellers, for example, proudly spread the word of their exploits on Dog Day, a big outdoor party sponsored by The Citadel's senior class. The two cadets told about the time they became enraged with their dates, followed them to the Portosans, and, after the women had entered, pushed the latrines over so they landed on the doors, trapping the occupants. The cadets left them there. Another cadet told Vergnolle that he had tacked a live hamster to a young woman's door. There was also the cadet who boasted widely that, as vengeance against an uncooperative young woman, he smashed the head of her cat against a window as she watched in horror. "The cat story," Vergnolle noted, "that was this guy's calling card."

Something of these attitudes shows up even in the ditties the cadets chant during their daily runs. Many of the chants are the usual military "jodies," well known for their misogynistic lyrics. But some are vintage Citadel and include lyrics about gouging out a woman's eyes, lopping off body parts, and evisceration. A cadence remembered by one Citadel cadet, sung to the tune of "The Candy Man," begins, "Who can take two jumper cables/Clip 'em to her tit/ Turn on the battery and watch the bitch twitch." Another verse starts with "Who can take an ice pick ..." and so on.

The day after last Thanksgiving, the phone rang at one-thirty in the morning in the home of Sandy and Ed Faulkner in Powdersville, South Carolina, a tiny community on the outskirts of Greenville. The caller was a neighbor. They had better come outside, he said—a car had been circling their block. Sandy and Ed, the parents of Shannon Faulkner, went out on their front lawn and looked around. At first, they saw nothing. Then, as they turned back to the house, they saw that across the white porch columns and along the siding of the house, painted in gigantic and what Sandy later recalled as "blood-red" letters, were the words, "Bitch," "Dyke," "Whore," and "Lesbo." Ed got up again at 6 A.M. and, armed with a bucket of white paint, hurried to conceal the message from his daughter.

A few days after the judge ordered The Citadel to admit Faulkner to the Corps of Cadets, morning rush-hour drivers in Charleston passed by a huge portable sign that read "Die Shannon." At least this threat wasn't home delivered. In the past year, instances of vandalism and harassment have mounted at the Faulkner home. Someone crawled under the house and opened the emergency exhaust valve on the water heater. The gas tank on Sandy's car was pried open. Someone driving a Ford Bronco mowed down the mailbox. Another motorist "did figure-eights through my flower bed," Sandy said. "This year, I didn't even plant flowers because I knew they would just tear them up." And someone with access to Southern Bell's voice-mail system managed, twice, to tap into their voice mail and change their greeting, both times to a recording featuring rap lyrics about a "bitch" with a "big butt." Callers phoned in the middle of the night with threatening messages. Sandy called the county sheriffs department about the vandalism, but in Anderson County, which has been home to many Citadel graduates, the deputy who arrived was not particularly helpful. He told them, Sandy recalled, "Well, if you're going to mess with The Citadel, you're just going to have to expect that."

Every trial has its rare moments of clarity, when the bramble of admissibility arguments and technicalities is cut away and we see the actual issue in dispute. One such moment came toward the end of the Faulkner-Citadel trial, when Alexander Astin, the director of the Higher Education Research Institute at the University of California at Los Angeles, took the stand. Astin, who is widely viewed as a leading surveyor of college-student performance and attitudes, found no negative effects on male students in nineteen all-male colleges he had studied which had gone coeducational.

"Can you tell me what kind of woman you would think would want to attend a coeducational Citadel?" Robert Patterson, the Citadel attorney who had previously represented V.M.I., asked Astin, his voice full of unflattering insinuation about the kind of woman he imagined her to be.

ASTIN: I suppose the same as the kind of men who want to go there.

PATTERSON: Would it be a woman that would not be all that different from men?

ASTIN: Yes.

To Patterson, this was a triumphant moment, and he closed on it: he had forced the government's witness to admit that a woman like Shannon Faulkner would have to be a mannish aberration from her gender. But in fact Astin's testimony expressed the precise point that the plaintiff's side had been trying to make all along, and that The Citadel strenuously resisted: that the sexes were, in the end, not all that different.

"I was considered the bitch of the band," Shannon Faulkner said, without embarrassment, of her four years in her high school's marching band—just stating a fact. She was lounging on the couch in her parents' living room, comfortable in an old T-shirt and shorts, one leg swung over an arm of the couch. "That's because I was the one who was mean and got it done." The phone rang, for the millionth time—another media call. "I'm not giving statements to the press right now," she said efficiently into the phone and hung up. She did not apologize for her brusqueness, as I was half expecting her to do, after she put down the receiver. There is nothing of the good girl about her. Not that she is disagreeable; Shannon Faulkner just doesn't see the point in false deference. "I never let anyone push me around, male or female," Faulkner said, and that fact had been exasperatingly obvious to reporters who covered the trial: they found that all the wheedling and cheap flatteries that usually prompt subjects to say more than they should didn't work with Faulkner.

One could scrounge around in Faulkner's childhood for the key to what made her take on The Citadel. You could say that it was because she was born six weeks premature, and her fierce struggle to live forged a "survivor." You could cite her memory that as a small child she preferred playing outside with the boys to playing with certain girls whom she deemed "too prissy." You could point to her sports career in high school and junior high: she lettered in softball for four years and kept stats for three of the schools' four basketball teams. You could note her ability to juggle tasks: she edited the yearbook, wrote for the school paper, and graduated with a 3.48 grade-point average. And you could certainly credit the sturdy backbone and outspokenness of both her mother and her maternal grandmother; this is a family where the women talk and the men keep a low profile. Her father, Ed, owns a small fence-building business. At thirty, a few years after Shannon's birth, Sandy returned to college to get her degree, a double major in psychology and education, and became a high-school teacher of psychology, sociology, United States history, and minority cultures. When a male professor had complained about certain "older women" in his class who asked "too many questions," Sandy hurled one of her wedge-heeled sandals at him. "I said, 'I'm paying for this class, and don't you ever tell me what I can ask.'" Shannon's maternal grandmother, sixty-seven-year-old Evelyn Richey, was orphaned at six and worked most of her life in textile factories, where, she noted, "women could do the job and men got the pay." Of her granddaughter's suit she said, "Women have got to come ahead. I say, let's get on with the show."

But there's little point in a detailed inspection of family history because there's no real mystery here. What is most striking about Shannon herself is that she's not particularly unusual. She reads novels by Tom Clancy and John Grisham, has worked in a local day-care center, is partial to places like Bennigan's. She wants a college education so she can support herself and have a career as a teacher or a journalist—she hasn't yet decided which. She might do a stint in the military, she might not. She is in many ways representative of the average striving lower-middle-class teenage girl, circa 1994, who intends to better herself and does not intend to achieve that betterment through a man—in fact, she has not for a moment entertained such a possibility.

Throughout the trial, cadets and Citadel alumni spoke of a feminist plot: she is "a pawn" of the National Organization for Women, or—a theory repeatedly posited to me by cadets—"Her mother put her up to it." Two Citadel alumni asked me in all seriousness if feminist organizations were paying Shannon Faulkner to take the stand. In truth, Shannon makes an unlikely feminist poster girl. She prefers to call herself "an individualist" and seems almost indifferent to feminist affairs; when I mentioned Gloria Steinem's name once in conversation, Shannon asked me, "Who's that?" After the judge issued his decision to admit her to the Corps, she told the *New York Times* that she didn't consider the ruling a victory "just for women"—only a confirmation of her belief that if you want something, "go for it." Shannon Faulkner's determination to enter The Citadel's Corps of Cadets was fuelled not so much by a desire to trailblaze as by a sense of amazement and indignation that this trail was barricaded in the first place. She had never, she told the court, encountered such a roadblock in all her nineteen years—a remark that perhaps only a young woman of her fortunate generation could make without perjuring herself.

Shannon Faulkner got the idea of attending The Citadel back in December of 1992. She was taking a preparatory education course at Wren High School, the local public school. Mike Hazel, the teacher, passed out articles for them to read and discuss, and Faulkner picked the article in *Sports Illustrated* about hazing at The Citadel. "It was almost as accidental as Rosa Parks," Hazel recalled. "I just held up *Sports Illustrated* and asked, 'Who wants to do this?'"

Faulkner told me she'd selected the article because "I had missed that issue." During the ensuing discussion, the class wandered off the subject of hazing and onto the question of what, exactly, a public state institution was doing barring women from its classrooms. After a while, Faulkner got up and went down to the counselor's office and returned with an application form from The Citadel. "I said, 'Hey, it doesn't even say 'Male/Female,'" she recalled. While she was sitting in class, she filled it out. "I didn't really make a big to-do about it."

Two weeks after Faulkner received her acceptance letter, The Citadel got word she was a woman and revoked her admission, and in August of 1993 she went off to spend a semester at the University of South Carolina at Spartanburg while the courts thrashed out the next move. As the lawyers filed papers, The Citadel's defenders delivered their own increasingly agitated personal beliefs to the plaintiff herself. Faulkner worked evenings as a waitress in a local bar called Chiefs Wings and Firewater until the nightly tirades from the many drunk Citadel-graduate customers got to be too much. Actually, Faulkner said, she wouldn't have quit if some of her male college friends hadn't felt the need to defend her honor. "I didn't want them getting hurt," she said. Her manner of dealing with the Citadel crowd was more good-humored. One day at the bar, she recalled, "a guy came up to me. 'Are you Shannon Faulkner?' he asked, and I said, 'Why?'—very casual. Then he got real huffy-puffy, madder and madder." Finally, she said, he stuck his ring in her face, then slammed his hand down on the table. "You will never wear *that!*" he yelled. Shannon saw him a few times in the bar after that, scowling at her from a far table. To lighten the mood, she once had the bartender send him a beer. He wouldn't drink it.

"I never show my true emotions in public," Shannon said. "I consider that weak." She can laugh at the cadets' threats, even when they turn ugly, because she doesn't see the reason for all the fuss. Whenever she is asked to sign the latest T-shirt inspired by the controversy, which depicts a group of male bulldogs (The Citadel's mascot) in cadet uniforms and one female bulldog in a red dress, above the caption "1,952 Bulldogs and 1 Bitch," Faulkner told me, "I always sign under the 'Bitch' part."

The first day that Shannon Faulkner attended classes, in January 1994, the cadets who had lined up by the academic building told the media the same thing over and over. "We were trained to be gentlemen, and that's what we'll be." But in Shannon's first class, biology, all three cadets assigned to sit in her row changed their seats. The teacher, Philippe Ross, had to threaten to mark them absent to get them to return to their places. (More than twenty unexcused absences a semester is grounds for failure.) Shortly thereafter, a rumor began to circulate that Faulkner was using a fake I.D. in the local bars. This summer, talk of a plot against Faulkner surfaced—to frame her, perhaps by planting drugs in her belongings. The threat seemed real enough for Faulkner to quit her summer job, in the Charleston area, and return home.

The *Brigadier's* column "Scarlet Pimpernel" took up the anti-Shannon cause with a vengeance. The columnist dubbed her "the divine bovine," likening her to a plastic revolving cow at a nearby mall (the mounting of which is a cadet tradition). The "Pimpernel" comments on an incident that occurred on

Faulkner's first day were particularly memorable. An African-American cadet named Von Mickle dared to shake her hand in front of the media and say, "It's time for women," and compared the exclusion of women to that of blacks. For this lone act, he was not only physically threatened by classmates but derided in the "Pimpernel." "The PIMP doth long to tame the PLASTIC COW on this most wondrous of nights," the anonymous author wrote, with the column's usual antique-English flourishes and coded references. "But it seems that we will have a live specimen, a home grown DAIRY QUEEN from the stables of Powdersville. Perhaps NON DICKLE will be the first to saddle up. He is DIVINE BOVINE's best friend after all."

More disturbing were cadet writings on Faulkner that were not for public consumption. Tom Lucas, a graduate student in The Citadel's evening program, told me about some "very harsh" graffiti that he'd found all over one of the men's rooms in The Citadel's academic building. The inscription that most stuck in his mind: "Let her in—then fuck her to death."

On the whole, The Citadel administrators to whom I spoke were defensive, evasive, or dismissive of the cadets' hostile words and deeds toward Faulkner. When I asked Citadel officials to respond to reports of barracks violence, harassment of women on staff, or verbal abuse of Faulkner, the responses were dismaying. Cases of violence and abuse were "aberrations"; cadets who spoke up were either "troublemakers" or "mama's boys"; and each complaint by a female faculty member was deemed a "private personnel matter" that could not be discussed further.

Certainly the administrators and trustees themselves are less than enthusiastic about Faulkner's arrival. William F. Prioleau, Jr., until recently a member of the Board of Visitors, implied on a radio talk show that abortions would go up as a result of the female invasion, as he claimed had happened at West Point. Meanwhile, in The Citadel's Math Department, all that was going up as a result of Shannon Faulkner's presence was the grade-point average. Faulkner's highest mark at the semester's end was in calculus, where she earned an A (prompting a surprised Dean Poole to comment to her that she was "certainly not the stereotypical woman"). The Math Department has in recent years invited A students to an annual party. But rather than include Faulkner, the department limited the guest list to math majors. Math professor David Trautman, who was in charge of invitations to the party, explained in an e-mail message to colleagues, "Her presence would put a damper on the evening."

Linda Ross, then a professor at The Citadel, was speaking one day with a seventy-six-year-old alumnus, and the talk turned to Faulkner's lawsuit. He asked her if she thought it possible that this young woman might prevail. "Well, it's probably an inevitable turning of the tide," Ross said, shrugging. To her amazement, the alumnus began to cry.

"I have the worst chance in society of getting a job, because I'm a white male," William H. Barnes, the senior platoon leader, shouted at me over the din in The Citadel's mess hall, a din created by the upperclassmen's tradition of berating knobs at mealtime. "And that's the major difference between me and my father." In a society where, at least since the Second World War, surpassing one's father has been an expected benchmark of American manhood, Barnes's point is a plangent one. But it's hard to say which Citadel generation is more undone by the loss of white male privilege—the young men who will never partake of a dreamed world of masculine advantage or the older men who are seeing that lived world split apart, shattered.

"I was in Vietnam in '63, and I'll defy you or Shannon or anyone else to hike through the rice paddies," the usually genial Colonel Harvey Dick, sixty-seven, a Board of Visitors member, an ex-marine, and an Army lieutenant colonel, was practically shouting from his recliner armchair in his Charleston home. He popped a Tums in his mouth. "There's just no way you can do that.... You can't pick up a ninety-five-pound projectile. There are certain things out there that are differences." On the wall above his head were seven bayonets. He was wearing his blue Citadel T-shirt, which matched the Citadel mementos that overwhelmed his den—Citadel mugs, hats, footballs, ceramic bulldogs. It was a room known in the Dick household as "Harvey's 'I Love Me' Room." Dick treated it as his command post—whenever the phone rang, he whipped it off the cradle and barked "Colonel Dick!"—but what he was commanding was unclear; he retired in 1993 from a sixteen-year stint as The Citadel's assistant commandant. Still, he at least knew that he was once in charge, that he once enjoyed lifetime job security as a career military man. This was something his son couldn't say: Harvey Dick II, a nuclear pipe fitter, had recently been laid off at the Charleston Naval Shipyard.

Colonel Dick wanted it known that he wasn't "one of those male-chauvinist pigs"; in fact, he believes that women are smarter than men. "Women used to let the men dominate," he said. "Maybe we need a male movement, since evidently we're coming out second on everything." He slipped another Tums from an almost empty roll. The sun was dropping as we spoke, and shadows fell across the Citadel hats and figurines in his room. "Go back and look at your Greek and Roman empires and why they fell," he said.

His wife cleared her throat. "This doesn't have anything to do with male-female," she said.

"I see a decline in this great nation of ours," Dick said. He crossed his arms and stared into the gathering darkness of the late summer afternoon. After a while, he said, "I guess I sound like a buffoon."

Unlike the cadets, the older male Citadel officials often have to face dissent from wives or daughters whose views and professional aspirations or accomplishments challenge their stand on women's proper place. Lewis Spearman, the assistant to the president, recently remarried, and his wife is a feminist paralegal who is now getting her master's degree in psychology. She says she engaged for more than a year in "shriekfests" with him over the Shannon Faulkner question before she halfheartedly came around to The Citadel party line on barring women. And, while the wife of Dean Poole may have sat on the Miss Citadel judging panel, their daughter, Mindy, had loftier ambitions. Despite the fact that she suffered from cystic fibrosis, she was an ardent skier, horseback rider, and college athlete, rising at 5 A.M. daily with her crew-team members at the University of Virginia. And, despite a double lung transplant during her junior year, she graduated in 1991 with honors and won a graduate fellowship. "She was an outstanding young lady," Poole said. "I was very proud of her." His eyes clouding over at the memory, he recalled that she had made him promise to take her to the big Corps Day parade on The Citadel's sesquicentennial. The day the father and daughter were to attend the parade was the day she died. "Sort of an interesting footnote," he said, wiping at his moist eyes. What if she had wanted to go to The Citadel? Well, actually, Poole said, she had talked about it. If she had persisted he would have tried to change her mind, he said, but he added, "I would never have stopped her from doing something she wanted to do."

One of the biggest spousal battles over Shannon Faulkner is waged nightly at the home of a man who might seem the least likely figure at The Citadel to wind up with a feminist wife. Probably The Citadel's most legendary elder, thanks to Pat Conroy's thinly veiled and admiring portrait of him in *The Lords of Discipline,* is Lieutenant Colonel T. Nugent Courvoisie, who, as an assistant commandant in the sixties, oversaw the admission of the first African-American cadet to The Citadel. A gravelly voiced and cigar-chomping tender tyrant, Courvoisie—or the Boo, as he is known, for obscure reasons—was a fixture at the school for more than two decades. There are two Citadel scholarships in his family name, and his visage peers down from two portraits on campus.

A courtly man, and still dapper at seventy-seven, the Boo, who has since given up cigars, insisted on picking me up at my hotel and driving me to his home, though I had a rental car sitting in the parking lot. On the drive over, he ticked off the differences between the sexes that he believed made it impossible for The Citadel to admit women—differences such as that "the average female is not as proficient athletically as the average male." When we were settled in the living room, the Boo on his recliner and his second wife, Margaret, who is also seventy-seven, in a straight-back chair, the subject of Shannon Faulkner was revisited. The first words out of Margaret's mouth were "The Citadel wants to chop the head off women." A low growl emanated from the Boo's corner. He lowered the recliner a notch. "We don't talk about it here," Margaret said—an obvious untruth. "We haven't come to blows yet, but—"

The Boo interrupted, "I have the correct view."

She retorted, "No one has the *correct* view." She turned and addressed me. "You have to understand him," she said of her husband of nine years. "This is a man who went to military prep schools and a church that was male-dominated, naturally."

The Boo interrupted. "J.C. picked twelve *men* as his disciples," he said.

Margaret rolled her eyes. "See? He even takes it into the church—and he's on such familiar ground with Christ he calls him J.C."

The Boo said, "J.C. never picked a woman, except his mother."

Margaret said, "Oh God, see, this is why we don't go into it."

But, as usual, go into it they did. As the words got batted back and forth, with Margaret doing most of the batting, the Boo levered his recliner progressively lower, until all I could see of him were the soles of his shoes.

MARGARET: You had plenty of good women soldiers in Saudi Arabia.

BOO: Plenty of pregnant ones....

MARGARET: What, do you think [the cadets] didn't get girls pregnant before? There've been plenty of abortions. And I know of a number of cases that, by the time [a cadet] graduated, there were four or five kids.

BOO: That's an exaggeration. Maybe two or three ... With women, there's going to be sexual harassment.

MARGARET: Oh, honey, those cadets are harassing each other right now, all the time.

BOO: That's different. That's standard operating procedure.

In the nineteen-sixties, Margaret worked in the library at The Citadel, where she would often see Charles Foster, the first African-American cadet (who died a few years ago), alone at one of the library desks. "He would just come to the library and sit there a lot. It's hard to be the only one, to be the groundbreaker. That's why I admire this girl."

Boo's voice boomed from the depths of his recliner: "But there's no need for her. She's ruining a good thing."

Margaret gave a mock groan. "This is the last vestige of male bastionship," she said, "and it's going to kill 'em when it crumbles." Boo raised his chair halfway back up and considered Margaret. "She has a good mind," he told me after a while.

Margaret smiled. "I'm a new experience for him. He's always been military. People didn't disagree with him."

The Boo showed the way upstairs, to the attic, where he has his own "Citadel room"—a collection of Citadel memorabilia vaster than but almost identical to Dick's. Around the house, there were sketches of Boo at various points in his Citadel career. He told me that, before he retired, the cadets commissioned a portrait of him that hangs in Jenkins Hall. "Man, I looked good in that," he said. "Like a man. A leader."

Margaret didn't think so. "No, it was horrible," she said. "It didn't look like you."

"If Shannon were in my class, I'd be fired by March for sexual harassment," Colonel James Rembert, an English professor, was saying as we headed toward his classroom. He had a ramrod bearing and a certain resemblance to Ted Turner (who, it happens, sent all three of his sons to The Citadel—Beau Turner among them—and donated twenty-five million dollars to the school earlier this year). The Colonel identifies himself as one of "the last white Remberts" in South Carolina, the Remberts being a Huguenot family of sufficiently ancient lineage to gain him admission to the St. John's Hunting Club of South Carolina—an all-male society chaired by a Citadel alumnus. Rembert, who has a Cambridge University doctorate and wrote a book on Jonathan Swift, said he preferred the company of men, in leisure and in learning. "I've dealt with young men all my life," he went on. "I know how to play with them. I have the freedom here to imply things I couldn't with women. I don't want to have to watch what I say."

The literary work under discussion that day was *Beowulf,* and the cadets agreed that it was all about "brotherhood loyalty" and, in the words of one student, "the most important characteristics of a man—glory and eternal fame." Then they turned to their papers on the topic.

"Mr. Rice," Rembert said in mock horror. "You turned in a single-spaced paper." This was a no-no. Rembert instructed him to take a pencil and "pen-e-trate"—Rembert drew the syllables out—the paper with the point. He shook his head. "What a pansy!" Rembert said. "Can't catch, can't throw, can't write." Another student was chastised for the use of the passive voice. "Never use the passive voice—it leads to effeminacy and homosexuality," Rembert told the class. "So next time you use the passive voice I'm going to make you lift up your limp wrist." Literary pointers concluded, Rembert floated the subject of Shannon Faulkner. The usual objections were raised. But then the class wandered into more interesting territory, provoked by a cadet's comment that "she would change the relationship between the men here." Just what is the nature of that relationship?

"When we are in the showers, it's very intimate," a senior cadet said. "We're one mass, naked together, and it makes us closer.... You're shaved, you're naked, you're afraid together. You can cry." Robert Butcher, another senior, said that the men take care of each classmate. "They'll help dress him, tuck in his shirt, shine his shoes." "You mean like a mother-child relationship?" I asked.

"That *is* what it is," another cadet said. "It's a family, even the way we eat—family style." A fourth cadet said, "Maybe it's a Freudian thing, but males feel more affection with each other when women are not around. Maybe we're all homosexuals."

The class groaned. "Speak for yourself, buddy," a number of cadets said, almost in a chorus.

Rembert said, "With no women, we can hug each other. There's nothing so nurturing as an infantry platoon."

The hooted-down cadet weighed in again: "When I used to wrestle in high school, we had this great tradition. Right before the game, the coach, he'd slap us really hard on the butt."

Rembert, a onetime paratrooper, said he and his skydiving buddies did that, too, right before they jumped. "First man out gets a pat right there."

Over lunch, Rembert returned to the theme of manly nurturance among Citadel men. "We hug each other," he said. One of his colleagues "always kisses me on the cheek," he went on. "It's like a true marriage. There's an affectionate intimacy that you will find between cadets. With this security they can, without being defensive, project tenderness to each other."

Months later, I was sitting in court watching Norman Doucet, the cadet regimental commander, testify. He was showing the judge a video of the Citadel experience and explaining the various scenes. First we were shown "one of the

Dependency is a main theme in cadet relationships. Colonel James Rembert says that the cadets' intimate bond is "like a true marriage." Illustration by Mark Zingarelli, originally published in *The New Yorker*. © Mark Zingarelli/House of Zing

great parts" of a knob's first day—the mothers looking weepy at the gate as their sons were led away. Doucet lingered over the head-shaving scene. "This is what does it, right here," he said. "Mothers can't even tell their sons apart after this." Thus shielded from the prying maternal eye, the cadets began their new life, and the video action shifted to a typical day in the life of the Corps. But the editing made it a day as heavy on early-morning domestic chores as it was on martial activity. Much of the film was devoted to housekeeping: scenes of cadets making beds, dressing each other, sweeping, taking out the trash, all of which Doucet described as "like some kind of a ballet or a dance that's going on." This is a dance where the most important moves took place before the show, in the dressing room. "What they are doing here is the Citadel shirt tuck," Doucet said. The tuck requires that a cadet unzip his pants halfway and fold down his waistband, then stand still while his helper approaches him from the back, puts his arms around the cadet's waist, pulls the loose shirt material firmly to the back, jams it as far down in the pants as he can, and then pulls the cadet's pants up. "If you watch closely right here, this is what the fourth-class system is all about," Doucet continued. "In order to get a proper shirt tuck, you can't do it yourself—you need your classmates to do it for you. There's really a lot of dependence upon your classmates." But, as Doucet's account suggested, cadets can experience that dependence only in concealment, away from mothers, away from all women.

When a Citadel attorney asked Doucet why female cadets would pose a problem on the campus, the only issue he raised was the humiliation that cadets feel if women observe the cadets' on-campus interactions. He spoke of the shame that knobs feel when, on occasion, a woman happened to be on the parade ground while upperclassmen were disciplining them. The cadets observing in the courtroom nodded in agreement.

It may seem almost paradoxical that the fourth-class system should be so solicitous of the emotional vulnerability of its wards—the same wards it subjects to such rigors. And yet the making of Whole Men evidently requires an initial stage of infantilization. Indeed, the objective of recapitulating childhood development is plainly spelled out in The Citadel's yearbook, known as "the Sphinx." The 1990 "Sphinx" explained, "As a freshman enters, he begins to release his childhood and takes the first steps to becoming a 'Citadel Man.'... As a 'knob,' every aspect of life is taught, a new way to walk.... Knobs are told how, where, and when to walk." Reentrance into manhood for the toddling knobs occurs on Recognition Day, when the upperclassmen force the knobs to do calisthenics until they drop, then gently lift up their charges and nurse them with cups of water. At that moment, for the first time in nine months, the older cadets call the knobs by their first names and embrace them.

The relationship between knobs and upperclassmen following Recognition Day, as they are integrated into the Corps, shifts from maternal to matrimonial. The yearbooks of the last several years picture Citadel men spending a lot of time embracing and kissing. Of course, this impulse, when it is captured on film, is always carefully disarmed with a jokey caption.

One afternoon, a group of cadets recounted for me the campus's many "nudity rituals," as they jokingly called them. There's "Senior Rip-Off Day," a spring rite in which three hundred seniors literally rip each other's clothes off, burn them in a bonfire, and hug and wrestle on the ground. There's "Nude Platoon," in which a group of juniors, unclad except for their cross-webbing, run around the quad yelling, "We love the Nude Platoon!" And there's the birthday ritual, in which the birthday boy is stripped, tied to a chair, and covered with shaving cream, while his groin is coated in liquid shoe polish.

During the fall semester before graduation, the seniors receive their "band of gold" (as it is called) in the Ring Ceremony. The chaplain blesses each class ring. (Receiving the ring, which I was constantly reminded is "the biggest class ring of any college," is a near-sacrament, and the yearbooks are filled with pictures of young men holding up their rings in fervor, as if clutching a crucifix before a vampire.) Then each senior walks through a ten-foot replica of the class ring with his mother on one arm and his "date" on the other. In a sort of reverse marriage ceremony, the mother gives the cadet away. Mother and date accompany him through the towering ring; then he kisses Mother farewell and marches under the arched swords of the Junior Sword Drill, a new bride of the Corps. Several cadets and alumni told me that when a Citadel graduate marries, it is a tradition to slide the class ring over the wedding band. Indeed, I saw such an ordering of priorities on the fingers of a number of Citadel men in the courtroom.

In the late-twentieth-century setting of The Citadel, in a time when extreme insecurity and confusion about masculinity's standing run rampant, the Corps of Cadets once again seeks to obscure a domestic male paradise with an intensifying of virile showmanship and violence. The result is a ruthless intimacy, in which physical abuse stands in for physical affection, and every display of affection must be counterbalanced by a display of sadism. Knobs told me that they were forced to run through the showers while the upperclassmen "guards" knocked the soap out of their hands and, when the knobs leaned over to retrieve it the upperclassmen would unzip their pants and yell, "Don't pick it up, don't pick it up! We'll use you like we used those girls!" A former Citadel Halloween tradition of upperclassmen dressing up—mostly in diapers and women's clothes—and collecting candy treats from knobs, has given way to "tricks" of considerable violence. (One upperclassman told me of cadets who knocked dressers over on candy-dispensing cadets and then walked on top of them.) The administration tried, unsuccessfully, to put a stop to the whole affair; too many freshmen were getting injured. And the playful pat on the butt that served to usher cadets into the brotherhood has degenerated into more invasive acts. According to a recent graduate, one company of cadets recently devised a regimen in which the older cadets tested sophomores nightly with increasingly painful treatments—beatings and stompings and so forth. The process, which they dubbed "Bananarama," culminated on a night in which an unpeeled banana was produced—and shoved into a cadet's anus.

Given this precarious dynamic, it is not surprising that in the past few years at The Citadel social rage has been directed toward any men who were perceived to be gay. Several young men who were suspected of homosexual inclinations were hounded out of the school. One cadet, Herbert Parker, who said that he was falsely accused of having a sexual encounter with a male janitor, recalled a year of total isolation—cadets refused to sit near him in the mess hall or in classes—and terror: incessant threatening phone calls and death threats. The cadets and the administration—which had responded to the report of his encounter by sending out a campus-security police car with lights flashing to question him—acted "like I had murdered someone."

The scapegoating reached such brutal proportions that the counseling center recently set up a sort of group-therapy session for the targeted young men, who are known as It, as in the game of tag.

One evening after the trial, I went over to the Treehouse, a "mixed" bar in Charleston, with an upstairs gay bar and nightly drag shows on the weekends. My intention was to ask about cadet violence against gay men. I presumed that on a campus where every second epithet was "faggot" such hate crimes were all but inevitable. There were indeed a few such cases, I learned, but the circumstances were different from what I had imagined. Nor were those cases the essence of my findings that evening.

"The proper terminology for The Citadel," a customer at the bar named Chris said, "is The Closet." Up and down the bar, heads bobbed in agreement. "They love faggots like me." What he meant by "like me," however, was not that he was gay. That night, he looked like a male model—sleek black hair and a handsome, chiseled face. But on the nights he was dressed for a performance he could pass for a woman. Arching an eyebrow, Chris said, "The cadets go for the drag queens."

Chris's observation was echoed in ensuing conversations in the bar. There are thousands of cadets, presumably, who have not dated drag queens, but in two visits to the Treehouse I could find only two drag queens, out of maybe a dozen, who did not tell me of dating a cadet—and that was only because these two found Citadel men "too emotional." Cadets can also occasionally be dangerous, Chris told me. "You can get the ones who are violent. They think they want it, then afterwards they turn on you, like you made them do it." Nonetheless, a drag queen who called himself Holly had been happily involved with a cadet for three years now. Marissa, another drag queen, the reigning "Miss Treehouse 1993–94," had gone out with one cadet, broken up, and was now in the throes of a budding romance with another. A third drag queen, who asked to be identified as Tiffany, was known to be a favorite of cadets.

As Chris and I were talking that first night, a drag queen called Lownie wandered in and settled on a bar stool. Lownie delighted in the Corps of Cadets pageantry—especially the Friday dress parades. "The parades are a big thing with the queers in Charleston," he said. "We'll have a cocktail party and go over and watch the boys. It's a very Southern-'lady' thing to do." Years ago, Lownie had been a student at the College of Charleston when he met *his* Citadel lover, and they had begun covert assignations—communicating through notes slipped in little-used books in the Citadel library. The only drawback, Lownie said, was dealing with his lover's constant emotional anxiety over making the grade at The Citadel. He was, in fact, a model macho cadet: a Junior Sword Drill member, a regimental officer, and a "hang king," who could dangle interminably from a closet rack by his fingertips. Lownie, who found such records more amusing than impressive, grinned, and said, "I used to make him wear his shako"—The Citadel's military cap—"when we were having sex. It's manhood at its most."

Lownie said he could begin to fathom his cadet's intense attachment to The Citadel—an emotion that he likened to a love affair—because he himself had spent four years in the Air Force. "The day-to-day aspect of being in a military environment is that you run around in a little bit of clothing and you are being judged as to how good a man you are by doing women's work—pressing pants, sewing, polishing shoes. You are a *better* man if you have mastery of womanly arts.... The camaraderie doesn't get any stronger than when you are in the barracks, sitting around at the end of the day in your briefs and T's and dogtags—like a bunch of hausfraus, talking and gossiping." The military stage set offers a false front and a welcome trapdoor—an escape hatch from the social burdens of traditional masculinity. Behind the martial backdrop, Lownie said, "you don't have to be a breadwinner. You don't have to be a leader. You can play back seat. It's a great relief. You can act like a human being and not have to act like a man."

"You know what the [cadet] I'm seeing now said to me?" Tiffany said. We were sitting in the dressing room a couple of hours before the night's performance, and as Tiffany spoke he peered into an elaborate mirror set illuminated with miniature movie-star lights, applying layer after layer of mascara and eyeliner with expert precision. "He said, 'You're more of a woman than a woman is.' And that's an exact quote." Tiffany stood up and struck a Southern belle pose by way of illustration. "I overexemplify everything a female is—my breasts, my hair, the way I hold myself." And who could better complete the hoopskirts picture than a fantasy gentleman in uniform?

Marissa, Miss Treehouse, looked up from his labors, painting row after row of fake nails with pink polish. "I love how they wear their caps slung low so you can't quite see their eyes," he said. "It's like all of us are female illusionists and they are male illusionists. A man in a uniform is a kind of dream."

Tiffany said, "For Halloween, you know what my cadet boyfriend wanted to dress as? A cadet."

The dressing-room scene before me, of a group of men tenderly helping each other get ready for the evening—an elaborate process of pinning and binding and stuffing—was not very different, in its way, from the footage in Norman Doucet's video of the cadets tucking in each other's shirts. As the drag queens conversed, they tossed stockings and Ace bandages and cosmetic bags back and forth. "Has anyone seen my mascara wand?" "O.K., who has the blush?" There was a homey comfort that reminded me of slumber parties when I was a girl, where we would put big pink spongy rollers in each other's hair and screech with laughter at the results. And suddenly it became obvious to me what was generating that void, that yearning, in the cadets' lives—and maybe in the lives of many American men. What was going on here was play—a kind of freedom and spontaneity that, in this culture, only women are permitted.

No wonder men found their Citadels, their Treehouses, where the rules of gender could be bent or escaped. For the drag queens of the Treehouse, the distinctions between the sexes are a goof, to be endlessly manipulated with fun-house-mirror glee. For cadets, despite the play set of The Citadel and the dress-up braids and ribbons, the guarding of their Treehouse is a dead-serious business. Still, undercover at The Citadel, the cadets have managed to create for themselves a world in which they get half the equation that Lownie described: they can "act like human beings" in the safety of the daily domestic life of the barracks. But, in return, the institution demands that they never cease to "act like a man"—a man of cold and rigid bearing, a man no more male than Tiffany's Southern belle is female, a man that no one, humanly, can be. That they must defend their inner humanity with outer brutality may say as much about the world outside The Citadel walls as about the world within them. The cadets feel called to defend those walls. Never mind that their true ideal may not be the vaunted one of martial masculinity, just as their true enemy is not Shannon Faulkner. The cadets at The Citadel feel that something about their life and routine is worthy on its merits and is endangered from without. And in that they may be right.

QUESTIONS FOR MAKING CONNECTIONS
WITHIN THE READING

1. In "The Naked Citadel," Susan Faludi provides a series of vignettes that describe life at the military school. Why does she present the vignettes in the order she does? Why does she start her article in Jane Bishop's classroom? Why does she then move to the courtroom? Make a chart that tracks the organization of Faludi's essay. What is the argument that Faludi is making by telling these vignettes in this order?

2. The sociologist Erving Goffman coined the term *total institutions* to describe places that become almost entirely self-enclosed and self-referential in their values and behaviors. Goffman's principal example was the mental asylum. Can we describe The Citadel accurately as a total institution? Are its values the product of its isolation, or does Faludi's account furnish evidence that the attitudes holding sway in The Citadel persist outside the institution as well? Is The Citadel just an aberration, or does it tell us certain truths about our own society?

3. Faludi offers this overview of The Citadel:

    > In the late-twentieth-century setting of The Citadel, in a time when extreme insecurity and confusion about masculinity's standing run rampant, the Corps of Cadets once again seeks to obscure a domestic male paradise with an intensifying of virile showmanship and violence. The result is a ruthless intimacy, in which physical abuse stands in for physical affection, and every display of affection must be counterbalanced by a display of sadism.

    On the basis of the evidence Faludi provides, is this a fair assessment of the culture of The Citadel? What evidence confirms this assessment? What evidence might be said to complicate or even contradict it? What other explanations might we offer for events at The Citadel? Does masculinity have to occupy the central place in our analysis, or might other factors be more important?

QUESTIONS FOR WRITING

1. In what sense is Susan Faludi a feminist? If we define a feminist as someone who is specifically concerned with defending the rights of women, does she qualify? Does she regard the rights of women as practically or theoretically distinct from the rights of men? How about the needs and aspirations of women? Are these fundamentally different from the needs and aspirations of men? Does Faludi see men as "oppressors of women"? Does she imply that our society systematically empowers men while systematically disempowering women, or does disempowerment cross gender lines?

2. "The Naked Citadel" might be described as a case study of the relations between sexuality and social structures. In what ways do social structures shape sexuality at The Citadel? Does Faludi's account call into question the belief in a single, natural form of male sexual expression? Is the problem with The Citadel that natural sexuality has been perverted by linking it to relations of power? Can sexuality and power ever be separated?

QUESTIONS FOR MAKING CONNECTIONS
BETWEEN READINGS

1. In "Immune to Reality," Daniel Gilbert sets out to create a theory of happiness, one that explains why humans, in general, are so unprepared to predict what things and accomplishments will lead to happiness. Does Gilbert's theory shed new light on the choices and the actions of the cadets at The Citadel? How would Gilbert's explanation for the cadets' behavior reinforce, extend, or contradict Faludi's understanding? Write an essay about the degree to which happiness, as Gilbert defines it, plays a role in education inside and outside The Citadel.

2. In "When I Woke Up Tuesday Morning, It Was Friday," from *The Myth of Sanity*, Martha Stout explores the psychological dynamics of dissociation. According to Stout, the experience of trauma "changes the brain itself." Under conditions of extreme pain or distress, the brain becomes unable to organize experience "usefully" or to integrate new experience with other, prior memories. Does it seem possible that dissociation plays a role in the training of cadets at The Citadel? What circumstantial evidence can you find to support this claim, or to dispute it? Does Stout's account of dissociation help to explain why so few cadets rebel against the treatment they receive? Is it possible that certain institutions use dissociation intentionally to weaken bonds sustained by affection and shared values? How might our society protect itself against the use of dissociation as a political instrument?

◆◆◆
_____

FRANKLIN FOER

FRANKLIN FOER (RHYMES WITH "LORE") is a writer long associated with the liberal magazine the *New Republic*, which was founded in 1914 by leaders of the Progressive movement. Impatient with the mainstream media, which these leaders saw as controlled by moneyed interests, they were hoping to create an independent journal of ideas. Since then, the *New Republic* has seen its ups and downs, but the near-collapse of the magazine during Foer's second stint as editor exposes the stubborn persistence of the problem it was founded to address: the survival of independent media in a highly unequal society like ours. In 1914, the elite owed their towering wealth to railroads, coal mines and oil wells; today they control the Internet and the "attention economy."

Foer was a casualty and not the cause of the magazine's decline. After a term as editor, he left to pursue other projects when he was lured back to the editor's post by Chris Hughes, then a boyish 28-year-old lucky enough to have shared a room with Facebook creator Mark Zuckerberg when the two were students at Harvard. As part of the original Facebook team, Hughes later sold his interest in the platform for an amount purportedly in excess of 700 million dollars. And that enormous wealth encouraged him to think that he could reshape the nation's cultural life in the ways he thought best. One of his first moves was to buy the *New Republic*, a respected but financially strapped print magazine.

At first, the *New Republic*'s journalists welcomed Hughes as a white knight who had arrived in the nick of time to save them from the problems created by the shift away from print to the Internet. They interpreted the return of Foer as a sign of Hughes' commitment to serious, hard-hitting analysis. But gradually the writers at the magazine realized that their owner had something else in mind, as Sarah Ellison reports in *Vanity Fair*, another mass-market periodical:

> Over time, one of the big flash points that developed between Hughes and his *New Republic* writers was their productivity. What that sometimes meant—despite Hughes's stated contempt for "superficial metrics of online virality"—was productivity measured in Web traffic.... The site's traffic did indeed double, but never got beyond that. "It was not just about traffic," another former staffer told me. "It was really about [Hughes] kind of feeling, 'These writers are taking my money, and they're coasting. They're sitting around in their office, intellectually masturbating, while I'm paying them.'"

"Mark Zuckerberg's War on Free Will" from A WORLD WITHOUT MIND: THE EXISTENTIAL THREAT OF BIG TECH by Franklin Foer, copyright © 2017 by Franklin Foer. Used by permission of Penguin Books, Ltd.

In the editorial offices of the *New Republic,* the older culture of ideas collided with the new culture of information. If ideas are measured by their quality, *information* can be quantified in metrics like "visits," "page views," and "downloads." Determined to increase the flow of traffic to the *New Republic*'s online site, Hughes eventually fired Foer, whose exit inspired two thirds the staff to resign in protest.

Just prior to Hughes' purchase of the magazine, sales had more than doubled, but on his watch, newsstand sales declined by 57% in 2013 and by another 20% in 2014. Today, the magazine limps along, a shadow of its former self. Hughes abandoned it in 2016, after deciding to devote his energies to venture capital.

Franklin Foer continues to write for some of the best magazines in the country, most recently the *Atlantic*. His latest book, *World Without Mind: The Existential Threat of Big Tech* (2017) tries to come to terms with dangers presented by the cultural clash that all but destroyed his magazine, and, quite possibly, many others in the years to come.

REFERENCES

Sarah Ellison, "The Complex Power Coupledom of Chris Hughes and Sean Eldridge." *Vanity Fair* July 2014. https://www.vanityfair.com/news/2015/06/chris-hughes-sean-eldridge-new-republic-congress-run

Katerina Eva Matsa and Michael Barthal, "The New Republic and the State of Niche News Magazines." Pew Research Center. FACTANK: News in the Numbers. 10 December 2014. http://www.pewresearch.org/fact-tank/2014/12/10/the-new-republic-and-the-state-of-niche-news-magazines/

Mark Zuckerberg's War on Free Will

Silicon valley graduated from the counterculture, but not really. All the values it professes are the values of the sixties. The big tech companies present themselves as platforms for personal liberation, just as Stewart Brand preached. Everyone has the right to speak their mind on social media, to fulfill their intellectual and democratic potential, to express their individuality. Where television had been a passive medium that rendered citizens inert, Facebook is participatory and empowering. It allows users to read widely, think for themselves, and form their own opinions.

We can't entirely dismiss this rhetoric. There are parts of the world, even in the United States, where Facebook emboldens citizens and enables them to organize themselves in opposition to power. But we shouldn't accept Facebook's self-conception as sincere, either. Facebook is a carefully managed top-down system, not a robust public square. It mimics some of the patterns of conversation, but that's a surface trail. In reality, Facebook is a tangle of rules and procedures for sorting information, rules devised by the corporation for the ultimate benefit of the corporation. Facebook is always surveilling users, always auditing them, using them as lab rats in its behavioral experiments. While it creates the impression that it offers choice, Facebook paternalistically nudges users in the direction it deems best for them, which also happens to be the direction that thoroughly addicts them. It's a phoniness most obvious in the compressed, historic career of Facebook's mastermind.

Mark Zuckerberg is a good boy, but he wanted to be bad, or maybe just a little bit naughty. The heroes of his adolescence were the original hackers. Let's be precise about the term. His idols weren't malevolent data thieves or cyber-terrorists. In the parlance of hacker culture, such ill-willed outlaws are known as crackers. Zuckerberg never put crackers on a pedestal. Still, his hacker heroes were disrespectful of authority. They were technically virtuosic, infinitely resourceful nerd cowboys, unbound by conventional thinking. In MIT's labs, during the sixties and seventies, they broke any rule that interfered with building the stuff of early computing, such marvels as the first video games and word processors. With their free time, they played epic pranks, which happened to draw further attention to their own cleverness—installing a living, breathing cow on the roof of a Cambridge dorm; launching a weather balloon, which miraculously emerged from beneath the turf, emblazoned with "MIT," in the middle of a Harvard-Yale football game.

The hackers' archenemies were the bureaucrats who ran universities, corporations, and governments. Bureaucrats talked about making the world more efficient, just like the hackers. But they were really small-minded paper-pushers who fiercely guarded the information they held, even when that information yearned to be shared. When hackers clearly engineered better ways of doing things—a box that enabled free long-distance calls, an instruction that might improve an operating system—the bureaucrats stood in their way, wagging an unbending finger. The hackers took aesthetic and comic pleasure in outwitting the men in suits.

When Zuckerberg arrived at Harvard in the fall of 2002, the heyday of the hackers had long passed. They were older guys now, the stuff of good tales, some stuck in twilight struggles against The Man. But Zuckerberg wanted to hack, too, and with that old-time indifference to norms. In high school—using the *nom de hack* Zuck Fader—he picked the lock that prevented outsiders from fiddling with AOL's code and added his own improvements to its instant messaging program. As a college sophomore he hatched a site called Facemash—with the high-minded purpose of determining the hottest kid on campus. Zuckerberg asked users to compare images of two students and then determine the better looking of the two. The winner of each pairing advanced to the next round of his hormonal tournament. To cobble this site together, Zuckerberg needed photos. He purloined those from the servers of the various Harvard houses that stockpiled them. "One thing is certain," he wrote on a blog as he put the finishing touches on his creation, "and it's that I'm a jerk for making this site. Oh well."

His brief experimentation with rebellion ended with his apologizing to a Harvard disciplinary panel, as well as campus women's groups, and mulling strategies to redeem his soiled reputation. In the years since, he's shown that defiance really wasn't his natural inclination. His distrust of authority was such that he sought out Don Graham, then the venerable chairman of the Washington Post company, as his mentor. After he started Facebook, he shadowed various giants of corporate America so that he could study their managerial styles up close. Though he hasn't fully shed his awkward ways, he has sufficiently overcome his introversion to appear at fancy dinner parties, Charlie Rose interviews, and *Vanity Fair* cover shoots.

Still, the juvenile fascination with hackers never did die, or rather he carried it forward into his new, more mature incarnation. When he finally had a corporate campus of his own, he procured a vanity address for it: One Hacker Way. He designed a plaza with h-a-c-k inlaid into the concrete. In the center of his office park, he created an open meeting space called Hacker Square. This is, of course, the venue where his employees join for all-night Hackathons. As he told a group of would-be entrepreneurs, "We've got this whole ethos that we want to build a hacker culture."

Plenty of companies have similarly appropriated hacker culture—hackers are the ur-disrupters—but none have gone as far as Facebook. Of course, that's not without risks. "Hacking" is a loaded term, and a potentially alienating one, at least to shareholders who crave sensible rule-abiding leadership. But by the time Zuckerberg began extolling the virtues of hacking, he'd stripped the name of most of its original meaning and distilled it into a managerial philosophy that contains barely a hint of rebelliousness. It might even be the opposite of rebelliousness. Hackers, he told one interviewer, were "just this group of computer scientists who were trying to quickly prototype and see what was possible. That's what I try to encourage our engineers to do here." To hack is to be a good worker, a responsible Facebook citizen—a microcosm of the way in which the company has taken the language of radical individualism and deployed it in the service of conformism.

Zuckerberg claimed to have distilled that hacker spirit into a motivational motto: "Move Fast and Break Things." Indeed, Facebook has excelled at that. The truth is, Facebook moved faster than Zuckerberg could ever have imagined. He hadn't really intended his creation. His company was, as we all know, a dorm room lark, a thing he ginned up in a Red Bull–induced fit of sleeplessness. As his creation grew, it needed to justify its new scale to its investors, to its users, to the world. It needed to grow up fast. According to Dustin Moskovitz, who cofounded the company with Zuckerberg at Harvard, "It was always very important for our brand to get away from the image of frivolity it had, especially in Silicon Valley." Over the span of its short life, the company has caromed from self-description to self-description. It has called itself a tool, a utility, and a platform. It has talked about openness and connectedness. And in all these attempts at defining itself, it has managed to clarify its intentions.

Though Facebook will occasionally talk about the transparency of governments and corporations, what it really wants to advance is the transparency of individuals—or what it has called, at various moments, "radical transparency" or "ultimate transparency." The theory holds that the sunshine of sharing our intimate details will disinfect the moral mess of our lives. Even if we don't intend for our secrets to become public knowledge, their exposure will improve society. With the looming threat that our embarrassing information will be broadcast, we'll behave better. And perhaps the ubiquity of incriminating photos and damning revelations will prod us to become more tolerant of one another's sins. Besides, there's virtue in living our lives truthfully. "The days of you having a different image for your work friends or co-workers and for the other people you know are probably coming to an end pretty quickly," Zuckerberg has said. "Having two identities for yourself is an example of a lack of integrity."

The point is that Facebook has a strong, paternalistic view on what's best for you, and it's trying to transport you there. "To get people to this point where there's more openness—that's a big challenge. But I think we'll do it," Zuckerberg has said. He has reason to believe that he will achieve that goal. With its size, Facebook has amassed outsized powers. These powers are so great that Zuckerberg doesn't bother denying that fact. "In a lot of ways Facebook is more like a government than a traditional company. We have this large community of people, and more than other technology companies we're really setting policies."

Without knowing it, Zuckerberg is the heir to a long political tradition. Over the last two hundred years, the West has been unable to shake an abiding fantasy, a dream sequence in which we throw out the bum politicians and replace them with engineers—rule by slide rule. The French were the first to entertain this notion in the bloody, world-churning aftermath of their revolution. A coterie of the country's most influential philosophers (notably, Henri de Saint-Simon and Auguste Comte) were genuinely torn about the course of the country. They hated all the old ancient bastions of parasitic power—the feudal lords, the priests, and the warriors—but they also feared the chaos of the mob. To split the difference, they proposed a form of technocracy—engineers and assorted technicians would rule with beneficent disinterestedness. Engineers would strip the old order of its power, while governing in the spirit of science. They would impose rationality and order.

This dream has captivated intellectuals ever since, especially Americans. The great sociologist Thorstein Veblen was obsessed with installing engineers in power and, in 1921, wrote a book making his case. His vision briefly became a reality. In the aftermath of World War I, American elites were aghast at all the irrational impulses unleashed by that conflict—the xenophobia, the racism, the urge to lynch and riot. What's more, the realities of economic life had grown so complicated, how could politicians possibly manage them? Americans of all persuasions began yearning for the salvific ascendance of the most famous engineer of his time: Herbert Hoover. During the war, Hoover had organized a system that managed to feed starving Europe, despite the seeming impossibility of that assignment. In 1920, Franklin Roosevelt—who would, of course, ultimately vanquish him from politics—organized a movement to draft Hoover for the presidency.

The Hoover experiment, in the end, hardly realized the happy fantasies about the Engineer King. A very different version of this dream, however, has come to fruition, in the form of the CEOs of the big tech companies. We're not ruled by engineers, not yet, but they have become the dominant force in American life, the highest, most influential tier of our elite. Marc Andreessen coined a famous aphorism that holds, "Software is eating the world." There's a bit of obfuscation in that formula—it's really the authors of software who are eating the world.

There's another way to describe this historical progression. Automation has come in waves. During the Industrial Revolution, machinery replaced manual workers. At first machines required human operators. Over time, machines came to function with hardly any human intervention. For centuries, engineers automated physical labor; our new engineering elite has automated thought. They have perfected technologies that take over intellectual processes, that render the brain redundant. Or as Marissa Mayer once argued, "You have to make *words* less human and more a piece of the *machine.*" Indeed, we have begun to outsource our intellectual work to companies that suggest what we should learn, the topics we should consider, and the items we ought to buy. These companies can justify their incursions into our lives with the very arguments that Saint-Simon and Comte articulated: They are supplying us with efficiency; they are imposing order on human life.

Nobody better articulates the modern faith in engineering's power to transform society than Zuckerberg. He told a group of software developers, "You know, I'm an engineer, and I think a key part of the engineering mindset is this hope and this belief that you can take any system that's out there and make it much, much better than it is today. Anything, whether it's hardware, or software, a company, a developer ecosystem, you can take anything and make it much, much better." The world will improve, if only Zuckerberg's reason can prevail—and it will.

THE PRECISE SOURCE OF FACEBOOK'S power is algorithms. That's a concept repeated dutifully in nearly every story about the tech giants, yet it remains fuzzy at best to users of those sites. From the moment of the algorithm's invention, it was possible to see its power, its revolutionary potential. The algorithm was developed in order to automate thinking, to remove difficult decisions from the hands of humans, to settle contentious debates. To understand the essence of the algorithm—and its utopian pretension—it's necessary to travel back to its birthplace, the brain of one of history's unimpeachable geniuses, Gottfried Leibniz.

Fifty years younger than Descartes, Leibniz grew up in the same world of religious conflict. His native Germany, Martin Luther's homeland, had become one of history's most horrific abattoirs, the contested territory at the center of the Thirty Years War. Although the battlefield made its own contribution to the corpse count, the aftermath of war was terrible, too. Dysentery, typhus, and plague conquered the German principalities. Famine and demographic collapse followed battle, some four million deaths in total. The worst-clobbered of the German states lost more than half of their population.

Leibniz was born as Europe negotiated the Peace of Westphalia ending the slaughter, so it was inevitable that he trained his prodigious intellectual energies on reconciling Protestants and Catholics, crafting schemes to unify humanity. Prodigious is perhaps an inadequate term to describe Leibniz's mental reserves. He produced schemes at, more or less, the rate he contracted his diaphragm. His archives, which still haven't been fully published, contain some two hundred thousand pages of his writing, filled with spectacular creations. Leibniz invented calculus—to be sure, he hadn't realized that Newton discovered the subject earlier, but it's his notation that we still use. He produced lasting treatises on metaphysics and theology, he drew up designs for watches and windmills, he advocated universal health care and the development of submarines. As a diplomat in Paris, he pressed Louis XIV to invade Egypt, a bank-shot ploy to divert Germany's mighty neighbor into an overseas adventure that might lessen the prospect of marching its armies east. Denis Diderot, no slouch, moaned, "When one compares . . . one's own small talents with those of a Leibniz, one is tempted to throw away one's books and go die peacefully in the depths of some dark corner."

Of all Leibniz's schemes, the dearest was a new lexicon he called the universal characteristic—and it, too, sprang from his desire for peace. Throughout history, fanciful thinkers have created languages from scratch in the hope that their concoctions would smooth communication between the peoples of the world, fostering the preconditions for global oneness. Leibniz created his language for that reason, too, but he also had higher hopes: He argued that a new set of symbols and expressions would lead science and philosophy to new truths, to a new age of reason, to a deeper appreciation of the universe's elegance and harmony, to the divine.

What he imagined was an alphabet of human thought. It was an idea that he first pondered as a young student, the basis for his doctoral dissertation at Altdorf. Over the years, he fleshed out a detailed plan for realizing his fantasy. A group of scholars would create an encyclopedia containing the fundamental, incontestably true concepts of the world, of physics, philosophy, geometry, everything really. He called these core concepts "primitives," and they would include things like the earth, the color red, and God. Each of the primitives would be assigned a numerical value, which allowed them to be combined to create new concepts or to express complex extant ones. And those numerical values would form the basis for a new calculus of thought, what he called the calculus ratiocinator.

Leibniz illustrated his scheme with an example. What is a human? A rational animal, of course. That's an insight that we can write like this:

rational x animal = man

But Leibniz translated this expression into an even more mathematical sentence. "Animal," he suggested, might be represented with the number two; "rational" with the number three. Therefore:

2 x 3 = 6

Thought had been turned into math—and this allowed for a new, foolproof method for adjudicating questions of truth. Leibniz asked, for instance, are all men monkeys? Well, he knew the number assigned to monkeys, ten. If ten can't be divided by six, and six can't be divided by ten, then we know: There's no element of monkey in man—and no element of man in monkey.

That was the point of his language: Knowledge, all knowledge, could ultimately be derived from computation. It would be an effortless process, *cogitatio caeca* or blind thought. Humans were no longer even needed to conceive new ideas. A machine could do that, by combining and dividing concepts. In fact, Leibniz built a prototype of such a machine, a gorgeous, intricate compilation of polished brass and steel, gears and dials. He called it the Stepped Reckoner. Leibniz spent a personal fortune building it. With a turn of the crank in one direction the Stepped Reckoner could multiply, in the other direction divide. Leibniz had designed a user interface so meticulous that Steve Jobs would have bowed down before it. Sadly, whenever he tested the machine for an audience, as he did before the Royal Society in London in 1673, it failed. The resilient Leibniz forgave himself these humiliating demonstrations. The importance of the universal characteristic demanded that he press forward. "Once this has been done, if ever further controversies should arise, there should be no more reason for disputes between two philosophers than between two calculators." Intellectual and moral argument could be settled with the disagreeing parties declaring, "Let's calculate!" There would be no need for wars, let alone theological controversy, because truth would be placed on the terra firma of math.

Leibniz was a prophet of the digital age, though his pregnant ideas sat in the waiting room for centuries. He proposed a numeric system that used only zeros and ones, the very system of binary on which computing rests. He explained how automation or white-collar jobs would enhance productivity. But his critical insight was mechanical thinking, the automation of reason, the very thing that makes the Internet so miraculous, and the power of the tech companies so potentially menacing.

Those procedures that enable mechanical thinking came to have a name. They were dubbed algorithms. The essence of the algorithm is entirely uncomplicated. The textbooks compare them to recipes—a series of precise steps that can be followed mindlessly. This is different from equations, which have one correct result. Algorithms merely capture the process for solving a problem and say nothing about where those steps ultimately lead.

These recipes are the crucial building blocks of software. Programmers can't simply order a computer to, say, search the Internet. They must give the computer a set of specific instructions for accomplishing that task. These instructions must take the messy human activity of looking for information and transpose that into an orderly process that can be expressed in code. First do this . . . then do that. . . . The process of translation, from concept to procedure to code, is inherently reductive. Complex processes must be subdivided into a series of binary choices. There's no equation to suggest a dress to wear, but an algorithm could easily be written for that—it will work its way through a series of either/or questions (morning or night, winter or summer, sun or rain), with each choice pushing to the next.

Mechanical thinking was exactly what Alan Turing first imagined as he collapsed on his run through the meadows of Cambridge in 1935 and daydreamed about a fantastical new calculating machine. For the first decades of computing, the term "algorithm" wasn't much mentioned. But as computer science departments began sprouting across campuses in the sixties, the term acquired a new cachet. Its vogue was the product of status anxiety. Programmers, especially in the academy, were anxious to show that they weren't mere technicians. They began to describe their work as algorithmic, in part because it tied them to one of the greatest of all mathematicians—the Persian polymath Muḥammad ibn Mūsā al-Khwārizmi, or as he was known in Latin, Algoritmi. During the twelfth century, translations of al-Khwārizmi introduced Arabic numerals to the West; his treatises pioneered algebra and trigonometry. By describing the algorithm as the fundamental element of programming, the computer scientists were attaching themselves to a grand history. It was a savvy piece of name dropping: See, we're not arriviste, we're working with abstractions and theories, just like the mathematicians!

There was sleight of hand in this self-portrayal. The algorithm may be the essence of computer science—but it's not precisely a scientific concept. An algorithm is a system, like plumbing or a military chain of command. It takes know-how, calculation, and creativity to make a system work properly. But some systems, like some armies, are much more reliable than others. A system is a human artifact, not a mathematical truism. The origins of the algorithm are unmistakably human, but human fallibility isn't a quality that we associate with it. When algorithms reject a loan application or set the price for an airline flight, they seem impersonal and unbending. The algorithm is supposed to be devoid of bias, intuition, emotion, or forgiveness. They call it a search engine, after all—a nod to pistons, gears, and twentieth-century industry, with the machinery wiped clean of human fingerprints.

Silicon Valley's algorithmic enthusiasts were immodest about describing the revolutionary potential of their objects of affection. Algorithms were always interesting and valuable, but advances in computing made them infinitely more powerful. The big change was the cost of computing. It collapsed, and just as the machines themselves sped up and were tied into a global network. Computers could stockpile massive piles of unsorted data—and algorithms could attack this data to find patterns and connections that would escape human analysts. In the hands of Google and Facebook, these algorithms grew ever more powerful. As they went about their searches, they accumulated more and more data. Their machines assimilated all the lessons of past searches, using these learnings to more precisely deliver the desired results.

For the entirety of human existence, the creation of knowledge was a slog of trial and error. Humans would dream up theories of how the world worked, then would examine the evidence to see whether their hypotheses survived or crashed upon their exposure to reality. Algorithms upend the scientific method—the patterns emerge from the data, from correlations, unguided by hypotheses. They remove humans from the whole process of inquiry. Writing in *Wired*, Chris Anderson argued: "We can stop looking for models. We can analyze the data without hypotheses about what it might show. We can throw the numbers into the biggest computing clusters the world has ever seen and let statistical algorithms find patterns where science cannot."

On one level, this is undeniable. Algorithms can translate languages without understanding words, simply by uncovering the patterns that undergird the construction of sentences. They can find coincidences that humans might never even think to seek. Walmart's algorithms found that people desperately buy strawberry Pop-Tarts as they prepare for massive storms. Still, even as an algorithm mindlessly implements its procedures—and even as it learns to see new patterns in the data—it reflects the minds of its creators, the motives of its trainers. Both Amazon and Netflix use algorithms to make recommendations about books and films. (One-third of purchases on Amazon come from these recommendations.) These algorithms seek to understand our tastes, and the tastes of like-minded consumers of culture. Yet the algorithms make fundamentally different recommendations. Amazon steers you to the sorts of books that you've seen before. Netflix directs users to the unfamiliar. There's a business reason for this difference. Blockbuster movies cost Netflix more to stream. Greater profit arrives when you decide to watch more obscure fare. Computer scientists have an aphorism that describes how algorithms relentlessly hunt for patterns: They talk about torturing the data until it confesses. Yet this metaphor contains unexamined implications. Data, like victims of torture, tells its interrogator what it wants to hear.

Sometimes, the algorithm reflects the subconscious of its creators. To take an extreme example: The Harvard professor Latanya Sweeney conducted a study that found that users with African American names were frequently targeted with Google ads that bluntly suggested that they had arrest records in need of expunging. ("Latisha Smith, Arrested?") Google is not particularly forthright about why such results appear. Their algorithm is a ferociously guarded secret. Yet, we know that Google has explicitly built its search engine to reflect values that it holds dear. It believes that the popularity of a Web site gives a good sense of its utility; it chooses to suppress pornography in its search results and not, say, anti-Semitic conspiracists; it believes that users will benefit from finding recent articles more than golden oldies. These are legitimate choices—and perhaps wise business decisions—but they are choices, not science.

Like economics, computer science has its preferred models and implicit assumptions about the world. When programmers are taught algorithmic thinking, they are told to venerate efficiency as a paramount consideration. This is perfectly understandable. An algorithm with an ungainly number of steps will gum up the machinery, and a molasseslike server is a useless one. But efficiency is also a value. When we speed things up, we're necessarily cutting corners, we're generalizing.

Algorithms can be gorgeous expressions of logical thinking, not to mention a source of ease and wonder. They can track down copies of obscure nineteenth-century tomes in a few milliseconds; they put us in touch with long-lost elementary school friends; they enable retailers to deliver packages to our doors in a flash. Very soon, they will guide self-driving cars and pinpoint cancers growing in our innards. But to do all these things, algorithms are constantly taking our measure. They make decisions about us and on our behalf. The problem is that when we outsource thinking to machines, we are really outsourcing thinking to the organizations that run the machines.

Mark Zuckerberg disingenuously poses as a friendly critic of algorithms. That's how he implicitly contrasts Facebook with his rivals across the way at Google.

Over in Larry Page's shop, the algorithm is king, a cold, pulseless ruler. There's not a trace of life force in its recommendations and very little apparent understanding of the person keying a query into its engine. Facebook, in his flattering self-portrait, is a respite from this increasingly automated, atomistic world. "Every product you use is better off with your friends," he says.

What he is referring to is Facebook's News Feed. Here's a brief explanation for the sliver of humanity who have apparently resisted Facebook: The News Feed provides a reverse chronological index of all the status updates, articles, and photos that your friends have posted to Facebook. The News Feed is meant to be fun, but also geared to solve one of the essential problems of modernity—our inability to sift through the evergrowing, always-looming mounds of information. Who better, the theory goes, to recommend what we should read and watch than our friends? Zuckerberg has boasted that the News Feed turned Facebook into a "personalized newspaper."

Unfortunately, our friends can do only so much to winnow things for us. Turns out, they like to share a lot. If we just read their musings and followed links to articles, we might be only a little less overwhelmed than before, or perhaps even deeper underwater. So Facebook makes its own choices about what should be read. The company's algorithms sort the thousands of things a Facebook user could possibly see down to a smaller batch of choice items. And then within those few dozen items, it decides what we might like to read first.

Algorithms are, by definition, invisibilia. But we can usually sense their presence—that somewhere in the distance, we're interacting with a machine. That's what makes Facebook's algorithm so powerful. Many users—60 percent, according to the best research—are completely unaware of its existence. But even if they know of its influence, it wouldn't really matter. Facebook's algorithm couldn't be more opaque. When the company concedes its existence to reporters, it manages to further cloud the algorithm in impenetrable descriptions. We know, for instance, that its algorithm was once called EdgeRank. But Facebook no longer uses that term. It's appropriate that the algorithm doesn't have a name. It has grown into an almost unknowable tangle of sprawl. The algorithm interprets more than one hundred thousand "signals" to make its decisions about what users see. Some of these signals apply to all Facebook users; some reflect users' particular habits and the habits of their friends. Perhaps Facebook no longer fully understands its own tangle of algorithms—the code, all sixty million lines of it, is a palimpsest, where engineers add layer upon layer of new commands. (This is hardly a condition unique to Facebook. The Cornell University computer scientist Jon Kleinberg cowrote an essay that argued, "We have, perhaps for the first time ever, built machines we do not understand. . . . At some deep level we don't even really understand how they're producing the behavior we observe. This is the essence of their incomprehensibility." What's striking is that the "we" in that sentence refers to the creators of code.)

Pondering the abstraction of this algorithm, imagine one of those earliest computers with its nervously blinking lights and long rows of dials. To tweak the algorithm, the engineers turn the knob a click or two. The engineers are constantly making small adjustments, here and there, so that the machine performs to their satisfaction. With even the gentlest caress of the metaphorical dial, Facebook changes what its users see and read. It can make our friends' photos more or less ubiquitous; it can punish posts filled with self-congratulatory musings and banish what it deems to be hoaxes; it can promote video rather than text; it can favor articles from the likes of the *New York Times* or BuzzFeed, if it so desires. Or if we want to be melodramatic about it, we could say Facebook is constantly tinkering with how its users view the world—always tinkering with the quality of news and opinion that it allows to break through the din, adjusting the quality of political and cultural discourse in order to hold the attention of users for a few more beats.

But how do the engineers know which dial to twist and how hard? There's a whole discipline, data science, to guide the writing and revision of algorithms. Facebook has a team, poached from academia, to conduct experiments on users. It's a statistician's sexiest dream—some of the largest data sets in human history, the ability to run trials on mathematically meaningful cohorts. When Cameron Marlow, the former head of Facebook's data science team, described the opportunity, he began twitching with ecstatic joy. "For the first time," Marlow said, "we have a microscope that not only lets us examine social behavior at a very fine level that we've never been able to see before but allows us to run experiments that millions of users are exposed to."

Facebook likes to boast of the fact of its experimentation more than the details of the actual experiments themselves. But there are examples that have escaped the confines of its laboratories. We know, for example, that Facebook sought to discover whether emotions are contagious. To conduct this trial, Facebook attempted to manipulate the mental state of its users. For one group, Facebook excised the positive words from the posts in the News Feed; for another group, it removed the negative words. Each group, it concluded, wrote posts that echoed the mood of the posts it had reworded. This study was roundly condemned as invasive, but it is not so unusual. As one member of Facebook's data science team confessed: "Anyone on that team could run a test. They're always trying to alter people's behavior."

There's no doubting the emotional and psychological power possessed by Facebook—at least Facebook doesn't doubt it. It has bragged about how it increased voter turnout (and organ donation) by subtly amping up the social pressures that compel virtuous behavior. Facebook has even touted the results from these experiments in peer-reviewed journals: "It is possible that more of the .60% growth in turnout between 2006 and 2010 might have been caused by a single message on Facebook." No other company has so precisely boasted about its ability to shape democracy like this—and for good reason. It's too much power to entrust to a corporation.

The many Facebook experiments add up. The company believes that it has unlocked social psychology and acquired a deeper understanding of its users than they possess of themselves. Facebook can predict users' race, sexual orientation, relationship status, and drug use on the basis of their "likes" alone. It's Zuckerberg's fantasy that this data might be analyzed to uncover the mother of all revelations, "a fundamental mathematical law underlying human social relationships that governs the balance of who and what we all care about." That is, of course, a goal in the distance. In the meantime, Facebook will probe—constantly testing to see what we crave and what we ignore, a never-ending campaign to improve Facebook's capacity to give us the things that we want and things that we don't even know we want. Whether the information is true or concocted, authoritative reporting or conspiratorial opinion, doesn't really seem to matter much to Facebook. The crowd gets what it wants and deserves.

The Automation of Thinking: We're in the earliest days of this revolution, of course. But we can see where it's heading. Algorithms have retired many of the bureaucratic, clerical duties once performed by humans—and they will soon begin to replace more creative tasks. At Netflix, algorithms suggest the genres of movies to commission. Some news wires use algorithms to write stories about crime, baseball games, and earthquakes, the most rote journalistic tasks. Algorithms have produced fine art and composed symphonic music, or at least approximations of them.

It's a terrifying trajectory, especially for those of us in these lines of work. If algorithms can replicate the process of creativity, then there's little reason to nurture human creativity. Why bother with the tortuous, inefficient process of writing or painting if a computer can produce something seemingly as good and in a painless flash? Why nurture the overinflated market for high culture, when it could be so abundant and cheap? No human endeavor has resisted automation, so why should creative endeavors he any different?

The engineering mind-set has little patience for the fetishization of words and images, for the mystique of art, for moral complexity and emotional expression. It views humans as data, components of systems, abstractions. That's why Facebook has so few qualms about performing rampant experiments on its users. The whole effort is to make human beings predictable—to anticipate their behavior, which makes them easier to manipulate. With this sort of cold-blooded thinking, so divorced from the contingency and mystery of human life, it's easy to see how long-standing values begin to seem like an annoyance—why a concept like privacy would carry so little weight in the engineer's calculus, why the inefficiencies of publishing and journalism seem so imminently disruptable.

Facebook would never put it this way, but algorithms are meant to erode free will, to relieve humans of the burden of choosing, to nudge them in the right direction. Algorithms fuel a sense of omnipotence, the condescending belief that our behavior can be altered, without our even being aware of the hand guiding us, in a superior direction. That's always been a danger of the engineering mind-set, as it moves beyond its roots in building inanimate stuff and begins to design a more perfect social world. We are the screws and rivets in the grand design.

QUESTIONS FOR MAKING CONNECTIONS
WITHIN THE READING

1. At times, Foer's argument seems to take the form of a personal attack on Mark Zuckerberg. Reread the chapter, noting all the moments where Foer turns our attention directly to him. What purpose do these moments serve? Is this simply an example of what philosophers call an argument *ad hominem*—an attack on a person rather than a fair evaluation of his ideas? Or does Foer see Zuckerberg as representative of the Internet in general, especially because Facebook has had such an outsized impact? To what degree does personality play an unusual role in the history of the Internet? Millions of people know Zuckerberg's name, but who knows the name of Wal-Mart's CEO or the Chairman of General Motors? Is there something about the Internet that makes it feel especially personal? How do algorithms contribute to the personal feel of the Web?

2. A key word in Foer's title is "free will." What does Foer mean by his phrase a "war on free will"? The use of Facebook clearly requires active attention and choice. Newsfeeds provide information nonstop, much of it eagerly consumed. Indeed, it is possible to spend many hours searching for a few absorbing posts. No one tells Facebook users what to read or what they should ignore. At every step, they seem to exercise control, and their decisions are guided by purpose and reflection. What does Foer mean, then, by alleging that the Internet—and Facebook in particular—undermines free will?

3. Why does Foer mention Leibnitz, the inventor of calculus? Is he simply showing off his historical knowledge? Or he is trying to demonstrate a long-term tendency in the West? What were Leibnitz's motives in his attempt to create a thinking machine which could process ideas automatically? What does Foer's knowledge of history add to our understanding of the Web, which claims to be completely new and unprecedented? Why is Foer so critical of engineers, including Mark Zuckerberg? If the purpose of engineering is to enhance the quality of life, why would anyone object to improvements in the flow of knowledge—improvements that actually hold back a deluge of unwanted information? Does Facebook's mechanical thinking give Zuckerberg more power, or has it moved beyond anyone's control?

QUESTIONS FOR WRITING

1. To what extent does the countercultural history of the Internet—its celebration of sixties-style openness—conflict with what Foer calls the "automation of thinking"? The hacker culture Foer references at the start of his chapter celebrates resistance to established sources of authority. And today, the Internet still seems to offer some of us the greatest freedom we enjoy anywhere. Yet Foer alleges that the masters of the Internet have created a system that controls everything—even the way we think—without our

noticing. Is Foer, an older journalist whose influence has declined along with print magazines, motivated by spite, or does he have a point about the way the Web's freewheeling rhetoric disguises authoritarian tendencies?

2. The title of Foer's book is *World Without Mind: The Existential Threat of Big Tech*. One key word in that title is "existential," which can simply imply that big tech represents a threat to our "existence." But the word "existential" carries with it richer connotations. A major school of modern philosophy is known as existentialism, which espouses the idea that humans have no reason to exist except for the ones they make for themselves. Existentialist philosophers like Jean-Paul Sartre rejected the idea that a god created us with a particular mission or task. Instead, the existentialists believe that we are ethically obligated to take full responsibility for the people we become and the world we have made. Pretending that we aren't responsible is what Sartre described as "bad faith"—intellectual dishonesty. Taking these ideas as your starting point, explain how and why "Big Tech" might be viewed as an existential threat. In what ways does it appear to free us from the work of creating ourselves? Does Big Tech encourage "bad faith"?

QUESTIONS FOR MAKING CONNECTIONS
BETWEEN READINGS

1. In "The End of Loyalty," Rick Wartzman chronicles the triumph of a new economic model, one based on cutting production costs instead of raising wages. This strategy has worked so far because Walmart and other retailers can import products manufactured overseas for wages so low that no American could survive on them. And here at home, these retailers have the ability to underprice everybody else. The problem is that with the loss of manufacturing jobs, wages here are eroding too. Walmart, then, has radically changed the character of social life in America, but so too has Facebook. Have they changed social life in the same way? Are they both producing the same trends, or are the two completely separate? Is Facebook helping to end the sense of community that used to bind workers and employers together? Or is it helping to reknit the torn social fabric?

2. Connecting present events to the past is a distinctive way of thinking known as "historicizing." Often, by turning to history, we can see our current situation in a new and revealing way. Both Foer in "Mark Zuckerberg's War on Free Will" and Ta-Nehisi Coates in "The First White President" historicize in order to gain deeper insight into their subjects. First, explain how and why they historicize. Then respond to this question: Is there something about our culture today that makes the past invisible? Does our obsession with the future blind us to the past? What advantages might be gained from historicizing?

BARBARA FREDRICKSON

AT THE END of the 1938 film, *The Wizard of Oz*, Dorothy Gale receives some sage advice about the importance of love. "A heart is not measured," the wizard says, "by how much you love but how much you are loved by others." These words echo notions expressed by countless writers long before the MGM studio was born. "Love is not love," William Shakespeare wrote, which "alters when it alteration finds … O no! It is an ever-fixed mark." But what exactly is this *love*? Is it an experience or is it an emotion? Does it change constantly or should it remain "ever-fixed," as Shakespeare says? Advice about love is so prevalent that we can easily overlook its vagueness, sentimentality, and inherent contradictions.

Psychologist Barbara Lee Fredrickson, author of the book *Love 2.0: How Our Supreme Emotion Affects Everything We Feel, Think, Do, and Become*, has no doubt that love is real, but she has tried to bring scientific rigor to the tangled discourse on the topic. Her recent writing about love might be seen as an extension of her earlier research in the field of positive psychology, a branch of psychology focused on positive emotions, as opposed to the disorders studied by previous researchers. Fredrickson's work on positive emotions culminated in what she describes as the "broaden-and-build theory," which suggests that positive emotions lead people to become more curious, outgoing, and creative. As she argues in an article from *American Psychologist* (2005), positive emotions probably evolved to improve our ancestors' odds for "survival and reproduction."

After completing her first book, *Positivity*, Fredrickson was quick to recognize one limitation of her argument: even if we know that positivity helps, how can those trapped by negative thinking ever change their habits of mind? How, in other words, can we apply the findings of positivity research? Toward an answer to these questions, Fredrickson's more recent studies focus on forms of human interaction that actively encourage positivity. Among these forms of interaction, Fredrickson sees love as the most important because it takes place in the "micro-moments" of our "resonance" with others: "Just as your body was designed to extract oxygen from the Earth's atmosphere, and nutrients from the foods you ingest, your body was designed to love." For the first time, research demonstrates that love can change our biochemistry and even the

"Survival and reproduction" from Barbara L. Fredrickson and Marcial F. Losada, "Positive Affect and the Complex Dynamics of Human Flourishing," *American Psychologist* 60(7), Oct 2005: 678–686.

expression of our DNA. But perhaps the most important implications are to be found in our social lives rather than in our biology. If love, for example, plays an essential role in our neural processing, why does society often seem to reflect our worst tendencies, not our best? If we are naturally hardwired to love, why does love sometimes seem hard to find?

Selections from Love 2.0: How Our Supreme Emotion Affects Everything We Feel, Think, Do, and Become

LOVE, OUR SUPREME EMOTION

The Eskimos had fifty-two names for snow because it was important to them: There ought to be as many for love.

—MARGARET ATWOOD

Longing. You know the feeling. It's that ache of sensing that something vital is missing from your life; a deep thirst for more. More meaning, more connection, more energy—more *something.* Longing is that feeling that courses through your body just before you decide that you're restless, lonely, or unhappy.

Longing like this is not just another mental state. It's deeply physical. Your body craves some essential nutrient that it's not getting, yet you can't quite put your finger on what it is. Sometimes you can numb this ache with a deep dive into work, gossip, television, or gaming. More often than not, though, these and other attempts to fill the aching void are merely temporary distractions. The longing doesn't let up. It trails you like a shadow, insistently, making distractions all the more appealing. And distractions abound—that second or third glass of wine, that stream of texts and tweets, that couch and remote control.

Odds are, food is abundant in your life. And clean drinking water is as close as the nearest faucet and virtually limitless. You have access to reasonably clean air and adequate shelter. Those basic needs have long been met. What you long for now is far more intangible.

What you long for is love. Whether you're single or not, whether you spend your days largely in isolation or steadily surrounded by the buzz of conversation, love is the essential nutrient that your cells crave: true positivity-charged connection with other living beings.

Love, as it turns out, nourishes your body the way the right balance of sunlight, nutrient-rich soil, and water nourishes plants and allows them to flourish. The more you experience it, the more you open up and grow, becoming wiser and more attuned, more resilient and effective, happier and healthier. You grow spiritually as well, better able to see, feel, and appreciate the deep interconnections that inexplicably tie you to others, that embed you within the grand fabric of life.

Just as your body was designed to extract oxygen from the earth's atmosphere and nutrients from the foods you ingest, your body was designed to love. Love—like taking a deep breath or eating an orange when you're depleted and thirsty—not only feels great but is also life-giving, an indispensable source of energy, sustenance, and health.

When I compare love to oxygen and food, I'm not just taking poetic license. I'm drawing on science: new science that illuminates for the first time how love, and its absence, fundamentally alters the biochemicals in which your body is steeped. They, in turn, can alter the very ways your DNA gets expressed within your cells. The love you do or do not experience today may quite literally change key aspects of your cellular architecture next season and next year—cells that affect your physical health, your vitality, and your overall well-being. In these ways and more, just as your supplies of clean air and nutritious food forecast how long you'll walk this earth—and whether you'll thrive or just get by—so does your supply of love.

It's Not What You Think

To absorb what the new science of love has to offer, you'll need to step back from "love" as you may now know it. Forget about the love that you typically hear on the radio, the one that's centered on desire and yearns for touch from a new squeeze. Set aside the take on love your family might have offered you, one that requires that you love your relatives unconditionally, regardless of whether their actions disturb you or their aloofness leaves you cold. I'm even asking you to set aside your view of love as a special bond or relationship, be it with your spouse, partner, or soul mate. And if you've come to view love as a commitment, promise, or pledge, through marriage or any other loyalty ritual, prepare for an about-face. I need you to step back from all of your preconceptions and consider an upgrade. *Love 2.0* offers a different perspective—your body's perspective.

If you were asked today, by a roving reporter or an inquisitive dinner party guest, to provide your own definition of love, your answer would likely reflect a mishmash of shared cultural messages and your own deeply personal experiences with intimacy. However compelling your answer, I'd wager that your body has its own—quite different—definition of love. That's what this book is about. Love is not sexual desire or the blood-ties of kinship. Nor is it a special bond or commitment. Sure enough, love is closely related to each of these important concepts. Yet none, I will argue, capture the true meaning of love as your body experiences it.

The vision of love that I offer here will require a radical shift, a departure from what you've come to believe. It's time to upgrade your view of love. Love is not a category of relationships. Nor is it something "out there" that you can fall into, or—years later—out of. Seeing love as a special bond is extraordinarily common, albeit misleading. A bond like this can endure for years—even a lifetime with proper commitment and effort. And having at least one close relationship like this is vital to your health and happiness, to be sure. Even so, that special bond and the commitments people often build around it are better taken as the *products* of love—the results of the many smaller moments in which love infuses you—rather than as love per se. When you equate love with intimate relationships, love can seem confusing. At times it feels great, while at other times it hurts like hell. At times it lifts you up with grand dreams for your future and at other times oppresses you with shame about your inadequacies, or guilt about your past actions. When you limit your view of love to relationships or commitment, love becomes a complex and bewildering thicket of emotions, expectations, and insecurities. Yet when you redirect your eyes toward your body's definition of love, a clear path emerges that cuts through that thicket and leads you to a better life.

There's still more ground to clear. I need to ask you to disengage from some of your most cherished beliefs about love as well: the notions that love is exclusive, lasting, and unconditional. These deeply held beliefs are often more wish than reality in people's lives. They capture people's daydreams about the love-of-their-life whom they've yet to meet. Love, as your body defines it, is not exclusive, not something to be reserved for your soul mate, your inner circle, your kin, or your so-called *loved ones*. Love's reach turns out to be far wider than we're typically coaxed to imagine. Even so, love's timescale is far shorter than we typically think. Love, as you'll see, is not lasting. It's actually far more fleeting than most of us would care to acknowledge. On the upside, though, love is forever renewable. And perhaps most challenging of all, love is not unconditional. It doesn't emerge no matter what, regardless of conditions. To the contrary, you'll see that the love your body craves is exquisitely sensitive to contextual cues. It obeys preconditions. Yet once you understand those preconditions, you can find love countless times each day.

It's difficult to speak of love in scientific terms, I've found, because listeners have so many preexisting and strong beliefs about it. Many of these beliefs reflect our shared cultural heritage, like all those proliferating songs and movies that equate love with infatuation or sexual desire, or with stories that end happily ever after, or even the realistic marriage ceremonies that celebrate love as an exclusive bond and commitment. Other beliefs about love are deeply personal. They reflect your own unique life history, with its interpersonal triumphs and scars, lessons about intimacy learned and not yet learned. Left unaddressed, these preconceptions can derail any serious intellectual discussion of love. They may even keep you from soaking up the full implications of the new findings on it....

LOVE'S BIOLOGY

The soul must always stand ajar, ready to welcome the ecstatic experience.

—EMILY DICKINSON

It's all too tempting, especially in Western culture, to take your body to be a noun, a thing. Sure, it's a living thing, but still, like other concrete things that you can see and touch, you typically describe your body with reference to its stable physical properties, like your height, your weight, your skin tone, your apparent age, and the like. A photo works well to convey these attributes. You recognize, of course, that five years from now, today's photo will seem a bit outdated. By then, your body's physical properties might shift a bit—you might, for instance, become a little shorter, a little heavier, a little paler, or look a little older. Still, you're comfortable with the idea that your body remains pretty much the same from day to day. It has constancy.

Yet constancy, ancient Eastern philosophies warn, is an illusion, a trick of the mind. Impermanence is the rule—constant change, the only constancy. True for all things, this is especially true for living things, which, by definition, change or adapt as needed in response to changes in context. Just as plants turn toward the sun and track its arc from dawn to dusk, your own heart alters its activity with each postural shift, each new emotion, even each breath you take. Seen in this light, your body is more verb than noun: It shifts, cascades, and pulsates; it connects and builds; it erodes and flushes. Mere photographs fail to capture these nonstop and mostly unseen churning dynamics. Instead, you need movies. Increasingly, scientists work to capture these and other dynamic changes as they unfurl within living, breathing, and interacting bodies. True, scientists need to understand form as well as function, anatomy as well as physiology, nouns as well as verbs. Yet when it comes to love, verbs rule. Positivity resonance lies in the action, the doing, the connecting. It wells up, like a wave forming in the ocean, and then dissipates, like that same wave, after its crash. To fully appreciate love's biology, you'll need to train your eye to see this ever-shifting ebb and flow.

Taking cues from what leading neuroscientist Stephen Porges calls the *social engagement system*, I describe love's biology as a system, a whole comprised of several interacting parts. You can think of love, or positivity resonance, as one of the more complex and recurrent *scenes* nested within the *act* of your day, which is in turn nested within the *play* of your life. As with any scene in a play, the drama of love has its own cast of characters. Here I turn the spotlight on three main biological characters: your brain; one particular hormone, oxytocin, which circulates throughout your brain and body; and your vagus nerve, the tenth cranial nerve that runs from deep within your brain stem down to your heart, lungs, and other internal organs. Other characters step onto the biological stage to deliver their own lines, to be sure, but these three are primary players in love's biology.

Although always on stage, these main characters deliver their lines quietly, most often fully outside of your conscious awareness. As you move through your day, these biological characters—your brain, your oxytocin, and your vagus nerve—are ever responsive to set changes. As you interact with one person after another, they gently nudge you to attend to these others more closely and forge connections when possible. They shape your motives and behaviors in subtle ways, yet ultimately, their actions serve to strengthen your relationships and knit you in closer to the social fabric of life. In the sections that follow, I'll shine the spotlight on each of these three main characters in turn, to help you see how each forges and supports those life-giving moments of positivity resonance for which your body thirsts.

Love on the Brain

When you and another truly connect, love reverberates between you. In the very moment that you experience positivity resonance, your brain syncs up with the other person's brain. Within each moment of love, you and the other [person] are on the same wavelength. As your respective brain waves mirror one another, each of you—moment by moment—changes the other's mind.

... How do you know it really happens? You can't see this brain synchrony surface in real time after all. What you'd need is some way to peer inside two people's heads while they chatted so that you could tell whether their respective brain activity really does march along in time together. This would tell you whether they really "click." Only with this sort of X-ray vision could you decide whether love is better described as a solo act—an emotion contained within the boundaries of the person feeling it—or a duet or ensemble, performed by a duo or group. That sort of X-ray vision sounds like science fiction.

Yet turning science fiction into science fact is what scientists and engineers love most. Breakthrough work by neuroscientist Uri Hasson, of Princeton University, has done just that. He and his team have found ways to measure multiple brains connecting through conversation. The obstacles they faced to do this were large. First, brain scanners are loud machines—no place to carry on actual conversations. Second, they're also extraordinarily expensive, both to buy and to use. Almost all brain imaging studies thus scan just one person's brain at a time. Yet with clever engineering and clever experimental logistics, Hasson's team cleared both obstacles. They created a custom optic microphone that canceled out the noise of the scanner without distorting the delicate brain signals his team sought to capture. The logistics feat was to mimic a natural conversation by pulling it apart in time.

Suppose, for a moment, you were stranded at the airport last week. Your plane to Miami was delayed for hours. Bored with your reading and web-browsing, you got to talking to another stranded passenger, a lively young college student on her way home for break. You'd been chatting back and forth for a while, every so often, meeting eyes and sharing smiles. The conversation was very natural, like you were friends already. Somehow or another, she got to telling you about her crazy high school prom experience. In great detail, she launched into how she happened to have two dates to the same prom; how she ended up having only five minutes to get dressed and ready for the prom after a full day of scuba diving; how, on her way to after-prom festivities, she crashed her boyfriend's car in the wee hours of the morning; and then how she completely lucked out of getting ticketed (or arrested!) by the officer who witnessed her accident. She's a good storyteller: You hung on her every word. Fifteen minutes melted away as she shared all the twists and turns of her hapless prom night. It's clear, too, that you both enjoyed the chance to connect, rather than read, while you waited for your plane together.

Okay, now it's time for a set change: Instead of in an airport terminal, this conversation actually unfolded in a brain imaging lab at Princeton University. And instead of you sitting side by side with your impromptu friend, Hasson's team actually invited her to visit the lab weeks ago, and they audio-recorded her entire prom story while scanning her brain's activity with functional magnetic resonance imaging (fMRI). You're here lying in the scanner today, listening to her story over fancy headphones, while Hasson's team records your own brain activity. After you get out of the scanner, they ask you to report on what you heard in as much detail as possible. This takes a while; hers was a long, circuitous story after all.

Hasson's team later looked at the extent to which your brain activity mirrored hers. They painstakingly matched up each specific brain area across the two of you, time-locked your respective scans, and looked for "coupling," or the degree to which your brains lit up in synchrony with each other, matched in both space and time.

It turns out that the brain coupling evident between you two is surprisingly widespread. In other words, speaking with and listening to the human voice appear to activate much of the exact same brain activity at pretty much the same time. Keep in mind that—despite your new friend's gift for storytelling—this was still a pretty artificial conversation. Isolated inside the brain scanner across different days, you never actually got to see each other's gestures, meet each other's eyes, or even take turns speaking. You only listened to her voice over headphones. The brain coupling that would emerge in real time with the full and animated dialogue that could well spring up between the two of you if you were in fact seated side by side in the airplane terminal is likely to be far more extensive. Yet hearing someone's voice offers an important channel of sensory and temporal connection, because voice can convey so much emotion. By contrast, consider how little brain coupling would emerge if the connection between the two of you were to be further reduced, for instance, if you only read her story, at your own pacing and presumed intonations, or only heard *about* her story, as in my thumbnail depiction of it a few paragraphs back.

Forget the idea of a few isolated mirror neurons. So-called mirror neurons refer to a microscopic brain area that Italian neurophysiologists found to "light up" both when a monkey reaches for a banana and when that same monkey sees a person reach for a banana. The discovery of mirror neurons was a huge breakthrough because it told us that taking some action and seeing someone else take that same action are far more alike than previously thought. This means that when you know something—like why that person who just walked into your office is smiling—you know it because your brain and body simulate being in that person's shoes, in their skin. Your knowing is not just abstract and conceptual; it's embodied and physical. Yet it seems now that the concept of isolated mirror neurons was just the tip of the unseen and enormous iceberg. What Hasson and his team uncovered was far more extensive neuronal coupling than previously imagined. Far from being isolated to one or two brain areas, really "clicking" with someone else appears to be a whole brain dance in a fully mirrored room. The reflections between the two of you are that penetrating and widespread.

It turns out that you weren't the only one listening to your new friend's prom story. Hasson's team invited ten other people to have their brains scanned while listening to the very same audio-recording of her story that you heard. Whereas you listened attentively to everything she said, others didn't so much. Those differences showed up clearly when you were each asked to recount her story afterward. By tallying up the matches between her original, impromptu prom story and each listener's retelling of it, Hasson's team rank-ordered the whole set of listeners by how well they understood the story. Those differences in comprehension reflect the success or failure of communication—how thoroughly information from her brain was transferred to your brain, and to the brains of the other listeners. Strikingly, Hasson's team discovered that the degree of success in communication predicted the degree of brain coupling between speaker and listener, and did so in surprising ways.

Most of the time, across most brain areas, listeners' brains mirrored the speaker's brain after a short time lag, around one to three seconds later. It only makes sense, after all, that the speaker leads this dance, since the story is hers and she chooses her words before you and the others hear them. In other cases, though, this neural pas de deux between speaker and listener showed hardly any lag at all—the respective changes in brain activity were virtually synchronized. Your particular case was different, however. Recall that you were the one who grasped your new friend's story better than anybody. You hung on every word and picked up every detail of it, even the seemingly inconsequential ones. Your more complete grasp of her story went hand in hand with something truly remarkable: Your brain activity actually *anticipated* her brain activity by a few seconds in several cortical areas. Excellent communication, it thus seems, doesn't simply involve following along very closely. It also involves forecasting. Once you were in sync and on the same page with your new friend, enjoying her and her story, you could even anticipate what she'd say next, or how she'd say it. Your brain could anticipate her brain's next move.

Brain coupling, Hasson argues, is the means by which we understand each other. He goes even further to claim that communication—a true meeting of the minds—is a single act, performed by two brains. Considering the positivity resonance of love, what I find most fascinating about these findings is that a key brain area that showed coupling in Hasson's speaker-listener study was the insula, an area linked with conscious feeling states. Evidence for synchrony in two people's insulae suggests that in good communication, two individuals come to feel a single, shared emotion as well, one that is distributed across their two brains.

Indeed, in other work, Hasson and colleagues have shown that people's brains come particularly into sync during emotional moments. Neural coupling, then—really understanding someone else—becomes all the more likely when you share the same emotion. Even more so than ordinary communication, a micro-moment of love is a single act, performed by two brains. Shared emotions, brain synchrony, and mutual understanding emerge together. And mutual understanding is just steps away from mutual care. Once two people understand each other—really "get" each other in any given moment—the benevolent concerns and actions of mutual care can flow forth unimpeded.

As you move through your day, quite naturally you move in and out of different scenes. Each scene, of course, has its own script. For perhaps most of your day, you're pretty much caught up in your own thoughts and plans, oblivious to the presence or feelings of anyone nearby. Your brain, in such moments, is doing its own thing. But in those rarer moments when you truly connect with someone else over positivity—by sharing a smile, a laugh, a common passion, or an engaging story—you become attuned, with genuine care and concern for the other. You empathize with what they're going through, as your two brains sync up and act as one, as a unified team.

Neural coupling like this is a biological manifestation of oneness. Laboratory studies have already shown that when positive emotions course through you, your awareness expands from your habitual focus on "me" to a more generous focus on "we." When you're feeling bad—afraid, anxious, or angry—even your best friend can seem pretty remote or separate from you. The same goes for when you're feeling nothing in particular. Not so, when you're feeling good. Under the influence of positive emotions, your sense of self actually expands to include others to greater degrees. Your best friend, in these lighthearted moments, simply seems like a bigger part of you.

Hasson's work suggests that when you share your positive emotions with others, when you experience positivity resonance together with this sense of expansion, it's also deeply physical, evident in your brain. The emotional understanding of true empathy recruits coinciding brain activity in both you and the person of your focus. Another telling brain imaging study, this one conducted by scientists in Taipei, Taiwan, illustrates self-other overlap at the neuronal level. Imagine for a moment being a participant in this study. While you are in the fMRI brain scanner, the researchers show you a number of short, animated scenes and ask you to picture yourself in these scenes. Some of these scenes depict painful events, like dropping something heavy on your toe or getting your fingers pinched in a closing door. What the brain images show is that, compared to imagining neutral, nonpainful situations, imagining yourself in these painful situations lights up the well-known network of brain areas associated with pain processing, including the insula, that area linked with conscious feeling states. When you are later asked to imagine these same painful events happening to a loved one—your spouse, your best friend, or your child, for instance—these same brain areas light up. By and large, then, your loved one's pain *is* your pain. By contrast, when you imagine these painful events happening to complete strangers, a different pattern of activation emerges altogether, one that shows little activation in the insula and more activation in areas linked with distinguishing and distancing yourself from others, and actively inhibiting or regulating emotions, as if to prevent their pain from becoming your pain. At the level of brain activity during imagined pain, you and your beloved are virtually indistinguishable.

Whereas the Taipei research team defined love to be a lasting loving relationship (what, for clarity's sake, I call a bond), the work from Hasson's team at Princeton tells me that neural synchrony and overlap can also unfold between you and a complete stranger—if you let it. Positivity resonance between brains, as it turns out, requires only connection, not the intimacy or shared history that comes with a special bond. Even so, the distinctions revealed in the Taipei study, between imagining your loved one's pain and imagining a stranger's pain, underscore that stifled emotions and guarded personal boundaries, while at times necessary and fully appropriate, can also function as obstacles to positivity resonance. As we'll see in the next section, your attunement to various opportunities for positive connection with others is supported not just by neural synchrony, but by the hormone oxytocin as well.

Biochemistries in Love

Oxytocin, which is nicknamed by some the "cuddle hormone" or the "love hormone," is actually more properly identified as a neuropeptide because it acts not just within your body but also within your brain. Oxytocin has long been known to play a key role in social bonding and attachment. Clear evidence of this first emerged from experiments with a monogamous breed of prairie voles: Oxytocin, when dripped into one animal's brain in the presence of the opposite sex, creates in that animal a long-lasting preference to remain together with the other, cuddled up side by side, behavior taken as evidence that oxytocin sparked the formation of a powerful social bond between them. In humans, oxytocin surges during sexual intercourse for both men and women, and, for women, during childbirth and lactation, pivotal interpersonal moments that stand to forge new social bonds or cement existing ones. The natural blasts of oxytocin during such moments are so large and powerful that for many years they all but blinded scientists to the more subtle ebb and flow of oxytocin during more typical day-to-day activities, like playing with your kids, getting to know your new neighbor, or striking a deal with a new business partner. Technical obstacles also needed to be cleared. Decades after oxytocin's role in monogamous prairie voles had been amply charted, scientists studying human biochemistry still struggled to find ways to reliably and noninvasively measure and manipulate oxytocin during natural behavior. Scientific understanding of oxytocin's role in your everyday social life could not advance without more practical research tools at hand.

Dramatic new evidence of oxytocin's power to shape your social life first surfaced in Europe, where laws permitted the use of a synthetic form of oxytocin, available as a nasal spray, for investigational purposes. Among the first of these studies was one in which 128 men from Zurich played the so-called trust game with real monetary outcomes on the line. At random, these men were assigned to either the role of "investor" or the role of "trustee," and each was given an equivalent pot of starting funds. Investors made the first move in the game. They could give some, all, or none of their allocated funds to the trustee. During the transfer of funds, the experimenter tripled their investment while letting the trustee know how much the investors had originally transferred. Trustees made the next move. They could give some, all, or none of their new allotment of funds (the investors' tripled investment plus their own original allocation) back to investors. The structure of the game puts investors, but not trustees, at risk. If an investor chose to entrust the other guy with his investment, he risked receiving nothing in return if the trustee chose to selfishly keep the entire monetary gain for himself. But if the trustee was fair, they could each double their money.

Prior to playing this trust game, using a double-blind research design, participants received either oxytocin or an inert placebo by nasal spray. The effect of this single intranasal blast of oxytocin on the outcome of the trust game was dramatic: The number of investors who trusted their entire allotment to their trustee more than doubled. Interestingly, related research using this same trust game showed that the mere act of being entrusted with another person's money raises the trustee's naturally occurring levels of oxytocin, and that the greater the trustee's oxytocin rise, the more of his recent windfall he sacrificed back to the investor. The neuropeptide oxytocin, then, steers the actions of both the investor and the trustee, shaping both trust and reciprocity. These findings suggest that through synchronous oxytocin surges, trust and cooperation can quickly become mutual.

Since the original study on oxytocin and the trust game was published in *Nature* in 2005, variations on it have abounded. We now know, for instance, that oxytocin doesn't simply make people more trusting with money, it also makes them far more trusting—a whopping 44 percent more trusting—with confidential information about themselves. Interestingly, the simple act of sharing an important secret from your life with someone you just met increases your naturally circulating levels of oxytocin, which in turn raises your confidence that you can trust that person to guard your privacy. Thankfully, we also know that oxytocin does not induce trust indiscriminately, making people gullible and therefore open to exploitation. The effects of oxytocin on trust turn out to be quite sensitive to interpersonal cues, like those subtle signs that tip you off that another may be the gambling type or irresponsible in other ways. Rest assured, then, if oxytocin spray were to be aerated through your workplace ventilation system, you'd still maintain your shrewd attunement to subtle signs that suggest whether someone is worthy of your trust or not.

Researchers have since moved on to examine the effects of oxytocin on people's sensitivities to the subtle social cues that signal whether or not trust is warranted. From this work, I can tell you that, under the influence of oxytocin, you attend more to people's eyes and become specifically more attuned to their smiles, especially subtle ones. Perhaps because of the closer attention you pay to peoples' smiles and eyes, you become a better judge of their feelings and view people on the whole as more attractive and trustworthy. You also become particularly sensitized to environmental cues linked to positive social connections—for instance, to words like *love* and *kissing*. Researchers who have combined the use of oxytocin nasal spray (versus placebo) with brain imaging have also learned that oxytocin modulates the activity of your amygdala, the subcortical structure deep within your brain linked to emotional processing. Specifically, under the influence of a single blast of oxytocin nasal spray, the parts of your amygdala that tune in to threats are muted, whereas the parts that tune in to positive social opportunities are amplified. Reflecting these negativity-dampening effects, a single shot of oxytocin can also help you glide through stressful social situations, like giving an impromptu speech or discussing a conflict-ridden topic with your spouse. If you were to face these difficulties under the influence of oxytocin, studies suggest, you'd have less cortisol, the so-called stress hormone, coursing through you, and you'd behave more positively, both verbally, by disclosing your feelings, and nonverbally, by making more eye contact and friendly gestures. Related research shows that behaving kindly in these ways also raises your naturally occurring levels of oxytocin, which in turn curbs stress-induced rises in heart rate and blood pressure, reduces feelings of depression, and increases your pain thresholds.

More generally, oxytocin has been cast as a lead character in the mammalian *calm-and-connect* response, a distinct cascade of brain and body responses best contrasted to the far more familiar *fight-or-flight* response. Let's face it, meeting new people can be a little scary at times. Think back to what it was like for you on your first day at a new school or in a new job. You're suddenly thrown in with people you'd never heard of before. Even if a new person seems friendly, it's hard to know his true motives. Will he help you? Or will he instead take advantage of you in one way or another? Human greed, after all, runs rampant and can yield all manner of exploitation. Oxytocin appears both to *calm* fears that might steer you away from interacting with strangers and also to sharpen your skills for *connection*. As I've mentioned, though, oxytocin is far from blind. It indeed heightens your attunement to cues that signal whether others are sincere or not. Through eye contact and close attention to all manner of smiles—and the embodied simulations such visual intake triggers—your gut instincts about whom to trust and whom not to trust become more reliable. Rather than avoid all new people out of fear and suspicion, oxytocin helps you pick up on cues that signal another person's goodwill and guides you to approach them with your own. Because all people need social connections, not just to reproduce, but to survive and thrive in this world, oxytocin has been dubbed "the great facilitator of life."

It, too, can jump the gap between people such that someone else's oxytocin flow can trigger your own. A biochemical synchrony can then emerge that supports mutual engagement, care, and responsiveness.

The clearest evidence that oxytocin rises and falls in synchrony between people comes from studies of infants and their parents. When an infant and a parent—either mom or dad—interact, sometimes they are truly captivated by each other, and other times not. When an infant and parent do click, their coordinated motions and emotions show lots of mutual positive engagement. Picture moms or dads showering their baby with kisses, tickling their baby's tiny fingers and toes, smiling at their baby, and speaking to him or her in that high-pitched, singsong tone that scientists call *motherese*. These parents are superattentive. As they tickle and coo they're also closely tracking their baby's face for signs that their delight is mutual. In step with their parent's affectionate antics, these attentive babies babble, coo, smile, and giggle. Positivity resonates back and forth between them. Micro-moments of love blossom.

Of course, not every infant-parent interaction is so rosy. Some pairs show little mutual engagement. Some moms and dads rarely make eye contact with their infants and emit precious little positivity, either verbally or nonverbally. These pairs are simply less attuned to each other, less connected. And in those rare moments when they are engaged, the vibe that joins them is distinctly more negative. They connect over mutual distress or indifference, rather than over mutual affection.

It turns out that positive behavioral synchrony—the degree to which an infant and a parent (through eye contact and affectionate touch) laugh, smile, and coo together—goes hand in hand with oxytocin synchrony. Researchers have measured oxytocin levels in the saliva of dads, moms, and infants both before and after a videotaped, face-to-face parent-infant interaction. For infant-parent pairs who show mutual positive engagement, oxytocin levels also come into sync. Without such engagement, however, no oxytocin synchrony emerges.

Positivity resonance, then, can be viewed as the doorway through which the exquisitely attuned biochemical tendencies of one generation influence those of the next generation to form lasting, often lifelong bonds. Knowing, too, that oxytocin can ebb and flow in unison among non-kin—even among brand-new acquaintances just learning to trust each other—micro-moments of love, of positivity resonance, can also be viewed as the doorways through which caring and compassionate communities are forged. Love, we know, builds lasting resources. Oxytocin, studies show, swings the hammer.

This core tenet of my broaden-and-build theory—that love builds lasting resources—finds support in a fascinating program of research on … rodents. It turns out that rat moms and their newborn pups show a form of positive engagement and synchrony analogous to that of human parents with their infants. Sensitive parenting in a rat mom, however, is conveyed by her attentively licking and grooming her newborn pups. When a rat mom licks and grooms her pup, it increases the pup's sensitivity to oxytocin, as indicated, for instance, by the number of oxytocin receptors deep within the pup's amygdala, as well as within other subcortical brain regions. Sure enough, these well-groomed—or I dare say well-*loved*—rat pups grow up to have calmer demeanors; they're less skittish, more curious. The researchers can be certain that it's the experiences of loving connection that determine the brain and behavioral profiles of the next generation (that is, their oxytocin receptors and calm demeanors)—and not simply shared genes—because cross-fostering studies show the same patterns of results. That is, even when a rat mom raises a newborn pup that is not her own, her maternal attention still forecasts that pup's brain sensitivity to oxytocin and whether it grows up to be anxious or calm.

Touring Vagus

Who you are today is also shaped by the third biological character that I want you to meet: your tenth cranial nerve. This key conduit connects your brain to your body and is also called your vagus nerve (sounds like Vegas, as in Las Vegas). It emerges from your brain stem deep within your skull and, although it makes multiple stops at your various internal organs, perhaps most significantly it connects your brain to your heart. You already know that your heart rate shoots up when you feel insulted or threatened—registering the ancestral fight-or-flight response—but you may not know that it's your vagus nerve that eventually soothes your racing heart, by orchestrating (together with oxytocin) the equally ancestral calm-and-connect response.

Keeping in mind that love *is* connection, you should know that your vagus nerve is a biological asset that supports and coordinates your experiences of love. Completely outside of your awareness, your vagus nerve stimulates tiny facial muscles that better enable you to make eye contact and synchronize your facial expressions with another person. It even adjusts the minuscule muscles of your middle ear so you can better track the other person's voice against any background noise. In these exquisitely subtle yet consequential ways, your vagus nerve increases the odds that the two of you will connect, upping your chances for positivity resonance.

Scientists can measure the strength of your vagus nerve—your biological aptitude for love—simply by tracking your heart rate in conjunction with your breathing rate. Specifically, I can look at the degree to which your heart rate, as tracked by sensors placed on your lowest ribs, is patterned by your breathing rate, as revealed by an expandable bellows that encircles your rib cage. This pattern is called *vagal tone*. Like muscle tone, the higher your vagal tone, the better.

In addition to putting the brakes on the big jumps in your heart rate that may be caused by stress, fear, or exertion, your vagus nerve also increases the routine efficiency of your heart, beat by beat, or more precisely, breath by breath. The human heart rate tends to run fairly high, as if we're always on guard for the next danger that might be hidden around the corner. When you're breathing in, a fast heart rate is an efficient heart rate. After all, each successive heartbeat during an in-breath circulates more freshly oxygenated blood throughout your brain and body. Yet when you're breathing out, a fast heart rate is not all that helpful because your supply of freshly oxygenated blood is waning. Here again, your vagus nerve steps in to help out. It can very gently apply the brake on your heart while you exhale, slowing your heart rate down a small degree. In turn your vagus nerve can gently let up on the brake while you inhale, letting your naturally high heart rate resume to grab all the oxygenated blood that it can get. This creates a subtle yet healthy pattern of cardiac arrhythmia: Your heart rate speeds up a bit when you inhale and slows down a bit when you exhale. This is the pattern that reflects your vagal tone, the strength or condition of your vagus nerve. It characterizes the nimbleness with which your primitive, nonconscious brain holds the reins on your galloping heart.

I give you this quick tour of vagus because this conduit within you, between your brain and your heart, has a story to tell about how attuned you are to sources of love in your midst. It even makes a quiet prediction about what illnesses may beset you and how long you're likely to live. Your biological propensities for love and health are intimately intertwined. Measured at rest, vagal tone also tends to be extraordinarily stable over time. For most people, it remains roughly the same year after year, rhythmically channeling them toward loneliness or social prosperity, sickness or health.

That's because people with higher vagal tone, science has shown, are more flexible across a whole host of domains—physical, mental, and social. They simply adapt better to their ever-shifting circumstances, albeit completely at nonconscious levels. Physically, they regulate their internal bodily processes more efficiently, like their glucose levels and inflammation. Mentally, they're better able to regulate their attention and emotions, even their behavior. Socially, they're especially skillful in navigating interpersonal interactions and in forging positive connections with others. By definition, then, they experience more micro-moments of love. It's as though the agility of the conduit between their brains and hearts—as reflected in their high vagal tone—allows them to be exquisitely agile, attuned, and flexible as they navigate the ups and downs of day-to-day life and social exchanges. High vagal tone, then, can be taken as high loving potential. Indeed, this is what doctoral student Bethany Kok and I have found: Compared to people with lower vagal tone, those with higher vagal tone experience more love in their daily lives, more moments of positivity resonance.

You might now be wondering whether you're one of the lucky ones blessed with high vagal tone. If you are, that's great. Yet even if you're not advantaged with high vagal tone today, the latest science gives plenty of reason for hope. Just as you can build muscle tone through regular physical exercises, you can build vagal tone…. The key, once again, is the power of love.

My students and I work together in what I call the PEP Lab, or the Positive Emotions and Psychophysiology Laboratory. Not long ago, we conducted an experiment on the effects of learning the ancient mind-training practice of loving-kindness meditation. Our study participants visited the PEP Lab at the University of North Carolina one by one, and we measured their vagal tone while they sat and relaxed for a few minutes. At the end of this initial laboratory testing session, we instructed participants how to log on to the study website each evening to record their emotions and social connections of the day. A few weeks later, by random assignment, we determined which participants would learn loving-kindness meditation and which would not. All would continue to monitor their day-to-day emotions and social connections using our study website. Months later, weeks after the meditation workshop ended, one by one we invited all participants back to the PEP Lab, where we again measured their vagal tone under the same resting conditions as before….

[It] was those study participants who had been assigned at random to learn loving-kindness meditation who changed the most. They devoted scarcely more than an hour of their time each week to the practice. Yet within a matter of months, completely unbeknownst to them, their vagus nerves began to respond more readily to the rhythms of their breathing, emitting more of that healthy arrhythmia that is the fingerprint of high vagal tone. Breath by breath—loving moment by loving moment—their capacity for positivity resonance matured. Moreover, through painstaking statistical analyses, we pinpointed that those who experienced the most frequent positivity resonance in connection with others showed the biggest increases in vagal tone. Love literally made people healthier.

Upward Spirals Unleashed

It's time now to step back from isolated scientific findings and take in the big picture. Recall that your body's positivity resonance operates within a much larger system. Along with love and all the other positive emotions, this system also includes your enduring resources—your physical health, your social bonds, your personality traits, and your resilience. Having assets like these certainly makes life easier, and more satisfying. In addition, though, such resources also serve as booster shots that increase the frequency and intensity of your micro-moments of positivity resonance. Love built those resources in you, and those resources in turn boost your experiences of love. This is not a simple case of cause and effect. The causal arrow instead runs in both directions at once, creating the dynamic and reciprocal causality that drives self-sustaining trajectories of growth. Through love, you become a better version of yourself. And as your better self, you experience love more readily. It is in this dance between your enduring resources and your micro-moments of love that life-giving upward spirals are born.

… By learning how to self-generate love, you can raise your vagal tone. And with higher vagal tone, your attention and actions become more agile, more attuned to the people in your midst. You become better able to forge the interpersonal connections that give rise to positivity resonance. Through vagal tone, then, love begets love.

Likewise, evidence suggests that positivity resonance raises your oxytocin levels. And under the influence of oxytocin, you grow calmer, more attuned to others, friendlier, and more open. Here, too, your skills for forging connections sharpen, which increases your ability to cultivate positivity resonance. Through oxytocin as well then, love begets love.

Recall, too, that positive connections with others create neural coupling, or synchronous brain activity between people. With repetition, positivity resonance also produces structural changes in the brain, for instance, rendering the threat-detecting amygdala more sensitive to the calming influence of oxytocin. While much of the work on neuroplasticity—the brain's capacity to change with experience—comes from research on nonhuman animals, tantalizing evidence has also recently emerged from studies of humans. Becoming a parent, for instance, not only opens the door for parent-infant positivity resonance but also appears to usher in structural changes in brain regions that facilitate positivity resonance. This research shows how love reroutes the neural wiring of your brain, making it more likely that you'll have healthy habits and healthy social bonds in the future. Through brain plasticity, too, then, love begets love.

Plasticity, or openness to change, characterizes your body's cells as well. New cells are born within you all the time. Even now, as you take time to read this book, new cells are coming online within you, taking their predetermined place within the massive orchestra of communication and mutual influence that you call your body. Yet not everything about the birth of your new cells is scripted in advance by your DNA. Some aspects are open to contextual influences signaled by the changing biochemicals that course through you. If you feel lonely and disconnected from others, for instance, your circulating levels of the stress hormone cortisol will rise. Your cortisol levels, in turn, signal your immune system to alter the way your genes are expressed in your next-generation white blood cells, specifically making them less sensitive to cortisol. When this happens, studies show, your inflammatory response becomes more chronic, less responsive to cues that a crisis situation has subsided. This is how, over time, chronic feelings of loneliness can weaken people's immune systems and open the door to inflammation-based chronic illnesses, like cardiovascular disease and arthritis. The data go further to suggest that *feeling* isolated or unconnected to others does more bodily damage than *actual* isolation, suggesting that painful emotions drive the bodily systems that in turn steer you toward dire health outcomes. By tracking how your emotions—and the biochemical changes they trigger—alter gene expression within your immune system, the tools of molecular biology now show how a lack of love compromises your immunity and your health.

Even so, there is ample reason for hope. In countless social exchanges each day, your potential to alleviate loneliness with love is enormous. Your biology, as we have seen in this chapter, enacts your experiences of love. Even so, you have more control over your biology than you realize. Once you grasp the pathways and common obstacles to love, you gain a measure of control over the biochemicals that bathe your cells. To a considerable extent, you orchestrate the messages that your cells hear, the messages that tell your cells whether to grow toward health or toward illness. My collaborators and I are just beginning to chart the ways that oxytocin and other ingredients that make up love's biochemistry trigger healthy changes in gene expression that may foster physical and mental well-being. Also through the plasticity of your cells, we hypothesize, love begets love.

All of love's unseen biological transformations—in your brain rhythms, your blood stream, your vagus nerve, and your cells—in turn ready you to become even more attuned to love, better equipped, biologically, to cultivate moments of positivity resonance with others. This latent biological upward spiral is a powerful force: Love can affect you so deeply that it reshapes you from the inside out and by doing so alters your destiny for further loving moments. With each micro-moment of love, then, you climb another rung on the spiraling ladder that lifts you up to your higher ground, to richer and more compassionate social relationships, to greater resilience and wisdom, and to better physical health.

NOTES

118 **The Eskimos had fifty-two names for snow:** Margaret Atwood (1972). *Surfacing.* New York: Simon and Schuster.

120 **having at least one close relationship like this is vital to your health and happiness, to be sure:** James S. House, Karl R. Landis, and Debra Umberson (1988). "Social relationships and health." *Science* 241(4865): 540–45. See also Ed Diener and Martin E. P. Seligman (2002). "Very happy people." *Psychological Science* 13(1): 81–84.

121 **The soul must always stand ajar, ready to welcome the ecstatic experience:** Emily Dickinson (1960). *The Complete Poems of Emily Dickinson.* Edited by Thomas Johnson. Boston: Little Brown.

121 **the *social engagement system:*** Stephen W. Porges (2003). "Social engagement and attachment: A phylogenetic perspective." *Annals of the New York Academy of Sciences* 1008: 31–47.

123 **the degree to which your brains lit up in synchrony with each other, matched in both space and time:** Greg J. Stephens, Lauren J. Silbert, and Uri Hasson (2010). "Speaker-listener neural coupling underlies successful communication." *Proceedings of the National Academy of Sciences (USA)* 107(32): 14425–30. See also Uri Hasson (2010). "I can make your brain look like mine." *Harvard Business Review,* December.

123 **voice can convey so much emotion:** Klaus R. Scherer, Tom Johnstone, and Gudrun Klasmeyer (2009). "Vocal expression of emotion." In *Handbook of Affective Sciences,* edited by Richard J. Davidson, Klaus R. Scherer, and Hill H. Goldsmith, pp. 433–56. New York: Oxford University Press; and Jo-Anne Bachorowski and Michael J. Owren (2008). "Vocal expressions of emotion." In *The Handbook of Emotions,* 3rd ed., edited by Michael Lewis, Jeanette M. Haviland-Jones, and Lisa Feldman Barrett, pp. 196–210.

124 **Your knowing is not just abstract and conceptual; it's embodied and physical:** Paula N. Niedenthal, Martial Mermillod, Marcus Maringer, and Ursula Hess (2010). "The Simulation of Smiles (SIMS) model: Embodied stimulation and the meaning of facial expressions." *Behavioral and Brain Sciences* 33(6): 417–80.

124 **Brain coupling, Hasson argues, is the means by which we understand each other:** You might be wondering how Hasson and his team can be so sure they've captured communication, a true transfer of information from one brain to another, and not simply matched responses to listening to the same sounds, like hearing your own voice, or the incomprehensible dialogue from a foreign-language film. They ruled this out by having listeners also hear a story in Russian (which none of them understood). In that case, virtually no neural coupling emerged.

124 **a single act, performed by two brains:** Hasson (2010), p. 1.

124 **the insula, an area linked with conscious feeling states:** A. D. (Bud) Craig (2009). "How do you feel—now? The anterior insula and human awareness." *Nature Reviews Neuroscience* 10: 59–70.

125 **people's brains come particularly into sync during emotional moments:** Uri Hasson, Yuval Nir, Ifat Levy, Galit Fuhrmann, and Rafael Malach (2004). "Intersubject synchronization of cortical activity during natural vision." *Science* 303: 1634–40.

125 **your awareness expands from your habitual focus on "me" to a more generous focus on "we":** This is work I described in my first book, *Positivity* (2009). See especially chapter 4.

126 **as if to prevent their pain from becoming your pain:** Yawei Cheng, Chenyi Chen, Ching-Po Lin, Kun-Hsien Chou, and Jean Decety (2010). "Love hurts: An fMRI study." *Neuroimage* 51: 923–29. See also work by Mary Helen Immordino-Yang, Andrea McColl, Hanna Damasio, and Antonio Damasio (2009). "Neural correlates of admiration and compassion." *Proceedings of the National Academy of Sciences (USA)* 106(19): 8021–26.

126 **stifled emotions ... can also function as obstacles to positivity resonance:** For support for this idea, see work by Iris Mauss and colleagues. It suggests that stifled positivity erodes social connection and thereby limits well-being. Iris B. Mauss, Amanda J. Shallcross, Allison S. Troy, Oliver P. John, Emilio Ferrer, Frank H. Wilhelm, and James J. Gross (2011). "Don't hide your happiness! Positive emotion dissociation, social connectedness, and psychological functioning." *Journal of Personality and Social Psychology* 100(4): 738–48.

126 **oxytocin sparked the formation of a powerful social bond between them:** Jessie R. Williams, Thomas R. Insel, Carroll R. Harbaugh, and C. Sue Carter (1994). "Oxytocin administered centrally facilitates formation of partner preference in female prairie voles (microtus ochrogaster)." *Journal of Neuroendocrinology* 6: 247–50. See also work by Mary M. Cho, A. Courtney DeVries, Jessie R. Williams, and C. Sue Carter (1999). "The effects of oxytocin and vasopressin on partner preferences in male and female prairie voles (microtus ochrogaster)." *Behavioral Neuroscience* 113(5): 1071–79.

126 **oxytocin surges during sexual intercourse:** Marie S. Carmichael, Richard Humbert, Jean Dixon, Glenn Palmisano, Walter Greenleaf, and Julian M. Davidson (1987). "Plasma oxytocin increases in the human sexual response." *Journal of Clinical Endocrinology and Metabolism* 64(1): 27–31.

126 **a synthetic form of oxytocin, available as a nasal spray, for investigational purposes:** Synthetic oxytocin has now been approved for limited investigational use within the United States by the U.S. Federal Drug Administration.

127 **a double-blind research design:** This is the gold standard in human science: Neither the researchers nor the participants are aware of who receives which nasal spray—the spray with the drug or the chemically inert spray that serves as the placebo control.

127 **trusted their entire allotment to their trustee more than doubled:** Michael Kosfeld, Markus Heinrichs, Paul J. Zak, Urs Fischbacher, and Ernst Fehr (2005). "Oxytocin increases trust in humans." *Nature* 435(2): 673–76.

127 **the mere act of being entrusted with another person's money raises the trustee's naturally occurring levels of oxytocin, and that the greater the trustee's oxytocin rise, the more of his recent windfall he sacrificed back to the investor:** Paul J. Zak, Robert Kurzban, and William T. Matzner (2005). "Oxytocin is associated with human trustworthiness." *Hormones and Behavior* 48: 522–27. Interestingly, the effect of being trusted on circulating oxytocin and monetary sacrifice is far higher if trustees have just had a shoulder massage. See Vera B. Morhenn, Jang Woo Park, Elisabeth Piper, and Paul J. Zak (2008). "Monetary sacrifice among strangers is mediated by endogenous oxytocin release after physical contact." *Evolution and Human Behavior* 29: 375–83.

127 **more trusting—a whopping 44 percent more trusting—with confidential information about themselves:** Moira Mikolajczak, Nicolas Pinon, Anthony Lane, Philippe de Timary, and Olivier Luminet (2010). "Oxytocin not only increases trust when money is at stake, but also when confidential information is in the balance." *Biological Psychology* 85: 182–84.

127 **sharing an important secret from your life with someone you just met increases your naturally circulating levels of oxytocin:** Szabolcs Keri and Imre Kiss (2011). "Oxytocin response in a trust game and habituation of arousal." *Physiology and Behavior* 102: 221–24. The effect of telling secrets on oxytocin holds unless you are diagnosed with schizophrenia; see Szabolcs Keri, Imre Kiss, and Oguz Keleman (2009). "Sharing secrets: Oxytocin and trust in schizophrenia." *Social Neuroscience* 4(4): 287–93.

127 **The effects of oxytocin on trust turn out to be quite sensitive to interpersonal cues:** Moiri Mikolajczak, James J. Gross, Anthony Lane, Olivier Corneille, Philippe de Timary, and Olivier Luminet (2010). "Oxytocin makes people trusting, not gullible." *Psychological Science* 21(8): 1072–74. Likewise, oxytocin seems to especially promote trust with in-group members; see Carsten K. W. De Dreu, Lidred L. Greer, Gerben A. Van Kleef, Shaul Shalvi, and Michel J. J. Handgraaf (2010). "Oxytocin promotes human ethnocentrism." *Proceedings of the National Academy of Sciences (USA)* 108(4): 1262–66.

127 **under the influence of oxytocin, you attend more to people's eyes:** Adam J. Guastella, Philip B. Mitchell, and Mark R. Dadds (2008). "Oxytocin increases gaze to the eye region of human faces." *Biological Psychiatry* 63: 3–5.

127 **more attuned to their smiles, especially subtle ones:** Abigail A. Marsh, Henry H. Yu, Daniel S. Pine, and R. J. R. Blair (2010). "Oxytocin improves specific recognition of positive facial expressions." *Psychopharmacology* 209: 225–32.

127 **a better judge of their feelings:** Gregor Domes, Markus Heinrichs, Andre Michel, Christoph Berger, and Sabine C. Herpertz (2007). "Oxytocin improves 'mind-reading' in humans." *Biological Psychiatry* 61: 731–33.

127 **view people on the whole as more attractive and trustworthy:** Angeliki Theodoridou, Angela C. Rowe, Ian S. Penton-Voak, and Peter J. Rogers (2009). "Oxytocin and social perception: Oxytocin increases perceived facial trustworthiness and attractiveness." *Hormones and Behavior* 56: 128–132.

127 **particularly sensitized to environmental cues linked to positive social connections—for instance, to words like** *love and kissing:* Christian Unkelback, Adam J. Guastella, and Joseph P. Forgas (2008). "Oxytocin selectively facilitates recognition of positive sex and relationship words." *Psychological Science* 19(11): 1092–94.

128 **the parts of your amygdala that tune in to threats are muted, whereas the parts that tune in to positive social opportunities are amplified:** Matthias Gamer, Bartosz Zurowski, and Christian Buchel (2010). "Different amygdala subregions mediate valence-related and attentional effects of oxytocin in humans." *Proceedings of the National Academy of Sciences (USA)* 107(20): 9400–9405. See also: Peter Kirsch, Christine Esslinger, Qiang Chen, et al. (2005). "Oxytocin modulates neural circuitry for social cognition and fear in humans." *Journal of Neuroscience* 25(49): 11489–93; and Predrag Petrovic, Raffael Kalisch, Tania Singer, and Raymond J. Dolan (2008). "Oxytocin attenuates affective evaluations of conditioned faces and amygdale activity." *Journal of Neuroscience* 28(26): 6607–15.

128 **If you were to face these difficulties under the influence of oxytocin, studies suggest:** Beate Ditzen, Marcel Schaer, Barbara Gabriel, et al. (2009). "Intranasal oxytocin increases positive communication and reduces cortisol levels during couple conflict." *Biological Psychiatry* 65: 728–731. See also work by Markus Heinrichs, Thomas Baumgartner, Clemens Kirschbaum, and Ulrike Ehlert (2003). "Social support and oxytocin interact to suppress cortisol and subjective responses to psychosocial stress." *Biological Psychiatry* 54: 1389–98.

128 **behaving kindly in these ways also raises your naturally occurring levels of oxytocin, which in turn curbs stress-induced rises in heart rate and blood pressure:** Julianne Holt-Lunstad, Wendy A. Birmingham, and Kathleen Light (2008). "Influence of a 'warm touch' support enhancement intervention among married couples on ambulatory blood pressure, oxytocin, alpha amylase, and cortisol." *Psychosomatic Medicine* 70: 976–85. See also forthcoming experimental work by Stephanie L. Brown, early versions of which she presented in a talk at the Society for Experimental Social Psychology meeting in October 2011 entitled "Prosocial behavior and health: Towards a biological model of a caregiving system."

128 **reduces feelings of depression, and increases your pain thresholds:** Kerstin Uvnäs-Moberg, E. Bjorkstrand, Viveka Hillegaart, and S. Ahlenius (1999). "Oxytocin as a possible mediator of SSRI-induced antidepressant effects." *Psychopharmacology* 142(1): 95–101. See also work by Maria Petersson, Pawel Alster, Thomas Lundeberg, and Kerstin Uvnäs-Moberg (1996). "Oxytocin increases nociceptive thresholds in a long-term perspective in female and male rats." *Neuroscience Letters* 212(2): 87–90.

128 **the mammalian *calm-and-connect* response:** Kerstin Uvnäs-Moberg, Ingemar Arn, and David Magnusson (2005). "The psychobiology of emotion: The role of the oxytocinergic system." *International Journal of Behavioral Medicine* 12(2): 59–65. See also Kerstin Uvnäs-Moberg's 2003 book written for a general audience, *The Oxytocin Factor: Tapping the Hormone of Calm, Love and Healing.* New York: Perseus.

128 **Human greed, after all, runs rampant and can yield all manner of exploitation:** Compelling new insights on the nature of greed can be drawn from new experimental research on social class. See work by Paul K. Piff, Daniel M. Stancato, Stephané Côté, Rodolfo Mendoza-Denton, and Dacher Keltner (2012). "Higher social class predicts increased unethical behavior." *Proceedings of the National Academy of Sciences (USA)* 109(11): 4086–91.

128 **Oxytocin appears both to calm fears that might steer you away from interacting with strangers and also to sharpen your skills for *connection:*** Anne Campbell (2009). "Oxytocin and human social behavior." *Personality and Social Psychological Review* 14(3): 281–95.

128 **your gut instincts about whom to trust and whom not to trust become more reliable:** Niedenthal et al. (2010).

128 **oxytocin has been dubbed "the great facilitator of life":** Heon-Jin Lee, Abbe H. Macbeth, Jerome H. Pagani, and W. Scott Young, III (2009). "Oxytocin: The great facilitator of life." *Progress in Neurobiology* 88(2): 127–51.

129 **Without such engagement, however, no oxytocin synchrony emerges:** Ruth Feldman, Ilanit Gordon, and Orna Zagoory-Sharon (2010). "The cross-generation transmission of oxytocin in humans." *Hormones and Behavior* 58: 669–76.

129 **When a rat mom licks and grooms her pup, it increases the pup's sensitivity to oxytocin:** Frances A. Champagne, Ian C. G. Weaver, Josie Diorio, Sergiy

Dymov, Moshe Szyf, and Michael J. Meaney (2006). "Maternal care associated with methylation of the estrogen receptor-α1b promoter and estrogen receptor-α1b expression in the medial preoptic area of female off-spring." *Endocrinology* 147(6): 2909–15.

130 **your vagus nerve increases the odds that the two of you will connect:** Porges (2003).

131 **regulate their internal bodily processes more efficiently, like their glucose levels and inflammation:** Julian F. Thayer and Esther Sternberg (2006). "Beyond heart rate variability: Vagal regulation of allostatic systems." *Annals of the New York Academy of Sciences* 1088: 361–72.

131 **better able to regulate their attention and emotions, even their behavior:** Stephen W. Porges, Jane A. Doussard-Roosevelt, and Ajit Maiti (1994), "Vagal tone and the physiological regulation of emotion." *Monographs of the Society for Research in Child Development* 59(2/3): 167–86.

131 **especially skillful in navigating interpersonal interactions and in forging positive connections with others:** Kok and Fredrickson (2010).

131 **those with higher vagal tone experience more love in their daily lives, more moments of positivity resonance:** Kok and Fredrickson (2010).

132 **their vagus nerves began to respond more readily to the rhythms of their breathing, emitting more of that healthy arrhythmia that is the fingerprint of high vagal tone:** Kok, et al. (in press).

132 **Having assets like these certainly makes life easier, and more satisfying:** Michael A. Cohn, Barbara L. Fredrickson, Stephanie L. Brown, et al. (2009). "Happiness unpacked: Positive emotions increase life satisfaction by building resilience." *Emotion* 9(3): 361–68.

132 **appears to usher in structural changes in brain regions that facilitate positivity resonance:** Pil Young Kim (2009). "The interplay of brain and experience in parental love." *Dissertation Abstracts International: Section B: The Sciences and Engineering* 70(6-B): 3810.

133 **your inflammatory response becomes more chronic, less responsive to cues that a crises situation has subsided:** Steve W. Cole (2009). "Social regulation of human gene expression." *Current Directions in Psychological Science* 18(3): 132–37.

133 *feeling* **isolated or unconnected to others does more bodily damage than** *actual* **isolation:** Steve W. Cole, Louise C. Hawkley, Jesusa M. Arevalo, et al. (2007). "Social regulation of gene expression in human leukocytes." *Genomic Biology* 8: R189.

133 **you orchestrate the messages that your cells hear, the messages that tell your cells whether to grow toward health or toward illness:** Of course, other forces are at work as well. You do not hold sole responsibility (or blame) for your health or illness via the emotions you experience. In other words, please do not use this science to blame those who suffer from illnesses for their own fate. For a sharp critique of how science can be misused in this manner, see Barbara Ehrenreich (2009). *Bright-Sided: How the Relentless Promotion of Positive Thinking Has Undermined America.* New York: Metropolitan Books.

133 **just beginning to chart the ways that oxytocin and other ingredients that make up love's biochemistry trigger healthy changes in gene expression:** In ongoing research funded by the U.S. National Institutes of Health (R01NR012899)

I've teamed up with Steve W. Cole, director of UCLA's Social Genomics Core Laboratory, to examine how learning loving-kindness meditation may alter people's patterns of gene expression. We are especially interested in changes that may occur in the cells that regulate inflammatory processes in the immune system.

QUESTIONS FOR MAKING CONNECTIONS
WITHIN THE READING

1. Fredrickson, a psychologist, claims to reveal the "true meaning of love as your body experiences it." What does she imply by distinguishing between your body and you? Are you identical to your body, and how do you normally think about your body's relation to yourself? How does the body's experience differ from the experience of the mind? In Fredrickson's account of love, what role does the body play? When Fredrickson instructs you to "set aside the take on love your family might have offered you" and to suspend the "view of love as a special bond or relationship," does she mean that such views of love are incorrect, or does she simply want us to approach the subject from a different angle?

2. Since the time of Plato, Western thinkers have been fascinated—and frustrated—by the relations between the mind and the body. The body was described as material—made of matter—whereas the mind was immaterial, supposedly *pure thought*. Does Fredrickson see body and mind as separate? Does her account suggest that emotions like love would exist at all without the body? If thoughts and feelings are impossible without the existence of the body, then what is the mind? Does Fredrickson suggest that our mental lives are completely determined by our biology, or do we have some degree of freedom?

3. What is gained by thinking about "love's biology" as a "system"? How is the body involved in the operation of this system? In what ways are other people part of the system? How much of the experience of love involves consciousness and how much happens below the threshold of our conscious minds? Does the self exist only by virtue of its relations to others in a system of some kind? What other systems can you think of, and how might they be compared to the one that creates the experience of love?

QUESTIONS FOR WRITING

1. A long tradition in many cultures represents suffering as redemptive. Suffering is believed to instill greater patience, endurance, and strength of will. To what degree does Fredrickson take issue with this view, at least implicitly? How can positive emotions, even if they are sometimes subtle and brief, help us become more flexible, attuned to others, and creative? If positive

emotions can have the powerful effects that Fredrickson describes, why has suffering enjoyed such prestige as a path to truth? Could it be the case that many of our traditional ideas about love as a form of self-sacrifice are bound up with a mistaken view of suffering as redemptive?

2.   If love is, as Fredrickson affirms, the "supreme" emotion, why do people frequently behave in a manner that seems far removed from "positivity resonance"? Instead of speculating broadly, look back over the selection for clues: where does Fredrickson's account reveal potential vulnerabilities in the system? For example, Uri Hasson's work suggests that just as people can share positive emotions, they can transmit negative emotions, as well. Because positivity is not guaranteed by our biology, Fredrickson's essay might be seen as an argument for a special kind of mental hygiene. If we understand our emotions more fully, can we live more happily? Can we change the world beyond ourselves by trying to be happier?

QUESTIONS FOR MAKING CONNECTIONS
BETWEEN READINGS

1.   In his essay "Wisdom," Robert Thurman argues that the existence of the self is only temporary and conditioned by its surroundings. "Realizing your selflessness," he writes, "does not mean that you become a nobody, it means that you become the type of somebody who is a viable, useful somebody, not a rigid, fixated, I'm-the-center-of-the-universe, isolated from others somebody. You become the type of somebody who is over the idea of a conceptually fixed and self-created 'self.'" Would Fredrickson agree that we are basically selfless? How does positivity resonance change our relations to others, and could it be said to take us beyond the limits of ourselves? Does love make us more "fixed" or more fluid? What can we learn about ourselves from the fact that love, according to Fredrickson, is not just one of the many positive emotions we experience from time to time but has a special status as "our supreme emotion"?

2.   Fredrickson's description of love is unreservedly positive. As the "supreme emotion," love lifts us up, connects us to others and even restores our bodies to robust health. But could love—or "positivity resonance," as Fredrickson calls it—have a darker side as well? Consider the role that it might play in the social lives of the undergraduates described by Karen Ho in "Biographies of Hegemony?" Feted by Wall Street recruiters and surrounded by fellow students eager to embrace a career in finance, they seldom encounter anyone who challenges their sense of belonging. But in what ways could this resonance prevent them from exploring alternatives that would seem painful and lonely at first but might lead to greater satisfaction later on? When does resonance become "groupthink," and when do our differences enrich our personal and collective lives?

◆◆◆

DANIEL GILBERT

HISTORICALLY, THE STUDY of human psychology has tended to emphasize the negative. Scholars and practitioners of mental health focused on the mysteries of schizophrenia, depression, and other forms of psychological distress. In recent years, however, an interdisciplinary cohort of psychologists and other researchers have directed their attention to what turns out to be an equally misunderstood area: human happiness.

Among the leaders of this movement—sometimes called "positive psychology," or, more informally, "happiness studies"—is Daniel Gilbert, a professor of social psychology at Harvard University. Gilbert pioneered the field of affective forecasting, or the study of the way that people try to predict their future emotional states based on their current situation. In fact, these predictions are often incorrect. Having dropped out of high school to travel and write science fiction, Gilbert is well suited to explore the role that the unexpected can play in our search for happiness. While living in Denver, Colorado, Gilbert tried to enroll in a creative writing course at a local community college. Turned away because the class was over enrolled, he decided to take the only open course: psychology. Realizing that psychology "wasn't about crazy people" but "about all of us," Gilbert "stumbled" onto the path that brought him to the present.

In his international bestseller *Stumbling on Happiness* (2006), Gilbert argues that people suffer from "illusions of prospection." Through his experimental research, he learned of a remarkable discrepancy: even though few people believe they can predict what the future will bring, many more are convinced they can foresee how they will feel when the future arrives. Yet our predictions are often subject to a high degree of "impact bias," which leads us to overestimate just how intense our feelings will be, whether they are negative or positive.

The chapter from *Stumbling on Happiness* included here, "Immune to Reality," offers just some of Gilbert's counterintuitive discoveries. For example, we meet experimental subjects who fail to predict their level of happiness just minutes into the future. While we might not be surprised by their inability to make these predictions, we probably remain confident that we understand ourselves well enough to avoid the same mistakes. Gilbert also explains the

Quotations are drawn from an interview conducted by Dave Weich of Powell's books at <http://www.powells.com/blog/interviews/daniel-gilbert-stumbles-onto-something-big-by-dave/>.

operations of the "psychological immune system," which protects us when we suffer wrenching setbacks but not when we try to cope with minor ones, imparting a surprising complacency in the face of significant blows but often leaving us quite helpless when we deal with trivial irritations. Gilbert's conclusions challenge the conventional ways we understand our mental well-being by showing just how poorly these conventions reflect the reality of our emotional lives. Through their work, Gilbert and the other champions of happiness studies are seeking to reshape how we go about the "pursuit of happiness."

Immune to Reality

Upon my back, to defend my belly; upon my wit, to defend my wiles; upon my secrecy, to defend mine honesty; my mask, to defend my beauty.

—SHAKESPEARE, *THE HISTORY OF TROILUS AND CRESSIDA*

Albert Einstein may have been the greatest genius of the twentieth century, but few people know that he came *this* close to losing that distinction to a horse. Wilhelm von Osten was a retired schoolteacher who in 1891 claimed that his stallion, whom he called Clever Hans, could answer questions about current events, mathematics, and a host of other topics by tapping the ground with his foreleg. For instance, when Osten would ask Clever Hans to add three and five, the horse would wait until his master had finished asking the question, tap eight times, then stop. Sometimes, instead of *asking* a question, Osten would write it on a card and hold it up for Clever Hans to read, and the horse seemed to understand written language every bit as well as it understood speech. Clever Hans didn't get *every* question right, of course, but he did much better than anyone else with hooves, and his public performances were so impressive that he soon became the toast of Berlin. But in 1904 the director of the Berlin Psychological Institute sent his student, Oskar Pfungst, to look into the matter more carefully, and Pfungst noticed that Clever Hans was much more likely to give the wrong answer when Osten was standing in back of the horse than in front of it, or when Osten himself did not know the answer to the question the horse had been asked. In a series of experiments, Pfungst was able to show that Clever Hans could indeed read—but that what he could read was Osten's body language. When Osten bent slightly, Clever Hans would start tapping, and when Osten straightened up, or tilted his head a bit, or faintly raised an eyebrow,

Clever Hans would stop. In other words, Osten was signaling Clever Hans to start and stop tapping at just the right moments to create the illusion of horse sense.

Clever Hans was no genius, but Osten was no fraud. Indeed, he'd spent years patiently talking to his horse about mathematics and world affairs, and he was genuinely shocked and dismayed to learn that he had been fooling himself, as well as everyone else. The deception was elaborate and effective, but it was perpetrated unconsciously, and in this Osten was not unique. When we expose ourselves to favorable facts, notice and remember favorable facts, and hold favorable facts to a fairly low standard of proof, we are generally no more aware of our subterfuge than Osten was of his. We may refer to the processes by which the psychological immune system does its job as "tactics" or "strategies," but these terms—with their inevitable connotations of planning and deliberation—should not cause us to think of people as manipulative schemers who are consciously *trying* to generate positive views of their own experience. On the contrary, research suggests that people are *typically unaware* of the reasons why they are doing what they are doing,[1] but when asked for a reason, they readily supply one.[2] For example, when volunteers watch a computer screen on which words appear for just a few milliseconds, they are unaware of seeing the words and are unable to guess which words they saw. But they are influenced by them. When the word *hostile* is flashed, volunteers judge others negatively.[3] When the word *elderly* is flashed, volunteers walk slowly.[4] When the word *stupid* is flashed, volunteers perform poorly on tests.[5] When these volunteers are later asked to explain *why* they judged, walked, or scored the way they did, two things happen: First, they don't know, and second, they do not say, "I don't know." Instead, their brains quickly consider the facts of which they *are* aware ("I walked slowly") and draw the same kinds of plausible but mistaken inferences about themselves that an observer would probably draw about them ("I'm tired").[6]

When we cook facts, we are similarly unaware of why we are doing it, and this turns out to be a good thing, because *deliberate* attempts to generate positive views ("There must be *something* good about bankruptcy, and I'm not leaving this chair until I discover it") contain the seeds of their own destruction. Volunteers in one study listened to Stravinsky's *Rite of Spring*.[7] Some were told to listen to the music, and others were told to listen to the music while consciously trying to be happy. At the end of the interlude, the volunteers who had tried to be happy were in a *worse* mood than were the volunteers who had simply listened to the music. Why? Two reasons. First, we may be able deliberately to generate positive views of our own experiences if we close our eyes, sit very still, and do nothing else,[8] but research suggests that if we become even slightly distracted, these deliberate attempts tend to backfire and we end up feeling worse than we did before.[9] Second, deliberate attempts to cook the facts are so transparent that they make us feel cheap. Sure, we *want* to believe that we're better off without the fiancée who left us standing at the altar, and we *will* feel better as soon as we begin to discover facts that support this conclusion ("She was never really right for me, was she, Mom?"), but the process by which we discover those facts must *feel* like a discovery and not like a snow job. If we *see* ourselves cooking the facts ("If I phrase the question just this way and ask nobody but Mom, I stand a pretty good chance of having my favored conclusion confirmed"), then the jig is up and *self-deluded* joins *jilted* in our list of pitiful qualities. For positive views to be credible, they must be based on facts that we believe we have come upon honestly. We accomplish this by unconsciously cooking the facts and then consciously consuming them. The diner is in the dining room, but the chef is in the basement. The benefit of all this unconscious cookery is that it works, but the cost is that it makes us strangers to ourselves. Let me show you how.

LOOKING FORWARD TO LOOKING BACKWARD

To my knowledge, no one has ever done a systematic study of people who've been left standing at the altar by a cold-footed fiancé. But I'm willing to bet a good bottle of wine that if you rounded up a healthy sample of almost brides and nearly grooms and asked them whether they would describe the incident as "the worst thing that ever happened to me" or "the best thing that ever happened to me," more would endorse the latter description than the former. And I'll bet an entire *case* of that wine that if you found a sample of people who'd never been through this experience and asked them to predict which of all their possible future experiences they are most likely to look back on as "the best thing that ever happened to me," not one of them will list "getting jilted." Like so many things, getting jilted is more painful in prospect and more rosy in retrospect. When we contemplate being hung out to dry this way, we naturally generate the most dreadful possible view of the experience; but once we've actually *been* heartbroken and humiliated in front of our family, friends, and florists, our brains begin shopping for a less dreadful view—and as we've seen, the human brain is one smart shopper. However, because our brains do their shopping unconsciously, we tend not to realize they will do it at all; hence, we blithely assume that the dreadful view we have when we look forward to the event is the dreadful view we'll have when we look back on it. In short, we do not realize that our views will change because we are normally unaware of the processes that change them.

This fact can make it quite difficult to predict one's emotional future. In one study, volunteers were given the opportunity to apply for a good-paying job that involved nothing more than tasting ice cream and making up funny names for it.[10] The application procedure required the volunteer to undergo an on-camera interview. Some of the volunteers were told that their interview would be seen by a judge who had sole discretionary authority to decide whether they would be hired (judge group). Other volunteers were told that their interview would be seen by a jury whose members would vote to decide whether the volunteer should be hired (jury group). Volunteers in the jury group were told that as long as one juror voted for them, they would get the job—and thus the only circumstance under which they would *not* get the job was if the jury voted unanimously against them. All of the volunteers then underwent an interview, and

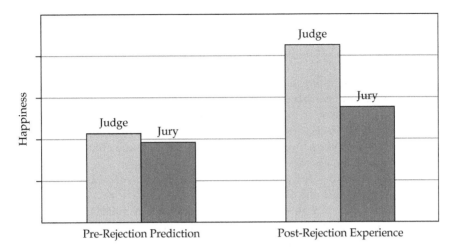

FIGURE Volunteers were happier when they were rejected by a capricious judge than by a unanimous jury (*bars on right*). But they could not foresee this moment before it happened (*bars on left*).

all predicted how they would feel if they didn't get the job. A few minutes later, the researcher came into the room and explained apologetically that after careful deliberation, the judge or jury had decided that the volunteer just wasn't quite right for the job. The researcher then asked the volunteers to report how they felt.

The results of the study are shown in the figure above. As the bars on the left show, volunteers in the two groups expected to feel equally unhappy. After all, rejection is a major whack on the nose, and we expect it to hurt whether the whacker is a judge, a jury, or a gang of Orthodox rabbis. And yet, as the bars on the right show, the whacks hurt more when they were administered by a jury than by a judge. Why? Well, just imagine that you've applied for a job as a swimsuit model, which requires that you don something skimpy and parade back and forth in front of some gimlet-eyed twit in a three-dollar suit. If the twit looked you over, shook his head, and said, "Sorry, but you're not model material," you'd probably feel bad. For a minute or two. But this is the sort of interpersonal rejection that everyone experiences from time to time, and after a few minutes, most of us get over it and go on with our lives. We do this quickly because our psychological immune systems have no trouble finding ways to exploit the ambiguity of this experience and soften its sting: "The guy wasn't paying attention to my extraordinary pivot," or "He's one of those weirdos who prefers height to weight," or "I'm supposed to take fashion advice from a guy with a suit like *that?*"

But now imagine that you've just modeled the skimpy thing for a whole roomful of people—some men, some women, some old, some young—and they all look you over and shake their heads in unison. You'd probably feel bad. Truly bad. Humiliated, hurt, and confused. You'd probably hurry offstage with a warm feeling in your ears, a tight feeling in your throat, and a wet feeling in your eyes. Being rejected by a large and diverse group of people is a demoralizing experience because it is so thoroughly unambiguous, and hence it is difficult for the psychological immune system to find a way to think about it that is both positive and credible. It's easy to blame failure on the eccentricities of a judge, but it's much more difficult to blame failure on the eccentricities of a unanimous jury. Claims such as "a synchronized mass blink caused ninety-four people to miss my pivot at precisely the same moment" are just not credible. Similarly, volunteers in this study found it easier to blame their rejection on an idiosyncratic judge than on a panel of jurors, which is why they felt worse when they were rejected by a jury.

Now, all this may seem painfully obvious to you as you contemplate the results of this study from the comfort of your sofa, but allow me to suggest that it is painfully obvious only after someone has taken pains to point it out to you. Indeed, if it were really painfully obvious, then why were a bunch of smart volunteers *unable to predict that it would happen just a few minutes before it did*? Why didn't the volunteers realize that they would have more success blaming a judge than a jury? Because when volunteers were asked to predict their emotional reactions to rejection, they imagined its sharp sting. Period. They did not go on to imagine how their brains might try to relieve that sting. Because they were unaware that they would alleviate their suffering by blaming those who caused it, it never occurred to them that they would be more successful if a single person were to blame rather than an entire group. Other studies have confirmed this general finding. For example, people *expect* to feel equally bad when a tragic accident is the result of human negligence as when it is the result of dumb luck, but they *actually* feel worse when luck is dumb and no one is blameworthy.[11]

Ignorance of our psychological immune systems causes us to mispredict the circumstances under which we will blame others, but it also causes us to mispredict the circumstances under which we will blame ourselves.[12] Who can forget the scene at the end of the 1942 film *Casablanca* in which Humphrey Bogart and Ingrid Bergman are standing on the tarmac as she tries to decide whether to stay in Casablanca with the man she loves or board the plane and leave with her husband? Bogey turns to Bergman and says: "Inside we both know you belong with Victor. You're part of his work, the thing that keeps him going. If that plane leaves the ground and you're not with him, you'll regret it. Maybe not today. Maybe not tomorrow. But soon and for the rest of your life."[13]

This thin slice of melodrama is among the most memorable scenes in the history of cinema—not because it is particularly well acted or particularly well written but because most of us have stood on that same runway from time to time. Our most consequential choices—whether to marry, have children, buy a house, enter a profession, move abroad—are often shaped by how we imagine our future regrets ("Oh no, I forgot to have a baby!"). Regret is an emotion we feel when we blame ourselves for unfortunate outcomes that might have been prevented had we only behaved differently in the past, and because that emotion is decidedly unpleasant, our behavior in the present is often designed to preclude it.[14] Indeed, most of us have elaborate theories about when and why people feel regret, and these theories allow us to avoid the experience. For instance, we expect to feel more regret when we learn about alternatives to our choices than when we don't,[15] when we accept bad advice than when we reject good advice,[16] when our bad choices are unusual rather than conventional,[17] and when we fail by a narrow margin rather than by a wide margin.[18]

But sometimes these theories are wrong. Consider this scenario. You own shares in Company A. During the past year you considered switching to stock in Company B but decided against it. You now find that you would have been better off by $1,200 if you had switched to the stock of Company B. You also owned shares in Company C. During the past year you switched to stock in Company D. You now find out that you'd have been better off by $1,200 if you kept your stock in Company C. Which error causes you more regret? Studies show that about nine out of ten people expect to feel more regret when they foolishly switch stocks than when they foolishly fail to switch stocks, because most people think they will regret foolish actions more than foolish inactions.[19] But studies also show that nine out of ten people are wrong. Indeed, in the long run, people of every age and in every walk of life seem to regret *not* having done things much more than they regret things they *did*, which is why the most popular regrets include not going to college, not grasping profitable business opportunities, and not spending enough time with family and friends.[20]

But why do people regret inactions more than actions? One reason is that the psychological immune system has a more difficult time manufacturing positive and credible views of inactions than of actions.[21] When our action causes us to accept a marriage proposal from someone who later becomes an axe murderer, we can console ourselves by thinking of all the things we learned from the experience ("Collecting hatchets is not a healthy hobby"). But when our inaction causes us to reject a marriage proposal from someone who later becomes a movie star, we can't console ourselves by thinking of all the things we learned from the experience because ... well, there wasn't one. The irony is all too clear: Because we do not realize that our psychological immune systems can rationalize an excess of courage more easily than an excess of cowardice, we hedge our bets when we should blunder forward. As students of the silver screen recall, Bogart's admonition about future regret led Bergman to board the plane and fly away with her husband. Had she stayed with Bogey in Casablanca, she would probably have felt just fine. Not right away, perhaps, but soon, and for the rest of her life.

LITTLE TRIGGERS

Civilized people have learned the hard way that a handful of iniquitous individuals can often cause more death and destruction than an invading army. If an enemy were to launch hundreds of airplanes and missiles against the United States, the odds are that none would reach its target because an offensive strike of that magnitude would trigger America's defensive systems, which are presumably adequate to quash the threat. On the other hand, were an enemy to launch seven guys with baggy pants and baseball caps, those men might well reach their targets and detonate bombs, release toxins, or fly hijacked airplanes into tall buildings. Terrorism is a strategy based on the idea that the best offense is the one that fails to trigger the best defense, and small-scale incursions are less likely to set off the alarm bells than are large-scale assaults. Although it is possible to design a defensive system that counters even the smallest threat (e.g., electrified borders, a travel ban, electronic surveillance, random searches), such systems are extraordinarily costly, in terms of both the resources required to run them and the number of false alarms they produce. A system like that would be an exercise in overkill. To be effective, a defensive system must respond to threats; but to be practical, it must respond only to threats that exceed some *critical threshold*—which means that threats that fall short of the critical threshold may have a destructive potential that belies their diminutive size. Unlike large threats, small threats can sneak in under the radar.

The Intensity Trigger

The psychological immune system is a defensive system, and it obeys this same principle. When experiences make us feel sufficiently unhappy, the psychological immune system cooks facts and shifts blame in order to offer us a more positive view. But it doesn't do this *every* time we feel the slightest tingle of sadness, jealousy, anger, or frustration. Failed marriages and lost jobs are the kinds of large-scale assaults on our happiness that trigger our psychological defenses, but these defenses are not triggered by broken pencils, stubbed toes, or slow elevators. Broken pencils may be annoying, but they do not pose a grave threat to our psychological well-being and hence do not trigger our psychological defenses. The paradoxical consequence of this fact is that it is sometimes more difficult to achieve a positive view of a *bad* experience than of a *very bad* experience.

For example, volunteers in one study were students who were invited to join an extracurricular club whose initiation ritual required that they receive three electric shocks.[22] Some of the volunteers had a truly dreadful experience because the shocks they received were quite severe (severe-initiation group), and others had a slightly unpleasant experience because the shocks they received were relatively mild (mild-initiation group). Although you might expect people to dislike anything associated with physical pain, the volunteers in the severe-initiation group actually liked the club more. Because these volunteers suffered greatly, the intensity of their suffering triggered their defensive systems, which immediately began working to help them achieve a credible and positive view of their experience. It isn't easy to find such a view, but it can be done. For example, physical suffering is bad ("Oh my God, that *really* hurt!"), but it isn't *entirely* bad if the thing one suffers for is extremely valuable ("But I'm joining a *very* elite group of *very* special people."). Indeed, research shows that when people are given electric shocks, they actually feel *less pain* when they believe they are suffering for something of great value.[23] The intense shocks were unpleasant enough to trigger the volunteers' psychological defenses, but the mild shocks were not, hence the volunteers valued the club most when its initiation was most painful.[24] If you've managed to forgive your spouse for some egregious transgression but still find yourself miffed about the dent in the garage door or the trail of dirty socks on the staircase, then you have experienced this paradox.

Intense suffering triggers the very processes that eradicate it, while mild suffering does not, and this counterintuitive fact can make it difficult for us to predict our emotional futures. For example, would it be worse if your best friend insulted you or insulted your cousin? As much as you may like your cousin, it's a pretty good bet that you like yourself more, hence you probably think that it would be worse if the epithet were hurled your way. And you're right. It *would* be worse. At first. But if intense suffering triggers the psychological immune system and mild suffering does not, then over time you should be more likely to generate a positive view of an insult that was directed at you ("Felicia called me a pea-brain ... boy, she can really crack me up sometimes") than one that was directed at your cousin ("Felicia called Cousin Dwayne a pea-brain ... I mean, she's *right*, of course, but it wasn't very nice of her to say"). The irony is that you may ultimately feel better when you are the *victim* of an insult than when you are a *bystander* to it.

This possibility was tested in a study in which two volunteers took a personality test and then *one* of them received feedback from a psychologist.[25] The feedback was professional, detailed, and unrelentingly negative. For example, it contained statements such as "You have few qualities that distinguish you from others," and "People like you primarily because you don't threaten their competence." Both of the volunteers read the feedback and then reported how much they liked the psychologist who had written it. Ironically, the volunteer who was the *victim* of the negative feedback liked the psychologist *more* than did the volunteer who was merely a *bystander* to it. Why? Because bystanders were miffed ("Man, that was a really crummy thing to do to the other volunteer."), but they were not devastated, hence their psychological immune systems did nothing to ameliorate their mildly negative feelings. But victims *were* devastated ("Yikes, I'm a certified loser!"), hence their brains quickly went shopping for a positive view of the experience ("But now that I think of it, that test could only provide a small glimpse into my very complex personality, so I rather doubt it means much.") Now here's the important finding: when a new group of volunteers was asked to *predict* how much they would like the psychologist, they predicted that they would like the psychologist *less* if they were victims than if they were bystanders. Apparently, people are not aware of the fact that their defenses are more likely to be triggered by intense rather than mild suffering, thus they mispredict their own emotional reactions to misfortunes of different sizes.

The Inescapability Trigger

Intense suffering is one factor that can trigger our defenses and thus influence our experiences in ways we don't anticipate. But there are others. For example, why do we forgive our siblings for behavior we would never tolerate in a friend? Why aren't we disturbed when the president does something that would have kept us from voting for him had he done it before the election? Why do we overlook an employee's chronic tardiness but refuse to hire a job seeker who is two minutes late for the interview? One possibility is that blood is thicker than water, flags were made to be rallied around, and first impressions matter most. But another possibility is that we are more likely to look for and find a positive view of the things we're *stuck with* than of the things we're not.[26] Friends come and go, and changing candidates is as easy as changing socks. But siblings and presidents are *ours*, for better or for worse, and there's not much we can do about it once they've been born or elected. When the experience we are having is not the experience we want to be having, our first reaction is to go out and have a different one, which is why we return unsatisfactory rental cars, check out of bad hotels, and stop hanging around with people who pick their noses in public. It is only when we cannot change the experience that we look for ways to change our view of the experience, which is why we love the clunker in the driveway, the shabby cabin that's been in the family for years, and Uncle Sheldon despite his predilection for nasal spelunking. We find silver linings only when we must, which is why people experience an increase in happiness when genetic tests reveal that they don't have a dangerous genetic defect, or when the tests reveal that they do have a dangerous genetic defect, but not when the tests are inconclusive.[27] We just can't make the best of a fate until it is inescapably, inevitably, and irrevocably ours.

Inescapable, inevitable, and irrevocable circumstances trigger the psychological immune system, but, as with the intensity of suffering, people do not always recognize that this will happen. For example, college students in one study signed up for a course in black-and-white photography.[28] Each student took a dozen photographs of people and places that were personally meaningful, then reported for a private lesson. In these lessons, the teacher spent an hour or two showing students how to print their two best photographs. When the prints were dry and ready, the teacher said that the student could keep one of the photographs but that the other would be kept on file as an example of student work. Some students (inescapable group) were told that once they had chosen a photograph to take home, they would not be allowed to change their minds. Other students (escapable group) were told that once they had chosen a photograph to take home, they would have several days to change their minds—and if they did, the teacher would gladly swap the photograph they'd taken home for the one they'd left behind. Students made their choices and took one of their photographs home. Several days later, the students responded to a survey asking them (among other things) how much they liked their photographs. The results showed that students in the escapable group liked their photograph *less* than did students in the inescapable group. Interestingly, when a new group of students was asked to *predict* how much they would like their photographs if they were or were not given the opportunity to change their minds, these students predicted that escapability would have no influence whatsoever on their satisfaction with the photograph. Apparently, inescapable circumstances trigger the psychological defenses that enable us to achieve positive views of those circumstances, but we do not anticipate that this will happen.

Our failure to anticipate that inescapability will trigger our psychological immune systems (hence promote our happiness and satisfaction) can cause us to make some painful mistakes. For example, when a new group of photography students was asked whether they would prefer to have or not to have the opportunity to change their minds about which photograph to keep, the vast majority preferred to have that opportunity—that is, the vast majority of students preferred to enroll in a photography course in which they would ultimately be dissatisfied with the photograph they produced. Why would anyone prefer less satisfaction to more? No one does, of course, but most people do seem to prefer more freedom to less. Indeed, when our freedom to make up our minds—or to change our minds once we've made them up—is threatened, we experience a strong impulse to re-assert it,[29] which is why retailers sometimes threaten your freedom to own their products with claims such as "Limited stock" or "You must order by midnight tonight."[30] Our fetish for freedom leads us to patronize expensive department stores that allow us to return merchandise rather than attend auctions that don't, to lease cars at a dramatic markup rather than buying them at a bargain, and so on.

Most of us will pay a premium today for the opportunity to change our minds tomorrow, and sometimes it makes sense to do so. A few days spent test-driving a little red roadster tells us a lot about what it might be like to own one, thus it is sometimes wise to pay a modest premium for a contract that includes a short refund period. But if keeping our options open has benefits, it also has costs. Little red roadsters are naturally cramped, and while the committed owner will find positive ways to view that fact ("Wow! It feels like a fighter jet!"), the buyer whose contract includes an escape clause may not ("This car is so tiny. Maybe I should return it."). Committed owners attend to a car's virtues and overlook its flaws, thus cooking the facts to produce a banquet of satisfaction, but the buyer for whom escape is still possible (and whose defenses have not yet been triggered) is likely to evaluate the new car more critically, paying special attention to its imperfections as she tries to decide whether to keep it. The costs and benefits of freedom are clear—but alas, they are not equally clear: We have no trouble anticipating the advantages that freedom may provide, but we seem blind to the joys it can undermine.[31]

EXPLAINING AWAY

If you've ever puked your guts out shortly after eating chili con carne and found yourself unable to eat it again for years, you have a pretty good idea of what it's like to be a fruit fly. No, fruit flies don't eat chili, and no, fruit flies don't puke. But they do associate their best and worst experiences with the circumstances that accompanied and preceded them, which allows them to seek or avoid those circumstances in the future. Expose a fruit fly to the odor of tennis shoes, give it a very tiny electric shock, and for the rest of its very tiny life it will avoid places that smell tennis-shoey. The ability to associate pleasure or pain with its circumstances is so vitally important that nature has installed that ability in every one of her creatures, from *Drosophila melanogaster* to Ivan Pavlov.

But if that ability is necessary for creatures like us, it certainly isn't sufficient because the kind of learning it enables is far too limited. If an organism can do no more than associate particular experiences with particular circumstances, then it can learn only a very small lesson, namely, to seek or avoid those particular circumstances in the future. A well-timed shock may teach a fruit fly to avoid the tennis-shoe smell, but it won't teach it to avoid the smell of snowshoes, ballet slippers, Manolo Blahniks, or a scientist armed with a miniature stun gun. To maximize our pleasures and minimize our pains, we must be able to associate our experiences with the circumstances that produced them, but we must also be able to *explain* how and why those circumstances produced the experiences they did. If we feel nauseous after a few turns on the Ferris wheel and our explanation involves poor equilibrium, then we avoid Ferris wheels in the future—just as a fruit fly would. But unlike a fruit fly, we also avoid some things that are *not* associated with our nauseating experience (such as bungee jumping and sailboats) and we do *not* avoid some things that *are* associated with our nauseating experience (such as hurdy-gurdy music and clowns). Unlike a mere association, an explanation allows us to identify particular aspects of a circumstance (spinning) as the *cause* of our experience, and other aspects (music) as irrelevant. In so doing, we learn more from our upchucks than a fruit fly ever could.

Explanations allow us to make full use of our experiences, but they also change the nature of those experiences. As we have seen, when experiences are unpleasant, we quickly move to explain them in ways that make us feel better ("I didn't get the job because the judge was biased against people who barf on Ferris wheels."). And indeed, studies show that the mere act of explaining an unpleasant event can help to defang it. For example, simply writing about a trauma—such as the death of a loved one or a physical assault—can lead to surprising improvements in both subjective well-being and physical health (e.g., fewer visits to the physician and improved production of viral antibodies).[32] What's more, the people who experience the greatest benefit from these writing exercises are those whose writing contains an *explanation* of the trauma.[33]

But just as explanations ameliorate the impact of *unpleasant* events, so too do they ameliorate the impact of *pleasant* events. For example, college students volunteered for a study in which they believed they were interacting in an online chat room with students from other universities.[34] In fact, they were actually interacting with a sophisticated computer program that simulated the presence of other students. After the simulated students had provided the real student with information about themselves ("Hi, I'm Eva, and I like to do volunteer work."), the researcher pretended to ask the simulated students to decide which of the people in the chat room they liked most, to write a paragraph explaining why, and then to send it to that person. In just a few minutes, something remarkable happened: the real student received e-mail messages from *every one* of the simulated students indicating that they liked the real student best! For example, one simulated message read: "I just felt that something clicked between us when I read your answers. It's too bad we're not at the same school!" Another read: "You stood out as the one I would like the most. I was especially interested in the way you described your interests and values." A third read: "I wish I could talk with you directly because ... I'd ask you if you like being around water (I love water-skiing) and if you like Italian food (it's my favorite)."

Now, here's the catch: Some real students (informed group) received e-mail that allowed them to know *which* simulated student wrote each of the messages, and other real students (uninformed group) received e-mail messages that had been stripped of that identifying information. In other words, every real student received exactly the same e-mail messages indicating that they had won the hearts and minds of all the simulated people in the chat room, but only real students in the informed group knew *which* simulated individual had written each of the messages. Hence, real students in the informed group were able to generate explanations for their good fortune ("Eva appreciates my values because we're both involved with Habitat for Humanity, and it makes sense that Catarina would mention Italian food."), whereas real students in the uninformed group were not ("Someone appreciates my values.... I wonder who? And why would anyone mention Italian food?"). The researchers measured how happy the real students were immediately after receiving these messages and then again fifteen minutes later. Although real students in both groups were initially delighted to have been chosen as everyone's best friend, only the real students in the uninformed group remained delighted fifteen minutes later. If you've ever had a secret admirer, then you understand why real students in the uninformed group remained on cloud nine while real students in the informed group quickly descended to clouds two through five.

Unexplained events have two qualities that amplify and extend their emotional impact. First, they strike us as rare and unusual.[35] If I told you that my brother, my sister, and I were all born on the same day, you'd probably consider that a rare and unusual occurrence. Once I explained that we were triplets, you'd find it considerably less so. In fact, just about *any* explanation I offered ("By *same day* I meant we were all born on a Thursday" or "We were all delivered by cesarean section, so Mom and Dad timed our births for maximum tax benefits") would tend to reduce the amazingness of the coincidence and make the event seem more probable. Explanations allow us to understand how and why an event happened, which immediately allows us to see how and why it might happen again. Indeed, whenever we say that something *can't* happen—for example, mind reading or levitation or a law that limits the power of incumbents—we usually just mean that we'd have no way to explain it if it did. Unexplained events seem rare, and rare events naturally have a greater emotional impact than common events do. We are awed by a solar eclipse but merely impressed by a sunset despite the fact that the latter is by far the more spectacular visual treat.

The second reason why unexplained events have a disproportionate emotional impact is that we are especially likely to keep thinking about them. People spontaneously try to explain events,[36] and studies show that when people do not complete the things they set out to do, they are especially likely to think about and remember their unfinished business.[37] Once we explain an event, we can fold it up like freshly washed laundry, put it away in memory's drawer, and move on to the next one; but if an event defies explanation, it becomes a *mystery* or a *conundrum*—and if there's one thing we all know about mysterious conundrums, it is that they generally refuse to stay in the back of our minds. Filmmakers and novelists often capitalize on this fact by fitting their narratives with mysterious endings, and research shows that people are, in fact, more likely to keep thinking about a movie when they can't explain what happened to the main character. And if they *liked* the movie, this morsel of mystery causes them to remain happy longer.[38]

Explanation robs events of their emotional impact because it makes them seem likely and allows us to stop thinking about them. Oddly enough, an explanation doesn't actually have to *explain* anything to have these effects—it merely needs to *seem* as though it does. For instance, in one study, a researcher approached college students in the university library, handed them one of two cards with a dollar coin attached, then walked away. You'd probably agree that this is a curious event that begs for explanation. Both cards stated that the researcher was a member of the "Smile Society," which was devoted to "random acts of kindness." But one card also contained two extra phrases: "Who are we?" and "Why do we do this?" These empty phrases didn't really provide any new information, of course, but they made students *feel* as though the curious event had been explained ("Aha, *now* I understand why they gave me a dollar!"). About five minutes later, a different researcher approached the student and claimed to be doing a class project on "community thoughts and feelings." The researcher asked the student to complete some survey questions, one of which was "How positive or negative are you feeling right now?" The results showed that those students who had received a card with the pseudo-explanatory phrases felt less happy than those who had received a card without them. Apparently, even a fake explanation can cause us to tuck an event away and move along to the next one.

Uncertainty can preserve and prolong our happiness, thus we might expect people to cherish it. In fact, the opposite is generally the case. When a new group of students was asked which of the two cards [offering a free dollar] would make them happier, 75-percent chose the one with the meaningless explanation. Similarly, when a group of students was asked whether they would prefer to know or not know which of the simulated students had written each of the glowing reports in the online chat-room study, 100-percent chose to know. In both cases, students chose certainty over uncertainty and clarity over mystery—despite the fact that in both cases clarity and certainty had been shown to diminish happiness. The poet John Keats noted that whereas great authors are "capable of being in uncertainties, mysteries, doubts, without any irritable reaching after fact and reason," the rest of us are "incapable of remaining content with half-knowledge."[39] Our relentless desire to explain everything that happens may well distinguish us from fruit flies, but it can also kill our buzz.

ONWARD

The eye and the brain are conspirators, and like most conspiracies, theirs is negotiated behind closed doors, in the back room, outside of our awareness. Because we do not realize that we have generated a positive view of our current experience, we do not realize that we will do so again in the future. Not only does our naïveté cause us to overestimate the intensity and duration of our distress in the face of future adversity, but it also leads us to take actions that may undermine the conspiracy. We are more likely to generate a positive and credible view of an action than an inaction, of a painful experience than of an annoying experience, of an unpleasant situation that we cannot escape than of one we can. And yet, we rarely choose action over inaction, pain over annoyance, and commitment over freedom. The processes by which we generate positive views are many: we pay more attention to favorable information, we surround ourselves with those who provide it, and we accept it uncritically. These tendencies make it easy for us to explain unpleasant experiences in ways that exonerate us and make us feel better. The price we pay for our irrepressible explanatory urge is that we often spoil our most pleasant experiences by making good sense of them.

NOTES

The notes contain references to the scientific research that supports the claims I make in the text. Occasionally they contain some extra information that may be of interest but that is not essential to the argument. If you don't care about sources, aren't interested in nonessentials, and are annoyed by books that make you flip back and forth all the time, then be assured that the only important note in [this chapter] is this one.

1. T. D. Wilson, *Strangers to Ourselves: Discovering the Adaptive Unconscious* (Cambridge, Mass.: Harvard University Press, 2002); and J. A. Bargh and T. L. Chartrand, "The Unbearable Automaticity of Being," *American Psychologist* 54: 462–79 (1999).

2. R. E. Nisbett and T. D. Wilson, "Telling More Than We Can Know: Verbal Reports on Mental Processes," *Psychological Review* 84: 231–59 (1977); D. J. Bem, "Self-Perception Theory," in *Advances in Experimental Social Psychology*, ed. L. Berkowitz, vol. 6 (New York: Academic Press, 1972), 1–62; M. S. Gazzaniga, *The Social Brain* (New York: Basic Books, 1985); and D. M. Wegner, *The Illusion of Conscious Will* (Cambridge, Mass.: MIT Press, 2003).

3. E. T. Higgings, W. S. Rholes, and C. R. Jones, "Category Accessibility and Impression Formation," *Journal of Experimental Social Psychology* 13: 141–54 (1977).

4. J. Bargh, M. Chen, and L. Burrows, "Automaticity of Social Behavior: Direct Effects of Trait Construct and Stereotype Activation on Action," *Journal of Personality and Social Psychology* 71: 230–44 (1996).

5. A. Dijksterhuis and A. van Knippenberg, "The Relation Between Perception and Behavior, or How to Win a Game of Trivial Pursuit," *Journal of Personality and Social Psychology* 74: 865–77 (1998).

6. Nisbett and Wilson, "Telling More Than We Can Know."

7. J. W. Schooler, D. Ariely, and G. Loewenstein, "The Pursuit and Assessment of Happiness Can Be Self-Defeating," in *The Psychology of Economic Decisions: Rationality and Well-Being*, eds. I. Brocas and J. Carillo, vol. 1 (Oxford: Oxford University Press, 2003).

8. K. N. Ochsner et al., "Rethinking Feelings: An fMRI Study of the Cognitive Regulation of Emotion," *Journal of Cognitive Neuroscience* 14: 1215–29 (2002).

9. D. M. Wegner, R. Erber, and S. Zanakos, "Ironic Processes in the Mental Control of Mood and Mood-Related Thought," *Journal of Personality and Social Psychology* 65: 1093–104 (1993); and D. M. Wegner, A. Broome, and S. J. Blumberg, "Ironic Effects of Trying to Relax Under Stress," *Behaviour Research and Therapy* 35: 11–21 (1997).

10. D. T. Gilbert et al., "Immune Neglect: A Source of Durability Bias in Affective Forecasting," *Journal of Personality and Social Psychology* 75: 617–38 (1998).

11. Ibid.

12. D. T. Gilbert et al., "Looking Forward to Looking Backward: The Misprediction of Regret," *Psychological Science* 15: 346–50 (2004).

13. M. Curtiz, *Casablanca*, Warner Bros., 1942.

14. T. Gilovich and V. H. Medvec, "The Experience of Regret: What, When, and Why," *Psychological Review* 102: 379–95 (1995); N. Roese, *If Only: How to Turn Regret into Opportunity* (New York: Random House 2004); G. Loomes and R. Sugden, "Regret Theory: An Alternative Theory of Rational Choice Under Uncertainty," *Economic Journal* 92: 805–24 (1982); and D. Bell, "Regret in Decision Making Under Uncertainty," *Operations Research* 20: 961–81 (1982).

15. I. Ritov and J. Baron, "Outcome Knowledge, Regret, and Omission Bias," *Organizational Behavior and Human Decision Processes* 64: 119–27 (1995); I. Ritov and J. Baron, "Probability of Regret: Anticipation of Uncertainty Resolution in Choice: Outcome Knowledge, Regret, and Omission Bias," *Organizational Behavior and Human Decision Processes* 66: 228–36 (1996); and M. Zeelenberg, "Anticipated Regret, Expected Feedback and Behavioral Decision Making," *Journal of Behavioral Decision Making* 12: 93–106 (1999).

16. M. T. Crawford et al., "Reactance, Compliance, and Anticipated Regret," *Journal of Experimental Social Psychology* 38: 56–63 (2002).

17. I. Simonson, "The Influence of Anticipating Regret and Responsibility on Purchase Decisions," *Journal of Consumer Research* 19: 105–18 (1992).

18. V. H. Medvec, S. F. Madey, and T. Gilovich, "When Less Is More: Counterfactual Thinking and Satisfaction Among Olympic Medalists," *Journal of Personality and Social Psychology* 69: 603–10 (1995); and D. Kahneman and A. Tversky, "Variants of Uncertainty," *Cognition* 11: 143–57 (1982).

19. D. Kahneman and A. Tversky, "The Psychology of Preferences," *Scientific American* 246: 160–73 (1982).

20. Gilovich and Medvec, "The Experience of Regret."

21. T. Gilovich, V. H. Medvec, and S. Chen, "Omission, Commission, and Dissonance Reduction: Overcoming Regret in the Monty Hall Problem," *Personality and Social Psychology Bulletin* 21: 182–90 (1995).

22. H. B. Gerard and G. C. Mathewson, "The Effects of Severity of Initiation on Liking for a Group: A Replication," *Journal of Experimental Social Psychology* 2: 278–87 (1966).

23. P. G. Zimbardo, "Control of Pain Motivation by Cognitive Dissonance," *Science* 151: 217–19 (1966).

24. See also E. Aronson and J. Mills, "The Effect of Severity of Initiation on Liking for a Group," *Journal of Abnormal and Social Psychology* 59: 177–81 (1958); J. L. Freedman, "Long-Term Behavioral Effects of Cognitive Dissonance," *Journal of Experimental Social*

Psychology 1: 145–55 (1965); D. R. Shaffer and C. Hendrick, "Effects of Actual Effort and Anticipated Effort on Task Enhancement," *Journal of Experimental Social Psychology* 7: 435–47 (1971); H. R. Arkes and C. Blumer, "The Psychology of Sunk Cost," *Organizational Behavior and Human Decision Processes* 35: 124–40 (1985); and J. T. Jost et al., "Social Inequality and the Reduction of Ideological Dissonance on Behalf of the System: Evidence of Enhanced System Justification Among the Disadvantaged," *European Journal of Social Psychology* 33: 13–36 (2003).

25. D. T. Gilbert et al., "The Peculiar Longevity of Things Not So Bad," *Psychological Science* 15: 14–19 (2004).

26. D. Frey et al., "Re-evaluation of Decision Alternatives Dependent upon the Reversibility of a Decision and the Passage of Time," *European Journal of Social Psychology* 14: 447–50 (1984); and D. Frey, "Reversible and Irreversible Decisions: Preference for Consonant Information as a Function of Attractiveness of Decision Alternatives," *Personality and Social Psychology Bulletin* 7: 621–26 (1981).

27. S. Wiggins et al., "The Psychological Consequences of Predictive Testing for Huntington's Disease," *New England Journal of Medicine* 327: 1401–5 (1992).

28. D. T. Gilbert and J. E. J. Ebert, "Decisions and Revisions: The Affective Forecasting of Changeable Outcomes," *Journal of Personality and Social Psychology* 82: 503–14 (2002).

29. J. W. Brehm, *A Theory of Psychological Reactance* (New York: Academic Press, 1966).

30. R. B. Cialdini, *Influence: Science and Practice* (Glenview, Ill.: Scott, Foresman, 1985).

31. S. S. Iyengar and M. R. Lepper, "When Choice Is Demotivating: Can One Desire Too Much of a Good Thing?" *Journal of Personality and Social Psychology* 79: 995–1006 (2000); and B. Schwartz, "Self-Determination: The Tyranny of Freedom," *American Psychologist* 55: 79–88 (2000).

32. J. W. Pennebaker, "Writing About Emotional Experiences as a Therapeutic Process," *Psychological Science* 8: 162–66 (1997).

33. J. W. Pennebaker, T. J. Mayne, and M. E. Francis, "Linguistic Predictors of Adaptive Bereavement," *Journal of Personality and Social Psychology* 72: 863–71 (1997).

34. T. D. Wilson et al., "The Pleasures of Uncertainty: Prolonging Positive Moods in Ways People Do Not Anticipate," *Journal of Personality and Social Psychology* 88: 5–21 (2005).

35. B. Fischoff, "Hindsight ≠ foresight: The Effects of Outcome Knowledge on Judgment Under Uncertainty," *Journal of Experimental Psychology: Human Perception and Performance* 1: 288–99 (1975); and C. A. Anderson, M. R. Lepper, and L. Ross, "Perseverance of Social Theories: The Role of Explanation in the Persistence of Discredited Information," *Journal of Personality and Social Psychology* 39: 1037–49 (1980).

36. B. Weiner, "'Spontaneous' Causal Thinking," *Psychological Bulletin* 97: 74–84 (1985); and R. R. Hassin, J. A. Bargh, and J. S. Uleman, "Spontaneous Causal Inferences," *Journal of Experimental Social Psychology* 38: 515–22 (2002).

37. B. Zeigarnik, "Das Behalten erledigter und unerledigter Handlungen," *Psychologische Forschung* 9: 1–85 (1927); and G. W. Boguslavsky, "Interruption and Learning," *Psychological Review* 58: 248–55 (1951).

38. Wilson et al., "Pleasures of Uncertainty."

39. J. Keats, letter to Richard Woodhouse, 27 October 1881, in *Selected Poems and Letters by John Keats*, ed. D. Bush (Boston: Houghton Mifflin, 1959).

QUESTIONS FOR MAKING CONNECTIONS
WITHIN THE READING

1. Throughout "Immune to Reality," Gilbert describes mental operations
    using terms from everyday life: the brain is "one smart shopper"; our brains
    are "conspirators"; once we come up with an explanation, "we can fold it
    up like freshly washed laundry, put it away in memory's drawer, and move
    on to the next one." Obviously, Gilbert is seeking to make his thoughts
    about human psychology readily accessible, but what exactly is he trying to
    convey with these descriptions? As you reread the essay, generate a list of the
    most significant images and analogies Gilbert uses to describe mental opera-
    tions. What does this list tell you about Gilbert's theory of mind?

2. On the basis of the experiments and studies Gilbert presents, would you say
    that happiness is fundamentally an illusion? Or is it the *pursuit* of happiness
    that deserves to be reconsidered? If happiness is not something that we can
    pursue consciously, then how do we go about becoming happy? Should we
    be pursuing something other than happiness?

3. What is the meaning of "reality" at the end of Gilbert's discussion of our
    "psychological immune system"? What exactly is it that this system is
    designed to protect us from? Is the psychological immune system analogous
    to our biological immune system, or does it operate according to a different
    logic? Is the reality from which this system protects us ultimately an illusion?
    Or are psychological realities fundamentally different from material realities?

QUESTIONS FOR WRITING

1. The Declaration of Independence proclaims that "all men" are "endowed by
    their Creator with certain unalienable Rights," among them "Life, Liberty
    and the pursuit of Happiness." What are the *political* implications of the
    research indicating that the pursuit of happiness is often misdirected because
    people typically fail to recognize the conditions that will really make them
    happy? Does Gilbert's work suggest that Thomas Jefferson's thinking in the
    Declaration was based on a false assumption? Can any government respon-
    sibly claim to make happiness available?

2. What are the *economic* implications of Gilbert's argument? If people began to
    choose "action over inaction, pain over annoyance, and commitment over
    freedom," would the consumer economy survive? That is, is consumerism
    dependent upon our collective ignorance about the path to happiness, or is
    the hope that one's life will be improved by increased purchasing power
    itself a path to happiness? Is trying to be happy with what one has a form of
    action or inaction? If Gilbert is right that "explanation robs events of their
    emotional impact," what role does explanation play in consumer economy?
    Is a healthy economy dependent upon consumers who are well informed or
    consumers who are "immune to reality"?

QUESTIONS FOR MAKING CONNECTIONS
BETWEEN READINGS

1. In "Son," Andrew Solomon writes about the experience of both children and parents who are challenged by the dissonance between what they expect from the future and what they actually get. Children feel trapped by parental expectations, and parents sometimes see their dreams destroyed by the adults their children become. In what ways do Solomon's reflections both confirm and complicate Gilbert's claims about the ways we "stumble" into happiness? Although Gilbert often makes a convincing case for the limitations of our ability to foresee the real sources of our happiness, he has less to say about our role in finding happiness at last. Do we really "stumble" into happiness, or is happiness an achievement that requires creativity on our part? Does Solomon himself get to happiness more or less by accident, or does it require him to actively become the author of his own life?

2. What are the connections between the quest for happiness as Gilbert describes it and the cultivation of wisdom that Robert Thurman outlines? Is the Buddhist experience of nothingness a way of freeing people from the hot states in which we overestimate our own capacity to find satisfaction through changes in external conditions? Or is the notion of wisdom itself an example of the kind of unconscious fact cooking Gilbert describes, which generates happiness only if it feels "like a discovery and not like a snow job"? Is there a way to determine, finally, if another person is happy or wise? Can one even know oneself with certainty if Gilbert is correct? How about if Thurman is correct?

$\blacklozenge\blacklozenge\blacklozenge$

KAREN HO

As KAREN HO's writing demonstrates, finance and education now intersect in a way few outsiders know much about: some of America's most powerful and prestigious universities have close ties with Wall Street firms. In 2007, the year before the recession began, more than half of Harvard's graduates chose careers in business or a related field. Two years later, thirty-six percent of Princeton's most recent graduates took a job in finance. Although the percentages have recently declined, the ties between the Ivy League and "the Street" have disturbing implications for the future of higher education in the United States.

For a long time colleges and universities played a special social role because the diversity of the curriculum reflected the rich development of culture over many centuries. History, literature, foreign languages, math and science, anthropology, sociology, psychology—these and other academic disciplines have given many generations of students the opportunity to broaden their minds while preparing them for their future work in a wide variety of fields. But now this ideal of higher education as an exploration of possibilities has come under intense pressure from the influence of "financialization." A number of observers have looked critically at this recent turn, but Karen Ho's writing is unique for several reasons. For one thing, the time she spent working on Wall Street gives her an insider's eye, but she is also an anthropologist who believes the Street has created a distinctive outlook that threatens to remake the whole society in its narrowing image:

> Wall Street shapes not just the stock market but also the very nature of employment and what kinds of workers are valued [everywhere]....
> The kind of worker they imagine is a worker like themselves. A worker who is constantly retraining, a worker who is constantly networked, a worker whose skill set is very interchangeable, a worker who thinks of downsizing as a challenge—a worker who thrives on this. This becomes the prototype, but in many ways that's quite removed from the daily lives of most American workers.

On Wall Street, rapid change and high risk hold the key to personal success, but for many other Americans, values of this kind have undermined their security and quality of life. If Ho is correct, then Americans need to rediscover or invent values of a different, more democratic kind. But where will this search for new values take place? Traditionally, such alternatives have come from colleges and universities. What will happen to the United States, however, if these institutions too are captured by the "ideology" of finance?

Biographies of Hegemony

When I began to conduct fieldwork in 1998 and 1999, delving into the network of contacts, coworkers, and friends I developed at Stanford, Princeton, and Bankers Trust (BT), it struck me how often my informants ranked and distinguished themselves according to their "smartness." The term seemed fundamental to the Wall Street lexicon. My informants proclaimed that the smartest people in the world came to work there; Wall Street, in their view, had created probably the most elite work-society ever to be assembled on the globe. Almost all the front-office workers that I encountered emphasized how smart their coworkers were, how "deep the talent" was at their particular bank, how if one just hired "the smartest people," then everything else fell into place. Chris Logan and Nicolas Bern, recent Princeton graduates working at BT and Merrill Lynch respectively, explained that from their relatively fresh perspective, what was most culturally unique about Wall Street was the experience of being surrounded by, as Bern put it, the "smartest and most ambitious people." Logan added that the three qualities of success on Wall Street are to be "smart, hardworking, and aggressive. Everything else is considered tangential." According to Kate Miller, a Spelman College graduate and former analyst at Morgan Stanley, interviewees are typically told they will be working with "the brightest people in the world. These are the greatest minds of the century."

Such sentiments were not confined to eager young analysts or investment banking representatives talking up their industry to overawed recruits. Julio Muñoz, who received his MBA from Harvard and was an associate in investment banking at Donaldson, Lufkin and Jenrette (DLJ), a prestigious boutique investment bank which has since been bought out by Credit Suisse First Boston (CSFB), claimed that the most distinguishing features of investment banks are their smartness and exclusivity:

> People are really smart. They really don't hire any—the hiring standards are pretty good. That's one thing they really focused on doing, and that differentiates investment banking from other working environments in that they really do target the experienced individuals with good academic background.... [This] really brings to the investment banks a very

elite society—somebody in society that had the means to study in
X universities. If you really narrowed down the universities where
the investment banks recruit, your number probably will not exceed
fifteen to twenty universities.

Similarly, John Carlton, a senior managing director at BT who had worked at multiple investment banks such as Kidder Peabody and CSFB, stated that the key characteristics of Wall Street investment bankers are their smartness, aggressiveness, and self-confidence: "There is always a premium on having smart people ... so, it is highly competitive. What happens is that a lot of people say, 'Look, some of the best and brightest people are going to Wall Street. I'm pretty smart myself; I should go [there] as well. And, by the way, I get paid very well.' " Remarking on how hedge funds attract the most brilliant minds from investment banks, Robert Hopkins, a vice president of mergers and acquisitions at Lehman Brothers, exclaimed, "We are talking about the smartest people in the world. We are! They are the smartest people in the world. If you [the average investor or the average corporation] don't know anything, why wouldn't you invest with the smartest people in the world? They must know what they are doing."[1]

The "culture of smartness" is central to understanding Wall Street's financial agency, how investment bankers are personally and institutionally empowered to enact their worldviews, export their practices, and serve as models for far-reaching socioeconomic change. On Wall Street, "smartness" means much more than individual intelligence; it conveys a naturalized and generic sense of "impressiveness," of elite, pinnacle status and expertise, which is used to signify, even prove, investment bankers' worthiness as advisors to corporate America and leaders of the global financial markets. To be considered "smart" on Wall Street is to be implicated in a web of situated practices and ideologies, coproduced through the interactions of multiple institutions, processes, and American culture at large, which confer authority and legitimacy on high finance and contribute to the sector's vast influence. The culture of smartness is not simply a quality of Wall Street, but a currency, a driving force productive of both profit accumulation and global prowess.

The key criterion of smartness is an ability to "wow" the clients—generally speaking, the top executives of Fortune 500 companies. In this sense, although technical skill and business savvy also help to constitute smartness on Wall Street, they are often considered secondary, learnable "on the job." "The best," "the greatest," and "the brightest" minds in the world are sorted and recognized through a credentialing process that is crucially bolstered by image and performance. In other words, smartness must be represented and reinforced by a specific appearance and bodily technique that dominantly signals that impressiveness; not surprisingly, such characteristics as being impeccably and smartly dressed, dashing appearance, mental and physical quickness, aggressiveness, and vigor reference the default upperclassness, maleness, whiteness, and heteronormativity of ideal investment bankers. Here I focus mainly on the specific elitism that is the key valence of smartness....

What allows investment bankers to claim smartness, what defines and legitimates them as smart in the first place, and what particular kind of smartness is being deployed? Where these questions become especially clear is during the process of investment banker identity and social formation: the recruiting, training, and orientation of freshly minted college graduates and MBAs, their initiation into the world of Wall Street. Here it is possible to discern, in starkest relief, Wall Street's cultural values in action, particularly the construction and maintenance of the hegemonic elitism that produces "expert" knowledge of financial markets. Through the continual praxis of recruitment and orientation, the Street enacts and regenerates the very foundations of its legitimacy.

Through the process of recruitment and orientation, investment banks define their notion of both what it takes and what it means to be a successful subject in an age of global capital. To play the role of "master of the universe" requires not only especially strong doses of self-confidence and institutional legitimation, but also a particular set of beliefs regarding Wall Street's role in the world and one's own role on Wall Street. Investment bankers, trained to view financial markets and corporate America through particular, highly ideological lenses, are also imbued with a sense of their own personal exemplariness as agents of *and models for* socioeconomic change—a sense that must be embodied, believed in, and continually "pumped up." In approaching the question of how investment bankers become empowered to advise and influence the direction of corporations in the United States and globally vis à vis their personal trajectories, qualities, connections, associations, and identities, I make the case for the importance of the biographical and the institutional in enacting global capitalist change. The building blocks of dominant capitalist practices are also personal and cultural; people's experiences, their university and career tracking and choices, are constitutive of capitalist hegemony; and the financial is cultural through and through.

In particular, I focus on the construction of "the smart investment banker": a member of an extended "family" network of elite university alumni and a living symbol of know-how and global agency. Their impressiveness and financial influence are further cemented and proven by surviving brutally intense hard work and an insecure job environment, which in turn allows them to internalize the merit of their analyses and recommendations. Through the institutional culture of Wall Street broadly conceived—where job experiences and workplace incentives map onto elite biographies—investment bankers not only imbibe a particular ideology of shareholder value and spread it across corporate America, but they are also pushed to refashion and reconstruct the working lives of millions in the image of their own.

By investigating investment bankers, as individuals and as collective agents of change, I do not assume a priori that "the market" always already exercises power, but rather that the particular biographies, experiences, and practices of investment bankers, who are both empowered and constrained by their cultural and institutional locations, create social change and financial hegemony on a daily basis. Just as "it is through the 'small stories' that one can begin to unravel and challenge homogenizing discourses embedded within concepts such as globalization, 'the' market, and 'the' state," it is possible to decenter the market as an abstract agent and powerful force by demonstrating that it is only through the small and the everyday that we can understand the creation of hegemony in all its particularity and contextuality. Otherwise, we risk privileging, homogenizing, or taking for granted the metanarratives of the market, the big stories (Crossa 2005, 29; S. 170).

RECRUITMENT

I first entered the cultural world of investment banks through the herculean recruiting efforts that Wall Street undertakes at the most elite universities. Despite my own ambivalence and feelings of mystification about Wall Street as an anthropology graduate student, this direct link—the pipeline between Princeton University and investment banks—enabled my very access to each step of the recruiting process, not to mention the field site itself. Wall Street, in a sense, came to me. Although I hardly recognized it at the time, Wall Street's ubiquity on campus, as well as the intensity of undergraduate interest in investment banking, meant that merely being a student at Princeton allowed, in a sense, automatic participant observation of this world. After fieldwork, I returned to Princeton to write the dissertation, thinking I would be getting away from Wall Street, retreating to an ivory-tower refuge in order to do some serious thinking and writing. Instead, it was more like reentering the belly of the beast. I was a graduate advisor at an undergraduate resident hall. Two weeks into the job, taking a walk after dinner I crossed paths with an undergraduate crowd (two of whom lived in my residence hall) headed toward Nassau Hall. Before I knew it, they had steered me into a Merrill Lynch presentation! The masses of students converging on these recruitment presentations and information sessions are akin to the campus traffic generated by the gatherings and dispersals of concert crowds. Already a veteran of the actual recruitment process back in 1996, now, almost four years later, after campus recruiting had even further intensified as a result of the bull market, I found myself participating in countless dining hall discussions about investment banking, attending still more presentations, and reading endless investment banking advertisements, updates, news, and opinion pieces in the pages of the *Daily Princetonian*. In 2000, I also had access on a regular basis to many of Wall Street's cultural representations and practices at Harvard University because my younger sister was an undergraduate there at the time. She introduced me to friends going through the recruiting process and kept me continually updated on how many of her acquaintances had suddenly, in their senior year, found their true calling as Wall Street investment bankers or management consultants. As many of my previous investment banking informants were also Harvard graduates, I have been able to make detailed observations of Wall Street's interactions with two elite universities.

More so than even the other Ivy League schools, Harvard and Princeton are the "prime recruiting ground for all of the most prestigious Wall Street, management consulting and other types of firms that offer the most sought after jobs.... The Princeton badge is a powerful currency that buys access" (Karseras 2006). As many of my informants have elaborated, "If you go to Harvard, Yale, or Princeton, there are really only two career fields presented: banking and consulting" (Duboff 2005). This shocking narrowness was verified throughout my time at Princeton and on Wall Street: I found not only that most bankers came from a few elite institutions, but also that most undergraduate and even many graduate students assumed that the only "suitable" destinations for life after Princeton—the only sectors offering a truly "Princeton-like job"—were, first, investment banking, and second, management consulting.[2] With its extensive alumni network and juggernaut recruitment machine, Wall Street is the "de facto home away from Princeton for recent graduates, many of whom continue living together even as they take on new responsibilities and lifestyles" (Hall 2005).

As perhaps the most important feeder school to Wall Street, Princeton sends astounding numbers of recruits into financial services in general, and in particular investment banking. According to the Office of Career Services, 30 percent of the class of 2001, 37 percent of the class of 2003, and 40 percent of the class of 2005 and 2006 entered financial services after graduation (Chan 2001; Creed 2003; Easton 2006; Henn 2001). Whereas from 2000 to 2005, 470 Princeton students pursued law or medical degrees, "520 Princeton students—about 40 percent of Princeton students choosing fulltime jobs directly after graduation—decided to work in the financial services sector," amounting to the largest percentage in a single industry (Hall 2005). At Harvard University, which rivals Princeton as the primary producer of Wall Street recruits, investment banking (as well as management consulting) also provides the majority of jobs for its students upon graduation (Lerer 1997). According to Harvard's Office of Career Services, in 2005, close to half of Harvard students go through "the recruiting process to vie for investment banking and consulting jobs" (Huber 2006).

As Devon Peterson, an undergraduate writing for the *Daily Princetonian*, observed in 2002, "It's been common knowledge that many of [Princeton's] undergraduates join the financial realm every year, creating a kind of light-hearted, self-deprecating joke about Philosophy majors becoming I-bankers and once hopeful novelists heading to Wall Street" (Peterson 2002). How do so many undergraduates who enter these institutions without any prior knowledge of investment banking, who once aspired to become, say writers or teachers, "realize" by the time they graduate that they have always wanted to go to Wall Street? How do these talented and well-connected students, with access to a wide range of possible futures, come to believe that investment banking is one of the *only* prestigious job options available post graduation? I argue that such changes in life courses and the attendant discursive transformations must be unpacked in order to understand the particular worldviews, cultural associations, and orientations the recruiting process demands and calls into being.

The forces that push these college students toward investment banking are obviously multiple: the particular college environment, the strength of alumni and peer networks, the cultural linking of success and smartness with Wall Street, the hierarchical narrowing of career options and what constitutes prestige, to name a few. Perhaps the most self-evident reason for Wall Street's recruiting monopoly is simply that its presence dominates campus life: recruiters visit the university virtually every week, even on weekends; they show up in the greatest numbers at career forums, panel discussions, and social events; their advertisements for information sessions "meet and greets," and free drinks and hors d'oeuvres dominate the campus newspapers daily; their company literature and application forms are easily accessible, either at campus locations or online.

The recruiting process saturates almost every aspect of campus life from the very first day of the academic year. Investment banks and consulting firms dominate the early fall career fairs, setting the terms for what constitutes a successful career (and what it looks like), and monopolize the attention of the student body by showing up with the most polish, fanfare, and numbers. They hand out the best goodie bags, the most titillating magnet sets, mugs, Frisbees, water bottles, caps, and t-shirts, and in a matter of days, thousands of students become walking advertisements as their logos disperse into campus life. At the 2006 Princeton Career Fair, 60 of the 104 firms represented were in financial services or consulting (Rampell 2006). At the 2003 Harvard Career Forum, more than half of the close to one hundred firms in attendance were in investment banking, general finance, and consulting (Urken and Habib 2003). Marketed as general career exploration meant to attract a diversity of students and pathways, these forums actually constitute "recruitment on a grand scale" for the investment banking and consulting industries *(Harvard Crimson* 1995). This early and intense branding of Wall Street careers as the symbol of arrival, the equating of investment banking with "career" in general, serves to narrow students' notions of success and gives the impression that for graduates, there's nothing else out there besides investment banking and consulting (N. Guyer 2003).

Taufiq Rahim, a *Daily Princetonian* columnist, wrote of what he called the "hunting season": "They're here. I can see them. I can smell them. They're in my inbox. They're in my mailbox. They're on my voicemail. They're outside my door. They're on campus, and they smell blood.... They're the investment banks, the consulting firms: McKinsey, Goldman Sachs, Bain and Company, Merrill Lynch" (Rahim 2003). Below I reproduce Goldman Sachs's "Recruitment Calendar" for Harvard undergraduates at the millennium (see Table 1). The recruitment schedule is painstakingly detailed, demonstrating the active pursuit of Harvard students: they will not fall through the cracks. As the director of Princeton's Career Services cautioned students about Wall Street recruiters: "They come after you. If you're hiding under the bed and you don't want to talk anymore, they'll come and get you" (Shapira 1998).

On the day of the recruitment presentation (and most investment banks usually have multiple campus events, as separate divisions will have their own presentations and interview timelines), a given bank's representatives descend in droves to central campus locations, usually the fanciest business hotel near campus. For Princeton, bankers will charter a bus, a few limos, and even some taxis to drive a group of thirty to fifty investment bankers, research analysts, and traders (usually alumni who will also serve as recruiters) from New York City to the Nassau Inn at Princeton. The same goes for Harvard. Elaborate recruitment presentations are held at the Charles Hotel in Cambridge or the Faculty Club; dozens of recent Harvard graduates and seasoned alumni currently working on Wall Street fill the rooms. Including recent hires from Harvard and Princeton allows potential recruits to witness former classmates as smart and successful, as having made the transition from undergraduate life onto the Wall Street fast track.

The very first Wall Street recruitment event I ever attended, in 1995 as a graduate student still contemplating research on Wall Street, was a session presented by Goldman Sachs, widely known among potential employees as the

T A B L E 1 **Goldman Sachs Recruitment Schedule at Harvard University, 2000–2001.**

Division	Date	Event
Firmwide	September 6, 2000	Thirteenth Annual Women's Leadership Conference Panel Discussion, 10:00–11:30 A.M.
Firmwide	September 14, 2000	HSA Business Leadership Dinner The Charles Hotel, 6:00–8:00 P.M.
Firmwide	September 27, 2000	Resume Writing Workshop Office of Career Services, 12:00–3:00 P.M.
Firmwide	September 27, 2000	Firmwide Information Session The Charles Hotel 6:00–8:00 P.M.
Investment Management	October 2, 2000	Divisional Presentation The Charles Hotel, 6:30–8:00 P.M.
Investment Banking	October 3, 2000	Divisional Presentation The Charles Hotel, 6:30–8:00 P.M.
Equities	October 5, 2000	Divisional Presentation Faculty Club, 8:00–9:30 P.M.
Firmwide	October 11, 2000	HSA Career Week Panel Discussion on "My Career"
Firmwide	October 13, 2000	Career Forum Gordon Track and Tennis Center
Sales and Trading	October 16, 2000	Divisional Presentation The Charles Hotel, 6:30–8:00 P.M.
All Divisions	October 19, 2000	Resume Drop
Corporate Treasury	October 25, 2000	Resume Drop (open)
Corporate Treasury	October 27, 2000	2 Open Full-time Analyst Interview Schedules
Firmwide	October 30, 2000	Minority Event (tentative)
Fixed Income, Currency & Commodities	October 30, 2000	Resume Drop (open)
Fixed Income, Currency & Commodities	November 1, 2000	1.5 Closed Full-Time Analyst Interview Schedules 1.5 Open Full-Time Analyst Interview Schedules
Investment Banking	November 2, 2000	3 Closed Full-Time Analyst Interview Schedules
Equities	November 3, 2000	3 Closed Full-Time Analyst Interview Schedules
Investment Research	November 9, 2000	2 Closed Full-Time Analyst Interview Schedules (1 Schedule for London)
Investment Management	November 9, 2000	2 Closed Full-Time Analyst Interview Schedules
Firmwide	December 4, 2000	Women's Event (tentative)

TABLE 1 Continued

Division	Date	Event
Firmwide	December 14, 2000	Resume Drop for Spring
The Hull Group	January 30, 2001	1 Closed Full-Time Analyst Interview Schedule
Equities	February 2, 2001	3 Closed Full-Time Analyst Interview Schedules
Fixed Income Research and Strategy	February 7, 2001	1 Closed Full-Time Analyst Interview Schedule
Fixed Income, Currency & Commodities	February 7, 2001	1.5 Closed Full-Time Analyst Interview Schedules 1.5 Open Summer Analyst Interview Schedules
Investment Banking	February 7, 2001	3 Closed Full-Time Analyst Interview Schedules
Investment Management	February 8, 2001	1 Closed Full-Time Analyst Interview Schedule 2 Closed Summer Analyst Interview Schedules
Equities	February 9, 2001	3 Closed Full-Time Analyst Interview Schedules
Investment Research	February 13, 2001	1 Closed Full-Time Analyst Interview Schedule
Investment Banking Training and Professional Development	February 21, 2001	1 Closed Full-Time Analyst Interview Schedule 1 Closed Summer Analyst Interview Schedule
Firmwide	TBD	IPO Case Study in conjunction with the Office of Career Services

most prestigious and exclusive investment bank on Wall Street. Arriving a little late at Princeton township's hallowed Nassau Inn, I was greeted by a sea of charcoal gray, navy, and black business suits. There must have been over 150 well-coiffed and starched, professionally driven undergraduates crowding the hotel's ballroom to hear a panel of sixteen Goldman Sachs executives, mostly Princeton grads. Apprehension and eagerness pervaded the room: this was not a time for socializing but rather for competitive vying for "face time" and searing first impressions with the recruiters. Instead of saying hello to friends, juniors and seniors surveyed the room and sought to get on their marks. As the only graduate student in the room, (as far as I could tell), awkwardly attempting to both observe and participate in the recruiting process, not to mention the fact that I was dressed in an old pair of slightly wrinkled gray slacks and a denim vest (of all things), I felt completely out of place.

The lights soon darkened for an introductory slide and video presentation. It was a recorded narration with sweeping views of Manhattan and fast-moving visuals of the globe, suit-clad workers traveling or walking briskly to corporate towers, and sharp-dressed bankers videoconferencing or huddled up in teams with their sleeves rolled up. The narrator explained that a Wall Street career was all about "dealing with change." "The world is going to continue to change faster and faster, so we need people like you." When the lights came on, we turned our attention to the panel. I counted eight white men, five white women, one Latino man, one South Asian woman, and one black man. A relatively older white man, a managing director (Princeton class of '82), began to speak in a tone of pride: "We are a Princeton family. I met my wife here. Princeton students make the best analysts, which is why we recruit heavily here." The other speakers who were recent graduates introduced themselves by naming the schools they had attended: Harvard, Williams, Harvard, Princeton, Wharton, Princeton, Princeton, Princeton. "I'm from the University of Chicago," said the south Asian woman wryly. "I'm not quite as bright as everyone else." The Princetonian managing director then got down to business. "The two-year program will go by in a flash. Your learning and growth curve will be exponential. You will get actual interaction with clients. You are part of the team at our firm; the last thing you should be doing is photocopying. We hire ten people to do that, and that's all they do. We need your intelligence." It quickly became apparent that this was the evening's guiding theme. "So why should you work here?" asked the recent white male alumnus from Harvard. "Because if you hang out with dumb people, you'll learn dumb things. In investment banking, the people are very smart; that's why they got the job. It's very fast, very challenging, and they'll teach as quickly as you can learn." Some speakers emphasized the access to power offered by a Goldman Sachs position. "Our analysts can go anywhere in the world," said one of the white male vice presidents who is an alumnus from Wharton. "We've got Hong Kong, we've got Sydney, we've got London." He returned, inevitably, to the presentation's central motif; with an admiring gaze at the audience, he exclaimed, "You are all so smart!" Finally, the Princetonian managing director got up and announced, "Let's break up, go to the Nassau Inn Tap Room; drinks are on us!" The swarm of undergraduates then beelined toward the panelists, eager for face time with actual Goldman Sachs executives while I was still lingering in my seat. Determined to join the fray, I surveyed the scene and realized that every investment banker was already surrounded by two to three semi-circle layers of undergraduates: as the first layer moved to impress and receive the business card of the banker holding court, the second layer would quickly move into "face-time" position. The only room in the crowd for me was actually behind the speaker's back where there was no waiting line! In that position, I mainly observed throughout the night, and the only person who turned around to talk to me was the young South Asian American analyst from the University of Chicago, and I held on dearly to her business card as a sign of my initiation into this grueling process.

During subsequent recruitment presentations, I experienced much of the same: well-suited alumnae declaring, "We only hire superstars," "We are only hiring from five different schools," "You are the cream of the crop." In these sessions, I was stuck by how proclamations of elitism (through "world-class" universities, the discourses of smartness and globalization) seemed foundational to the very core of how investment bankers see themselves, the world, and their place in it. Representing a world of "collective smartness" and exclusivity seemed fundamentally connected not only to the criteria for becoming an investment banker but also to the very nature of what they do. What precisely were the links between elitism and the enactments of their financial expertise and global dreams, between Wall Street's claims to smartness and their promises of global prowess? Motivated in large part by these compelling presentations, I decided that to understand these grandiose, even mystifying, pronouncements, I had to get a job on Wall Street. I took a leave of absence from graduate school to participate "for real" in this process.

The "vigorous college recruiting season" is usually capped off with elaborate "sell days" to encourage seniors to accept the job. Such perks include "ski trips to Utah and dinners at Lahiere's" (Princeton's four-star restaurant) (Easton 2006; Shapira 1998). Every junior and senior that I interviewed spoke about the allure of recruiting, the constant wining and dining, the fancy spreads at upscale hotels and clubs. According to the *Daily Princetonian* staff writer Alice Easton:

> After months of dressing up in suits and ties, making their way to New York or the Nassau Inn and trying to impress panels of interviewers with their technical and social skills, juniors applying for summer internships in finance and consulting can now reap the benefits of their work: elaborate "sell days" to convince them to accept the job.... "They paid for two nights at a fancy hotel in New York.... They rented out a museum and had a cocktail party, and then rented out the VIP room in a nightclub in Soho."... The company later sent him chocolates in the mail.... [They showed recruits] a whole lifestyle. (Easton 2006)

The obvious implication is that if Harvard and Princeton students join these firms, then in a few years, they too can have it all.

During one of my visits to Harvard University to see my sister in 2000, I sat down with Kendra Lin, a premed student who was not planning to go into investment banking but wanted to understand "what the hype was all about" and possessed a genuine curiosity about why her classmates were so obsessed with Wall Street. In addition to attending the various career forums and participating formally in the recruiting process by signing up with the Office of Career Services (ocs), many Harvard students also participate in immersion programs to educate them about Wall Street and management consulting. Therefore, at the time, at the onset of recruiting season, Harvard Student Agencies, in collaboration with Harvard Business School and leading investment banks and management consulting firms, sponsored the Harvard Business Leadership Program (blp), a week of recruitment, training, socializing, and general orientation to Wall Street financial institutions, management consulting, and general business practices. Being chosen to participate in blp was itself a competitive process to search for "business leaders," and as the president of various student associations, Lin made the cut.

Describing her impressions of the BLP events, Lin said that the speakers who made the greatest impression were the representatives of Goldman Sachs. "They're this really elite investment bank that advises many leaders in corporate America on their mergers and acquisitions and securities offerings. They talked about how they managed the privatizations of the largest corporations in China and Spain, to name a few." While some of the non-investment-banking financial firms and smaller start-up corporations (who were in the minority) appeared "homely" to Lin, firms like J. P. Morgan and Goldman Sachs and management consulting groups like Boston Consulting Group "looked very accomplished" and "thought very highly of themselves." As a result, all the Harvard students flocked to talk to them. During the cocktail and dinner hour after the presentations, investment banks proclaimed that Harvard produced the most stellar recruits. Lin talked at length about her favorable impression of Goldman Sachs:

> I really enjoyed Goldman—as a side note, all of these firms are really talented in recruiting students. They make Harvard students feel like they are the cream of the crop. We have the best minds. This image of the Harvard student runs thick through recruiters and through people at the business school. I have heard this many times over the course of the week: that Harvard students are the best business people because you can give them any problem and they will be the ones to come up with the solution most quickly.... I left his speech believing that Goldman is the Harvard of all investment banks, but they all sure know how to sell themselves well.

Goldman Sachs, as Lin described, worked very hard to position itself as an extension of Harvard and, in doing so, confirmed Harvard as the progenitor of the best.

According to Lin, investment bankers emphasized how they "had the perfect life." One executive talked about how "he lives in the burbs, has a minivan, a dog, and two kids. Seriously! His wife graduated from Pritzker [the University of Chicago's business school] and is now a Harvard Medical School professor, and he is a rich VP." After hearing Lin's initial impressions on Wall Street recruiting presentations, I asked her what she thought about her week-long experience with BLP—the dinners, the socials, the business school case studies. What did she like and dislike?

KL: It's all a schmooze fest. You have to schmooze your recruiters. You have to master rounds of interviews followed by more schmoozing, and then once you get there, you have to "live the lifestyle" of a business person. Be social, drink, go to parties, and schmooze some more. Also … there is no commitment really to social change.

KH: Interesting observations. How did you realize just from this week, so early on, that people have to "live the lifestyle"? How were you clued into this point?

KL: I think it was the set up of the whole BLP that first clued me in to that: I mean, they cater *all* of our meals, our dinners are all at the Charles hotel, and they are quite extravagant for a bunch of college kids. Hey, I love duck and sushi! Before we go into the hotel for dinner, there is a social hour where they serve juice and soda, and that's where it hit me. Basically you see all these students huddled around the bankers and consultants and kissing their ass. Everyone's all dressed up—it's a different culture. Put that together with stereotypes of businessmen from movies, you see that it really is pretty much like that.

This conflation of elite universities with investment banking and "the perfect lifestyle" is crucial to the recruitment process, reproducing as it does the ambience of Wall Street cocktail parties, where investment bankers "schmooze clients" in lavish, impeccably catered settings. These norms are enacted for and demonstrated to students, and like Lin, they immediately pick up on the importance of performing "smartness," not to mention how Wall Street business success is premised on pedigree, competitive consumption, and heteronormativity.

Not surprisingly, Wall Street's intense focus and persistence at Princeton, Harvard, and a few other campuses have repercussions for student culture. Newspapers and dorms overflow with debates about the pros and cons of investment banking work life, excited discussions of what investment bankers "actually do," and romanticized tales of high-roller life in Manhattan. Students begin to see "i-banking" as a "mysterious, glamorous, and relatively undefined world" (Hall 2005). A glance at the campus publications at Princeton and Harvard demonstrates what amounts to a communal obsession, with constant news and opinion articles on "recruiting insanity," "avoiding the i-banking shadow," "schmoozing at Nassau Inn," "defending the indefensible career," "the dangerous allure of recruiting," "aspiring Gordon Gekkos," "new recruits," "future financiers flock to a Darwinian fete," "banking on pain," "i-banking ire," "how investment banking consumed my life," and "is there more to life than investment banking?" Heated campus panel discussions debate the relative merits of banking and consulting, as panelists (firm representatives, usually former students) face off with a cost-benefit analysis of the two career choices and use the platform to further recruit students to their side. It is hardly surprising, then, that the much-mythologized field of investment banking often presents itself as the solution to anxieties about postgraduation life.

Although most of my recruitment participation was with undergraduates (as I myself went through the college analyst recruitment program), the process for elite business schools for the recruitment of MBAS for associate positions (one level higher than analyst) has similar components. For the most part, many graduate students at prestigious business schools, such as Harvard Business School (HBS), Wharton, Sloan (MIT Business School), Columbia Business School, and so forth, have had financial experience. Most have worked as analysts at investment banks or in management consulting firms; those who do not have a financial background have plenty of opportunity to study finance as a "concentration" in business schools. All MBAs are literally bombarded by recruitment presentations and information sessions sponsored by their school's own student finance clubs and associations as well as Wall Street investment banks themselves.

Starting the first year, MBA students realize that to work on Wall Street after graduating from the two-year masters program, they must intern on Wall Street their first summer and receive a job offer thirteen weeks into the internship. As Bill Hayes, a recent MIT Sloan alumnus and an associate at Goldman Sachs, described the process in 2001:

> Within a month of school starting, everyone starts coming. Hotel presentations; meet and greets. They invite you out for drinks in the effort to get the best and brightest to apply. The bulge bracket firms don't have to sell themselves (the smaller banks do) since all the students gravitate toward them. I guess only they can afford it. They'll have a reception, and you have to meet people and hope you make some sort of connection. For Merrill, I went to a presentation, sent in my resume, and they called. Goldman came in with a whole crew of Wharton alumni, and then went to HBS afterwards. At the same time this is all happening, we have smaller events where the school Finance Club has receptions with bankers from top firms, where half of the MBA class shows up, or these clubs have information "learning" sessions like "Investment Banking 101" and "Day on the Job," which is a smaller setting, and you hope to make a contact with a recent grad to give you an "in." You have to send follow-up e-mails and thank-you's to every contact. Our Finance Club also organized mock interviews, resume workshops, and "trips to Wall Street" where anyone can go and visit all the banks. I met with Morgan and Goldman and Lehman. You go to their offices and try to distinguish yourself.... They only hire from these elite schools because they are already prefiltered. It makes you feel good; you've already been nominated. Bankers will say, "You might ask why we ask about GPA and test scores. Because we've done the correlation between top GPA and test scores from top schools and performance in the organization, and we know you will succeed."

Wall Street saturation of business school life is certainly equal to that of the general university population. The difference is that elite MBA programs explicitly represent themselves as channels to and of Wall Street; they are not emphasizing a general liberal arts education. Students often enter these institutions precisely to get a job in finance, and just a few months into the scramble for a job at top Wall Street investment banks, the first-round interview slots are full.

For MBAs, the selling of "the perfect lifestyle" is, on the one hand, expected and taken for granted, and on the other, understood as ironic, as most MBAs, having worked on Wall Street as college graduates, have experienced their "lifestyle" as simultaneously grueling and exploitative. What is more seductive is the forecasting of elite social networking and Wall Street influence over corporate America. Such an anointing was unmistakable at the Harvard Business School Women's Panel, an event catered for young professional women to network and apply to business schools, sponsored by Harvard Business School and held at Citigroup's Headquarters in New York City in 1999. Although designed as an open career forum, the HBS alumnae panelists talked almost exclusively about finance and management consulting: "For HBS women, 30 percent go into consulting and about 40 percent go into finance and investment banking." "Banking internships come pretty quickly into the process. You receive one-on-one counseling before your internship decision. Recruiters are there pretty early." What struck me the most was panelist Jordan Thompson's parallel between Harvard and Wall Street: "I've never been to so many black tie parties. I was invited to so many parties and you see that people bring their intensity, enthusiasm, and ambitions as much in their work as in their social lives. I organized pub nights and cross-section mixes. When you are social chair at HBS, you have a certain carte blanche to talk to and call up the CEOs of companies." What Thompson experienced as social chair of her class mirrored the Wall Street's relationship with corporate America. Wall Street, armed with HBS graduates, has "carte blanche" to advise CEOs on the latest deals and expectations.

THE CROSS-POLLINATION OF ELITISM

They are declared to be "the best and the brightest." They quickly become used to the respect, status, and impressive nods from peers, parental figures, job prospectors, and society at large. Those most enamored of, or dependent on, their putative membership in "the cream of the crop" seek ways to maintain and continue the high status to which they have become accustomed, especially as graduation looms near. As Devon Peterson, an undergraduate writer for the *Daily Princetonian*, observed about the "the allures and drawbacks of elite jobs": "For four years we have enjoyed being the most elite college-aged kids in one of the most elite, unilaterally powerful nations ever to exist.... These banking firms provide us with a way to maintain our elite status in society by providing avenues to wealth and power that other professions do not" (Peterson 2002). Peterson's reference to himself as being at the pinnacle of power is a crucial window into the identity formation of bankers-to-be. Dafna Hochman, an undergraduate writer for the *Harvard Crimson*, similarly recognizes, not only the central importance of being the best, as defined by prestige, status, and smartness, to Harvard students, but also that what gives Wall Street crucial competitive advantage in recruiting is its acute understanding of this phenomena. Wall Streeters are able to sell themselves so effectively because they know what attracts these students: it is also precisely what investment banks themselves seek. Hochman (1999) observes, "The business world is obviously desperate to milk our minds, youth, creativity and work ethic. And they have correctly assessed what it takes to attract us: appear competitive, prestigious, and upwardly mobile.... They know that four years ago, we wanted the absolute best. We did not settle for number three or four on the college rankings. They prey on our desire to find the 'Harvard' of everything: activities, summer jobs, relationships and now careers."

Elite Students and Life after Graduation

Implicit in this transformation from undergraduate to investment banker is Wall Street's notion that if students do not choose Wall Street postgraduation, they are somehow "less smart," as smartness is defined by continued aggressive striving to perpetuate elite status. The cultivation of a particular kind of banker and the privileging of an elite norm, insidiously racialized, are nowhere better illustrated than with this event in Kate Miller's work life. In 1997, Miller, former analyst at Morgan Stanley, was one of its first recruits from a historically black college. In the following narrative describing her experience with a senior manager, Miller further demonstrates that what constitutes "smartness" is explicitly dependent on school pedigree as well as race.

> Well, there were a couple of officers that were known for being really good guys and being fair to people of color. And it was very interesting because I was in Word Processing [an actual floor of the bank where all the documents investment banks use to pitch deals are professionally printed]. I was trying to work on a document with some of the assistants there, and a principal [equivalent to senior vice president] came into Word Processing and was talking about his experiences recruiting that year. And he turned to me, well, he was saying to another analyst, "Well, you know, I just really have problems with the idea of us recruiting at historically black colleges. I mean, I know people say that the students that attend those schools are smart enough to attend Harvard and Stanford and get into these great institutions, but actually choose to attend the black college. Well, I have a problem with that. If they're that smart, and they're turning down one of the top institutions in the country, then I think that shows poor judgment, and we should really rethink whether or not these are the type of people that we want working at our company." He said this so that I overheard, and I guess he had assumed that I had gone to an Ivy League school because he then sort of turned to me and said, "Well, what do you think, Kate?" And I said, "Well, I went to a black college; I went to Spelman." And he just sort of looked at me and realized he made an incredible mistake and just said, "Well, I guess I lost my case. I guess you proved your point against me." So I just sort of shrugged my shoulders. Well, what do you say? You've been there for five months. You never really worked with the guy. It's not like you two have a rapport. But it was awkward, especially to think that this was one of the cool guys who really thought that it was important to increase diversity within the company.

By virtue of "choosing" Spelman College, Miller demonstrated a lack of judgment; she was not only quantitatively "less smart" because she chose not to attend Harvard or Stanford, but she was also more provincial, less global. The complete equating of smartness with these institutions, the identification of historically white colleges as global, universal institutions, as well as the wholesale erasure of the white upper-class male privilege embedded in these universities are part and parcel of how excellence is understood. Central to Wall Street's construction of its own superiority is the corollary assumption that other corporations and industries are "less than"—less smart, less efficient, less competitive, less global, less hardworking—and thus less likely to survive the demands of global capitalism unless they restructure their cultural values and practices according to the standards of Wall Street. In a meritocratic feedback loop, their growing influence itself becomes further evidence that they are, in fact, "the smartest."

It is important to pause here to acknowledge that many of these students are of course quite aware of how the culture of smartness, as coproduced by elite universities, students, and Wall Street, capitalizes on, monopolizes, and narrows students' interests. Katherine Reilly, an undergraduate *Daily Princetonian* columnist, asked her fellow students to find "the courage to buck a system that has served us so well": "We should not let our type-A drive for success, money, or power or our fear of ending up outside the realm of 'acceptable' Princeton accomplishment dictate what we do with our lives" (Reilly 2003). Similarly, Dafna Hochman indicted Harvard for portraying the Wall Street recruiting process as every student's career process: this conflation "reflects Harvard's subtle and not so subtle attempts to challenge our values, delude our personal goals and to generally morph our diverse interests and talents into its ideal type of a respectable alum" (Hochman 1999). Fellow undergraduate *Harvard Crimson* writer Matthew Siegel wondered, "Could it be at all possible that the culture of success at Harvard drives people to skip right over the most important part of cognition—getting to know themselves and what they want and need—and instead, sends them straight into the outstretched arms of J. P. Morgan's H.R. department?" (Siegel 2003). Interestingly enough, his answer to why investment banking has so seduced Harvard undergraduates does not centrally implicate investment banking as the culprit: "It's not about investment banking. It is about the possibility that with all our running around trying to impress everyone all the time, it becomes hard to know what we really want" (Siegel 2003). Many students recognize the monopolistic hold that banking and consulting have on their future aspirations and that the very act of participating in recruiting precludes the questioning of "our place and privilege in the world" because the desire to hold on to privilege is naturalized vis à vis recruiting (Suleiman 1998). It is one thing if one's goal in life is to make "multi-million-dollar corporations even richer" or if one "cannot be happy unless you work for Goldman," but the crux of the problem is that students hardly question or ponder what they might truly be passionate about, much less the contradictions of their own privilege (Graham-Felsen 2003). Instead, these students more than likely continue with "the absurd impression that there is only one thing to do next year," that is, resort to the already-laid-out "typical Princeton job," the next step toward continued upward mobility, the surefire sign that one truly is the best and the brightest (Suleiman 1998).

Certainly, the pinnacle of meritocracy is necessarily precarious: it is shot through with class, race, and gender hierarchies; with the constant and anxious performance of smartness; and with a prestigious branding so dependent on the singularity of the apex that it cannot help but degrade. The fact that American culture, as Katherine Newman presciently pointed out long ago, has virtually no cultural repertoire that helps make sense of downward mobility for the middle class is perhaps doubly true for the elite, for whom expanding or diverging from the narrow path of status maintenance is understood and experienced as slippage or corrosion (Newman 1999). Where to find Harvard after Harvard? The push to replicate is excruciatingly intense. As Devon Peterson (2002) observed: "Perhaps most difficult to overcome is the naturally difficult task of giving up social status and an elite way of life."

"Wall Street University": Kinship Networks and Elite Extension

Wall Street and elite universities work together to foster and exploit this need to "find the next Harvard," in the process creating a symbiotic relationship that furthers each institution's dreams, goals, and practices. Wall Street has enjoyed long-standing historical ties with status-heavy Ivy League universities, ties that have produced generations of financiers and advisors to American industry. Since the 1980s, at precisely the time that Wall Street worked to solidify its expert influence over most U.S. corporations, these historical ties have been transformed into massive feeder relationships. Investment banks have naturalized themselves as the primary destinations for elite graduates as part of a program to consolidate and justify Wall Street's domination of corporate America, regardless of the "quality" of advice. In addition, over the past twenty-five years, student anxieties over preserving their elite status have increased, making Wall Street, at least until mid-2008, a much more attractive possibility than before. These developments, I argue, have converged to create a culture of "survival of the smartest."

Wall Street did not begin to recruit in droves at elite East Coast schools until the early 1980s. Throughout the mid-twentieth century, elite university graduates interested in business careers looked to management training programs with industrial, aerospace, or chemical corporations, rather than Wall Street firms (*Harvard Crimson* 1963; Wilentz 1975). For decades, general, "open" recruiting was not a standard practice for most businesses: Ivy League graduates relied on family wealth and networks, entered graduate school, or were approached via the "old boys' network" for financial or industrial fast-track grooming; and most Ivy League faculty, determined to perpetuate the ivory tower model, were "outraged by recruiting" (Beniger 1967). At Harvard in the 1950s, Wall Street financiers recruited a relatively small number of men directly from the well-established residential houses at Harvard College by holding small panels and conferences in intimate settings such as the Lowell House common room and the Eliot House dining hall (*Harvard Crimson* 1953, 1957). These efforts were small-scale as interest in the securities markets had plummeted after the Great Depression, and Wall Street was not necessarily the first choice for dynamic, ambitious college graduates. Furthermore, Wall Street and many other businesses searched for managers from business schools, not undergraduate programs (Masters 1986). In general, because of economic stability in the postwar era for the upper-middle and upper classes, the postgraduation job search lacked the anxiety so often associated with it later. Most elite graduates had "job futures so well established that they never have to go seek" recruiting (Wilentz 1975). Remarking on a "trend" toward "working right after college," *Harvard Crimson* writer Jeffrey Senger (1984) reported that it was not until 1984 that a majority of Harvard, Yale, and Princeton graduates sought jobs after graduation; in 1974, only one-third, and in 1959, only one-tenth. For example, with surprisingly little angst, the *Harvard Crimson*, in an article headlined "The Jobless Class of '72," said that "by choice or by chance, over half of the Class of 1972 found themselves with nowhere to go and nothing to do after graduation." The culprit was not so much economic hard times as the fact that "students who were planning on business careers were unwilling to make long-term commitments" and that those going to graduate schools "also wanted to take a breather from the academic regimen" (Bennett 1972). It is also important to remember that campus culture in the Vietnam Era was much more hostile to big business in general than in subsequent years, as evidenced (for example) by student protests against napalm manufacturer Dow Chemical Corporation's attempt to recruit at Harvard in 1967 (Beniger 1967).

As Wall Street investment banks profited exorbitantly from their increasing influence over corporate America in the 1980s, they began to recruit at elite universities on a grand scale, creating the two-year analyst programs for the express purpose of targeting undergraduates directly out of college. This new cadre of workers, no longer handpicked through small-scale networks of family, friends, and close business associates, was legitimated by placing even greater cachet on the universities where they were recruited. In place of the elite, individualized family of men came the elite "Princeton" or "Harvard" family, which relied on a new variant of kinship based on alumni rather than "old boys'" networks. Recall my own initiation into "the Princeton family" in my very first recruitment presentation in 1995 when a Goldman Sachs managing director and Princeton alumnus addressed the audience as "the Princeton family" to establish both connection with "us" and to delineate an elite selectivity—just as not everyone can be a student at Princeton, investment banking is not a profession in which all can participate. "Princeton alumnae make the best analysts." That women and minorities were not explicitly excluded in this process was a crucial part of this new ideology of meritocracy.

What made this central glue of elite-institution-alumni stick to Wall Street despite the possible dilution of elitism caused by this extension of exclusivity to all alumni, ostensibly, was the formation of a generic culture of "the best" which pervaded and extended from, say, Wharton to Wall Street. By attracting masses of elite university alumni to Wall Street, investment banks and universities coproduce an extension and transferal of elitism via what I call a human kinship bridge. For example, in 2004, when Goldman Sachs CEO Hank Paulson gave a keynote speech to Wharton MBA students, the first point he made "after stating

Goldman Sachs's $23 billion in revenue in 2004" was "the importance his firm places on 'hiring and retaining the best people' in order to maintain a 'culture of excellence'." Paulson then emphasized the strong, intimate relationship his firm has with Wharton, "saying that more people were hired from the University to work at Goldman Sachs in 2004 than from any other school in the country" (Siegal 2005).

When a Harvard or Princeton education is seen as the normative "baseline" pedigree, it becomes ordinary as well as collective, encompassing, even universal. Wall Street smartness is, in a sense, "generic," and it is precisely this notion of elitism so pervasive as to be commonplace, smartness so sweeping as to become generic, that reinforces Wall Street's claims of extraordinariness. Specifically, the assumption is that everyone on Wall Street is smart and comes from Princeton or Harvard; as such, this smartness generically applies to *all members of this class* or kind in a way that is naturalized and comprehensively descriptive of this entire group of workers. The notion of Wall Street smartness is so ingrained that it does not have to be emphasized as "special" or qualified; as such, smartness is not a "brand name" or external label, but a blanket, sweeping generalization about all investment bankers. Wall Street's generic smartness is so comprehensive as to connote a global application to all members. Of course, while Princeton and Harvard are pinnacle "brand names," their generic status on Wall Street further attests to how special the accumulation of merit is at investment banks.

The kinship of generically smart investment bankers guarantees the extension and reinforcement of all the social particularities of those universities' positions in American culture, while simultaneously rendering invisible its normative, unmarked privilege. Marked investment bankers, who usually strive to be generically kin (and generically smart), feel the brunt of these contradictions daily. Kate Miller observed that she "never felt like more of a black woman with all of the negative stereotypes attached than I did when I was working at Morgan Stanley." She chose not to pursue a career in investment banking (or was discouraged from doing so), so her narratives illustrate a certain level of what might be called alienation from Wall Street culture and values. She described her initial experiences this way:

> I felt like the first thing people saw when they looked at me was not a bright person who had been admitted to the analyst class but a black woman. And most of the people that I worked with really had very little exposure to other races. I'm sure some of the men had very little exposure to women on a professional basis. Even though the industry has made a lot of strides to be more inclusive of women, I still think that white male officers prefer to work with white male analysts.

This pattern of exclusion, where white male vice presidents pick white male analysts to be on their team, where Yale graduates seek to work with other Yale graduates, greatly influenced Miller's opportunity to work on "higher profile" deals and to make connections with potential mentors. Many first-year analysts get to know senior-level bankers through various formal and informal alma mater networking events. Miller poignantly observed, "If you're an analyst from Dartmouth and there are fifteen managing directors who also went to Dartmouth, then you get to know those fifteen managing directors. Well, Spelman College grad, guess what? There are no MDs, VPs, even associates that graduated from Spelman." Given that smartness and membership in a financial kin network that drives business and social opportunities are intimately dependent on both elite institutions and one's closeness to the unmarked, generic norm, Miller's various identities as a black woman from Spelman renders her less smart, less kin, and by extension, less of an investment banker.

Creating Pinnacle Status and Generic Smartness

Solidifying Wall Street as "the" extension of hyperelite universities requires the convergence of student aspirations, cultural pressures of elite upward mobility, Wall Street reframing of alumni kinship, and its marketing and monopoly of the recruitment process. In this section, I demonstrate one concrete way in which these entanglements of elitism are "operationalized" by even further narrowing the space at the top such that the most coveted investment banks and the "most" prestigious universities are not only associated singularly with each other but also distinguished from (and desired more than) the "regularly" prestigious ones. I argue that by painstakingly differentiating and creating hierarchies between and within elite universities through the recruitment process, investment bankers further intertwine their identities with the most elite universities, create demand for their jobs and institutions, and solidify their association with smartness.

As I have described, the two universities from which the prestigious Wall Street investment banks most actively recruit all students without restriction to major or department are Harvard and Princeton. It turns out that recruitment at other elite universities is not approached in a similar manner. For example, although investment banks also widely recruit at Yale, often included with Harvard and Princeton as one of the "top three" schools for banking or consulting, Yale, however, lags behind the other two in its reputation on Wall Street. According to one Yale alumnus who works on Wall Street, "because investment bankers perceive hostility" from many students at Yale, "they concentrate their recruitment energies at Princeton and Harvard.... They're looking to hire a larger portion of students from Harvard and Princeton, despite the fact that the number of applicants from each school is relatively similar" (Tanenbaum 2005). Yale is perceived by many of my investment banker informants to be more "liberal and 'artsy'," less free-market oriented in a sense, and perhaps even tainted by New Haven, a largely working-class, majority African American city. Instead of recruiting universally at Yale, as happens at Harvard and Princeton, banks might require Yale students to demonstrate their quantitative ability, by, say, majoring in economics or undergoing a financial internship (Engler 2006).[3]

A similar phenomenon occurs at the University of Pennsylvania. There, again, investment banks do not recruit as actively from the general undergraduate population as a whole, although undergraduates and graduates from Penn's renowned Wharton School of Business are among the most highly sought-after recruits. "Some college seniors said it was difficult to find investment banking and consulting opportunities without a Wharton pedigree. It's harder to [secure financial jobs] if you are in the College" (Miley 2000). "Wharton may be the reason big-name investment banks are attracted to ... Penn." In 2005, over half of Wharton graduates went into investment banking (Steinbery 2006). Similar to Yale, non-Wharton undergraduates at Penn report that they need to demonstrate technical or financial expertise in order to attract Wall Street investment banks.

By contrast, investment banking recruiters at Princeton and Harvard explicitly express how they *do not care* if undergraduates are trained in finance because a skilled background or already-acquired technical expertise is *not* really what they are looking for. As Gia Moron, a media and recruiting spokesperson at Goldman Sachs, told *The Harvard Crimson*, "We have found that financial know-how is easy to teach—in fact, training is an important part of a new hire's orientation—but the skills that the most successful candidates possess are beyond teaching: Energy, a history of excellence and achievement, leadership and interpersonal skills are some of the stand-outs" (Ho 2003). According to a Princeton undergraduate, Kate Daviau ('06), "They understand that interns come in knowing basically nothing—but if you're smart and personable, it's worth it to them to hire you." The *Daily Princetonian* writer Catherine Rampell observed that from all her interactions with potential Wall Street employees during her years at Princeton, most do not even know what "financial services" is. "Most are going into finance because they haven't figured out what else they could do," yet "finance employers are seeking them out, telling them they're qualified for finance" no matter what their training, major, or department—as long as they are from Princeton. "They bombard us with food, mail, Princeton alumni connection, and they keep telling us we're qualified, we're perfectly qualified even though we've never 'held a real job' " (Rampell 2006).

This open-ended, "generic" recruitment at Princeton and Harvard not only naturalizes the students there as "the best," the elite among the elite, but also sheds light on what actually constitutes smartness for Wall Street. Being the best and the brightest, especially for college graduates, does not mean possessing actual technical skills, a background in finance, or even a specific aptitude for banking. Instead, Princeton and Harvard recruits bring to the table just the right mix of general qualities and associations: they are not too technical or geeky (MIT), not too liberal (Yale), not too far away (Stanford), and their universities carry more historical prestige than the remaining Ivies (Brown, Columbia, Cornell, Dartmouth, University of Pennsylvania). Possessed of a combination of traditional cachet, class standing, and pedigree, they can show prima facie evidence of their "excellence" by virtue of their schools' (presumably) exclusive selection processes; and they demonstrate a constant striving for further "excellence" by virtue of their participation in the intense process of recruiting and their evident desire for a high-status, upper-crust lifestyle.

NOTES

1. Certainly, this idea has currency beyond Wall Street, though I would argue that, as evidenced by Bethany McLean's and Peter Elkind's *The Smartest Guys in the Room* (2003) on the Enron executives and Wall Street advisors, these financiers are so convinced of their own brilliance that they created illusory businesses for short-term stock price appreciation while scamming small investors and their own employees. The culture of smartness is particularly heralded, utilized, and valued in finance capital as productive of spectacular profit accumulation and global dominance.

2. Management consulting is considered a professional service where consulting firms advise corporate America on such "strategic" matters as entering a new business, streamlining existing departments, restructuring and downsizing, outsourcing, and so forth. Projects might include figuring out how to increase a company's market share, how to exit a certain business, where to move and relocate a particular division. At elite universities, becoming a management consulting analyst for some of the top consulting firms such as McKinsey and Bain is almost as highly sought after as investment banking, though not quite as prestigious or lucrative. The fact that one of the most popular debates on Harvard's and Princeton's campuses are panel sessions entitled "Investment Banking vs. Consulting" is evidence, not only of the production of narrow career "choices," but also of the limiting of what constitutes an acceptable job after graduation. That there are heated debates and panel discussions on campus about whether or not to choose "investment banking or consulting" (not to mention the fact that literally hundreds of students pack auditoriums to hear this topic) is a culturally specific phenomenon. Usually, panelists composed of firm representatives (usually former students) face off about the pros and cons of the two career choices, and use the platform to further recruit students to their "side." Discussion usually ranges from talk of compensation and the "caliber of people" to work hours and the amount of "strategic" responsibility an entry-level employee can have over corporate America. In a *Harvard Crimson* opinion piece, "Avoiding a Path to Nowhere," J. Mehta, a Harvard undergraduate, called attention to this oddness, in a sense, as well as the narrowness of such a debate. He writes, "I-banking and consulting. Consulting and I-banking. I-banking vs. consulting. What more could be on a Harvard senior's mind?" He continues, "We are caught in a vicious cycle, in which the brightest and most ambitious enter fields that most solidify the social status quo—blazing a path to nowhere in which the next generation of equally smart and energetic Harvard graduates are bound to follow" (Mehta 1998).

3. Yale numbers are significantly lower that that of Princeton and Harvard. According to their recruitment office, "30 percent of Yale students chose jobs in non-profits, 30 percent go to graduate or professional school, and 40 percent choose corporate careers in finance, consulting, publishing, communications, manufacturing, even brewing" (Tanenbaum 2005). A survey by the Office of Institutional Research showed that ordinarily around 20 percent of Yale students enter finance, but only 13 percent did in 2002 with the financial downturn (Pryor 2006).

REFERENCES

Beniger, James. 1967. "Smithies, Walzer, and Peretz Discuss the Five R's: Recruitment, ROTC, Ranking, Research, and Relationship." *Harvard Crimson*, 11 November, www.thecrimson.com (accessed 11 May 2007).

Bennett, Amanda. 1972. "The Jobless Class of '72." *Harvard Crimson*, 16 December, www.thecrimson.com (accessed 11 May 2007).

Chan, Kai. 2001. "A Cacophony of Career Choices." *Daily Princetonian*, 13 February, www.dailyprincetonian.com (accessed 27 February 2007).

Creed, Jesse. 2003. "Students Face Weak Job Market despite Improvements." *Daily Princetonian*, 26 September, www.dailyprincetonian.com (accessed 27 February 2007).

Crossa, Veronica. 2005. "Converting the 'Small Stories' into 'Big' Ones: A Response to Susan Smith's 'States, Markets and an Ethic of Care'." *Political Geography* 24, 29–34.

Duboff, Josh. 2005. "Six College Students Create Job-Search Site." *Yale Daily News*, 11 February, www.yaledailynews.com (accessed 19 March 2007).

Easton, Alice. 2006. "Firms Lure Students with Extravagance." *Daily Princetonian*, 13 March, www.dailyprincetonian.com (accessed 27 February 2007).

Engler, Steve. 2006. "Don't Let Job Frenzy Overwhelm Your Life." *Yale Daily News*, 18 October, www.yaledailynews.com (accessed 19 March 2007).

Guyer, Nora. 2003. "There Is More to Life Than I-Banking." *Harvard Crimson*, 28 April, www.thecrimson.com (accessed 27 February 2007).

Hall, Cailey. 2005. "Wall Street: Paradise Found?" *Daily Princetonian*, 25 September, www.dailyprincetonian.com (accessed 27 February 2007).

Harvard Crimson. 1953. "Finance Industry Needs Graduates, Businessmen Say." 25 February, www.thecrimson.com (accessed 11 May 2007).

Henn, Brian. 2001. "Fewer Jobs in Financial Services Worry Class of '02." *Daily Princetonian*, 9 November, www.dailyprincetonian.com (accessed 27 February 2007).

Ho, Margaret. 2003. "Campus Recruiting Rates Inch Upward." *Harvard Crimson*, 26 September, www.thecrimson.com (accessed 27 February 2007).

Hochman, Dafna V. 1999. "Recruiting Your Career." *Harvard Crimson*, 15 October, www.thecrimson.com (accessed 27 February 2007).

Huber, H. Max. 2006. "Careers 'R Us: Online Recruiting Isn't Just for Aspiring Gordon Gekkos Anymore." *Harvard Crimson*, 5 October, www.thecrimson.com (accessed 27 February 2007).

Karseras, Hugh. 2006. "Starting Out on the Right Foot." *Daily Princetonian*, 21 November, www.dailyprincetonian.com (accessed 27 February 2007).

Mehta, Jal D. 1998. "Avoiding a Path to Nowhere." *Harvard Crimson*, 16 October, www.theharvardcrimson.com (accessed 27 February 2007).

Miley, Marissa. 2000. "Career Fair Provides Exposure for Students and Companies." *Daily Pennsylvanian*, 9 October, www.dailypennsylvanian.com (accessed 27 February 2007).

Newman, Katherine 1999. Falling from Grace: Downward Mobility in the Age of Affluence. Berkeley: University of California Press.

Peterson, Devon. 2002. "Careers at Princeton: The Allure and Drawbacks of Elite Jobs." *Daily Princetonian*, 16 October, www.dailyprincetonian.com (accessed 27 February 2007).

Pryor, Christina. 2006. "Future I-bankers Face Grueling Interview Cycle." *Yale Daily News*, 1 November, www.yaledailynews.com (accessed 19 March 2007).

Rahim, Taufiq. 2003. "Recruiting Insanity." *Daily Princetonian*, 15 October, www.dailyprincetonian.com (accessed 27 February 2007).

Rampell, Catherine. 2006. "In the Nation's Financial Service." *Daily Princetonian*, 6 October, www.dailyprincetonian.com (accessed 27 February 2007).

Reilly, Katherine. 2003. "Courage to Buck a System That Has Served Us So Well." *Daily Princetonian*, 23 April, www.dailyprincetonian.com (accessed 27 February 2007).

Senger, Jeffrey. 1984. "A Stampede to the Work Place." *Harvard Crimson*, 7 June, www.thecrimson.com (accessed 11 May 2007).

Shapira, Ian. 1998. "Companies Use Aggressive Tactics to Bolster Employee Recruitment." *Daily Princetonian*, 19 February, www.dailyprincetonian.com (accessed 27 February 2007).

Siegel, Matthew L. 2003. "Dress for Success: The I-Banker Has No Clothes." *Harvard Crimson*, 20 October, www.thecrimson.com (accessed 27 February 2007).

Smith, Susan J. 2005. "States, Markets and an Ethic of Care." *Political Geography* 24, 1–20.

Tanenbaum, Jessica. 2005. "I-Banking for Dummies." *Yale Daily News*, 6 October, www.yaledailynews.com (accessed 19 March 2007).

Wilentz, Amy. 1975. "The Class, Leaving." *Harvard Crimson*, 12 June, www.thecrimson .com (accessed 11 May 2007).

QUESTIONS FOR MAKING CONNECTIONS
WITHIN THE READING

1. Ho points out that a future in finance has not always been the preferred goal of students at Harvard and other elite universities. Before the 1980s, she writes, "Ivy League graduates relied on family wealth and networks ... for financial or industrial fast-track grooming." How do the values of Ivy League students seem to have changed over time? What factors might explain how Wall Street became so pervasive a presence in the lives of Ivy League undergraduates? How might the growing influence of finance on university campuses reflect changes in the larger culture?

2. Why does Ho see "smartness" as an "ideology" and not an empirical fact? Clearly, many students come to the Ivies with excellent grades, well-developed skills, and broad-based general knowledge, but does "smartness" actually refer to qualities like these? Or does "smartness" signify something more complex? How does "smartness" help to create a sense of group solidarity and exclusiveness, and in what ways might it accentuate the students' fears about not fitting in? If students like Princeton's Katherine Reilly understand that "smartness" exerts pressure on people to embrace a narrow set of expectations, why does hers remain the minority view?

3. One of Ho's most important terms is *hegemony*, which refers to the use of culture rather than force as an instrument of domination (political, social, or economic). How does the elite educational system create hegemony, and who, exactly, dominates whom? Does the hegemony that Ho describes

reach beyond the university? Is the university itself dominated by *the Street*? Within the system of hegemony, should we see all Ivy League students as equal? Are all being groomed for membership in the elite? Or do we find within the Ivy League itself a division between the future elite and those destined to become subordinate?

QUESTIONS FOR WRITING

1. When Ho describes investment bankers, she often uses the word *power*. For example, she writes, "I do not assume a priori [automatically] that 'the market' always already exercises power, but rather that the particular biographies, experiences, and practices of investment bankers, who are both empowered and constrained by their cultural and institutional locations, create social change and financial hegemony on a daily basis." Should we think of power as something possessed by individuals or groups, or does it have to be created and sustained by the actions of the powerful? How does Wall Street use the Ivy Leagues to create its power? Why is it necessary for financiers to recruit so relentlessly? Is the presence of Wall Street on campus a sign of its strength or its weakness?

2. Using the evidence that Ho provides, can we say that Wall Street qualifies as a true meritocracy—that is, an elite system whose success has been achieved by virtue of ability, strength of character, and hard work? Or, conversely, do investment bankers represent an example of unearned privilege? One measure of a meritocracy is the degree to which its members are required to compete in order to gain entry into the ranks of the elite. Are the Ivy Leaguers recruited by Wall Street subjected to rigorous competition, or would you say they have been protected from competing by the process of recruitment? What other evidence can you provide to support the case for meritocracy, or the case for special privilege?

QUESTIONS FOR MAKING CONNECTIONS
BETWEEN READINGS

1. In "Immune to Reality," Daniel Gilbert makes the claim that people are surprisingly inept at predicting what will make them happy in the future. Gilbert argues that we stumble into happiness because it turns up inadvertently, and he suggests that our conscious intentions to realize long-held dreams are just as likely to end in frustration as in felicity. What might Gilbert say to the students recruited by the investment banking firms? Even if those students had read Gilbert (who teaches at Harvard, by the way), would they be likely to step off the fast track to "success"? If they

understood Gilbert's argument but still persisted in careers on the Street, what motives might explain their choice?

2.   In what ways might the ideology of "smartness" contribute to the growing inequality that Joseph Stiglitz examines in "Rent Seeking and the Making of an Unequal Society"? As you develop your response, you might pay particular attention to his distinction between the supposed "geniuses of business" like Steve Jobs and Mark Zuckerberg, and the "giant" Stiglitz celebrates, Tim Berners-Lee, inventor of the World Wide Web, who could have become a billionaire but instead chose to make his idea freely available. Would it be fair to say that the recruitment programs in the Ivy League are designed to create a culture of rent-seeking? And does the existence of this culture complicate Stiglitz's call for systemic reform? How might the ideology of "smartness" work against the prospects for greater equality?

STEVEN JOHNSON

STEVEN JOHNSON, THE founder and editor of one of the Web's earliest magazines, *Feed*, is the author of many books, including *Emergence: The Connected Lives of Ants, Brains, Cities, and Software* (2001), from which "The Myth of the Ant Queen" is drawn; *Mind Wide Open: Your Brain and the Neuroscience of Everyday Life* (2004); *Everything Bad Is Good for You: How Today's Popular Culture Is Actually Making Us Smarter* (2005); and *The Invention of Air: A Story of Science, Faith, Revolution, and the Birth of America* (2009).

Johnson's preoccupation in all these books, most controversially in *Everything Bad Is Good for You*, is with reconceiving the nature of intelligence. Although it is common to think of intelligence as located in the individual—the outstanding student, the creative genius, the scientist at work in his lab—Johnson proposes that intelligence is not an attribute of individuals at all, but a property that emerges out of a system working as a whole. To illustrate this new view of intelligence, Johnson looks at complex systems like ant colonies, cities, and software programs to argue that in these contexts intelligence emerges in the absence of any central form of leadership or authority. The intelligence of the whole is created by individual agents—ants, people, "subroutines"—following what Johnson terms "local rules." By showing how decentralized, adaptive, self-organizing systems use lower-level thinking to solve higher-order problems, Johnson asks his readers to see the advent of the Internet not simply as an extension of human intelligence but also as a new frontier where the very nature of human intelligence is being transformed, one hyperlink at a time.

Johnson acknowledges the difficulties involved in imagining intelligence along these lines. When filmmakers try to depict artificial intelligence, for example, they envision a future where cyborgs look and think just like ordinary humans. Johnson predicts, however, that when there is a breakthrough in the effort to create artificial intelligence (AI), the result "won't quite look like human intelligence. It'll have other properties in it, and it may be hard for us to pick up on the fact that it is intelligent because our criteria [are] different."

Johnson's 2012 book *Future Perfect: The Case for Progress in a Networked Age* asks readers to consider how the Web might be used to address our society's most urgent challenges. His proposal deviates from classic liberalism, with its faith in activist government, but also from the libertarian spirit popular among many Internet entrepreneurs. Instead, Johnson identifies himself as a "peer progressive" who is convinced that "peer networks" represent a new and more democratic way of organizing our collective creativity.

The Myth of the Ant Queen

It's early fall in Palo Alto, and Deborah Gordon and I are sitting in her office in Stanford's Gilbert Biological Sciences building, where she spends three-quarters of the year studying behavioral ecology. The other quarter is spent doing fieldwork with the native harvester ants of the American Southwest, and when we meet, her face still retains the hint of a tan from her last excursion to the Arizona desert.

I've come here to learn more about the collective intelligence of ant colonies. Gordon, dressed neatly in a white shirt, cheerfully entertains a few borderline-philosophical questions on group behavior and complex systems, but I can tell she's hankering to start with a hands-on display. After a few minutes of casual rumination, she bolts up out of her chair. "Why don't we start with me showing you the ants that we have here," she says. "And then we can talk about what it all means."

She ushers me into a sepulchral room across the hallway, where three long tables are lined up side by side. The initial impression is that of an underpopulated and sterilized pool hall, until I get close enough to one of the tables to make out the miniature civilization that lives within each of them. Closer to a Habitrail than your traditional idea of an ant farm, Gordon's contraptions house an intricate network of plastic tubes connecting a dozen or so plastic boxes, each lined with moist plaster and coated with a thin layer of dirt.

"We cover the nests with red plastic because some species of ants don't see red light," Gordon explains. "That seems to be true of this species, too." For a second, I'm not sure what she means by "this species"—and then my eyes adjust to the scene, and I realize with a start that the dirt coating the plastic boxes is, in fact, thousands of harvester ants, crammed so tightly into their quarters that I had originally mistaken them for an undifferentiated mass. A second later, I can see that the whole simulated colony is wonderfully alive, the clusters of ants pulsing steadily with movement. The tubing and cramped conditions and surging crowds bring one thought immediately to mind: the New York subway system, rush hour.

At the heart of Gordon's work is a mystery about how ant colonies develop, a mystery that has implications extending far beyond the parched earth of the Arizona desert to our cities, our brains, our immune systems—and increasingly, our technology. Gordon's work focuses on the connection between the microbehavior of individual ants and the overall behavior of the colonies themselves, and part of that research involves tracking the life cycles of individual colonies, following them year after year as they scour the desert floor for food, competing with other colonies for territory, and—once a year—mating with them. She is a student, in other words, of a particular kind of emergent, self-organizing system.

Dig up a colony of native harvester ants and you'll almost invariably find that the queen is missing. To track down the colony's matriarch, you need to examine the bottom of the hole you've just dug to excavate the colony: you'll find a narrow, almost invisible passageway that leads another two feet underground, to a tiny vestibule burrowed out of the earth. There you will find the queen. She will have been secreted there by a handful of ladies-in-waiting at the first sign of disturbance. That passageway, in other words, is an emergency escape hatch, not unlike a fallout shelter buried deep below the West Wing.

But despite the Secret Service-like behavior, and the regal nomenclature, there's nothing hierarchical about the way an ant colony does its thinking. "Although *queen* is a term that reminds us of human political systems," Gordon explains, "the queen is not an authority figure. She lays eggs and is fed and cared for by the workers. She does not decide which worker does what. In a harvester ant colony, many feet of intricate tunnels and chambers and thousands of ants separate the queen, surrounded by interior workers, from the ants working outside the nest and using only the chambers near the surface. It would be physically impossible for the queen to direct every worker's decision about which task to perform and when." The harvester ants that carry the queen off to her escape hatch do so not because they've been ordered to by their leader; they do it because the queen ant is responsible for giving birth to all the members of the colony, and so it's in the colony's best interest—and the colony's gene pool—to keep the queen safe. Their genes instruct them to protect their mother, the same way their genes instruct them to forage for food. In other words, the matriarch doesn't train her servants to protect her, evolution does.

Popular culture trades in Stalinist ant stereotypes—witness the authoritarian colony regime in the animated film *Antz*—but in fact, colonies are the exact opposite of command economies. While they are capable of remarkably coordinated feats of task allocation, there are no Five-Year Plans in the ant kingdom. The colonies that Gordon studies display some of nature's most mesmerizing decentralized behavior: intelligence and personality and learning that emerges from the bottom up.

I'm still gazing into the latticework of plastic tubing when Gordon directs my attention to the two expansive white boards attached to the main colony space, one stacked on top of the other and connected by a ramp. (Imagine a two-story parking garage built next to a subway stop.) A handful of ants meander across each plank, some porting crumblike objects on their backs, others apparently just out for a stroll. If this is the Central Park of Gordon's ant metropolis, I think, it must be a workday.

Gordon gestures to the near corner of the top board, four inches from the ramp to the lower level, where a pile of strangely textured dust—littered with tiny shells and husks—presses neatly against the wall. "That's the midden," she says. "It's the town garbage dump." She points to three ants marching up the ramp, each barely visible beneath a comically oversize shell. "These ants are on midden duty: they take the trash that's left over from the food they've collected—in this case, the seeds from stalk grass—and deposit it in the midden pile."

Gordon takes two quick steps down to the other side of the table, at the far end away from the ramp. She points to what looks like another pile of dust. "And this is the cemetery." I look again, startled. She's right: hundreds of ant carcasses are piled atop one another, all carefully wedged against the table's corner. It looks brutal, and yet also strangely methodical.

I know enough about colony behavior to nod in amazement. "So they've somehow collectively decided to utilize these two areas as trash heap and cemetery," I say. No individual ant defined those areas, no central planner zoned one area for trash, the other for the dead. "It just sort of happened, right?"

Gordon smiles, and it's clear that I've missed something. "It's better than that," she says. "Look at what actually happened here: they've built the cemetery at exactly the point that's furthest away from the colony. And the midden is even more interesting: they've put it at precisely the point that maximizes its distance from both the colony *and* the cemetery. It's like there's a rule they're following: put the dead ants as far away as possible, and put the midden as far away as possible without putting it near the dead ants."

I have to take a few seconds to do the geometry myself, and sure enough, the ants have got it right. I find myself laughing out loud at the thought: it's as though they've solved one of those spatial math tests that appear on standardized tests, conjuring up a solution that's perfectly tailored to their environment, a solution that might easily stump an eight-year-old human. The question is, who's doing the conjuring?

It's a question with a long and august history, one that is scarcely limited to the collective behavior of ant colonies. We know the answer now because we have developed powerful tools for thinking about—and modeling—the emergent intelligence of self-organizing systems, but that answer was not always so clear. We know now that systems like ant colonies don't have real leaders, that the very idea of an ant "queen" is misleading. But the desire to find pacemakers in such systems has always been powerful—in both the group behavior of the social insects, and in the collective human behavior that creates a living city.

Records exist of a Roman fort dating back to A.D. 76 situated at the confluence of the Medlock and Irwell Rivers, on the northwestern edge of modern England, about 150 miles from London. Settlements persisted there for three centuries, before dying out with the rest of the empire around A.D. 400. Historians believe that the site was unoccupied for half a millennium, until a town called Manchester began to take shape there, the name derived from the Roman settlement Mamucium—Latin for "place of the breastlike hill."

Manchester subsisted through most of the millennium as a nondescript northern-England borough: granted a charter in 1301, the town established a college in the early 1400s, but remained secondary to the neighboring town of Salford for hundreds of years. In the 1600s, the Manchester region became a node for the wool trade, its merchants shipping goods to the Continent via the great ports of London. It was impossible to see it at the time, but Manchester—and indeed the entire Lancashire region—had planted itself at the very center of a technological and commercial revolution that would irrevocably alter the future of the planet. Manchester lay at the confluence of several world-historical rivers: the nascent industrial technologies of steam-powered looms; the banking system of commercial London; the global markets and labor pools of the British Empire. The story of that convergence has been told many times, and the debate over its consequences continues to this day. But beyond the epic effects that it had on the global economy, the industrial takeoff that occurred in Manchester between 1700 and 1850 also created a new kind of city, one that literally exploded into existence.

The statistics on population growth alone capture the force of that explosion: a 1773 estimate had 24,000 people living in Manchester; the first official census in 1801 found 70,000. By the midpoint of the century, there were more than 250,000 people in the city proper—a tenfold increase in only seventy-five years. That growth rate was as unprecedented and as violent as the steam engines themselves. In a real sense, the city grew too fast for the authorities to keep up with it. For five hundred years, Manchester had technically been considered a "manor," which meant, in the eyes of the law, it was run like a feudal estate, with no local government to speak of—no city planners, police, or public health authorities. Manchester didn't even send representatives to Parliament until 1832, and it wasn't incorporated for another six years. By the early 1840s, the newly formed borough council finally began to institute public health reforms and urban planning, but the British government didn't officially recognize Manchester as a city until 1853. This constitutes one of the great ironies of the Industrial Revolution, and it captures just how dramatic the rate of change really was: the city that most defined the future of urban life for the first half of the nineteenth century didn't legally become a city until the great explosion had run its course.

The result of that discontinuity was arguably the least planned and most chaotic city in the six-thousand-year history of urban settlements. Noisy, polluted, massively overcrowded, Manchester attracted a steady stream of intellectuals and public figures in the 1830s, traveling north to the industrial magnet in search of the modern world's future. One by one, they returned with stories of abject squalor and sensory overload, their words straining to convey the immensity and uniqueness of the experience. "What I have seen has disgusted and astonished me beyond all measure," Dickens wrote after a visit in the fall of 1838. "I mean to strike the heaviest blow in my power for these unfortunate creatures." Appointed to command the northern districts in the late 1830s, Major General Charles James Napier wrote: "Manchester is the chimney of the world. Rich rascals, poor rogues, drunken ragamuffins and prostitutes form the moral.... What a place! The entrance to hell, realized." De Tocqueville visited Lancashire in 1835 and described the landscape in language that would be echoed throughout the next two centuries: "From this foul drain the greatest stream of human industry flows out to fertilize the whole world. From this filthy sewer pure gold flows. Here humanity attains its most complete development and its most brutish; here civilization works its miracles, and civilized man is turned back almost into a savage."

But Manchester's most celebrated and influential documentarian was a young man named Friedrich Engels, who arrived in 1842 to help oversee the family cotton plant there, and to witness firsthand the engines of history bringing the working class closer to self-awareness. While Engels was very much on the payroll of his father's firm, Ermen and Engels, by the time he arrived in Manchester he was also under the sway of the radical politics associated with the Young Hegelian school. He had befriended Karl Marx a few years before and had been encouraged to visit Manchester by the socialist Moses Hess, whom he'd met in early 1842. His three years in England were thus a kind of scouting mission for the revolution, financed by the capitalist class. The book that Engels eventually wrote, *The Condition of the Working Class in England,* remains to this day one of the classic tracts of urban history and stands as the definitive account of nineteenth-century Manchester life in all its tumult and dynamism. Dickens, Carlyle, and Disraeli had all attempted to capture Manchester in its epic wildness, but their efforts were outpaced by a twenty-four-year-old from Prussia.

But *The Condition* is not, as might be expected, purely a document of Manchester's industrial chaos, a story of all that is solid melting into air, to borrow a phrase Engels's comrade would write several years later. In the midst of the city's insanity, Engels's eye is drawn to a strange kind of order, in a wonderful passage where he leads the reader on a walking tour of the industrial capital, a tour that reveals a kind of politics built into the very topography of the city's streets. It captures Engels's acute powers of observation, but I quote from it at length because it captures something else as well—how difficult it is to think in models of self-organization, to imagine a world without pacemakers.

> The town itself is peculiarly built, so that someone can live in it for years and travel into it and out of it daily without ever coming into contact with a working-class quarter or even with workers—so long, that is to say, as one confines himself to his business affairs or to strolling about for pleasure. This comes about mainly in the circumstances that through an unconscious, tacit agreement as much as through conscious, explicit intention, the working-class districts are most sharply separated from the parts of the city reserved for the middle class....
>
> I know perfectly well that this deceitful manner of building is more or less common to all big cities. I know as well that shopkeepers must in the nature of the business take premises on the main thoroughfares. I know in such streets there are more good houses than bad ones, and that the value of land is higher in their immediate vicinity than in neighborhoods that lie at a distance from them. But at the same time I have never come across so systematic a seclusion of the working class from the main streets as in Manchester. I have never elsewhere seen a concealment of such fine sensibility of everything that might offend the eyes and nerves of the middle classes. And yet it is precisely Manchester that has been built less according to a plan and less within the limitations of official regulations—and indeed more through accident—than any other town. Still ... I cannot help feeling that the liberal industrialists, the Manchester "bigwigs," are not so altogether innocent of this bashful style of building.

You can almost hear the contradictions thundering against each other in this passage, like the "dark satanic mills" of Manchester itself. The city has built a *cordon sanitaire* to separate the industrialists from the squalor they have unleashed on the world, concealing the demoralization of Manchester's working-class districts—and yet that disappearing act comes into the world without "conscious, explicit intention." The city seems artfully planned to hide its atrocities, and yet it "has been built less according to a plan" than any city in history. As Steven Marcus puts it in his history of the young Engels's sojourn in Manchester, "The point to be taken is that this astonishing and outrageous arrangement cannot fully be understood as the result of a plot, or even a deliberate design, although those in whose interests it works also control it. It is indeed too huge and too complex a state of organized affairs ever to have been *thought up* in advance, to have preexisted as an idea."

Those broad, glittering avenues, in other words, suggest a Potemkin village without a Potemkin. That mix of order and anarchy is what we now call emergent behavior. Urban critics since Lewis Mumford and Jane Jacobs have known that cities have lives of their own, with neighborhoods clustering into place without any Robert Moses figure dictating the plan from above. But that understanding has entered the intellectual mainstream only in recent years—when Engels paced those Manchester streets in the 1840s, he was left groping blindly, trying to find a culprit for the city's fiendish organization, even as he acknowledged that the city was notoriously unplanned. Like most intellectual histories, the development of that new understanding—the sciences of complexity and self-organization—is a complicated, multithreaded tale, with many agents interacting over its duration. It is probably better to think of it as less a linear narrative and more an interconnected web, growing increasingly dense over the century and a half that separates us from Engels's first visit to Manchester.

Complexity is a word that has frequently appeared in critical accounts of metropolitan space, but there are really two kinds of complexity fundamental to the city, two experiences with very different implications for the individuals trying to make sense of them. There is, first, the more conventional sense of complexity as sensory overload, the city stretching the human nervous system to its very extremes, and in the process teaching it a new series of reflexes—and leading the way for a complementary series of aesthetic values, which develop out like a scab around the original wound. The German cultural critic Walter Benjamin writes in his unfinished masterpiece, *The Arcades Project:*

> Perhaps the daily sight of a moving crowd once presented the eye with a spectacle to which it first had to adapt…. [T]hen the assumption is not impossible that, having mastered this task, the eye welcomed opportunities to confirm its possession of its new ability. The method of impressionist painting, whereby the picture is assembled through a riot of flecks of color, would then be a reflection of experience with which the eye of a big-city dweller has become familiar.

There's a long tributary of nineteenth- and twentieth-century urban writing that leads into this passage, from the London chapters of Wordsworth's *Prelude* to the ambulatory musings of Joyce's *Dubliners:* the noise and the senselessness somehow transformed into an aesthetic experience. The crowd is something you throw yourself into, for the pure poetry of it all. But complexity is not solely a matter of sensory overload. There is also the sense of complexity as a self-organizing system—more Santa Fe Institute than Frankfurt School. This sort of complexity lives up one level: it describes the system of the city itself, and not its experiential reception by the city dweller. The city is complex because it overwhelms, yes, but also because it has a coherent personality, a personality that self-organizes out of millions of individual decisions, a global order built out of local interactions. This is the "systematic" complexity that Engels glimpsed on the boulevards of Manchester: not the overload and anarchy he documented elsewhere, but instead a strange kind of order, a pattern in the streets that furthered the political values of Manchester's elite without being deliberately planned by them. We know now from computer models and sociological studies—as well as from the studies of comparable systems generated by the social insects, such as Gordon's harvester ants—that larger patterns can emerge out of uncoordinated local actions. But for Engels and his contemporaries, those unplanned urban shapes must have seemed like a haunting. The city appeared to have a life of its own.

A hundred and fifty years later, the same techniques translated into the language of software ... trigger a similar reaction: the eerie sense of something life-like, something organic forming on the screen. Even those with sophisticated knowledge about self-organizing systems still find these shapes unnerving—in their mix of stability and change, in their capacity for open-ended learning. The impulse to build centralized models to explain that behavior remains almost as strong as it did in Engels's day. When we see repeated shapes and structure emerging out of apparent chaos, we can't help looking for pacemakers.

Understood in the most abstract sense, what Engels observed are *patterns* in the urban landscape, visible because they have a repeated structure that distinguishes them from the pure noise you might naturally associate with an unplanned city. They are patterns of human movement and decision-making that have been etched into the texture of city blocks, patterns that are then fed back to the Manchester residents themselves, altering their subsequent decisions. (In that sense, they are the very opposite of the traditional sense of urban complexity—they are signals emerging where you would otherwise expect only noise.) A city is a kind of pattern-amplifying machine: its neighborhoods are a way of measuring and expressing the repeated behavior of larger collectivities— capturing information about group behavior, and sharing that information with the group. Because those patterns are fed back to the community, small shifts in behavior can quickly escalate into larger movements: upscale shops dominate the main boulevards, while the working class remains clustered invisibly in the alleys and side streets; the artists live on the Left Bank, the investment bankers in the Eighth Arrondissement. You don't need regulations and city planners deliberately creating these structures. All you need are thousands of individuals and a few simple rules of interaction. The bright shop windows attract more bright shop windows and drive the impoverished toward the hidden core. There's no need for a Baron Haussmann in this world, just a few repeating patterns of movement, amplified into larger shapes that last for lifetimes: clusters, slums, neighborhoods.

Not all patterns are visible to every city dweller, though. The history of urbanism is also the story of more muted signs, built by the collective behavior of smaller groups and rarely detected by outsiders. Manchester harbors several such secret clusters, persisting over the course of many generations, like a "standing wave in front of a rock in a fast-moving stream." One of them lies just north of Victoria University, at a point where Oxford Road becomes Oxford Street. There are reports dating back to the mid-nineteenth century of men cruising other men on these blocks, looking for casual sex, more lasting relationships, or even just the camaraderie of shared identity at a time when that identity dared not speak its name. Some historians speculate that Wittgenstein visited these streets during his sojourn in Manchester in 1908. Nearly a hundred years later, the area has christened itself the Gay Village and actively promotes its coffee bars and boutiques as a must-see Manchester tourist destination, like Manhattan's Christopher Street and San Francisco's Castro. The pattern is now broadcast to a wider audience, but it has not lost its shape.

But even at a lower amplitude, that signal was still loud enough to attract the attention of another of Manchester's illustrious immigrants: the British polymath Alan Turing. As part of his heroic contribution to the war effort, Turing had been a student of mathematical patterns, designing the equations and the machines that cracked the "unbreakable" German code of the Enigma device. After a frustrating three-year stint at the National Physical Laboratory in London, Turing moved to Manchester in 1948 to help run the university's embryonic computing lab. It was in Manchester that Turing began to think about the problem of biological development in mathematical terms, leading the way to the "Morphogenesis" paper, published in 1952, that Evelyn Fox Keller would rediscover more than a decade later. Turing's war research had focused on detecting patterns lurking within the apparent chaos of code, but in his Manchester years, his mind gravitated toward a mirror image of the original code-breaking problem: how complex patterns could come into being by following simple rules. How does a seed know how to build a flower?

Turing's paper on morphogenesis—literally, "the beginning of shape"—turned out to be one of his seminal works, ranking up there with his more publicized papers and speculations: his work on Gödel's undecidability problem, the Turing Machine, the Turing Test—not to mention his contributions to the physical design of the modern digital computer. But the morphogenesis paper was only the beginning of a shape—a brilliant mind sensing the outlines of a new problem, but not fully grasping all its intricacies. If Turing had been granted another few decades to explore the powers of self-assembly—not to mention access to the number-crunching horsepower of non-vacuum-tube computers—it's not hard to imagine his mind greatly enhancing our subsequent understanding of emergent behavior. But the work on morphogenesis was tragically cut short by his death in 1954.

Alan Turing was most likely a casualty of the brutally homophobic laws of postwar Britain, but his death also intersected with those discreet patterns of life on Manchester's sidewalks. Turing had known about that stretch of Oxford Road since his arrival in Manchester; on occasion, he would drift down to the neighborhood, meeting other gay men—inviting some of them back to his flat for conversation, and presumably some sort of physical contact. In January of 1952, Turing met a young man named Arnold Murray on those streets, and the two embarked on a brief relationship that quickly turned sour. Murray—or a friend of Murray's—broke into Turing's house and stole a few items. Turing reported the theft to the police and, with his typical forthrightness, made no effort to conceal the affair with Murray when the police visited his flat. Homosexuality was a criminal offense according to British law, punishable by up to two years' imprisonment, and so the police promptly charged both Turing and Murray with "gross indecency."

On February 29, 1952, while the Manchester authorities were preparing their case against him, Turing finished the revisions to his morphogenesis paper, and he argued over its merits with Ilya Prigogine, the visiting Belgian chemist whose work on nonequilibrium thermodynamics would later win him a Nobel Prize. In one day, Turing had completed the text that would help engender the discipline of biomathematics and inspire Keller and Segel's slime mold discoveries fifteen years later, and he had enjoyed a spirited exchange with the man who would eventually achieve world fame for his research into self-organizing systems. On that winter day in 1952, there was no mind on the face of the earth better prepared to wrestle with the mysteries of emergence than Alan Turing's. But the world outside that mind was conspiring to destroy it. That very morning, a local paper broke the story that the war-hero savant had been caught in an illicit affair with a nineteen-year-old boy.

Within a few months Turing had been convicted of the crime and placed on a humiliating estrogen treatment to "cure" him of his homosexuality. Hounded by the authorities and denied security clearance for the top-secret British computing projects he had been contributing to, Turing died two years later, an apparent suicide.

Turing's career had already collided several times with the developing web of emergence before those fateful years in Manchester. In the early forties, during the height of the war effort, he had spent several months at the legendary Bell Laboratories on Manhattan's West Street, working on a number of encryption schemes, including an effort to transmit heavily encoded wave forms that could be decoded as human speech with the use of a special key. Early in his visit to Bell Labs, Turing hit upon the idea of using another Bell invention, the Vocoder—later used by rock musicians such as Peter Frampton to combine the sounds of a guitar and the human voice—as a way of encrypting speech. (By early 1943, Turing's ideas had enabled the first secure voice transmission to cross the Atlantic, unintelligible to German eavesdroppers.) Bell Labs was the home base for another genius, Claude Shannon, who would go on to found the influential discipline of information theory, and whose work had explored the boundaries between noise and information. Shannon had been particularly intrigued by the potential for machines to detect and amplify patterns of information in noisy communication channels—a line of inquiry that promised obvious value to a telephone company, but could also save thousands of lives in a war effort that relied so heavily on the sending and breaking of codes. Shannon and Turing immediately recognized that they had been working along parallel tracks: they were both code-breakers by profession at that point, and in their attempts to build automated machines that could recognize patterns in audio signals or numerical sequences, they had both glimpsed a future populated by even more intelligence machines. Shannon and Turing passed many an extended lunchtime at the Bell Labs, trading ideas on an "electronic brain" that might be capable of humanlike feats of pattern recognition.

Turing had imagined his thinking machine primarily in terms of its logical possibilities, its ability to execute an infinite variety of computational routines. But Shannon pushed him to think of the machine as something closer to an actual human brain, capable of recognizing more nuanced patterns. One day over lunch at the lab, Turing exclaimed playfully to his colleagues, "Shannon wants to feed not just data to a brain, but *cultural* things! He wants to play music to it!" Musical notes were patterns, too, Shannon recognized, and if you could train an electronic brain to understand and respond to logical patterns of zeros and ones, then perhaps sometime in the future we could train our machines to appreciate the equivalent patterns of minor chord progressions and arpeggios. The idea seemed fanciful at the time—it was hard enough getting a machine to perform long division, much less savor Beethoven's Ninth. But the pattern recognition that Turing and Shannon envisioned for digital computers has, in recent years, become a central part of our cultural life, with machines both generating music for our entertainment and recommending new artists for us to enjoy. The connection between musical patterns and our neurological wiring would play a central role in one of the founding texts of modern artificial intelligence, Douglas Hofstadter's *Gödel, Escher, Bach.* Our computers still haven't developed a genuine ear for music, but if they ever do, their skill will date back to those lunchtime conversations between Shannon and Turing at Bell Labs. And that learning, too, will be a kind of emergence, a higher-level order forming out of relatively simple component parts.

Five years after his interactions with Turing, Shannon published a long essay in the *Bell System Technical Journal* that was quickly repackaged as a book called *The Mathematical Theory of Communication.* Dense with equations and arcane chapter titles such as "Discrete Noiseless Systems," the book managed to become something of a cult classic, and the discipline it spawned—information theory—had a profound impact on scientific and technological research that followed, on both a theoretical and practical level. *The Mathematical Theory of Communication* contained an elegant, layman's introduction to Shannon's theory, penned by the esteemed scientist Warren Weaver, who had early on grasped the significance of Shannon's work. Weaver had played a leading role in the Natural Sciences division of the Rockefeller Foundation since 1932, and when he retired in the late fifties, he composed a long report for the foundation looking back at the scientific progress that had been achieved over the preceding quarter century. The occasion suggested a reflective look backward, but the document that Weaver produced (based loosely on a paper he had written for *American Scientist*) was far more prescient, more forward-looking. In many respects, it deserves to be thought of as the founding text of complexity theory—the point at which the study of complex systems began to think of itself as a unified field. Drawing upon research in molecular biology, genetics, physics, computer science, and Shannon's information theory, Weaver divided the last few centuries of scientific inquiry into three broad camps. First, the study of simple systems: two- or three-variable problems, such as the rotation of planets, or the connection between an electric current and its voltage and resistance. Second, problems of "disorganized complexity": problems characterized by millions or billions of variables that can only be approached by the methods of statistical mechanics and probability theory. These tools helped explain not only the behavior of molecules in a gas, or the patterns of heredity in a gene pool, but also helped life insurance companies turn a profit despite their limited knowledge about any individual human's future health. Thanks to Claude Shannon's work, the statistical approach also helped phone companies deliver more reliable and intelligible long-distance service.

But there was a third phase to this progression, and we were only beginning to understand. "This statistical method of dealing with disorganized complexity, so powerful an advance over the earlier two-variable methods, leaves a great field untouched," Weaver wrote. There was a middle region between two-variable equations and problems that involved billions of variables. Conventionally, this region involved a "moderate" number of variables, but the size of the system was in fact a secondary characteristic:

> Much more important than the mere number of variables is the fact that these variables are all interrelated.... These problems, as contrasted with the disorganized situations with which statistics can cope, *show the essential feature of organization*. We will therefore refer to this group of problems as those of *organized complexity*.

Think of these three categories of problems in terms of [a] billiards table analogy.... A two- or three-variable problem would be an ordinary billiards table, with balls bouncing off one another following simple rules: their velocities, the friction of the table. That would be an example of a "simple system"—and indeed, billiard balls are often used to illustrate basic laws of physics in high school textbooks. A system of disorganized complexity would be that same table enlarged to include a million balls, colliding with one another millions of times a second. Making predictions about the behavior of any individual ball in that mix would be difficult, but you could make some accurate predictions about the overall behavior of the table. Assuming there's enough energy in the system at the outset, the balls will spread to fill the entire table, like gas molecules in a container. It's complex because there are many interacting agents, but it's disorganized because they don't create any higher-level behavior other than broad statistical trends. Organized complexity, on the other hand, is like [a] motorized billiards table, where the balls follow specific rules and through their various interactions create a distinct macrobehavior, arranging themselves in a specific shape, or forming a specific pattern over time. That sort of behavior, for Weaver, suggested a problem of organized complexity, a problem that suddenly seemed omnipresent in nature once you started to look for it:

> What makes an evening primrose open when it does? Why does salt water fail to satisfy thirst? … What is the description of aging in bio-chemical terms? … What is a gene, and how does the original genetic constitution of a living organism express itself in the developed charac-teristics of the adult?
>
> All these are certainly complex problems. But they are not problems of disorganized complexity, to which statistical methods hold the key. They are all problems which involve dealing simultaneously with a siz-able number of factors which are interrelated into an organic whole.

Tackling such problems required a new approach: "The great central con-cerns of the biologist … are now being approached not only from *above,* with the broad view of the natural philosopher who scans the whole living world, but also from *underneath,* by the quantitative analyst who measures the underlying facts." This was a genuine shift in the paradigm of research, to use Thomas Kuhn's language—a revolution not so much in the interpretations that science built in its attempt to explain the world, but rather in the types of questions it asked. The paradigm shift was more than just a new mind-set, Weaver recog-nized; it was also a by-product of new tools that were appearing on the horizon. To solve the problems of organized complexity, you needed a machine capable of churning through thousands, if not millions, of calculations per second—a rate that would have been unimaginable for individual brains running the numbers with the limited calculating machines of the past few centuries. Because of his connection to the Bell Labs group, Weaver had seen early on the promise of digital computing, and he knew that the mysteries of organized complexity would be much easier to tackle once you could model the behavior in close-to-real time. For millennia, humans had used their skills at observation and clas-sification to document the subtle anatomy of flowers, but for the first time they were perched on the brink of answering a more fundamental question, a ques-tion that had more to do with patterns developing over time than with static structure: why does an evening primrose open when it does? And how does a simple seed know how to make a primrose in the first place? …

"Organized complexity" proved to be a constructive way of thinking … but … was it possible to model and explain the behavior of self-organizing systems using more rigorous methods? Could the developing technology of digital computing be usefully applied to this problem? Partially thanks to Shannon's work in the late forties, the biological sciences … made a number of significant breakthroughs in understanding pattern recognition and feedback…. Shortly after his appointment to the Harvard faculty in 1956, the entomologist Edward O. Wilson convinc-ingly proved that ants communicate with one another—and coordinate overall colony behavior—by recognizing patterns in pheromone trails left by fellow ants…. At the Free University of Brussels in the fifties, Ilya Prigogine was making steady advances in his understanding of nonequilibrium thermodynamics, envir-onments where the laws of entropy are temporarily overcome, and higher-level order may spontaneously emerge out of underlying chaos. And at MIT's Lincoln Laboratory, a twenty-five-year-old researcher named Oliver Selfridge was experimenting with a model for teaching a computer how to learn.

There is a world of difference between a computer that passively receives the information you supply and a computer that actively learns on its own. The very first generation of computers such as ENIAC had processed information fed to them by their masters, and they had been capable of performing various calculations with that data, based on the instruction sets programmed into them. This was a startling enough development at a time when "computer" meant a person with a slide rule and an eraser. But even in those early days, the digital visionaries had imagined a machine capable of more open-ended learning. Turing and Shannon had argued over the future musical tastes of the "electronic brain" during lunch hour at Bell Labs, while their colleague Norbert Wiener had written a best-selling paean to the self-regulatory powers of feedback in his 1949 manifesto *Cybernetics.*

"Mostly my participation in all of this is a matter of good luck for me," Selfridge says today, sitting in his cramped, windowless MIT office. Born in England, Selfridge enrolled at Harvard at the age of fifteen and started his doctorate three years later at MIT, where Norbert Wiener was his dissertation adviser. As a precocious twenty-one-year-old, Selfridge suggested a few corrections to a paper that his mentor had published on heart flutters, corrections that Wiener graciously acknowledged in the opening pages of *Cybernetics.* "I think I now have the honor of being one of the few living people mentioned in that book," Selfridge says, laughing.

After a sojourn working on military control projects in New Jersey, Selfridge returned to MIT in the mid-fifties. His return coincided with an explosion of interest in artificial intelligence (AI), a development that introduced him to a then-junior fellow at Harvard named Marvin Minsky. "My concerns in AI," Selfridge says now, "were not so much the actual processing as they were in how systems change, how they evolve—in a word, how they learn." Exploring the possibilities of machine learning brought Selfridge back to memories of his own education in England. "At school in England I had read John Milton's *Paradise Lost,*" he says, "and I'd been struck by the image of Pandemonium—it's Greek for 'all the demons.' Then after my second son, Peter, was born, I went over *Paradise Lost* again, and the shrieking of the demons awoke something in me." The pattern recognizer in Selfridge's brain had hit upon a way of teaching a computer to recognize patterns.

"We are proposing here a model of a process which we claim can adaptively improve itself to handle certain pattern-recognition problems which cannot be adequately specified in advance." These were the first words Selfridge delivered at a symposium in late 1958, held at the very same National Physical Laboratory from which Turing had escaped a decade before. Selfridge's presentation had the memorable title "Pandemonium: A Paradigm for Learning," and while it had little impact outside the nascent computer-science community, the ideas Selfridge outlined that day would eventually become part of our everyday life—each time we enter a name in our Palm Pilots or use voice-recognition software to ask for information over the phone. Pandemonium, as Selfridge outlined it in his talk, was not so much a specific piece of software as it was a way of approaching a problem. The problem was an ambitious one, given the limited computational resources of the day: how to teach a computer to recognize patterns that were ill-defined or erratic, like the sound waves that comprise spoken language.

The brilliance of Selfridge's new paradigm lay in the fact that it relied on a distributed, bottom-up intelligence, and not a unified, top-down one. Rather than build a single smart program, Selfridge created a swarm of limited miniprograms, which he called demons. "The idea was, we have a bunch of these demons shrieking up the hierarchy," he explains. "Lower-level demons shrieking to higher-level demons shrieking to higher ones."

To understand what that "shrieking" means, imagine a system with twenty-six individual demons, each trained to recognize a letter of the alphabet. The pool of demons is shown a series of words, and each demon "votes" as to whether each letter displayed represents its chosen letter. If the first letter is *a,* the *a*-recognizing demon reports that it is highly likely that it has recognized a match. Because of the similarities in shape, the *o*-recognizer might report a possible match, while the *b*-recognizer would emphatically declare that the letter wasn't intelligible to it. All the letter-recognizing demons would report to a master demon, who would tally up the votes for each letter and choose the demon that expressed the highest confidence. Then the software would move on to the next letter in the sequence, and the process would begin again. At the end of the transmission, the master demon would have a working interpretation of the text that had been transmitted, based on the assembled votes of the demon democracy.

Of course, the accuracy of that interpretation depended on the accuracy of the letter recognizers. If you were trying to teach a computer how to read, it was cheating to assume from the outset that you could find twenty-six accurate letter recognizers. Selfridge was after a larger goal: how do you teach a machine to recognize letters—or vowel sounds, minor chords, fingerprints—in the first place? The answer involved adding another layer of demons, and a feedback mechanism whereby the various demon guesses could be graded. This lower level was populated by even less sophisticated miniprograms, trained only to recognize raw physical shapes (or sounds, in the case of Morse code or spoken language). Some demons recognized parallel lines, others perpendicular ones. Some demons looked for circles, others for dots. None of these shapes were associated with any particular letter; these bottom-dwelling demons were like two-year-old children—capable of reporting on the shapes they witnessed, but not perceiving them as letters or words.

Using these minimally equipped demons, the system could be trained to recognize letters, without "knowing" anything about the alphabet in advance. The recipe was relatively simple: present the letter *b* to the bottom-level demons, and see which ones respond, and which ones don't. In the case of the letter *b,* the vertical-line recognizers might respond, along with the circle recognizers. Those lower-level demons would report to a letter-recognizer one step higher in the chain. Based on the information gathered from its lieutenants, that recognizer would make a guess as to the letter's identity. Those guesses are then "graded"

by the software. If the guess is wrong, the software learns to dissociate those particular lieutenants from the letter in question; if the guess happens to be right, it
strengthens the connection between the lieutenants and the letter.

The results are close to random at first, but if you repeat the process a thousand times, or ten thousand, the system learns to associate specific assemblies of
shape-recognizers with specific letters and soon enough is capable of translating
entire sentences with remarkable accuracy. The system doesn't come with any
predefined conceptions about the shapes of letters—you train the system to associate letters with specific shapes in the grading phase. (This is why handwriting-
recognition software can adapt to so many different types of penmanship, but
can't adapt to penmanship that changes day to day.) That mix of random beginnings organizing into more complicated results reminded Selfridge of another
process, whose own underlying code was just then being deciphered in the
form of DNA. "The scheme sketched is really a natural selection on the processing demons," Selfridge explained. "If they serve a useful function they survive
and perhaps are even the source for other subdemons who are themselves judged
on their merits. It is perfectly reasonable to conceive of this taking place on a
broader scale.... [I]nstead of having but one Pandemonium we might have
some crowd of them, all fairly similarly constructed, and employ natural selection
on the crowd of them."

The system Selfridge described—with its bottom-up learning, and its evalu-
ating feedback loops—belongs in the history books as the first practical description of an emergent software program. The world now swarms with millions of
his demons.

QUESTIONS FOR MAKING CONNECTIONS
WITHIN THE READING

1. Do you accept Johnson's analogy between the behavior of harvester ants and
    the emergence of cities like Manchester? Does Johnson mean that instinct
    guides human builders in much the same way as it guides the ants? Does he
    mean that in both cases an order has emerged entirely by accident? Or does
    he mean that there is something about "systems" in general—ant colonies as
    well as sprawling conurbations—that makes them self-organizing? What
    exactly is a self-organizing system, and how do both the ant colony and
    the city qualify as equally appropriate examples? How does each system
    organize itself?

2. The idea of self-organizing systems might seem to suggest that order
    automatically and smoothly arises as ants and human beings go about their
    private business. Can Manchester in the nineteenth century, when Napier,
    Dickens, and Engels each observed it, be described as orderly? Was there
    an order behind the apparent disorder? How can we distinguish between a
    self-organizing system and results that are produced entirely by chance?

3. One could say that there are three different parts to "The Myth of the Ant Queen." The first deals with the colony of harvester ants. The second deals with the city of Manchester. The third deals with the emergence of complexity theory. In what ways are these three parts connected? Why doesn't Johnson make the connections more explicit—why does he leave them for the reader to work out? Could the structure of his chapter in some way reflect the nature of his argument about self-organization?

QUESTIONS FOR WRITING

1. What role does intelligence play in self-organizing systems? This question might be more complex than it seems at first because intelligence may exist on multiple levels. The intelligence demonstrated by an ant colony may be much greater than the intelligence of an individual ant. On any particular day during the 1880s, life in Manchester must have seemed to many people very close to absolute chaos, but could it be said that the city as a whole possessed a certain intelligence? Does Johnson mean to suggest that the ideas and aspirations of individuals do not matter? Are we, from the standpoint of complexity theory, intelligent beings? What is intelligence, anyway?

2. Families, communities, schools, religious groups, circles of friends, political parties, public service organizations—all of these qualify as social institutions, and there are many others. Choose one institution and, drawing on Johnson's chapter, decide whether it qualifies as truly self-organizing. If it does not, can you imagine how it might be reorganized in a bottom-up fashion? In what ways do our customs and traditions encourage or discourage self-organization? What do you conclude from the importance of kings, presidents, generals, CEOs, bosses, coaches, principals, and other leaders in our culture?

QUESTIONS FOR MAKING CONNECTIONS
BETWEEN READINGS

1. Johnson's purpose in writing "The Myth of the Ant Queen" is to teach us to see complex systems in a new and decentered way that is, he suggests, more consistent with the way nature really works. Instead of trying to identify structures of leadership or basic laws and rules, we need to understand the principle of self-organization, which creates order from the ground up instead of from the top down. In his discussion of the rise of the city of Manchester, Johnson implies that self-organization will produce the optimum results. But what would Joseph Stiglitz say about Johnson's proposition? Would he agree that self-organization always leads to the best results,

or does he think that the consequences can be quite destructive? What might Stiglitz say to Johnson about the limitations and dangers of decentralized economies?

2. At first glance, Robert Thurman's claim that we have no permanent or essential self may seem like sheer nonsense, since, clearly, each of us is a self or has one. But does "the self," as we call it, actually represent a self-organizing system, more like an ant colony than a single ant, or more like a city than a single neighborhood? As you work through this question, you should move beyond the two texts to consider your own experience. Are you always the same person from one moment to the next? To what degree is your identity at any particular time shaped by your interactions with others? Can you accurately predict what you will be like ten years from now? Ten months? Ten days?

NAOMI KLEIN

Wʜᴀᴛ ᴅᴏ ᴡᴇ ᴍᴇᴀɴ when we talk about "sustainability"—a term often used in discussions of economics as well as the environment? How exactly is our financial well-being—as reflected in the basics of health care, education, food, and housing—dependent on a healthy natural environment? How can we transition from a narrow focus on profits for the few to "a caring economy" that yields quality lives for the many?

In *This Changes Everything: Capitalism vs. the Climate* (2014), from which this selection is drawn, Klein takes a close look at the way neoliberal orthodoxies have thwarted various attempts to lower carbon emissions worldwide since the 1980s. Defining neoliberalism as the "privatization of the public sphere, deregulation of the corporate sector, and the lowering of income and corporate taxes," Klein documents the impact of trade agreements such as NAFTA and of international regulators such as the World Trade Organization (WTO), which have undercut successful renewable energy programs in other countries. They do this by portraying these programs, and the many local jobs they support, as protectionist violations of free trade agreements. Her analysis ventures still more deeply to consider how a neoliberal economic model, which claims to generate prosperity for all, actually compromises efforts at sustainable economic growth in the Global South. According to Klein, neoliberal development continues a cycle of exploitation reaching back to the heyday of eighteenth- and nineteenth-century colonial regimes in Africa, Asia, and Latin America.

Klein argues that neoliberalism's commitment to "indiscriminate economic growth" encourages a "frenetic," competitive consumption that not only degrades the environment but also unravels the social fabric. To counter this devastation, Klein proposes a program of "massive de-growth" that will replace the myth of endless economic growth with a sharing economy. She argues that "humane, fulfilling lifestyles" are indeed achievable, provided we are willing to distribute social goods more equitably.

Growing up in suburban Toronto as the child of a highly regarded feminist filmmaker and a physician, Naomi Klein devoted her free time as a teenager to shopping in the malls. She describes her behavior during this period as a reaction against her activist parents, who had moved to Canada to protest the U.S. war in

Biographical information comes from <http://www.naomiklein.org/main>; and https://www.theguardian.com/books/2017/jun/11/naomi-klein-donald-trump-no-is-not-enough-interview>.

Vietnam. But as Klein remembers, one event that turned her life around was her mother's stroke when she was only 17. To help her family, Klein postponed her first year of studies at the University of Toronto and had her first real encounter with human frailty and suffering. Then, a second life-changing event took place.

On a cold December day in 1989 at Quebec's Ecole Polytechnique de Montréal, a young male student armed with a 223-calibre Sturm-Ruger rifle entered an engineering classroom and ordered the women to move to the back of room. Before killing six of them, he announced, "You're all a bunch of feminists, I hate feminists." Returning to the hallway, he eventually murdered six other female engineering students, an office clerk and a nursing student.

These events made Klein decide to become an activist, and she chose writing as her métier. While at Toronto, she reported for *The Varsity*, the student newspaper, and eventually became its editor-in-chief. In her third year, she went to work at one of Canada's leading newspapers, *The Globe and Mail*, followed by a term as editor of *This Magazine*.

Since then, Klein has produced a series of highly acclaimed, impressively researched exposés of the destructive effects of globalization and expanding corporate power. *No Logo* (1999), *Fences and Windows* (2002), *The Shock Doctrine* (2007), and *No Is Not Enough: Resisting Trump's Shock Politics and Winning the World We Need* (2017), have each spent time on the bestseller lists.

Hot Money
How Free Market Fundamentalism
Helped Overheat the Planet

We always had hope that next year was gonna be better. And even this year was gonna be better. We learned slowly, and what didn't work, you tried it harder the next time. You didn't try something different You just tried harder, the same thing that didn't work.
—Wayne Lewis, Dust Bowl survivor, 2012

As leaders we have a responsibility to fully articulate the risks our people face. If the politics are not favorable to speaking truthfully, then clearly we must devote more energy to changing the politics.
—Marlene Moses, Ambassador to the United
Nations for Nauru, 2012

During the globalization wars of the late nineties and early 2000s, I used to follow international trade law extremely closely. But I admit that as I immersed myself in the science and politics of climate change, I stopped paying attention to trade. I told myself that there was only so much abstract, bureaucratic jargon one person could be expected to absorb, and my quota was filled up with emission mitigation targets, feed-in tariffs, and the United Nations' alphabet soup of UNFCCCs and IPCCs.

Then about three years ago, I started to notice that green energy programs—the strong ones that are needed to lower global emissions fast—were increasingly being challenged under international trade agreements, particularly the World Trade Organization's rules.

In 2010, for instance, the United States challenged one of China's wind power subsidy programs on the grounds that it contained supports for local industry considered protectionist. China, in turn, filed a complaint in 2012 targeting various renewable energy programs in the European Union, singling out Italy and Greece (it has also threatened to bring a dispute against renewables subsidies in five U.S. states). Washington, meanwhile, has launched a World Trade Organization attack on India's ambitious Jawaharlal Nehru National Solar Mission, a large, multiphase solar support program—once again, for containing provisions, designed to encourage local industry, considered to be protectionist. As a result, brand-new factories that should be producing solar panels are now contemplating closure. Not to be outdone, India has signaled that it might take aim at state renewable energy programs in the U.S.

This is distinctly bizarre behavior to exhibit in the midst of a climate emergency. Especially because these same governments can be counted upon to angrily denounce each other at United Nations climate summits for not doing enough to cut emissions, blaming their own failures on the other's lack of commitment. Yet rather than compete for the best, most effective supports for green energy, the biggest emitters in the world are rushing to the WTO to knock down each other's windmills.

As one case piled on top of another, it seemed to me that it was time to delve back into the trade wars. And as I explored the issue further, I discovered that one of the key, precedent-setting cases pitting "free trade" against climate action was playing out in Ontario, Canada—my own backyard. Suddenly, trade law became a whole lot less abstract.

Sitting at the long conference table overlooking his factory floor, Paolo Maccario, an elegant Italian businessman who moved to Toronto to open a solar factory, has the proud, resigned air of a captain determined to go down with his ship. He makes an effort to put on a brave face: True, "the Ontario market is pretty much gone," but the company will find new customers for its solar panels, he tells me, maybe in Europe, or the United States. Their products are good, best in class, and "the cost is competitive enough."

As chief operating officer of Silfab Ontario, Maccario has to say these things; anything else would be a breach of fiduciary duty. But he is also frank that the last few months have been almost absurdly bad. Old customers are convinced the factory is going to close down and won't be able to honor the twenty-five-year warranty on the solar panels they purchased. New customers aren't placing orders over the same concerns, opting to go with Chinese companies that are selling less efficient but cheaper modules.* Suppliers who had been planning to set up their own factories nearby to cut down on transport costs are now keeping their distance.

Even his own board back home in Italy (Silfab is owned by Silfab SpA, whose founder was a pioneer in Italian photovoltaic manufacturing) seemed to be jumping ship. The parent company had committed to invest around $7 million on a custom piece of machinery that, according to Maccario, would have created solar modules that "have an efficiency that has not been reached by any manufacturer in China and in the Western world." But at the last minute, and after all the research and design for the machinery was complete, "It was decided that we cannot spend the money to bring the technology here," Maccario explains. We put on hair nets and lab coats and he shows me an empty rectangle in the middle of the factory floor, the space set aside for equipment that is not coming.

What are the chances he would choose to open this factory here today, given all that has happened, I ask. At this, all attempts at PR drop away and he replies, "I would say below zero if such a number exists."

With his finely tailored wool suit and trim salt and pepper goatee, Maccario looks as if he should be sipping espresso in a piazza in Turin, working for Fiat perhaps—not stuck in this concrete box with an unopened yogurt on his desk, across the street from Imperial Chilled Juice and down the road from the ass end of an AMC multiplex.

And yet in 2010, the decision to locate the company's first North American solar manufacturing plant in Ontario seemed to make a great deal of sense. Back then the mood in Ontario's renewable sector was positively giddy. One year earlier, at the peak of the Wall Street financial crisis, the province had unveiled its climate action plan, the Green Energy and Green Economy Act, centered on a bold pledge to wean Canada's most populous province completely off coal by 2014.

The plan was lauded by energy experts around the world, particularly in the U.S., where such ambition was lagging. On a visit to Toronto, Al Gore offered his highest blessing, proclaiming it "widely recognized now as the single best green energy [program] on the North American continent." And Michael T. Eckhart, then president of the American Council on Renewable Energy, described it as "the most comprehensive renewable energy policy entered anywhere around the world."

The legislation created what is known as a feed-in tariff program, which allowed renewable energy providers to sell power back to the grid, offering long-term contracts with guaranteed premium prices. It also contained a variety of provisions to ensure that the developers weren't all big players but that local municipalities, co-ops, and Indigenous communities could all get into the renewable energy market and benefit from those premium rates. The catch was that in order for most of the energy providers to qualify, they had to ensure that a minimum percentage of their workforces and materials were local to Ontario.

---

* China has of course emerged as the world's dominant supplier of inexpensive modules, and in that role has helped to drive dramatic drops in solar prices. It has also flooded the market with cheap panels in recent years, contributing to a global oversupply that has outpaced demand.

And the province set the bar high: solar energy developers had to source at least 40–60 percent of their content from within the province.

The provision was an attempt to revive Ontario's moribund manufacturing sector, which had long been centered on the Big Three U.S. automakers (Chrysler, Ford, and General Motors) and was, at that time, reeling from the near bankruptcy of General Motors and Chrysler. Compounding these challenges was the fact that Alberta's tar sands oil boom had sent the Canadian dollar soaring, making Ontario a much costlier place to build anything.

In the years that followed the announcement, Ontario's efforts to get off coal were plagued by political blunders. Large natural gas and wind developers ran roughshod over local communities, while the government wasted hundreds of millions (at least) trying to clean up the unnecessary messes. Yet even with all these screwups, the core of the program was an undeniable success. By 2012, Ontario was the largest solar producer in Canada and by 2013, it had only one working coal-fired power plant left. The local content requirements—as the "buy local" and "hire local" provisions are called—were also proving to be a significant boost to the ailing manufacturing sector: by 2014, more than 31,000 jobs had been created and a wave of solar and wind manufacturers had set up shop.

Silfab is a great example of how it worked. The Italian owners had already decided to open a solar panel plant in North America. The company had considered Mexico but was leaning toward the United States. The obvious choices, Maccario told me, were California, Hawaii, and Texas, all of which offered lots of sunshine and corporate incentives, as well as large and growing markets for their product. Ontario—overcast and cold a lot of the year—wasn't "on the radar screen," he admitted. That changed when the province introduced the green energy plan with its local-content provisions, which Maccario described as a "very gutsy and very well intended program." The provisions meant that in communities that switched to renewable energy, companies like his could count on a stable market for their products, one that was protected from having to compete head-to-head with cheaper solar panels from China. So Silfab chose Toronto for its first North American solar plant.

Ontario's politicians loved Silfab. It helped that the building the company purchased to produce its panels was an abandoned auto parts factory, then sitting idle like so many others. And many of the workers the company hired also came from the auto sector—men and women from Chrysler and the autoparts giant Magna, who had years of experience working with the kind of robotic arms that are used to assemble Silfab's high-tech panels. When the plant opened, Wayne Wright, a laid-off autoworker who landed a job as a production operator on the Silfab line, spoke movingly about his seventeen-year-old son, who told him that "finally" his dad's new job would be "creating a better future for all the younger kids."

And then things started to go very wrong. Just as the U.S. has acted against local renewable supports in China and India, so Japan and then the European Union let it be known that they considered Ontario's local-content requirement to be a violation of World Trade Organization rules. Specifically, they claimed that the requirement that a fixed percentage of renewable energy equipment be made in Ontario would "discriminate against equipment for renewable energy generation facilities produced outside Ontario."

The WTO ruled against Canada, determining that Ontario's buy-local provisions were indeed illegal. And the province wasted little time in nixing the local-content rules that had been so central to its program. It was this, Maccario said, that led his foreign investors to pull their support for factory expansion. "Seeing all those, for lack of a better term, mixed messages . . . was the straw that broke the camel's back."

It was also why many plants like his could well close, and others have decided not to open in the first place.

TRADE TRUMPS CLIMATE

From a climate perspective, the WTO ruling was an outrage: if there is to be any hope of meeting the agreed-upon 2 degree Celsius target, wealthy economies like Canada must make getting off fossil fuels their top priority. It is a moral duty, one that the federal government undertook when it signed the Kyoto Protocol in 1997. Ontario was putting real policies in place to honor that commitment (unlike the Canadian government as a whole, which has allowed emissions to balloon, leading it to withdraw from the Kyoto Protocol rather than face international censure). Most importantly, the program was working. How absurd, then, for the WTO to interfere with that success—to let trade trump the planet itself.

And yet from a strictly legal standpoint, Japan and the EU were perfectly correct. One of the key provisions in almost all free trade agreements involves something called "national treatment," which requires governments to make no distinction between goods produced by local companies and goods produced by foreign firms outside their borders. Indeed, favoring local industry constitutes illegal "discrimination." This was a flashpoint in the free trade wars back in the 1990s, precisely because these restrictions effectively prevent governments from doing what Ontario was trying to do: create jobs by requiring the sourcing of local goods as a condition of government support. This was just one of the many fateful battles that progressives lost in those years.

Defenders of these trade deals argue that protections like Ontario's buy-local provisions distort the free market and should be eliminated. Some green energy entrepreneurs (usually those that purchase their products from China) have made similar arguments, insisting that it doesn't matter where solar panel and wind turbines are produced: the goal should be to get the cheapest products to the consumer so that the green transition can happen as quickly as possible.

The biggest problem with these arguments is the notion that there is any free market in energy to be protected from distortion. Not only do fossil fuel companies receive $775 billion to $1 trillion in annual global subsidies, but they pay nothing for the privilege of treating our shared atmosphere as a free waste dump—a fact that has been described by the *Stem Review on the Economics of Climate Change* as "the greatest market failure the world has ever seen." That freebie is the real distortion, that theft of the sky the real subsidy.

In order to cope with these distortions (which the WTO has made no attempt to correct), governments need to take a range of aggressive steps—from price guarantees to straight subsidies—so that green energy has a fair shot at competing. We know from experience that this works: Denmark has among the most successful renewable energy programs in the world, with 40 percent of its electricity coming from renewables, mostly wind. But it's significant that the program was rolled out in the 1980s, before the free trade era began, when there was no one to argue with the Danish government's generous subsidies to the community-controlled energy projects putting up wind turbines (in 1980, new installations were subsidized by up to 30 percent).

As Scott Sinclair of the Canadian Centre for Policy Alternatives has pointed out, "many of the policies Denmark used to launch its renewable energy industry would have been inconsistent with ... international trade and investment agreements," since favoring "locally owned cooperatives would conflict with non-discrimination rules requiring that foreign companies be treated no less favourably than domestic suppliers."

And Aaron Cosbey, a development economist and trade and climate expert who is generally supportive of the WTO, rightly notes that the promise of local job creation has been key to the political success of renewable energy programs. "In many cases the green jobs argument is the deciding factor that convinces governments to dole out support. And such requirements, if attached to subsidies or investment privileges, violate WTO obligations."

Which is why governments adopting these tried-and-tested policies—of which there have been far too few—are the ones getting dragged into trade court, whether China, India, Ontario, or the European Union.

Worse, it's not only critical supports for renewable energy that are at risk of these attacks. Any attempt by a government to regulate the sale or extraction of particularly dirty kinds of fossil fuels is also vulnerable to similar trade challenges. The European Union, for instance, is considering new fuel quality standards that would effectively restrict the sales of oil derived from such high-carbon sources as the Alberta tar sands. It's excellent climate policy of the kind we need much more, but the effort has been slowed down by Canada's not so subtle threats of trade retaliation. Meanwhile, the European Union is using bilateral trade talks to try to circumvent longstanding U.S. restrictions on oil and gas exports, including a decades-old export ban on crude oil. In July 2014, a leaked negotiating document revealed that Europe is pushing for a "legally binding commitment" that would guarantee its ability to import fracked gas and oil from North Dakota's Bakken formation and elsewhere.

Almost a decade ago, a WTO official claimed that the organization enables challenges against "almost any measure to reduce greenhouse gas emissions"—there was little public reaction at the time, but clearly there should have been. And the WTO is far from the only trade weapon that can be used in such battles—so too can countless bilateral and regional free trade and investment agreements.

As we will see later on, these trade deals may even give multinationals the power to overturn landmark grassroots victories against highly controversial extractive activities like natural gas fracking: in 2012, an oil company began taking steps to use NAFTA to challenge Quebec's hard-won fracking moratorium, claiming it robbed the company of its right to drill for gas in the province. (The case is ongoing.) As more activist victories are won, more such legal challenges should be expected.

In some of these cases, governments may successfully defend their emission-reducing activities in trade court. But in too many others, they can be relied upon to cave in early, not wanting to appear anti-free trade (which is likely what is behind Ontario's quiet acceptance of the WTO's ruling against its green energy plan). These challenges aren't killing renewable energy; in the U.S. and China, for instance, the solar market continues to grow impressively. But it is not happening fast enough. And the legal uncertainty that now surrounds some of the most significant green energy programs in the world is bogging us down at the very moment when science is telling us we need to leap ahead. To allow arcane trade law, which has been negotiated with scant public scrutiny, to have this kind of power over an issue so critical to humanity's future is a special kind of madness. As Nobel Prize-winning economist Joseph Stiglitz puts it, "Should you let a group of foolish lawyers, who put together something before they understood these issues, interfere with saving the planet?"

Clearly not. Steven Shrybman, an international trade and public interest lawyer who has worked with a broad range of civil society groups to defend against these trade challenges, says that the problem is structural. "If the trade rules don't permit all kinds of important measures to deal with climate change—and they don't—then the trade rules obviously have to be rewritten. Because there is no way in the world that we can have a sustainable economy and maintain international trade rules as they are. There's no way at all."

This is exactly the sort of commonsense conclusion that has the Heartlanders so very scared of climate change. Because when people wake up to the fact that our governments have locked us into dozens of agreements that make important parts of a robust climate change response illegal, they will have an awfully powerful argument to oppose any such new deals until the small matter of our planet's habitability is satisfactorily resolved.

The same goes for all kinds of free market orthodoxies that threaten our capacity to respond boldly to this crisis, from the suffocating logic of austerity that prevents governments from making the necessary investments in low-carbon infrastructure (not to mention firefighting and flood response), to the auctioning off of electric utilities to private corporations that, in many cases, refuse to switch over to less profitable renewables.

Indeed the three policy pillars of the neoliberal age—privatization of the public sphere, deregulation of the corporate sector, and the lowering of income and corporate taxes, paid for with cuts to public spending—are each incompatible with many of the actions we must take to bring our emissions to safe levels. And together these pillars form an ideological wall that has blocked a serious response to climate change for decades. Before delving more deeply into the ways the climate crisis calls for dismantling that wall, it's helpful to look a little more closely at the epic case of bad timing that landed us where we are today.

A WALL COMES DOWN, EMISSIONS GO UP

If the climate movement had a birthday, a moment when the issue pierced the public consciousness and could no longer be ignored, it would have to be June 23, 1988. Global warming had been on the political and scientific radar long before that, however. The basic insights central to our current understanding date back to the beginning of the second half of the nineteenth century, and first scientific breakthroughs demonstrating that burning carbon could be warming the planet were made in the late 1950s. In 1965, the concept was so widely accepted among specialists that president Lyndon B. Johnson was given a report from his Science Advisory Committee warning that, "Through his worldwide industrial civilization, Man is unwittingly conducting a vast geophysical experiment . . . The climatic changes that may be produced by the increased CO_2 content could be deleterious from the point of view of human beings."

But it wasn't until James Hansen, then director of NASA's Goddard Institute for Space Studies, testified before a packed congressional hearing on June 23, 1988, that global warming became the stuff of chat shows and political speeches. With temperatures in Washington, D.C. a sweltering 98 degrees Fahrenheit (still a record for that day), and the building's air conditioning on the fritz, Hansen told a room filled with sweaty lawmakers that he had "99 percent confidence" in "a real warming trend" linked to human activity. In a comment to *The New York Times* he added that it was "time to stop waffling" about the science. Later that same month, hundreds of scientists and policymakers held the historic World Conference on the Changing Atmosphere in Toronto where the first emission reductions were discussed. The United Nations' Intergovernmental Panel on Climate Change (IPCC), the premier scientific body advising governments on the climate threat, held its first session that November. By the following year, 79 percent of Americans had heard of the greenhouse effect—a leap from just 38 percent in 1981.

The issue was so prominent that when the editors of *Time* magazine announced their 1988 "Man of the Year," they went for an unconventional choice: "Planet of the Year: Endangered Earth," read the magazine's cover line, over an image of the globe held together with twine, the sun setting ominously in the background. "No single individual, no event, no movement captured imaginations or dominated headlines more," journalist Thomas Sancton explained, "than the clump of rock and soil and water and air that is our common home."

More striking than the image was Sancton's accompanying essay. "This year the earth spoke, like God warning Noah of the deluge. Its message was loud and clear, and suddenly people began to listen, to ponder what portents the message held." That message was so profound, so fundamental, he argued, that it called into question the founding myths of modern Western culture. Here it is worth quoting Sancton at length as he described the roots of the crisis:

> In many pagan societies, the earth was seen as a mother, a fertile giver
> of life. Nature—the soil, forest, sea—was endowed with divinity, and
> mortals were subordinate to it. The Judeo-Christian tradition introduced
> a radically different concept. The earth was the creation of a monotheistic

God, who, after shaping it, ordered its inhabitants, in the words of Genesis: "Be fruitful and multiply, and replenish the earth and subdue it: and have dominion over the fish of the sea and over the fowl of the air and over every living thing that moveth upon the earth." The idea of dominion could be interpreted as an invitation to use nature as a convenience.

The diagnosis wasn't original—indeed it was a synthesis of the founding principles of ecological thought. But to read these words in America's most studiously centrist magazine was nothing short of remarkable. For this reason and others, the start of 1989 felt to many in the environmental movement like a momentous juncture, as if the thawing of the Cold War and the warming of the planet were together helping to birth a new consciousness, one in which cooperation would triumph over domination, and humility before nature's complexity would challenge technological hubris.

As governments came together to debate responses to climate change, strong voices from developing countries spoke up, insisting that the core of the problem was the high-consumption lifestyle that dominated in the West. In a speech in 1989, for instance, India's President R.Venkataraman argued that the global environmental crisis was the result of developed countries'"excessive consumption of all materials and through large-scale industrialization intended to support their styles of life." If wealthy countries consumed less, then everyone would be safer.

But if that was the way 1989 began, it would end very differently. In the months that followed, popular uprisings would spread across the Soviet controlled Eastern Bloc, from Poland to Hungary and finally to East Germany where, in November 1989, the Berlin Wall collapsed. Under the banner "the End of History," right-wing ideologues in Washington seized on this moment of global flux to crush all political competition, whether socialism, Keynesianism, or deep ecology. They waged a frontal attack on political experimentation, on the idea that there might be viable ways of organizing societies other than deregulated capitalism.

Within a decade, all that would be left standing would be their own extreme, pro-corporate ideology. Not only would the Western consumer lifestyle survive intact, it would grow significantly more lavish, with credit card debt per household increasing fourfold between 1980 and 2010. Simultaneously, that voracious lifestyle would be exported to the middle and upper classes in every corner of the globe—including, despite earlier protestations, India, where it would wreak environmental damage on a scale difficult to fathom.The victories in the new era would be faster and bigger than almost anyone predicted; and the armies of losers would be left to pick through the ever-growing mountains of methane-spewing waste.

TRADE AND CLIMATE: TWO SOLITUDES

Throughout this period of rapid change, the climate and trade negotiations closely paralleled one another, each winning landmark agreements within a couple of years of each other. In 1992, governments met for the first United Nations Earth

Summit in Rio, where they signed the United Nations Framework Convention on Climate Change (UNFCCC), the document that formed the basis for all future climate negotiations. That same year, the North American Free Trade Agreement was signed, going into effect two years later. Also in 1994, negotiations establishing the World Trade Organization concluded, and the new global trade body made its debut the next year. In 1997, the Kyoto Protocol was adopted, containing the first binding emission reduction targets. In 2001, China gained full membership in the WTO, the culmination of a trade and investment liberalization process that had begun decades earlier.

What is most remarkable about these parallel processes—trade on the one hand, climate on the other—is the extent to which they functioned as two solitudes. Indeed, each seemed to actively pretend that the other did not exist, ignoring the most glaring questions about how one would impact the other. Like, for example: how would the vastly increased distances that basic goods would now travel—by carbon-spewing container ships and jumbo jets, as well as diesel trucks—impact the carbon emissions that the climate negotiations were aiming to reduce? How would the aggressive protections for technology patents enshrined under the WTO impact the demands being made by developing nations in the climate negotiations for free transfers of green technologies to help them develop on a low-carbon path? And perhaps most critically, how would provisions that allowed private companies to sue national governments over laws that impinged on their profits dissuade governments from adopting tough antipollution regulations, for fear of getting sued?

These questions were not debated by government negotiators, nor was any attempt made to resolve their obvious contradictions. Not that there was ever any question about which side would win should any of the competing pledges to cut emissions and knock down commercial barriers ever come into direct conflict: the commitments made in the climate negotiations all effectively functioned on the honor system, with a weak and unthreatening mechanism to penalize countries that failed to keep their promises. The commitments made under trade agreements, however, were enforced by a dispute settlement system with real teeth, and failure to comply would land governments in trade court, often facing harsh penalties.

In fact, the hierarchy was so clear that the climate negotiators formally declared their subservience to the trading system from the start. When the U.N. climate agreement was signed at the Rio Earth Summit in 1992, it made clear that "measures taken to combat climate change, including unilateral ones, should not constitute . . . a disguised restriction on international trade." (Similar language appears in the Kyoto Protocol.) As Australian political scientist Robyn Eckersley puts it, this was "the pivotal moment that set the shape of the relationship between the climate and trade regimes" because, "Rather than push for the recalibration of the international trade rules to conform with the requirements of climate protection . . . the Parties to the climate regime have ensured that liberalized trade and an expanding global economy have been protected against trade-restrictive climate policies." This practically guaranteed that the negotiating process would be unable to reckon with the kinds of bold but "trade-restrictive" policy options that could have been coordinated internationally—from buy-local renewable energy programs to restrictions on trade in goods produced with particularly high carbon footprints.

A few isolated voices were well aware that the modest gains being made in the negotiations over "sustainable development" were being actively unmade by the new trade and investment architecture. One of those voices belonged to Martin Khor, then director of the Third World Network, which has been a key advisor to developing country governments in both trade and climate talks. At the end of the 1992 Rio Earth Summit, Khor cautioned that there was a "general feeling among Southern country delegates . . . that events outside the [summit] process were threatening to weaken the South further and to endanger whatever positive elements exist in" the Rio agenda. The examples he cited were the austerity policies being pushed at the time by the World Bank and the International Monetary Fund, as well as the trade negotiations that would soon result in the creation of the WTO.

Another early warning was sounded by Steven Shrybman, who observed a decade and a half ago that the global export of industrial agriculture had already dealt a devastating blow to any possible progress on emissions. In a paper published in 2000, Shrybman argued that "the globalization of agricultural systems over recent decades is likely to have been one of the most important causes of overall increases in greenhouse gas emissions."

This had far less to do with current debates about the "food miles" associated with imported versus local produce than with the way in which the trade system, by granting companies like Monsanto and Cargill their regulatory wish list— from unfettered market access to aggressive patent protection to the maintenance of their rich subsidies has helped to entrench and expand the energy-intensive, higher-emissions model of industrial agriculture around the world. This, in turn, is a major explanation for why the global food system now accounts for between 19 and 29 percent of world greenhouse gas emissions. "Trade policy and rules actually drive climate change in a very structural way in respect of food systems," Shrybman stressed in an interview.

The habit of willfully erasing the climate crisis from trade agreements continues to this day: for instance, in early 2014, several negotiating documents for the proposed Trans-Pacific Partnership, a controversial new NAFTA-style trade deal spanning twelve countries, were released to the public via WikiLeaks and the Peruvian human rights group RedGE. A draft of the environment chapter had contained language stating that countries "acknowledge climate change as a global concern that requires collective action and recognize the importance of implementation of their respective commitments under the United Nations Framework Convention on Climate Change (UNFCCC)." The language was vague and non-binding, but at least it was a tool that governments could use to defend themselves should their climate policies be challenged in a trade tribunal, as Ontario's plan was. But a later document showed that U.S. negotiators had proposed an edit: take out all the stuff about climate change and UNFCCC commitments. In other words, while trade has repeatedly been allowed to trump climate, under no circumstances would climate be permitted to trump trade.

Nor was it only the trade negotiators who blocked out the climate crisis as they negotiated agreements that would send emissions soaring and make many solutions to this problem illegal. The climate negotiations exhibited their own special form of denial. In the early and mid-1990s, while the first climate protocol was being drafted, these negotiators, along with the Intergovernmental Panel on Climate Change, hashed out the details of precisely how countries should measure and monitor how much carbon they were emitting—a necessary process since governments were on the verge of pledging their first round of emission reductions, which would need to be reported and monitored.

The emissions accounting system on which they settled was an odd relic of the pre-free trade era that took absolutely no account of the revolutionary changes unfolding right under their noses regarding how (and where) the world's goods were being manufactured. For instance, emissions from the transportation of goods across borders—all those container ships, whose traffic has increased by nearly 400 percent over the last twenty years—are not formally attributed to any nation-state and therefore no one country is responsible for reducing their polluting impact. (And there remains little momentum at the U.N. for changing that, despite the reality that shipping emissions are set to double or even triple by 2050.)

And fatefully, countries are responsible only for the pollution they create inside their own borders not for the pollution produced in the manufacturing of goods that are shipped to their shores; those are attributed to the countries where the goods were produced. This means that the emissions that went into produc-ing, say, the television in my living room, appear nowhere on Canada's emissions ledger, but rather are attributed entirely to China's ledger, because that is where the set was made. And the international emissions from the container ship that carried my TV across the ocean (and then sailed back again) aren't entered into anyone's account book.

This deeply flawed system has created a vastly distorted picture of the drivers of global emissions. It has allowed rapidly de-industrializing wealthy states to claim that their emissions have stabilized or even gone down when, in fact, the emissions embedded in their consumption have soared during the free trade era. For in-stance, in 2011, the *Proceedings of the National Academy of Sciences* published a study of the emissions from industrialized countries that signed the Kyoto Protocol. It found that while their emissions had stopped growing, that was partly because international trade had allowed these countries to move their dirty production overseas. The researchers concluded that the rise in emissions from goods pro-duced in developing countries but consumed in industrialized ones was *six times* greater than the emissions savings of industrialized countries.

CHEAP LABOR, DIRTY ENERGY: A PACKAGE DEAL

As the free trade system was put in place and producing offshore became the rule, emissions did more than move—they multiplied. As mentioned earlier, before the neoliberal era, emissions growth had been slowing, from 4.5 percent annual increases in the 1960s to about 1 percent a year in the 1990s. But the new millennium was a watershed: between 2000 and 2008, the growth rate reached 3.4 percent a year, shooting past the highest IPCC projections of the day. In 2009, it dipped due to the financial crisis, but made up for lost time with the historic 5.9 percent increase in 2010 that left climate watchers reeling. (In mid-2014, two decades after the creation of the WTO, the IPCC finally acknowledged the reality of globalization and noted in its Fifth Assessment Report, "A growing share of total anthropogenic CO_2 emissions is released in the manufacture of products that are traded across international borders.")

The reason for what Andreas Malm—a Swedish expert on the history of coal—describes as "the early 21st Century emissions explosion" is straightforward enough. When China became the "workshop of the world" it also became the coal-spewing "chimney of the world." By 2007, China was responsible for two thirds of the annual increase in global emissions. Some of that was the result of China's own internal development—bringing electricity to rural areas, and building roads. But a lot of it was directly tied to foreign trade: according to one study, between 2002 and 2008, 48 percent of China's total emissions was related to producing goods for export.

"One of the reasons why we're in the climate crisis is because of this model of globalization," says Margrete Strand Rangnes, executive vice president at Public Citizen, a Washington-based policy institute that has been at the forefront of the fight against free trade. And that, she says, is a problem that requires "a pretty fundamental re-formation of our economy, if we're going to do this right."

International trade deals were only one of the reasons that governments embraced this particular model of fast-and-dirty, export-led development, and every country had its own peculiarities. In many cases (though not China's), the conditions attached to loans from the International Monetary Fund and World Bank were a major factor, so was the economic orthodoxy imparted to elite students at schools like Harvard and the University of Chicago. All of these and other factors played a role in shaping what was (never ironically) referred to as the Washington Consensus. Underneath it all is the constant drive for endless economic growth, a drive that, as will be explored later on, goes much deeper than the trade history of the past few decades. But there is no question that the trade architecture and the economic ideology embedded within it played a central role in sending emissions into hyperdrive.

That's because one of the primary driving forces of the particular trade system designed in the 1980s and 1990s was always to allow multinationals the freedom to scour the globe in search of the cheapest and most exploitable labor force. It was a journey that passed through Mexico and Central America's sweatshop maquiladoras and had a long stopover in South Korea. But by the end of the 1990s, virtually all roads led to China, a country where wages were extraordinarily low, trade unions were brutally suppressed, and the state was willing to spend seemingly limitless funds on massive infrastructure projects—modern ports, sprawling highway systems, endless numbers of coal-fired power plants, massive dams—all to ensure that the lights stayed on in the factories and the goods made it from the assembly lines onto the container ships on time. A free trader's dream, in other words—and a climate nightmare.

A nightmare because there is a close correlation between low wages and high emissions, or as Malm puts it, "a causal link between the quest for cheap and disciplined labor power and rising CO_2 emissions." And why wouldn't there be? The same logic that is willing to work laborers to the bone for pennies a day will burn mountains of dirty coal while spending next to nothing on pollution controls because it's the cheapest way to produce. So when the factories moved to China, they also got markedly dirtier. As Malm points out, Chinese coal use was declining slightly between 1995 and 2000, only for the explosion in manufacturing to send it soaring once again. It's not that the companies moving their production to China wanted to drive up emissions: they were after the cheap labor, but exploited workers and an exploited planet are, it turns out, a package deal. A destabilized climate is the cost of deregulated, global capitalism, its unintended, yet unavoidable consequence.

This connection between pollution and labor exploitation has been true since the earliest days of the Industrial Revolution. But in the past, when workers organized to demand better wages, and when city dwellers organized to demand cleaner air, the companies were pretty much forced to improve both working and environmental standards. That changed with the advent of free trade: thanks to the removal of virtually all barriers to capital flows, corporations could pick up and leave every time labor costs started rising. That's why many large manufacturers left South Korea for China in the late 1990s, and it's why many are now leaving China, where wages are climbing, for Bangladesh, where they are significantly lower. So while our clothes, electronics, and furniture may be made in China, the economic model was primarily made in the U.S.A.

And yet when the subject of climate change comes up in discussion in wealthy, industrialized countries, the instant response, very often, is that it's all China's fault (and India's fault and Brazil's fault and so on). Why bother cutting our own emissions when everyone knows that the fast developing economies are the real problem, opening more coal plants every month than we could ever close? This argument is made as if we in the West are mere spectators to this reckless and dirty model of economic growth. As if it was not our governments and our multinationals that pushed a model of export-led development that made all of this possible. It is said as if it were not our own corporations who, with single-minded determination (and with full participation from China's autocratic rulers), turned the Pearl River Delta into their carbon-spewing special economic zone, with the goods going straight onto container ships headed to our superstores. All in the name of feeding the god of economic growth (via the altar of hyper-consumption) in every country in the world.

The victims in all this are regular people: the workers who lose their factory jobs in Juárez and Windsor; the workers who get the factory jobs in Shenzhen and Dhaka, jobs that are by this point so degraded that some employers install nets along the perimeters of roofs to catch employees when they jump, or where safety codes are so lax that workers are killed in the hundreds when buildings collapse. The victims are also the toddlers mouthing lead-laden toys; the Walmart employee expected to work over the Thanksgiving holiday only to be trampled by a stampede of frenzied customers, while still not earning a living wage. And the Chinese villagers whose water is contaminated by one of those coal plants we use as our excuse for inaction, as well as the middle class of Beijing and Shanghai whose kids are forced to play inside because the air is so foul.

A MOVEMENT DIGS ITS OWN GRAVE

The greatest tragedy of all is that so much of this was eminently avoidable. We knew about the climate crisis when the rules of the new trade system were being written. After all, NAFTA was signed just one year after governments, including the United States, signed the United Nations Framework Convention on Climate Change in Rio. And it was by no means inevitable that these deals would go though. A strong coalition of North American labor and environmental groups opposed NAFTA precisely because they knew it would drive down labor and environmental standards. For a time it even looked as if they would win.

Public opinion in all three countries was deeply divided, so much so that when Bill Clinton ran for president in 1992, he pledged that he would not sign NAFTA until it substantively reflected those concerns. In Canada Jean Chrétien campaigned for prime minister against the deal in the election of 1993. Once both were in office, however, the deal was left intact and two toothless side agreements were tacked on, one for labor and one for environmental standards. The labor movement knew better than to fall for this ploy and continued to forcefully oppose the deal, as did many Democrats in the U.S. But for a complex set of reasons that will be explored later, having to do with a combination of reflexive political centrism and the growing influence of corporate "partners" and donors, the leadership of many large environmental organizations decided to play ball. "One by one, former NAFTA opponents and skeptics became enthusiastic supporters, and said so publicly," writes journalist Mark Dowie in his critical history of the U.S. environmental movement, *Losing Ground*. These Big Green groups even created their own pro-NAFTA organization, the Environmental Coalition for NAFTA— which included the National Wildlife Federation, the Environmental Defense Fund, Conservation International, the National Audubon Society, the Natural Resources Defense Council, and the World Wildlife Fund—which, according to Dowie, provided its "unequivocal support to the agreement." Jay Hair, then head of the National Wildlife Federation, even flew to Mexico on an official U.S. trade mission to lobby his Mexican counterparts, while attacking his critics for "putting their protectionist polemics ahead of concern for the environment."

Not everyone in the green movement hopped on the pro-trade bandwagon: Greenpeace, Friends of the Earth, and the Sierra Club, as well as many small organizations, continued to oppose NAFTA. But that didn't matter to the Clinton administration, which had what it wanted—the ability to tell a skeptical public that "groups representing 80 percent of national [environmental] group membership have endorsed NAFTA." And that was important, because Clinton faced an uphill battle getting NAFTA through Congress, with many in his own party pledging to vote against the deal. John Adams, then director of the Natural Resources Defense Council, succinctly described the extraordinarily helpful role played by groups like his: "We broke the back of the environmental opposition to NAFTA. After we established our position Clinton only had labor to fight. We did him a big favor."

Indeed when the president signed NAFTA into law in 1993, he made a special point of thanking "the environmental people who came out and worked through this—many of them at great criticism, particularly in the environmental movement." Clinton also made it clear that this victory was about more than one agreement. "Today we have the chance to do what our parents did before us. We have the opportunity to remake the world." He explained that, "We are on the verge of a global economic expansion.... Already the confidence we've displayed by ratifying NAFTA has begun to bear fruit. We are now making real progress toward a worldwide trade agreement so significant that it could make the material gains of NAFTA for our country look small by comparison." He was referring to the World Trade Organization. And just in case anyone was still worried about the environmental consequences, Clinton offered his personal assurance. "We will seek new institutional arrangements to ensure that trade leaves the world cleaner than before."

Standing by the president's side was his vice president, Al Gore, who had been largely responsible for getting so many Big Green groups on board. Given this history, it should hardly come as a surprise that the mainstream environmental movement has been in no rush to draw attention to the disastrous climate impacts of the free trade era. To do so would only highlight their own active role in helping the U.S. government to, in Clinton's words, "remake the world." Much better, as we will see later on, to talk about light bulbs and fuel efficiency.

The significance of the NAFTA signing was indeed historic, tragically so. Because if the environmental movement had not been so agreeable, NAFTA might have been blocked or renegotiated to set a different kind of precedent. A new trade architecture could have been built that did not actively sabotage the fragile global climate change consensus. Instead—as had been the promise and hope of the 1992 Rio Earth Summit—this new architecture could have been grounded in the need to fight poverty and reduce emissions at the same time. So for example, trade access to developing countries could have been tied to transfers of resources and green technology so that critical new electricity and transit infrastructure was low carbon from the outset. And the deals could have been written to ensure that any measures taken to support renewable energy would not be penalized and, in fact, could be rewarded. The global economy might not have grown as quickly as it did, but it also would not be headed rapidly off the climate cliff.

The errors of this period cannot be undone, but it is not too late for a new kind of climate movement to take up the fight against so-called free trade and build this needed architecture now. That doesn't—and never had—meant an end to economic exchange across borders. It does, however, mean a far more thoughtful and deliberate approach to why we trade and whom it serves. Encouraging the frenetic and indiscriminate consumption of essentially disposable products can no longer be the system's goal. Goods must once again be made to last, and the use of energy-intensive long-haul transport will need to be rationed—reserved for those cases where goods cannot be produced locally or where local production is more carbon-intensive. (For example, growing food in greenhouses in cold parts of the United States is often more energy intensive than growing it in warmer regions and shipping it by light rail.)

According to Ilana Solomon, trade analyst for the Sierra Club, this is not a fight that the climate movement can avoid. "In order to combat climate change, there's a real need to start localizing our economies again, and thinking about how and what we're purchasing and how it's produced. And the most basic rule of trade law is you can't privilege domestic over foreign. So how do you tackle the idea of needing to incentivize local economies, tying together local green jobs policies with clean energy policies, when that is just a no-go in trade policy? . . . If we don't think about how the economy is structured, then we're actually never going to the real root of the problem."

These kinds of economic reforms would be good news—for unemployed workers, for farmers unable to compete with cheap imports, for communities that have seen their manufacturers move offshore and their local businesses replaced with big box stores. And all of these constituencies would be needed to fight for these policies, since they represent the reversal of the thirty-year trend of removing every possible limit on corporate power.

FROM FRENETIC EXPANSION TO STEADY STATES

Challenging free trade orthodoxy is a heavy lift in our political culture; anything that has been in place for that long takes on an air of inevitability. But, critical as these shifts are, they are not enough to lower emissions in time. To do that, we will need to confront a logic even more entrenched than free trade—the logic of indiscriminate economic growth. This idea has understandably inspired a good deal of resistance among more liberal climate watchers, who insist that the task is merely to paint our current growth-based economic model green, so it's worth examining the numbers behind the claim.

It is Kevin Anderson of the Tyndall Centre for Climate Change Research, and one of Britain's top climate experts, who has most forcefully built the case that our growth-based economic logic is now in fundamental conflict with atmospheric limits. Addressing everyone from the U.K. Department for International Development to the Manchester City Council, Anderson has spent more than a decade patiently translating the implications of the latest climate science to politicians, economists, and campaigners. In clear and understandable language, the spiky-haired former mechanical engineer (who used to work in the petrochemical sector) lays out a rigorous road map for cutting our emissions down to a level that provides a decent shot at keeping global temperature rise below 2 degrees Celsius.

But in recent years Anderson's papers and slide shows have become more alarming. Under titles such as "Climate Change: Going Beyond Dangerous . . . Brutal Numbers and Tenuous Hope," he points out that the chances of staying within anything like safe temperature levels are diminishing fast. With his colleague Alice Bows-Larkin, an atmospheric physicist and climate change mitigation expert at the Tyndall Centre, Anderson argues that we have lost so much time to political stalling and weak climate policies—all while emissions ballooned—that we are now facing cuts so drastic that they challenge the core expansionist logic at the heart of our economic system.

They argue that, if the governments of developed countries want a fifty-fifty chance of hitting the agreed-upon international target of keeping warming below 2 degrees Celsius, and if reductions are to respect any kind of equity principle between rich and poor nations, then wealthy countries need to start cutting their greenhouse gas emissions by something like 8 to 10 percent a year—and they need to start right now. The idea that such deep cuts are required used to be controversial in the mainstream climate community, where the deadlines for steep reductions always seemed to be far off in the future (an 80 percent cut by 2050, for instance). But as emissions have soared and as tipping points loom, that is changing rapidly. Even Yvo de Boer, who held the U.N.'s top climate position until 2009, remarked recently that "the only way" negotiators "can achieve a 2-degree goal is to shut down the whole global economy."

That is a severe overstatement, yet it underlines Anderson and Bows-Larkin's point that we cannot achieve 8 to 10 percent annual cuts with the array of modest carbon-pricing or green tech solutions usually advocated by Big Green. These measures will certainly help, but they are simply not enough. That's because an 8 to 10 percent drop in emissions, year after year, is virtually unprecedented since we started powering our economies with coal. In fact, cuts above 1 percent per year "have historically been associated only with economic recession or upheaval," as the economist Nicholas Stem put it in his 2006 report for the British government.

Even after the Soviet Union collapsed, reductions of this duration and depth did not happen (the former Soviet countries experienced average annual reductions of roughly 5 percent over a period of ten years). Nor did this level of reduction happen beyond a single-year blip after Wall Street crashed in 2008. Only in the immediate aftermath of the great market crash of 1929 did the United States see emissions drop for several consecutive years by more than 10 percent annually, but that was the worst economic crisis of modern times.

If we are to avoid that kind of carnage while meeting our science-based emissions targets, carbon reduction must be managed carefully through what Anderson and Bows-Larkin describe as "radical and immediate de-growth strategies in the US, EU and other wealthy nations."*

Now, I realize that this can all sound apocalyptic—as if reducing emissions requires economic crises that result in mass suffering. But that seems so only because we have an economic system that fetishizes GDP growth above all else, regardless of the human or ecological consequences, while failing to place value on those things that most of us cherish above all—a decent standard of living, a measure of future security, and our relationships with one another. So what Anderson and Bows-Larkin are really saying is that there is still time to avoid catastrophic warming, but not within the rules of capitalism as they are currently constructed. Which is surely the best argument there has ever been for changing those rules.

Rather than pretending that we can solve the climate crisis without rocking the economic boat, Anderson and Bows-Larkin argue, the time has come to tell the truth, to "liberate the science from the economics, finance and astrology, stand by the conclusions however uncomfortable . . . we need to have the audacity to think differently and conceive of alternative futures."

Interestingly, Anderson says that when he presents his radical findings in climate circles, the core facts are rarely disputed. What he hears most often are confessions from colleagues that they have simply given up hope of meeting the 2 degree temperature target, precisely because reaching it would require such a profound challenge to economic growth. "This position is shared by many senior scientists and economists advising government," Anderson reports.

In other words, changing the earth's climate in ways that will be chaotic and disastrous is easier to accept than the prospect of changing the fundamental, growth-based, profit-seeking logic of capitalism. We probably shouldn't be surprised that some climate scientists are a little spooked by the radical implications of their own research. Most of them were quietly measuring ice cores, running global climate models, and studying ocean acidification, only to discover, as Australian climate expert and author Clive Hamilton puts it, that in breaking the news of the depth of our collective climate failure, they "were unwittingly destabilizing the political and social order."

Nonetheless, that order has now been destabilized, which means that the rest of us are going to have to quickly figure out how to turn "managed degrowth" into something that looks a lot less like the Great Depression and a lot more like what some innovative economic thinkers have taken to calling "The Great Transition."

Over the past decade, many boosters of green capitalism have tried to gloss over the clashes between market logic and ecological limits by touting the wonders of green tech, or the "decoupling" of environmental impacts from economic activity. They paint a picture of a world that can continue to

---

*And they don't let developing countries like China and India off the hook. According to their projections, developing countries can have just one more decade to continue to increase their emissions to aid their efforts to pull themselves out of poverty while switching over to green energy sources. By 2025, they would need to be cutting emissions "at an unprecedented 7 per cent" a year as well.

function pretty much as it does now, but in which our power will come from renewable energy and all of our various gadgets and vehicles will become so much more energy-efficient that we can consume away without worrying about the impact.

If only humanity's relationship with natural resources was that simple. While it is true that renewable technologies hold tremendous promise to lower emissions, the kinds of measures that would do so on the scale we need involve building vast new electricity grids and transportation systems, often from the ground up. Even if we started construction tomorrow, it would realistically take many years, perhaps decades, before the new systems were up and running. Moreover, since we don't yet have economies powered by clean energy, all that green construction would have to burn a lot of fossil fuels in the interim—a necessary process, but one that wouldn't lower our emissions fast enough. Deep emission cuts in the wealthy nations have to start immediately. That means that if we wait for what Bows-Larkin describes as the "whiz-bang technologies" to come online "it will be too little too late."

So what to do in the meantime? Well, we do what we can. And what we can do—what doesn't require a technological and infrastructure revolution—is to consume less, right away. Policies based on encouraging people to consume less are far more difficult for our current political class to embrace than policies that are about encouraging people to consume green. Consuming green just means substituting one power source for another, or one model of consumer goods for a more efficient one. The reason we have placed all of our eggs in the green tech and green efficiency basket is precisely because these changes are safely within market logic—indeed, they encourage us to go out and buy more new, efficient, green cars and washing machines.

Consuming less, however, means changing how much energy we actually use: how often we drive, how often we fly, whether our food has to be flown to get to us, whether the goods we buy are built to last or to be replaced in two years, how large our homes are. And these are the sorts of policies that have been neglected so far. For instance, as researchers Rebecca Willis and Nick Eyre argue in a report for the U.K.'s Green Alliance, despite the fact that groceries represent roughly 12 percent of greenhouse gas emissions in Britain, "there is virtually no government policy which is aimed at changing the way we produce, incentivising farmers for low energy farming, or how we consume, incentivising consumption of local and seasonal food." Similarly, "there are incentives to drive more efficient cars, but very little is done to discourage car dependent settlement patterns."

Plenty of people are attempting to change their daily lives in ways that do reduce their consumption. But if these sorts of demand-side emission reductions are to take place on anything like the scale required, they cannot be left to the lifestyle decisions of earnest urbanites who like going to farmers' markets on Saturday afternoons and wearing up-cycled clothing. We will need comprehensive policies and programs that make low-carbon choices easy and convenient for everyone. Most of all, these policies need to be fair, so that the people already struggling to cover the basics are not being asked to make additional sacrifice to offset the excess consumption of the rich. That means cheap public transit and clean light rail accessible to all; affordable, energy-efficient housing along those transit lines; cities planned for high-density living; bike lanes in which riders aren't asked to risk their lives to get to work; land management that discourages sprawl and encourages local, low-energy forms of agriculture; urban design that clusters essential services like schools and health care along transit routes and in pedestrian-friendly areas; programs that require manufacturers to be responsible for the electronic waste they produce, and to radically reduce built-in redundancies and obsolescences.*

And as hundreds of millions gain access to modern energy for the first time, those who are consuming far more energy than they need would have to consume less. How much less? Climate change deniers like to claim that environmentalists want to return us to the Stone Age. The truth is that if we want to live within ecological limits, we would need to return to a lifestyle similar to the one we had in the 1970s, before consumption levels wont crazy in the 1980s. Not exactly the various forms of hardship and deprivation evoked at Heartland conferences. As Kevin Anderson explains: "We need to give newly industrializing countries in the world the space to develop and improve the welfare and well-being of their people. This means more cuts in energy use by the developed world. It also means lifestyle changes which will have most impact on the wealthy. . . . We've done this in the past. In the 1960s and 1970s we enjoyed a healthy and moderate lifestyle and we need to return to this to keep emissions under control. It is a matter of the well-off 20 percent in a population taking the largest cuts. A more even society might result and we would certainly benefit from a lower carbon and more sustainable way of life."

There is no doubt that these types of policies have countless benefits besides lower emissions. They encourage civic space, physical activity, community building, as well as cleaner air and water. They also do a huge amount to reduce inequality, since it is low-income people, often people of color, who benefit most from improvements in public housing and public transit. And if strong living-wage and hire-local provisions were included in transition plans, they could also benefit most from the jobs building and running those expanded services, while becoming less dependent on jobs in dirty industries that have been disproportionately concentrated in low-income communities of color.

As Phaedra Ellis-Lamkins of the environmental justice organization Green for All puts it, "The tools we use to combat climate change are the same tools we can use to change the game for low-income Americans and people of color. . . . We need Congress to make the investments necessary to upgrade and repair our crumbling infrastructure—from building seawalls that protect shoreline communities to fixing our storm-water systems. Doing so will create family-sustaining, local jobs. Improving our storm-water infrastructure alone

---

*A law passed by the European Parliament that would require that all cell phone manufacturers offer a common battery charger is a small step in the right direction. Similarly, requiring that electronics manufacturers use recycled metals like copper could save a great many communities from one of the most toxic mining processes in the world.

would put 2 million Americans to work. We need to make sure that people of color are a part of the business community and workforce building these new systems."

Another way of thinking about this is that what is needed is a fundamental reordering of the component parts of Gross Domestic Product. GDP is traditionally understood to consist of *consumption* plus *investment* plus *government spending* plus *net exports*. The free market capitalism of the past three decades has put the emphasis particularly on consumption and trade. But as we remake our economies to stay within our global carbon budget, we need to see less consumption (except among the poor), less trade (as we relocalize our economies), and less private investment in producing for excessive consumption. These reductions would be offset by increased government spending, and increased public and private investment in the infrastructure and alternatives needed to reduce our emissions to zero. Implicit in all of this is a great deal more redistribution, so that more of us can live comfortably within the planet's capacity.

Which is precisely why, when climate change deniers claim that global warming is a plot to redistribute wealth, it's not (only) because they are paranoid. It's also because they are paying attention.

GROWING THE CARING ECONOMY, SHRINKING THE CARELESS ONE

A great deal of thought in recent years has gone into how reducing our use of material resources could be managed in ways that actually improve quality of life overall—what the French call "selective degrowth."* Policies like luxury taxes could be put in place to discourage wasteful consumption. The money raised could be used to support those parts of our economics that are already low-carbon and therefore do not need to contract. Obviously a huge number of jobs would be created in the sectors that are part of the green transition— in mass transit, renewable energy, weatherization, and ecosystem restoration. And those sectors that are not governed by the drive for increased yearly profit (the public sector, co-ops, local businesses, nonprofits) would expand their share of overall economic activity, as would those sectors with minimal ecological impact (such as the caregiving professions, which tend to be occupied by women and people of color and therefore underpaid). "Expanding our economies in these directions has all sorts of advantages," Tim Jackson, an economist at the University of Surrey and author of *Prosperity Without Growth*, has written. "In the first place, the time spent by these professions directly improves the quality of our lives. Making them more and more efficient is not, after a certain point, actually desirable. What sense does it make to ask our teachers to teach ever bigger classes? Our doctors to treat more and more patients per hour?"

---

*In French, "decroissance" has the double meaning of challenging both growth, *croissance*, and *croire*, to believe—invoking the idea of choosing not to believe in the fiction of perpetual growth on a finite planet.

There could be other benefits too, like shorter work hours, in part to create more jobs, but also because overworked people have less time to engage in low-consumption activities like gardening and cooking (because they are just too busy). Indeed, a number of researchers have analyzed the very concrete climate benefits of working less. John Stutz, a senior fellow at the Boston-based Tellus Institute, envisions that "hours of paid work and income could converge worldwide at substantially lower levels than is seen in the developed countries today." If countries aimed for somewhere around three to four days a week, introduced gradually over a period of decades, he argues, it could offset much of the emissions growth projected through 2030 while improving quality of life.

Many degrowth and economic justice thinkers also call for the introduction of a basic annual income, a wage given to every person, regardless of income, as a recognition that the system cannot provide jobs for everyone and that it is counterproductive to force people to work in jobs that simply fuel consumption. As Alyssa Battistoni, an editor at the journal *Jacobin*, writes, "While making people work shitty jobs to 'earn' a living has always been spiteful, it's now starting to seem suicidal."

A basic income that discourages shitty work (and wasteful consumption) would also have the benefit of providing much-needed economic security in the front-line communities that are being asked to sacrifice their health so that oil companies can refine tar sands oil or gas companies can drill another fracking well. Nobody wants to have their water contaminated or have their kids suffer from asthma. But desperate people can be counted on to do desperate things—which is why we all have a vested interest in taking care of one another so that many fewer communities are faced with those impossible choices. That means rescuing the idea of safety net that ensures that everyone has the basics covered: health care, education, food, and clean water. Indeed, fighting inequality on every front and through multiple means must be understood as a central strategy in the battle against climate change.

This kind of carefully planned economy holds out the possibility of much more humane, fulfilling lifestyles than the vast majority of us at experiencing under our current system, which is what makes the idea of massive social movement coalescing behind such demands a real possibility But these policies are also the most politically challenging.

Unlike encouraging energy efficiency, the measures we must take to secure a just, equitable, and inspiring transition away from fossil fuels clash directly with our reigning economic orthodoxy at every level. As we will see, such a shift breaks all the ideological rules—it requires visionary long-term planning, tough regulation of business, higher levels of taxation for the affluent, big public sector expenditure, and in many cases reversals of core privatizations in order to give communities the power to make the changes they desire. In short, it means changing everything about how we think about the economy so that our pollution doesn't change everything about our physical world.

QUESTIONS FOR MAKING CONNECTIONS
WITHIN THE READING

1. Klein describes economic and environmental concerns as "two solitudes." Her point is that twentieth- and twenty-first thinking about global trade has evolved in almost complete isolation from thinking about climate change. Looking back over her chapter, retrace the development of each "solitude," paying particular attention to the motivations driving them. What agendas are responsible for international treaties like NAFTA? Who are the key players; who gets included and who gets excluded from the process of decision-making? Now, do the same for the movement to reduce emissions and create truly renewable energy. How might we explain the continued isolation of these two "solitudes" from one another? Is the problem created by unnecessary misunderstandings, or by fundamentally incompatible ways of thinking?

2. What *political* lessons can be learned from the situation Klein describes? Is there such a thing as a global political community? What role does the United Nations play, if any? What role do multinational corporations play? To what extent are the key decision-makers the wealthiest and most powerful nations, and what role do the smaller and less developed countries play? Who, exactly, defines the rules of the game when it comes to trade and energy policy? Can we say that our decisions about the fate of the earth have been democratic, autocratic, oligarchic or anarchistic? According to Klein, what can be achieved by the collaboration of individual citizens? What might be the limits to such collaboration?

3. Discuss the relationship between growth and degrowth. As you define the two terms, consider the ways of life that each aspires to create. What are the key objectives of growth? Of degrowth? Would it be fair to say that accepting the idea of degrowth requires us to part ways with our desire for material security and personal happiness? Or is it the case, instead, that degrowth would offer us security and happiness in a new and different way? Are growth and degrowth different paths to the same destination, or do they lead in fundamentally opposing directions?

QUESTIONS FOR WRITING

1. What is the relation between fact and opinion in Klein's chapter—not only Klein's own opinions but those of the figures she discusses: Paulo Maccario, Al Gore, Joseph Stiglitz, Bill Clinton, and others? How can different people, looking at the same evidence, reach different conclusions? To what extent is our interpretation of the evidence predetermined by the assumptions we bring to it? Based on your understanding of global climate change, would you be willing to say that everything is a matter of perspective? Or is there a point at which certain viewpoints become unsustainable? Is personal experience more powerful than fact in changing opinions?

2. As Klein observes, "Challenging free trade orthodoxy is a heavy lift in our political culture." Why do economic calculations so readily trump all other concerns—political, ethical, religious, psychological, medical, and aesthetic? Some contemporary theorists have argued that politics no longer really exists, if we mean by that word the ability of citizens to determine their own destiny through deliberation and debate. Is our failure to protect the environment really a political failure? Or is it really a deeper, cultural failure—an inability to imagine an alternative way of life? What brings us the greatest sense of wellbeing? Consumer goods? Texting? Interacting with friends? Where does the natural world fit in?

QUESTIONS FOR MAKING CONNECTIONS
BETWEEN READINGS

1. Klein suggests that one milestone in popular awareness about the environmental crisis was *Time* magazine's decision to name our planet, the Earth, its 1988 "Man of the Year." She also quotes at length from journalist Thomas Sancton's article in that edition of *Time*. There, Sancton connects the crisis to Western religious ideas:

    > In many pagan societies, the earth was seen as a mother, a fertile giver of life. Nature—the soil, forest, sea—was endowed with divinity, and mortals were subordinate to it. The Judeo-Christian tradition introduced a radically different concept. The earth was the creation of a monotheistic God, who, after shaping it, ordered its inhabitants, in the words of Genesis: "Be fruitful and multiply, and replenish the earth and subdue it: and have dominion over the fish of the sea and over the fowl of the air and over every living thing that moveth upon the earth." The idea of dominion could be interpreted as an invitation to use nature as a convenience.

    To what extent do we find Sancton's argument confirmed by Karen Armstrong's "*Homo religiosus*"? Do experiences like *kenosis* encourage people to the view nature as "as a convenience"? Do they connect people to nature or distance them from it? Using Klein's discussion as your guide, discuss the values and attitudes that underlie the global economy. Are those the same values that Armstrong sees as fundamental to religious experience? If people today rediscovered *kenosis*, would they feel differently about protecting the natural world?

2. In "Immune to Reality," the psychologist Daniel Gilbert makes the case that we all fare poorly when it comes to what he calls "affective forecasting." Our tendency to "cook the facts," along with other unconscious reactions to events—the inescapability trigger or explaining away, for example—prevent us from predicting accurately what will actually make us happy in the long run. To what extent is our pursuit of unlimited growth, as Klein describes it in her chapter, also "immune to reality"? Can the mechanisms Gilbert describes help explain why we have so far failed to address the problem of global climate change? Would Gilbert support Klein's plan for "degrowth" and a "steady state" economy as better a better strategy for "stumbling into happiness"?

JONATHAN LETHEM

CRITICS OFTEN USE the word *prolific* to describe Jonathan Lethem. He has published nine novels, five collections of stories, two essay volumes, a novella, and a comic book. But a better word for him might be *protean*. In the religion of the ancient Greeks, Proteus was a god of the sea who presided over unexpected change, a power that gave him the ability to alter his shape whenever humans tried to compel him to foretell events. Like the mythical Proteus, Lethem is a shape-shifter whose work threads across boundaries of all kinds—the boundaries between detective fiction, for example, and the "serious" literature of ideas. What Lethem has written about New York might be said to encapsulate his view of both life and art:

> To live in Manhattan is to be persistently amazed at the worlds squirreled inside one another, like those lines of television cable and fresh water and steam heat and outgoing sewage and telephone wire and whatever else which cohabit in the same intestinal holes that pavement-demolishing workmen periodically wrench open.... We only pretend to live on something as orderly as a grid.

For Lethem, the writer's task is to look beneath the reassuring surface. He believes the truth is seldom found by stopping with the obvious or respecting conventions. Indeed, he sees the act of writing as fundamentally promiscuous.

Perhaps it is not at all surprising that Lethem would have some unexpected ideas about what it means to be creative. Normally we think of creativity as the ability to say or do something completely original, but the isolation implied by this belief strikes Lethem as unappealing. Instead, he celebrates what he calls the "ecstasy of influence." If we wish, we can treat words, ideas, and images as somebody's private property, but we can also view them as available for everyone to use. Nothing, he suggests, is totally original: everything is bound up with everything else, if not on the surface, then underneath, like the "lines of television cable and fresh water" hidden by the "grid." Once we give up the idea of the private ownership of culture, writing and thinking take on a new life, as acts of generosity that place us in debt to everyone who has made our creativity possible.

Lethem's argument is powerful, and many writers, artists, and scientists have experienced the *ecstasy* he describes. But where does that leave the writing done in the university itself? Most universities impose harsh penalties on plagiarists, the people who use the words of others without attribution—that is, without an acknowledgment of someone's prior ownership. Indeed, your own college or university might expel students found guilty of cheating. Where does cheating start and creativity stop?

The Ecstasy of Influence: A Plagiarism

> All mankind is of one author, and is one volume; when one man dies, one chapter is not torn out of the book, but translated into a better language; and every chapter must be so translated....
>
> —JOHN DONNE

Love and Theft

Consider this tale: a cultivated man of middle age looks back on the story of an *amour fou,* one beginning when, traveling abroad, he takes a room as a lodger. The moment he sees the daughter of the house, he is lost. She is a preteen, whose charms instantly enslave him. Heedless of her age, he becomes intimate with her. In the end she dies, and the narrator—marked by her forever—remains alone. The name of the girl supplies the title of the story: *Lolita.*

The author of the story I've described, Heinz von Lichberg, published his tale of Lolita in 1916, forty years before Vladimir Nabokov's novel. Lichberg later became a prominent journalist in the Nazi era, and his youthful works faded from view. Did Nabokov, who remained in Berlin until 1937, adopt Lichberg's tale consciously? Or did the earlier tale exist for Nabokov as a hidden, unacknowledged memory? The history of literature is not without examples of this phenomenon, called cryptomnesia. Another hypothesis is that Nabokov, knowing Lichberg's tale perfectly well, had set himself to that art of quotation that Thomas Mann, himself a master of it, called "higher cribbing." Literature has always been a crucible in which familiar themes are continually recast. Little of what we admire in Nabokov's *Lolita* is to be found in its predecessor; the former is in no way deducible from the latter. Still: did Nabokov consciously borrow and quote?

"When you live outside the law, you have to eliminate dishonesty." The line comes from Don Siegel's 1958 film noir, *The Lineup,* written by Stirling

Silliphant. The film still haunts revival houses, likely thanks to Eli Wallach's blazing portrayal of a sociopathic hit man and to Siegel's long, sturdy auteurist career. Yet what were those words worth—to Siegel, or Silliphant, or their audience—in 1958? And again: what was the line worth when Bob Dylan heard it (presumably in some Greenwich Village repertory cinema), cleaned it up a little, and inserted it into "Absolutely Sweet Marie"? What are they worth now, to the culture at large?

Appropriation has always played a key role in Dylan's music. The songwriter has grabbed not only from a panoply of vintage Hollywood films but from Shakespeare and F. Scott Fitzgerald and Junichi Saga's *Confessions of a Yakuza.* He also nabbed the title of Eric Lott's study of minstrelsy for his 2001 album *Love and Theft.* One imagines Dylan liked the general resonance of the title, in which emotional misdemeanors stalk the sweetness of love, as they do so often in Dylan's songs. Lott's title is, of course, itself a riff on Leslie Fiedler's *Love and Death in the American Novel,* which famously identifies the literary motif of the interdependence of a white man and a dark man, like Huck and Jim or Ishmael and Queequeg—a series of nested references to Dylan's own appropriating, minstrel-boy self. Dylan's art offers a paradox: while it famously urges us not to look back, it also encodes a knowledge of past sources that might otherwise have little home in contemporary culture, like the Civil War poetry of the Confederate bard Henry Timrod, resuscitated in lyrics on Dylan's newest record, *Modern Times.* Dylan's originality and his appropriations are as one.

The same might be said of *all* art. I realized this forcefully when one day I went looking for the John Donne passage quoted above. I know the lines, I confess, not from a college course but from the movie version of *84, Charing Cross Road* with Anthony Hopkins and Anne Bancroft. I checked out *84, Charing Cross Road* from the library in the hope of finding the Donne passage, but it wasn't in the book. It's alluded to in the play that was adapted from the book, but it isn't reprinted. So I rented the movie again, and there was the passage, read in voice-over by Anthony Hopkins but without attribution. Unfortunately, the line was also abridged so that, when I finally turned to the Web, I found myself searching for the line "all mankind is of one volume" instead of "all mankind is of one author, and is one volume."

My Internet search was initially no more successful than my library search. I had thought that summoning books from the vasty deep was a matter of a few keystrokes, but when I visited the website of the Yale library, I found that most of its books don't yet exist as computer text. As a last-ditch effort I searched the seemingly more obscure phrase "every chapter must be so translated." The passage I wanted finally came to me, as it turns out, not as part of a scholarly library collection but simply because someone who loves Donne had posted it on his homepage. The lines I sought were from Meditation 17 in *Devotions upon Emergent Occasions,* which happens to be the most famous thing Donne ever wrote, containing as it does the line "never send to know for whom the bell tolls; it tolls for thee." My search had led me from a movie to a book to a play to a website and back to a book. Then again, those words may be as famous as they are only because Hemingway lifted them for his book title.

Literature has been in a plundered, fragmentary state for a long time. When I was thirteen I purchased an anthology of Beat writing. Immediately, and to my very great excitement, I discovered one William S. Burroughs, author of something called *Naked Lunch,* excerpted there in all its coruscating brilliance. Burroughs was then as radical a literary man as the world had to offer. Nothing, in all my experience of literature since, has ever had as strong an effect on my sense of the sheer possibilities of writing. Later, attempting to understand this impact, I discovered that Burroughs had incorporated snippets of other writers' texts into his work, an action I knew my teachers would have called plagiarism. Some of these borrowings had been lifted from American science fiction of the Forties and Fifties, adding a secondary shock of recognition for me. By then I knew that this "cut-up method," as Burroughs called it, was central to whatever he thought he was doing, and that he quite literally believed it to be akin to magic. When he wrote about his process, the hairs on my neck stood up, so palpable was the excitement. Burroughs was interrogating the universe with scissors and a paste pot, and the least imitative of authors was no plagiarist at all.

Contamination Anxiety

In 1941, on his front porch, Muddy Waters recorded a song for the folklorist Alan Lomax. After singing the song, which he told Lomax was entitled "Country Blues," Waters described how he came to write it. "I made it on about the eighth of October '38," Waters said. "I was fixin' a puncture on a car. I had been mistreated by a girl. I just felt blue, and the song fell into my mind and it come to me just like that and I started singing." Then Lomax, who knew of the Robert Johnson recording called "Walkin' Blues," asked Waters if there were any other songs that used the same tune. "There's been some blues played like that," Waters replied. "This song comes from the cotton field and a boy once put a record out—Robert Johnson. He put it out as named 'Walkin' Blues.' I heard the tune before I heard it on the record. I learned it from Son House." In nearly one breath, Waters offers five accounts: his own active authorship: he "made it" on a specific date. Then the "passive" explanation: "it come to me just like that." After Lomax raises the question of influence, Waters, without shame, misgivings, or trepidation, says that he heard a version by Johnson, but that his mentor, Son House, taught it to him. In the middle of that complex genealogy, Waters declares that "this song comes from the cotton field."

Blues and jazz musicians have long been enabled by a kind of "open source" culture, in which pre-existing melodic fragments and larger musical frameworks are freely reworked. Technology has only multiplied the possibilities; musicians have gained the power to *duplicate* sounds literally rather than simply approximate them through allusion. In Seventies Jamaica, King Tubby and Lee "Scratch" Perry deconstructed recorded music, using astonishingly primitive pre-digital hardware, creating what they called "versions." The recombinant nature of their means of production quickly spread to DJs in New York and London. Today an endless, gloriously impure, and fundamentally social process generates countless hours of music.

Visual, sound, and text collage—which for many centuries were relatively fugitive traditions (a cento here, a folk pastiche there)—became explosively central to a series of movements in the twentieth century: futurism, cubism, Dada, musique concrète, situationism, pop art, and appropriationism. In fact, collage, the common denominator in that list, might be called *the* art form of the twentieth century, never mind the twenty-first. But forget, for the moment, chronologies, schools, or even centuries. As examples accumulate—Igor Stravinsky's music and Daniel Johnston's, Francis Bacon's paintings and Henry Darger's, the novels of the Oulipo group and of Hannah Crafts (the author who pillaged Dickens's *Bleak House* to write *The Bondwoman's Narrative),* as well as cherished texts that become troubling to their admirers after the discovery of their "plagiarized" elements, like Richard Condon's novels or Martin Luther King Jr.'s sermons—it becomes apparent that appropriation, mimicry, quotation, allusion, and sublimated collaboration consist of a kind of sine qua non of the creative act, cutting across all forms and genres in the realm of cultural production.

In a courtroom scene from *The Simpsons* that has since entered into the television canon, an argument over the ownership of the animated characters Itchy and Scratchy rapidly escalates into an existential debate on the very nature of cartoons. "Animation is built on plagiarism!" declares the show's hot-tempered cartoon-producer-within-a-cartoon, Roger Meyers Jr. "You take away our right to steal ideas, where are they going to come from?" If nostalgic cartoonists had never borrowed from *Fritz the Cat,* there would be no *Ren & Stimpy Show;* without the Rankin/Bass and Charlie Brown Christmas specials, there would be no *South Park;* and without *The Flintstones*—more or less *The Honeymooners* in cartoon loincloths—*The Simpsons* would cease to exist. If those don't strike you as essential losses, then consider the remarkable series of "plagiarisms" that links Ovid's "Pyramus and Thisbe" with Shakespeare's *Romeo and Juliet* and Leonard Bernstein's *West Side Story,* or Shakespeare's description of Cleopatra, copied nearly verbatim from Plutarch's life of Mark Antony and also later nicked by T. S. Eliot for *The Waste Land.* If these are examples of plagiarism, then we want more plagiarism.

Most artists are brought to their vocation when their own nascent gifts are awakened by the work of a master. That is to say, most artists are converted to art by art itself. Finding one's voice isn't just an emptying and purifying oneself of the words of others but an adopting and embracing of filiations, communities, and discourses. Inspiration could be called inhaling the memory of an act never experienced. Invention, it must be humbly admitted, does not consist in creating out of void but out of chaos. Any artist knows these truths, no matter how deeply he or she submerges that knowing.

What happens when an allusion goes unrecognized? A closer look at *The Waste Land* may help make this point. The body of Eliot's poem is a vertiginous mélange of quotation, allusion, and "original" writing. When Eliot alludes to Edmund Spenser's "Prothalamion" with the line "Sweet Thames, run softly, till I end my song," what of readers to whom the poem, never one of Spenser's most popular, is unfamiliar? (Indeed, the Spenser is now known largely because of Eliot's use of it.) Two responses are possible: grant the line to Eliot, or later discover the source and understand the line as plagiarism. Eliot evidenced no small anxiety about these matters; the notes he so carefully added to *The Waste Land* can be read as a symptom of modernism's contamination anxiety. Taken from this angle, what exactly is postmodernism, except modernism without the anxiety?

Surrounded by Signs

The surrealists believed that objects in the world possess a certain but unspecifiable intensity that had been dulled by everyday use and utility. They meant to reanimate this dormant intensity, to bring their minds once again into close contact with the matter that made up their world. André Breton's maxim "Beautiful as the chance encounter of a sewing machine and an umbrella on an operating table" is an expression of the belief that simply placing objects in an unexpected context reinvigorates their mysterious qualities.

This "crisis" the surrealists identified was being simultaneously diagnosed by others. Martin Heidegger held that the essence of modernity was found in a certain technological orientation he called "enframing." This tendency encourages us to see the objects in our world only in terms of how they can serve us or be used by us. The task he identified was to find ways to resituate ourselves vis-à-vis these "objects," so that we may see them as "things" pulled into relief against the ground of their functionality. Heidegger believed that art had the great potential to reveal the "thingness" of objects.

The surrealists understood that photography and cinema could carry out this reanimating process automatically; the process of framing objects in a lens was often enough to create the charge they sought. Describing the effect, Walter Benjamin drew a comparison between the photographic apparatus and Freud's psychoanalytic methods. Just as Freud's theories "isolated and made analyzable things which had heretofore floated along unnoticed in the broad stream of perception," the photographic apparatus focuses on "hidden details of familiar objects," revealing "entirely new structural formations of the subject."

It's worth noting, then, that early in the history of photography a series of judicial decisions could well have changed the course of that art: courts were asked whether the photographer, amateur or professional, required permission before he could capture and print an image. Was the photographer *stealing* from the person or building whose photograph he shot, pirating something of private and certifiable value? Those early decisions went in favor of the pirates. Just as Walt Disney could take inspiration from Buster Keaton's *Steamboat Bill, Jr.,* the Brothers Grimm, or the existence of real mice, the photographer should be free to capture an image without compensating the source. The world that meets our eye through the lens of a camera was judged to be, with minor exceptions, a sort of public commons, where a cat may look at a king.

Novelists may glance at the stuff of the world too, but we sometimes get called to task for it. For those whose ganglia were formed pre-TV, the mimetic deployment of pop-culture icons seems at best an annoying tic and at worst a dangerous vapidity that compromises fiction's seriousness by dating it out of the

Platonic Always, where it ought to reside. In a graduate workshop I briefly passed through, a certain gray eminence tried to convince us that a literary story should always eschew "any feature which serves to date it" because "serious fiction must be Timeless." When we protested that, in his own well-known work, characters moved about electrically lit rooms, drove cars, and spoke not Anglo-Saxon but postwar English—and further, that fiction he'd himself ratified as great, such as Dickens, was liberally strewn with innately topical, commercial, and timebound references—he impatiently amended his proscription to those explicit references that would date a story in the "frivolous Now." When pressed, he said of course he meant the "trendy mass-popular-media" reference. Here, trans-generational discourse broke down.

I was born in 1964; I grew up watching Captain Kangaroo, moon landings, zillions of TV ads, the Banana Splits, *M*A*S*H*, and *The Mary Tyler Moore Show*. I was born with words in my mouth—"Band-Aid," "Q-tip," "Xerox"—object-names as fixed and eternal in my logosphere as "taxicab" and "toothbrush." The world is a home littered with pop-culture products and their emblems. I also came of age swamped by parodies that stood for originals yet mysterious to me—I knew Monkees before Beatles, Belmondo before Bogart, and "remember" the movie *Summer of '42* from a *Mad* magazine satire, though I've still never seen the film itself. I'm not alone in having been born backward into an incoherent realm of texts, products, and images, the commercial and cultural environment with which we've both supplemented and blotted out our natural world. I can no more claim it as "mine" than the sidewalks and forests of the world, yet I do dwell in it, and for me to stand a chance as either artist or citizen, I'd probably better be permitted to name it.

Consider Walker Percy's *The Moviegoer*:

> Other people, so I have read, treasure memorable moments in their
> lives: the time one climbed the Parthenon at sunrise, the summer night
> one met a lonely girl in Central Park and achieved with her a sweet
> and natural relationship, as they say in books. I too once met a girl in
> Central Park, but it is not much to remember. What I remember is the
> time John Wayne killed three men with a carbine as he was falling to
> the dusty street in *Stagecoach*, and the time the kitten found Orson
> Welles in the doorway in *The Third Man*.

Today, when we can eat Tex-Mex with chopsticks while listening to reggae and watching a YouTube rebroadcast of the Berlin Wall's fall—i.e., when damn near *everything* presents itself as familiar—it's not a surprise that some of today's most ambitious art is going about trying to *make the familiar strange*. In so doing, in reimagining what human life might truly be like over there across the chasms of illusion, mediation, demographics, marketing, imago, and appearance, artists are paradoxically trying to restore what's taken for "real" to three whole dimensions, to reconstruct a univocally round world out of disparate streams of flat sights.

Whatever charge of tastelessness or trademark violation may be attached to the artistic appropriation of the media environment in which we swim, the alternative—to flinch, or tiptoe away into some ivory tower of irrelevance—is far worse. We're surrounded by signs; our imperative is to ignore none of them.

Usemonopoly

The idea that culture can be property—*intellectual* property—is used to justify everything from attempts to force the Girl Scouts to pay royalties for singing songs around campfires to the infringement suit brought by the estate of Margaret Mitchell against the publishers of Alice Randall's *The Wind Done Gone*. Corporations like Celera Genomics have filed for patents for human genes, while the Recording Industry Association of America has sued music downloaders for copyright infringement, reaching out-of-court settlements for thousands of dollars with defendants as young as twelve. ASCAP bleeds fees from shop owners who play background music in their stores; students and scholars are shamed from placing texts facedown on photocopy machines. At the same time, copyright is revered by most established writers and artists as a birthright and bulwark, the source of nurture for their infinitely fragile practices in a rapacious world. Plagiarism and piracy, after all, are the monsters we working artists are taught to dread, as they roam the woods surrounding our tiny preserves of regard and remuneration.

A time is marked not so much by ideas that are argued about as by ideas that are taken for granted. The character of an era hangs upon what needs no defense. In this regard, few of us question the contemporary construction of copyright. It is taken as a law, both in the sense of a universally recognizable moral absolute, like the law against murder, and as naturally inherent in our world, like the law of gravity. In fact, it is neither. Rather, copyright is an ongoing social negotiation, tenuously forged, endlessly revised, and imperfect in its every incarnation.

Thomas Jefferson, for one, considered copyright a necessary evil: he favored providing just enough incentive to create, nothing more, and thereafter allowing ideas to flow freely, as nature intended. His conception of copyright was enshrined in the Constitution, which gives Congress the authority to "promote the Progress of Science and useful Arts, by securing for limited Times to Authors and Inventors the exclusive Right to their respective Writings and Discoveries." This was a balancing act between creators and society as a whole; second comers might do a much better job than the originator with the original idea.

But Jefferson's vision has not fared well, has in fact been steadily eroded by those who view the culture as a market in which everything of value should be owned by someone or other. The distinctive feature of modern American copyright law is its almost limitless bloating—its expansion in both scope and duration. With no registration requirement, every creative act in a tangible medium is now subject to copyright protection: your email to your child or your child's finger painting, both are automatically protected. The first Congress to grant copyright gave authors an initial term of fourteen years, which could be renewed for another fourteen if the author still lived. The current term is the life of the author plus seventy years. It's only a slight exaggeration to say that each time Mickey Mouse is about to fall into the public domain, the mouse's copyright term is extended.

Even as the law becomes more restrictive, technology is exposing those restrictions as bizarre and arbitrary. When old laws fixed on reproduction as the compensable (or actionable) unit, it wasn't because there was anything fundamentally invasive of an author's rights in the making of a copy. Rather it was because copies were once easy to find and count, so they made a useful bench-mark for deciding when an owner's rights had been invaded. In the contempo-rary world, though, the act of "copying" is in no meaningful sense equivalent to an infringement—we make a copy every time we accept an emailed text, or send or forward one—and is impossible anymore to regulate or even describe.

At the movies, my entertainment is sometimes lately preceded by a dire trailer, produced by the lobbying group called the Motion Picture Association of America, in which the purchasing of a bootleg copy of a Hollywood film is compared to the theft of a car or a handbag—and, as the bullying supertitles remind us, "You wouldn't steal a handbag!" This conflation forms an incitement to quit thinking. If I were to tell you that pirating DVDs or downloading music is in no way different from loaning a friend a book, my own arguments would be as ethically bankrupt as the MPAA's. The truth lies somewhere in the vast gray area between these two overstated positions. For a car or a handbag, once stolen, no longer is available to its owner, while the appropriation of an article of "intellectual property" leaves the original untouched. As Jefferson wrote, "He who receives an idea from me, receives instruction himself without lessening mine; as he who lights his taper at mine, receives light without darkening me."

Yet industries of cultural capital, who profit not from creating but from distrib-uting, see the sale of culture as a zero-sum game. The piano-roll publishers fear the record companies, who fear the cassette-tape manufacturers, who fear the online vendors, who fear whoever else is next in line to profit most quickly from the intan-gible and infinitely reproducible fruits of an artist's labor. It has been the same in every industry and with every technological innovation. Jack Valenti, speaking for the MPAA: "I say to you that the VCR is to the American film producer and the American public as the Boston Strangler is to the woman home alone."

Thinking clearly sometimes requires unbraiding our language. The word "copyright" may eventually seem as dubious in its embedded purposes as "family values," "globalization," and, sure, "intellectual property." Copyright is a "right" in no absolute sense; it is a government-granted monopoly on the use of creative results. So let's try calling it that—not a right but a *monopoly on use,* a "usemonopoly"—and then consider how the rapacious expansion of monopoly rights has always been counter to the public interest, no matter if it is Andrew Carnegie controlling the price of steel or Walt Disney managing the fate of his mouse. Whether the monopolizing beneficiary is a living artist or some artist's heirs or some corporation's shareholders, the loser is the community, including living artists who might make splendid use of a healthy public domain.

The Beauty of Second Use

A few years ago someone brought me a strange gift, purchased at MoMA's down-town design store: a copy of my own first novel, *Gun, With Occasional Music,* expertly cut into the contours of a pistol. The object was the work of Robert The, an artist whose specialty is the reincarnation of everyday materials. I regard my first book as an old friend, one who never fails to remind me of the spirit with which I entered into this game of art and commerce—that to be allowed to insert the materials of my imagination onto the shelves of bookstores and into the minds of readers (if only a handful) was a wild privilege. I was paid $6,000 for three years of writing, but at the time I'd have happily published the results for nothing. Now my old friend had come home in a new form, one I was unlikely to have imagined for it myself. The gun-book wasn't readable, exactly, but I couldn't take offense at that. The fertile spirit of stray connection this appropriated object conveyed back to me—the strange beauty of its second use—was a reward for being a published writer I could never have fathomed in advance. And the world makes room for both my novel and Robert The's gun-book. There's no need to choose between the two.

In the first life of creative property, if the creator is lucky, the content is sold. After the commercial life has ended, our tradition supports a second life as well. A newspaper is delivered to a doorstep, and the next day wraps fish or builds an archive. Most books fall out of print after one year, yet even within that period they can be sold in used bookstores and stored in libraries, quoted in reviews, parodied in magazines, described in conversations, and plundered for costumes for kids to wear on Halloween. The demarcation between various possible uses is beautifully graded and hard to define, the more so as artifacts distill into and repercuss through the realm of culture into which they've been entered, the more so as they engage the receptive minds for whom they were presumably intended.

Active reading is an impertinent raid on the literary preserve. Readers are like nomads, poaching their way across fields they do not own—artists are no more able to control the imaginations of their audiences than the culture industry is able to control second uses of its artifacts. In the children's classic *The Velveteen Rabbit,* the old Skin Horse offers the Rabbit a lecture on the practice of textual poaching. The value of a new toy lies not in its material qualities (not "having things that buzz inside you and a stick-out handle"), the Skin Horse explains, but rather in how the toy is used. "Real isn't how you are made.... It's a thing that happens to you. When a child loves you for a long, long time, not just to play with, but REALLY loves you, then you become Real." The Rabbit is fearful, recognizing that consumer goods don't become "real" without being actively reworked: "Does it hurt?" Reassuring him, the Skin Horse says: "It doesn't happen all at once.... You become. It takes a long time.... Generally, by the time you are Real, most of your hair has been loved off, and your eyes drop out and you get loose in the joints and very shabby." Seen from the perspective of the toy-maker, the Velveteen Rabbit's loose joints and missing eyes represent vandalism, signs of misuse and rough treatment; for others, these are marks of its loving use.

Artists and their surrogates who fall into the trap of seeking recompense for every possible second use end up attacking their own best audience members for the crime of exalting and enshrining their work. The Recording Industry Association of America prosecuting their own record-buying public makes as little sense as the novelists who bristle at autographing used copies of their books for collectors. And artists, or their heirs, who fall into the trap of attacking the collagists and satirists and digital samplers of their work are attacking the next generation of creators for the crime of being influenced, for the crime of responding with the same mixture of intoxication, resentment, lust, and glee that characterizes all artistic successors. By doing so they make the world smaller, betraying what seems to me the primary motivation for participating in the world of culture in the first place: to make the world larger.

Source Hypocrisy, or, Disnial

The Walt Disney Company has drawn an astonishing catalogue from the work of others: *Snow White and the Seven Dwarfs, Fantasia, Pinocchio, Dumbo, Bambi, Song of the South, Cinderella, Alice in Wonderland, Robin Hood, Peter Pan, Lady and the Tramp, Mulan, Sleeping Beauty, The Sword in the Stone, The Jungle Book,* and, alas, *Treasure Planet,* a legacy of cultural sampling that Shakespeare, or De La Soul, could get behind. Yet Disney's protectorate of lobbyists has policed the resulting cache of cultural materials as vigilantly as if it were Fort Knox—threatening legal action, for instance, against the artist Dennis Oppenheim for the use of Disney characters in a sculpture, and prohibiting the scholar Holly Crawford from using any Disney-related images—including artwork by Lichtenstein, Warhol, Oldenburg, and others—in her monograph *Attached to the Mouse: Disney and Contemporary Art.*

This peculiar and specific act—the enclosure of commonwealth culture for the benefit of a sole or corporate owner—is close kin to what could be called *imperial plagiarism,* the free use of Third World or "primitive" artworks and styles by more privileged (and better-paid) artists. Think of Picasso's *Les Demoiselles d'Avignon,* or some of the albums of Paul Simon or David Byrne: even without violating copyright, those creators have sometimes come in for a certain skepticism when the extent of their outsourcing became evident. And, as when Led Zeppelin found themselves sued for back royalties by the bluesman Willie Dixon, the act can occasionally be an expensive one. *To live outside the law, you must be honest:* perhaps it was this, in part, that spurred David Byrne and Brian Eno to recently launch a "remix" website, where anyone can download easily disassembled versions of two songs from *My Life in the Bush of Ghosts,* an album reliant on vernacular speech sampled from a host of sources. Perhaps it also explains why Bob Dylan has never refused a request for a sample.

Kenneth Koch once said, "I'm a writer who likes to be influenced." It was a charming confession, and a rare one. For so many artists, the act of creativity is intended as a Napoleonic imposition of one's uniqueness upon the universe—*après moi le déluge* of copycats! And for every James Joyce or Woody Guthrie or Martin Luther King Jr., or Walt Disney, who gathered a constellation of voices in his work, there may seem to be some corporation or literary estate eager to stopper the bottle: cultural debts flow in, but they don't flow out. We might call this tendency "source hypocrisy." Or we could name it after the most pernicious source hypocrites of all time: Disnial.

You Can't Steal a Gift

My reader may, understandably, be on the verge of crying, "Communist!" A large, diverse society cannot survive without property; a large, diverse, and modern society cannot flourish without some form of intellectual property. But it takes little reflection to grasp that there is ample value that the term "property" doesn't capture. And works of art exist simultaneously in two economies, a market economy and a *gift economy*.

The cardinal difference between gift and commodity exchange is that a gift establishes a feeling-bond between two people, whereas the sale of a commodity leaves no necessary connection. I go into a hardware store, pay the man for a hacksaw blade, and walk out. I may never see him again. The disconnectedness is, in fact, a virtue of the commodity mode. We don't want to be bothered, and if the clerk always wants to chat about the family, I'll shop elsewhere. I just want a hacksaw blade. But a gift makes a connection. There are many examples, the candy or cigarette offered to a stranger who shares a seat on the plane, the few words that indicate goodwill between passengers on the late-night bus. These tokens establish the simplest bonds of social life, but the model they offer may be extended to the most complicated of unions—marriage, parenthood, mentorship. If a value is placed on these (often essentially unequal) exchanges, they degenerate into something else.

Yet one of the more difficult things to comprehend is that the gift economies—like those that sustain open-source software—coexist so naturally with the market. It is precisely this doubleness in art practices that we must identify, ratify, and enshrine in our lives as participants in culture, either as "producers" or "consumers." Art that matters to us—which moves the heart, or revives the soul, or delights the senses, or offers courage for living, however we choose to describe the experience—is received as a gift is received. Even if we've paid a fee at the door of the museum or concert hall, when we are touched by a work of art something comes to us that has nothing to do with the price. The daily commerce of our lives proceeds at its own constant level, but a gift conveys an uncommodifiable surplus of inspiration.

The way we treat a thing can change its nature, though. Religions often prohibit the sale of sacred objects, the implication being that their sanctity is lost if they are bought and sold. We consider it unacceptable to sell sex, babies, body organs, legal rights, and votes. The idea that something should never be commodified is generally known as *inalienability* or *unalienability*—a concept most famously expressed by Thomas Jefferson in the phrase "endowed by their Creator with certain unalienable Rights ..." A work of art seems to be a hardier breed; it can be sold in the market and still emerge a work of art. But if it is true that in the essential commerce of art a gift is carried by the work from the artist to his audience, if I am right to say that where there is no gift there is no art, then it may be possible to destroy a work of art by converting it into a pure commodity. I don't maintain that art can't be bought and sold, but that the gift portion of the work places a constraint upon our merchandising. This is the reason why even a really beautiful, ingenious, powerful ad (of which there are a lot) can never be any kind of real art: an ad has no status as gift; i.e., it's never really *for* the person it's directed at.

The power of a gift economy remains difficult for the empiricists of our market culture to understand. In our times, the rhetoric of the market presumes that everything should be and can be appropriately bought, sold, and owned—a tide of alienation lapping daily at the dwindling redoubt of the unalienable. In free-market theory, an intervention to halt propertization is considered "paternalistic," because it inhibits the free action of the citizen, now reposited as a "potential entrepreneur." Of course, in the real world, we know that child-rearing, family life, education, socialization, sexuality, political life, and many other basic human activities require insulation from market forces. In fact, paying for many of these things can ruin them. We may be willing to peek at *Who Wants to Marry a Multimillionaire* or an eBay auction of the ova of fashion models, but only to reassure ourselves that some things are still beneath our standards of dignity.

What's remarkable about gift economies is that they can flourish in the most unlikely places—in rundown neighborhoods, on the Internet, in scientific communities, and among members of Alcoholics Anonymous. A classic example is commercial blood systems, which generally produce blood supplies of lower safety, purity, and potency than volunteer systems. A gift economy may be superior when it comes to maintaining a group's commitment to certain extra-market values.

The Commons

Another way of understanding the presence of gift economies—which dwell like ghosts in the commercial machine—is in the sense of a *public commons*. A commons, of course, is anything like the streets over which we drive, the skies through which we pilot airplanes, or the public parks or beaches on which we dally. A commons belongs to everyone and no one, and its use is controlled only by common consent. A commons describes resources like the body of ancient music drawn on by composers and folk musicians alike, rather than the commodities, like "Happy Birthday to You," for which ASCAP, 114 years after it was written, continues to collect a fee. Einstein's theory of relativity is a commons. Writings in the public domain are a commons. Gossip about celebrities is a commons. The silence in a movie theater is a transitory commons, impossibly fragile, treasured by those who crave it, and constructed as a mutual gift by those who compose it.

The world of art and culture is a vast commons, one that is salted through with zones of utter commerce yet remains gloriously immune to any overall commodification. The closest resemblance is to the commons of a *language:* altered by every contributor, expanded by even the most passive user. That a language is a commons doesn't mean that the community owns it; rather it belongs *between* people, possessed by no one, not even by society as a whole.

Nearly any commons, though, can be encroached upon, partitioned, enclosed. The American commons include tangible assets such as public forests and minerals, intangible wealth such as copyrights and patents, critical infrastructures such as the Internet and government research, and cultural resources such as the broadcast airwaves and public spaces. They include resources we've paid for as taxpayers and inherited from previous generations. They're not just an inventory of marketable assets; they're social institutions and cultural traditions that define us as Americans and enliven us as human beings. Some invasions of the commons are sanctioned because we can no longer muster a spirited commitment to the public sector. The abuse goes unnoticed because the theft of the commons is seen in glimpses, not in panorama. We may occasionally see a former wetland paved; we may hear about the breakthrough cancer drug that tax dollars helped develop, the rights to which pharmaceutical companies acquired for a song. The larger movement goes too much unremarked. The notion of a *commons of cultural materials* goes more or less unnamed.

Honoring the commons is not a matter of moral exhortation. It is a practical necessity. We in Western society are going through a period of intensifying belief in private ownership, to the detriment of the public good. We have to remain constantly vigilant to prevent raids by those who would selfishly exploit our common heritage for their private gain. Such raids on our natural resources are not examples of enterprise and initiative. They are attempts to take from all the people just for the benefit of a few.

Undiscovered Public Knowledge

Artists and intellectuals despondent over the prospects for originality can take heart from a phenomenon identified about twenty years ago by Don Swanson, a library scientist at the University of Chicago. He called it "undiscovered public knowledge." Swanson showed that standing problems in medical research may be significantly addressed, perhaps even solved, simply by systematically survey-ing the scientific literature. Left to its own devices, research tends to become more specialized and abstracted from the real-world problems that motivated it and to which it remains relevant. This suggests that such a problem may be tack-led effectively not by commissioning more research but by assuming that most or all of the solution can already be found in various scientific journals, waiting to be assembled by someone willing to read across specialties. Swanson himself did this in the case of Raynaud's syndrome, a disease that causes the fingers of young women to become numb. His finding is especially striking—perhaps even scandalous—because it happened in the ever-expanding biomedical sciences.

Undiscovered public knowledge emboldens us to question the extreme claims to originality made in press releases and publishers' notices: Is an intellec-tual or creative offering truly novel, or have we just forgotten a worthy precur-sor? Does solving certain scientific problems really require massive additional funding, or could a computerized search engine, creatively deployed, do the same job more quickly and cheaply? Lastly, does our appetite for creative vitality require the violence and exasperation of another avant-garde, with its wearisome killing-the-father imperatives, or might we be better off ratifying *the ecstasy of influence*—and deepening our willingness to understand the commonality and timelessness of the methods and motifs available to artists?

Give All

A few years ago, the Film Society of Lincoln Center announced a retrospective of the works of Dariush Mehrjui, then a fresh enthusiasm of mine. Mehrjui is one of Iran's finest filmmakers, and the only one whose subject was personal relationships among the upper-middle-class intelligentsia. Needless to say, opportunities to view his films were—and remain—rare indeed. I headed uptown for one, an adaptation of J. D. Salinger's *Franny and Zooey,* titled *Pari,* only to discover at the door of the Walter Reade Theater that the screening had been canceled: its announcement had brought threat of a lawsuit down on the Film Society. True, these were Salinger's rights under the law. Yet why would he care that some obscure Iranian filmmaker had paid him homage with a meditation on his heroine? Would it have damaged his book or robbed him of some crucial remuneration had the screening been permitted? The fertile spirit of stray connection—one stretching across what is presently seen as the direst of international breaches—had in this case been snuffed out. The cold, undead hand of one of my childhood literary heroes had reached out from its New Hampshire redoubt to arrest my present-day curiosity.

A few assertions, then:

Any text that has infiltrated the common mind to the extent of *Gone With the Wind* or *Lolita* or *Ulysses* inexorably joins the language of culture. A map-turned-to-landscape, it has moved to a place beyond enclosure or control. The authors and their heirs should consider the subsequent parodies, refractions, quotations, and revisions an honor, or at least the price of a rare success.

A corporation that has imposed an inescapable notion—Mickey Mouse, Band-Aid—on the cultural language should pay a similar price.

The primary objective of copyright is not to reward the labor of authors but "to promote the Progress of Science and useful Arts." To this end, copyright assures authors the right to their original expression, but encourages others to build freely upon the ideas and information conveyed by a work. This result is neither unfair nor unfortunate.

Contemporary copyright, trademark, and patent law is presently corrupted. The case for perpetual copyright is a denial of the essential gift-aspect of the creative act. Arguments in its favor are as un-American as those for the repeal of the estate tax.

Art is sourced. Apprentices graze in the field of culture.

Digital sampling is an art method like any other, neutral in itself.

Despite hand-wringing at each technological turn—radio, the Internet—the future will be much like the past. Artists will sell some things but also give some things away. Change may be troubling for those who crave less ambiguity, but the life of an artist has never been filled with certainty.

The dream of a perfect systematic remuneration is nonsense. I pay rent with the price my words bring when published in glossy magazines and at the same moment offer them for almost nothing to impoverished literary quarterlies, or speak them for free into the air in a radio interview. So what are they worth? What would they be worth if some future Dylan worked them into a song? Should I care to make such a thing impossible?

Any text is woven entirely with citations, references, echoes, cultural languages, which cut across it through and through in a vast stereophony. The citations that go to make up a text are anonymous, untraceable, and yet *already read;* they are quotations without inverted commas. The kernel, the soul—let us go further and say the substance, the bulk, the actual and valuable material of all human utterances—is plagiarism. For substantially all ideas are secondhand, consciously and unconsciously drawn from a million outside sources, and daily used by the garnerer with a pride and satisfaction born of the superstition that he originated them; whereas there is not a rag of originality about them anywhere except the little discoloration they get from his mental and moral caliber and his temperament, and which is revealed in characteristics of phrasing. Old and new make the warp and woof of every moment. There is no thread that is not a twist of these two strands. By necessity, by proclivity, and by delight, we all quote. Neurological study has lately shown that memory, imagination, and consciousness itself is stitched, quilted, pastiched. If we cut-and-paste our selves, might we not forgive it of our artworks?

Artists and writers—and our advocates, our guilds and agents—too often subscribe to implicit claims of originality that do injury to these truths. And we too often, as hucksters and bean counters in the tiny enterprises of our selves, act to spite the gift portion of our privileged roles. People live differently who treat a portion of their wealth as a gift. If we devalue and obscure the gift-economy function of our art practices, we turn our works into nothing more than advertisements for themselves. We may console ourselves that our lust for subsidiary rights in virtual perpetuity is some heroic counter to rapacious corporate interests. But the truth is that with artists pulling on one side and corporations pulling on the other, the loser is the collective public imagination from which we were nourished in the first place, and whose existence as the ultimate repository of our offerings makes the work worth doing in the first place.

As a novelist, I'm a cork on the ocean of story, a leaf on a windy day. Pretty soon I'll be blown away. For the moment I'm grateful to be making a living, and so must ask that for a limited time (in the Thomas Jefferson sense) you please respect my small, treasured usemonopolies. Don't pirate my editions; do plunder my visions. The name of the game is Give All. You, reader, are welcome to my stories. They were never mine in the first place, but I gave them to you. If you have the inclination to pick them up, take them with my blessing.

KEY: I IS ANOTHER

This key to the preceding essay names the source of every line I stole, warped, and cobbled together as I "wrote" (except, alas, those sources I forgot along the way). First uses of a given author or speaker are highlighted in bold type. Nearly every sentence I culled I also revised, at least slightly—for necessities of space, in order to produce a more consistent tone, or simply because I felt like it.

Title

The phrase "the ecstasy of influence," which embeds a rebuking play on Harold Bloom's "anxiety of influence," is lifted from spoken remarks by Professor **Richard Dienst** of Rutgers.

Love and Theft

"… a cultivated man of middle age …" to "… hidden, unacknowledged memory?" These lines, with some adjustments for tone, belong to the **anonymous editor** or **assistant** who wrote the dust-flap copy of **Michael Maar's** *The Two Lolitas*. Of course, in my own experience, dust-flap copy is often a collaboration between author and editor. Perhaps this was also true for Maar.

"The history of literature …" to "… borrow and quote?" comes from Maar's book itself.

"Appropriation has always …" to "… Ishmael and Queequeg …" This paragraph makes a hash of remarks from an interview with **Eric Lott** conducted by **David McNair** and **Jayson Whitehead**, and incorporates both interviewers' and interviewee's observations. (The text-interview form can be seen as a commonly accepted form of multivocal writing. Most interviewers prime their subjects with remarks of their own—leading the witness, so to speak—and gently refine their subjects' statements in the final printed transcript.)

"I realized this …" to "… for a long time." The anecdote is cribbed, with an elision to avoid appropriating a dead grandmother, from **Jonathan Rosen**'s *The Talmud and the Internet.* I've never seen *84, Charing Cross Road,* nor searched the Web for a Donne quote. For me it was through Rosen to Donne, Hemingway, website, et al.

"When I was thirteen …" to "… no plagiarist at all." This is from **William Gibson**'s "God's Little Toys," in *Wired* magazine. My own first encounter with William Burroughs, also at age thirteen, was less epiphanic. Having grown up with a painter father who, during family visits to galleries or museums, approvingly noted collage and appropriation techniques in the visual arts (Picasso, Claes Oldenburg, Stuart Davis), I was gratified, but not surprised, to learn that literature could encompass the same methods.

Contamination Anxiety

"In 1941, on his front porch …" to "… 'this song comes from the cotton field.'" **Siva Vaidhyanathan**, *Copyrights and Copywrongs.*

"… enabled by a kind … freely reworked." **Kembrew McLeod**, *Freedom of Expression.* In *Owning Culture,* McLeod notes that, as he was writing, he

> happened to be listening to a lot of old country music, and in my casual listening I noticed that *six* country songs shared *exactly* the same vocal melody, including Hank Thompson's "Wild Side of Life," the Carter Family's "I'm Thinking Tonight of My Blue Eyes," Roy Acuff's "Great Speckled Bird," Kitty Wells's "It Wasn't God Who Made Honky Tonk Angels," Reno & Smiley's "I'm Using My Bible for a Roadmap," and Townes Van Zandt's "Heavenly Houseboat Blues."… In his extensively researched book, *Country: The Twisted Roots of Rock 'n' Roll,* Nick Tosches documents that the melody these songs share is both "ancient and British." There were no recorded lawsuits stemming from these appropriations….

"... musicians have gained ... through allusion." **Joanna Demers**, *Steal This Music.*

"In Seventies Jamaica ..." to "... hours of music." Gibson.

"Visual, sound, and text collage ..." to "... realm of cultural production." This plunders, rewrites, and amplifies paragraphs from McLeod's *Owning Culture,* except for the line about collage being the art form of the twentieth and twenty-first centuries, which I heard filmmaker **Craig Baldwin** say, in defense of sampling, in the trailer for a forthcoming documentary, *Copyright Criminals.*

"In a courtroom scene ..." to "... would cease to exist." **Dave Itzkoff**, *New York Times.*

"... the remarkable series of 'plagiarisms' ..." to "... we want more plagiarism." **Richard Posner**, combined from The Becker-Posner Blog and *The Atlantic Monthly.*

"Most artists are brought ..." to "... by art itself." These words, and many more to follow, come from **Lewis Hyde**'s *The Gift.* Above any other book I've here plagiarized, I commend *The Gift* to your attention.

"Finding one's voice ... filiations, communities, and discourses." Semanticist **George L. Dillon**, quoted in **Rebecca Moore Howard**'s "The New Abolitionism Comes to Plagiarism."

"Inspiration could be ... act never experienced." **Ned Rorem**, found on several "great quotations" sites on the Internet.

"Invention, it must be humbly admitted ... out of chaos." **Mary Shelley**, from her introduction to *Frankenstein.*

"What happens ..." to "... contamination anxiety." **Kevin J. H. Dettmar**, from "The Illusion of Modernist Allusion and the Politics of Postmodern Plagiarism."

Surrounded By Signs

"The surrealists believed ..." to the Walter Benjamin quote. **Christian Keathley**'s *Cinephilia and History, or the Wind in the Trees,* a book that treats fannish fetishism as the secret at the heart of film scholarship. Keathley notes, for instance, Joseph Cornell's surrealist-influenced 1936 film *Rose Hobart,* which simply records "the way in which Cornell himself watched the 1931 Hollywood potboiler *East of Borneo,* fascinated and distracted as he was by its B-grade star"—the star, of course, being Rose Hobart herself. This, I suppose, makes Cornell a sort of father to computer-enabled fan-creator re-workings of Hollywood product, like the version of George Lucas's *The Phantom Menace* from which the noxious Jar Jar Binks character was purged; both incorporate a viewer's subjective preferences into a revision of a filmmaker's work.

"... early in the history of photography" to "... without compensating the source." From *Free Culture,* by **Lawrence Lessig**, the greatest of public advocates for copyright reform, and the best source if you want to get radicalized in a hurry.

"For those whose ganglia ..." to "... discourse broke down." From **David Foster Wallace**'s essay "E Unibus Pluram," reprinted in A *Supposedly Fun Thing I'll Never Do Again.* I have no idea who Wallace's "gray eminence" is or was.

I inserted the example of Dickens into the paragraph; he strikes me as overlooked in the lineage of authors of "brand-name" fiction.

"I was born ... *Mary Tyler Moore Show.*" These are the reminiscences of **Mark Hosler** from Negativland, a collaging musical collective that was sued by U2's record label for their appropriation of "I Still Haven't Found What I'm Looking For." Although I had to adjust the birth date, Hosler's cultural menu fits me like a glove.

"The world is a home ... pop-culture products ..." McLeod.

"Today, when we can eat ..." to "... flat sights." Wallace.

"We're surrounded by signs, ignore none of them." This phrase, which I unfortunately rendered somewhat leaden with the word "imperative," comes from **Steve Erickson**'s novel *Our Ecstatic Days.*

Usemonopoly

"... everything from attempts ..." to "defendants as young as twelve." **Robert Boynton**, *The New York Times Magazine,* "The Tyranny of Copyright?"

"A time is marked ..." to "...what needs no defense." Lessig, this time from *The Future of Ideas.*

"Thomas Jefferson, for one ..." to "'... respective Writings and Discoveries.'" Boynton.

"... second comers might do a much better job than the originator ..." I found this phrase in Lessig, who is quoting Vaidhyanathan, who himself is characterizing a judgment written by **Learned Hand**.

"But Jefferson's vision ... owned by someone or other." Boynton.

"The distinctive feature ..." to "... term is extended." Lessig, again from *The Future of Ideas.*

"When old laws ..." to "... had been invaded." **Jessica Litman**, *Digital Copyright.*

"'I say to you ... woman home alone.'" I found the Valenti quote in Mcleod. Now fill in the blank: Jack Valenti is to the public domain as _____ is to _____.

The Beauty of Second Use

"In the first ..." to "... builds an archive." Lessig.

"Most books ... one year ..." Lessig.

"Active reading is ..." to "... do not own ..." This is a mashup of **Henry Jenkins**, from his *Textual Poachers: Television Fans and Participatory Culture,* and **Michel de Certeau**, whom Jenkins quotes.

"In the children's classic ..." to "... its loving use." Jenkins. (Incidentally, have the holders of the copyright to *The Velveteen Rabbit* had a close look at *Toy Story?* There could be a lawsuit there.)

Source Hypocrisy, or, Disnial

"The Walt Disney Company ... alas, *Treasure Planet* ..." Lessig.

"Imperial Plagiarism" is the title of an essay by **Marilyn Randall**.

"... spurred David Byrne ... *My Life in the Bush of Ghosts* ..." **Chris Dahlen**, *Pitchfork*—though in truth by the time I'd finished, his words were so utterly dissolved within my own that had I been an ordinary cutting-and-pasting journalist it never would have occurred to me to give Dahlen a citation. The effort of preserving another's distinctive phrases as I worked on this essay was sometimes beyond my capacities; this form of plagiarism was oddly hard work.

"Kenneth Koch ..." to "... *déluge* of copycats!" **Emily Nussbaum**, *The New York Times Book Review*.

You Can't Steal a Gift

"You can't steal a gift." Dizzy Gillespie, defending another player who'd been accused of poaching Charlie Parker's style: "You can't steal a gift. Bird gave the world his music, and if you can hear it you can have it."

"A large, diverse society ... intellectual property." Lessig.

"And works of art ..." to "... marriage, parenthood, mentorship." Hyde.

"Yet one ... so naturally with the market." **David Bollier**, *Silent Theft*.

"Art that matters ..." to "... bought and sold." Hyde.

"We consider it unacceptable ..." to "'... certain unalienable Rights ...'" Bollier, paraphrasing **Margaret Jane Radin**'s *Contested Commodities*.

"A work of art ..." to "... constraint upon our merchandising." Hyde.

"This is the reason ... person it's directed at." Wallace.

"The power of a gift ..." to "... certain extra-market values." Bollier, and also the sociologist Warren O. Hagstrom, whom Bollier is paraphrasing.

The Commons

"Einstein's theory ..." to "... public domain are a commons." Lessig.

"That a language is a commons ... society as a whole." **Michael Newton**, in the *London Review of Books,* reviewing a book called *Echolalias: On the Forgetting of Language* by **Daniel Heller-Roazen**. The paraphrases of book reviewers are another covert form of collaborative culture; as an avid reader of reviews, I know much about books I've never read. To quote Yann Martel on how he came to be accused of imperial plagiarism in his Booker-winning novel *Life of Pi,*

> Ten or so years ago, I read a review by John Updike in the *New York Times Review of Books* [sic]. It was of a novel by a Brazilian writer, Moacyr Scliar. I forget the title, and John Updike did worse: he clearly thought the book as a whole was forgettable. His review—one of those that makes you suspicious by being mostly descriptive ... oozed indifference. But one thing about it struck me: the premise.... Oh, the wondrous things I could do with this premise.

Unfortunately, no one was ever able to locate the Updike review in question.

"The American commons ..." to "... for a song." Bollier.

"Honoring the commons ..." to "... practical necessity." Bollier.

"We in Western ... public good." **John Sulston**, Nobel Prize–winner and co-mapper of the human genome.

"We have to remain ..." to "... benefit of a few." **Harry S Truman**, at the opening of the Everglades National Park. Although it may seem the height of presumption to rip off a president—I found claiming Truman's stolid advocacy as my own embarrassing in the extreme—I didn't rewrite him at all. As the poet Marianne Moore said, "If a thing had been said in the *best* way, how can you say it better?" Moore confessed her penchant for incorporating lines from others' work, explaining, "I have not yet been able to outgrow this hybrid method of composition."

Undiscovered Public Knowledge

"... intellectuals despondent ..." to "... quickly and cheaply?" **Steve Fuller**, *The Intellectual.* There's something of Borges in Fuller's insight here; the notion of a storehouse of knowledge waiting passively to be assembled by future users is suggestive of both "The Library of Babel" and "Kafka and his Precursors."

Give All

"... one of Iran's finest ..." to "... meditation on his heroine?" **Amy Taubin**, *Village Voice,* although it was me who was disappointed at the door of the Walter Reade Theater.

"The primary objective ..." to "... unfair nor unfortunate." **Sandra Day O'Connor**, 1991.

"... the future will be much like the past" to "... give some things away." Open-source film archivist **Rick Prelinger**, quoted in McLeod.

"Change may be troubling ... with certainty." McLeod.

"... woven entirely ..." to "... without inverted commas." **Roland Barthes**.

"The kernel, the soul ..." to "... characteristics of phrasing." **Mark Twain**, from a consoling letter to Helen Keller, who had suffered distressing accusations of plagiarism (!). In fact, her work included unconsciously memorized phrases; under Keller's particular circumstances, her writing could be understood as a kind of allegory of the "constructed" nature of artistic perception. I found the Twain quote in the aforementioned *Copyrights and Copywrongs,* by Siva Vaidhyanathan.

"Old and new ..." to "... we all quote." **Ralph Waldo Emerson**. These guys all sound alike!

"People live differently ... wealth as a gift." Hyde.

"... I'm a cork ..." to "... blown away." This is adapted from The Beach Boys song "'Til I Die," written by **Brian Wilson**. My own first adventure with song-lyric permissions came when I tried to have a character in my second novel quote the lyrics "There's a world where I can go and/Tell my secrets to/In my room/In my room." After learning the likely expense, at my editor's suggestion I replaced those with "You take the high road/I'll take the low road/I'll be in Scotland before you," a lyric in the public domain. This capitulation always bugged me, and in the subsequent British publication of the same book I restored the Brian Wilson lyric, without permission. *Ocean of Story* is the title of a collection of **Christina Stead**'s short fiction.

Saul Bellow, writing to a friend who'd taken offense at Bellow's fictional use of certain personal facts, said: "The name of the game is Give All. You are welcome to all my facts. You know them, I give them to you. If you have the strength to pick them up, take them with my blessing." I couldn't bring myself to retain Bellow's "strength," which seemed presumptuous in my new context, though it is surely the more elegant phrase. On the other hand, I was pleased to invite the suggestion that the gifts in question may actually be light and easily lifted.

Key to the Key

The notion of a collage text is, of course, not original to me. **Walter Benjamin**'s incomplete *Arcades Project* seemingly would have featured extensive interlaced quotations. Other precedents include **Graham Rawle**'s novel *Diary of an Amateur Photographer,* its text harvested from photography magazines, and **Eduardo Paolozzi**'s collage-novel *Kex,* cobbled from crime novels and newspaper clippings. Closer to home, my efforts owe a great deal to the recent essays of **David Shields**, in which diverse quotes are made to closely intertwine and reverberate, and to conversations with editor **Sean Howe** and archivist **Pamela Jackson**. Last year **David Edelstein**, in *New York* magazine, satirized the Kaavya Viswanathan plagiarism case by creating an almost completely plagiarized column denouncing her actions. Edelstein intended to demonstrate, through ironic example, how bricolage such as his own was ipso facto facile and unworthy. Although Viswanathan's version of "creative copying" was a pitiable one, I differ with Edelstein's conclusions.

The phrase *Je est un autre,* with its deliberately awkward syntax, belongs to **Arthur Rimbaud**. It has been translated both as "I is another" and "I is someone else," as in this excerpt from Rimbaud's letters:

> For *I* is someone else. If brass wakes up a trumpet, it is not its fault. To me this is obvious: I witness the unfolding of my own thought: I watch it, I listen to it: I make a stroke of the bow: the symphony begins to stir in the depths, or springs on to the stage.
>
> If the old fools had not discovered only the *false* significance of the Ego, we should not now be having to sweep away those millions of skeletons which, since time immemorial, have been piling up the fruits of their one-eyed intellects, and claiming to be, themselves, the authors!

QUESTIONS FOR MAKING CONNECTIONS
WITHIN THE READING

1. Discuss the relationship between the two economies that Lethem describes—the economy of the market and the economy of the gift. What is the role of property in the two economies, and what role do culture and the arts play in each? At first glance the two economies might appear to be antithetical, but Lethem suggests that the two of them can actually coexist. How is such coexistence possible, and in what ways might the two economies sustain and revitalize each other? How would the disappearance of the *public commons* damage the whole society? In what respects does private property depend on the health of the commons?

2. In your own words, explain the following passage: "A time is marked not so much by ideas that are argued about as by ideas that are taken for granted. The character of an era hangs upon what needs no defense. In this regard, few of us question the contemporary construction of copyright." How might it be possible that ideas which seem to require no defense are actually the most revealing ones? Why aren't the most discussed ideas the ones of greatest consequence? If the justness of the copyright appears to be self-evident, what can we conclude about the blindnesses of our own historical period? In what ways do our copyright laws reflect deeper anxieties about our relations to others? Does the common sense of our time prevent us from enjoying more creative lives?

3. Explain Lethem's point when he declares, "When damn near everything presents itself as familiar ... it's not a surprise that some of today's most ambitious art is going about trying to make the familiar strange." What does Lethem mean when he claims that "everything presents itself as familiar"? And what might be involved in making the familiar strange? What effect does the familiar have on us, and what effect does strangeness have? How do the artists Lethem discusses make the familiar seem strange? How might taking the words of someone else and putting them to a new use illustrate the value of estrangement? Does Lethem himself manage to make the familiar strange, and why is doing so important to his argument?

QUESTIONS FOR WRITING

1. The anthropologist David Graeber has made the claim that all societies, even those that have developed sophisticated forms of private property, still observe an implicit communism on the level of basic human interactions. For example, if your father asks you for a wrench while he is repairing a faucet, you would not normally respond with the question, "What's in it for me?" If the word *communism* actually refers to the owning of things in common, does Lethem seem to accept the argument that something like

common ownership is required for the health of a society? In what ways might communism in this sense actually contribute to democracy as well as personal freedom? In what ways might the open source movement represent a rebellion against the dominant ways of thinking about property as fundamentally private?

2. Does Lethem want students to cheat? When he writes that plagiarism is the soul of all human utterances, does he really mean it? Does he believe that you should feel free to learn from the *ideas* of others, while still respecting the principle of private ownership when it comes to *words*? Would he approve of your submitting a paper purchased from an Internet company? Would he approve of splicing into your next essay sentences or whole paragraphs taken from someone else's work, all without proper attribution? Does Lethem do the same thing himself? Is Lethem's argument *amoral*—that is, is it indifferent to ethical concerns? Is his view actually immoral— calculated to do harm? Or is Lethem trying to promote a different set of values? What might those values include?

QUESTIONS FOR MAKING CONNECTIONS
BETWEEN READINGS

1. In what ways might the "ecstasy of influence" celebrated by Lethem qualify as a form of "love" in the sense explored by Barbara Fredrickson in *Love 2.0*? With its detailed attention to the brain, Fredrickson's argument might seem quite far removed from Lethem's literary concerns, but can biological science shed light on the process Lethem explores? Look, for example, at Fredrickson's discussion of "brain coupling":

    > Communication—a true meeting of the minds—is a single act, performed by two brains. Considering the positivity resonance of love, what I find most fascinating about these findings is that a key brain area that showed coupling in [the] speaker-listener study was the insula, an area linked with conscious feeling states.

    Does making someone else's language your own qualify as *brain coupling* too, and does it produce a change in your conscious emotional state? Can we think of sharing language as a form of *positivity resonance*? If love as Fredrickson defines it helps to expand the boundaries of the self, does the ecstasy of influence do the same?

2. In his defense of the freedom to use culture creatively, Lethem levels criticism at a major player on the entertainment scene:

    > The Walt Disney Company has drawn an astonishing catalogue from the work of others: *Snow White and the Seven Dwarfs*, *Fantasia*, *Pinocchio*, *Dumbo*, *Bambi*, *Song of the South*, *Cinderella*, *Alice in*

Wonderland, Robin Hood, Peter Pan, Lady and the Tramp, Mulan, Sleeping Beauty, The Sword in the Stone, The Jungle Book .... Yet Disney's protectorate of lobbyists has policed the resulting cache of cultural materials as vigilantly as if it were Fort Knox—threatening legal action.

As you explain and explore the reasoning behind Lethem's critique, consider Joseph Stiglitz's discussion of economic monopolies in "Rent Seeking and the Making of an Unequal Society." Is the Disney Company guilty of *rent seeking* in the sphere of culture? Does such behavior contribute to inequalities of access to cultural capital? Does Stiglitz want to bring open access to the economic sphere—access akin to the commons Lethem extols in the realm of culture? Or does Stiglitz argue for a change less sweeping in its scope?

MICHAEL MOSS

EVEN MORE THAN shelter and clothing, food occupies a special place in our lives. Needless to say, our existence would be unsustainable without it, but food is unique in another way: its appearance in the store, the campus cafeteria, or the restaurant down the street represents the work of countless people, most of whom we will never know. The food system, vast and enormously complex, ultimately operates on trust. But what happens when that trust is betrayed? This is the question journalist Michael Moss has set out to answer. In the course of his detailed investigation of the food industry, Moss learned that many corporations use the findings of contemporary science to create addictions that undermine the health of millions of Americans—while raking in enormous profits.

Investigative journalism of this kind is Moss's stock-in-trade. A winner of a Pulitzer Prize in 2010, he wrote for the *Wall Street Journal,* the *Atlanta Journal-Constitution,* and *New York Newsday* before becoming a reporter for the *New York Times.* In 2006, three years into the U.S. occupation of Iraq, he brought to light a disturbing truth about the conduct of the war. A study done by the Pentagon—and later concealed—found that as many as 80 percent of the marines who died from upper body wounds could have survived if they had only been given extra protective armor. Simply by enlarging the existing plates, without adding new protection, the leadership would have prevented about a third of the fatal injuries. As early as 2003, Army General Richard A. Cody recognized the problem and made serious efforts to scale up production, but the ensuing missteps clearly showed a fatal lack of coordination between the Pentagon, the manufacturers, and their various suppliers.

Moss's reporting on the armor saved lives, and lives are at stake in his book, *Salt Sugar Fat: How the Food Giants Hooked Us* (2013). Once again he acknowledges that certain people on the inside recognized a problem and set out to correct it. In the following selection, he recounts a meeting in 1999 where the head of Kraft Foods, Michael Mudd, warned his fellow CEOs that their industry was largely to blame for the obesity crisis. The failure of the industry to respond to his candid warning suggests that the problem cannot be understood by focusing on the ethical decisions of a few powerful individuals. Moss's article strongly

Body armor article: Michael Moss, "Pentagon Study Links Fatalities to Body Armor," *New York Times,* January 7, 2006. Reference to General Cody comes from Michael Moss, "Many Missteps Tied to Delay in Armor for Troops in Iraq," *New York Times,* March 7, 2005.

implies instead that real change requires us to start with the systemic nature of the threat to public health. Again and again the people Moss interviews are hard-working, intelligent men and women who have spent many years perfecting their expertise. But these same people often fail to think about the large-scale social implications of their work.

The Extraordinary Science of Addictive Junk Food

On the evening of April 8, 1999, a long line of Town Cars and taxis pulled up to the Minneapolis headquarters of Pillsbury and discharged 11 men who controlled America's largest food companies. Nestlé was in attendance, as were Kraft and Nabisco, General Mills and Procter & Gamble, Coca-Cola and Mars. Rivals any other day, the C.E.O.s and company presidents had come together for a rare, private meeting. On the agenda was one item: the emerging obesity epidemic and how to deal with it. While the atmosphere was cordial, the men assembled were hardly friends. Their stature was defined by their skill in fighting one another for what they called "stomach share"—the amount of digestive space that any one company's brand can grab from the competition.

James Behnke, a 55-year-old executive at Pillsbury, greeted the men as they arrived. He was anxious but also hopeful about the plan that he and a few other food-company executives had devised to engage the C.E.O.s on America's growing weight problem. "We were very concerned, and rightfully so, that obesity was becoming a major issue," Behnke recalled. "People were starting to talk about sugar taxes, and there was a lot of pressure on food companies." Getting the company chiefs in the same room to talk about anything, much less a sensitive issue like this, was a tricky business, so Behnke and his fellow organizers had scripted the meeting carefully, honing the message to its barest essentials. "C.E.O.s in the food industry are typically not technical guys, and they're uncomfortable going to meetings where technical people talk in technical terms about technical things," Behnke said. "They don't want to be embarrassed. They don't want to make commitments. They want to maintain their aloofness and autonomy."

A chemist by training with a doctoral degree in food science, Behnke became Pillsbury's chief technical officer in 1979 and was instrumental in creating a long line of hit products, including microwaveable popcorn. He deeply admired Pillsbury but in recent years had grown troubled by pictures of obese children suffering from diabetes and the earliest signs of hypertension and heart disease. In the months leading up to the C.E.O. meeting, he was engaged in conversation with a group of food-science experts who were painting an increasingly grim picture of the public's ability to cope with the industry's formulations—from the body's fragile controls on overeating to the hidden power of some processed foods to make people feel hungrier still. It was time, he and a handful of others felt, to warn the C.E.O.s that their companies may have gone too far in creating and marketing products that posed the greatest health concerns.

The discussion took place in Pillsbury's auditorium. The first speaker was a vice president of Kraft named Michael Mudd. "I very much appreciate this opportunity to talk to you about childhood obesity and the growing challenge it presents for us all," Mudd began. "Let me say right at the start, this is not an easy subject. There are no easy answers—for what the public health community must do to bring this problem under control or for what the industry should do as others seek to hold it accountable for what has happened. But this much is clear: For those of us who've looked hard at this issue, whether they're public health professionals or staff specialists in your own companies, we feel sure that the one thing we shouldn't do is nothing."

As he spoke, Mudd clicked through a deck of slides—114 in all—projected on a large screen behind him. The figures were staggering. More than half of American adults were now considered overweight, with nearly one-quarter of the adult population—40 million people—clinically defined as obese. Among children, the rates had more than doubled since 1980, and the number of kids considered obese had shot past 12 million. (This was still only 1999; the nation's obesity rates would climb much higher.) Food manufacturers were now being blamed for the problem from all sides—academia, the Centers for Disease Control and Prevention, the American Heart Association and the American Cancer Society. The Secretary of Agriculture, over whom the industry had long held sway, had recently called obesity a "national epidemic."

Mudd then did the unthinkable. He drew a connection to the last thing in the world the C.E.O.s wanted linked to their products: cigarettes. First came a quote from a Yale University professor of psychology and public health, Kelly Brownell, who was an especially vocal proponent of the view that the processed-food industry should be seen as a public health menace: "As a culture, we've become upset by the tobacco companies advertising to children, but we sit idly by while the food companies do the very same thing. And we could make a claim that the toll taken on the public health by a poor diet rivals that taken by tobacco."

"If anyone in the food industry ever doubted there was a slippery slope out there," Mudd said, "I imagine they are beginning to experience a distinct sliding sensation right about now."

Mudd then presented the plan he and others had devised to address the obesity problem. Merely getting the executives to acknowledge some culpability was an important first step, he knew, so his plan would start off with a small but crucial move: the industry should use the expertise of scientists—its own and others—to gain a deeper understanding of what was driving Americans to overeat. Once this was achieved, the effort could unfold on several fronts. To be sure, there would be no getting around the role that packaged foods and drinks play in overconsumption. They would have to pull back on their use of salt, sugar and fat, perhaps by imposing industrywide limits. But it wasn't just a matter of these three ingredients; the schemes they used to advertise and market their products were critical, too. Mudd proposed creating a "code to guide the nutritional aspects of food marketing, especially to children."

"We are saying that the industry should make a sincere effort to be part of the solution," Mudd concluded. "And that by doing so, we can help to defuse the criticism that's building against us."

What happened next was not written down. But according to three participants, when Mudd stopped talking, the one C.E.O. whose recent exploits in the grocery store had awed the rest of the industry stood up to speak. His name was Stephen Sanger, and he was also the person—as head of General Mills—who had the most to lose when it came to dealing with obesity. Under his leadership, General Mills had overtaken not just the cereal aisle but other sections of the grocery store. The company's Yoplait brand had transformed traditional unsweetened breakfast yogurt into a veritable dessert. It now had twice as much sugar per serving as General Mills' marshmallow cereal Lucky Charms. And yet, because of yogurt's well-tended image as a wholesome snack, sales of Yoplait were soaring, with annual revenue topping $500 million. Emboldened by the success, the company's development wing pushed even harder, inventing a Yoplait variation that came in a squeezable tube—perfect for kids. They called it Go-Gurt and rolled it out nationally in the weeks before the C.E.O. meeting. (By year's end, it would hit $100 million in sales.)

According to the sources I spoke with, Sanger began by reminding the group that consumers were "fickle." (Sanger declined to be interviewed.) Sometimes they worried about sugar, other times fat. General Mills, he said, acted responsibly to both the public and shareholders by offering products to satisfy dieters and other concerned shoppers, from low sugar to added whole grains. But most often, he said, people bought what they liked, and they liked what tasted good. "Don't talk to me about nutrition," he reportedly said, taking on the voice of the typical consumer. "Talk to me about taste, and if this stuff tastes better, don't run around trying to sell stuff that doesn't taste good."

To react to the critics, Sanger said, would jeopardize the sanctity of the recipes that had made his products so successful. General Mills would not pull back. He would push his people onward, and he urged his peers to do the same. Sanger's response effectively ended the meeting.

"What can I say?" James Behnke told me years later. "It didn't work. These guys weren't as receptive as we thought they would be." Behnke chose his words deliberately. He wanted to be fair. "Sanger was trying to say, 'Look, we're not going to screw around with the company jewels here and change the formulations because a bunch of guys in white coats are worried about obesity.'"

The meeting was remarkable, first, for the insider admissions of guilt. But I was also struck by how prescient the organizers of the sit-down had been.

Today, one in three adults is considered clinically obese, along with one in five kids, and 24 million Americans are afflicted by type 2 diabetes, often caused by poor diet, with another 79 million people having pre-diabetes. Even gout, a painful form of arthritis once known as "the rich man's disease" for its associations with gluttony, now afflicts eight million Americans.

The public and the food companies have known for decades now—or at the very least since this meeting—that sugary, salty, fatty foods are not good for us in the quantities that we consume them. So why are the diabetes and obesity and hypertension numbers still spiraling out of control? It's not just a matter of poor willpower on the part of the consumer and a give-the-people-what-they-want attitude on the part of the food manufacturers. What I found, over four years of research and reporting, was a conscious effort—taking place in labs and marketing meetings and grocery-store aisles—to get people hooked on foods that are convenient and inexpensive. I talked to more than 300 people in or formerly employed by the processed-food industry, from scientists to marketers to C.E.O.s. Some were willing whistle-blowers, while others spoke reluctantly when presented with some of the thousands of pages of secret memos that I obtained from inside the food industry's operations. What follows is a series of small case studies of a handful of characters whose work then, and perspective now, sheds light on how the foods are created and sold to people who, while not powerless, are extremely vulnerable to the intensity of these companies' industrial formulations and selling campaigns.

I. 'IN THIS FIELD, I'M A GAME CHANGER.'

John Lennon couldn't find it in England, so he had cases of it shipped from New York to fuel the "Imagine" sessions. The Beach Boys, ZZ Top and Cher all stipulated in their contract riders that it be put in their dressing rooms when they toured. Hillary Clinton asked for it when she traveled as first lady, and ever after her hotel suites were dutifully stocked.

What they all wanted was Dr Pepper, which until 2001 occupied a comfortable third-place spot in the soda aisle behind Coca-Cola and Pepsi. But then a flood of spinoffs from the two soda giants showed up on the shelves—lemons and limes, vanillas and coffees, raspberries and oranges, whites and blues and clears—what in food-industry lingo are known as "line extensions," and Dr Pepper started to lose its market share.

Responding to this pressure, Cadbury Schweppes created its first spin-off, other than a diet version, in the soda's 115-year history, a bright red soda with a very un-Dr Pepper name: Red Fusion. "If we are to re-establish Dr Pepper back to its historic growth rates, we have to add more excitement," the company's president, Jack Kilduff, said. One particularly promising market, Kilduff pointed out, was the "rapidly growing Hispanic and African-American communities."

But consumers hated Red Fusion. "Dr Pepper is my all-time favorite drink, so I was curious about the Red Fusion," a California mother of three wrote on a blog to warn other Peppers away. "It's disgusting. Gagging. Never again."

Stung by the rejection, Cadbury Schweppes in 2004 turned to a food-industry legend named Howard Moskowitz. Moskowitz, who studied mathematics and holds a Ph.D. in experimental psychology from Harvard, runs a consulting firm in White Plains, where for more than three decades he has "optimized" a variety of products for Campbell Soup, General Foods, Kraft and PepsiCo. "I've optimized soups," Moskowitz told me. "I've optimized pizzas. I've optimized salad dressings and pickles. In this field, I'm a game changer."

In the process of product optimization, food engineers alter a litany of variables with the sole intent of finding the most perfect version (or versions) of a product. Ordinary consumers are paid to spend hours sitting in rooms where they touch, feel, sip, smell, swirl and taste whatever product is in question. Their opinions are dumped into a computer, and the data are sifted and sorted through a statistical method called conjoint analysis, which determines what features will be most attractive to consumers. Moskowitz likes to imagine that his computer is divided into silos, in which each of the attributes is stacked. But it's not simply a matter of comparing Color 23 with Color 24. In the most complicated projects, Color 23 must be combined with Syrup 11 and Packaging 6, and on and on, in seemingly infinite combinations. Even for jobs in which the only concern is taste and the variables are limited to the ingredients, endless charts and graphs will come spewing out of Moskowitz's computer. "The mathematical model maps out the ingredients to the sensory perceptions these ingredients create," he told me, "so I can just dial a new product. This is the engineering approach."

Moskowitz's work on Prego spaghetti sauce was memorialized in a 2004 presentation by the author Malcolm Gladwell at the TED conference in Monterey, Calif.: "After ... months and months, he had a mountain of data about how the American people feel about spaghetti sauce.... And sure enough, if you sit down and you analyze all this data on spaghetti sauce, you realize that all Americans fall into one of three groups. There are people who like their spaghetti sauce plain. There are people who like their spaghetti sauce spicy. And there are people who like it extra-chunky. And of those three facts, the third one was the most significant, because at the time, in the early 1980s, if you went to a supermarket, you would not find extra-chunky spaghetti sauce. And Prego turned to Howard, and they said, 'Are you telling me that one-third of Americans crave extra-chunky spaghetti sauce, and yet no one is servicing their needs?' And he said, 'Yes.' And Prego then went back and completely reformulated their spaghetti sauce and came out with a line of extra-chunky that immediately and completely took over the spaghetti-sauce business in this country.... That is Howard's gift to the American people.... He fundamentally changed the way the food industry thinks about making you happy."

Well, yes and no. One thing Gladwell didn't mention is that the food industry already knew some things about making people happy—and it started with sugar. Many of the Prego sauces—whether cheesy, chunky or light—have one feature in common: The largest ingredient, after tomatoes, is sugar. A mere half-cup of Prego Traditional, for instance, has the equivalent of more than two teaspoons of sugar, as much as two-plus Oreo cookies. It also delivers one-third of the sodium recommended for a majority of American adults for an entire day.

In making these sauces, Campbell supplied the ingredients, including the salt, sugar and, for some versions, fat, while Moskowitz supplied the optimization. "More is not necessarily better," Moskowitz wrote in his own account of the Prego project. "As the sensory intensity (say, of sweetness) increases, consumers first say that they like the product more, but eventually, with a middle level of sweetness, consumers like the product the most (this is their optimum, or 'bliss,' point)."

I first met Moskowitz on a crisp day in the spring of 2010 at the Harvard Club in Midtown Manhattan. As we talked, he made clear that while he has worked on numerous projects aimed at creating more healthful foods and insists the industry could be doing far more to curb obesity, he had no qualms about his own pioneering work on discovering what industry insiders now regularly refer to as "the bliss point" or any of the other systems that helped food companies create the greatest amount of crave. "There's no moral issue for me," he said. "I did the best science I could. I was struggling to survive and didn't have the luxury of being a moral creature. As a researcher, I was ahead of my time."

Moskowitz's path to mastering the bliss point began in earnest not at Harvard but a few months after graduation, 16 miles from Cambridge, in the town of Natick, where the U.S. Army hired him to work in its research labs. The military has long been in a peculiar bind when it comes to food: how to get soldiers to eat more rations when they are in the field. They know that over time, soldiers would gradually find their meals-ready-to-eat so boring that they would toss them away, half-eaten, and not get all the calories they needed. But what was causing this M.R.E.-fatigue was a mystery. "So I started asking soldiers how frequently they would like to eat this or that, trying to figure out which products they would find boring," Moskowitz said. The answers he got were inconsistent. "They liked flavorful foods like turkey tetrazzini, but only at first; they quickly grew tired of them. On the other hand, mundane foods like white bread would never get them too excited, but they could eat lots and lots of it without feeling they'd had enough."

This contradiction is known as "sensory-specific satiety." In lay terms, it is the tendency for big, distinct flavors to overwhelm the brain, which responds by depressing your desire to have more. Sensory-specific satiety also became a guiding principle for the processed-food industry. The biggest hits—be they Coca-Cola or Doritos—owe their success to complex formulas that pique the taste buds enough to be alluring but don't have a distinct, overriding single flavor that tells the brain to stop eating.

Thirty-two years after he began experimenting with the bliss point, Moskowitz got the call from Cadbury Schweppes asking him to create a good line extension for Dr Pepper. I spent an afternoon in his White Plains offices as he and his vice president for research, Michele Reisner, walked me through the Dr Pepper campaign. Cadbury wanted its new flavor to have cherry and vanilla on top of the basic Dr Pepper taste. Thus, there were three main components to play with. A sweet cherry flavoring, a sweet vanilla flavoring and a sweet syrup known as "Dr Pepper flavoring."

Finding the bliss point required the preparation of 61 subtly distinct formulas—31 for the regular version and 30 for diet. The formulas were then subjected to 3,904 tastings organized in Los Angeles, Dallas, Chicago and Philadelphia. The Dr Pepper tasters began working through their samples, resting five minutes between each sip to restore their taste buds. After each sample, they gave numerically ranked answers to a set of questions: How much did they like it overall? How strong is the taste? How do they feel about the taste? How would they describe the quality of this product? How likely would they be to purchase this product?

Moskowitz's data—compiled in a 135-page report for the soda maker—is tremendously fine-grained, showing how different people and groups of people feel about a strong vanilla taste versus weak, various aspects of aroma and the powerful sensory force that food scientists call "mouth feel." This is the way a product interacts with the mouth, as defined more specifically by a host of related sensations, from dryness to gumminess to moisture release. These are terms more familiar to sommeliers, but the mouth feel of soda and many other food items, especially those high in fat, is second only to the bliss point in its ability to predict how much craving a product will induce.

In addition to taste, the consumers were also tested on their response to color, which proved to be highly sensitive. "When we increased the level of the Dr Pepper flavoring, it gets darker and liking goes off," Reisner said. These preferences can also be cross-referenced by age, sex and race.

On Page 83 of the report, a thin blue line represents the amount of Dr Pepper flavoring needed to generate maximum appeal. The line is shaped like an upside-down U, just like the bliss-point curve that Moskowitz studied 30 years earlier in his Army lab. And at the top of the arc, there is not a single sweet spot but instead a sweet range, within which "bliss" was achievable. This meant that Cadbury could edge back on its key ingredient, the sugary Dr Pepper syrup, without falling out of the range and losing the bliss. Instead of using 2 milliliters of the flavoring, for instance, they could use 1.69 milliliters and achieve the same effect. The potential savings is merely a few percentage points, and it won't mean much to individual consumers who are counting calories or grams of sugar. But for Dr Pepper, it adds up to colossal savings. "That looks like nothing," Reisner said. "But it's a lot of money. A lot of money. Millions."

The soda that emerged from all of Moskowitz's variations became known as Cherry Vanilla Dr Pepper, and it proved successful beyond anything Cadbury imagined. In 2008, Cadbury split off its soft-drinks business, which included Snapple and 7-Up. The Dr Pepper Snapple Group has since been valued in excess of $11 billion.

II. 'LUNCHTIME IS ALL YOURS.'

Sometimes innovations within the food industry happen in the lab, with scientists dialing in specific ingredients to achieve the greatest allure. And sometimes, as in the case of Oscar Mayer's bologna crisis, the innovation involves putting old products in new packages.

The 1980s were tough times for Oscar Mayer. Red-meat consumption fell more than 10 percent as fat became synonymous with cholesterol, clogged arteries, heart attacks, and strokes. Anxiety set in at the company's headquarters in Madison, Wis., where executives worried about their future and the pressure they faced from their new bosses at Philip Morris.

Bob Drane was the company's vice president for new business strategy and development when Oscar Mayer tapped him to try to find some way to reposition bologna and other troubled meats that were declining in popularity and sales. I met Drane at his home in Madison and went through the records he had kept on the birth of what would become much more than his solution to the company's meat problem. In 1985, when Drane began working on the project, his orders were to "figure out how to contemporize what we've got."

Drane's first move was to try to zero in not on what Americans felt about processed meat but on what Americans felt about lunch. He organized focus-group sessions with the people most responsible for buying bologna—mothers—and as they talked, he realized the most pressing issue for them was time. Working moms strove to provide healthful food, of course, but they spoke with real passion and at length about the morning crush, that nightmarish dash to get breakfast on the table and lunch packed and kids out the door. He summed up their remarks for me like this: "It's awful. I am scrambling around. My kids are asking me for stuff. I'm trying to get myself ready to go to the office. I go to pack these lunches, and I don't know what I've got." What the moms revealed to him, Drane said, was "a gold mine of disappointments and problems."

He assembled a team of about 15 people with varied skills, from design to food science to advertising, to create something completely new—a convenient prepackaged lunch that would have as its main building block the company's sliced bologna and ham. They wanted to add bread, naturally, because who ate bologna without it? But this presented a problem: There was no way bread could stay fresh for the two months their product needed to sit in warehouses or in grocery coolers. Crackers, however, could—so they added a handful of cracker rounds to the package. Using cheese was the next obvious move, given its increased presence in processed foods. But what kind of cheese would work? Natural Cheddar, which they started off with, crumbled and didn't slice very well, so they moved on to processed varieties, which could bend and be sliced and would last forever, or they could knock another two cents off per unit by using an even lesser product called "cheese food," which had lower scores than processed cheese in taste tests. The cost dilemma was solved when Oscar Mayer merged with Kraft in 1989 and the company didn't have to shop for cheese anymore; it got all the processed cheese it wanted from its new sister company, and at cost.

Drane's team moved into a nearby hotel, where they set out to find the right mix of components and container. They gathered around tables where bagfuls of meat, cheese, crackers and all sorts of wrapping material had been dumped, and they let their imaginations run. After snipping and taping their way through a host of failures, the model they fell back on was the American TV dinner—and after some brainstorming about names (Lunch Kits? Go-Packs? Fun Mealz?), Lunchables were born.

The trays flew off the grocery-store shelves. Sales hit a phenomenal $218 million in the first 12 months, more than anyone was prepared for. This only brought Drane his next crisis. The production costs were so high that they were losing money with each tray they produced. So Drane flew to New York, where he met with Philip Morris officials who promised to give him the money he needed to keep it going. "The hard thing is to figure out something that will sell," he was told. "You'll figure out how to get the cost right." Projected to lose $6 million in 1991, the trays instead broke even; the next year, they earned $8 million.

With production costs trimmed and profits coming in, the next question was how to expand the franchise, which they did by turning to one of the cardinal rules in processed food: When in doubt, add sugar. "Lunchables With Dessert is a logical extension," an Oscar Mayer official reported to Philip Morris executives in early 1991. The "target" remained the same as it was for regular Lunchables—"busy mothers" and "working women," ages 25 to 49—and the "enhanced taste" would attract shoppers who had grown bored with the current trays. A year later, the dessert Lunchable morphed into the Fun Pack, which would come with a Snickers bar, a package of M&M's or a Reese's Peanut Butter Cup, as well as a sugary drink. The Lunchables team started by using Kool-Aid and cola and then Capri Sun after Philip Morris added that drink to its stable of brands.

Eventually, a line of the trays, appropriately called Maxed Out, was released that had as many as nine grams of saturated fat, or nearly an entire day's recommended maximum for kids, with up to two-thirds of the max for sodium and 13 teaspoons of sugar.

When I asked Geoffrey Bible, former C.E.O. of Philip Morris, about this shift toward more salt, sugar and fat in meals for kids, he smiled and noted that even in its earliest incarnation, Lunchables was held up for criticism. "One article said something like, 'If you take Lunchables apart, the most healthy item in it is the napkin.'"

Well, they did have a good bit of fat, I offered. "You bet," he said. "Plus cookies."

The prevailing attitude among the company's food managers—through the 1990s, at least, before obesity became a more pressing concern—was one of supply and demand. "People could point to these things and say, 'They've got too much sugar, they've got too much salt,'" Bible said. "Well, that's what the consumer wants, and we're not putting a gun to their head to eat it. That's what they want. If we give them less, they'll buy less, and the competitor will get our market. So you're sort of trapped." (Bible would later press Kraft to reconsider its reliance on salt, sugar and fat.)

When it came to Lunchables, they did try to add more healthful ingredients. Back at the start, Drane experimented with fresh carrots but quickly gave up on that, since fresh components didn't work within the constraints of the processed-food system, which typically required weeks or months of transport and storage before the food arrived at the grocery store. Later, a low-fat version of the trays was developed, using meats and cheese and crackers that were formulated with less fat, but it tasted inferior, sold poorly and was quickly scrapped.

When I met with Kraft officials in 2011 to discuss their products and policies on nutrition, they had dropped the Maxed Out line and were trying to improve the nutritional profile of Lunchables through smaller, incremental changes that were less noticeable to consumers. Across the Lunchables line, they said they had reduced the salt, sugar and fat by about 10 percent, and new versions, featuring mandarin-orange and pineapple slices, were in development. These would be promoted as more healthful versions, with "fresh fruit," but their list of ingredients—containing upward of 70 items, with sucrose, corn syrup, high-fructose corn syrup and fruit concentrate all in the same tray—have been met with intense criticism from outside the industry.

One of the company's responses to criticism is that kids don't eat the Lunchables every day—on top of which, when it came to trying to feed them more healthful foods, kids themselves were unreliable. When their parents packed fresh carrots, apples and water, they couldn't be trusted to eat them. Once in school, they often trashed the healthful stuff in their brown bags to get right to the sweets.

This idea—that kids are in control—would become a key concept in the evolving marketing campaigns for the trays. In what would prove to be their greatest achievement of all, the Lunchables team would delve into adolescent psychology to discover that it wasn't the food in the trays that excited the kids; it was the feeling of power it brought to their lives. As Bob Eckert, then the C.E.O. of Kraft, put it in 1999: "Lunchables aren't about lunch. It's about kids being able to put together what they want to eat, anytime, anywhere."

Kraft's early Lunchables campaign targeted mothers. They might be too distracted by work to make a lunch, but they loved their kids enough to offer them this prepackaged gift. But as the focus swung toward kids, Saturday-morning cartoons started carrying an ad that offered a different message: "All day, you gotta do what they say," the ads said. "But lunchtime is all yours."

With this marketing strategy in place and pizza Lunchables—the crust in one compartment, the cheese, pepperoni and sauce in others—proving to be a runaway success, the entire world of fast food suddenly opened up for Kraft to pursue. They came out with a Mexican-themed Lunchables called Beef Taco Wraps; a Mini Burgers Lunchables; a Mini Hot Dog Lunchable, which also happened to provide a way for Oscar Mayer to sell its wieners. By 1999, pancakes—which included syrup, icing, Lifesavers candy and Tang, for a whopping 76 grams of sugar—and waffles were, for a time, part of the Lunchables franchise as well.

Annual sales kept climbing, past $500 million, past $800 million; at last count, including sales in Britain, they were approaching the $1 billion mark. Lunchables was more than a hit; it was now its own category. Eventually, more than 60 varieties of Lunchables and other brands of trays would show up in the grocery stores. In 2007, Kraft even tried a Lunchables Jr. for 3- to 5-year-olds.

In the trove of records that document the rise of the Lunchables and the sweeping change it brought to lunchtime habits, I came across a photograph of Bob Drane's daughter, which he had slipped into the Lunchables presentation he showed to food developers. The picture was taken on Monica Drane's wedding day in 1989, and she was standing outside the family's home in Madison, a beautiful bride in a white wedding dress, holding one of the brand-new yellow trays.

During the course of reporting, I finally had a chance to ask her about it. Was she really that much of a fan? "There must have been some in the fridge," she told me. "I probably just took one out before we went to the church. My mom had joked that it was really like their fourth child, my dad invested so much time and energy on it."

Monica Drane had three of her own children by the time we spoke, ages 10, 14 and 17. "I don't think my kids have ever eaten a Lunchable," she told me. "They know they exist and that Grandpa Bob invented them. But we eat very healthfully."

Drane himself paused only briefly when I asked him if, looking back, he was proud of creating the trays. "Lots of things are trade-offs," he said. "And I do believe it's easy to rationalize anything. In the end, I wish that the nutritional profile of the thing could have been better, but I don't view the entire project as anything but a positive contribution to people's lives."

Today Bob Drane is still talking to kids about what they like to eat, but his approach has changed. He volunteers with a nonprofit organization that seeks to build better communications between school kids and their parents, and right in the mix of their problems, alongside the academic struggles, is childhood obesity. Drane has also prepared a précis on the food industry that he used with medical students at the University of Wisconsin. And while he does not name his Lunchables in this document, and cites numerous causes for the obesity epidemic, he holds the entire industry accountable. "What do University of Wisconsin M.B.A.s learn about how to succeed in marketing?" his presentation to the med students asks. "Discover what consumers want to buy and give it to them with both barrels. Sell more, keep your job! How do marketers often translate these 'rules' into action on food? Our limbic brains love sugar, fat, salt.... So formulate products to deliver these. Perhaps add low-cost ingredients to boost profit margins. Then 'supersize' to sell more.... And advertise/promote to lock in 'heavy users.' Plenty of guilt to go around here!"

III. 'IT'S CALLED VANISHING CALORIC DENSITY.'

At a symposium for nutrition scientists in Los Angeles on Feb. 15, 1985, a professor of pharmacology from Helsinki named Heikki Karppanen told the remarkable story of Finland's effort to address its salt habit. In the late 1970s, the Finns were consuming huge amounts of sodium, eating on average more than two teaspoons of salt a day. As a result, the country had developed significant issues with high blood pressure, and men in the eastern part of Finland had the highest rate of fatal cardiovascular disease in the world. Research showed that this plague was not just a quirk of genetics or a result of a sedentary lifestyle—it was also owing to processed foods. So when Finnish authorities moved to address the problem, they went right after the manufacturers. (The Finnish response worked. Every grocery item that was heavy in salt would come to be marked prominently with the warning "High Salt Content." By 2007, Finland's per capita consumption of salt had dropped by a third, and this shift—along with improved medical care—was accompanied by a 75 to 80 percent decline in the number of deaths from strokes and heart disease.)

Karppanen's presentation was met with applause, but one man in the crowd seemed particularly intrigued by the presentation, and as Karppanen left the stage, the man intercepted him and asked if they could talk more over dinner. Their conversation later that night was not at all what Karppanen was expecting. His host did indeed have an interest in salt, but from quite a different vantage point: the man's name was Robert I-San Lin, and from 1974 to 1982, he worked as the chief scientist for Frito-Lay, the nearly $3-billion-a-year manufacturer of Lay's, Doritos, Cheetos and Fritos.

Lin's time at Frito-Lay coincided with the first attacks by nutrition advocates on salty foods and the first calls for federal regulators to reclassify salt as a "risky" food additive, which could have subjected it to severe controls. No company took this threat more seriously—or more personally—than Frito-Lay, Lin explained to Karppanen over their dinner. Three years after he left Frito-Lay, he was still anguished over his inability to effectively change the company's recipes and practices.

By chance, I ran across a letter that Lin sent to Karppanen three weeks after that dinner, buried in some files to which I had gained access. Attached to the letter was a memo written when Lin was at Frito-Lay, which detailed some of the company's efforts in defending salt. I tracked Lin down in Irvine, Calif., where we spent several days going through the internal company memos, strategy papers and handwritten notes he had kept. The documents were evidence of the concern that Lin had for consumers and of the company's intent on using science not to address the health concerns but to thwart them. While at Frito-Lay, Lin and other company scientists spoke openly about the country's excessive consumption of sodium and the fact that, as Lin said to me on more than one occasion, "people get addicted to salt."

Not much had changed by 1986, except Frito-Lay found itself on a rare cold streak. The company had introduced a series of high-profile products that failed miserably. Toppels, a cracker with cheese topping; Stuffers, a shell with a variety of fillings; Rumbles, a bite-size granola snack—they all came and went in a blink, and the company took a $52 million hit. Around that time, the marketing team was joined by Dwight Riskey, an expert on cravings who had been a fellow at the Monell Chemical Senses Center in Philadelphia, where he was part of a team of scientists that found that people could beat their salt habits simply by refraining from salty foods long enough for their taste buds to return to a normal level of sensitivity. He had also done work on the bliss point, showing how a product's allure is contextual, shaped partly by the other foods a person is eating, and that it changes as people age. This seemed to help explain why Frito-Lay was having so much trouble selling new snacks. The largest single block of customers, the baby boomers, had begun hitting middle age. According to the research, this suggested that their liking for salty snacks—both in the concentration of salt and how much they ate—would be tapering off. Along with the rest of the snack-food industry, Frito-Lay anticipated lower sales because of an aging population, and marketing plans were adjusted to focus even more intently on younger consumers.

Except that snack sales didn't decline as everyone had projected, Frito-Lay's doomed product launches notwithstanding. Poring over data one day in his home office, trying to understand just who was consuming all the snack food, Riskey realized that he and his colleagues had been misreading things all along.

They had been measuring the snacking habits of different age groups and were seeing what they expected to see, that older consumers ate less than those in their 20s. But what they weren't measuring, Riskey realized, is how those snacking habits of the boomers compared to *themselves* when they were in their 20s. When he called up a new set of sales data and performed what's called a cohort study, following a single group over time, a far more encouraging picture—for Frito-Lay, anyway—emerged. The baby boomers were not eating fewer salty snacks as they aged. "In fact, as those people aged, their consumption of all those segments—the cookies, the crackers, the candy, the chips—was going up," Riskey said. "They were not only eating what they ate when they were younger, they were eating more of it." In fact, everyone in the country, on average, was eating more salty snacks than they used to. The rate of consumption was edging up about one-third of a pound every year, with the average intake of snacks like chips and cheese crackers pushing past 12 pounds a year.

Riskey had a theory about what caused this surge: Eating real meals had become a thing of the past. Baby boomers, especially, seemed to have greatly cut down on regular meals. They were skipping breakfast when they had early-morning meetings. They skipped lunch when they then needed to catch up on work because of those meetings. They skipped dinner when their kids stayed out late or grew up and moved out of the house. And when they skipped these meals, they replaced them with snacks. "We looked at this behavior, and said, 'Oh, my gosh, people were skipping meals right and left,'" Riskey told me. "It was amazing." This led to the next realization, that baby boomers did not represent "a category that is mature, with no growth. This is a category that has huge growth potential."

The food technicians stopped worrying about inventing new products and instead embraced the industry's most reliable method for getting consumers to buy more: the line extension. The classic Lay's potato chips were joined by Salt & Vinegar, Salt & Pepper and Cheddar & Sour Cream. They put out Chili-Cheese-flavored Fritos, and Cheetos were transformed into 21 varieties. Frito-Lay had a formidable research complex near Dallas, where nearly 500 chemists, psychologists, and technicians conducted research that cost up to $30 million a year, and the science corps focused intense amounts of resources on questions of crunch, mouth feel, and aroma for each of these items. Their tools included a $40,000 device that simulated a chewing mouth to test and perfect the chips, discovering things like the perfect break point: people like a chip that snaps with about four pounds of pressure per square inch.

To get a better feel for their work, I called on Steven Witherly, a food scientist who wrote a fascinating guide for industry insiders titled, "Why Humans Like Junk Food." I brought him two shopping bags filled with a variety of chips to taste. He zeroed right in on the Cheetos. "This," Witherly said, "is one of the most marvelously constructed foods on the planet, in terms of pure pleasure." He ticked off a dozen attributes of the Cheetos that make the brain say more. But the one he focused on most was the puff's uncanny ability to melt in the mouth. "It's called vanishing caloric density," Witherly said. "If something melts down quickly, your brain thinks that there's no calories in it ... you can just keep eating it forever."

As for their marketing troubles, in a March 2010 meeting, Frito-Lay executives hastened to tell their Wall Street investors that the 1.4 billion boomers worldwide weren't being neglected; they were redoubling their efforts to understand exactly what it was that boomers most wanted in a snack chip. Which was basically everything: great taste, maximum bliss but minimal guilt about health, and more maturity than puffs. "They snack a lot," Frito-Lay's chief marketing officer, Ann Mukherjee, told the investors. "But what they're looking for is very different. They're looking for new experiences, real food experiences." Frito-Lay acquired Stacy's Pita Chip Company, which was started by a Massachusetts couple who made food-cart sandwiches and started serving pita chips to their customers in the mid-1990s. In Frito-Lay's hands, the pita chips averaged 270 milligrams of sodium—nearly one-fifth a whole day's recommended maximum for most American adults—and were a huge hit among boomers.

The Frito-Lay executives also spoke of the company's ongoing pursuit of a "designer sodium," which they hoped, in the near future, would take their sodium loads down by 40 percent. No need to worry about lost sales there, the company's C.E.O., Al Carey, assured their investors. The boomers would see less salt as the green light to snack like never before.

There's a paradox at work here. On the one hand, reduction of sodium in snack foods is commendable. On the other, these changes may well result in consumers eating more. "The big thing that will happen here is removing the barriers for boomers and giving them permission to snack," Carey said. The prospects for lower-salt snacks were so amazing, he added, that the company had set its sights on using the designer salt to conquer the toughest market of all for snacks: schools. He cited, for example, the school-food initiative championed by Bill Clinton and the American Heart Association, which is seeking to improve the nutrition of school food by limiting its load of salt, sugar and fat. "Imagine this," Carey said. "A potato chip that tastes great and qualifies for the Clinton-A.H.A. alliance for schools.... We think we have ways to do all of this on a potato chip, and imagine getting that product into schools, where children can have this product and grow up with it and feel good about eating it."

Carey's quote reminded me of something I read in the early stages of my reporting, a 24-page report prepared for Frito-Lay in 1957 by a psychologist named Ernest Dichter. The company's chips, he wrote, were not selling as well as they could for one simple reason: "While people like and enjoy potato chips, they feel guilty about liking them.... Unconsciously, people expect to be punished for 'letting themselves go' and enjoying them." Dichter listed seven "fears and resistances" to the chips: "You can't stop eating them; they're fattening; they're not good for you; they're greasy and messy to eat; they're too expensive; it's hard to store the leftovers; and they're bad for children." He spent the rest of his memo laying out his prescriptions, which in time would become widely used not just by Frito-Lay but also by the entire industry. Dichter suggested that Frito-Lay avoid using the word "fried" in referring to its chips and adopt instead the more healthful-sounding term "toasted." To counteract the "fear of letting oneself go," he suggested repacking the chips into smaller bags. "The more-anxious consumers, the ones who have the deepest fears about their capacity to control their appetite, will tend to sense the function of the new pack and select it," he said.

Dichter advised Frito-Lay to move its chips out of the realm of between-meals snacking and turn them into an ever-present item in the American diet. "The increased use of potato chips and other Lay's products as a part of the regular fare served by restaurants and sandwich bars should be encouraged in a concentrated way," Dichter said, citing a string of examples: "potato chips with soup, with fruit or vegetable juice appetizers; potato chips served as a vegetable on the main dish; potato chips with salad; potato chips with egg dishes for breakfast; potato chips with sandwich orders."

In 2011, *The New England Journal of Medicine* published a study that shed new light on America's weight gain. The subjects—120,877 women and men—were all professionals in the health field, and were likely to be more conscious about nutrition, so the findings might well understate the overall trend. Using data back to 1986, the researchers monitored everything the participants ate, as well as their physical activity and smoking. They found that every four years, the participants exercised less, watched TV more and gained an average of 3.35 pounds. The researchers parsed the data by the caloric content of the foods being eaten, and found the top contributors to weight gain included red meat and processed meats, sugar-sweetened beverages and potatoes, including mashed and French fries. But the largest weight-inducing food was the potato chip. The coating of salt, the fat content that rewards the brain with instant feelings of pleasure, the sugar that exists not as an additive but in the starch of the potato itself—all of this combines to make it the perfect addictive food. "The starch is readily absorbed," Eric Rimm, an associate professor of epidemiology and nutrition at the Harvard School of Public Health and one of the study's authors, told me. "More quickly even than a similar amount of sugar. The starch, in turn, causes the glucose levels in the blood to spike"—which can result in a craving for more.

If Americans snacked only occasionally, and in small amounts, this would not present the enormous problem that it does. But because so much money and effort have been invested over decades in engineering and then relentlessly selling these products, the effects are seemingly impossible to unwind. More than 30 years have passed since Robert Lin first tangled with Frito-Lay on the imperative of the company to deal with the formulation of its snacks, but as we sat at his dining-room table, sifting through his records, the feelings of regret still played on his face. In his view, three decades had been lost, time that he and a lot of other smart scientists could have spent searching for ways to ease the addiction to salt, sugar and fat. "I couldn't do much about it," he told me. "I feel so sorry for the public."

IV. 'THESE PEOPLE NEED A LOT OF THINGS, BUT THEY DON'T NEED A COKE.'

The growing attention Americans are paying to what they put into their mouths has touched off a new scramble by the processed-food companies to address health concerns. Pressed by the Obama administration and consumers, Kraft, Nestlé, Pepsi, Campbell and General Mills, among others, have begun to trim the loads of salt, sugar and fat in many products. And with consumer advocates pushing for more government intervention, Coca-Cola made headlines in January by releasing ads that promoted its bottled water and low-calorie drinks as a way to counter obesity. Predictably, the ads drew a new volley of scorn from critics who pointed to the company's continuing drive to sell sugary Coke.

One of the other executives I spoke with at length was Jeffrey Dunn, who, in 2001, at age 44, was directing more than half of Coca-Cola's $20 billion in annual sales as president and chief operating officer in both North and South America. In an effort to control as much market share as possible, Coke extended its aggressive marketing to especially poor or vulnerable areas of the U.S., like New Orleans—where people were drinking twice as much Coke as the national average—or Rome, Ga., where the per capita intake was nearly three Cokes a day. In Coke's headquarters in Atlanta, the biggest consumers were referred to as "heavy users." "The other model we use was called 'drinks and drinkers,' " Dunn said. "How many drinkers do I have? And how many drinks do they drink? If you lost one of those heavy users, if somebody just decided to stop drinking Coke, how many drinkers would you have to get, at low velocity, to make up for that heavy user? The answer is a lot. It's more efficient to get my existing users to drink more."

One of Dunn's lieutenants, Todd Putman, who worked at Coca-Cola from 1997 to 2001, said the goal became much larger than merely beating the rival brands; Coca-Cola strove to outsell every other thing people drank, including milk and water. The marketing division's efforts boiled down to one question, Putman said: "How can we drive more ounces into more bodies more often?" (In response to Putman's remarks, Coke said its goals have changed and that it now focuses on providing consumers with more low- or no-calorie products.)

In his capacity, Dunn was making frequent trips to Brazil, where the company had recently begun a push to increase consumption of Coke among the many Brazilians living in *favelas*. The company's strategy was to repackage Coke into smaller, more affordable 6.7-ounce bottles, just 20 cents each. Coke was not alone in seeing Brazil as a potential boon; Nestlé began deploying battalions of women to travel poor neighborhoods, hawking American-style processed foods door to door. But Coke was Dunn's concern, and on one trip, as he walked through one of the impoverished areas, he had an epiphany. "A voice in my head says, 'These people need a lot of things, but they don't need a Coke.' I almost threw up."

Dunn returned to Atlanta, determined to make some changes. He didn't want to abandon the soda business, but he did want to try to steer the company into a more healthful mode, and one of the things he pushed for was to stop marketing Coke in public schools. The independent companies that bottled Coke viewed his plans as reactionary. A director of one bottler wrote a letter to Coke's chief executive and board asking for Dunn's head. "He said what I had done was the worst thing he had seen in 50 years in the business," Dunn said. "Just to placate these crazy leftist school districts who were trying to keep people from having their Coke. He said I was an embarrassment to the company, and I should be fired." In February 2004, he was.

Dunn told me that talking about Coke's business today was by no means easy and, because he continues to work in the food business, not without risk.

"You really don't want them mad at you," he said. "And I don't mean that, like, I'm going to end up at the bottom of the bay. But they don't have a sense of humor when it comes to this stuff. They're a very, very aggressive company."

When I met with Dunn, he told me not just about his years at Coke but also about his new marketing venture. In April 2010, he met with three executives from Madison Dearborn Partners, a private-equity firm based in Chicago with a wide-ranging portfolio of investments. They recently hired Dunn to run one of their newest acquisitions—a food producer in the San Joaquin Valley. As they sat in the hotel's meeting room, the men listened to Dunn's marketing pitch. He talked about giving the product a personality that was bold and irreverent, conveying the idea that this was the ultimate snack food. He went into detail on how he would target a special segment of the 146 million Americans who are regular snackers—mothers, children, young professionals—people, he said, who "keep their snacking ritual fresh by trying a new food product when it catches their attention."

He explained how he would deploy strategic storytelling in the ad campaign for this snack, using a key phrase that had been developed with much calculation: "Eat 'Em Like Junk Food."

After 45 minutes, Dunn clicked off the last slide and thanked the men for coming. Madison's portfolio contained the largest Burger King franchise in the world, the Ruth's Chris Steak House chain, and a processed-food maker called AdvancePierre whose lineup includes the Jamwich, a peanut-butter-and-jelly contrivance that comes frozen, crustless and embedded with four kinds of sugars.

The snack that Dunn was proposing to sell: carrots. Plain, fresh carrots. No added sugar. No creamy sauce or dips. No salt. Just baby carrots, washed, bagged, then sold into the deadly dull produce aisle.

"We act like a snack, not a vegetable," he told the investors. "We exploit the rules of junk food to fuel the baby-carrot conversation. We are pro-junk-food behavior but anti-junk-food establishment."

The investors were thinking only about sales. They had already bought one of the two biggest farm producers of baby carrots in the country, and they'd hired Dunn to run the whole operation. Now, after his pitch, they were relieved. Dunn had figured out that using the industry's own marketing ploys would work better than anything else. He drew from the bag of tricks that he mastered in his 20 years at Coca-Cola, where he learned one of the most critical rules in processed food: The selling of food matters as much as the food itself.

Later, describing his new line of work, Dunn told me he was doing penance for his Coca-Cola years. "I'm paying my karmic debt," he said.

QUESTIONS FOR MAKING CONNECTIONS
WITHIN THE READING

1. In the course of Moss's reporting, we meet executives and scientists who try to reform the food industry: James Behnke, Michael Mudd, Robert Lin, and Jeffrey Dunn. Why have their efforts proven to be largely unsuccessful? Does

their failure indicate that the problem with the food industry cannot be corrected or even explained by pointing to "bad people," individuals who make personal decisions? If the problem really lies with the system as a whole, does Moss regard personal responsibility as irrelevant? In what ways does his account suggest that individuals have the capacity to make a genuine difference? How did the reformers come to change their minds? Does Moss's narrative suggest that change is now taking place, and if so, what factors might explain why?

2. The last executive interviewed by Moss is Jeffrey Dunn of Coca-Cola, who eventually lost his job as the company's president and chief operating officer because he made an effort to curtail the sales of soft drinks in the public schools. At the close of the article we learn that Dunn has tried to pay his "karmic debt" by promoting baby carrots as a healthy snack, now marketed with the slogan, "Eat 'Em Like Junk Food." Does a shift from junk food to more healthful items solve the larger problems suggested by Moss's article? Does the new slogan really help to change the culture of consumption created by junk food marketers? Will Dunn's initiative bring about a change in the system itself?

3. How do corporations work? Use Moss's article to explain the corporate culture of the food industry. What factors shape its thinking and behavior? How does it conceive of its relationship to its customers? What forms of knowledge does it employ to achieve its ends, and what mechanisms does it use to communicate with the general public? Based on the evidence, would you say that the food industry exists to *meet* our needs, or does it actively *create* them? Would you describe the industry's influence as beneficial, benign, coercive, deceptive? When you finished reading Moss's article, were you surprised, offended, alarmed? Why might some readers have no reaction? Does Moss's article give any hints as to why the narrative he relates might simply seem like business as usual?

QUESTIONS FOR WRITING

1. What lessons can be learned from Moss's article about the relations between the general public and specialists? Many of the specialists interviewed by Moss, including the legendary Howard Moskowitz, do their work with a high degree of intelligence, creativity, and professionalism, yet the larger enterprise they contribute to may do damage that they largely ignore or never recognize at all. In what ways might the food industry illuminate the problems with specialization? On the basis of your reading of this article, would you say that professionals in every field have a responsibility to think about the social impacts of their work? Does education overemphasize specialization at the expense of other forms of understanding and development?

2. Where should we draw the line between addictions and genuine needs? Is the difference a matter of degree—how much we consume—or is the

defining element our inability to control our appetites? Or could it be that the word *addiction* refers to a particular social relationship connecting addicts to their pushers, or users to their enablers? Building on Moss, explore the possibility that addiction is indeed a form of social interaction. If addiction is social in this way, are addicts individually to blame for their lack of self-control? Does Moss's work on the food industry suggest that ending addiction means imposing restraints on the supplier? To what extent does our whole economy—not only in the food sector but in electronics and other areas—actively encourage addiction?

QUESTIONS FOR MAKING CONNECTIONS
BETWEEN READINGS

1. Both Moss and Susan Faludi in "The Naked Citadel" shine a light on tensions inside communities that have become isolated from the larger outside world. The Citadel, according to Faludi, is an island of male privilege at a time when women have come closer to equality almost everywhere else, but, perhaps surprisingly, the food industry might also be described as insular and increasingly at odds with the values of the larger public. No less than The Citadel, the food industry appears to be unwelcoming to agents of change who have tried to bring new values from outside. Even though the word *community* normally carries positive connotations, the two authors might be used to explore the ways in which communities become destructive or stultifying. What benefits do we derive from our communities, and what potential problems do they create? Can the strengths of a community also become its greatest weakness?

2. In his essay, Moss criticizes the American food industry for refusing to accept some responsibility for the adverse effects that its products have on consumers. How does he characterize the executives in charge? In what ways are the food companies like the countries Naomi Klein discusses that have chosen free trade over environmentalism? How is the targeted advertising that the food companies use similar to the ways in which countries have attacked the local requirements of clean energy initiatives? How do both texts characterize capitalism? Do both texts imply that corporations are unethical? How do Klein and Moss indicate their perspectives on ethics? What judgments do Klein and Moss make against the people, countries, and corporations that choose profit over the greater good? What responsibility do Moss and Klein argue these entities should take?

AZAR NAFISI

Azar Nafisi rose to international prominence in 2003 with the publication of her critically acclaimed bestseller, *Reading* Lolita *in Tehran: A Memoir in Books.* A professor of aesthetics, culture, and literature, Dr. Nafisi was expelled from the University of Tehran in 1981 for refusing to comply with the Ayatollah Khomeini's mandate that women wear the *chador,* or Muslim veil. Nafisi resumed teaching in 1987, but resigned eight years later in protest over the Iranian government's increasingly harsh treatment of women. *Reading Lolita in Tehran* provides an account of the seminar that Nafisi then went on to hold in her home from 1995 to 1997, in which seven of her best students joined her to discuss some of the classic texts of Western literature. Nafisi saw the change in her circumstances as an opportunity to fulfill a dream of working with "a group of students who just love literature, who are in it not for the grades, not just to graduate and get a job but just want to read Nabokov and Austen." That Nafisi and her students persisted in this activity, despite the obvious dangers it posed, has come to symbolize for readers around the world how the struggle against totalitarianism is waged on the level of everyday human experience.

Nafisi is no stranger to politics, or to political repression. Her mother was one of the first women to serve in the Iranian parliament, while her father, appointed by the Shah to serve as Tehran's mayor, was later jailed when he fell from favor. Currently Nafisi is the Executive Director of Cultural Conversations and a Visiting Professor at the Johns Hopkins University's Paul H. Nitze School of Advanced International Studies in Washington, D.C. Until 2008 she directed the Dialogue Project, "a multiyear initiative designed to promote—in a primarily cultural context—the development of democracy and human rights in the Muslim world." For Nafisi, the freedom to talk and think together in small groups, in a context where the ideas raised and the topics of conversation are not determined in advance, is the litmus test for a true democracy. To engage in this act, she believes, is to embrace a shared humanity that extends beyond the boundaries of national and religious differences. More recently, she has begun to explore tyranny of another kind—not in a totalitarian state but in the habits of

Biographical information comes from Azar Nafisi's website at <http://azarnafisi.com/about-azar/>; the quotation about the Dialogue Project comes from <http://www.middle-east-studies.net/?page_id=1642>.

self-censorship and repression that are taught by the family. In *Things I Have Been Silent About: Memories of a Prodigal Daughter* (2008), Nafisi explores her complicated struggles with a mother whose overwhelming expectations virtually ensured that her daughter's future life would be successful but unhappy.

Selections from Reading Lolita in Tehran

A Memoir in Books

1. In the fall of 1995, after resigning from my last academic post, I decided to indulge myself and fulfill a dream. I chose seven of my best and most committed students and invited them to come to my home every Thursday morning to discuss literature. They were all women—to teach a mixed class in the privacy of my home was too risky, even if we were discussing harmless works of fiction. One persistent male student, although barred from our class, insisted on his rights. So he, Nima, read the assigned material, and on special days he would come to my house to talk about the books we were reading.

I often teasingly reminded my students of Muriel Spark's *The Prime of Miss Jean Brodie* and asked, Which one of you will finally betray me? For I am a pessimist by nature and I was sure at least one would turn against me. Nassrin once responded mischievously, You yourself told us that in the final analysis we are our own betrayers, playing Judas to our own Christ. Manna pointed out that I was no Miss Brodie, and they, well, they were what they were. She reminded me of a warning I was fond of repeating: *do not*, under *any* circumstances, belittle a work of fiction by trying to turn it into a carbon copy of real life; what we search for in fiction is not so much reality but the epiphany of truth. Yet I suppose that if I were to go against my own recommendation and choose a work of fiction that would most resonate with our lives in the Islamic Republic of Iran, it would not be *The Prime of Miss Jean Brodie* or even *1984* but perhaps Nabokov's *Invitation to a Beheading* or better yet, *Lolita.*

A couple of years after we had begun our Thursday-morning seminars, on the last night I was in Tehran, a few friends and students came to say good-bye and to help me pack. When we had deprived the house of all its items, when the objects had vanished and the colors had faded into eight gray suitcases, like errant genies evaporating into their bottles, my students and I stood against the bare white wall of the dining room and took two photographs.

I have the two photographs in front of me now. In the first there are seven women, standing against a white wall. They are, according to the law of the land, dressed in black robes and head scarves, covered except for the oval of their faces and their hands. In the second photograph the same group, in the same position, stands against the same wall. Only they have taken off their coverings. Splashes of color separate one from the next. Each has become distinct through the color and style of her clothes, the color and the length of her hair; not even the two who are still wearing their head scarves look the same.

The one to the far right in the second photograph is our poet, Manna, in a white T-shirt and jeans. She made poetry out of things most people cast aside. The photograph does not reflect the peculiar opacity of Manna's dark eyes, a testament to her withdrawn and private nature.

Next to Manna is Mahshid, whose long black scarf clashes with her delicate features and retreating smile. Mahshid was good at many things, but she had a certain daintiness about her and we took to calling her "my lady." Nassrin used to say that more than defining Mahshid, we had managed to add another dimension to the word *lady*. Mahshid is very sensitive. She's like porcelain, Yassi once told me, easy to crack. That's why she appears fragile to those who don't know her too well; but woe to whoever offends her. As for me, Yassi continued good-naturedly, I'm like good old plastic; I won't crack no matter what you do with me.

Yassi was the youngest in our group. She is the one in yellow, bending forward and bursting with laughter. We used to teasingly call her our comedian. Yassi was shy by nature, but certain things excited her and made her lose her inhibitions. She had a tone of voice that gently mocked and questioned not just others but herself as well.

I am the one in brown, standing next to Yassi, with one arm around her shoulders. Directly behind me stands Azin, my tallest student, with her long blond hair and a pink T-shirt. She is laughing like the rest of us. Azin's smiles never looked like smiles; they appeared more like preludes to an irrepressible and nervous hilarity. She beamed in that peculiar fashion even when she was describing her latest trouble with her husband. Always outrageous and outspoken, Azin relished the shock value of her actions and comments, and often clashed with Mahshid and Manna. We nicknamed her the wild one.

On my other side is Mitra, who was perhaps the calmest among us. Like the pastel colors of her paintings, she seemed to recede and fade into a paler register. Her beauty was saved from predictability by a pair of miraculous dimples, which she could and did use to manipulate many an unsuspecting victim into bending to her will.

Sanaz, who, pressured by family and society, vacillated between her desire for independence and her need for approval, is holding on to Mitra's arm. We are all laughing. And Nima, Manna's husband and my one true literary critic—if only he had had the perseverance to finish the brilliant essays he started to write—is our invisible partner, the photographer.

There was one more: Nassrin. She is not in the photographs—she didn't make it to the end. Yet my tale would be incomplete without those who could not or did not remain with us. Their absences persist, like an acute pain that seems to have no physical source. This is Tehran for me: its absences were more real than its presences.

When I see Nassrin in my mind's eye, she's slightly out of focus, blurred, somehow distant. I've combed through the photographs my students took with me over the years and Nassrin is in many of them, but always hidden behind something—a person, a tree. In one, I am standing with eight of my students in the small garden facing our faculty building, the scene of so many farewell photographs over the years. In the background stands a sheltering willow tree. We are laughing, and in one corner, from behind the tallest student, Nassrin peers out, like an imp intruding roguishly on a scene it was not invited to. In another I can barely make out her face in the small V space behind two other girls' shoulders. In this one she looks absentminded; she is frowning, as if unaware that she is being photographed.

How can I describe Nassrin? I once called her the Cheshire cat, appearing and disappearing at unexpected turns in my academic life. The truth is I can't describe her: she was her own definition. One can only say that Nassrin was Nassrin.

For nearly two years, almost every Thursday morning, rain or shine, they came to my house, and almost every time, I could not get over the shock of seeing them shed their mandatory veils and robes and burst into color. When my students came into that room, they took off more than their scarves and robes. Gradually, each one gained an outline and a shape, becoming her own inimitable self. Our world in that living room with its window framing my beloved Elburz Mountains became our sanctuary, our self-contained universe, mocking the reality of black-scarved, timid faces in the city that sprawled below.

The theme of the class was the relation between fiction and reality. We read Persian classical literature, such as the tales of our own lady of fiction, Scheherazade, from *A Thousand and One Nights,* along with Western classics—*Pride and Prejudice, Madame Bovary, Daisy Miller, The Dean's December* and, yes, *Lolita.* As I write the title of each book, memories whirl in with the wind to disturb the quiet of this fall day in another room in another country.

Here and now in that other world that cropped up so many times in our discussions, I sit and reimagine myself and my students, my girls as I came to call them, reading *Lolita* in a deceptively sunny room in Tehran. But to steal the words from Humbert, the poet/criminal of *Lolita,* I need you, the reader, to imagine us, for we won't really exist if you don't. Against the tyranny of time and politics, imagine us the way we sometimes didn't dare to imagine ourselves: in our most private and secret moments, in the most extraordinarily ordinary instances of life, listening to music, falling in love, walking down the shady streets or reading *Lolita* in Tehran. And then imagine us again with all this confiscated, driven underground, taken away from us.

If I write about Nabokov today, it is to celebrate our reading of Nabokov in Tehran, against all odds. Of all his novels I choose the one I taught last, and the one that is connected to so many memories. It is of *Lolita* that I want to write, but right now there is no way I can write about that novel without also writing about Tehran. This, then, is the story of *Lolita* in Tehran, how *Lolita* gave a different color to Tehran, and how Tehran helped redefine Nabokov's novel, turning it into this *Lolita,* our *Lolita.*

2. And so it happened that one Thursday in early September we gathered in my living room for our first meeting. Here they come, one more time. First I hear the bell, a pause, and the closing of the street door. Then I hear footsteps coming up the winding staircase and past my mother's apartment. As I move towards the front door, I register a piece of sky through the side window. Each girl, as soon as she reaches the door, takes off her robe and scarf, sometimes shaking her head from side to side. She pauses before entering the room. Only there is no room, just the teasing void of memory.

More than any other place in our home, the living room was symbolic of my nomadic and borrowed life. Vagrant pieces of furniture from different times and places were thrown together, partly out of financial necessity, and partly because of my eclectic taste. Oddly, these incongruous ingredients created a symmetry that the other, more deliberately furnished rooms in the apartment lacked.

My mother would go crazy each time she saw the paintings leaning against the wall and the vases of flowers on the floor and the curtainless windows, which I refused to dress until I was finally reminded that this was an Islamic country and windows needed to be dressed. I don't know if you really belong to me, she would lament. Didn't I raise you to be orderly and organized? Her tone was serious, but she had repeated the same complaint for so many years that by now it was an almost tender ritual. Azi—that was my nickname—Azi, she would say, you are a grown-up lady now; act like one. Yet there was something in her tone that kept me young and fragile and obstinate, and still, when in memory I hear her voice, I know I never lived up to her expectations. I never did become the lady she tried to will me into being.

That room, which I never paid much attention to at that time, has gained a different status in my mind's eye now that it has become the precious object of memory. It was a spacious room, sparsely furnished and decorated. At one corner was the fireplace, a fanciful creation of my husband, Bijan. There was a love seat against one wall, over which I had thrown a lace cover, my mother's gift from long ago. A pale peach couch faced the window, accompanied by two matching chairs and a big square glass-topped iron table.

My place was always in the chair with its back to the window, which opened onto a wide cul-de-sac called Azar. Opposite the window was the former American Hospital, once small and exclusive, now a noisy, overcrowded medical facility for wounded and disabled veterans of the war. On "weekends"— Thursdays and Fridays in Iran—the small street was crowded with hospital visitors who came as if for a picnic, with sandwiches and children. The neighbor's front yard, his pride and joy, was the main victim of their assaults, especially in summer, when they helped themselves to his beloved roses. We could hear the sound of children shouting, crying and laughing, and, mingled in, their mothers' voices, also shouting, calling out their children's names and threatening them with punishments. Sometimes a child or two would ring our doorbell and run away, repeating their perilous exercise at intervals.

From our second-story apartment—my mother occupied the first floor, and my brother's apartment, on the third floor, was often empty, since he had left for England—we could see the upper branches of a generous tree and, in the distance, over the buildings, the Elburz Mountains. The street, the hospital and its visitors were censored out of sight. We felt their presence only through the disembodied noises emanating from below.

I could not see my favorite mountains from where I sat, but opposite my chair, on the far wall of the dining room, was an antique oval mirror, a gift from my father, and in its reflection, I could see the mountains capped with snow, even in summer, and watch the trees change color. That censored view intensified my impression that the noise came not from the street below but from some far-off place, a place whose persistent hum was our only link to the world we refused, for those few hours, to acknowledge.

That room, for all of us, became a place of transgression. What a wonderland it was! Sitting around the large coffee table covered with bouquets of flowers, we moved in and out of the novels we read. Looking back, I am amazed at how much we learned without even noticing it. We were, to borrow from Nabokov, to experience how the ordinary pebble of ordinary life could be transformed into a jewel through the magic eye of fiction.

3.   Six A.M.: the first day of class. I was already up. Too excited to eat breakfast, I put the coffee on and then took a long, leisurely shower. The water caressed my neck, my back, my legs, and I stood there both rooted and light. For the first time in many years, I felt a sense of anticipation that was not marred by tension: I would not need to go through the torturous rituals that had marked my days when I taught at the university—rituals governing what I was forced to wear, how I was expected to act, the gestures I had to remember to control. For this class, I would prepare differently.

Life in the Islamic Republic was as capricious as the month of April, when short periods of sunshine would suddenly give way to showers and storms. It was unpredictable: the regime would go through cycles of some tolerance, followed by a crackdown. Now, after a period of relative calm and so-called liberalization, we had again entered a time of hardships. Universities had once more become the targets of attack by the cultural purists who were busy imposing stricter sets of laws, going so far as to segregate men and women in classes and punishing disobedient professors.

The University of Allameh Tabatabai, where I had been teaching since 1987, had been singled out as the most liberal university in Iran. It was rumored that someone in the Ministry of Higher Education had asked, rhetorically, if the faculty at Allameh thought they lived in Switzerland. *Switzerland* had somehow become a byword for Western laxity: any program or action that was deemed un-Islamic was reproached with a mocking reminder that Iran was by no means Switzerland.

The pressure was hardest on the students. I felt helpless as I listened to their endless tales of woe. Female students were being penalized for running up the stairs when they were late for classes, for laughing in the hallways, for talking to members of the opposite sex. One day Sanaz had barged into class near the end of the session, crying. In between bursts of tears, she explained that she was late because the female guards at the door, finding a blush in her bag, had tried to send her home with a reprimand.

Why did I stop teaching so suddenly? I had asked myself this question many times. Was it the declining quality of the university? The ever-increasing indifference among the remaining faculty and students? The daily struggle against arbitrary rules and restrictions?

I smiled as I rubbed the coarse loofah over my skin, remembering the reaction of the university officials to my letter of resignation. They had harassed and limited me in all manner of ways, monitoring my visitors, controlling my actions, refusing a long-overdue tenure; and when I resigned, they infuriated me by suddenly commiserating and by refusing to accept my resignation. The students had threatened to boycott classes, and it was of some satisfaction to me to find out later that despite threats of reprisals, they in fact did boycott my replacement. Everyone thought I would break down and eventually return.

It took two more years before they finally accepted my resignation. I remember a friend told me, You don't understand their mentality. They won't accept your resignation because they don't think you have the right to quit. *They* are the ones who decide how long you should stay and when you should be dispensed with. More than anything else, it was this arbitrariness that had become unbearable.

What will you do? my friends had asked. Will you just stay home now? Well, I could write another book, I would tell them. But in truth I had no definite plans. I was still dealing with the aftershocks of a book on Nabokov I had just published, and only vague ideas, like vapors, formed when I turned to consider the shape of my next book. I could, for a while at least, continue the pleasant task of studying Persian classics, but one particular project, a notion I had been nurturing for years, was uppermost in my mind. For a long time I had dreamt of creating a special class, one that would give me the freedoms denied me in the classes I taught in the Islamic Republic. I wanted to teach a handful of selected students wholly committed to the study of literature, students who were not handpicked by the government, who had not chosen English literature simply because they had not been accepted in other fields or because they thought an English degree would be a good career move.

Teaching in the Islamic Republic, like any other vocation, was subservient to politics and subject to arbitrary rules. Always, the joy of teaching was marred by diversions and considerations forced on us by the regime—how well could one teach when the main concern of university officials was not the quality of one's work but the color of one's lips, the subversive potential of a single strand of hair? Could one really concentrate on one's job when what preoccupied the faculty was how to excise the word *wine* from a Hemingway story, when they decided not to teach Brontë because she appeared to condone adultery?

I was reminded of a painter friend who had started her career by depicting scenes from life, mainly deserted rooms, abandoned houses, and discarded photographs of women. Gradually, her work became more abstract, and in her last exhibition, her paintings were splashes of rebellious color, like the two in my living room, dark patches with little droplets of blue. I asked about her progress from modern realism to abstraction. Reality has become so intolerable, she said, so bleak, that all I can paint now are the colors of my dreams.

The colors of my dreams, I repeated to myself, stepping out of the shower and onto the cool tiles. I liked that. How many people get a chance to paint the colors of their dreams? I put on my oversize bathrobe—it felt good to move from the security of the embracing water to the protective cover of a bathrobe wrapped around my body. I walked barefoot into the kitchen, poured some coffee into my favorite mug, the one with red strawberries, and sat down forgetfully on the divan in the hall.

This class was the color of my dreams. It entailed an active withdrawal from a reality that had turned hostile. I wanted very badly to hold on to my rare mood of jubilance and optimism. For in the back of my mind, I didn't know what awaited me at the end of this project. You are aware, a friend had said, that you are more and more withdrawing into yourself, and now that you have cut your relations with the university, your whole contact with the outside world will be mainly restricted to one room. Where will you go from here? he had asked. Withdrawal into one's dreams could be dangerous, I reflected, padding into the bedroom to change; this I had learned from Nabokov's crazy dreamers, like Kinbote and Humbert.

In selecting my students, I did not take into consideration their ideological or religious backgrounds. Later, I would count it as the class's great achievement that such a mixed group, with different and at times conflicting backgrounds, personal as well as religious and social, remained so loyal to its goals and ideals.

One reason for my choice of these particular girls was the peculiar mixture of fragility and courage I sensed in them. They were what you would call loners, who did not belong to any particular group or sect. I admired their ability to survive not despite but in some ways because of their solitary lives. We can call the class "a space of our own," Manna had suggested, a sort of communal version of Virginia Woolf's room of her own.

I spent longer than usual choosing my clothes that first morning, trying on different outfits, until I finally settled on a red-striped shirt and black corduroy jeans. I applied my makeup with care and put on bright red lipstick. As I fastened my small gold earrings, I suddenly panicked. What if it doesn't work? What if they won't come?

Don't, don't do that! Suspend all fears for the next five or six hours at least. Please, please, I pleaded with myself, putting on my shoes and going into the kitchen.

4.   I was making tea when the doorbell rang. I was so preoccupied with my thoughts that I didn't hear it the first time. I opened the door to Mahshid. I thought you weren't home, she said, handing me a bouquet of white and yellow daffodils. As she was taking off her black robe, I told her, There are no men in the house—you can take that off, too. She hesitated before uncoiling her long black scarf. Mahshid and Yassi both observed the veil, but Yassi of late had become more relaxed in the way she wore her scarf. She tied it with a loose knot under her throat, her dark brown hair, untidily parted in the middle, peeping out from underneath. Mahshid's hair, however, was meticulously styled and curled under. Her short bangs gave her a strangely old-fashioned look that struck me as more European than Iranian. She wore a deep blue jacket over her white shirt, with a huge yellow butterfly embroidered on its right side. I pointed to the butterfly: did you wear this in honor of Nabokov?

I no longer remember when Mahshid first began to take my classes at the university. Somehow, it seems as if she had always been there. Her father, a devout Muslim, had been an ardent supporter of the revolution. She wore the scarf even before the revolution, and in her class diary, she wrote about the lonely mornings when she went to a fashionable girls' college, where she felt neglected and ignored—ironically, because of her then-conspicuous attire. After the revolution, she was jailed for five years because of her affiliation with a dissident religious organization and banned from continuing her education for two years after she was out of jail.

I imagine her in those pre-revolutionary days, walking along the uphill street leading to the college on countless sunny mornings. I see her walking alone, her head to the ground. Then, as now, she did not enjoy the day's brilliance. I say "then, as now" because the revolution that imposed the scarf on others did not relieve Mahshid of her loneliness. Before the revolution, she could in a sense take pride in her isolation. At that time, she had worn the scarf as a testament to her faith. Her decision was a voluntary act. When the revolution forced the scarf on others, her action became meaningless.

Mahshid is proper in the true sense of the word: she has grace and a certain dignity. Her skin is the color of moonlight, and she has almond-shaped eyes and jet-black hair. She wears pastel colors and is soft-spoken. Her pious background should have shielded her, but it didn't. I cannot imagine her in jail.

Over the many years I have known Mahshid, she has rarely alluded to her jail experiences, which left her with a permanently impaired kidney. One day in class, as we were talking about our daily terrors and nightmares, she mentioned that her jail memories visited her from time to time and that she had still not found a way to articulate them. But, she added, everyday life does not have fewer horrors than prison.

I asked Mahshid if she wanted some tea. Always considerate, she said she'd rather wait for the others and apologized for being a little early. Can I help? she asked. There's really nothing to help with. Make yourself at home, I told her as I stepped into the kitchen with the flowers and searched for a vase. The bell rang again. I'll get it, Mahshid cried out from the living room. I heard laughter; Manna and Yassi had arrived.

Manna came into the kitchen holding a small bouquet of roses. It's from Nima, she said. He wants to make you feel bad about excluding him from the class. He says he'll carry a bouquet of roses and march in front of your house during class hours, in protest. She was beaming; a few brief sparkles flashed in her eyes and died down again.

Putting the pastries onto a large tray, I asked Manna if she envisioned the words to her poems in colors. Nabokov writes in his autobiography that he and his mother saw the letters of the alphabet in color, I explained. He says of himself that he is a painterly writer.

The Islamic Republic coarsened my taste in colors, Manna said, fingering the discarded leaves of her roses. I want to wear outrageous colors, like shocking pink or tomato red. I feel too greedy for colors to see them in carefully chosen words of poetry. Manna was one of those people who would experience ecstasy but not happiness. Come here, I want to show you something, I said, leading her into our bedroom. When I was very young, I was obsessed with the colors of places and things my father told me about in his nightly stories. I wanted to know the color of Scheherazade's dress, her bedcover, the color of the genie and the magic lamp, and once I asked him about the color of paradise. He said it could be any color I wanted it to be. That was not enough. Then one day when we had guests and I was eating my soup in the dining room, my eyes fell on a painting I had seen on the wall ever since I could remember, and I instantly knew the color of my paradise. And here it is, I said, proudly pointing to a small oil painting in an old wooden frame: a green landscape of lush, leathery leaves with two birds, two deep red apples, a golden pear and a touch of blue.

My paradise is swimming-pool blue! Manna shot in, her eyes still glued to the painting. We lived in a large garden that belonged to my grandparents, she said, turning to me. You know the old Persian gardens, with their fruit trees, peaches, apples, cherries, persimmons and a willow or two. My best memories are of swimming in our huge irregularly shaped swimming pool. I was a swimming champion at our school, a fact my dad was very proud of. About a year after the revolution, my father died of a heart attack, and then the government confiscated our house and our garden and we moved into an apartment. I never swam again. My dream is at the bottom of that pool. I have a recurring dream of diving in to retrieve something of my father's memory and my childhood, she said as we walked to the living room, for the doorbell had rung again.

Azin and Mitra had arrived together. Azin was taking off her black kimono-like robe—Japanese-style robes were all the rage at the time—revealing a white peasant blouse that made no pretense of covering her shoulders, big golden earrings and pink lipstick. She had a branch of small yellow orchids— from Mitra and myself, she said in that special tone of hers that I can only describe as a flirtatious pout.

Nassrin came in next. She had brought two boxes of nougats: presents from Isfahan, she declared. She was dressed in her usual uniform—navy robe, navy scarf and black heelless shoes. When I had last seen her in class, she was wearing a huge black chador, revealing only the oval of her face and two restless hands, which, when she was not writing or doodling, were constantly in motion, as if trying to escape the confines of the thick black cloth. More recently, she had exchanged the chador for long, shapeless robes in navy, black or dark brown, with thick matching scarves that hid her hair and framed her face. She had a small, pale face, skin so transparent you could count the veins, full eyebrows, long lashes, lively eyes (brown), a small straight nose and an angry mouth: an unfinished miniature by some master who had suddenly been called away from his job and left the meticulously drawn face imprisoned in a careless splash of dark color.

We heard the sound of screeching tires and sudden brakes. I looked out the window: a small old Renault, cream-colored, had pulled up on the curb. Behind the wheel, a young man with fashionable sunglasses and a defiant profile rested his black-sleeved arm on the curve of the open window and gave the impression that he was driving a Porsche. He was staring straight in front of him as he talked to the woman beside him. Only once did he turn his head to his right, with what I could guess was a cross expression, and that was when the woman got out of the car and he angrily slammed the door behind her. As she walked to our front door, he threw his head out and shouted a few words, but she did not turn back to answer. The old Renault was Sanaz's; she had bought it with money saved from her job.

I turned towards the room, blushing for Sanaz. That must be the obnoxious brother, I thought. Seconds later the doorbell rang and I heard Sanaz's hurried steps and opened the door to her. She looked harassed, as if she had been running from a stalker or a thief. As soon as she saw me, she adjusted her face into a smile and said breathlessly: I hope I am not too late?

There were two very important men dominating Sanaz's life at the time. The first was her brother. He was nineteen years old and had not yet finished high school and was the darling of their parents, who, after two girls, one of whom had died at the age of three, had finally been blessed with a son. He was spoiled, and his one obsession in life was Sanaz. He had taken to proving his masculinity by spying on her, listening to her phone conversations, driving her car around, and monitoring her actions. Her parents had tried to appease Sanaz and begged her, as the older sister, to be patient and understanding, to use her motherly instincts to see him through this difficult period.

The other was her childhood sweetheart, a boy she had known since she was eleven. Their parents were best friends, and their families spent most of their time and vacations together. Sanaz and Ali seemed to have been in love forever. Their parents encouraged this union and called it a match made in heaven. When Ali went away to England six years ago, his mother took to calling Sanaz his bride. They wrote to each other, sent photographs, and recently, when the number of Sanaz's suitors increased, there were talks of engagement and a reunion in Turkey, where Iranians did not require entrance visas. Any day now it might happen, an event Sanaz looked forward to with some fear and trepidation.

I had never seen Sanaz without her uniform, and stood there almost transfixed as she took off her robe and scarf. She was wearing an orange T-shirt tucked into tight jeans and brown boots, yet the most radical transformation was the mass of shimmering dark brown hair that now framed her face. She shook her magnificent hair from side to side, a gesture that I later noticed was a habit with her; she would toss her head and run her fingers through her hair every once in a while, as if making sure that her most prized possession was still there. Her features looked softer and more radiant—the black scarf she wore in public made her small face look emaciated and almost hard.

I'm sorry I'm a little late, she said breathlessly, running her fingers through her hair. My brother insisted on driving me, and he refused to wake up on time. He never gets up before ten, but he wanted to know where I was going. I might be off on some secret tryst, you know, a date or something.

I have been worrying in case any of you would get into trouble for this class, I said, inviting them all to take their seats around the table in the living room. I hope your parents and spouses feel comfortable with our arrangement.

Nassrin, who was wandering around the room, inspecting the paintings as if seeing them for the first time, paused to say offhandedly, I mentioned the idea very casually to my father, just to test his reaction, and he vehemently disapproved.

How did you convince him to let you come? I asked. I lied, she said. You lied? What else can one do with a person who's so dictatorial he won't let his daughter, at *this age*, go to an all-female literature class? Besides, isn't this how we treat the regime? Can we tell the Revolutionary Guards the truth? We lie to them; we hide our satellite dishes. We tell them we don't have illegal books and alcohol in our houses. Even my venerable father lies to them when the safety of his family is at stake, Nassrin added defiantly.

What if he calls me to check on you? I said, half teasingly. He won't. I gave a brilliant alibi. I said Mahshid and I had volunteered to help translate Islamic texts into English. And he believed you? Well, he had no reason not to. I hadn't lied to him before—not really—and it was what he wanted to believe. And he trusts Mahshid completely.

So if he calls me, I should lie to him? I persisted. It's up to you, Nassrin said after a pause, looking down at her twisting hands. Do *you* think you should tell him? By now I could hear a note of desperation in her voice. Am I getting you into trouble?

Nassrin always acted so confident that sometimes I forgot how vulnerable she really was under that tough-girl act. Of course I would respect your confidence, I said more gently. As you said, you are a big girl. You know what you're doing.

I had settled into my usual chair, opposite the mirror, where the mountains had come to stay. It is strange to look into a mirror and see not yourself but a view so distant from you. Mahshid, after some hesitation, had taken the chair to my right. On the couch, Manna settled to the far right and Azin to the far left; they instinctively kept their distance. Sanaz and Mitra were perched on the love seat, their heads close together as they whispered and giggled.

At this point Yassi and Nassrin came in and looked around for seats. Azin patted the empty part of the couch, inviting Yassi with her hand. Yassi hesitated for a moment and then slid between Azin and Manna. She slumped into place and seemed to leave little room for her two companions, who sat upright and a little stiff in their respective corners. Without her robe, she looked a little overweight, as if she had not as yet lost her baby fat. Nassrin had gone to the dining room in search of a chair. We can squeeze you in here, said Manna. No, thank you, I actually prefer straight-backed chairs. When she returned, she placed her chair between the couch and Mahshid.

They kept that arrangement, faithfully, to the end. It became representative of their emotional boundaries and personal relations. And so began our first class.

5. "Upsilamba!" I heard Yassi exclaim as I entered the dining room with a tray of tea. Yassi loved playing with words. Once she told us that her obsession with words was pathological. As soon as I discover a new word, I have to use it, she said, like someone who buys an evening gown and is so eager that she wears it to the movies, or to lunch.

Let me pause and rewind the reel to retrace the events leading us to Yassi's exclamation. This was our first session. All of us had been nervous and inarticulate. We were used to meeting in public, mainly in classrooms and in lecture halls. The girls had their separate relationships with me, but except for Nassrin and Mahshid, who were intimate, and a certain friendship between Mitra and Sanaz, the rest were not close; in many cases, in fact, they would never have chosen to be friends. The collective intimacy made them uncomfortable.

I had explained to them the purpose of the class: to read, discuss, and respond to works of fiction. Each would have a private diary, in which she should record her responses to the novels, as well as ways in which these works and their discussions related to her personal and social experiences. I explained that I had chosen them for this class because they seemed dedicated to the study of literature. I mentioned that one of the criteria for the books I had chosen was their authors' faith in the critical and almost magical power of literature, and reminded them of the nineteen-year-old Nabokov, who, during the Russian Revolution, would not allow himself to be diverted by the sound of bullets. He kept on writing his solitary poems while he heard the guns and saw the bloody fights from his window. Let us see, I said, whether seventy years later our disinterested faith will reward us by transforming the gloomy reality created of this other revolution.

The first work we discussed was *A Thousand and One Nights*, the familiar tale of the cuckolded king who slew successive virgin wives as revenge for his queen's betrayal, and whose murderous hand was finally stayed by the entrancing storyteller Scheherazade. I formulated certain general questions for them to consider, the most central of which was how these great works of imagination could help us in our present trapped situation as women. We were not looking for blueprints, for an easy solution, but we did hope to find a link between the open spaces the novels provided and the closed ones we were confined to. I remember reading to my girls Nabokov's claim that "readers were born free and ought to remain free."

What had most intrigued me about the frame story of *A Thousand and One Nights* were the three kinds of women it portrayed—all victims of a king's unreasonable rule. Before Scheherazade enters the scene, the women in the story are divided into those who betray and then are killed (the queen) and those who are killed before they have a chance to betray (the virgins). The virgins, who, unlike Scheherazade, have no voice in the story, are mostly ignored by the critics. Their silence, however, is significant. They surrender their virginity, and their lives, without resistance or protest. They do not quite exist, because they leave no trace in their anonymous death. The queen's infidelity does not rob the king of his absolute authority; it throws him off balance. Both types of women—the queen and the virgins—tacitly accept the king's public authority by acting within the confines of his domain and by accepting its arbitrary laws.

Scheherazade breaks the cycle of violence by choosing to embrace different terms of engagement. She fashions her universe not through physical force, as does the king, but through imagination and reflection. This gives her the courage to risk her life and sets her apart from the other characters in the tale.

Our edition of *A Thousand and One Nights* came in six volumes. I, luckily, had bought mine before it was banned and sold only on the black market, for exorbitant prices. I divided the volumes among the girls and asked them, for the next session, to classify the tales according to the types of women who played central roles in the stories.

Once I'd given them their assignment, I asked them each to tell the rest of us why they had chosen to spend their Thursday mornings here, discussing Nabokov and Jane Austen. Their answers were brief and forced. In order to break the ice, I suggested the calming distraction of cream puffs and tea.

This brings us to the moment when I enter the dining room with eight glasses of tea on an old and unpolished silver tray. Brewing and serving tea is an aesthetic ritual in Iran, performed several times a day. We serve tea in transparent glasses, small and shapely, the most popular of which is called slim-waisted: round and full at the top, narrow in the middle and round and full at the bottom. The color of the tea and its subtle aroma are an indication of the brewer's skill.

I step into the dining room with eight slim-waisted glasses whose honey-colored liquid trembles seductively. At this point, I hear Yassi shout triumphantly, "Upsilamba!" She throws the word at me like a ball, and I take a mental leap to catch it.

Upsilamba!—the word carries me back to the spring of 1994, when four of my girls and Nima were auditing a class I was teaching on the twentieth-century novel. The class's favorite book was Nabokov's *Invitation to a Beheading*. In this novel, Nabokov differentiates Cincinnatus C., his imaginative and lonely hero, from those around him through his originality in a society where uniformity is not only the norm but also the law. Even as a child, Nabokov tells us, Cincinnatus appreciated the freshness and beauty of language, while other children "understood each other at the first word, since they had no words that would end in an unexpected way, perhaps in some archaic letter, an upsilamba, becoming a bird or catapult with wondrous consequences."

No one in class had bothered to ask what the word meant. No one, that is, who was properly taking the class—for many of my old students just stayed on and sat in on my classes long after their graduation. Often, they were more interested and worked harder than my regular students, who were taking the class for credit. Thus it was that those who audited the class—including Nassrin, Manna, Nima, Mahshid, and Yassi—had one day gathered in my office to discuss this and a number of other questions.

I decided to play a little game with the class, to test their curiosity. On the midterm exam, one of the questions was "Explain the significance of the word *upsilamba* in the context of *Invitation to a Beheading*. What does the word mean, and how does it relate to the main theme of the novel?" Except for four or five students, no one had any idea what I could possibly mean, a point I did not forget to remind them of every once in a while throughout the rest of that term.

The truth was that *upsilamba* was one of Nabokov's fanciful creations, possibly a word he invented out of *upsilon*, the twentieth letter in the Greek alphabet, and *lambda*, the eleventh. So that first day in our private class, we let our minds play again and invented new meanings of our own.

I said I associated *upsilamba* with the impossible joy of a suspended leap. Yassi, who seemed excited for no particular reason, cried out that she always thought it could be the name of a dance—you know, "C'mon, baby, do the Upsilamba with me." I proposed that for the next time, they each write a sentence or two explaining what the word meant to them.

Manna suggested that *upsilamba* evoked the image of small silver fish leaping in and out of a moonlit lake. Nima added in parentheses, Just so you won't forget me, although you have barred me from your class: an upsilamba to you, too! For Azin it was a sound, a melody. Mahshid described an image of three girls jumping rope and shouting "Upsilamba!" with each leap. For Sanaz, the word was a small African boy's secret magical name. Mitra wasn't sure why the word reminded her of the paradox of a blissful sigh. And to Nassrin it was the magic code that opened the door to a secret cave filled with treasures.

Upsilamba became part of our increasing repository of coded words and expressions, a repository that grew over time until gradually we had created a secret language of our own. That word became a symbol, a sign of that vague sense of joy, the tingle in the spine Nabokov expected his readers to feel in the act of reading fiction; it was a sensation that separated the good readers, as he called them, from the ordinary ones. It also became the code word that opened the secret cave of remembrance.

6.   In his foreword to the English edition of *Invitation to a Beheading* (1959), Nabokov reminds the reader that his novel does not offer *"tout pour tous."* Nothing of the kind. "It is," he claims, "a violin in the void." And yet, he goes on to say, "I know ... a few readers who will jump up, ruffling their hair." Well, absolutely. The original version, Nabokov tells us, was published in installments in 1935. Almost six decades later, in a world unknown and presumably unknowable to Nabokov, in a forlorn living room with windows looking out towards distant white-capped mountains, time and again I would stand witness to the unlikeliest of readers as they lost themselves in a madness of hair-ruffling.

Invitation to a Beheading begins with the announcement that its fragile hero, Cincinnatus C., has been sentenced to death for the crime of "gnostic turpitude": in a place where all citizens are required to be transparent, he is opaque. The principal characteristic of this world is its arbitrariness; the condemned man's only privilege is to know the time of his death—but the executioners keep even this from him, turning every day into a day of execution. As the story unfolds, the reader discovers with increasing discomfort the artificial texture of this strange place. The moon from the window is fake; so is the spider in the corner, which, according to convention, must become the prisoner's faithful companion. The director of the jail, the jailer, and the defense lawyer are all the same man, and keep changing places. The most important character, the executioner, is first introduced to the prisoner under another name and as a fellow prisoner: M'sieur Pierre. The executioner and the condemned man must learn to love each other and cooperate in the act of execution, which will be celebrated in a gaudy feast. In this staged world, Cincinnatus's only window to another universe is his writing.

The world of the novel is one of empty rituals. Every act is bereft of substance and significance, and even death becomes a spectacle for which the good citizens buy tickets. It is only through these empty rituals that brutality becomes possible. In another Nabokov novel, *The Real Life of Sebastian Knight*, Sebastian's brother discovers two seemingly incongruous pictures in his dead brother's library: a pretty, curly-haired child playing with a dog and a Chinese man in the act of being beheaded. The two pictures remind us of the close relation between banality and brutality. Nabokov had a special Russian term for this: *poshlust.*

Poshlust, Nabokov explains, "is not only the obviously trashy but mainly the falsely important, the falsely beautiful, the falsely clever, the falsely attractive." Yes, there are many examples you can bring from everyday life, from the politicians' sugary speeches to certain writers' proclamations to chickens. Chickens? You know, the ones the street vendors sell nowadays—if you lived in Tehran, you couldn't possibly miss them. The ones they dip in paint—shocking pink, brilliant red, or turquoise blue—in order to make them more attractive. Or the plastic flowers, the bright pink-and-blue artificial gladiolas carted out at the university both for mourning and for celebration.

What Nabokov creates for us in *Invitation to a Beheading* is not the actual physical pain and torture of a totalitarian regime but the nightmarish quality of living in an atmosphere of perpetual dread. Cincinnatus C. is frail, he is passive, he is a hero without knowing or acknowledging it: he fights with his instincts, and his acts of writing are his means of escape. He is a hero because he refuses to become like all the rest.

Unlike in other utopian novels, the forces of evil here are not omnipotent; Nabokov shows us their frailty as well. They are ridiculous and they can be defeated, and this does not lessen the tragedy—the waste. *Invitation to a Beheading* is written from the point of view of the victim, one who ultimately sees the absurd sham of his persecutors and who must retreat into himself in order to survive.

Those of us living in the Islamic Republic of Iran grasped both the tragedy and absurdity of the cruelty to which we were subjected. We had to poke fun at our own misery in order to survive. We also instinctively recognized poshlust—not just in others, but in ourselves. This was one reason that art and literature became so essential to our lives: they were not a luxury but a necessity. What Nabokov captured was the texture of life in a totalitarian society, where you are completely alone in an illusory world full of false promises, where you can no longer differentiate between your savior and your executioner.

We formed a special bond with Nabokov despite the difficulty of his prose. This went deeper than our identification with his themes. His novels are shaped around invisible trapdoors, sudden gaps that constantly pull the carpet from under the reader's feet. They are filled with mistrust of what we call everyday reality, an acute sense of that reality's fickleness and frailty.

There was something, both in his fiction and in his life, that we instinctively related to and grasped, the possibility of a boundless freedom when all options are taken away. I think that was what drove me to create the class. My main link with the outside world had been the university, and now that I had severed that link, there on the brink of the void, I could invent the violin or be devoured by the void.

7. The two photographs should be placed side by side. Both embody the "fragile unreality"—to quote Nabokov on his own state of exile—of our existence in the Islamic Republic of Iran. One cancels the other, and yet without one, the other is incomplete. In the first photograph, standing there in our black robes and scarves, we are as we had been shaped by someone else's dreams. In the second, we appear as we imagined ourselves. In neither could we feel completely at home.

The second photograph belonged to the world inside the living room. But outside, underneath the window that deceptively showcased only the mountains and the tree outside our house, was the other world, where the bad witches and furies were waiting to transform us into the hooded creatures of the first.

The best way I can think of explaining this self-negating and paradoxical inferno is through an anecdote, one that, like similar anecdotes, defies fiction to become its own metaphor.

The chief film censor in Iran, up until 1994, was blind. Well, nearly blind. Before that, he was the censor for theater. One of my playwright friends once described how he would sit in the theater wearing thick glasses that seemed to hide more than they revealed. An assistant who sat by him would explain the action onstage, and he would dictate the parts that needed to be cut.

After 1994, this censor became the head of the new television channel. There, he perfected his methods and demanded that the scriptwriters give him their scripts on audiotape; they were forbidden to make them attractive or dramatize them in any way. He then made his judgments about the scripts based on the tapes. More interesting, however, is the fact that his successor, who was not blind—not physically, that is—nonetheless followed the same system.

Our world under the mullahs' rule was shaped by the colorless lenses of the blind censor. Not just our reality but also our fiction had taken on this curious coloration in a world where the censor was the poet's rival in rearranging and reshaping reality, where we simultaneously invented ourselves and were figments of someone else's imagination.

We lived in a culture that denied any merit to literary works, considering them important only when they were handmaidens to something seemingly more urgent—namely ideology. This was a country where all gestures, even the most private, were interpreted in political terms. The colors of my head scarf or my father's tie were symbols of Western decadence and imperialist tendencies. Not wearing a beard, shaking hands with members of the opposite sex, clapping or whistling in public meetings, were likewise considered Western and therefore decadent, part of the plot by imperialists to bring down our culture.

A few years ago some members of the Iranian Parliament set up an investigative committee to examine the content of national television. The committee issued a lengthy report in which it condemned the showing of *Billy Budd*, because, it claimed, the story promoted homosexuality. Ironically, the Iranian television programmers had mainly chosen that film because of its lack of female characters. The cartoon version of *Around the World in Eighty Days* was also castigated, because the main character—a lion—was British and the film ended in that bastion of imperialism, London.

Our class was shaped within this context, in an attempt to escape the gaze of the blind censor for a few hours each week. There, in that living room, we rediscovered that we were also living, breathing human beings; and no matter how repressive the state became, no matter how intimidated and frightened we were, like Lolita we tried to escape and to create our own little pockets of freedom. And like Lolita, we took every opportunity to flaunt our insubordination: by showing a little hair from under our scarves, insinuating a little color into the drab uniformity of our appearances, growing our nails, falling in love, and listening to forbidden music.

An absurd fictionality ruled our lives. We tried to live in the open spaces, in the chinks created between that room, which had become our protective cocoon, and the censor's world of witches and goblins outside. Which of these two worlds was more real, and to which did we really belong? We no longer knew the answers. Perhaps one way of finding out the truth was to do what we did: to try to imaginatively articulate these two worlds and, through that process, give shape to our vision and identity.

8.   How can I create this other world outside the room? I have no choice but to appeal once again to your imagination. Let's imagine one of the girls, say Sanaz, leaving my house and let us follow her from there to her final destination. She says her goodbyes and puts on her black robe and scarf over her orange shirt and jeans, coiling her scarf around her neck to cover her huge gold earrings. She directs wayward strands of hair under the scarf, puts her notes into her large bag, straps it on over her shoulder, and walks out into the hall. She pauses a moment on top of the stairs to put on thin lacy black gloves to hide her nail polish.

We follow Sanaz down the stairs, out the door, and into the street. You might notice that her gait and her gestures have changed. It is in her best interest not to be seen, not be heard or noticed. She doesn't walk upright, but bends her head towards the ground and doesn't look at passersby. She walks quickly and with a sense of determination. The streets of Tehran and other Iranian cities are patrolled by militia, who ride in white Toyota patrols, four gun-carrying men and women, sometimes followed by a minibus. They are called the Blood of God. They patrol the streets to make sure that women like Sanaz wear their veils properly, do not wear makeup, do not walk in public with men who are not their fathers, brothers, or husbands. She will pass slogans on the walls, quotations from Khomeini, and a group called the Party of God: MEN WHO WEAR TIES ARE U.S. LACKEYS. VEILING IS A WOMAN'S PROTECTION. Beside the slogan is a charcoal drawing of a woman: her face is featureless and framed by a dark chador. MY SISTER, GUARD YOUR VEIL. MY BROTHER, GUARD YOUR EYES.

If she gets on a bus, the seating is segregated. She must enter through the rear door and sit in the back seats, allocated to women. Yet in taxis, which accept as many as five passengers, men and women are squeezed together like sardines, as the saying goes, and the same goes with minibuses, where so many of my students complain of being harassed by bearded and God-fearing men.

You might well ask, What is Sanaz thinking as she walks the streets of Tehran? How much does this experience affect her? Most probably, she tries to distance her mind as much as possible from her surroundings. Perhaps she is thinking of her brother, or of her distant boyfriend and the time when she will meet him in Turkey. Does she compare her own situation with her mother's when she was the same age? Is she angry that women of her mother's generation could walk the streets freely, enjoy the company of the opposite sex, join the police force, become pilots, live under laws that were among the most progressive in the world regarding women? Does she feel humiliated by the new laws, by the fact that after the revolution, the age of marriage was lowered from eighteen to nine, that stoning became once more the punishment for adultery and prostitution?

In the course of nearly two decades, the streets have been turned into a war zone, where young women who disobey the rules are hurled into patrol cars, taken to jail, flogged, fined, forced to wash the toilets, and humiliated, and as soon as they leave, they go back and do the same thing. Is she aware, Sanaz, of her own power? Does she realize how dangerous she can be when her every stray gesture is a disturbance to public safety? Does she think how vulnerable the Revolutionary Guards are who for over eighteen years have patrolled the streets of Tehran and have had to endure young women like herself, and those of other generations, walking, talking, showing a strand of hair just to remind them that they have not converted?

We have reached Sanaz's house, where we will leave her on her doorstep, perhaps to confront her brother on the other side and to think in her heart of her boyfriend.

These girls, my girls, had both a real history and a fabricated one. Although they came from very different backgrounds, the regime that ruled them had tried to make their personal identities and histories irrelevant. They were never free of the regime's definition of them as Muslim women.

Whoever we were—and it was not really important what religion we belonged to, whether we wished to wear the veil or not, whether we observed certain religious norms or not—we had become the figment of someone else's dreams. A stern ayatollah, a self-proclaimed philosopher-king, had come to rule our land. He had come in the name of a past, a past that, he claimed, had been stolen from him. And he now wanted to re-create us in the image of that illusory past. Was it any consolation, and did we even wish to remember, that what he did to us was what we allowed him to do?

QUESTIONS FOR MAKING CONNECTIONS
WITHIN THE READING

1. Why does Nafisi spend so much time describing the members of her reading group? What different motives may have brought these readers to Nafisi's apartment? We might normally think of reading as a solitary activity, unlike watching movies or sports; why was it so important for the women to meet together as a group?

2. Judging from the information that Nafisi provides, why do you think her reading group selected the particular works she mentions: *A Thousand and*

One Nights, as well as *Invitation to a Beheading, Lolita*, and other novels by Nabokov? Why might religious authorities, not only in Iran but also in the United States, object to the teaching of such works?

3. Early in Chapter 10 of *Reading Lolita in Tehran*, Nafisi writes, "*Lolita* was *not* a critique of the Islamic Republic, but it went against the grain of all total-itarian perspectives." Without consulting a dictionary, and drawing instead on Nafisi's account, try to define *totalitarian*. What social and psychological effects does the totalitarian regime have on Nafisi and her students? In what sense might Lolita or other books you know pose a challenge to totalitari-anism? How are literature and the other arts—music, painting, sculpture, dance—inherently liberating? Is it possible for art itself to be totalitarian?

QUESTIONS FOR WRITING

1. Does Nafisi present a theory of interpretation? In other words, what does she see as the *real* or *correct* meaning of a work of art? Does she accept Nabokov's claims that "readers were born free and ought to remain free"? Would Nafisi say a work of art can mean anything we want? What is the value of art if it has no determinate or *correct* meaning? If art has a value, is its value simply personal? Does it also have social, political, and cultural value?

2. Nafisi and her students read Nabokov against the backdrop of the Islamic Republic of Iran. In that setting, what does the experience offer them? Would their reading of the novel provide the same experience if it took place in the United States? Does literature serve a different function in our society? How might reading a novel in a private group differ from the experience of reading the same novel in an American high school or college classroom?

QUESTIONS FOR MAKING CONNECTIONS
BETWEEN READINGS

1. Nafisi is convinced that reading groups like hers posed a real challenge to the regime. One important part of their effectiveness lay in the ability of litera-ture to sustain human connectedness in spite of isolating policies. But taking off the black chador and speaking face to face were only the beginning. Still more powerfully, perhaps, literature gave the members of the reading group permission to become the creators of themselves. Starting with Cathy Davidson's "Project Classroom Makeover," would you say that the new electronic media—the Web and iPods, for example—pose a challenge to the established order in much the same way as Nabokov's writing did in Iran? Or are the new media here in the West actually helping to erode the culture of books that allowed Nafisi and her students to resist an oppressive regime?

Are the new media truly liberating? Do they heighten our sense of connectedness, or do they make individuals feel invisible and insignificant?

2. In "Darwin's *Really* Dangerous Idea," Richard Prum argues that beauty plays a crucial role in the evolution of species, and he suggests that his colleagues may have resisted this idea because it recognizes women's agency—their ability to control their own lives, and, beyond that, to influence nothing less than the future of our species, *Homo sapiens*. Aesthetic experience, he argues, is distinct from natural selection with its logic of "survival of the fittest," operating by a different set of laws—laws, we could say, of attraction rather than of competition and conflict. To what extent does the account of Nafisi's reading group lend support to Prum's argument? What role does aesthetic experience play among Nafisi and her students? In what ways does it pose a challenge to the way of life imposed on them by the Islamic Republic?

◆◆◆

MAGGIE NELSON

AMERICAN SOCIETY IS SATURATED with violence—and not just the violence horrifically displayed in early December 2012 at the Sandy Hook Elementary School, where a former student returned to shoot 20 children and 6 adults before he trained his rifle on himself. In 2011, the homicide rate in the United States was more than four times greater than Germany's and more than eight times Japan's. But violence here is not just a social fact—it's also a cultural phenomenon, as poet, critic, and essayist Maggie Nelson understands. Anyone who watches television and YouTube, or spends hours playing video games, will recognize its pervasiveness. But Nelson finds violence in a place we might never think to look—in the high arts, especially the cutting-edge tradition known as the avant-garde.

Past defenders of the artistic avant-garde celebrated the possibilities opened up by "aesthetic shock," the experience produced by radical disorientation. But they have tended to soft-pedal its complicity with sadism and terror. At times, Nelson herself seems to be thrilled by the avant-garde's liberating openness, but she tries to nudge artists and art lovers toward what one reviewer, writing in the *New York Times*, calls a "post-avant-garde aesthetics." Such an aesthetics—a new framework for the arts—might, as Nelson claims, "deliver us to a more sensitive, perceptive, insightful, enlivened, collaborative and just way of inhabiting the earth." Nelson's shift from art to "inhabiting the earth" might seem to give too much importance to what goes on in galleries, museums, and film festivals. But the sadism of the avant-garde has never stopped at the museum door: in fact, its influence reaches everywhere: into popular films and magazines, architecture, television, fashion, and design—the entire "cultural imaginary." When Nelson questions the pieties of past art criticism, she does so because she understands that the arts help to create the texture and the shape of our experience.

Nelson, who received a Ph.D. in English from the Graduate Center of the City University of New York, has taught writing and literature at the Pratt Institute, Wesleyan University, and the New School. Since 2005 she has been on the faculty of the California Institute of the Arts (CALARTS). While Nelson's essays on culture explore new directions in the arts, she also speaks for a post-Boomer generation of writers and artists who have had to live without stable jobs at marquee newspapers

---

The *New York Times* quotation is from Laura Kipnis, "Why Is Contemporary Art Addicted to Violence?" *New York Times*, July 14, 2011. The quotation on inhabiting the earth is from *The Art of Cruelty: A Reckoning*, 265 and the quotation from the interview in the online journal comes from "Pathos: Maggie Nelson," *Full Stop*, January 24, 2013 <http://www.full-stop.net/2013/01/24/interviews/the-editors-pathos-maggie-nelson/>.

or tenured professorships at universities. As she told an interviewer for the online journal *Full Stop* about the difficulties of the writer's life today, "I don't think the world owes anyone anything. I think we owe the world more stewardship and vision and respect than we currently are giving it, and as fellow humans we owe each other more care than our current system impels us to give."

Great to Watch

In her moving, influential anti–capital punishment memoir, *Dead Man Walking*, Sister Helen Prejean asserts, "I know that it is not a question of malice or ill will or meaness of spirit that prompts our citizens to support executions. It is, quite simply, that people don't know the truth of what is going on." Prejean is convinced that if executions were made public, "the torture and violence would be unmasked, and we would be shamed into abolishing executions."

Alas, if only it were so. For if the bad news from Abu Ghraib made anything clear in recent years, it is that this model of shaming-us-into-action-by-unmasking-the-truth-of-our-actions cannot hold a candle to our capacity to assimilate horrific images, and to justify or shrug off horrific behavior. Not to mention the fact that the United States has a long history—as do many countries and individuals—of reveling in the spectacle of public executions and gruesome torture. (On this account, I unhappily recommend to you the 2000 book of documentary photography *Without Sanctuary: Lynching Photography in America*.)

Prejean's conviction that it is simple, blameless ignorance that prompts so many Americans to support executions (or the torture of detainees in the so-called war on terror, and so on) may be goodhearted. But unfortunately it leaves us but one option: know the truth, and ye shall be redeemed. But "knowing the truth" does not come with redemption as a guarantee, nor does a feeling of redemption guarantee an end to a cycle of wrongdoing. Some would even say it is key to maintaining it, insofar as it can work as a reset button—a purge that cleans the slate, without any guarantee of change at the root. Placing all one's eggs in "the logic of exposure," as Eve Kosofsky Sedgwick has put it (in *Touching Feeling*), may also simply further the logic of paranoia. "Paranoia places its faith in exposure," Sedgwick observes—which is to say that the exposure of a disturbing fact or situation does not necessarily alter it, but in fact may further the circular conviction that *one can never be paranoid enough*.

Prejean's logic relies on the hope that shame, guilt, and even simple embarrassment are still operative principles in American cultural and political life—and that such principles can fairly trump the forces of desensitization and self-justification. Such a presumption is sorely challenged by the seeming unembarrassability of the military, the government, corporate CEOs, and others repetitively caught in monstrous acts of irresponsibility and malfeasance. This unembarrassability has proved difficult to contend with, as it has had a literally stunning effect on the citizenry. *They ought to be ashamed of themselves!* we cry, over and over again, to no avail. But they are not ashamed, and they are not going to become so.

Also difficult to contend with: the fact that we ourselves have ample and wily reserves of malice, power-mongering, self-centeredness, fear, sadism, or simple meanness of spirit that we ourselves, our loved ones, our enemies, skillful preachers, politicians, and rhetoricians of all stripes can whip into a hysterical, destructive froth at any given moment, if we allow for it.

To this list, one should surely add television producers. In 1982, Stephen King published a sci-fi novel called *The Running Man,* set in the not-so-distant future. In the novel, "The Running Man" is the country's most popular TV game show, and features a contestant who agrees to run for his life while being trailed by a group of "Hunters" charged with killing him. The network engages the populace by paying civilians for confirmed sightings of the runner, which it then passes along to the Hunters. If the runner survives for thirty days, he gets a billion dollars. If he is caught, he is killed by the Hunters on live TV.

As others have noted, the dystopic plot of *The Running Man* turned out to be more prophetic than dissuasive. So-called reality television has been foraying into this territory for over a decade now, churning out show after show that draws on some combination of surveillance; self-surveillance; "interactivity" with the home audience; techniques associated with torture, interrogation, or incarceration; and rituals of humiliation, sadism, and masochism (of the I'll-do-anything-for-fame-or-money variety, not the I-do-this-because-it-gives-me-pleasure variety: outing one's pleasures, it seems, remains more taboo than outing one's ambition or avarice).

The international craze for reality programming has, to date, given us shows such as the United Kingdom's *Shattered* (2004), in which contestants are deprived of sleep for many days in a row, and *Unbreakable* (2008), in which contestants undergo various forms of torture (including being waterboarded, buried alive, or made to cross the Sahara Desert while wearing suffocating gas masks), and whose motto is "Pain Is Glory, Pain Is Pride, Pain Is Great to Watch." In the United States, reality TV has at times joined forces with soft-core journalism and law enforcement to produce shows like Dateline/NBC's *To Catch a Predator. To Catch a Predator*—which operates in questionable legal conjunction with not only the police but also a vigilante "anti-predator" group called "Perverted Justice"—hires decoys who pretend to be underage teens. These decoys attempt to entice adults into online sex chats; if and when one of the adults agrees to meet his online pen pal at the "decoy house," he (and it is always a he) is there greeted by the show's host, Chris Hansen, who first verbally humiliates him by reading him the most tawdry excerpts of his online sex chatter, then turns him over to the police, who are waiting nearby with handcuffs.

The legal, ethical, and psychological ramifications of such shows have occasioned quite a bit of debate, as these effects have often proved unmanageable. On November 5, 2006, for example, after a SWAT team trailed by TV cameras forced its way into the home of Louis Conradt Jr., a longtime county prosecutor in Murphy, Texas, Conradt said, "I'm not going to hurt anybody," before firing a single bullet from a semiautomatic handgun into his brain, thereby ending his life. (There had been no pressing reason to break into Conradt's home—Conradt had, in fact, refused to meet the decoy at the decoy house—but the show's producers were anxious to capture the arrest of a prominent public figure on tape, as it promised to make compelling TV. In the end, Dateline refrained from airing the death itself, but it did run a segment on the case.) As one newspaper columnist writing about the incident acidly put it, "When a TV show makes you feel sorry for potential child rapists, you know it's doing something wrong." (Or right, depending on your point of view; To Catch a Predator was one of NBC's hit shows for some time.)

As if a test were needed of how much sadism reality television participants, audiences, and producers are willing to indulge, on March 17, 2010, French TV broadcast something called Le jeu de la mort, or The Game of Death, a faux game show which re-performed the Milgram experiment on eighty unknowing contestants. The contestants had been told that they were taking part in a game-show pilot, in which they were to administer electric shocks to other contestants when they answered questions incorrectly. A smiling host and vociferous studio audience, rather than a taciturn guy in a lab coat (as was the case in Stanley Milgram's experiment), urged the behavior on, but the results were remarkably similar: sixty-four of the eighty contestants were willing to deliver shocks that could have killed their recipients, had there been any actual receivers.

But beyond prime time, which the digital age may be rendering a quaint outpost, more literal renditions of the Running Man scenario—and ones that offer their viewers slightly more participation than that of armchair schadenfreude—are now available via a few strokes of your computer keyboard. Consider, for example, the Texas Virtual Border Watch Program, in which "The Texas Border Sheriff's Coalition (TBSC) has joined BlueServo[SM] in a public-private partnership to deploy the Virtual Community Watch, an innovative real-time surveillance program designed to empower the public to proactively participate in fighting border crime." In other words, the TBSC has placed cameras along the U.S.-Mexican border in Texas at so-called high-threat spots for border crossing or drug trafficking, and now invites the home viewer to log on, pick a spot, and start "directly monitoring suspicious criminal activity via this virtual fence[SM]." Viewers can watch the live feed from one of the "virtual stake outs" for as long as they like—the New York Times recently interviewed a housewife from Rochester, New York, who reported watching for at least four hours a day.

While controversial, the BlueServo[SM] project should come as no surprise to anyone familiar with the Minutemen and its offshoots, whose volunteers have been (non-virtually) patrolling the U.S.-Mexican border, looking for "illegals," since 1995. "It's just like hunting," explained Chuck Stonex, a prominent member. "If you're going out hunting deer, you want to scout around and get an idea what their pattern is, what trails they use." Stonex, along with Minuteman founder Jim Gilchrist and other leading figures, has since taken a more defensive stance, after one of their principal associates, Shawna Forde, was arrested in June 2009 in connection with the murder of two members of a Hispanic family in their home in Arivaca, Arizona; one of those killed was a nine-year-old girl. But the chilling new anti-immigration law signed by Governor Jan Brewer of Arizona on April 23, 2010, which authorizes police to demand proof of any person's immigration status should "reasonable suspicion exist that the person is an alien," has breathed new life into the "hunt 'em down" mindset, in both Arizona and the nation at large.

With BlueServo^{SM}, the condition of spectatorship is not so much abolished as it is recast as a form of empowerment: you, too, can defend the homeland, without ever having to leave your home! The project eerily combines the appeal of a spectator sport with language more typically reserved for left wing–sounding community activism: *Innovative. Proactive. Participation. Partnership. Coalition. Community. Empowerment.* (Especially poignant: "public-private partnership"—in the age of Blackwater [now called Xe] or the Tea Party, every vigilante need be prepared for a trademark!) Last time I visited the BlueServo^{SM} site, there were fifteen cameras rolling on scenes of bucolic calm. My favorites were Camera 5, which featured a still patch of golden weeds with the directive, "During the day watch for subjects on foot carrying large bags," and Camera 10, which featured a swiftly moving river alongside the directive, "During the day if you see four or five men in a boat report this activity. At night if you see vehicle, boat, or people movement report this activity." The static, unending nature of the footage bears a weird resemblance to the endurance-based, art house aesthetic of, say, Andy Warhol's *Empire* (1964)—a film that consists of eight hours and five minutes of continuous footage of the Empire State Building—or that of a virtual yule log, albeit one of a more sinister variety.

On the flip side of such a "if you see something, say something" policing projects lies a human rights organization such as the Hub, which describes itself as "the world's first participatory media site for human rights." I'm thinking in particular of the Hub's Witness project, whose motto is "See It, Film It, Change It," and which aims to use "video and online technologies to open the eyes of the world to human rights violations." The operation of Witness is twofold: one, to give people cameras and train them to videotape atrocities or injustices they may be suffering or witnessing; two, to invent a circuitry by which one can upload one's own videos and view those of others, presumably as a prelude to taking a form of action after viewing. For convenience, one can scroll through the videos by category (armed conflict, children's rights, discrimination, violence, women's rights, and so on), or by "most viewed" (Japanese sexual slavery during World War II has occupied this slot for some time now).

As the creators of the Hub well know, the employment of image or moving image in service of mobilizing an individual or a populace is tricky business. For this reason, the Hub aims to zero in on the little window of time between an upsurge of outrage or sympathy and the onset of apathy—to hurl an otherwise fleeting emotion into action before it dissolves. (What action consists of is a difficult, debatable question—right now the "take action" tab on the Hub's Web site links to "a growing portfolio of advocacy tools to help allies and users call for action," ranging from signing email petitions to writing members of Congress to sending money to a variety of organizations to creating "offline events.")

I mean it as no slight to the Hub when I say that I find the smorgasbord of human suffering offered on its site repellent. Not because "it is difficult to look" (though sometimes, of course, it is), but because the physical and mental activity of Web surfing, which consists of rapid image flow, the distillation of long, complex stories and situations to 2-inch-high, four-minute snippets, one-click decision-making, happenstance isolations, juxtapositions, and linkages that have an eerily leveling effect on content and context, is, in my experience, an exceptionally poor means by which to contemplate the horrors of human trafficking, child prostitution, landmines, and the like. For better or worse, one's experience of surfing the Hub is shaped by the do-I-or-don't-I-want-to-watch-this question, as in: Do I or don't I want to watch a Tibetan pilgrim being shot dead by the Chinese police at Nangpa La Pass? How about cell phone footage of a man being hung upside down and sodomized with a rod in an Egyptian prison? Or the testimony of women in Bangladesh whose faces have been disfigured by acid? Well-intentioned and effective as the operation may be, scrolling through such choices makes me feel as though I've arrived at the hub of a problem rather than its solution.

Insofar as "image flow" isn't going away any time soon, it certainly makes sense to try to harness the powers of YouTube for all kinds of social causes as well as for entertainment. But there are also perils. And one is that in a cultural moment defined (by some, for some) by image flow, the question of what one should look at, along with attendant inquiries into the nature and effect of the images blowing by, has a creepy way of overtaking almost all other questions. This may in fact be part of the so-called image regime's raison d'etre, rather than a puzzling side effect. In any case, it can lead to cul-de-sacs, red herrings, or distractions fatal to the primary issue at hand.

For example, in a director's statement about his Abu Ghraib documentary, *Standard Operating Procedure,* filmmaker Errol Morris names the principal question posed by his film as, "Is it possible for a photograph to change the world?" But what could the answer to this question—be it in the negative or the affirmative—really mean? As Sontag puts it in *Regarding the Pain of Others,* "The image as shock and the image as cliché are two aspects of the same presence"—a notion that partially explains how the iconic image of the hooded prisoner at Abu Ghraib forced to hold a foreboding wire in each hand could literally sicken one's stomach when first viewed, then move on to become a much-parodied image (e.g., on the satirical posters that appeared throughout the New York subways not long after the Abu Ghraib story broke, posters that borrowed the distinctive design of Apple's iPod campaign, but substituted the word "iRaq" for "iPod," and featured the silhouette of the hooded man in lieu of the iPod's silhouetted dancer). It isn't that this photograph played no role in the unfolding of human events—clearly, it did. But after nearly 200 years of photography, it may be that we are closer than ever to understanding that an image—be it circulated in a newspaper, on YouTube, or in an art gallery—is an exceptionally poor platform on which to place the unending, arduous, multifaceted, and circuitous process of "changing the world."

In his April 2008 *Artforum* review of *Standard Operating Procedure,* critic Paul Arthur noted something of the same. In thinking about Morris's focus on the revelation that the man who identified himself publicly as the hooded prisoner turned out *not* to be the actual victim, Arthur writes, "Morris finds this revelation telling because it shows how massively disseminated pictures can mask their own provenance or 'attract false beliefs.' Really? I thought the images under consideration, especially when supplemented by salient verbal contexts, revealed more about policy than about epistemology, more about state-sponsored barbarity than about media deception." In other words, one need not immerse oneself in horrific images or a debate about their epistemological status in order to apprehend and protest barbarities wherever they are to be found. Nor does one need to distract oneself with rehashings of the Milgram experiment, which uselessly reiterate what we already know about our capacity to cause harm under pressure (or, as the case may be, at simple invitation).

One does, however, need to know what barbarities have taken place: there's the rub. Enter President Obama, speaking about his administration's May 2009 decision to suppress the release of a new spate of photographs that depict the abuse, rape, and torture of Afghan and Iraqi prisoners in American custody. "The most direct consequence of releasing [these photos]," Obama said, "would be to further inflame anti-American opinion and to put our troops in greater danger." Mark down one vote for the idea that images have the power to cause injury—though to warn against such a thing in this case smells pretty rotten, given that the suppressed photos presumably depict our troops injuring others.

Obama also skips over the most obvious direct consequence of releasing the photos: that Americans would see—along with the rest of the world—more evidence of the barbarities that have been committed in their name, on their supposed behalf, and on their dime. To state the obvious but oft-repressed or denied point, it isn't the act of releasing photos that inflames anti-American sentiment; it's the behavior captured by the photos. In the age of "the torturer with the Toshiba," as art historian T.J. Clark has put it, no image flow can be fully marshaled. Nor can survivors and witnesses be unilaterally silenced. If you don't want to inflame via images of the behavior, then you have to stop the behavior.

Of course, it isn't entirely clear that the United States meant to keep the news of its use of torture a secret. No regime hoping to gain power from its use of such violence (an impossibility, according to Hannah Arendt) ever has. Certainly the revelations from Abu Ghraib appeared as a mistake, a rip in the fabric; certainly the U.S. government has employed intense secrecy, censorship, and denial about everything from the Red Cross Torture Report to the exact interrogation methods used to the operations of "black sites" around the world. Certainly journalists from Seymour Hersh to Jane Mayer to Mark Danner to Scott Horton have had an enormously difficult time obtaining the information they need to inform the public about what, exactly, has gone on; certainly the CIA has classified and egregiously destroyed pivotal evidence, such as the videotapes depicting the 2002 interrogations of several terrorism suspects—tapes the CIA outrageously destroyed in 2005, in the midst of a federal investigation.

And yet. On a parallel track run the monologues of Dick Cheney, who, since leaving office, has toured the talk shows, speaking with candor and pride about his role in "The Program." Then there's the ongoing consideration of the topic in the bright glare of television and the blogosphere, in which everyone from Bill O'Reilly to Andrew Sullivan to Christopher Hitchens to Elisabeth Hasselbeck openly debates the efficacy of torture, and the effect its use has had on our country—not whether or not we have done it. The Bush/Cheney dyad of denial/justification represents two sides of a single coin: Bush spoke the voice of delusion (it never happened, it will never happen); Cheney, the voice of justification (we had to do it, we should still be doing it). The average citizen can then ricochet between these two irreconcilable, collaborative poles until desensitization sets in, and with it, a begrudging (or, for some, an enthusiastic) acceptance of the practice.

Back in 1965, Sontag declared that we live in "an age of extremity," characterized by "the continual threat of two equally fearful, but seemingly opposed destinies: unremitting banality and inconceivable terror." Much of the art produced under the influence of [Antonin] Artaud—such as [Hermann] Nitsch's—proceeds from this premise, and attempts to replace the crush of banality with some form of brutal, sensory overload. Even quieter works such as [Alfredo] Jaar's *Untitled (Newsweek)* depend on this by-now familiar dichotomy—one that places benumbing banality on one side, and unthinkable, rupturing calamity on the other.

The moral of this dichotomy is that distraction by the banal obviates a necessary focus on the all-too-real-calamitous. This equation became ubiquitous in the weeks and months after 9/11, when media commentator after commentator lamented the fact that instead of focusing on the real threat from Al Qaeda, Americans spent the summer of 2001 unforgivably obsessing over the latest incarnation of Britney Spears. But really this is a self-flagellating, essentially non-sensical diagnosis, especially in its supposition that Americans would have been better off spending more of their time worrying about an impending terrorist attack, the shape of which they could have had no foreknowledge. (The next seven years and four months of the Bush administration provided a good picture of what a populace in thrall to such anxiety might look like—and what it might tolerate from its leaders—and it wasn't pretty.)

After 9/11, Sontag's formulation would seem to have more adherents than ever, on both the right and the left. See, for example, the leftist collective RETORT's *Afflicted Powers: Capital and Spectacle in a New Age of War* (2005), which repeatedly pits the eviscerating "false depth" of consumerism (i.e., unremitting banality) against claims that "we have never been closer to hell on earth" (i.e., inconceivable terror). But is it true? Or more precisely, for whom is it true, and who presumes it to be true for others? Do we really live under the aegis of these opposing threats, or is it the very reiteration of them as our two primary ontological options (and our unthinking acquiescence to such a formulation) that acts as a truer threat to our enlivenment, to our full experience of the vast space between these two poles—a space which, after all, is where the great majority of many of our lives takes place? And if, as David Graeber has suggested, revolutionary action is "not a form of grim self-sacrifice," but rather "the defiant insistence on acting as if one is already free," what good does it do us to charge those who refuse to live under the aegis of these two grim choices with false consciousness, with not truly understanding the stakes of the age?

Compare, for example, the "troughs of blood and wine," the "extreme noise from the orchestras" of Nitsch's *Six-Day Play* with John Cage's Zen-inspired *4′33″,* first composed in 1952, in which Cage famously asks audience members to sit in complete silence for four minutes and thirty-three seconds, in order to awaken to the sounds going on around them, to hear all the ambient noise of which they would have otherwise been unaware. In light of the heightened state of perception conjured by Cage's piece—its profound capacity to "return us to our senses" via an emptying out of input rather than an overload of it—one may begin to wonder whose interests it serves to keep us believing in, and riveted by, the mythos of this "age of extremity," which focuses on knocking oneself out rather than tuning in.

Perhaps more controversially still, given our inarguable complicity in all kinds of systemic forms of global injustice: is there any space left for *not* watching, *not* focusing, *not* keeping abreast of all the events and atrocities unfolding in the world, as an ethically viable option? "Why are we watching the news, reading the news, keeping up with the news?" asks Annie Dillard in *For the Time Being,* a book that sets forth the deeply unfashionable argument that our times are not uniquely grievous—that they are, in fact, not unique at all—and further, that their vicissitudes may make no intrinsic demand on our attention, or on our conscience. That enlivenment may consist of quiet, even monastic retreat, rather than bombardment or disembowelment. "Who can bear to hear this, or who will consider it?" Dillard wonders.

In completely disparate circles—such as those of leftist political philosophy, for example—a distinct but not wholly unrelated idea of "engaged withdrawal" has also begun to hold sway. Rather than fixate on revolution, this strategy privileges orchestrated and unorchestrated acts of exodus. As Italian political philosopher Paolo Virno has put it, "Nothing is less passive that the act of fleeing, of exiting." In anarchist circles, this withdrawal bears a relationship to the idea of the "TAZ," or "temporary autonomous zones" (as elaborated by writer Hakim Bey; Graeber prefers the term "provisional autonomous zones"): ephemeral but crucial gaps in an otherwise suffocating global capitalist order, gaps that, at the very least, make other forms of social organization and perception seem momentarily possible.

In short, after decades of critical focus on the evils of spectatorship, the gaze, and the presumably passive role of the audience, an increasing chorus of critical voices is currently arguing that we have somehow gotten wildly off course by treating the condition of spectatorship as a problem, or at least as *the* problem. There's Jacques Rancière, who argues in 2009's *The Emancipated Spectator* that spectatorship is not "the passivity that has to be turned into activity," but rather "our normal situation." Then, of course, there's Sontag, whose final book, *Regarding the Pain of Others,* argues that to impugn the sense of sight for allowing us to "stand back from the aggressiveness of the world" and to free us up "for observation and for elective attention" is to impugn the function of the mind itself. Sontag concludes, "There's nothing wrong with standing back and thinking. To paraphrase several sages: 'Nobody can think and hit someone at the same time.'" In a culture obsessed with pitting thought against action (in order to privilege the latter), not to mention a culture perpetually dubious of the cash value of rumination, these are fighting words. In 2006, T.J. Clark—who is known as much for his fierce political convictions as his insights into Picasso (he is, in fact, a member of RETORT)—published *The Sight of Death*, a 242-page meditation on two works by seventeenth-century painter Nicolas Poussin, in which Clark aims to honor the slow work of "this focusing, this staying still, this allowing oneself to respond to the *picture's* stillness—everything hidden and travestied, in short, by the current word 'gaze.'" Clark also rebukes those scholars of "visual culture" who, in his words, are "chained to their image-displacement machines like lab animals to dispensers of morphine," and whose knee-jerk response to an expansive, devoted, patient contemplation of classical painting (such as his) would be to dismiss it as nostalgic, or elitist, or "some such canting parrot-cry."

The above-mentioned writers have dedicated their lives to slow seeing, slow thinking, measured articulation, and radical dissent or defection from any *doxa* that stifles existence or adds injustice to it. I am inclined to listen to them. Rather than lambast that which mediates as our enemy, each makes a concerted effort to reclaim the value of the "third term." "In the logic of emancipation," Rancière writes, "there is always a third thing—a book or some other piece of writing—alien to both [teacher and student] and to which they can refer to verify in common what the pupil has seen, what she says about it and what she thinks about it." The emancipatory value of this third thing, as Rancière sees it, lies in the fact that no one can own it; no one can own its meaning. Its function is to mediate, but not in the sense of imitating or representing a reality from which spectators are barred. Here, "the mediate" relates people to each other, with *relation* signifying the process of being brought together and given a measure of space from each other at the same time.

This is essentially a spatial construct—a diagram, or, as [Francis] Bacon might have it, a ring of action—that constructs both distance and association (or, if you like, individuality and collectivity). Its construction demarcates some sort of boundary, but it does not follow that the function of that boundary need be a constrictive or restrictive one. In fact, the function of the boundary may be wildly variable and even liberating, especially insofar as it creates sub-spaces, and guarantees that there can be a game. As philosopher Ludwig Wittgenstein puts it, "If I surround an area with a fence or a line or otherwise, the purpose may be to prevent someone from getting in or out; but it may also be part of a game and the players supposed, say, to jump over the boundary; or it may show where the property of one man ends and that of another begins; and so on. So if I draw a boundary line that is not yet to say what I am drawing it for." Given that "breaking down boundaries" has come to act as a synonym for innovative or progressive action, be it in art, social justice, or beyond, Wittgenstein's distinctions bear some repeating. Not all boundaries or mediating forces are created equal; not all serve the same purpose. Neither politics nor art is served if and when the distinctions between them are willingly or unthinkingly smeared out.

Rancière's veneration of this third term also echoes certain remarks Hannah Arendt made over fifty years ago, in speaking about the importance of the public realm (which, Arendt makes clear, is definitively *not* the same as the social realm). "The public realm, as the common world," Arendt wrote, "gathers us together and yet prevents our falling over each other, so to speak. What makes mass society so difficult to bear is not the number of people involved, or at least not primarily, but the fact that the world between them has lost its power to gather them together, to relate and separate them. The weirdness of this situation resembles a spiritualistic séance where a number of people gathered round a table might suddenly, through some magic trick, see the table vanish from their midst, so that two persons sitting opposite each other were no longer separated but also would be entirely unrelated to each other by anything tangible."

For Arendt, this collapse signifies a deep and dangerous failure in human relations. (God only knows what she would have made of the vast social realm of the Internet, and its creation of a wholly different type of séance—one in which the table remains, but the human bodies are disappeared.) For others, this collapse serves as the gateway to ecstatic, unmediated union. Others still, seeing this fantasized union as utopian nonsense, but who are equally troubled by the forms of alienation that ostensibly prohibit it, offer up satirical or cynical dystopias in its place. And others—especially younger others—simply ignore both the promises and the perils of the whole communion/alienation dyad, as one typically ignores any binaries that no longer speak to the defining conditions and possibilities of one's time. The mind-bending work of an artist such as Ryan Trecartin offers a particularly gripping example of the latter.

Trecartin's 2007 feature-length video, *I-Be Area*, while nominally based on the concept of "virtual reality," is a riotous exploration of what kinds of space, identity, physicality, language, sexuality, and consciousness might be possible once one leaves the dichotomy of the virtual and the real behind, along with a whole host of other need-not-apply binaries (the everyday and the apocalyptic, the public and the private, the utopic and the dystopic, male and female, gay and straight, among them). The hyperactive cloning, frenetic strobing of characters, and post-identity verbiage of *I-Be Area* make James Cameron's *Avatar* (2009) or the Internet game Second Life look like relics from the Stone Age. "I love the idea of technology and culture moving faster than the understanding of those mediums by people," Trecartin has said, and his works aim to immerse viewers in this failed-to-upload state. The disorientation of this state is not that of grandpa befuddled by a fistful of printer cables, but rather the sort of psychological and physiological stupefaction more often associated with acid overdoses and schizoid breakdowns.

I-Be Area takes incapacity—to absorb, to make sense, to cohere, to sort, to concentrate—as its starting point. ("It's like the jumper being jumped before the onset of 'jump,'" Trecartin explains, both helpfully and unhelpfully.) Then it amplifies this incapacity by turning up the speed, the color, the hysteria, the flicker. Image or speech overflow is no longer a problem, and certainly not one that art could or should aid in solving. It is where we live, at least while watching Trecartin; it is our "abstract plot of now," as he calls it. Trecartin's ability to sustain us here for some real time often feels like a miracle, in that such an ability seems as if it should be, by definition, also beyond the artist. That is to say, the art often feels as if it is moving faster than Trecartin himself could be—which is likely why his films, when combined with his youth (*I-Be Area* was finished when he was twenty-six), have had something of an awe-inducing effect on the art world. "All I can do is generalize about this world and point to it with a yearning, stumped pleasure," writes Wayne Koestenbaum about Trecartin's work. "My pointing finger is the gesture of an outsider, a tourist, gawking at a radioactive carnival I can't domesticate or quarantine."

Koestenbaum notes that Trecartin's work is about radical distraction—that dreaded, proliferate state that leads to dazzlingly high numbers of cell phone–related car crashes each day, or that leads otherwise progressive professors to shake their heads in despair as their students text each other under the classroom table. But Trecartin's brand of distraction doesn't rely on any simple use of the imitative fallacy—that is, "contemporary life is mind-scrambling, fragmented, and distracted, so my art must be mind-scrambling, fragmented, and distracted, too." It is too tightly orchestrated for that—too layered, too well-performed, too purposefully edited, too intelligently perverse. However bawdy and hysterical, Trecartin's videos draw tight rings of actions: they are condensed, fast-moving world creations that make an intense demand on our attention. And the animating paradox of this world, as Koestenbaum has put it, is that "*Trecartin's characters concentrate on distraction.*" However frenetic *I-Be Area* may be, its distraction is not of the same order as that of, say, the idiotic pop-up balloons and crawling tickers that have become staples of the television screen. To stay with *I-Be Area* all the way through—to listen to every word, to follow every decision and cut—requires a keen effort. You'll get the most out of it if you, too, can concentrate on distraction.

Of course, you may not remember much of what happened; you may not remember any of the characters; you may not even be left with an image. If your experience resembles mine, you'll be left with something far more amorphous—a kind of vibrating memory of the unnerving psychic state the work induced, or captured, or invented (and, perhaps, a notebook full of scrawled lines that sounded great at the time, such as, "My personal really concise pussy is developing a very inner monologue which I will not reveal to you as I become dynamic"). In his lucid, compelling book on craft, *Unbalancing Acts: Foundations for a Theater,* famed avant-garde dramatist Richard Foreman articulates this aesthetics-of-amnesia quite well: "The image of the Marlboro man riding his horse and smoking his cigarette has stuck with me for many years—and so what? It's garbage. It's kitsch. All it means is that the image seduced me, that it pushed a button that was ready to be pushed, and I responded. It didn't widen my sensibilities, compassion, or intuition. Whereas an art that affects you in the moment, but which you then find hard to remember, is straining to bring you to another level. It offers images or ideas from that other level, that other way of being, which is why you find them hard to remember. But it has opened you to the possibility of growing into what you are not yet, which is exactly what art should do."

Foreman is a bit more sanguine about the possibility of "growing into what you are not yet" than Trecartin, whose enthusiasm about new technologies and their relationship to human consciousness has a decidedly who-cares-where-we're-headed-let's-party vibe. I don't think, for example, that Trecartin is explicitly setting out to make work that offers his viewers "artistic structures—models of consciousness—that might evolve into a new kind of lucidity and self-possession, which would enable us to navigate the rapids of our times," as Foreman says he has been trying to do for upward of forty years now. In short, critics and viewers who look to Trecartin as an idiot savant emissary from the next generation who has come to answer the question *Are we going to be alright?* are not likely to feel reassured.

But in the end, it may not matter. Both Foreman and Trecartin work from a conception of the human, or the "real," borne out of contradiction, fluctuation, incoherence, and perversity; both offer immersion in their vision without rehashing the avant-garde fetish of terrorizing the audience or the mainstream one of chaperoning it. "We abide by cultural directives that urge us: clarify each thought, each experience, so you can cull from them their single, dominant meaning and, in the process, become a responsible adult who knows what he or she thinks," Foreman has said. "But what I try to show is the opposite: how at every moment, the world presents us with a composition in which a multitude of meanings and realities are available, and you are able to swim, lucid and self-contained, in that turbulent sea of multiplicity." After an hour or so of watching *I-Be Area,* or of watching a Foreman play, you start to swim in such a sea. The experience seems to me at least a start on a worthwhile sense of human freedom.

BIBLIOGRAPHY

Arendt, Hannah. *On Violence.* New York: Harvest Books/Harcourt Brace, 1969, 1970.

Arthur, Paul. "The Horror: Paul Arthur on Errol Morris's Standard Operating Procedure." *Artforum* April 2008. <http://artforum.com/inprint/issue=200804&id=19738>.

Bachman, Richard (King, Stephen). *The Running Man.* New York: Signet Books, 1982.

Bey, Hakim. *The Temporary Autonomous Zone, Ontological Anarchy, Poetic Terrorism.* New York: Autonomedia, 1985.

Clark, T. J. *The Sight of Death: An Experiment in Art Writing.* New Haven, CT: Yale University Press, 2006.

Dillard, Annie. *For the Time Being.* New York: Vintage, 2000.

Foreman, Richard. *Unbalancing Acts: Foundations for a Theater.* New York: Theater Communications Group, 1993.

Graeber, Donald. *Possibilities: Essays on Hierarchy, Rebellion, and Desire.* Oakland, CA: AK Press, 2007.

Koestenbaum, Wayne. *Andy Warhol* (Penguin Lives). New York: Viking, 2001.

Prejean, Sister Helen. *Dead Man Walking: An Eyewitness Account of the Death Penalty in the United States.* New York: Vintage, 1994.

Rancière, Jacques. *The Emancipated Spectator.* Trans. Gregory Elliott. New York: Verso, 2009.

RETORT. *Afflicted Powers: Capital and Spectacle in a New Age of War.* New York: Verso, 2005.

Sedgwick, Eve Kosofsky. *Touching Feeling: Affect, Pegagogy, Performativity.* Durham, NC: Duke University Press, 2003.

Sontag, Susan. *Regarding the Pain of Others.* New York: Picador, 2004.

Virno, Paolo. *A Grammar of the Multitude: For an Analysis of Contemporary Forms of Life.* Trans. Isabella Bertoletti, James Cascaito, and Andrea Casson. New York: Semiotext(e), 2004.

Wittgenstein, Ludwig. *Culture and Value.* Ed. G. H. von Wright. Trans. Peter Winch. Chicago, IL: University of Chicago Press, 1980.

QUESTIONS FOR MAKING CONNECTIONS
WITHIN THE READING

1. When you read Nelson, you might feel like a stranger who has entered a room full of unfamiliar people, all of whom have known one another for years and are eager to discuss subjects you know little about. But the truth is that few of Nelson's readers will understand all her references. Why, then, does she add so many? Assuming Nelson's game is something other than parading her erudition, what purpose might her many references serve? What is Nelson trying to do by drawing together so many different ideas from so many different thinkers? Is she trying to dramatize how it feels to live in the information age? Or would you say that she is simply thinking—learning new things and then following connections to see wherever they might lead?

2. *Dead Man Walking,* Abu Ghraib, the Milgram experiment, black sites, Blackwater, RETORT, Zen, 4'33''—these are just some of Nelson's references, along with a long list of people that includes Eve Kosofsky Sedgwick, Stephen King, Susan Sontag, Ludwig Wittgenstein, Hannah Arendt, Seymour Hersh, and Wayne Koestenbaum. Pick one name from the essay and do some online research which you can later report to the class, explaining how the person and his or her work connect to Nelson's larger argument. After everyone in the class has made a presentation, collectively try to identify the common interests and agendas that might tie these different people together. If the names weren't chosen at random—and they weren't—how do they intersect?

3. Nelson quotes Susan Sontag who famously described her time as an "age of extremity." According to Sontag, living in such an age provides only "two equally fearful, but seemingly opposed, destinies: unremitting banality and inconceivable terror." What might Sontag have meant when she made this declaration—in particular, what "extremities" could she have had in mind? In what ways does the term *banality* describe the media environment today? Think, for example, about the latest coverage of figures like Lady Gaga or Beyoncé. In what ways does "terror" also play a role, and what is the relation between terror and banality? Does Nelson agree with Sontag's claim that only two "destinies" are now available to us? Could slowing down and staying still offer an alternative to both banality and terror? How?

QUESTIONS FOR WRITING

1. Nelson begins her essay by arguing that Sister Helen Prejean was naive to think "that it is simple, blameless ignorance that prompts so many Americans to support executions (or the torture of detainees in the so called war on terror, and so on)." If our entanglement with violence were just a matter of "simple, blameless ignorance," then new knowledge should indeed be an adequate solution. But Nelson seems to doubt that knowledge by itself has the power to set us free. For her, *how* we know may be even more

important than *what* we know. What is the relation between violence and "watching"—between violence and the habit of spectatorship created by the constant presence of the media? Are we so busy watching violence that we neglect to act in ways that might bring it to an end? Do we need to change the things we watch? Do we need to watch more critically?

2. At one moment in her essay Nelson asks us to compare the work of two artists: the Austrian avant-garde filmmaker Hermann Nitsch, whose multimedia creations routinely include scenes of mutilated humans and animals, and John Cage's Zen-inspired *4′33″*. Examples of the work of both artists are available online. On YouTube, for example, you can listen to Cage's *Dream* or *In a Landscape*, and you can hear some of Nitsch's work—but you should do an image search as well. Prepare to be surprised and possibly revulsed. Using Cage and Nitsch as a starting point, discuss the dangers and the possibilities offered by the arts in our time. In what ways are Cage and Nitsch in opposition? What objectives and methods do they share despite their differences? Can art point the way beyond our current dilemmas, or does it simply mirror our confusions?

QUESTIONS FOR MAKING CONNECTIONS
BETWEEN READINGS

1. Like Cathy Davidson, Nelson asks us to explore how our attention is influenced by contemporary culture, including the new media. Of the two writers, which of them seems to be more receptive to the possibilities of technology? How does Nelson's thinking complicate Davidson's optimism about the uses of attention in our times? What role does distraction play in the ideas of each writer? In what ways might Nelson's essay be said to inject an ethical dimension into the debate over the influence of new media? That is, in what ways does she urge us to consider the "dark side" as well as the positives? Would Nelson agree with Davidson's critics, who allege that she is naively optimistic?

2. Nelson's subject is a violence that often goes unnoticed because it has become so ubiquitous. Few Americans, apparently, think it strange that people should enjoy watching real or simulated torture on their TVs and computer screens. We often say we want a less violent society, but we find violence fascinating, stimulating, liberating, beautiful—or so Nelson's evidence would suggest. In what ways does the violence at the Citadel compare to the violence Nelson describes? Do they meet different needs or provide different forms of satisfaction? When the violence at the Citadel is so open, oppressive, and brutal, why don't the cadets revolt? What clues to their behavior does Nelson's essay provide? Does violence become most powerful when we have failed to find other ways of "being in the world"? Do Nelson and Faludi provide any sense of what those other "ways of being" might involve?

TIM O'BRIEN

In 1968, DURING the war in Vietnam, Tim O'Brien graduated from college and was served a draft notice. An avowed opponent of the war, he considered fleeing to Canada but ultimately reported for basic training and was stationed near the hamlet of My Lai shortly after the shocking massacre there, when American soldiers slaughtered three- to five-hundred unarmed civilians, including women and children. Investigators later produced evidence of torture, gang rape, and the dismemberment of the bodies of villagers. O'Brien returned to the United States in 1970, having received injuries that earned him a Purple Heart. Since then he has published dozens of stories and books, both fiction and nonfiction, exploring the themes of war and violence, including the National Book Award-winning *Going After Cacciato* (1978). He has received many other prestigious awards as well, among them the O. Henry Award, the National Book Critics Circle Award, and the Pulitzer Prize. He holds an endowed chair at Texas State University in San Marcos, where he teaches in the creative writing program.

"How to Tell a True War Story," from O'Brien's collection *The Things They Carried* (1998), is, paradoxically, a work of fiction. In the shadow of events like My Lai, the choice of fiction might appear to offer readers a comforting distance from a troubled history. But O'Brien's decision to present his narrative in the form of fiction is actually a sign of his continued engagement with a puzzle that has shaped his work for almost three decades. For O'Brien, fiction is sometimes the most faithful way of getting at the truth, especially in accounts of war, where the experience outstrips the resources of language. In O'Brien's work, the cost of war is not measured only in the loss of life, but also in the loss of moral certainty. As he told one interviewer, "What we see accurately with our eyes can sometimes be very deceptive. We don't see everything. No historian can fit into a textbook the thoughts of every single soldier in every single war and every single episode. Much is being selected and generalized. So in *The Things They Carried*, I'm trying to get at this sense of how difficult it is to pin down the truth with a capital 'T.' In a way, it's a warning against absolutism, against black and white declarations of what's true and what's not true. So part of the effort is trying to display through fiction the ambiguous, blurry, complicated, grayish fog of even the most plainly historical events."

Biographical information comes from <http://illyria.com/tob/tobbio.html>; quotation comes from "An Interview with Tim O'Brien," *The Big Read*, <http://www.neabigread.org/books/thethingstheycarried/readers-guide/about-the-author/>.

How to Tell a True War Story

This is true.

I had a buddy in Vietnam. His name was Bob Kiley, but everybody called him Rat.

A friend of his gets killed, so about a week later Rat sits down and writes a letter to the guy's sister. Rat tells her what a great brother she had, how together the guy was, a number one pal and comrade. A real soldier's soldier, Rat says. Then he tells a few stories to make the point, how her brother would always volunteer for stuff nobody else would volunteer for in a million years, dangerous stuff, like doing recon or going out on these really badass night patrols. Stainless steel balls, Rat tells her. The guy was a little crazy, for sure, but crazy in a good way, a real daredevil, because he liked the challenge of it, he liked testing himself, just man against gook. A great, great guy, Rat says.

Anyway, it's a terrific letter, very personal and touching. Rat almost bawls writing it. He gets all teary telling about the good times they had together, how her brother made the war seem almost fun, always raising hell and lighting up villes and bringing smoke to bear every which way. A great sense of humor, too. Like the time at this river when he went fishing with a whole damn crate of hand grenades. Probably the funniest thing in world history, Rat says, all that gore, about twenty zillion dead gook fish. Her brother, he had the right attitude. He knew how to have a good time. On Halloween, this real hot spooky night, the dude paints up his body all different colors and puts on this weird mask and hikes over to a ville and goes trick-or-treating almost stark naked, just boots and balls and an M-16. A tremendous human being, Rat says. Pretty nutso sometimes, but you could trust him with your life.

And then the letter gets very sad and serious. Rat pours his heart out. He says he loved the guy. He says the guy was his best friend in the world. They were like soul mates, he says, like twins or something, they had a whole lot in common. He tells the guy's sister he'll look her up when the war's over.

So what happens?

Rat mails the letter. He waits two months. The dumb cooze never writes back.

A true war story is never moral. It does not instruct, nor encourage virtue, nor suggest models of proper human behavior, nor restrain men from doing the things men have always done. If a story seems moral, do not believe it. If at the end of a war story you feel uplifted, or if you feel that some small bit of rectitude has been salvaged from the larger waste, then you have been made the victim of a very old and terrible lie. There is no rectitude whatsoever. There is no virtue. As a first rule of thumb, therefore, you can tell a true war story by its absolute and uncompromising allegiance to obscenity and evil. Listen to Rat Kiley.

Cooze, he says. He does not say bitch. He certainly does not say woman, or girl. He says cooze. Then he spits and stares. He's nineteen years old—it's too much for him—so he looks at you with those big sad gentle killer eyes and says cooze, because his friend is dead, and because it's so incredibly sad and true: she never wrote back.

You can tell a true war story if it embarrasses you. If you don't care for obscenity, you don't care for the truth; if you don't care for the truth, watch how you vote. Send guys to war, they come home talking dirty.

Listen to Rat: "Jesus Christ, man, I write this beautiful fuckin' letter, I slave over it, and what happens? The dumb cooze never writes back."

The dead guy's name was Curt Lemon. What happened was, we crossed a muddy river and marched west into the mountains, and on the third day we took a break along a trail junction in deep jungle. Right away, Lemon and Rat Kiley started goofing. They didn't understand about the spookiness. They were kids; they just didn't know. A nature hike, they thought, not even a war, so they went off into the shade of some giant trees—quadruple canopy, no sunlight at all—and they were giggling and calling each other yellow mother and playing a silly game they'd invented. The game involved smoke grenades, which were harmless unless you did stupid things, and what they did was pull out the pin and stand a few feet apart and play catch under the shade of those huge trees. Whoever chickened out was a yellow mother. And if nobody chickened out, the grenade would make a light popping sound and they'd be covered with smoke and they'd laugh and dance around and then do it again.

It's all exactly true.

It happened, to *me,* nearly twenty years ago, and I still remember that trail junction and those giant trees and a soft dripping sound somewhere beyond the trees. I remember the smell of moss. Up in the canopy there were tiny white blossoms, but no sunlight at all, and I remember the shadows spreading out under the trees where Curt Lemon and Rat Kiley were playing catch with smoke grenades. Mitchell Sanders sat flipping his yo-yo. Norman Bowker and Kiowa and Dave Jensen were dozing, or half dozing, and all around us were those ragged green mountains.

Except for the laughter things were quiet.

At one point, I remember, Mitchell Sanders turned and looked at me, not quite nodding, as if to warn me about something, as if he already *knew,* then after a while he rolled up his yo-yo and moved away.

It's hard to tell you what happened next.

They were just goofing. There was a noise, I suppose, which must've been the detonator, so I glanced behind me and watched Lemon step from the shade into bright sunlight. His face was suddenly brown and shining. A handsome kid, really. Sharp gray eyes, lean and narrow-waisted, and when he died it was almost beautiful, the way the sunlight came around him and lifted him up and sucked him high into a tree full of moss and vines and white blossoms.

In any war story, but especially a true one, it's difficult to separate what happened from what seemed to happen. What seems to happen becomes its own happening and has to be told that way. The angles of vision are skewed. When a booby trap explodes, you close your eyes and duck and float outside yourself. When a guy dies, like Curt Lemon, you look away and then look back for a moment and then look away again. The pictures get jumbled; you tend to miss a lot. And then afterward, when you go to tell about it, there is always that surreal seemingness, which makes the story seem untrue, but which in fact represents the hard and exact truth as it *seemed*.

In many cases a true war story cannot be believed. If you believe it, be skeptical. It's a question of credibility. Often the crazy stuff is true and the normal stuff isn't, because the normal stuff is necessary to make you believe the truly incredible craziness.

In other cases you can't even tell a true war story. Sometimes it's just beyond telling.

I heard this one, for example, from Mitchell Sanders. It was near dusk and we were sitting at my foxhole along a wide muddy river north of Quang Ngai. I remember how peaceful the twilight was. A deep pinkish red spilled out on the river, which moved without sound, and in the morning we would cross the river and march west into the mountains. The occasion was right for a good story.

"God's truth," Mitchell Sanders said. "A six-man patrol goes up into the mountains on a basic listening-post operation. The idea's to spend a week up there, just lie low and listen for enemy movement. They've got a radio along, so if they hear anything suspicious—anything—they're supposed to call in artillery or gunships, whatever it takes. Otherwise they keep strict field discipline. Absolute silence. They just listen."

Sanders glanced at me to make sure I had the scenario. He was playing with his yo-yo, dancing it with short, tight little strokes of the wrist.

His face was blank in the dusk.

"We're talking regulation, by-the-book LP. These six guys, they don't say boo for a solid week. They don't got tongues. *All* ears."

"Right," I said.

"Understand me?"

"Invisible."

Sanders nodded.

"Affirm," he said. "Invisible. So what happens is, these guys get themselves deep in the bush, all camouflaged up, and they lie down and wait and that's all they do, nothing else, they lie there for seven straight days and just listen. And man, I'll tell you—it's spooky. This is mountains. You don't *know* spooky till you been there. Jungle, sort of, except it's way up in the clouds and there's always this fog—like rain, except it's not raining—everything's all wet and swirly and tangled up and you can't see jack, you can't find your own pecker to piss with. Like you don't even have a body. Serious spooky. You just go with the vapors—the fog sort of takes you in.... And the sounds, man. The sounds carry forever. You hear stuff nobody should *ever* hear."

Sanders was quiet for a second, just working the yo-yo, then he smiled at me.

"So after a couple days the guys start hearing this real soft, kind of wacked-out music. Weird echoes and stuff. Like a radio or something, but it's not a radio, it's this strange gook music that comes right out of the rocks. Faraway, sort of, but right up close, too. They try to ignore it. But it's a listening post, right? So they listen. And every night they keep hearing that crazyass gook concert. All kinds of chimes and xylophones. I mean, this is wilderness—no way, it can't be real—but there it *is*, like the mountains are tuned in to Radio fucking Hanoi. Naturally they get nervous. One guy sticks Juicy Fruit in his ears. Another guy almost flips. Thing is, though, they can't report music. They can't get on the horn and call back to base and say, 'Hey, listen, we need some firepower, we got to blow away this weirdo gook rock band.' They can't do that. It wouldn't go down. So they lie there in the fog and keep their mouths shut. And what makes it extra bad, see, is the poor dudes can't horse around like normal. Can't joke it away. Can't even talk to each other except maybe in whispers, all hush-hush, and that just revs up the willies. All they do is listen."

Again there was some silence as Mitchell Sanders looked out on the river. The dark was coming on hard now, and off to the west I could see the mountains rising in silhouette, all the mysteries and unknowns.

"This next part," Sanders said quietly, "you won't believe."

"Probably not," I said.

"You won't. And you know why?" He gave me a long, tired smile. "Because it happened. Because every word is absolutely dead-on true."

Sanders made a sound in his throat, like a sigh, as if to say he didn't care if I believed him or not. But he did care. He wanted me to feel the truth, to believe by the raw force of feeling. He seemed sad, in a way.

"These six guys," he said, "they're pretty fried out by now, and one night they start hearing voices. Like at a cocktail party. That's what it sounds like, this big swank gook cocktail party somewhere out there in the fog. Music and chitchat and stuff. It's crazy, I know, but they hear the champagne corks. They hear the actual martini glasses. Real hoity-toity, all very civilized, except this isn't civilization. This is Nam.

"Anyway, the guys try to be cool. They just lie there and groove, but after a while they start hearing—you won't believe this—they hear chamber music. They hear violins and cellos. They hear this terrific mama-san soprano. Then after a while they hear gook opera and a glee club and the Haiphong Boys Choir and a barbershop quartet and all kinds of weird chanting and Buddha-Buddha stuff. And the whole time, in the background, there's still that cocktail party going on. All these different voices. Not human voices, though. Because it's the mountains. Follow me? The rock—it's *talking*. And the fog, too, and the grass and the goddamn mongooses. Everything talks. The trees talk politics, the monkeys talk religion. The whole country: Vietnam. The place talks. It talks. Understand? Nam—it truly *talks*.

"The guys can't cope. They lose it. They get on the radio and report enemy movement—a whole army, they say—and they order up the firepower. They get arty and gunships. They call in air strikes. And I'll tell you, they fuckin' crash that cocktail party. All night long, they just smoke those mountains. They make jungle juice. They blow away trees and glee clubs and whatever else there is to blow away. Scorch time. They walk napalm up and down the ridges.

They bring in the Cobras and F-4s, they use Willie Peter and HE and incendiaries. It's all fire. They make those mountains burn.

"Around dawn things finally get quiet. Like you never even *heard* quiet before. One of those real thick, real misty days—just clouds and fog, they're off in this special zone—and the mountains are absolutely dead-flat silent. Like *Brigadoon*—pure vapor, you know? Everything's all sucked up inside the fog. Not a single sound, except they still *hear* it.

"So they pack up and start humping. They head down the mountain, back to base camp, and when they get there they don't say diddly. They don't talk. Not a word, like they're deaf and dumb. Later on this fat bird colonel comes up and asks what the hell happened out there. What'd they hear? Why all the ordnance? The man's ragged out, he gets down tight on their case. I mean, they spent six trillion dollars on firepower, and this fatass colonel wants answers, he wants to know what the fuckin' story is.

"But the guys don't say zip. They just look at him for a while, sort of funny like, sort of amazed, and the whole war is right there in that stare. It says everything you can't ever say. It says, man, you got *wax* in your ears. It says, poor bastard, you'll never know—wrong frequency—you don't *even* want to hear this. Then they salute the fucker and walk away, because certain stories you don't ever tell."

You can tell a true war story by the way it never seems to end. Not then, not ever. Not when Mitchell Sanders stood up and moved off into the dark.

It all happened.

Even now, at this instant, I remember that yo-yo. In a way, I suppose, you had to be there, you had to hear it, but I could tell how desperately Sanders wanted me to believe him, his frustration at not quite getting the details right, not quite pinning down the final and definitive truth.

And I remember sitting at my foxhole that night, watching the shadows of Quang Ngai, thinking about the coming day and how we would cross the river and march west into the mountains, all the ways I might die, all the things I did not understand.

Late in the night Mitchell Sanders touched my shoulder. "Just came to me," he whispered. "The moral, I mean. Nobody listens. Nobody hears nothin'. Like that fatass colonel. The politicians, all the civilian types. Your girlfriend. My girlfriend. Everybody's sweet little virgin girlfriend. What they need is to go out on LP. The vapors, man. Trees and rocks—you got to *listen* to your enemy."

And then again, in the morning, Sanders came up to me. The platoon was preparing to move out, checking weapons, going through all the little rituals that preceded a day's march. Already the lead squad had crossed the river and was filing off toward the west.

"I got a confession to make," Sanders said. "Last night, man, I had to make up a few things."

"I know that."

"The glee club. There wasn't any glee club."

"Right."

"No opera."

"Forget it, I understand."

"Yeah, but listen, it's still true. Those six guys, they heard wicked sound out there. They heard sound you just plain won't believe."

Sanders pulled on his rucksack, closed his eyes for a moment, then almost smiled at me. I knew what was coming.

"All right," I said, "what's the moral?"

"Forget it."

"No, go ahead."

For a long while he was quiet, looking away, and the silence kept stretching out until it was almost embarrassing. Then he shrugged and gave me a stare that lasted all day.

"Hear that quiet, man?" he said. "That quiet—just listen. There's your moral."

In a true war story, if there's a moral at all, it's like the thread that makes the cloth. You can't tease it out. You can't extract the meaning without unraveling the deeper meaning. And in the end, really, there's nothing much to say about a true war story, except maybe "Oh."

True war stories do not generalize. They do not indulge in abstraction or analysis.

For example: War is hell. As a moral declaration the old truism seems perfectly true, and yet because it abstracts, because it generalizes, I can't believe it with my stomach. Nothing turns inside.

It comes down to gut instinct. A true war story, if truly told, makes the stomach believe.

This one does it for me. I've told it before—many times, many versions—but here's what actually happened.

We crossed that river and marched west into the mountains. On the third day, Curt Lemon stepped on a booby-trapped 105 round. He was playing catch with Rat Kiley, laughing, and then he was dead. The trees were thick; it took nearly an hour to cut an LZ for the dustoff.

Later, higher in the mountains, we came across a baby VC water buffalo. What it was doing there I don't know—no farms or paddies—but we chased it down and got a rope around it and led it along to a deserted village where we set up for the night. After supper Rat Kiley went over and stroked its nose.

He opened up a can of C rations, pork and beans, but the baby buffalo wasn't interested.

Rat shrugged.

He stepped back and shot it through the right front knee. The animal did not make a sound. It went down hard, then got up again, and Rat took careful aim and shot off an ear. He shot it in the hindquarters and in the little hump at its back. He shot it twice in the flanks. It wasn't to kill; it was to hurt. He put the rifle muzzle up against the mouth and shot the mouth away. Nobody said much. The whole platoon stood there watching, feeling all kinds of things, but there wasn't a great deal of pity for the baby water buffalo. Curt Lemon was dead. Rat Kiley had lost his best friend in the world. Later in the week he would write a long personal letter to the guy's sister, who would not write back, but for now it was a question of pain. He shot off the tail. He shot away chunks of meat below the ribs. All around us there was the smell of smoke and filth and deep greenery, and the evening was humid and very hot. Rat went to automatic. He shot randomly, almost casually, quick little spurts in the belly and butt. Then he reloaded, squatted down, and shot it in the left front knee. Again the animal fell hard and tried to get up, but this time it couldn't quite make it. It wobbled and went down sideways. Rat shot it in the nose. He bent forward and whispered something, as if talking to a pet, then he shot it in the throat. All the while the baby buffalo was silent, or almost silent, just a light bubbling sound where the nose had been. It lay very still. Nothing moved except the eyes, which were enormous, the pupils shiny black and dumb.

Rat Kiley was crying. He tried to say something, but then cradled his rifle and went off by himself.

The rest of us stood in a ragged circle around the baby buffalo. For a time no one spoke. We had witnessed something essential, something brand-new and profound, a piece of the world so startling there was not yet a name for it.

Somebody kicked the baby buffalo.

It was still alive, though just barely, just in the eyes.

"Amazing," Dave Jensen said. "My whole life, I never seen anything like it."

"Never?"

"Not hardly. Not once."

Kiowa and Mitchell Sanders picked up the baby buffalo. They hauled it across the open square, hoisted it up, and dumped it in the village well.

Afterward, we sat waiting for Rat to get himself together.

"Amazing," Dave Jensen kept saying. "A new wrinkle. I never seen it before."

Mitchell Sanders took out his yo-yo. "Well, that's Nam," he said. "Garden of Evil. Over here, man, every sin's real fresh and original."

How do you generalize?

War is hell, but that's not the half of it, because war is also mystery and terror and adventure and courage and discovery and holiness and pity and despair and longing and love. War is nasty; war is fun. War is thrilling; war is drudgery. War makes you a man; war makes you dead.

The truths are contradictory. It can be argued, for instance, that war is grotesque. But in truth war is also beauty. For all its horror, you can't help but gape at the awful majesty of combat. You stare out at tracer rounds unwinding through the dark like brilliant red ribbons. You crouch in ambush as a cool, impassive moon rises over the nighttime paddies. You admire the fluid symmetries of troops on the move, the harmonies of sound and shape and proportion, the great sheets of metal-fire streaming down from a gunship, the illumination rounds, the white phosphorus, the purply orange glow of napalm, the rocket's red glare. It's not pretty, exactly. It's astonishing. It fills the eye. It commands you. You hate it, yes, but your eyes do not. Like a killer forest fire, like cancer under a microscope, any battle or bombing raid or artillery barrage has the aesthetic purity of absolute moral indifference—a powerful, implacable beauty—and a true war story will tell the truth about this, though the truth is ugly.

To generalize about war is like generalizing about peace. Almost every-thing is true. Almost nothing is true. At its core, perhaps, war is just another name for death, and yet any soldier will tell you, if he tells the truth, that prox-imity to death brings with it a corresponding proximity to life. After a firefight, there is always the immense pleasure of aliveness. The trees are alive. The grass, the soil—everything. All around you things are purely living, and you among them, and the aliveness makes you tremble. You feel an intense, out-of-the-skin awareness of your living self—your truest self, the human being you want to be and then become by the force of wanting it. In the midst of evil you want to be a good man. You want decency. You want justice and courtesy and human concord, things you never knew you wanted. There is a kind of largeness to it, a kind of godliness. Though it's odd, you're never more alive than when you're almost dead. You recognize what's valuable. Freshly, as if for the first time, you love what's best in yourself and in the world, all that might be lost. At the hour of dusk you sit at your foxhole and look out on a wide river turning pinkish red, and at the mountains beyond, and although in the morning you must cross the river and go into the mountains and do terrible things and maybe die, even so, you find yourself studying the fine colors on the river, you feel wonder and awe at the setting of the sun, and you are filled with a hard, aching love for how the world could be and always should be, but now is not.

Mitchell Sanders was right. For the common soldier, at least, war has the feel—the spiritual texture—of a great ghostly fog, thick and permanent. There is no clarity. Everything swirls. The old rules are no longer binding, the old truths no longer true. Right spills over into wrong. Order blends into chaos, love into hate, ugliness into beauty, law into anarchy, civility into savagery. The vapors suck you in. You can't tell where you are, or why you're there, and the only certainty is overwhelming ambiguity.

In war you lose your sense of the definite, hence your sense of truth itself, and therefore it's safe to say that in a true war story nothing is ever absolutely true.

Often in a true war story there is not even a point, or else the point doesn't hit you until twenty years later, in your sleep, and you wake up and shake your wife and start telling the story to her, except when you get to the end you've forgotten the point again. And then for a long time you lie there watching the story happen in your head. You listen to your wife's breathing. The war's over. You close your eyes. You smile and think, Christ, what's the *point*?

This one wakes me up.

In the mountains that day, I watched Lemon turn sideways. He laughed and said *something* to Rat Kiley. Then he took a peculiar half step, moving from shade into bright sunlight, and the booby-trapped 105 round blew him into a tree. The parts were just hanging there, so Dave Jensen and I were ordered to shinny up and peel him off. I remember the white bone of an arm. I remember pieces of skin and something wet and yellow that must've been the intestines. The gore was horrible, and stays with me. But what wakes me up twenty years later is Dave Jensen singing "Lemon Tree" as we threw down the parts.

You can tell a true war story by the questions you ask. Somebody tells a story, let's say, and afterward you ask, "Is it true?" and if the answer matters, you've got your answer.

For example, we've all heard this one. Four guys go down a trail. A grenade sails out. One guy jumps on it and takes the blast and saves his three buddies.

Is it true?

The answer matters.

You'd feel cheated if it never happened. Without the grounding reality, it's just a trite bit of puffery, pure Hollywood, untrue in the way all such stories are untrue. Yet even if it did happen—and maybe it did, anything's possible—even then you know it can't be true, because a true war story does not depend upon that kind of truth. Absolute occurrence is irrelevant. A thing may happen and be a total lie; another thing may not happen and be truer than the truth. For example: Four guys go down a trail. A grenade sails out. One guy jumps on it and takes the blast, but it's a killer grenade and everybody dies anyway. Before they die, though, one of the dead guys says, "The fuck you do *that* for?" and the jumper says, "Story of my life, man," and the other guy starts to smile but he's dead.

That's a true story that never happened.

Twenty years later, I can still see the sunlight on Lemon's face. I can see him turning, looking back at Rat Kiley, then he laughed and took that curious half step from shade into sunlight, his face suddenly brown and shining, and when his foot touched down, in that instant, he must've thought it was the sunlight that was killing him. It was not the sunlight. It was a rigged 105 round. But if I could ever get the story right, how the sun seemed to gather around him and pick him up and lift him high into a tree, if I could somehow re-create the fatal whiteness of that light, the quick glare, the obvious cause and effect, then you would believe the last thing Curt Lemon believed, which for him must've been the final truth.

Now and then, when I tell this story, someone will come up to me afterward and say she liked it. It's always a woman. Usually it's an older woman of kindly temperament and humane politics. She'll explain that as a rule she hates war stories; she can't understand why people want to wallow in all the blood and gore. But this one she liked. The poor baby buffalo, it made her sad. Sometimes, even, there are little tears. What I should do, she'll say, is put it all behind me. Find new stories to tell.

I won't say it but I'll think it.

I'll picture Rat Kiley's face, his grief, and I'll think, *You dumb cooze*.

Because she wasn't listening.

It *wasn't* a war story. It was a *love* story.

But you can't say that. All you can do is tell it one more time, patiently, adding and subtracting, making up a few things to get at the real truth. No Mitchell Sanders, you tell her. No Lemon, no Rat Kiley. No trail junction. No baby buffalo. No vines or moss or white blossoms. Beginning to end, you tell her, it's all made up. Every goddamn detail—the mountains and the river and especially that poor dumb baby buffalo. None of it happened. *None* of it.

And even if it did happen, it didn't happen in the mountains, it happened in this little village on the Batangan Peninsula, and it was raining like crazy, and one night a guy named Stink Harris woke up screaming with a leech on his tongue. You can tell a true war story if you just keep on telling it.

And in the end, of course, a true war story is never about war. It's about sunlight. It's about the special way that dawn spreads out on a river when you know you must cross the river and march into the mountains and do things you are afraid to do. It's about love and memory. It's about sorrow. It's about sisters who never write back and people who never listen.

QUESTIONS FOR MAKING CONNECTIONS
WITHIN THE READING

1. Tim O'Brien's "How to Tell a True War Story" is part of a collection of stories by the author entitled *The Things They Carried*. Although the ostensible subject of this particular short story is a series of events that may have actually happened, the subtitle of the entire collection is "A Work of Fiction." "How to Tell a True War Story" begins with the explicit statement "This is true," but what sort of truth does it manage to convey? As you consider possible answers, please remember that the narrator warns us, "In many cases a true war story cannot be believed. If you believe it, be skeptical." Why is the issue of truth so important to a story about what happens in war? Does O'Brien really mean that there is no such thing as truth when we are talking about war? If everything about war is subjective, is it ever possible for one person to judge another person's military conduct?

2. Why does Rat Kiley write a letter to Curt Lemon's sister? What do you make of the details of his letter? Conventionally, such a letter would praise a fallen fellow combatant as a "hero," someone of exemplary character who had chosen to make the "ultimate sacrifice." Instead, Rat writes about the times he and Curt were "raising hell and lighting up villes and bringing smoke to bear every which way." Is Rat trying to insult the sister? Seduce her? Destroy her positive memories of her brother? When she fails to write back to him, why does Rat refer to her as a "dumb cooze"? For that matter, why does he refer to the Vietnamese as "gooks"? Is this simply an example of crude prejudice? If Rat began to think of the Vietnamese as people, much like his own family back home, how would such a change influence his behavior? If he thought of Lemon's sister as nothing more than a "cooze," why did he bother to write to her at all?

3. Why does Rat Kiley kill the baby water buffalo? And why is it that "the whole platoon stood there watching, feeling all kinds of things, but [not] a great deal of pity for the baby water buffalo"? How do you explain the reaction of Mitchell Sanders: "Well, that's Nam. Garden of Evil. Over here ... every sin's fresh and original"? If the men view Rat's killing of the buffalo as a "sin," why do they make no effort to stop him? Why do they appear to

feel no remorse afterward? Do they displace onto the buffalo their desire to get back at the Vietnamese, or is their behavior even more complicated? When they kill the buffalo, are they killing something in themselves? What part of themselves might they be killing, and why might they want to do so?

QUESTIONS FOR WRITING

1. Readers might perceive O'Brien's story to be a powerfully realistic evocation of war as people actually live it. On the other hand, in spite of its realistic qualities, the story sometimes becomes highly poetic, as in passages like this one:

    > Twenty years later, I can still see the sunlight on Lemon's face. I can see him turning, looking back at Rat Kiley, then he laughed and took the curious half step from shade into sunlight, his face suddenly brown and shining, and when his foot touched down, in that instant, he must've thought it was the sunlight that was killing him.

    Is O'Brien guilty of aestheticizing war—that is, of making it seem more beautiful, romantic, or exotic than it really is? Do you think that your reading of his account has made you less likely or more likely to regard war as necessary and noble? Has O'Brien's account made it less likely or more likely that you will think of war as a natural and even indispensable part of life as a human being?

2. What is the connection in O'Brien's short story between experience and language? Does he believe that our language predetermines the nature of our experience, or does he suggest, instead, that our experience is often more complex than our language can accommodate? Toward the end of the story, the narrator describes the kind of exchange he has, after reading his short stories in public, often with "an older woman of kindly temperament and humane politics." What sense can you make of the narrator's remarks about this exchange? Is it ever possible to describe our experience to others? Would listeners who had served in Vietnam be more likely to understand the narrator's account than those who had never been there? How about someone who had served in a different war? How much experience must people share in order to understand one another?

QUESTIONS FOR MAKING CONNECTIONS
BETWEEN READINGS

1. Would O'Brien's narrator be comfortable at The Citadel as described by Susan Faludi? Does the form of camaraderie we find at The Citadel correspond to the love felt by the men who served with the narrator

of O'Brien's story? Can we understand the rituals performed at The Citadel as forging bonds similar to those forged by war, or do you see significant differences? In what ways does O'Brien's story suggest that the culture of The Citadel is likely to prove more enduring than Faludi suggests? Is the culture of The Citadel really the culture of war itself? If you think so, then why have some distinguished military leaders tried to reform that institution?

2. Maggie Nelson, the author of "Great to Watch," probes our obsession with violence. After she has taken a critical look at popular books like Stephen King's *Running Man*, the reality television show *To Catch a Predator*, and Errol Morris's documentary *Standard Operating Procedure*, Nelson reflects on the possibility of some other way of life. Does O'Brien's "How to Tell a True War Story" belong in the company of *Running Man?* Does it actually embrace the violence it appears to reject? Or does it rise to the status of "art" as defined by Richard Foreman, the dramatist Nelson quotes:

> [Kitsch] means ... that the image seduced me, that it pushed a button that was ready to be pushed, and I responded. It didn't widen my sensibilities, compassion, or intuition. Whereas an art that affects you in the moment ... is straining to bring you to another level.... [It] has opened you to the possibility of growing into what you are not yet.

Does O'Brien push our buttons or does he strain to bring us to another level? Is his story "kitsch" or does it qualify as art when measured by Foreman's standard?

RICHARD O. PRUM

When most people hear the name Charles Darwin, one term in particular comes to mind: "natural selection." Darwin introduced the term in his revolutionary book, *On the Origin of Species*, first published in 1859. He used "natural selection" to describe the way environmental forces shape species over time. Just as a farmer might breed horses to produce lighter, faster foals, so, for almost five billion years, nature has "bred" plants and animals, selecting for the traits most conducive to their survival under changing conditions. One point often misunderstood about natural selection is that nobody controls it: it has no purpose or design other than reproductive success. Starting with a single organism, life on earth has achieved its diversity simply because the varied natural environments selected for different traits at different times. Or so Darwin thought at first.

Darwin's careful observations of life in places as far away from Britain as the Galapagos Islands convinced him that natural selection was real, but gradually he began to doubt that this single mechanism could account for all biological change. How can we explain, for example, traits that appear to contribute nothing to a species' adaptation to the environment—such as the colorful plumage of birds? This question led Darwin later to conclude that sexual selection—the choice of a mate—operated as a second evolutionary force, equal in importance to natural selection but also quite distinct. Darwin presented this argument in a subsequent book, *The Descent of Man, and Selection in Relation to Sex*.

Looking back on Darwin now, after more than a century, we can see a puzzling response to this idea. While scientists have eagerly embraced the idea of natural selection, an embarrassed or contemptuous silence surrounds the role played by sexual selection. How can we explain this inconsistency?

One answer comes to us from Richard O. Prum, a Yale-based ornithologist, museum curator, and 2009 MacArthur Fellowship "genius grant" awardee in his book *The Evolution of Beauty: How Darwin's Forgotten Theory of Mate Choice Shapes the Animal World* (2017). There Prum makes a powerful argument for the importance of sexual selection, and he faults many of his fellow scientists for what he views as their narrowmindedness.

But he also takes his criticism an additional step, alleging that scientists and philosophers have neglected sexual selection because of its dangerous *social* implications. For one thing, it threatens the longstanding view that conflict and struggle—typically male concerns—are more important biologically than love and cooperation, often viewed as women's preoccupations. What's more, by ignoring the importance of mating and mate choice, many scientists have been able to dismiss most of human culture as "soft" or irrelevant: beauty, pleasure, creativity, and the arts in general. According to Prum, Darwin's most brilliant insight was to trace all of these back to the strategies employed in attracting a mate. Prum argues that the strategies associated with sexual selection have played an essential role in our evolution as a species—and not only the evolution of our species but of all life on earth.

This rethinking of evolutionary theory has other implications as well. Over time, the aesthetic as a fundamental element in reproduction privileges female choice in determining which biological and social traits will prosper or falter. But perhaps the most sweeping consequence of Prum's revival of "Darwin's really dangerous idea" is the importance of agency. Evolution, it appears, is shaped as much by the choices we make as by forces over which we have no control.

Darwin's *Really* Dangerous Idea

Adaptation by natural selection is among the most successful and influential ideas in the history of science, and rightly so. It unifies the entire field of biology and has had a profound influence on many other disciplines, including anthropology, psychology, economics, sociology, and even the humanities. The singular genius behind the theory of natural selection, Charles Darwin, is at least as famous as his most famous idea.

You might think that my contrarian view of the limited power of adaptation by natural selection would mean that I am "over" Darwin, that I am ready to denigrate the cultural/scientific personality cult that surrounds Darwin's legacy. Quite to the contrary. I hope to celebrate that legacy but also to transform the popular understanding of it by shedding new light on Darwinian ideas that have been neglected, distorted, ignored, and almost forgotten for nearly a century and a half. It's not that I'm interested in doing a Talmudic-style investigation of Darwin's every word; rather, my focus is on the science of today, and I believe that Darwin's ideas have a value to contemporary science that has yet to be fully exploited.

Trying to communicate the richness of Darwin's ideas puts scientists in the unenviable position of having to convince people that we don't actually know the real Darwin and that he was an even greater, more creative, and more insightful thinker than he has been given credit for. I am convinced that most of those who think of themselves as Darwinians today—the neo-Darwinists—have gotten Darwin all wrong. The real Darwin has been excised from modern scientific hagiography.

The philosopher Daniel Dennett referred to evolution by natural selection— the subject of Darwin's first great book, *On the Origin of Species by Means of Natural Selection*—as "Darwin's dangerous idea." Here I propose that Darwin's *really* dangerous idea is the concept of aesthetic evolution by mate choice, which he explored in his second great book, *The Descent of Man, and Selection in Relation to Sex.*

Why is the idea of Darwinian mate choice so dangerous? First and foremost, Darwinian mate choice really *is* dangerous—to the neo-Darwinists—because it acknowledges that there are limits to the power of natural selection as an evolutionary force and as a scientific explanation of the biological world. Natural selection cannot be the only dynamic at work in evolution, Darwin maintained in *Descent*, because it cannot fully account for the extraordinary diversity of ornament we see in the biological world.

It took Darwin a long time to grapple with this dilemma. He famously wrote, "The sight of a feather in a peacock's tail, whenever I gaze at it, makes me sick!" Because the extravagance of its design seemed of no survival value whatsoever, unlike other heritable features that are the result of natural selection, the peacock's tail seemed to challenge everything that he had said in *Origin*. The insight he eventually arrived at, that there was another evolutionary force at work, was considered an unforgivable apostasy by Darwin's orthodox adaptationist followers. As a consequence, the Darwinian theory of mate choice has largely been suppressed, misinterpreted, redefined, and forgotten ever since.

Aesthetic evolution by mate choice is an idea so dangerous that it had to be laundered out of Darwinism itself in order to preserve the omnipotence of the explanatory power of natural selection. Only when Darwin's aesthetic view of evolution is restored to the biological and cultural mainstream will we have a science capable of explaining the diversity of beauty in nature.

Charles Darwin, a member of England's nineteenth-century rural gentry, led a privileged life within the most elite class of an expanding global empire. Yet Darwin was no idle member of the upper class. A man of careful habits and a steady, hardworking disposition, he used his privilege (and his generous independent income) to support the searching of a stubbornly relentless intellect. By following where his interests took him, he ultimately discovered the fundamentals of modern evolutionary biology. He thus delivered a fatal blow to the hierarchical Victorian world-view, which put man on a pedestal above, and totally removed from, the rest of the animal kingdom. Charles Darwin became a radical despite himself. Even today the full creative impact of his intellectual radicalism—its implications for science and for the culture at large—has yet to be appreciated.

The traditional image of Darwin as a young man portrays him as an indifferent and undisciplined student who mostly liked to roam around outside collecting beetles. He dropped out of his original course of medical education and bounced aimlessly among various interests with little outward commitment to any of them until he was offered the opportunity to go on his famous *Beagle* voyage. According to legend, Darwin was transformed by his world travels and became the revolutionary scientist we remember today.

I think it more likely that Darwin had the same voracious, quiet, but stubborn intellect as a young man that he displayed later in life, an intellect that would have given him an instinctive sense of what good science looked like. Just prior to publishing *On the Origin of Species* in 1859, Darwin characterized the giant creationist masterwork of the world-famous Harvard professor Louis Agassiz, the *Essay on Classification*, as "utterly impracticable rubbish!" As a medical student, Darwin, I think, likely came to the same conclusion about most of his biological education. And he would have been right. Most of what was taught as medicine in the 1820s *was* impracticable rubbish. There was no central mechanistic understanding of the workings of the body and no broader scientific concept of the causes of disease. Medical treatments were a grab bag of irrelevant placebos, powerful poisons, and dangerous quackery. It would be hard to identify more than a handful of professional medical treatments from that time that would be recognized today as being likely to do any patient any good whatsoever. Indeed, in his autobiography Darwin describes his experience of attending lectures at the Royal Medical Society in Edinburgh: "Much rubbish was talked there." I suspect that it was only when Darwin went all the way to the unexplored reaches of the Southern Hemisphere that he found an intellectual space free enough from the hidebound dogmas of his day to allow him the full play of his far-reaching, brilliant, and ever-curious mind.

Once he could make his own unfiltered observations, what he saw led him to the two great biological discoveries he revealed in *Origin:* the mechanism of evolution by natural selection, and the concept that all organisms are historically descended from a single common ancestor and thus related to one another in a "great Tree of Life." The enduring debates in some corners over whether these ideas should be taught in public schools give us some sense of how profoundly they must have challenged Darwin's readers a century and a half ago.

In confronting the fierce attacks that were mounted against *Origin* after its publication, Darwin had three gnawing problems. The first problem was the absence of any working theory of genetics. Not knowing the work of Mendel, Darwin struggled and failed to develop a functioning theory of inheritance, which was fundamental to the mechanism of natural selection. Darwin's second problem was the evolutionary origin of human beings, human nature, and human diversity. When it came to human evolution, Darwin pulled his punches in *Origin* and evasively concluded only that "light will be thrown on the origin of man and his history."

Darwin's third big problem was the origin of impracticable beauty. If natural selection was driven by the differential survival of heritable variations, what could explain the elaborate beauty of that peacock's tail that troubled him so much? The tail obviously did not help the male peacock to survive; if anything, the huge tail would be a hindrance, slowing him down and making him much more vulnerable to predators. Darwin was particularly obsessed with the eyespots on the peacock's tail. He had argued that the perfection of the human eye could be explained by the evolution of many incremental advances over time. Each evolutionary advance would have produced slight improvements in the ability of the eye to detect light, to distinguish shadows from light, to focus, to create images, to differentiate among colors, and so on, all of which would have contributed to the animal's survival. But what purpose could the intermediate stages in the evolution of the peacock's eyespots have served? Indeed, what purpose do the "perfect" eyespots of a peacock serve today? If the problem of explaining the evolution of the human eye was an intellectual challenge, the problem of explaining the peacock's eyespot was an intellectual nightmare. Darwin lived this nightmare. It was in that context that in 1860 he wrote that oft-quoted line to his American friend the Harvard botanist Asa Gray: "The sight of a feather in a peacock's tail, whenever I gaze at it, makes me sick!"

In 1871, with the publication of *The Descent of Man, and Selection in Relation to Sex,* Darwin boldly addressed both the problem of human origins and the evolution of beauty. In this book he proposed a second, independent mechanism of evolution—sexual selection—to account for armaments and ornaments, battle and beauty. If the results of natural selection were determined by the differential survival of heritable variations, then the results of sexual selection were determined by their differential sexual success—that is, by those heritable features that contribute to success at obtaining mates.

Within sexual selection, Darwin envisioned two distinct and potentially opposing evolutionary mechanisms at work. The first mechanism, which he called the law of battle, was the struggle between individuals of one sex—often male—for sexual control over the individuals of the other sex. Darwin hypothesized that the battle for sexual control would result in the evolution of large body size, weapons of aggression like horns, antlers, and spurs, and mechanisms of physical control. The second sexual selection mechanism, which he called the taste for the beautiful, concerned the process by which the members of one sex—often female—choose their mates on the basis of their own innate preferences. Darwin hypothesized that mate choice had resulted in the evolution of many of those traits in nature that are so pleasing and beautiful. These ornamental traits included everything from the songs, colorful plumages, and displays of birds to the brilliant blue face and hindquarters of the Mandrill *(Mandrillus sphinx)*. In an exhaustive survey of animal life from spiders and insects to birds and mammals, Darwin reviewed the evidence for sexual selection in many different species. Using the law of battle and the taste for the beautiful, he proposed to explain the evolution of both armament and ornament in nature.

In *The Descent of Man,* Darwin finally presented the explicit theory of the evolutionary origins of humans that he had avoided articulating in *Origin.* The book begins with a long discussion of the continuity between human beings and other animals, slowly and incrementally chipping away at the edifice of human uniqueness and exceptionalism. Because of the obvious cultural sensitivity of the subject, Darwin proceeded at a very deliberate pace to build the argument for this evolutionary continuity. He put off until his final chapter, "General Summary and Conclusion," the incendiary conclusion to which all this was leading: "We thus learn that man is descended from a hairy quadruped."

Then, after discussing how sexual selection worked in the animal world, Darwin analyzed its impact on human evolution. From our furless bodies, to the enormous geographic, ethnic, and tribal diversity in human appearance, to our highly social character, to language and music, Darwin made a powerful case that sexual selection had played a critical role in the shaping of the human species:

> Courage, pugnacity, perseverance, strength and size of body, weapons of all kinds, musical organs, both vocal and instrumental, bright colors, stripes and marks, and ornamental appendages, have all been indirectly gained . . . through the influence of love and jealousy, through the appreciation of the beautiful . . . and through the exertion of a choice.

Although tackling two subjects as complex and controversial as the evolution of beauty and the origins of humankind in one volume was an intellectually daring feat, *Descent* is generally considered a difficult, or even flawed, work. By building his argument so slowly and incrementally, writing in such dry, discursive prose, and citing so many learned authorities in support of the ideas he was advancing, Darwin might have thought he could draw any reasonable reader to accept the inevitability of his radical conclusions. But his rhetorical tactics failed, and in the end *Descent* was criticized by both creationist opponents of the very concept of evolution and fellow scientists who accepted natural selection but were adamantly opposed to sexual selection. To this day, *Descent* has never had the same intellectual impact as *Origin*.

The most notable and revolutionary feature of Darwin's theory of mate choice is that it was explicitly *aesthetic*. He described the evolutionary origin of beauty in nature as a consequence of the fact that animals had evolved to be beautiful to *themselves*. What was so radical about this idea was that it positioned organisms— especially female organisms—as active agents in the evolution of their own species. Unlike natural selection, which emerges from external forces in nature, such as competition, predation, climate, and geography, acting on the organism, sexual selection is a potentially independent, self-directed process in which the organisms themselves (mostly female) were in charge. Darwin described females as having a "taste for the beautiful" and an "aesthetic faculty." He described males as trying to "charm" their mates:

> With the great majority of animals ... the taste for the beautiful is confined to the attractions of the opposite sex. The sweet strains poured forth by many male birds during the season of love are certainly admired by the females, of which fact evidence will hereafter be given. If female birds had been incapable of appreciating the beautiful colours, the ornaments, and voices of their male partners, all the labour and anxiety by the latter in displaying their charms before the females would have been thrown away; and this is impossible to admit ...
>
> On the whole, birds appear to be the most aesthetic of all animals, excepting of course man, and they have nearly the same taste for the beautiful as we have ... [Male birds] charm the female by vocal and instrumental music of the most varied kinds.

From the scientific and cultural perspectives of today, Darwin's choice of aesthetic language may seem quaint, anthropomorphic, and possibly even embarrassingly silly. And that may help to account for why Darwin's aesthetic view of mate choice is treated today like the crazy aunt in the evolutionary attic; she is not to be spoken of. Clearly, Darwin did not have our contemporary fear of anthropomorphism. Indeed, because he was vitally engaged in breaking down the previously unquestioned barrier between humans and other forms of life, his use of aesthetic language was not just a curious mannerism or a quaint Victorian affectation. It was an integral feature of his scientific argument about the nature of evolutionary process. Darwin was making explicit claims about the sensory and cognitive abilities of animals and the evolutionary consequences of those abilities. Having put humans and all other organisms on different branches of the same great Tree of Life, Darwin used ordinary language to make an extraordinary scientific claim: that the subjective sensory experiences of humans can be compared scientifically to those of animals.

The first implication of Darwin's language was that animals are choosing among their prospective mates on the basis of judgments about their aesthetic appeal. To many Victorian readers, even those sympathetic to evolution, this was patently absurd. It seemed impossible that animals could make fine aesthetic judgments. Even if they were able to *observe* differences in the color of their suitors' plumage or the musical notes of their songs, the notion that they could cognitively distinguish among them, and then demonstrate a specific preference for one or another variation, was considered ludicrous.

These Victorian-era objections have been definitively rejected. Darwin's hypothesis that animals are able to make sensory evaluations and exercise mate preferences is now supported by volumes of evidence and is universally accepted. There have been numerous experiments across the animal kingdom—from birds to fishes, grasshoppers to moths—showing that animals have the capacity to make sensory evaluations that influence their mate choices.

Although Darwin's proposal of animal cognitive choice is now the accepted wisdom, the second implication of his aesthetic theory of sexual selection remains as revolutionary today, and as controversial, as when he first proposed it. By using the words "beauty," "taste," "charm," "appreciate," "admire," and "love," Darwin was suggesting that mating preferences could evolve for displays that had no utilitarian value at all to the chooser, only aesthetic value. In short, Darwin hypothesized that beauty evolves primarily because it is *pleasurable* to the observer.

Darwin's views on this issue developed over time. In an early discussion of sexual selection in *Origin,* Darwin wrote, "Amongst many animals, sexual selection will give its aid to ordinary [natural] selection by assuring to the most vigorous and best adaptive of all males the greatest number of offspring."

In other words, in *Origin,* Darwin saw sexual selection as simply the handmaiden of natural selection, another means of guaranteeing the perpetuation of the most vigorous and best-adapted mates. This view still prevails today. By the time he wrote *Descent,* however, Darwin had embraced a much broader concept of sexual selection that may have nothing to do with a potential mate's being more vigorous or better adapted per se, but only with being aesthetically appealing, as he stated clearly for the mesmerizing example of the Argus Pheasant: "The case of the male Argus pheasant is eminently interesting, because it affords good evidence that the most refined beauty may serve as a sexual charm, *and for no other purpose* [emphasis added]."

Moreover, in *Descent,* Darwin viewed sexual selection and natural selection as two distinct and frequently independent evolutionary mechanisms. Thus, the concept of two distinct but potentially interacting and even conflicting sources of selection is a fundamental and vital component of an authentically Darwinian vision of evolutionary biology. As we will see, however, this view has been rejected by most modern evolutionary biologists in favor of Darwin's earlier view of sexual selection as just another variant on natural selection.

Another distinctive feature of Darwin's theory of mate choice was that it was *coevolutionary*. Darwin hypothesized that the specific display traits and the "standards of beauty" used to select a mate evolved together, mutually influencing and reinforcing each other—as demonstrated again by the Argus Pheasant:

> The male Argus Pheasant acquired his beauty gradually through the preference of the females during many generations for the more highly ornamented males; the aesthetic capacity of females advanced through exercise or habit just as our own taste is gradually improved.

Here, Darwin envisions an evolutionary process in which each species coevolves its own, unique, cognitive "standards of beauty" in concert with the elaboration of the display traits that meet those standards. According to this hypothesis, behind every biological ornament is an equally elaborate, coevolved cognitive preference that has driven, shaped, and been shaped by that ornament's evolution. By modern scientific criteria, Darwin's description of the coevolutionary process in the Argus Pheasant is rather hazy, but it is no less substantive than his explanations of the mechanism of natural selection, which are viewed today as being brilliantly prescient, despite his ignorance of genetics.

Within Darwin's argument for mate choice in *Descent* was another revolutionary idea: that animals are not merely subject to the extrinsic forces of ecological competition, predation, climate, geography, and so on that create natural selection. Rather, animals can play a distinct and vital role in their *own* evolution through their sexual and social choices. Whenever the opportunity evolves to enact sexual preferences through mate choice, a new and distinctively *aesthetic* evolutionary phenomenon occurs. Whether it occurs within a shrimp or a swan, a moth or a human, individual organisms wield the potential to evolve arbitrary and useless beauty completely independent of (and sometimes in opposition to) the forces of natural selection.

In some species—like penguins and puffins—there is mutual mate choice, and both sexes exhibit the same displays and coevolved mating preferences. In polyandrous species, like the phalaropes *(Phalaropus)* and lily-trodding jacanas (Jacanidae), successful females may take multiple mates. These females are larger and brighter than the males, and they're the ones who perform courtship displays and sing songs to attract mates, while the males are the ones who exhibit mate choice, build the nests, and care for the young. But Darwin observed that in many of the most highly ornamented species the evolutionary force of sexual selection acted predominantly through female mate choice, which is why this-book focuses largely on female mate choice. If *female* aesthetic preferences drove the process, then *female* sexual desire was responsible for creating, defining, and shaping the most extreme forms of sexual display that we see in nature. Ultimately, it is female sexual autonomy that is predominantly responsible for the evolution of natural beauty. This was a very unsettling concept in Darwin's time—as it is to many today.

Because the concept of sexual autonomy has not been well-explored in evolutionary biology, it is worthwhile to define it and understand its far-reaching implications. Whether in ethics, political philosophy, sociology, or biology, autonomy is the capacity of an individual agent to make an informed, independent, and uncoerced decision. So, sexual autonomy is the capacity for an individual organism to exercise an informed, independent, and uncoerced *sexual* choice about whom to mate with. The individual elements of the Darwinian concept of sexual autonomy—that is, sensory perception, cognitive capacities for sensory evaluation and mate choice, the potential for independence from sexual coercion, and so on—are all common concepts in evolutionary biology today. Yet few evolutionary biologists since Darwin have aligned these dots as clearly as he did.

In *Descent,* Darwin presented his hypothesis that female sexual autonomy—the taste for the beautiful—is an independent and transformative evolutionary force in the history of life. He also hypothesized that it can sometimes be matched, counterbalanced, or even overwhelmed by an independent force of male sexual control: the law of battle, the combat among members of one sex for control over mating with the other sex. In some species, one evolutionary mechanism or the other may dominate the outcome of sexual selection, but in other species—ducks, for example, as we shall see—female choice and male competition and coercion will both be operative and can give rise to an escalating process of sexual conflict. Darwin did not have the intellectual framework to fully describe the dynamics of sexual conflict, but he clearly understood that it existed—in humans and in other animals.

In short, *Descent* was as mechanistically innovative and analytically thoughtful as *Origin,* but to most of Darwin's contemporaries it was a bridge too far.

Upon publication in 1871, Darwin's theory of sexual selection was swiftly and brutally attacked. Or more precisely, part of it was. Darwin's concept of male-male competition—the law of battle—was immediately and almost universally accepted. Clearly, the notion of male-male competition for dominance over female sexuality was not a hard sell in the patriarchal Victorian culture of Darwin's time. For example, in an initially anonymous review of *Descent* that appeared soon after the book was published, the biologist St. George Mivart wrote,

> Under the head of sexual selection, Darwin put two very distinct
> processes. One of these consists in the action of superior strength or
> activity, by which one male succeeds in obtaining possession of mates
> and in keeping away rivals. This is, undoubtedly, a *vera causa;* but may be
> more conveniently reckoned as one kind of "natural selection" than as a
> branch of "sexual selection."

In these few words, Mivart established an intellectual gambit that is still operative today. He took the element of Darwin's sexual selection theory that he agreed with—male-male competition—and declared it to be just another form of natural selection, rather than an independent force, in direct opposition to Darwin's own view. But at least he acknowledged that it existed. Not so the other aspect of Darwin's sexual selection theory.

When he came to a consideration of female mate choice, Mivart launched an all-out attack: "The second process consists in the alleged preference or choice, exercised freely by the female in favour of particular males on account of some attractiveness or beauty of form, colour, odor, or voice which the males may possess."

By referring to "choice, exercised freely," Mivart documents that Darwin's theory implied female sexual autonomy to his Victorian readers. However, the notion of an animal's exercising any kind of choice was a complete impossibility to Mivart:

> Even in Mr. Darwin's specially-selected instances, there is not a tittle of evidence tending, however slightly, to show that any brute possesses the representative reflective faculties .... It cannot be denied that, looking broadly over the whole animal kingdom, there is no evidence of advance in mental power on the part of brutes.

Mivart asserts that animals lack the requisite sensory powers, cognitive capacity, and free will necessary to make sexual choices based on display traits. Therefore, they could not possibly be active players, or selective agents, in their own evolution. Moreover, in discussing the role of the peahen in the evolution of the peacock's tail, Mivart found the idea of choice being exercised by female "brutes" particularly preposterous: "such is the instability of *vicious femi-nine caprice,* [emphasis added] that no constancy of coloration could be produced by its selective actions."

To Mivart, female sexual whims were so malleable—that is, fickle females preferring one thing one minute, and another the next—that they could never lead to the evolution of something as marvelously complex as the peacock's tail.

We need to take a closer look at Mivart's language because the meanings of some of his words have changed in common English usage over the past 140 years. Today, the word "vicious" means intentionally violent or ferocious, but its original meaning was immoral, depraved, or wicked—literally, characterized by vice. Likewise, today "caprice" refers to a delightful, lighthearted whim, but in Victorian times it had the less-appealing meaning of an arbitrary "turn of mind made without apparent or adequate motive." Thus, to Mivart, the concept of female mate choice and autonomy had overtones not just of fickleness but of unjustifiable immorality and sin.

Mivart did concede that display might play a role in sexual arousal: "The display of the male may be useful in supplying the necessary degree of stimulation to her nervous system, and to that of the male. Pleasurable sensations, perhaps very keen in intensity, may thence result to both."

Mivart's evocation of "stimulation" that creates "pleasurable sensations" reads like advice for a fulfilling sex life from a Victorian marriage manual. In this view, females merely require sufficient stimulation in order to elicit an appropriate sexual response and coordinate their sexual behavior with that of the male.

But if the purpose of sexual display is simply to supply "the necessary degree of stimulation," then females do not have their own individual, autonomous sexual desires. Rather, females should inevitably, and in due time, respond to the workmanlike stimulatory efforts of their suitors. This autonomy-denying conception of female sexual desire would reverberate throughout the next century, reaching its apogee in Freud's theory of human sexual response. According to this physiological interpretation of female sexual pleasure, men need never entertain the possibility that "maybe she's just not that into you." Absence of female sexual response always means that there is something wrong with *her* physiology—in short, that she's frigid. As we will see, it is probably not an accident that the rediscovery of the biological theory of evolution by mate choice, the broad acknowledgment in Western culture of female autonomy, and the collapse of the Freudian conception of female sexuality all occurred during a short period of time that coincided with the advent of the women's liberation movement in the 1970s.

Mivart's review of *Descent* also established another enduring intellectual trend. He was the very first person to portray Darwin as a traitor to his own great legacy—a traitor to *true* Darwinism: "The assignment of the law of 'natural selection' to a subordinate position is virtually an abandonment of the Darwinian theory; for the one distinguishing feature of that theory was *the all-sufficiency of 'natural selection'* [emphasis added]."

Mere weeks after publication of *Descent,* Mivart mounted an attack against it that is still in use—citing *Origin* to argue against *Descent.* To Mivart, Darwin's signature achievement had been the creation of a single, "all-sufficient" theory of biological evolution. By diluting the theory of natural selection with a mechanism that rested largely on the power of aesthetic subjective experiences—*vicious feminine caprice*—Darwin had gone beyond the pale of what was acceptable. Many evolutionary biologists would still agree.

Mivart's attacks on sexual selection set many others in motion. But the most consistent, relentless, and effective critique of sexual selection came from Alfred Russel Wallace. Wallace was famous as the co-discoverer of the theory of natural selection. In 1859, he sent Darwin a manuscript from the jungles of Indonesia in which he set down a theory quite similar to Darwin's, and he asked for his advice and assistance with the manuscript. Fearful of being preempted by the younger man after decades of private work on his theory of natural selection, Darwin quickly published Wallace's article along with a short article summarizing his own theory. Then he rushed the full manuscript of *On the Origin of Species* into publication. By the time Wallace returned to England, Darwin and his theory were world famous.

There is no evidence that Wallace ever held this against Darwin, nor could he. Darwin had been working away on the idea of natural selection for more than twenty years, while Wallace was just beginning to think it through. But Darwin and Wallace never agreed on the subject of mate choice, and Wallace soon mounted a relentless attack on it. The two men debated their opposing views in a series of publications and in private letters that continued until Darwin's death in 1882, with neither man ever changing his mind. In what turned out to be his last scientific publication, Darwin wrote, "I may perhaps be here permitted to say that, after having carefully weighed to the best of my ability the various arguments which have been advanced against the principle of sexual selection, I remain firmly convinced of its truth."

In contrast to Darwin's always polite and understated expression of his views, Wallace's attack on evolution by mate choice grew ever more strident after Darwin's death and continued until his own death in 1913. Ultimately, Wallace was so successful that the subject of sexual selection was almost completely marginalized and forgotten within evolutionary biology until the 1970s.

Wallace expended an enormous amount of energy arguing that the "ornamental" differences between the sexes that Darwin described were not ornaments at all and that Darwin's theory of mate choice was unnecessary to explain animal diversity. Like Mivart, Wallace was skeptical about the possibility that animals had sensory and cognitive capacities to make mate choices. Wallace believed that humans had been specially created by God and divinely endowed with cognitive capacities that animals lacked. Thus, Darwin's concept of mate choice violated Wallace's spiritual theory of human exceptionalism.

However, faced with overwhelming evidence in the form of elaborate ornaments and displays, especially among birds, Wallace was never able to reject evolution by mate choice entirely. But when forced to admit the possibility, he insisted that sexual ornaments could only have evolved because they had an adaptive, utilitarian value. Thus, in his 1878 book, *Tropical Nature, and Other Essays,* under the heading "Natural Selection as Neutralizing Sexual Selection," Wallace wrote, "The only way in which we can account for the observed facts is by supposing that colour and ornament are strictly correlated with health, vigor, and general fitness to survive."

Here, Wallace articulates the idea that sexual displays constitute "honest" indicators of quality and condition—an entirely orthodox view in sexual selection today. But how can it be that Wallace, the man justly credited with having destroyed sexual selection theory for over a century, actually wrote a statement that would be entirely at home in any modern biology textbook, or practically any contemporary paper on mate choice? The answer is that today's mainstream views of mate choice are as stridently anti-Darwinian as Wallace's critiques.

Wallace was the first to propose the now exceedingly popular BioMatch .com hypothesis, which holds that all beauty provides a rich profile of practical information about the adaptive qualities of potential mates. This view of evolution has become so pervasive that it even found its way into the 2013 Princeton University graduation speech by the Federal Reserve chairman, Ben Bernanke, who admonished the graduates to "remember that physical beauty is evolution's way of assuring us that the other person doesn't have too many intestinal parasites."

Today, most researchers agree with Wallace that all of sexual selection is simply a form of natural selection. But Wallace went further than they do and rejected the term "sexual selection" entirely. In that same passage, he continued,

> If there is (as I maintain) such a correlation [between ornament and
> health, vigor, and fitness to survive], then the sexual selection of color
> or ornament, for which there is little or no evidence, becomes needless,

because natural selection, which is the admitted *vera causa,* will itself produce all the results …. Sexual selection becomes as unnecessary as it would certainly be ineffective.

Of course, it was the arbitrary and aesthetic components of Darwin's theory of sexual selection that Wallace rejected as "needless," "unnecessary," and "ineffective." Today, most evolutionary biologists would still agree.

Like Mivart, Wallace, who saw Darwin's aesthetic heresy as a threat to their shared intellectual legacy, took steps to fix what he perceived as Darwin's error. In the introduction to his 1889 book *Darwinism,* Wallace wrote,

In rejecting that phase of sexual selection depending on female choice, I insist on the greater efficacy of natural selection. This is pre-eminently the Darwinian doctrine, and I therefore claim for my book the position of being the advocate of pure Darwinism.

Here, Wallace claims to be more Darwinian than Darwin! After wrangling unsuccessfully over mate choice with the living Darwin, within just a few years of Darwin's death Wallace has begun to reshape Darwinism in his *own* image.

In these passages, we witness the birth of adaptationism—the belief that adaptation by natural selection is a universally strong force that will *always* be predominant in the evolutionary process. Or, as Wallace put it in a strikingly absolutist statement, "Natural selection acts perpetually and on an enormous scale"—so enormous that it would "neutralise" any other evolutionary mechanisms.

Wallace set in motion the transformation of Darwin's fertile, creative, and diverse intellectual legacy into the monolithic and intellectually impoverished theory with which he is almost universally associated today. Notably, Wallace also invented the characteristic style of adaptationist argument—mere stubborn insistence.

This is kind of a big deal. The Darwin we have inherited, through the filter of Wallace's outsized influence on evolutionary biology in the twentieth century, has been laundered, retailored, and cleaned up for ideological purity. The true breadth and creativity of Darwin's ideas, especially his aesthetic view of evolution, have been written out of history. Alfred Russel Wallace might have lost the battle for credit over the discovery of natural selection, but he won the war over what evolutionary biology and Darwinism would become in the twentieth century. More than one hundred years later, I am still pissed about it.

In the century following the publication of Darwin's *Descent of Man,* the theory of sexual selection was almost entirely eclipsed. Despite a few scattered attempts to revive the topic, Wallace's hatchet job on mate choice was so successful that generation after generation would turn exclusively to natural selection to account for sexual ornament and display behavior.

During the century-long dark age of mate choice theory, however, one man did make a fundamental contribution to the field. In a 1915 paper and a 1930 book, Ronald A. Fisher proposed a genetic mechanism for the evolution of mate choice that built on and extended Darwin's aesthetic view. Unfortunately, however, Fisher's ideas on sexual selection would be mostly ignored for the next fifty years.

Fisher was a gifted mathematician who had a huge effect on the sciences through his fundamental work developing both the basic tools and the intellectual structure underlying modern statistics. However, he was first and foremost a biologist, and his statistical research grew directly from his desire for a more rigorous understanding of the workings of genetics and evolution in nature, agriculture, and human populations. His interest in genetics and evolution was motivated in part by his ardent support for eugenics—the now disgraced theory and social movement that advocated the use of social, political, and legal regulation of reproduction in order to genetically improve the human species and maintain "racial purity." Appalling as his beliefs were, Fisher's investigations led him to some brilliant scientific conclusions—conclusions that, in the end, conflicted with his eugenic beliefs.

Fisher permanently reframed the sexual selection debate with a critical observation: Explaining the evolution of sexual ornaments is easy; all other things being equal, display traits should evolve to match the prevailing mating preferences. The more critical scientific question is, why and how do mating preferences evolve? This insight remains fundamental to all contemporary discussions of evolution by sexual selection.

Fisher actually proposed a two-stage evolutionary model: one phase for the initial origin of mating preferences, and a second, subsequent phase for the coevolutionary elaboration of trait and preference. The first phase, which is solidly Wallacean, holds that preferences initially evolve for traits that are honest and accurate indices of health, vigor, and survival ability. Natural selection would ensure that mate choice based on these traits would lead to objectively better mates and to genetically based mating preferences for these better mates. But then, after the origin of mating preference, Fisher hypothesized in his second-phase model that the very existence of mate choice would *unhinge* the display trait from its original honest, quality information by creating a new, unpredictable, aesthetically driven evolutionary force: sexual attraction to the trait itself. When the honest indicator trait becomes disconnected from its correlation with quality, that doesn't make the trait any less attractive to a potential mate; it will continue to evolve and to be elaborated merely because it is preferred.

In the end, according to the Fisher phase-two model, the force that drives the subsequent evolution of mate choice is mate *choice* itself. In an exact reversal of the Wallacean view of natural selection as neutralizing sexual selection, arbitrary aesthetic choices (per Darwin) trump choices made for adaptive advantage (per Wallace) because the trait that was originally preferred for some adaptive reason has become a source of attraction in its own right. Once the trait is attractive, its attractiveness and popularity become ends in themselves. According to Fisher, mating preference is like a Trojan horse. Even if mate choice originally acts to enhance traits that carry adaptive information, desire for the preferred trait will eventually undermine the ability of natural selection to dictate the evolutionary outcome. Desire for beauty will endure and undermine the desire for truth.

How does this happen? Fisher hypothesized that a positive feedback loop between the sexual ornament and the mating preference for that ornament will evolve through genetic covariation (that is, correlated genetic variation) between the two. To understand how this could work, imagine a population of birds with genetic variation for a display trait—say tail length—and for mating preferences for different tail lengths. Females who prefer males with long tails will find mates with those longer tails. Likewise, females who prefer males with shorter tails will find mates with shorter tails. The action of mate choice means that variation in genes for traits and preferences will no longer be found randomly in the population. Rather, most individuals will soon carry genes for correlated traits and preferences—that is, genes for long tails *and* preferences for long tails, or genes for short tails *and* preferences for short tails. Likewise, there will be fewer and fewer individuals who carry genes for short tails and preferences for long tails, or vice versa. The very action of mate choice will distill and concentrate genetic variation for trait and preference into correlated combinations. To Fisher, this observation was merely a mathematical fact. This outcome is what mating preference means.

As a consequence of genetic covariation, genes for a given trait and the preference for that trait will coevolve with each other. When females exercise their mate choices based on particular displays—for example, a long tail—they will *also* be selecting *indirectly* particular mate choice genes because they will be choosing mates whose *mothers* likely also had genes for preferring long tails.

The result is a strong, positive feedback loop in which mate choice becomes the selective agent in the evolution of mate preference itself. Fisher called this self-reinforcing sexual selection mechanism "a runaway process." Selection of specific display traits creates evolutionary change in mating preferences, and evolutionary change in mating preferences will create further evolutionary change in display traits, and so on. The form of beauty, and the desire for it, shape each other through a coevolutionary process. In this way, Fisher provided an explicit genetic mechanism for how the display trait and the mating preference can "advance together," as Darwin first envisioned for the Argus Pheasant.

Fisher's coevolutionary mechanism also explains the potential evolutionary benefit of mating preference. If the female chooses a mate with a sexually attractive trait—again let's say a long tail—her male offspring will be more likely to inherit this sexually attractive trait. If other females in the population also prefer long tails, then the female will end up with a greater number of descendants because her male offspring will be sexually attractive to them. This evolutionary advantage is the indirect, genetic benefit of mate choice alone. We call it indirect because it does not accrue *directly* to the chooser's own survival or fecundity (that is, her capacity to have and raise offspring), or even to the survival of her offspring. Rather, the benefit accrues through the reproductive success of her sexually attractive sons, which will result in a wider propagation of her genes (that is, more grandkids).

Fisher's runaway process works something like the Dutch tulip bulb craze of the 1630s, the speculative financial market bubble of the 1920s, or, to take something much more recent, the overvalued housing markets that led to the near collapse of the entire world banking system in 2008. All of these are examples of what happens when the value of something becomes unhinged from its "actual" worth and continues not only to be valued but to increase in value. What drives speculative market bubbles is desire itself. That is, something is desirable because it is desired, popular because it's popular. Thus, Fisherian mate choice is the genetic version of the "irrational exuberance" of a market bubble.

Fisher asserted that mating preferences do not continue to evolve because the particular male that the female chooses is any better than any other male. In fact, sexually successful males could sometimes evolve to be *worse* at survival or *poorer* in health or condition. If a display trait becomes disconnected from any other, extrinsic measure of mate quality—that is, overall genetic quality, disease resistance, diet quality, or ability to make parental investments—then we say that that display trait is arbitrary. Arbitrary does not mean accidental, random, or unexplainable; it means only that the display trait communicates no other information than its presence. It simply exists to be observed and evaluated. Arbitrary traits are neither honest nor dishonest because they do not encode any information that can be lied about. They are merely attractive, or *merely beautiful.*

This evolutionary mechanism is rather like high fashion. The difference between successful and unsuccessful clothes is determined not by variation in function or objective quality (really) but by evanescent ideas about what is subjectively appealing—the style of the season. Fisher's model of mate choice results in the evolution of traits that lack any functional advantages and may even be disadvantageous to the displayer—like stylish shoes that hurt one's feet, or garments so skimpy that they fail to protect the body from the elements. In a Fisherian world, animals are slaves to evolutionary fashion, evolving extravagant and arbitrary displays and tastes that are all "meaningless"; they do not involve anything other than perceivable qualities.

Fisher never presented an explicit mathematical model of his runaway process (something that later biologists did). Some have conjectured that he was such a skilled mathematician that he thought the results were obvious and needed no further explication. If so, then Fisher was sorely mistaken because there were plenty of discoveries still to be made. Actually, I think Fisher probably knew there was more work to do. So why didn't he do it? I think Fisher did not pursue his runaway model any further because he realized that the implications of this evolutionary mechanism were completely antithetical to his personal support for the eugenics movement. Fisher's runaway model implied that adaptive mate choice—the kind of choice required to eugenically "improve" the species—was evolutionarily unstable and would almost inevitably be undermined by arbitrary mate choice, the irrational desire that beauty inspires. And he was right!

The Darwin versus Wallace, aesthetic versus adaptationist debate remains vital to science today. Whenever we study mate choice, we are using intellectual tools that were shaped by this debate, and we need to be aware of the history of our tools.

Among those tools is the language we use to define concepts in evolutionary biology. For example, let's examine the history of the word "fitness." To Darwin, fitness had the ordinary language meaning of physical fitness. Fitness meant fit to do a task. Darwinian fitness was the physical capacity to do the tasks necessary to ensure one's survival and capacity for reproduction. However, during the development of population genetics in the early twentieth century, fitness was redefined mathematically as the differential success of one's genes in subsequent generations. This broader and more general new definition combined all sources of differential genetic success—survival, fecundity, *and* mating/fertilization success—into a single variable under the common label of "adaptive natural selection." The redefinition of fitness was accomplished precisely during the period when sexual selection by mate choice had been entirely rejected as irrelevant to evolutionary biology. Thus, the effect of redefining fitness was to flatten and eliminate the original, subtle, Darwinian distinction between *natural selection* on traits that ensured survival and fecundity and *sexual selection* on traits that resulted in differential mating and fertilization success. Ever since, this mathematically convenient but intellectually muddled new concept of fitness has reshaped how people think evolution works and made it difficult to even articulate the possibility of a distinct, independent, nonadaptive sexual selection mechanism. *If it contributes to fitness, it must be adaptive, right?* The Darwinian/Fisherian concept of sexual selection by mate choice has been essentially written out of the language of biology. It has become linguistically impossible to be an authentic Darwinian.

The flattening of the intellectual complexity of aesthetic Darwinism was motivated, at least in part, by the belief that conceptual unification is a general scientific virtue, that the development of fewer, more powerful, more broadly applicable, singular theories, laws, and frameworks is a fundamental goal of science itself. Sometimes unification in science works great, but it is doomed to fail when the distinctive, emergent properties of particular phenomena are reduced, eliminated, or ignored in the process. This loss of intellectual content is exactly what happens when something complex is *explained away* instead of being *explained* in its own right.

By claiming that evolution by mate choice was a special process with its own, distinctive internal logic, Darwin fought against the powerful scientific and intellectual bias toward simplicity and unification. Of course, many of Darwin's Victorian antagonists were recent converts from religious monotheism to materialist evolutionism. Their historic monotheism might have predisposed them to adopt a powerful new monoideism; they replaced a single omnipotent God with a single omnipotent idea—natural selection. Indeed, contemporary adaptationists should question why *they* feel it is necessary to explain all of nature with a single powerful theory or process. Is the desire for scientific unification simply the ghost of monotheism lurking within contemporary scientific explanation? This is another implication of Darwin's *really* dangerous idea.

If evolutionary biology is to adopt an authentically Darwinian view, it must recognize, as he did, that natural selection and sexual selection are *independent* evolutionary mechanisms. In this framework, adaptive mate choice is a process that occurs through the *interaction* of sexual selection and natural selection.

To better understand the evolution of beauty and how to study it, we will now take a look at the sex lives of birds. There can be no better place to start than with Darwin's "eminently interesting" Great Argus pheasant.

QUESTIONS FOR MAKING CONNECTIONS
WITHIN THE READING

1. One of Prum's concerns is unexamined bias in evolutionary science, including gender bias. Most male scientists do not intend, of course, to marginalize women, and many women have become prominent figures in the sciences. According to Prum, the problem is not the result of any conscious decision but of the way most scientists have understood evolution itself. By focusing exclusively on natural selection, they have largely overlooked what Prum calls women's "agency" or power to act. What roles do females play in traditional thinking about evolution? Is it fair to say that natural selection reduces women to a purely reproductive role? By contrast, what roles do men play? Are they seen as endowed with greater agency than women? How does this balance of power change if we add sexual selection as a second evolutionary force, equal to natural selection? If females often choose their mates based on aesthetic factors, how does that alter the way we understand the process of evolution? And how might it change the way we think about gender differences in general?

2. What does Prum mean in this passage by "co-evolutionary"?

> Another distinctive feature of Darwin's theory of mate choice was that it was coevolutionary. Darwin hypothesized that the specific display traits and "standards of beauty" used to select a mate evolved together, mutually influencing and reinforcing each other.... Darwin envisions an evolutionary process in which each species coevolves its own, unique, cognitive "standards of beauty" in concert with the elaboration of display traits that meet those standards.

How does the addition of the *co-* prefix change the way we think of evolution? If the females and males of a species co-evolve, is evolution entirely beyond the control of the animals themselves? Is one gender more in charge than the other? Is "survival of the fittest" guaranteed? Does co-evolution call into doubt the "survival of the fittest" idea?

3. At the end of Prum's essay, he claims that the "loss of intellectual content is exactly what happens when something complex is *explained away* instead of being explained in its own right" (emphasis in the original). The "something" in his chapter is beauty. How has beauty been "explained away" rather than explained, and what "intellectual content" has been lost? In particular, how has this loss distorted Charles Darwin's legacy as well as evolution itself? By leaving beauty out of evolution, how have scientists made other animals seem less like us—less human—than they really are? How does ignoring beauty make humans look less natural?

QUESTIONS FOR WRITING

1. Richard O. Prum's book, from which this chapter is drawn, is entitled *The Evolution of Beauty*. The idea that beauty can evolve is actually quite radical. The traditional humanities have often viewed beauty as an intangible idea, like "truth" and "goodness." Some thinkers—Plato, for example—have even described it as eternal. Others, like the German philosopher Immanuel Kant, have described beauty as universal and "disinterested"—ultimately without any purpose, like play. For these thinkers, beauty that can evolve will no longer qualify as true beauty. On the other hand, science has generally ignored beauty altogether. For scientists who view natural selection as the only form of evolution, beauty is just a means to one end: the "survival of the fittest." Using this chapter from Prum's book, explain how it might be possible for beauty to evolve. What factors, according to Prum, have led to changes in the nature of beauty, not only for humans but for other species as well? And, conversely, what role does beauty play in the evolutionary process?

2. Prum's chapter helps us understand how knowledge grows through controversy. "In the century following the publication of Darwin's *Descent of Man*," he writes, "the theory of sexual selection was almost entirely eclipsed." But before it was almost eclipsed, as he shows, sexual selection was hotly debated. Carefully retrace this debate. How did key figures like St. George Mivart and Alfred Russell Wallace interpret the ideas presented in *On the Origin of Species*? How did they react to Darwin's later book, *The Descent of Man*? In retracing this history, be sure to explain how it evolved as genuine debate—a back-and-forth, an exchange of views—rather than a clash of convictions, private and unchanging.

QUESTIONS FOR MAKING CONNECTIONS
BETWEEN THE READINGS

1. Prum criticizes past scientists for their misunderstanding of Darwin. But his criticisms actually possess a coherence that elevates them into something bigger—not just criticisms but a *critique*. Instead of rejecting this idea or that, Prum calls into question an entire way of thinking, and his goal is to replace it with an alternative that he calls "aesthetic Darwinism." Although Karen Ho's subject is education rather than biology, her "Biographies of Hegemony" also offers a critique—of higher education under the influence of big Wall Street firms. Imagine if Prum and Ho were to meet at a hypothetical conference. What areas of commonality would they share, and what could they learn from each other about how to change established ways of thinking? Why might their critiques carry more weight than simple criticisms?

2. Prum's book has the word "beauty" in the title. And Barbara Fredrickson's has the word "love." Both beauty and love have been trivialized in romance novels and the clichéd romcoms that Hollywood cranks out. And both have been profoundly misunderstood by ignoring their roots in our biology. Prum, writing on beauty, and Fredrickson, on love, have each set out to correct that neglect by using science to provide new and deeper understandings. But to what extent have they met with success and to what extent have they left out crucial elements of their subjects? Can science—even the best science—have the last word about our experience, especially experience we think of as subjective, personal, and idiosyncratic?

◆◆◆

CHARLES SIEBERT

HAVING CLAIMED DOMINANCE over the planet for centuries, human beings have, by and large, made use of the earth without much consideration for the environmental and social needs of other animals. As a result, the areas in which animals are free to move about without danger from humans have steadily declined both in size and number. Overall, most of the animal kingdom has acquiesced without substantial resistance. But what happens when an animal community responds to the destruction of its natural habitat by turning against people, other species, and themselves? Charles Siebert addresses these questions in "An Elephant Crackup?," an article that first appeared in the *New York Times Magazine*.

An essayist, a novelist, and a poet, Siebert has published numerous articles in the *New York Times Magazine*, the *New Yorker, Harpers*, and other periodicals. He has published four books, *A Man After His Own Heart* (2004), a meditation on the human heart (literally); *Angus: A Novel* (2000), an account of the inner life of a Jack Russell terrier; *Wickerby: An Urban Pastoral* (1998), which explores the fluid relationship between the urban and the rural worlds; and *The Wauchula Woods Accord: Toward a New Understanding of Animals* (2009).

"An Elephant Crackup?" is a further example of the sympathy for the emotional lives of animals that Siebert first explored in *Angus*. Here, he conducts research across Africa, India, and parts of southeastern Asia on the new phenomenon called "human–elephant conflict," which has resulted in hundreds of human deaths since the year 2000. This is especially troubling, Siebert feels, because elephants possess "a highly developed sensibility" and "a deep-rooted sense of family" that is nowhere in evidence during these violent rampages. Drawing on research into the fabric of animal society and the similarities between the emotional brains of elephants and the emotional brains of humans, Siebert weaves a compelling narrative of conflict between a species that once enjoyed dominance over its territory and the species that has the upper hand now.

If "An Elephant Crackup?" explores the surprisingly "human" psychology of elephants in distress, *The Wauchula Woods Accord* suggests that we feel ambivalence toward animals because we fear the animal in ourselves. As Siebert told an interviewer in 2009, "The more we begin to see and understand ourselves as one more extension of the greater biological forces that created and control

Lisa G. Brown, "An Interview with Author Charles Siebert about his new book, The Wauchula Woods Accord," *Animal Inventory Blog*, June 22, 2009.

all life on earth, rather than as beings apart [from other species, or as] entities anointed by some higher authority, the more the 'inter-species empathy' I speak of … will be allowed to flourish."

An Elephant Crackup?

"We're not going anywhere," my driver, Nelson Okello, whispered to me one morning this past June, the two of us sitting in the front seat of a jeep just after dawn in Queen Elizabeth National Park in southwestern Uganda. We'd origi-nally stopped to observe what appeared to be a lone bull elephant grazing in a patch of tall savanna grasses off to our left. More than one "rogue" crossed our path that morning—a young male elephant that has made an overly strong power play against the dominant male of his herd and been banished, sometimes permanently. This elephant, however, soon proved to be not a rogue but part of a cast of at least thirty. The ground vibrations registered just before the emer-gence of the herd from the surrounding trees and brush. We sat there watching the elephants cross the road before us, seeming, for all their heft, so light on their feet, soundlessly playing the wind-swept savanna grasses like land whales adrift above the floor of an ancient, waterless sea.

Then, from behind a thicket of acacia trees directly off our front left bum-per, a huge female emerged—"the matriarch," Okello said softly. There was a small calf beneath her, freely foraging and knocking about within the secure cribbing of four massive legs. Acacia leaves are an elephant's favorite food, and as the calf set to work on some low branches, the matriarch stood guard, her vast back flank blocking the road, the rest of the herd milling about in the brush a short distance away.

After fifteen minutes or so, Okello started inching the jeep forward, revving the engine, trying to make us sound as beastly as possible. The matriarch, how-ever, was having none of it, holding her ground, the fierce white of her eyes as bright as that of her tusks. Although I pretty much knew the answer, I asked Okello if he was considering trying to drive around. "No," he said, raising an index finger for emphasis. "She'll charge. We should stay right here."

I'd have considered it a wise policy even at a more peaceable juncture in the course of human-elephant relations. In recent years, however, those relations have become markedly more bellicose. Just two days before I arrived, a woman was killed by an elephant in Kazinga, a fishing village nearby. Two months ear-lier, a man was fatally gored by a young male elephant at the northern edge of the park, near the village of Katwe. African elephants use their long tusks to forage through dense jungle brush. They've also been known to wield them, however, with the ceremonious flash and precision of gladiators, pinning down a victim with one knee in order to deliver the decisive thrust. Okello told me that a young Indian tourist was killed in this fashion two years ago in Murchison Falls National Park, just north of where we were.

These were not isolated incidents. All across Africa, India, and parts of Southeast Asia, from within and around whatever patches and corridors of their natural habitat remain, elephants have been striking out, destroying villages and crops, attacking and killing human beings. In fact, these attacks have become so commonplace that a whole new statistical category, known as Human-Elephant Conflict, or HEC, was created by elephant researchers in the mid-1990s to monitor the problem. In the Indian state Jharkhand near the western border of Bangladesh, 300 people were killed by elephants between 2000 and 2004. In the past twelve years, elephants have killed 605 people in Assam, a state in northeastern India, 239 of them since 2001; 265 elephants have died in that same period, the majority of them as a result of retaliation by angry villagers, who have used everything from poison-tipped arrows to laced food to exact their revenge. In Africa, reports of human-elephant conflicts appear almost daily, from Zambia to Tanzania, from Uganda to Sierra Leone, where 300 villagers evacuated their homes last year because of unprovoked elephant attacks.

Still, it is not only the increasing number of these incidents that is causing alarm but also the singular perversity—for want of a less anthropocentric term—of recent elephant aggression. Since the early 1990s, for example, young male elephants in Pilanesberg National Park and the Hluhluwe-Umfolozi Game Reserve in South Africa have been raping and killing rhinoceroses; this abnormal behavior, according to a 2001 study in the journal *Pachyderm*, has been reported in "a number of reserves" in the region. In July of last year, officials in Pilanesberg shot three young male elephants who were responsible for the killings of sixty-three rhinos, as well as attacks on people in safari vehicles. In Addo Elephant National Park, also in South Africa, up to ninety percent of male elephant deaths are now attributable to other male elephants, compared with a rate of six percent in more stable elephant communities.

In a coming book on this phenomenon, Gay Bradshaw, a psychologist at the environmental sciences program at Oregon State University, notes that in India, where the elephant has long been regarded as a deity, a recent headline in a leading newspaper warned, "To Avoid Confrontation, Don't Worship Elephants." "Everybody pretty much agrees that the relationship between elephants and people has dramatically changed," Bradshaw told me recently. "What we are seeing today is extraordinary. Where for centuries humans and elephants lived in relative peaceful coexistence, there is now hostility and violence. Now, I use the term 'violence' because of the intentionality associated with it, both in the aggression of humans and, at times, the recently observed behavior of elephants."

For a number of biologists and ethologists who have spent their careers studying elephant behavior, the attacks have become so abnormal in both number and kind that they can no longer be attributed entirely to the customary factors. Typically, elephant researchers have cited, as a cause of aggression, the high levels of testosterone in newly matured male elephants or the competition for land and resources between elephants and humans. But in "Elephant Breakdown," a 2005 essay in the journal *Nature*, Bradshaw and several colleagues argued that today's elephant populations are suffering from a form of chronic stress, a kind of species-wide trauma. Decades of poaching and culling and habitat loss, they claim, have so disrupted the intricate web of familial and societal relations by which young elephants have traditionally been raised in the wild, and by which established elephant herds are governed, that what we are now witnessing is nothing less than a precipitous collapse of elephant culture.

It has long been apparent that every large, land-based animal on this planet is ultimately fighting a losing battle with humankind. And yet entirely befitting of an animal with such a highly developed sensibility, a deep-rooted sense of family and, yes, such a good long-term memory, the elephant is not going out quietly. It is not leaving without making some kind of statement, one to which scientists from a variety of disciplines, including human psychology, are now beginning to pay close attention.

Once the matriarch and her calf were a comfortable distance from us that morning, Okello and I made the twenty-minute drive to Kyambura, a village at the far southeastern edge of the park. Back in 2003, Kyambura was reportedly the site of the very sort of sudden, unprovoked elephant attack I'd been hearing about. According to an account of the event in the magazine *New Scientist*, a number of huts and fields were trampled, and the townspeople were afraid to venture out to surrounding villages, either by foot or on their bikes, because elephants were regularly blocking the road and charging out at those who tried to pass.

Park officials from the Uganda Wildlife Authority with whom I tried to discuss the incident were reluctant to talk about it or any of the recent killings by elephants in the area. Ecotourism is one of Uganda's major sources of income, and the elephant and other wildlife stocks of Queen Elizabeth National Park are only just now beginning to recover from years of virtually unchecked poaching and habitat destruction. Tom Okello, the chief game warden at the park (and no relation to my driver), and Margaret Driciru, Queen Elizabeth's chief veterinarian, each told me that they weren't aware of the attack in Kyambura. When I mentioned it to the executive director of the wildlife authority, Moses Mapesa, upon my initial arrival in the capital city, Kampala, he eventually admitted that it did happen, but he claimed that it was not nearly as recent as reported. "That was fourteen years ago," he said. "We have seen aggressive behavior from elephants, but that's a story of the past."

Kyambura did look, upon our arrival, much like every other small Ugandan farming community I'd passed through on my visit. Lush fields of banana trees, millet, and maize framed a small town center of pastel-colored, single-story cement buildings with corrugated-tin roofs. People sat on stoops out front in the available shade. Bicyclers bore preposterously outsize loads of bananas, firewood, and five-gallon water jugs on their fenders and handlebars. Contrary to what I had read, the bicycle traffic along the road in and out of Kyambura didn't seem impaired in the slightest.

But when Okello and I asked a shopkeeper named Ibrah Byamukama about elephant attacks, he immediately nodded and pointed to a patch of maize and millet fields just up the road, along the edges of the surrounding Maramagambo Forest. He confirmed that a small group of elephants charged out one morning two years earlier, trampled the fields and nearby gardens, knocked down a few huts, and then left. He then pointed to a long orange gash in the earth between the planted fields and the forest: a fifteen-foot-deep, twenty-five-foot-wide trench that had been dug by the wildlife authority around the perimeter of Kyambura in an attempt to keep the elephants at bay. On the way out of town, Okello and I took a closer look at the trench. It was filled with stacks of thorny shrubs for good measure.

"The people are still worried," Byamukama said, shaking his head. "The elephants are just becoming more destructive. I don't know why."

Three years ago, Gay Bradshaw, then working on her graduate degree in psychology at the Pacifica Graduate Institute outside Santa Barbara, California, began wondering much the same thing: was the extraordinary behavior of elephants in Africa and Asia signaling a breaking point? With the assistance of several established African-elephant researchers, including Daphne Sheldrick and Cynthia Moss, and with the help of Allan Schore, an expert on human trauma disorders at the department of psychiatry and biobehavioral sciences at UCLA, Bradshaw sought to combine traditional research into elephant behavior with insights about trauma drawn from human neuroscience. Using the few remaining relatively stable elephant herds in places like Amboseli National Park in Kenya as control groups, Bradshaw and her colleagues analyzed the far more fractious populations found in places like Pilanesberg in South Africa and Queen Elizabeth National Park in Uganda. What emerged was a portrait of pervasive pachyderm dysfunction.

Elephants, when left to their own devices, are profoundly social creatures. A herd of them is, in essence, one incomprehensibly massive elephant: a somewhat loosely bound and yet intricately interconnected, tensile organism. Young elephants are raised within an extended, multitiered network of doting female caregivers that includes the birth mother, grandmothers, aunts, and friends. These relations are maintained over a life span as long as seventy years. Studies of established herds have shown that young elephants stay within fifteen feet of their mothers for nearly all of their first eight years of life, after which young females are socialized into the matriarchal network, while young males go off for a time into an all-male social group before coming back into the fold as mature adults.

When an elephant dies, its family members engage in intense mourning and burial rituals, conducting weeklong vigils over the body, carefully covering it with earth and brush, revisiting the bones for years afterward, caressing the bones with their trunks, often taking turns rubbing their trunks along the teeth of a skull's lower jaw, the way living elephants do in greeting. If harm comes to a member of an elephant group, all the other elephants are aware of it. This sense of cohesion is further enforced by the elaborate communication system that elephants use. In close proximity they employ a range of vocalizations, from low-frequency rumbles to higher-pitched screams and trumpets, along with a variety of visual signals, from the waving of their trunks to subtle anglings of the head, body, feet, and tail. When communicating over long distances—in order to pass along, for example, news about imminent threats, a sudden change of plans or, of the utmost importance to elephants, the death of a community member—they use patterns of subsonic vibrations that are felt as far as several miles away by exquisitely tuned sensors in the padding of their feet.

This fabric of elephant society, Bradshaw and her colleagues concluded, had effectively been frayed by years of habitat loss and poaching, along with systematic culling by government agencies to control elephant numbers and translocations of herds to different habitats. The number of older matriarchs and female caregivers (or "allomothers") had drastically fallen, as had the number of elder bulls, who play a significant role in keeping younger males in line. In parts of Zambia and Tanzania, a number of the elephant groups studied contained no adult females whatsoever. In Uganda, herds were often found to be "semipermanent aggregations," as a paper written by Bradshaw describes them, with many females between the ages of fifteen and twenty-five having no familial associations.

As a result of such social upheaval, calves are now being born to and raised by ever younger and inexperienced mothers. Young orphaned elephants, meanwhile, that have witnessed the death of a parent at the hands of poachers are coming of age in the absence of the support system that defines traditional elephant life. "The loss of elephants' elders," Bradshaw told me, "and the traumatic experience of witnessing the massacres of their family, impairs normal brain and behavior development in young elephants."

What Bradshaw and her colleagues describe would seem to be an extreme form of anthropocentric conjecture if the evidence that they've compiled from various elephant researchers, even on the strictly observational level, wasn't so compelling. The elephants of decimated herds, especially orphans who've watched the death of their parents and elders from poaching and culling, exhibit behavior typically associated with post-traumatic stress disorder and other trauma-related disorders in humans: abnormal startle response, unpredictable asocial behavior, inattentive mothering, and hyperaggression. Studies of the various assaults on the rhinos in South Africa, meanwhile, have determined that the perpetrators were in all cases adolescent males that had witnessed their families being shot down in cullings. It was common for these elephants to have been tethered to the bodies of their dead and dying relatives until they could be rounded up for translocation to, as Bradshaw and Schore describe them, "locales lacking traditional social hierarchy of older bulls and intact natal family structures."

In fact, even the relatively few attempts that park officials have made to restore parts of the social fabric of elephant society have lent substance to the elephant-breakdown theory. When South African park rangers recently introduced a number of older bull elephants into several destabilized elephant herds in Pilanesburg and Addo, the wayward behavior—including unusually premature hormonal changes among the adolescent elephants—abated.

But according to Bradshaw and her colleagues, the various pieces of the elephant-trauma puzzle really come together at the level of neuroscience, or what might be called the physiology of psychology, by which scientists can now map the marred neuronal fields, snapped synaptic bridges, and crooked chemical streams of an embattled psyche. Though most scientific knowledge of trauma is still understood through research on human subjects, neural studies of elephants are now under way. (The first functional MRI scan of an elephant brain, taken this year, revealed, perhaps not surprisingly, a huge hippocampus, a seat of memory in the mammalian brain, as well as a prominent structure in the limbic system, which processes emotions.) Allan Schore, the UCLA psychologist and neuroscientist who for the past fifteen years has focused his research on early human brain development and the negative impact of trauma on it, recently wrote two articles with Bradshaw on the stress-related neurobiological underpinnings of current abnormal elephant behavior.

"We know that these mechanisms cut across species," Schore told me. "In the first years of humans as well as elephants, development of the emotional brain is impacted by these attachment mechanisms, by the interaction that the infant has with the primary caregiver, especially the mother. When these early experiences go in a positive way, it leads to greater resilience in things like affect regulation, stress regulation, social communication, and empathy. But when these early experiences go awry in cases of abuse and neglect, there is a literal thinning down of the essential circuits in the brain, especially in the emotion-processing areas."

For Bradshaw, these continuities between human and elephant brains resonate far outside the field of neuroscience. "Elephants are suffering and behaving in the same ways that we recognize in ourselves as a result of violence," she told me. "Elephant behavior is entirely congruent with what we know about humans and other mammals. Except perhaps for a few specific features, brain organization and early development of elephants and humans are extremely similar. That's not news. What is news is when you start asking, What does this mean beyond the science? How do we respond to the fact that we are causing other species like elephants to psychologically break down? In a way, it's not so much a cognitive or imaginative leap anymore as it is a political one."

Eve Abe says that in her mind, she made that leap before she ever left her mother's womb. An animal ethologist and wildlife-management consultant now based in London, Abe (pronounced AH-bay) grew up in northern Uganda. After several years of studying elephants in Queen Elizabeth National Park, where decades of poaching had drastically reduced the herds, Abe received her doctorate at Cambridge University in 1994 for work detailing the parallels she saw between the plight of Uganda's orphaned male elephants and the young male orphans of her own people, the Acholi, whose families and villages have been decimated by years of civil war. It's work she proudly proclaims to be not only "the ultimate act of anthropomorphism" but also what she was destined to do.

"My very first encounter with an elephant was a fetal one," Abe told me in June in London as the two of us sipped tea at a cafe in Paddington Station. I was given Abe's contact numbers earlier in the spring by Bradshaw, who is currently working with Abe to build a community center in Uganda to help both elephants and humans in their recovery from violence. For more than a month before my departure from New York, I had been trying without luck to arrange with the British Home Office for Abe, who is still waiting for permanent residence status in England, to travel with me to Uganda as my guide through Queen Elizabeth National Park without fear of her being denied re-entry to England. She was to accompany me that day right up to the departure gate at Heathrow, the two of us hoping (in vain, as it turned out) for a last-minute call that would have given her leave to use the ticket I was holding for her in my bag.

"My dad was a conservationist and a teacher," explained Abe, a tall, elegant woman with a trilling, nearly girlish voice. "He was always out in the parks. One of my aunts tells this story about us passing through Murchison Park one day. My dad was driving. My uncle was in the front seat. In the back were my aunt and my mom, who was very pregnant with me. They suddenly came upon this huge herd of elephants on the road, and the elephants just stopped. So my dad stopped. He knew about animals. The elephants just stood there, then they started walking around the car, and looking into the car. Finally, they walked off. But my father didn't start the car then. He waited there. After an hour or more, a huge female came back out onto the road, right in front of the car. It reared up and trumpeted so loudly, then followed the rest of the herd back into the bush. A few days later, when my mom got home, I was born."

Abe began her studies in Queen Elizabeth National Park in 1982, as an undergraduate at Makerere University in Kampala, shortly after she and her family, who'd been living for years as refugees in Kenya to escape the brutal violence in Uganda under the dictatorship of Idi Amin, returned home in the wake of Amin's ouster in 1979. Abe told me that when she first arrived at the park, there were fewer than 150 elephants remaining from an original population of nearly 4,000. The bulk of the decimation occurred during the war with Tanzania that led to Amin's overthrow: soldiers from both armies grabbed all the ivory they could get their hands on—and did so with such cravenness that the word "poaching" seems woefully inadequate. "Normally when you say 'poaching,'" Abe said, "you think of people shooting one or two and going off. But this was war. They'd just throw hand grenades at the elephants, bring whole families down, and cut out the ivory. I call that mass destruction."

The last elephant survivors of Queen Elizabeth National Park, Abe said, never left one another's side. They kept in a tight bunch, moving as one. Only one elderly female remained; Abe estimated her to be at least sixty-two. It was this matriarch who first gathered the survivors together from their various hideouts on the park's forested fringes and then led them back out as one group into open savanna. Until her death in the early 90s, the old female held the group together, the population all the while slowly beginning to rebound. In her yet-to-be-completed memoir, *My Elephants and My People,* Abe writes of the prominence of the matriarch in Acholi society; she named the park's matriarchal elephant savior Lady Irene, after her own mother. "It took that core group of survivors in the park about five or six years," Abe told me, "before I started seeing whole new family units emerge and begin to split off and go their own way."

In 1986, Abe's family was forced to flee the country again. Violence against Uganda's people and elephants never completely abated after Amin's regime collapsed, and it drastically worsened in the course of the full-fledged war that developed between government forces and the rebel Lord's Resistance Army. For years, that army's leader, Joseph Kony, routinely "recruited" from Acholi villages, killing the parents of young males before their eyes, or sometimes having them do the killings themselves, before pressing them into service as child soldiers. The Lord's Resistance Army has by now been largely defeated, but Kony, who is wanted by the International Criminal Court for numerous crimes against humanity, has hidden with what remains of his army in the mountains of Murchison Falls National Park, and more recently in Garamba National Park in northern Congo, where poaching by the Lord's Resistance Army has continued to orphan more elephants.

"I started looking again at what has happened among the Acholi and the elephants," Abe told me. "I saw that it is an absolute coincidence between the two. You know we used to have villages. We still don't have villages. There are over 200 displaced people's camps in present-day northern Uganda. Everybody lives now within these camps, and there are no more elders. The elders were systematically eliminated. The first batch of elimination was during Amin's time, and that set the stage for the later destruction of northern Uganda. We are among the lucky few, because my mom and dad managed to escape. But the families there are just broken. I know many of them. Displaced people are living in our home now. My mother said let them have it. All these kids who have grown up with their parents killed—no fathers, no mothers, only children looking after them. They don't go to schools. They have no schools, no hospitals. No infrastructure. They form these roaming, violent, destructive bands. It's the same thing that happens with the elephants. Just like the male war orphans, they are wild, completely lost."

On the ride from Paddington that afternoon out to Heathrow, where I would catch a flight to Uganda, Abe told me that the parallel between the plight of Ugandans and their elephants was in many ways too close for her to see at first. It was only after she moved to London that she had what was, in a sense, her first full, adult recognition of the entwinement between human and elephant that she says she long ago felt in her mother's womb.

"I remember when I first was working on my doctorate," she said. "I mentioned that I was doing this parallel once to a prominent scientist in Kenya. He looked amazed. He said, 'How come nobody has made this connection before?' I told him because it hadn't happened this way to anyone else's tribe before. To me it's something I see so clearly. Most people are scared of showing that kind of anthropomorphism. But coming from me it doesn't sound like I'm inventing something. It's there. People know it's there. Some might think that the way I describe the elephant attacks makes the animals look like people. But people are animals."

Shortly after my return from Uganda, I went to visit the Elephant Sanctuary in Tennessee, a 2,700-acre rehabilitation center and retirement facility situated in the state's verdant, low-rolling southern hill country. The sanctuary is a kind of asylum for some of the more emotionally and psychologically disturbed former zoo and circus elephants in the United States—cases so bad that the people who profited from them were eager to let them go. Given that elephants in the wild are now exhibiting aberrant behaviors that were long observed in captive elephants, it perhaps follows that a positive working model for how to ameliorate the effects of elephant breakdown can be found in captivity.

Of the nineteen current residents of the sanctuary, perhaps the biggest hard-luck story was that of a forty-year-old, five-ton Asian elephant named Misty. Originally captured as a calf in India in 1966, Misty spent her first decade in captivity with a number of American circuses and finally ended up in the early 80s at a wild-animal attraction known as Lion Country Safari in Irvine, California. It was there, on the afternoon of July 25, 1983, that Misty, one of four performing elephants at Lion Country Safari that summer, somehow managed to break free of her chains and began madly dashing about the park, looking to make an escape. When one of the park's zoologists tried to corner and contain her, Misty killed him with one swipe of her trunk.

There are, in the long, checkered history of human-elephant relations, countless stories of lethal elephantine assaults, and almost invariably of some gruesomely outsize, animalistic form of retribution exacted by us. It was in the very state of Tennessee, back in September 1916, that another five-ton Asian circus elephant, Mary, was impounded by a local sheriff for the killing of a young hotel janitor who'd been hired to mind Mary during a stopover in the northeast Tennessee town of Kingsport. The janitor had apparently taken Mary for a swim at a local pond, where, according to witnesses, he poked her behind the left ear with a metal hook just as she was reaching for a piece of floating watermelon rind. Enraged, Mary turned, swiftly snatched him up with her trunk, dashed him against a refreshment stand, and then smashed his head with her foot.

With cries from the townspeople to "Kill the elephant!" and threats from nearby town leaders to bar the circus if "Murderous Mary," as newspapers quickly dubbed her, remained a part of the show, the circus's owner, Charlie Sparks, knew he had to do something to appease the public's blood lust and save his business. Among the penalties he is said to have contemplated was electrocution, a ghastly precedent for which had been set thirteen years earlier, on the grounds of the nearly completed Luna Park in Coney Island. A longtime circus elephant named Topsy, who'd killed three trainers in as many years—the last one after he tried to feed her a lighted cigarette—would become the largest and most prominent victim of Thomas Edison, the father of direct-current electricity, who had publicly electrocuted a number of animals at that time using his rival George Westinghouse's alternating current, in hopes of discrediting it as being too dangerous.

Sparks ultimately decided to have Mary hanged and shipped her by train to the nearby town of Erwin, Tennessee, where more than 2,500 people gathered at the local rail yard for her execution. Dozens of children are said to have run off screaming in terror when the chain that was suspended from a huge industrial crane snapped, leaving Mary writhing on the ground with a broken hip. A local rail worker promptly clambered up Mary's bulk and secured a heavier chain for a second, successful hoisting.

Misty's fate in the early 80s, by contrast, seems a triumph of modern humanism. Banished, after the Lion Safari killing, to the Hawthorn Corporation, a company in Illinois that trains and leases elephants and tigers to circuses, she would continue to lash out at a number of her trainers over the years. But when Hawthorn was convicted of numerous violations of the Animal Welfare Act in 2003, the company agreed to relinquish custody of Misty to the Elephant Sanctuary. She was loaded onto a trailer transport on the morning of November 17, 2004, and even then managed to get away with one final shot at the last in her long line of captors.

"The details are kind of sketchy," Carol Buckley, a founder of the Elephant Sanctuary, said to me one afternoon in July, the two of us pulling up on her all-terrain four-wheeler to a large grassy enclosure where an extremely docile and contented-looking Misty, trunk high, ears flapping, waited to greet us. "Hawthorn's owner was trying to get her to stretch out so he could remove her leg chains before loading her on the trailer. At one point he prodded her with a bull hook, and she just knocked him down with a swipe of her trunk. But we've seen none of that since she's been here. She's as sweet as can be. You'd never know that this elephant killed anybody."

In the course of her nearly two years at the Elephant Sanctuary—much of it spent in quarantine while undergoing daily treatment for tuberculosis—Misty has also been in therapy, as in psychotherapy. Wild-caught elephants often witness as young calves the slaughter of their parents, just about the only way, shy of a far more costly tranquilization procedure, to wrest a calf from elephant parents, especially the mothers. The young captives are then dispatched to a foreign environment to work either as performers or laborers, all the while being kept in relative confinement and isolation, a kind of living death for an animal as socially developed and dependent as we now know elephants to be.

And yet just as we now understand that elephants hurt like us, we're learning that they can heal like us as well. Indeed, Misty has become a testament to the Elephant Sanctuary's signature "passive control" system, a therapy tailored in many ways along the lines of those used to treat human sufferers of posttraumatic stress disorder. Passive control, as a sanctuary newsletter describes it, depends upon "knowledge of how elephants process information and respond to stress" as well as specific knowledge of each elephant's past response to stress. Under this so-called nondominance system, there is no discipline, retaliation, or withholding of food, water, and treats, which are all common tactics of elephant trainers. Great pains are taken, meanwhile, to afford the elephants both a sense of safety and freedom of choice—two mainstays of human trauma therapy—as well as continual social interaction.

Upon her arrival at the Elephant Sanctuary, Misty seemed to sense straight off the different vibe of her new home. When Scott Blais of the sanctuary went to free Misty's still-chained leg a mere day after she'd arrived, she stood peaceably by, practically offering her leg up to him. Over her many months of quarantine, meanwhile, with only humans acting as a kind of surrogate elephant family, she has consistently gone through the daily rigors of her tuberculosis treatments—involving two caregivers, a team of veterinarians, and the use of a restraining chute in which harnesses are secured about her chest and tail—without any coaxing or pressure. "We'll shower her with praise in the barn afterwards," Buckley told me as Misty stood by, chomping on a mouthful of hay, "and she actually purrs with pleasure. The whole barn vibrates."

Of course, Misty's road to recovery—when viewed in light of her history and that of all the other captive elephants, past and present—is as harrowing as it is heartening. She and the others have suffered, we now understand, not simply because of us, but because they are, by and large, us. If as recently as the end of the Vietnam War people were still balking at the idea that a soldier, for example, could be physically disabled by a psychological harm—the idea, in other words, that the mind is not an entity apart from the body and therefore just as woundable as any limb—we now find ourselves having to make an equally profound and, for many, even more difficult leap: that a fellow creature as ostensibly unlike us in every way as an elephant is as precisely and intricately woundable as we are. And while such knowledge naturally places an added burden upon us, the keepers, that burden is now being greatly compounded by the fact that sudden violent outbursts like Misty's can no longer be dismissed as the inevitable isolated revolts of a restless few against the constraints and abuses of captivity.

They have no future without us. The question we are now forced to grapple with is whether we would mind a future without them, among the more mindful creatures on this earth and, in many ways, the most devoted. Indeed, the manner of the elephants' continued keeping, their restoration and conservation, both in civil confines and what's left of wild ones, is now drawing the attention of everyone from naturalists to neuroscientists. Too much about elephants, in the end—their desires and devotions, their vulnerability and tremendous resilience—reminds us of ourselves to dismiss out of hand this revolt they're currently staging against their own dismissal. And while our concern may ultimately be rooted in that most human of impulses—the preservation of our own self-image—the great paradox about this particular moment in our history with elephants is that saving them will require finally getting past ourselves; it will demand the ultimate act of deep, interspecies empathy.

On a more immediate, practical level, as Gay Bradshaw sees it, this involves taking what has been learned about elephant society, psychology, and emotion and inculcating that knowledge into the conservation schemes of researchers and park rangers. This includes doing things like expanding elephant habitat to what it used to be historically and avoiding the use of culling and translocations as conservation tools. "If we want elephants around," Bradshaw told me, "then what we need to do is simple: learn how to live with elephants. In other words, in addition to conservation, we need to educate people how to live with wild animals like humans used to do, and to create conditions whereby people can live on their land and live with elephants without it being this life-and-death situation."

The other part of our newly emerging compact with elephants, however, is far more difficult to codify. It requires nothing less than a fundamental shift in the way we look at animals and, by extension, ourselves. It requires what Bradshaw somewhat whimsically refers to as a new "trans-species psyche," a commitment to move beyond an anthropocentric frame of reference and, in effect, be elephants. Two years ago, Bradshaw wrote a paper for the journal *Society and Animals,* focusing on the work of the David Sheldrick Wildlife Trust in Kenya, a sanctuary for orphaned and traumatized wild elephants—more or less the wilderness-based complement to Carol Buckley's trauma therapy at the Elephant Sanctuary in Tennessee. The trust's human caregivers essentially serve as surrogate mothers to young orphan elephants, gradually restoring their psychological and emotional well-being to the point at which they can be reintroduced into existing wild herds. The human "allomothers" stay by their adopted young orphans' sides, even sleeping with them at night in stables. The caregivers make sure, however, to rotate from one elephant to the next so that the orphans grow fond of all the keepers. Otherwise an elephant would form such a strong bond with one keeper that whenever he or she was absent, that elephant would grieve as if over the loss of another family member, often becoming physically ill itself.

To date, the Sheldrick Trust has successfully rehabilitated more than sixty elephants and reintroduced them into wild herds. A number of them have periodically returned to the sanctuary with their own wild-born calves in order to reunite with their human allomothers and to introduce their offspring to what— out on this uncharted frontier of the new "trans-species psyche"—is now being recognized, at least by the elephants, it seems, as a whole new subspecies: the human allograndmother. "Traditionally, nature has served as a source of healing for humans," Bradshaw told me. "Now humans can participate actively in the healing of both themselves and nonhuman animals. The trust and the sanctuary are the beginnings of a mutually benefiting interspecies culture."

On my way back to New York via London, I contacted Felicity de Zulueta, a psychiatrist at Maudsley Hospital in London, who treats victims of extreme trauma, among them former child soldiers from the Lord's Resistance Army. De Zulueta, an acquaintance of Eve Abe's, grew up in Uganda in the early 1960s on the outskirts of Queen Elizabeth National Park, near where her father, a malaria doctor, had set up camp as part of a malaria-eradication program. For a time she had her own elephant, orphaned by poaching, that local villagers had given to her father, who brought it home to the family garage, where it immediately bonded with an orphan antelope and dog already residing there.

"He was doing fine," de Zulueta told me of the pet elephant. "My mother was loving it and feeding it, and then my parents realized, How can we keep this elephant that is going to grow bigger than the garage? So they gave it to who they thought were the experts. They sent him to the Entebbe Zoo, and although they gave him all the right food and everything, he was a lonely little elephant, and he died. He had no attachment."

For de Zulueta, the parallel that Abe draws between the plight of war orphans, human and elephant, is painfully apt, yet also provides some cause for hope, given the often startling capacity of both animals for recovery. She told me that one Ugandan war orphan she is currently treating lost all the members of his family except for two older brothers. Remarkably, one of those brothers, while serving in the Ugandan Army, rescued the younger sibling from the Lord's Resistance Army; the older brother's unit had captured the rebel battalion in which his younger brother had been forced to fight.

The two brothers eventually made their way to London, and for the past two years, the younger brother has been going through a gradual process of recovery in the care of Maudsley Hospital. Much of the rehabilitation, according to de Zulueta, especially in the early stages, relies on the basic human trauma therapy principles now being applied to elephants: providing decent living quarters, establishing a sense of safety and of attachment to a larger community, and allowing freedom of choice. After that have come the more complex treatments tailored to the human brain's particular cognitive capacities: things like reliving the original traumatic experience and being taught to modulate feelings through early detection of hyperarousal and through breathing techniques. And the healing of trauma, as de Zulueta describes it, turns out to have physical correlatives in the brain just as its wounding does.

"What I say is, we find bypass," she explained. "We bypass the wounded areas using various techniques. Some of the wounds are not healable. Their scars remain. But there is hope because the brain is an enormous computer, and you can learn to bypass its wounds by finding different methods of approaching life. Of course there may be moments when something happens and the old wound becomes unbearable. Still, people do recover. The boy I've been telling you about is eighteen now, and he has survived very well in terms of his emotional health and capacities. He's a lovely, lovely man. And he's a poet. He writes beautiful poetry."

On the afternoon in July that I left the Elephant Sanctuary in Tennessee, Carol Buckley and Scott Blais seemed in particularly good spirits. Misty was only weeks away from the end of her quarantine, and she would soon be able to socialize with some of her old cohorts from the Hawthorn Corporation: eight female Asians that had been given over to the sanctuary. I would meet the lot of them that day, driving from one to the next on the back of Buckley's four-wheeler across the sanctuary's savannalike stretches. Buckley and Blais refer to them collectively as the Divas.

Buckley and Blais told me that they got word not long ago of a significant breakthrough in a campaign of theirs to get elephants out of entertainment and zoos: the Bronx Zoo, one of the oldest and most formidable zoos in the country, had announced that upon the death of the zoo's three current elephant inhabitants, Patty, Maxine, and Happy, it would phase out its elephant exhibit on social-behavioral grounds—an acknowledgment of a new awareness of the elephant's very particular sensibility and needs. "They're really taking the lead," Buckley told me. "Zoos don't want to concede the inappropriateness of keeping elephants in such confines. But if we as a society determine that an animal like this suffers in captivity, if the information shows us that they do, hey, we are the stewards. You'd think we'd want to do the right thing."

Four days later, I received an e-mail message from Gay Bradshaw, who consults with Buckley and Blais on their various stress-therapy strategies. She wrote that one of the sanctuary's elephants, an Asian named Winkie, had just killed a thirty-six-year-old female assistant caretaker and critically injured the male caretaker who'd tried to save her.

People who work with animals on a daily basis can tell you all kinds of stories about their distinct personalities and natures. I'd gotten, in fact, an elaborate breakdown from Buckley and Blais on the various elephants at the sanctuary and their sociopolitical maneuverings within the sanctuary's distinct elephant culture, and I went to my notebook to get a fix again on Winkie. A forty-year-old, 7,600-pound female from Burma, she came to the sanctuary in 2000 from the Henry Vilas Zoo in Madison, Wisconsin, where she had a reputation for lashing out at keepers. When Winkie first arrived at the sanctuary, Buckley told me, she used to jump merely upon being touched and then would wait for a confrontation. But when it never came, she slowly calmed down. "Has never lashed out at primary keepers," my last note on Winkie reads, "but has at secondary ones."

Bradshaw's e-mail message concludes: "A stunning illustration of trauma in elephants. The indelible etching."

I thought back to a moment in Queen Elizabeth National Park this past June. As Nelson Okello and I sat waiting for the matriarch and her calf to pass, he mentioned to me an odd little detail about the killing two months earlier of the man from the village of Katwe, something that, the more I thought about it, seemed to capture this particularly fraught moment we've arrived at with the elephants. Okello said that after the man's killing, the elephant herd buried him as it would one of its own, carefully covering the body with earth and brush and then standing vigil over it.

Even as we're forcing them out, it seems, the elephants are going out of their way to put us, the keepers, in an ever more discomfiting place, challenging us to preserve someplace for them, the ones who in many ways seem to regard the matter of life and death more devoutly than we. In fact, elephant culture could be considered the precursor of our own, the first permanent human settlements having sprung up around the desire of wandering tribes to stay by the graves of their dead. "The city of the dead," as Lewis Mumford once wrote, "antedates the city of the living."

When a group of villagers from Katwe went out to reclaim the man's body for his family's funeral rites, the elephants refused to budge. Human remains, a number of researchers have observed, are the only other ones that elephants will treat as they do their own. In the end, the villagers resorted to a tactic that has long been etched in the elephant's collective memory, firing volleys of gunfire into the air at close range, finally scaring the mourning herd away.

QUESTIONS FOR MAKING CONNECTIONS
WITHIN THE READING

1. What evidence does Siebert provide to support the claim there is such a thing as an "elephant culture"? In making this claim, is Siebert guilty of anthropomorphism? That is, does he ascribe to animals the thoughts and emotions that only humans have? Or is he guilty of the opposite mistake,

the error of anthropocentrism—treating human beings as the standard by which all other species should be measured? Is it possible that these "mistakes" are really not mistakes at all, especially because we *Homo sapiens* are in fact animals, too? Would you agree that understanding other minds—human or otherwise—requires us to start with what we know about own mental processes? Can we even prove that our fellow human beings have thoughts and emotions like our own?

2. As Siebert's discussion unfolds, he describes elephants who experience acute trauma and then become deliberately aggressive. He also shows that they respond to psychotherapies that were initially developed to assist human beings. Do you find these developments surprising? Is Siebert seeking to establish that humans and elephants are part of a continuum? Does he mean to imply that the minds of the two species are identical? Or does he see them on parallel paths?

3. Siebert's essay ends with two acts of violence: a caretaker killed by an elephant in captivity, and a villager killed and buried by an elephant herd. Why does he structure the piece in this way? Since he also began by describing violence, has Siebert come full circle? Or has he put his readers in a better position to understand the violence?

QUESTIONS FOR WRITING

1. Throughout "An Elephant Crackup?" Siebert gestures towards modes of consciousness that differ significantly from the model of an individual thinking. He describes a herd of elephants as "in essence, one incomprehensibly massive elephant." He observes that saving elephants from extinction "will demand the ultimate act of deep, interspecies empathy." And he cites Gay Bradshaw's call for the development of a "trans-species psyche" that will allow humans to "be elephants." How would one go about creating these new modes of consciousness? Does Siebert's narrative provide any hints about how the two species might begin to share the same conceptual world?

2. Siebert notes that those who are concerned with the effects of trauma on the elephant population are now focusing on the "physiology of psychology"—that is, on the neurological foundation for psychological development. Based on the preliminary results of these studies, would you say that the turn to neurology provides cause for optimism about the possibilities of overcoming trauma? Or does the fact that trauma during the formative years results in "a literal thinning down of the essential circuits in the brain" mean that there's no saving young victims of trauma, be they elephant or human?

QUESTIONS FOR MAKING CONNECTIONS
BETWEEN READINGS

1. In Selections from *Love 2.0*, Barbara Fredrickson describes the way our brains operate below the level of consciousness to produce our conscious experience of resonating with others. In what ways does Fredrickson's account complicate our tendency to think about the mental life of *Homo sapiens* as fundamentally different from the mental lives of animals like the elephants whose decline Siebert chronicles? Does Fredrickson's account of our emotions justify Gay Bradshaw's willingness to violate the rule in animal studies against anthropomorphism—against imposing on animal behavior the thoughts and motivations of humans? In view of the possible parallels between displaced humans and the young elephants raised without the guidance of adults, would you agree that our way of life might be doing damage to us?

2. In Selections from *Alone Together*, Sherry Turkle contemplates the ways that contemporary children interact with their Tamagotchis and Furbies. She describes her own experience, as well:

   > My Tamagotchi liked to eat at particular intervals. I thought it prospered best with only small doses of amusement. I worked hard at keeping it happy. I did not anticipate how bad I would feel when it died. I immediately hit the reset button. Somewhat to my surprise, I had no desire to take care of the new infant Tamagotchi that appeared on my screen.

   Will our embrace of technology make us more receptive, or less, to the predicament of the elephants? If we should lose the ability to distinguish between biological life and its simulations, will the extinction of species matter to us at all? Does the belief that a "singularity" that will free our minds from all material constraints express an unacknowledged loathing for our humanity and, perhaps, even for life itself?

ANDREW SOLOMON

WHO ARE YOU—REALLY? What does "me" indicate? We count on our ability to understand ourselves, but what do we know for certain?

Questions about identity lie at the heart of Andrew Solomon's writing. By all accounts, Solomon was raised in a happy home with loving parents. Once he graduated from Yale, he went to Cambridge University, which awarded him the top first-class degree, the only time the honor had ever been bestowed on a foreign student. After Solomon met with such success, happiness should have been his lot in life, but when he was only 25, his mother died from cancer. It would be conventional to say that Solomon "fell into a deep depression," but the malady that overcame him unfolded in such a strange, oblique way that he had no sense of what was happening: "A loss of feeling, a numbness, infected all my human relations. I didn't care about love, my work, family, friends. My writing slowed, then stopped.... I was losing my self and that scared me." This experience of losing himself led to Solomon's third book, *The Noonday Demon: An Atlas of Depression* (2001), which won the National Book Award for Nonfiction and has been translated into 24 languages. The story it tells is quite harrowing, but depression gave Solomon a much deeper sense of what it means to be or to have a self. As he told one interviewer, "It seems to me that who other people are is always mysterious. What I realized in the wake of depression is that who I am is fully mysterious to me."

Solomon's book *Far from the Tree: Parents, Children, and the Search for Identity* (2012), from which the following selection is taken, might be read as an attempt to explore the self in another way, not through the labyrinth of the mind but through our relations to others. As a gay man, Solomon is fascinated by how we each create ourselves, sometimes in ways our parents dislike. Most prospective parents start out convinced their children will embrace the lives mapped out for them, but the unexpected often happens. Solomon's own mother could never accept his sexuality, and his experience of her disapproval brought him closer to other children whose arrival in the world thwarted parental expectations: deaf people, dwarves, those born with Down syndrome, autism,

Biographical details are from Andrew Solomon's site <http://andrewsolomon.com>. Quotation on depression is from Andrew Solomon, *The Noonday Demon: An Atlas of Depression* (New York: Scribner, 2001) 45. Quotation on the self is from "The Soul in Depression," *On Being*, February 26, 2009 <http://www.onbeing.org/program/soul-depression/transcript/1332>.

schizophrenia. Solomon understands that many loving parents want their children to be "normal," but he argues that our differences can teach us all how to think and love more inclusively.

Son

There is no such thing as reproduction. When two people decide to have a baby, they engage in an act of production, and the widespread use of the word *reproduction* for this activity, with its implication that two people are but braiding themselves together, is at best a euphemism to comfort prospective parents before they get in over their heads. In the subconscious fantasies that make conception look so alluring, it is often ourselves that we would like to see live forever, not someone with a personality of his own. Having anticipated the onward march of our selfish genes, many of us are unprepared for children who present unfamiliar needs. Parenthood abruptly catapults us into a permanent relationship with a stranger, and the more alien the stranger, the stronger the whiff of negativity. We depend on the guarantee in our children's faces that we will not die. Children whose defining quality annihilates that fantasy of immortality are a particular insult; we must love them for themselves, and not for the best of ourselves in them, and that is a great deal harder to do. Loving our own children is an exercise for the imagination.

Yet blood, in modern as in ancient societies, is thicker than water. Little is more gratifying than successful and devoted children, and few situations are worse than filial failure or rejection. Our children are not us: they carry throwback genes and recessive traits and are subject right from the start to environmental stimuli beyond our control. And yet we are our children; the reality of being a parent never leaves those who have braved the metamorphosis. The psychoanalyst D. W. Winnicott once said, "There is no such thing as a baby—meaning that if you set out to describe a baby, you will find you are describing a *baby and someone*. A baby cannot exist alone but is essentially part of a relationship." Insofar as our children resemble us, they are our most precious admirers, and insofar as they differ, they can be our most vehement detractors. From the beginning, we tempt them into imitation of us and long for what may be life's most profound compliment: their choosing to live according to our own system of values. Though many of us take pride in how different we are from our parents, we are endlessly sad at how different our children are from us.

Because of the transmission of identity from one generation to the next, most children share at least some traits with their parents. These are *vertical* identities.

Attributes and values are passed down from parent to child across the generations not only through strands of DNA, but also through shared cultural norms. Ethnicity, for example, is a vertical identity. Children of color are in general born to parents of color; the genetic fact of skin pigmentation is transmitted across generations along with a self-image as a person of color, even though that self-image may be subject to generational flux. Language is usually vertical, since most people who speak Greek raise their children to speak Greek, too, even if they inflect it differently or speak another language much of the time. Religion is moderately vertical: Catholic parents will tend to bring up Catholic children, though the children may turn irreligious or convert to another faith. Nationality is vertical, except for immigrants. Blondness and myopia are often transmitted from parent to child, but in most cases do not form a significant basis for identity—blondness because it is fairly insignificant, and myopia because it is easily corrected.

Often, however, someone has an inherent or acquired trait that is foreign to his or her parents and must therefore acquire identity from a peer group. This is a *horizontal* identity. Such horizontal identities may reflect recessive genes, random mutations, prenatal influences, or values and preferences that a child does not share with his progenitors. Being gay is a horizontal identity; most gay kids are born to straight parents, and while their sexuality is not determined by their peers, they learn gay identity by observing and participating in a subculture outside the family. Physical disability tends to be horizontal, as does genius. Psychopathy, too, is often horizontal; most criminals are not raised by mobsters and must invent their own treachery. So are conditions such as autism and intellectual disability. A child conceived in a rape is born into emotional challenges that his own mother cannot know, even though they spring from her trauma.

In 1993, I was assigned to investigate Deaf culture for the *New York Times*. My assumption about deafness was that it was a deficit and nothing more. Over the months that followed, I found myself drawn into the Deaf world. Most deaf children are born to hearing parents, and those parents frequently prioritize functioning in the hearing world, expending enormous energy on oral speech and lipreading. Doing so, they can neglect other areas of their children's education. While some deaf people are good at lipreading and produce comprehensible speech, many do not have that skill, and years go by as they sit endlessly with audiologists and speech pathologists instead of learning history and mathematics and philosophy. Many stumble upon Deaf identity in adolescence, and it comes as a great liberation. They move into a world that validates Sign as a language and discover themselves. Some hearing parents accept this powerful new development; others struggle against it.

The whole situation felt arrestingly familiar to me because I am gay. Gay people usually grow up under the purview of straight parents who feel that their children would be better off straight and sometimes torment them by pressing them to conform. Those gay people often discover gay identity in adolescence or afterward, finding great relief there. When I started writing about the deaf, the cochlear implant, which can provide some facsimile of hearing, was a recent innovation. It had been hailed by its progenitors as a miraculous cure for a terrible defect and was deplored by the Deaf community as a genocidal attack on a vibrant community. Both sides have since moderated their rhetoric, but the issue is complicated by the fact that cochlear implants are most effective when they are surgically implanted early—in infants, ideally—so the decision is often made by parents before the child can possibly have or express an informed opinion. Watching the debate, I knew that my own parents would gamely have consented to a parallel early procedure to ensure that I would be straight, had one existed. I do not doubt that the advent of such a thing even now could wipe out most of gay culture. I am saddened by the idea of such a threat, and yet as my understanding of Deaf culture deepened, I realized that the attitudes I had found benighted in my parents resembled my own likely response to producing a deaf child. My first impulse would have been to do whatever I could to fix the abnormality.

Then a friend had a daughter who was a dwarf. She wondered whether she should bring up her daughter to consider herself just like everyone else, only shorter; whether she should make sure her daughter had dwarf role models; or whether she should investigate surgical limb-lengthening. As she narrated her bafflement, I saw a familiar pattern. I had been startled to note my common ground with the Deaf, and now I was identifying with a dwarf; I wondered who else was out there waiting to join our gladsome throng. I thought that if gayness, an identity, could grow out of homosexuality, an illness, and Deafness, an identity, could grow out of deafness, an illness, and if dwarfism as an identity could emerge from an apparent disability, then there must be many other categories in this awkward interstitial territory. It was a radicalizing insight. Having always imagined myself in a fairly slim minority, I suddenly saw that I was in a vast company. Difference unites us. While each of these experiences can isolate those who are affected, together they compose an aggregate of millions whose struggles connect them profoundly. The exceptional is ubiquitous; to be entirely typical is the rare and lonely state.

As my parents had misapprehended who I was, so other parents must be constantly misapprehending their own children. Many parents experience their child's horizontal identity as an affront. A child's marked difference from the rest of the family demands knowledge, competence, and actions that a typical mother and father are unqualified to supply, at least initially. The child is expressly different from most of his or her peers as well, and therefore broadly less understood or accepted. Abusive fathers visit less abuse on children who resemble them physically; if you are born to a bully, pray that you bear his features. Whereas families tend to reinforce vertical identities from earliest childhood, many will oppose horizontal ones. Vertical identities are usually respected as identities; horizontal ones are often treated as flaws.

One could argue that black people face many disadvantages in the United States today, but there is little research into how gene expression could be altered to make the next generation of children born to black parents come out with straight, flaxen hair and creamy complexions. In modern America, it is sometimes hard to be Asian or Jewish or female, yet no one suggests that Asians,

Jews, or women would be foolish not to become white Christian men if they could. Many vertical identities make people uncomfortable, and yet we do not attempt to homogenize them. The disadvantages of being gay are arguably no greater than those of such vertical identities, but most parents have long sought to turn their gay children straight. Anomalous bodies are usually more frightening to people who witness them than to people who have them, yet parents rush to normalize physical exceptionalism, often at great psychic cost to themselves and their children. Labeling a child's mind as diseased—whether with autism, intellectual disabilities, or transgenderism—may reflect the discomfort that mind gives parents more than any discomfort it causes their child. Much gets corrected that might better have been left alone.

Defective is an adjective that has long been deemed too freighted for liberal discourse, but the medical terms that have supplanted it—*illness, syndrome, condition*—can be almost equally pejorative in their discreet way. We often use *illness* to disparage a way of being, and *identity* to validate that same way of being. This is a false dichotomy. In physics, the Copenhagen interpretation defines energy/matter as behaving sometimes like a wave and sometimes like a particle, which suggests that it is both, and posits that it is our human limitation to be unable to see both at the same time. The Nobel Prize–winning physicist Paul Dirac identified how light appears to be a particle if we ask a particle-like question, and a wave if we ask a wavelike question. A similar duality obtains in this matter of self. Many conditions are both illness and identity, but we can see one only when we obscure the other. Identity politics refutes the idea of illness, while medicine shortchanges identity. Both are diminished by this narrowness.

Physicists gain certain insights from understanding energy as a wave, and other insights from understanding it as a particle, and use quantum mechanics to reconcile the information they have gleaned. Similarly, we have to examine *illness* and *identity,* understand that observation will usually happen in one domain or the other, and come up with a syncretic mechanics. We need a vocabulary in which the two concepts are not opposites, but compatible aspects of a condition. The problem is to change how we assess the value of individuals and of lives, to reach for a more ecumenical take on *healthy.* Ludwig Wittgenstein said, "All I know is what I have words for." The absence of words is the absence of intimacy; these experiences are starved for language.

The children I describe here have horizontal conditions that are alien to their parents. They are deaf or dwarfs; they have Down syndrome, autism, schizophrenia, or multiple severe disabilities; they are prodigies; they are people conceived in rape or who commit crimes; they are transgender. The timeworn adage says that the apple doesn't fall far from the tree, meaning that a child resembles his or her parents; these children are apples that have fallen elsewhere—some a couple of orchards away, some on the other side of the world. Yet myriad families learn to tolerate, accept, and finally celebrate children who are not what they originally had in mind. This transformative process is often eased and sometimes confounded by identity politics and medical progress—both of which have infiltrated households to a degree that would have been inconceivable even twenty years ago.

All offspring are startling to their parents; these most dramatic situations are merely variations on a common theme. Much as we learn the properties of a medication by studying its effect at extremely high doses, or look at the viability of a construction material by exposing it to unearthly supertemperatures, so we can understand the universal phenomenon of difference within families by looking at these extreme cases. Having exceptional children exaggerates parental tendencies; those who would be bad parents become awful parents, but those who would be good parents often become extraordinary. I take the anti-Tolstoyan view that the unhappy families who reject their variant children have much in common, while the happy ones who strive to accept them are happy in a multitude of ways.

Because prospective parents have ever-increasing options to choose against having children with horizontal challenges, the experiences of those who have such children are critical to our larger understanding of difference. Parents' early responses to and interactions with a child determine how that child comes to view himself. These parents are also profoundly changed by their experiences. If you have a child with a disability, you are forever the parent of a disabled child; it is one of the primary facts about you, fundamental to the way other people perceive and decipher you. Such parents tend to view aberrance as illness until habituation and love enable them to cope with their odd new reality—often by introducing the language of identity. Intimacy with difference fosters its accommodation.

Broadcasting these parents' learned happiness is vital to sustaining identities that are now vulnerable to eradication. Their stories point a way for all of us to expand our definitions of the human family. It's important to know how autistic people feel about autism, or dwarfs about dwarfism. Self-acceptance is part of the ideal, but without familial and societal acceptance, it cannot ameliorate the relentless injustices to which many horizontal identity groups are subject and will not bring about adequate reform. We live in xenophobic times, when legislation with majority support abrogates the rights of women, LGBT people, illegal immigrants, and the poor. Despite this crisis in empathy, compassion thrives at home, and most of the parents I have profiled love across the divide. Understanding how they came to think well of their own children may give the rest of us motive and insight to do the same. To look deep into your child's eyes and see in him both yourself and something utterly strange, and then to develop a zealous attachment to every aspect of him, is to achieve parenthood's self-regarding, yet unselfish, abandon. It is astonishing how often such mutuality has been realized—how frequently parents who had supposed that they couldn't care for an exceptional child discover that they can. The parental predisposition to love prevails in the most harrowing of circumstances. There is more imagination in the world than one might think.

I had dyslexia as a child; indeed, I have it now. I still cannot write by hand without focusing on each letter as I form it, and even when I do so, some letters are out of order or omitted. My mother, who identified the dyslexia early, began to work on reading with me when I was two. I spent long afternoons in her lap, learning to sound out words, training like an Olympic athlete in phonetics; we practiced letters as though no shapes could ever be lovelier than theirs. To keep my attention, she gave me a notebook with a yellow felt cover on which Winnie-the-Pooh and Tigger were sewn; we made flash cards and played games with them in the car. I reveled in the attention, and my mother taught with a sense of fun, as though it was the best puzzle in the world, a private game between us. When I was six, my parents applied for my admission to eleven schools in New York City, and all eleven turned me down on grounds that I would never learn to read and write. A year later, I was enrolled in a school where the principal grudgingly allowed my advanced reading skills to overrule test scores that predicted I would never learn to read at all. The standards of perpetual triumph were high in our house, and that early victory over dyslexia was formative: with patience, love, intelligence, and will, we had trounced a neurological abnormality. Unfortunately, it set the stage for our later struggles by making it hard to believe that we couldn't reverse the creeping evidence of another perceived abnormality—my being gay.

People ask when I knew I was gay, and I wonder what that knowledge entails. It took some time for me to become aware of my sexual desires. The realization that what I wanted was exotic, and out of step with the majority, came so early that I cannot remember a time preceding it. Recent studies have shown that as early as age two, male children who will grow up to be gay are averse to certain types of rough-and-tumble play; by age six, most will behave in obviously gender-nonconforming ways. Because I could tell early on that many of my impulses were unmasculine, I embarked on further acts of self-invention. When, in first grade, each of us was asked to name his favorite food and everyone else said ice cream or hamburgers or French toast, I proudly chose *ekmek kadayiff* with *kaymak*, which I used to order at an Armenian restaurant on East Twenty-Seventh Street. I never traded a baseball card, but I did recount the plots of operas on the school bus. None of this made me popular.

I was popular at home, but I was subject to corrections. My mother, my brother, and I were at Indian Walk Shoes when I was seven, and as we were leaving, the salesman asked what color balloons we'd like. My brother wanted a red balloon. I wanted a pink one. My mother countered that I didn't want a pink balloon and reminded me that my favorite color was blue. I said I really wanted the pink, but under her glare, I took the blue one. That my favorite color is blue but I am still gay is evidence of both my mother's influence and its limits. She once said, "When you were little, you didn't like to do what other kids liked to do, and I encouraged you to be yourself." She added, only half-ironically, "I sometimes think I let things go too far." I have sometimes thought she didn't let them go far enough. But her encouragement of my individuality, although doubtless ambivalent, has shaped my life.

My new school had quasi-liberal ideas and was supposed to be integrated—which meant that our class included a few black and Latino kids on scholarship who mostly socialized with one another. My first year there, Debbie Camacho had a birthday party in Harlem, and her parents, unacquainted with the logic of New York private education, scheduled it for the same weekend as homecoming. My mother asked how I would feel if no one attended my birthday party, and insisted that I attend. I doubt many kids in my class would have gone to the party even if there hadn't been such a convenient excuse, but in fact, only two white kids went out of a class of forty. I was frankly terrified of being there. The birthday girl's cousins tried to get me to dance; everyone spoke Spanish; there were unfamiliar fried foods; and I had something of a panic attack and went home in tears.

I drew no parallels between everyone's avoidance of Debbie's party and my own unpopularity, even when, a few months later, Bobby Finkel had a birthday party and invited everyone in the class but me. My mother called his mother on the assumption that there had been a mistake; Mrs. Finkel said that her son didn't like me and didn't want me at his party. My mother picked me up at school on the day of the party and took me to the zoo, and for a hot fudge sundae at Old-Fashioned Mr. Jennings. It's only in retrospect that I imagine how hurt my mother was on my behalf—more hurt than I was, or let myself notice I was. I didn't guess then that her tenderness was a bid to compensate for the insults of the world. When I contemplate my parents' discomfort with my gayness, I can see how vulnerable my vulnerabilities made her, and how much she wanted to preempt my sadness with the assurance that we were our own good time. Forbidding the pink balloon must be held as partly a protective gesture.

I'm glad my mother made me go to Debbie Camacho's birthday party—because I think it was the right thing to do and because, though I couldn't see it at the time, it was the beginning of an attitude of tolerance that allowed me to stomach myself and find happiness in adulthood. It's tempting to paint myself and my family as beacons of liberal exceptionalism, but we weren't. I teased one African-American student in my elementary school by claiming he resembled a picture in our social studies book of a tribal child in an African *rondavel*. I didn't think that this was racist; I thought it was funny, and vaguely true. When I was older, I remembered my behavior with deep regret, and when the person in question found me on Facebook, I apologized profusely. I said that my only excuse was that it was not easy to be gay at the school, and that I'd acted out the prejudice I experienced in the form of prejudice toward others. He accepted my apology, and mentioned that he was also gay; I was humbled that he had survived, where so much of both kinds of bias were in play.

I floundered in the tricky waters of elementary school, but at home, where bias was never tinged with cruelty, my more intractable deficits were minimized and my quirks were mostly humored. When I was ten, I became fascinated by the tiny principality of Liechtenstein. A year later, my father took us along on a business trip to Zürich, and one morning my mother announced that she'd arranged for us all to drive to Liechtenstein's capital, Vaduz. I remember the thrill that the whole family was going along with what was clearly my wish and mine alone. In retrospect, the Liechtenstein preoccupation seems peculiar, but the same mother who forbade the pink balloon thought up and arranged that day: lunch in a charming café, a tour of the art museum, a visit to the printing office where they make the country's distinctive postage stamps. Although I did not always feel approved of, I always felt acknowledged and was given the latitude of my eccentricity. But there were limits, and pink balloons fell on the wrong side of them. Our family rule was to be interested in otherness from within a pact of sameness. I wanted to stop merely observing the wide world and inhabit its wideness: I wanted to dive for pearls, memorize Shakespeare, break the sound barrier, learn to knit. From one angle, the desire to transform myself can be seen as an attempt to unshackle myself from an undesirable way of being. From another, it was a gesture toward my essential self, a crucial pivot toward who I was to become.

Even in kindergarten, I spent recess making conversation with my teachers because other children didn't get it; the teachers probably didn't get it, either, but they were old enough to be polite. By seventh grade, I ate lunch most days in the office of Mrs. Brier, secretary of the head of the lower school. I graduated from high school without visiting the cafeteria, where I would have sat with the girls and been laughed at for doing so, or with the boys and been laughed at for being the kind of boy who should really sit with the girls. The impulse to conformity that so often defines childhood never existed for me, and when I began to think about sexuality, the nonconformity of same-sex desires thrilled me—the realization that what I wanted was even more different and forbidden than all sex is to the young. Homosexuality felt to me like an Armenian dessert or a day in Liechtenstein. I nonetheless thought that if anyone found out I was gay, I would have to die.

My mother didn't want me to be gay because she thought it wouldn't be the happiest course for me, but equally, she didn't like the image of herself as the mother of a gay son. The problem wasn't that she wanted to control *my* life—although she did, like most parents, genuinely believe that her way of being happy was the best way of being happy. The problem was that she wanted to control *her* life, and it was her life as the mother of a homosexual that she wished to alter. Unfortunately, there was no way for her to fix her problem without involving me.

I learned to hate this aspect of my identity profoundly and early because that crouching posture echoed a family response to a vertical identity. My mother thought it was undesirable to be Jewish. She had learned this view from my grandfather, who kept his religion secret so he could hold a high-level job in a company that did not employ Jews. He belonged to a suburban country club where Jews were not welcome. In her early twenties, my mother was briefly engaged to a Texan, but he broke it off when his family threatened to disinherit him if he married a Jew. For her, it was a trauma of self-recognition, because until then she had not thought of herself as a designated Jew; she had thought she could be whomever she appeared to be. Five years later, she chose to marry my Jewish father and live in a largely Jewish world, but she carried the anti-Semitism within her. She would see people who fit certain stereotypes and say, "Those are the people who give us a bad name." When I asked her what she thought of the much sought-after beauty of my ninth-grade class, she said, "She looks very Jewish." Her method of rueful self-doubt was organized for me around being gay: I inherited her gift for discomfort.

Long after childhood, I clung to childish things as a dam against sexuality. This willful immaturity was overlaid with an affected Victorian prudery, aimed not at masking but at obliterating desire. I had some farfetched idea that I would be Christopher Robin forever in the Hundred Acre Wood; indeed, the final chapter of the *Winnie-the-Pooh* books felt so much like my story that I couldn't bear to hear it, though I had my father read me all the other chapters hundreds of times. *The House at Pooh Corner* ends, "Wherever they go, and whatever happens to them on the way, in that enchanted place on top of the Forest, a little boy and his Bear will always be playing." I decided that I would be that boy and that bear, that I would freeze myself in puerility, because what growing up portended for me was too humiliating. At thirteen, I bought a copy of *Playboy* and spent hours studying it, trying to resolve my discomfort with female anatomy; it was much more grueling than my homework. By the time I reached high school, I knew I had to have sex with women sooner or later and felt that I couldn't do so, and thought often about dying. The half of me that wasn't planning to be Christopher Robin playing forever in an enchanted place was planning to be Anna Karenina throwing myself in front of a train. It was a ludicrous duality.

When I was in eighth grade at the Horace Mann School in New York, an older kid nicknamed me Percy as a shorthand for my demeanor. We were on the same school-bus route, and each day when I boarded, he and his cohort would chant, "Percy! Percy! Percy!" I sometimes sat with a Chinese-American student who was too shy to talk to anyone else (and turned out to be gay himself), and sometimes with a nearly blind girl who was also the object of considerable cruelty. Sometimes, everyone on the bus chanted that provocation the entire ride. "Per-cy! Per-cy! Per-cy! Per-cy!" at the top of their lungs for forty-five minutes: all the way up Third Avenue, along the FDR Drive, across the Willis Avenue Bridge, the length of the Major Deegan Expressway, and onto 246th Street in Riverdale. The blind girl kept repeating that I should "just ignore it," and so I sat there pretending unconvincingly that it wasn't happening.

Four months after it began, I came home one day and my mother asked, "Has something been happening on the school bus? Have other students been calling you Percy?" A classmate had told his mother, who in turn had called mine. When I admitted it, she hugged me for a long time, then asked why I hadn't told her. It had never occurred to me: partly because talking about something so degrading seemed only to reify it, partly because I thought there was nothing to be done, and partly because I felt that the qualities for which I was being tortured would be abhorrent to my mother, too, and I wanted to protect her from disappointment.

Thereafter, a chaperone rode on the school bus and the chanting stopped. I was merely called "faggot" on the bus and at school, often within hearing distance of teachers who raised no objections. That same year, my science teacher told us that homosexuals developed fecal incontinence because their anal sphincters were destroyed. Homophobia was ubiquitous in the 1970s, but the smug culture of my school delivered a sharply honed version of it.

In June of 2012, the *New York Times Magazine* published an article by Horace Mann alumnus Amos Kamil about some male faculty members' predatory abuse of boys at the school while I was a student there. The article quoted students who developed addiction issues and other self-destructive behavior in the wake of such episodes; one man had committed suicide in middle age as the culmination of despair that his family traced to the youthful exploitation. The article made me profoundly sad—and confused, because some teachers accused of such acts had been kinder to me than anyone else at my school during a desolate time. My beloved history teacher took me out to dinner, gave me a copy of the Jerusalem Bible, and talked with me during free periods when other students wanted nothing to do with me. The music teacher awarded me concert solos, let me call him by his first name and hang out in his office, and led the glee club trips that were among my happiest adventures. They seemed to recognize who I was and thought well of me anyway. Their implicit acknowledgment of my sexuality helped me not to become an addict or a suicide.

When I was in ninth grade the school's art teacher (who was also a football coach) kept trying to strike up a conversation with me about masturbation. I was paralyzed: I thought it might be a form of entrapment, and that if I responded, he'd tell everyone that I was gay, and I'd be even more of a laughingstock than I already was. No other faculty member ever made a move on me—perhaps because I was a skinny, socially awkward kid with glasses and braces, perhaps because my parents had a reputation for protective vigilance, perhaps because I assumed a self-insulating arrogance that made me less vulnerable than some others.

The art teacher was removed when allegations against him emerged soon after my conversations with him. The history teacher was let go and committed suicide a year later. The music teacher, who was married, survived the ensuing "reign of terror," as one gay faculty member later called it, when many gay teachers were ousted. Kamil wrote to me that the firings of nonpredatory gay teachers grew out of "a misguided attempt to root our pedophilia by falsely equating it with homosexuality." Students spoke monstrously of and even to gay teachers because their prejudice was so obviously endorsed by the school community.

The head of the theater department, Anne MacKay, was a lesbian who quietly survived the recriminations. Twenty years after I graduated, she and I began corresponding by e-mail. I drove to the east end of Long Island to visit her a decade later when I learned she was dying. We had both been contacted by Amos Kamil, who was then researching his article, and had both been unsettled by the allegations he shared. Miss MacKay had been the wise teacher who once explained gently that I was teased because of how I walked, and tried to show me a more confident stride. She staged *The Importance of Being Earnest* my senior year so that I could have a star turn as Algernon. I had come to thank her. But she had invited me to apologize.

At a previous job, she explained, word had got around that she lived with another woman, parents had complained, and she'd gone into a kind of hiding for the rest of her career. Now she regretted the formal distance she'd sustained and felt she had failed the gay students to whom she might have been a beacon—although I knew, and she did, too, that if she'd been more open, she'd have lost her job. When I was her student, I never thought to wonder about greater intimacy than we had, but talking decades later, I realized how forlorn we'd both been. I wish we could have been the same age for a while, because who I am at forty-eight would be a good friend for who she was when she was teaching young me. Off campus, Miss MacKay was a gay activist; now, I am, too. When I was in high school, I knew she was gay; she knew I was gay; yet each of us was imprisoned by our homosexuality in a way that made direct conversation impossible, leaving us with only kindness to give each other instead of truth. Seeing her after so many years stirred up my old loneliness, and I was reminded of how isolating an exceptional identity can be unless we resolve it into horizontal solidarity.

In the unsettling online reunion of Horace Mann alumni that followed the publication of Amos Kamil's story, one man wrote of his sadness for both the abuse victims and the perpetrators, saying of the latter, "They were wounded, confused people trying to figure out how to function in a world that taught them that their homosexual desire was sick. Schools mirror the world we live in. They can't be perfect places. Not every teacher will be an emotionally balanced person. We can condemn these teachers. But this deals with a symptom only, not the original problem, which is that an intolerant society creates self-hating people who act out inappropriately." Sexual contact between teachers and students is unacceptable because it exploits a power differential that clouds the demarcation between coercion and consent. It often causes irrecoverable trauma. It clearly did so for the students Kamil interviewed and described. Wondering how my teachers could have done this, I thought that someone whose core being is deemed a sickness and an illegality may struggle to parse the distinction between that and a much greater crime. Treating an identity as an illness invites real illness to make a braver stand.

Sexual opportunity comes often to young people, especially in New York. One of my chores was to walk our dog before bedtime, and when I was fourteen, I discovered two gay bars near our apartment: Uncle Charlie's Uptown and Camp David. I would walk Martha, our Kerry Blue terrier, on a circuit that included these two emporiums of denimed flesh, watching the guys spill out into Lexington Avenue while Martha tugged gently on the leash. One man who said his name was Dwight followed me and pulled me into a doorway. I couldn't go home with Dwight or the others because if I did, I'd be turned into someone else. I don't remember what Dwight looked like, but his name makes me wistful. When I eventually had sex with a man, at seventeen, I felt that I was severing myself forever from the normal world. I went home and boiled my clothes, then took a scalding, hour-long shower, as though my transgression could be sterilized away.

When I was nineteen, I read an ad in the back of *New York* magazine that offered surrogate therapy for people who had issues with sex. I still believed that the problem of whom I wanted was subsidiary to the problem of whom I didn't want. I knew the back of a magazine was not a good place to find treatment, but my condition was too embarrassing to reveal to anyone who knew me. Taking my savings to a walk-up office in Hell's Kitchen, I subjected myself to long conversations about my sexual anxieties, unable to admit to myself or the so-called therapist that I was actually just not interested in women. I didn't mention the busy sexual life I had by this time with men. I began "counseling" with people I was encouraged to call "doctors," who would prescribe "exercises" with my "surrogates"—women who were not exactly prostitutes but who were also not exactly anything else. In one protocol, I had to crawl around naked on all fours pretending to be a dog while the surrogate pretended to be a cat; the metaphor of enacting intimacy between mutually averse species is more loaded than I noticed at the time. I became curiously fond of these women, one of whom, an attractive blonde from the Deep South, eventually told me that she was a necrophiliac and had taken this job after she got into trouble down at the morgue. You were supposed to keep switching girls so your ease was not limited to one sexual partner; I remember the first time a Puerto Rican woman climbed on top of me and began to bounce up and down, crying ecstatically, "You're in me! You're in me!" and how I lay there wondering with anxious boredom whether I had finally achieved the prize and become a qualified heterosexual.

Cures seldom work swiftly and completely for anything other than bacterial infections, but it can be hard to see that when social and medical realities are in rapid flux. My own recovery has been from the perception of illness. That office on Forty-Fifth Street shows up in my dreams: the necrophiliac who found my pale, sweaty form close enough to a corpse to float her boat; the mission-driven Latino woman who introduced me to her body with so much jubilation. My treatment took only two hours a week for about six months, and it gave me an ease with women's bodies that was vital to subsequent heterosexual experiences I'm glad to have had. I truly loved some of the women with whom I later had relationships, but when I was with them, I could never forget that my "cure" was a distilled manifestation of self-loathing, and I have never entirely forgiven the circumstances that disposed me to make the obscene effort. Stretching my psyche between Dwight and those catwomen made romantic love almost impossible for me during my early adulthood.

My interest in profound differences between parents and children arose from a need to investigate the locus of my regret. While I'd like to blame my parents, I have come to believe that a lot of my pain came from the larger world around me, and some of it came from me. In the heat of an argument, my mother once told me, "Someday you can go to a therapist and tell him all about how your terrible mother ruined your life. But it will be *your* ruined life you're talking about. So make a life for yourself in which you can feel happy, and in which you can love and be loved, because that's what's actually important." You can love someone but not accept him; you can accept someone but not love him. I wrongly felt the flaws in my parents' acceptance as deficits in their love. Now, I think their primary experience was of having a child who spoke a language they'd never thought of studying.

How is any parent to know whether to erase or celebrate a given characteristic? When I was born in 1963, homosexual activity was a crime; during my childhood, it was a symptom of illness. When I was two, *Time* magazine wrote, "Even in purely nonreligious terms, homosexuality represents a misuse of the sexual faculty. It is a pathetic little second-rate substitute for reality, a pitiable flight from life. As such it deserves fairness, compassion, understanding and, when possible, treatment. But it deserves no encouragement, no glamorization, no rationalization, no fake status as minority martyrdom, no sophistry about simple difference in taste—and, above all, no pretense that it is anything but a pernicious sickness."

When I was growing up, we nonetheless had close family friends who were gay—neighbors, and surrogate great-uncles to my brother and me, who spent holidays with us because their own families would not have them. I was always bewildered that Elmer had gone off to World War II halfway through medical school, fought on the Western Front, and then opened a gift shop when he came home. For years, I heard that the terrible things he saw in the war had changed him, and that he didn't have the stomach for medicine after his return. It was only after Elmer died that Willy, his partner of fifty years, explained to me that no one would have considered going to an openly gay doctor in 1945. The horrors of war had propelled Elmer into integrity, and he paid its price by spending his adulthood painting amusing bar stools and selling crockery. Elmer and Willy were a great romance in many ways, but an undertone of sadness for what might have been informed their lives. The gift shop was an apology for medicine; Christmas with us was an apology for family. I am humbled by Elmer's choice; I do not know that I would have had the courage to choose likewise, nor the discipline to keep regret from undermining my love had I done so. Though Elmer and Willy would never have seen themselves as activists, their galvanizing sorrow and that of others like them was the precondition of my happiness and that of others like me. When I understood their story more richly, I recognized that my parents' fears for me were not simply the product of overactive imaginations.

In my adulthood, being gay is an identity; the tragic narrative my parents feared for me is no longer inevitable. The happy life I now lead was unimaginable when I was asking for pink balloons and *ekmek kadayiff*—even when I was being Algernon. Yet, the trifecta view of homosexuality as a crime, an illness, and a sin remains potent. I sometimes felt that it was easier for me to ask people about their disabled children, their children conceived in rape, their children who committed crimes, than it would have been to look squarely at how many parents still respond to having children like me. Ten years ago, a *New Yorker* poll asked parents whether they would prefer to see their child gay, happily partnered, fulfilled, and with children, or straight, single or unhappily partnered, and childless. One out of three chose the latter. You cannot hate a horizontal identity much more explicitly than to wish unhappiness and likeness for your children over happiness and difference. In the United States, new anti-gay laws emerge with monotonous regularity; in December 2011, Michigan enacted the Public Employee Domestic Partner Benefit Restriction Act, which bars gay employees' partners from health-care coverage, despite allowing city and county employers to provide health-care coverage to all other family members, including uncles, nieces, and cousins. Meanwhile, in much of the larger world, the identity I inhabit remains unimaginable. In 2011, Uganda came close to passing a bill that would have made some homosexual acts punishable by death. An article in *New York* magazine about gay people in Iraq includes this information: "The bodies of gay men, often mutilated, began turning up on the street.

Hundreds of men are believed to have been killed. Gay men's rectums had been glued shut, and they had been force-fed laxatives and water until their insides exploded."

Much of the debate around sexual-orientation laws has turned on the idea that if you choose homosexuality, it should not be protected, but if you are born with it, perhaps it should. Members of minority religions are protected not because they are born that way and can't do anything about it, but because we affirm their right to discover, declare, and inhabit the faith with which they identify. Activists got homosexuality removed from the official list of mental illnesses in 1973, yet gay rights remain contingent on claims that the condition is involuntary and fixed. This cripple-like model of sexuality is depressing, but as soon as anyone posits that homosexuality is chosen or mutable, lawmakers and religious leaders try to cure and disenfranchise the gay people in their purview. Today, men and women continue to be "treated" for homosexuality at religious reform camps and in the offices of unscrupulous or misguided psychiatrists. The ex-gay movement in evangelical Christianity deranges gay people by the tens of thousands by seeking to persuade them, contrary to their experience, that desire is wholly volitional. The founder of the antihomosexual organization MassResistance has argued that gays should be made specific targets of discrimination, due to the supposedly voluntary nature of their ostensible perversion.

Those who think that a biological explanation of gayness will improve the sociopolitical position of gay people are also sadly mistaken, as the response to recent scientific findings makes clear. The sexologist Ray Blanchard has described a "fraternal birth order effect," which holds that the chance of producing gay sons goes up steadily with each male fetus a mother carries. Within weeks of publishing this data, he was called by a man who had decided against hiring a surrogate who had borne previous boys, saying to Blanchard, "That's not really what I want … especially if I'm paying for it." The arthritis drug dexamethasone is used off-label to treat women at risk for producing daughters with a condition that partially masculinizes their genitalia. Maria New, a researcher at Mount Sinai Hospital in New York, has suggested that dexamethasone given in early pregnancy will also reduce the chances that such babies will grow up to be lesbian; indeed, she has described the treatment as making girls more interested in childbearing and homemaking, less aggressive, and more shy. It has been posited that such therapy might curb lesbianism even in the general population. In animal studies, prenatal exposure to dexamethasone seems to cause many health problems, but if any medication can actually limit lesbianism, researchers will come up with a safer one. Medical findings such as these will continue to have serious social implications. If we develop prenatal markers for homosexuality, many couples will abort their gay children; if we come up with a viable preventative drug, many parents will be willing to try it.

I would no more insist that parents who don't want gay children must have them than I would that people who don't want children at all must have them. Nonetheless, I cannot think about Blanchard's and New's research without feeling like the last quagga. I am not evangelical. I don't need to verticalize my identity onto my children, but I would hate for my horizontal identity to vanish. I would hate it for those who share my identity, and for those who lie outside it.

I hate the loss of diversity in the world, even though I sometimes get a little worn out by being that diversity. I don't wish for anyone in particular to be gay, but the idea of no one's being gay makes me miss myself already.

All people are both the objects and the perpetrators of prejudice. Our understanding of the prejudice directed against us informs our responses to others. Universalizing from the cruelties we have known, however, has its limits, and the parents of a child with a horizontal identity often fail at empathy. My mother's issues with Judaism didn't make her much better at dealing with my being gay; my being gay wouldn't have made me a good parent to a deaf child until I'd discerned the parallels between the Deaf experience and the gay one. A lesbian couple I interviewed who had a transgender child told me they approved of the murder of George Tiller, the abortion provider, because the Bible said that abortion was wrong, and yet they were astonished and frustrated at the intolerance they had encountered for their identity and their child's. We are overextended in the travails of our own situation, and making common cause with other groups is an exhausting prospect. Many gay people will react negatively to comparisons with the disabled, just as many African-Americans reject gay activists' use of the language of civil rights. But comparing people with disabilities to people who are gay implies no negativity about gayness or disability. Everyone is flawed and strange; most people are valiant, too. The reasonable corollary to the queer experience is that everyone has a defect, that everyone has an identity, and that they are often one and the same.

It's terrifying to me to think that without my mother's sustained intervention, I might never have learned fluency in letters; I am grateful every day for the sufficient resolution of my dyslexia. Conversely, while I might have had an easier life if I had been straight, I am now wedded to the idea that without my struggles, I would not be myself, and that I like being myself better than I like the idea of being someone else—someone I have neither the ability to imagine nor the option of being. Nevertheless, I have often wondered whether I could have ceased to hate my sexual orientation without Gay Pride's Technicolor fiesta, of which this writing is one manifestation. I used to think that I would be mature when I could simply be gay without emphasis. I have decided against this viewpoint, in part because there is almost nothing about which I feel neutral, but more because I perceive those years of self-loathing as a yawning void, and celebration needs to fill and overflow it. Even if I adequately address my private debt of melancholy, there is an outer world of homophobia and prejudice to repair. Someday, I hope this identity may devolve into a simple fact, free of both party hats and blame, but that's some ways off. A friend who thought Gay Pride was getting a bit carried away with itself once suggested we organize Gay Humility Week. It's a good idea, but its time has not yet come. Neutrality, which appears to lie halfway between shame and rejoicing, is in fact the endgame, reached only when activism becomes unnecessary.

It is a surprise to me to like myself; among all the elaborate possibilities I contemplated for my future, that never figured. My hard-won contentment reflects the simple truth that inner peace often hinges on outer peace. In the gnostic gospel of St. Thomas, Jesus says, "If you bring forth what is within you, what is within you will save you. If you do not bring forth what is within you, what is within you will destroy you." When I run up against the antigay positions of modern religious bodies, I often wish that St. Thomas's words were canonical because his message embraces many of us with horizontal identities. Keeping the homosexuality locked away within me nearly destroyed me, and bringing it forth has nearly saved me.

Although men who murder usually target people not related to them, nearly 40 percent of women who inflict death kill their own babies. Reports of human children discarded in dumpsters and the overburdened foster-care network point to the ability of human beings to detach. Oddly, this seems to have at least as much to do with the infant's appearance as with its health or character. Parents will usually take home a child with a life-threatening internal defect, but not one with a minor visible defect; at a later stage, some parents will reject even children with severe burn scars. Manifest disabilities affront parents' pride and their need for privacy; everyone can see that this child isn't what you wanted, and you must either accept the world's pity or insist on your own pride. At least half of the children available for adoption in the United States have disabilities of some kind. Half of those available for adoption, however, still constitutes only a small proportion of disabled children.

Modern love comes with more and more options. For most of history, people married only members of the opposite sex, from their own class, race, denomination, and geographical location—all increasingly disputed boundaries. Similarly, people were supposed to accept the children given to them because one could do little to choose or change them. Birth control and fertility technologies have severed the bond between sex and procreation: intercourse does not necessarily engender babies, nor is it requisite to produce them. The analysis of embryos prior to implantation and the expanding domain of prenatal testing give parents access to a wealth of information to help them decide whether to initiate, continue, or terminate a pregnancy. The choices are broadening every day. People who believe in the right to opt for healthy, normative children refer to *selective abortion*; people to whom that idea is anathema refer to *commercial eugenics,* evoking a world stripped of variety and vulnerability. A vast industry of pediatric medicine implies that responsible parents should revamp their children in various ways, and parents expect doctors to correct their children's perceived defects: to administer human growth hormone to make the short ones taller, to fix a cleft lip, to normalize ambiguous genitalia. These optimizing interventions are not exactly cosmetic, but they are not necessary for survival. They have led social theorists such as Francis Fukuyama to speak of a "post-human future" in which we will eliminate the variety within mankind.

Yet while medicine promises to normalize us, our social reality remains a miscellany. If the cliché is that modernity makes people more similar, as tribal headdresses and frock coats alike give way to T-shirts and jeans, the reality is that modernity comforts us with trivial uniformities even as it allows us to become more far-flung in our desires and our ways of realizing them. Social mobility and the Internet allow anyone to find others who share his quiddities.

No closed circle of French aristocrats or farm boys from Iowa has been tighter than these new clusters of the electronic age. As the line between illness and identity is challenged, the strength of these online supports is a vital setting for the emergence of true selves. Modern life is lonely in many ways, but the ability of everyone with access to a computer to find like-minded people has meant that no one need be excluded from social kinship. If the physical or psychic place to which you were born wants no more of you, an infinitude of locales of the spirit beckons. Vertical families are famously breaking down in divorce, but horizontal ones are proliferating. If you can figure out who you are, you can find other people who are the same. Social progress is making disabling conditions easier to live with just as medical progress is eliminating them. There is something tragic about this confluence, like those operas in which the hero realizes he loves the heroine just as she expires.

Parents willing to be interviewed are a self-selecting group; those who are bitter are less likely to tell their stories than those who have found value in their experience and want to help others in similar circumstances to do the same. No one loves without reservation, however, and everyone would be better off if we could destigmatize parental ambivalence. Freud posits that any declaration of love masks some degree of odium, any hatred at least a trace of adoration. All that children can properly require of their parents is that they tolerate their own muddled spectrum—that they neither insist on the lie of perfect happiness nor lapse into the slipshod brutality of giving up. One mother who lost a child with a serious disability worried in a letter to me that if she felt relieved, her grief was not real. There is no contradiction between loving someone and feeling burdened by that person; indeed, love tends to magnify the burden. These parents need space for their ambivalence, whether they can allow it for themselves or not. For those who love, there should be no shame in being exhausted—even in imagining another life....

In 2011, gay marriage became legal in New York State after several Republicans in the state Senate agreed to support it. One of them, Roy J. McDonald, said that he had changed his stance on gay marriage because he had two autistic grandchildren, which had caused him "to rethink several issues." Jared Spurbeck, an autistic adult, thought his own quirks were "a sign of sinfulness" when he was growing up in the Mormon faith; when he started reading about gay Mormons, he found their experience much the same as his. "I couldn't ignore the parallels between autism and homosexuality. Once I'd accepted the one, I couldn't not accept the other."

I encountered activists of every stripe while I did this research and admired them even when I occasionally found their rhetoric expedient. The changes they sought seemed, individually, restricted to their particular province and experience, but as a group, they represent a rethinking of humanity. Most parents who become activists do so because they want to spur social change, but that impulse is never unalloyed. Some find it a relief because it gets them out of the house and away from their child without their having to feel guilty about it. Some use activism to distract themselves from grief; parents often laud what they rue most about their children to defend against despair. But just as belief can result in action, action can result in belief. You can gradually fall in love with your child, and by extension with that child's disabilities, and by further extension with all the world's brave disadvantages. Many of the activists I met were determined to help other people because they couldn't help themselves. Activism successfully displaced their pain. By teaching their learned optimism or strength to parents reeling from a recent diagnosis, they fortified it in their own families.

I understand this strategy firsthand, because writing this book addressed a sadness within me and—somewhat to my surprise—has largely cured it. The best way to get through these horizontalities is to find coherence, and in the wake of these stories, I recast my own narrative. I have a horizontal experience of being gay and a vertical one of the family that produced me, and the fact that they are not fully integrated no longer seems to undermine either. Some impulse toward anger at my parents evaporated, leaving only trace residue. In absorbing stories of strangers' clemency, I realized that I had demanded that my parents accept me but had resisted accepting them. Once I did, I was glad to have their ubiquitous company. The playwright Doug Wright once said that family inflicts the deepest wounds, then salves them the most tenderly. When I realized there was no refuge from my parents' meddling, I learned to value it over loneliness and call it love. I started my research aggrieved; I ended it forbearing. I set off to understand myself and ended up understanding my parents. Unhappiness is a constant grudging, and in these pages, happiness served as a spur to amnesty. Their love always forgave me; mine came to forgive them, too.

I know that who I was appalled my mother and concerned my father, and I used to be furious at them for not embracing this horizontal part of me, for not embracing the early evidence of it. Writing has been a lesson in absolution, because I have seen the valiance love takes. Acceptance was always easier for my father than it was for my mother, but that was not particular to me; he accepts himself more readily than she did herself. In her own mind, she always fell short; in my father's own mind, he is victorious. The interior daring of becoming myself was my mother's gift to me, while the outer audacity to express that self came from my father.

I wish I'd been accepted sooner and better. When I was younger, not being accepted made me enraged, but now, I am not inclined to dismantle my history. If you banish the dragons, you banish the heroes—and we become attached to the heroic strain in our personal history. We choose our own lives. It is not simply that we decide on the behaviors that construct our experience; when given our druthers, we elect to be ourselves. Most of us would like to be more successful or more beautiful or wealthier, and most people endure episodes of low self-esteem or even self-hatred. We despair a hundred times a day. But we retain the startling evolutionary imperative of affection for the fact of ourselves, and with that splinter of grandiosity we redeem our flaws. These parents have, by and large, chosen to love their children, and many of them have chosen to value their own lives, even though they carry what much of the world considers an intolerable burden. Children with horizontal identities alter your self painfully; they also illuminate it. They are receptacles for rage and joy—even for salvation.

When we love them, we achieve above all else the rapture of privileging what exists over what we have merely imagined.

A follower of the Dalai Lama who had been imprisoned by the Chinese for decades was asked if he had ever been afraid in jail, and he said his fear was that he would lose compassion for his captors. Parents often think that they've captured something small and vulnerable, but the parents I've profiled have been captured, locked up with their children's madness or genius or deformity, and the quest is never to lose compassion. A Buddhist scholar once explained to me that most Westerners mistakenly think that nirvana is what you arrive at when your suffering is over and only an eternity of happiness stretches ahead. But such bliss would always be shadowed by the sorrow of the past and would therefore be imperfect. Nirvana occurs when you not only look forward to rapture, but also gaze back into the times of anguish and find in them the seeds of your joy. You may not have felt that happiness at the time, but in retrospect it is incontrovertible.

For some parents of children with horizontal identities, acceptance reaches its apogee when parents conclude that while they supposed that they were pinioned by a great and catastrophic loss of hope, they were in fact falling in love with someone they didn't yet know enough to want. As such parents look back, they see how every stage of loving their child has enriched them in ways they never would have conceived, ways that are incalculably precious. Rumi said that the light enters you at the bandaged place. This book's conundrum is that most of the families described here have ended up grateful for experiences they would have done anything to avoid.

NOTES

1. Winnicott's statement is in the paper "Anxiety associated with insecurity," on page 98 of *Through Paediatrics to Psycho-analysis* (1958).

2. My investigation of Deaf culture resulted in an article, "Defiantly deaf," *New York Times Magazine,* August 29, 1994.

3. The Cochlear corporation website (http://www.cochlear.com) contains numerous instances of the word *miracle;* see also, for example, Aaron and Nechama Parnes's report from the 2007 Cochlear Celebration, "Celebrating the miracle of the cochlear implant," at http://www.hearingpocket.com/celebration1.shtml. For the other side of the story, see Paddy Ladd, *Understanding Deaf Culture: In Search of Deafhood* (2003), page 415: "In the 1990s, genetic engineering has initiated the process of trying to identify 'the deaf gene,' thus bringing within theoretical reach what might be termed the 'final solution'—that of eradicating Deaf people altogether." Harlan Lane likened attempts to eliminate deafness to attempts to eliminate ethnic groups in Paul Davies, "Deaf culture clash," *Wall Street Journal,* April 25, 2005.

4. Studies establishing a heightened risk of abuse for children who do not resemble their fathers include Rebecca Burch and George Gallup, "Perceptions of paternal resemblance predict family violence," *Evolution & Human Behavior* 21, no. 6 (November 2000); and Hongli Li and Lei Chang, "Paternal harsh parenting in relation to paternal versus child characteristics: The moderating effect of paternal resemblance belief," *Acta Psychologica Sinica* 39, no. 3 (2007).

5. The theologian John Polkinghorne reported this interpretation in keeping with what he had learned from Dirac. From page 31 of Polkinghorne, *Science and Theology: An Introduction* (1998): "Ask a quantum entity a particle-like question and you will get a particle-like answer; ask a wave-like question and you will get a wave-like answer."

6. "All I know is what I have words for" comes from part 5.6 of Ludwig Wittgenstein, *Tractatus Logico-Philosophicus* (1922): "Die Grenzen meiner Sprache bedeuten die Grenzen meiner Welt." C.K. Ogden translates the sentence as "The limits of my language mean the limits of my world"; that version occurs on page 149 of Ludwig Wittgenstein, *Tractatus Logico-Philosophicus,* translated by C.K. Ogden (1922).

7. From the entry "apple" in *The Oxford Dictionary of Proverbs,* edited by Jennifer Speake (2009): "The apple never falls far from the tree: Apparently of Eastern origin, it is frequently used to assert the continuity of family characteristics. Cf. 16th cent. Ger *der Apfel fellt nicht gerne weit vom Baume.*"

8. From the opening of Leo Tolstoy, *Anna Karenina*: "Happy families are all alike; each unhappy family is unhappy in its own way." The line is the first in the book and occurs on page 5 of the following edition: Leo Tolstoy, *Anna Karenina,* translated by Constance Garnett (2004).

9. Early development of gay children is discussed on pages 16–21 of Richard C. Friedman, *Male Homosexuality: A Contemporary Psychoanalytic Perspective* (1990).

10. For more information on gender-atypical color preference as a predictor of homosexuality, see Vanessa LoBue and Judy S. DeLoache, "Pretty in pink: The early development of gender-stereotyped colour preferences," *British Journal of Developmental Psychology* 29, no. 3 (September 2011).

11. The unforgettable last line, "Wherever they go, and whatever happens to them on the way, in that enchanted place on the top of the Forest a little boy and his Bear will always be playing," occurs on pages 179–80 of A.A. Milne, *The House at Pooh Corner* (1961).

12. See Amos Kamil, "Prep-school predators: The Horace Mann School's secret history of sexual abuse," *New York Times Magazine,* June 6, 2012.

13. The quotation about "wounded, confused people" is from a Facebook post by Peter Lappin.

14. For more information on surrogate partner therapy, see the website of the International Professional Surrogates Association, http://surrogatetherapy.org/.

15. The gay-damning quotation comes from "The homosexual in America," *Time,* January 21, 1966.

16. Hendrik Hertzberg, "The Narcissus survey," *New Yorker,* January 5, 1998.

17. On December 22, 2011, Michigan governor Rick Snyder signed House Bill 4770 (now Public Act 297 of 2011), the Public Employee Domestic Partner Benefit Restriction Act. The text and legislative history of House Bill 4770 can be found on the website of the Michigan legislature, http://www.legislature.mi.gov/mileg.aspx?page=getobject&objectname=2011-HB-4770.

18. On Uganda, see Josh Kron, "Resentment toward the West bolsters Uganda's anti-gay bill," *New York Times,* February 29, 2012; and Clar Ni Chonghaile, "Uganda anti-gay bill resurrected in parliament," *Guardian,* February 8, 2012; see also, three notes down, reference to Scott Lively.

19. The description of torture and murder of gays in Iraq comes from Matt McAllester, "The hunted," *New York,* October 4, 2009.

20. The *This American Life* episode "81 Words" at (http://www.thisamericanlife.org/ radio-archives/episode/204/81-Words) is an absorbing account of the removal of homosexuality from the *Diagnostic and Statistical Manual of Mental Disorders;* see also Ronald Bayer, *Homosexuality and American Psychiatry: The Politics of Diagnosis* (1981).

21. The passage references Scott Lively, *Redeeming the Rainbow: A Christian Response to the "Gay" Agenda* (2009). Scott Lively has recently been sued by a Ugandan gay rights group, who have accused him of fomenting persecution of gays in their country; see Laurie Goodstein, "Ugandan gay rights group sues U.S. evangelist," *New York Times,* March 14, 2012.

22. The response of the surrogate-shopper to Ray Blanchard appears in "Fraternal birth order and the maternal immune hypothesis of male homosexuality," *Hormones & Behavior* 40, no. 2 (September 2001), and is described in Alice Domurat Dreger, "Womb gay," *Hastings Center Bioethics Forum,* December 4, 2008.

23. The debate over Maria Iandolo New's administration of dexamethasone to expectant mothers is chronicled in Shari Roan, "Medical treatment carries possible side effect of limiting homosexuality," *Los Angeles Times,* August 15, 2010.

24. For an example of African-American objections to the language of civil rights being used by gay people, see this statement by North Carolina minister Rev. Patrick Wooden, quoted in David Kaufman, "Tensions between black and gay groups rise anew in advance of anti-gay marriage vote in N.C.," *Atlantic,* May 4, 2012: "African-Americans are appalled that their Civil Rights movement has been co-opted by the so-called Civil Rights movement of the homosexuals. It is an insult, it is angering when LGBT groups say there is no difference between being black and being homosexual."

25. "If you bring forth what is within you ..." is Saying 70 in Elaine H. Pagels, *Beyond Belief: The Secret Gospel of Thomas* (2003), page 53.

26. Maternal infanticide statistics occur on page 42 of James Alan Fox and Marianne W. Zawitz, "Homicide trends in the United States" (2007), in the chart "Homicide Type by Gender, 1976–2005." See also Steven Pinker, "Why they kill their newborns," *New York Times,* November 2, 1997.

27. Parental rejection of visibly disabled children is discussed on pages 152–54 of Meira Weiss, *Conditional Love: Parents' Attitudes Toward Handicapped Children* (1994). For a dated, albeit useful, review of literature on familial adjustment to severe burn scars in children, see Dale W. Wisley, Frank T. Masur, and Sam B. Morgan, "Psychological aspects of severe burn injuries in children," *Health Psychology* 2, no. 1 (Winter 1983).

28. A recent study from the CDC found that the majority of adopted children have significant health problems and disabilities. The report was put together by Matthew D. Bramlett, Laura F. Radel. and Stephen J. Blumberg and published as "The health and well-being of adopted children," *Pediatrics* 119, suppl. 1 (February 1, 2007).

29. The first occurrence of the term *commercial eugenics* appears to occur in M. MacNaughton, "Ethics and reproduction," *American Journal of Obstetrics & Gynecology* 162, no. 4 (April 1990).

30. Personal communication with Doug Wright.

31. See Ann Whitcher-Gentzke, "Dalai Lama brings message of compassion to UB," *UB Reporter,* September 21, 2006.

32. This Western naïveté about nirvana was explained to me by Robert Thurman in 2006.

33. Jalāl al-Dīn Rūmī (Maulana), *The Essential Rumi* (1995), page 142: "Don't turn away. Keep your gaze on the bandaged place. That's where the light enters you."

BIBLIOGRAPHY

Blanchard, Ray. "Fraternal birth order and the maternal immune hypothesis of male homosexuality." *Hormones & Behavior* 40, no. 2 (September 2001): 105–14.

Freud, Sigmund. Mourning and Melancholia. In *The Standard Edition of the Complete Psychological Works of Sigmund Freud.* Trans. Joan Riviere. Ed. James Strachey. Vol. 14, *1914–1916.* London: Hogarth Press, 1955.

Fukuyama, Francis. *Our Posthuman Future: Consequences of the Biotechnology Revolution.* New York: Farrar, Straus & Giroux, 2002.

Kamil, Amos. "Prep-school predators: The Horace Mann School's secret history of sexual abuse." *New York Times Magazine,* June 6, 2012.

Spurbeck, Jared. "NY senator's grandkids made him realize 'gay is OK.'" *Yahoo! News,* June 26, 2011.

Wittgenstein, Ludwig. *Tractatus Logico-Philosophicus.* Trans. C. K. Ogden. London: Routledge & Kegan Paul, 1922.

QUESTIONS FOR MAKING CONNECTIONS
WITHIN THE READING

1. "Son" explores two different kinds of identity—vertical identities like the ones that connect us to the members of our families, and the horizontal identities we form on the basis of characteristics we share with our contemporaries. Why do the two so often seem to conflict, and how do they conflict in Solomon's own life? What solutions does he find? As you re-read, pay particular attention to what Solomon observes about illness and identity. Can we apply to identities his analogy to the physics principle known as the Copenhagen interpretation, which holds that energy can be described as either a particle or a wave but not both at once? Must we choose between our vertical and horizontal identities, or can they somehow be combined? Do all identities actually include vertical and horizontal elements?

2. "Parenthood," Solomon writes, "abruptly catapults us into a permanent relationship with a stranger, and the more alien the stranger, the stronger the whiff of negativity." What role does negativity play in Solomon's development, and what role does it often play in cross-generational encounters? How does Solomon account for the pervasiveness of negativity? In what

ways was he disapproved of by his family, his friends, and his fellow students? Did Solomon disapprove of himself? Can negativity ultimately lead to a deeper understanding of others and our own nature? Can you identify distinct stages in the journey from negativity to acceptance?

3. Leo Tolstoy's novel *Anna Karenina* famously begins with the declaration, "Happy families are all alike; every unhappy family is unhappy in its own way." But Solomon declares his position to be anti-Tolstoyan. Why? What reasoning does he supply in defense of the conclusion that happy families will embrace their differences, whereas unhappy families insist on a single, definitive identity? If families are not defined by one basic identity, are they really families at all? Does "Son" offer an implicit argument for seeing families in a different light?

QUESTIONS FOR WRITING

1. Do we have a right to our identities, and, conversely, does society have a right to limit the ways we choose to define ourselves? Does Solomon's thinking imply that we have no obligations to society, to the past, or to tradition? How would you respond to the claim that he had made an argument for the principle that "Anything goes"—for the idea that any way of life is permitted and should be acceptable? Does "Son" elevate the author's personal desires above the good of the whole society, or is Solomon's celebration of differences a profoundly ethical stance? What role does understanding play in the encounter with differences? Is Solomon arguing for tolerance, or something deeper?

2. A key insight of "Son" has to do with the possibilities for freedom and fulfillment in an unsupportive or even hostile world. "My hard-won contentment," Solomon writes, "reflects the simple truth that inner peace often hinges on outer peace." Even though we might prefer to think that we hold the key to our own happiness, to what degree do we actually depend on the support of our whole society? If our happiness depends on supportive conditions, what might be the social or political implications? In order to make the world a better place, do we have a responsibility to bring our personal search for happiness into public view? Can inner peace survive without the proper outer conditions?

QUESTIONS FOR MAKING CONNECTIONS
BETWEEN READINGS

1. How might Solomon respond to Susan Faludi's "The Naked Citadel"? Think about The Citadel in terms of the potential conflicts between vertical

and horizontal identities. Would it be accurate to say that The Citadel only tolerates identities of a vertical kind, and if so, what effects follow from such systematic repression? Does the culture of The Citadel drive horizontal identities underground? Why haven't the cadets undergone the same learning process that Solomon experienced in his life? Given the conspicuous failure of most cadets to change or evolve, how might Faludi's narrative complicate Solomon's thinking? Can a way of life grow so rigid that transformation becomes impossible?

2.   Solomon's family appears to be an extremely healthy and supportive one, despite his mother's reluctance to embrace her son's gay identity. But in what ways might the experience of trauma, as described by Martha Stout in her discussions of Julia and Seth, have made Solomon's insights far more difficult to achieve—perhaps even unattainable? In your discussion you might take note of the way that repetition weakens our capacity for change:

> Deepening the mire of our divided awareness, in the course of a lifetime ... "protective" mental reactions acquire tremendous *habit strength*. These over-exercised muscles can take us away even when traumatic memory fragments have not been evoked. Sometimes dissociation can occur when we are simply confused or frustrated or nervous.

Does Stout's argument suggest that Solomon is overly sanguine about the prospects for personal and social change? Does his narrative suggest that Stout is too pessimistic? Or does Stout's narrative confirm Solomon's claim that "inner peace" requires a conducive environment?

JOSEPH E. STIGLITZ

ANYONE WHO THINKS OF academic knowledge as dry and irrelevant simply hasn't studied economics. And anyone who thinks of economics as an impartial discipline, plodding on modestly without controversy, simply hasn't heard of Joseph Stiglitz, winner of the 2001 Sveriges Riksbank Prize in Economic Sciences in Memory of Alfred Nobel. After Stiglitz left Stanford University to serve as a senior vice-president and chief economist of the World Bank, his appointment came to a premature end when, in 2000, he published an article excoriating the International Monetary Fund (IMF). Stiglitz, a "neo-Keynesian," targeted the IMF because it had imposed harsh austerity on the East Asian economies after a real estate bubble there collapsed. Even though many economists agreed with Stiglitz's criticisms, so notorious did the article become that the leadership of the World Bank pressured him to leave. After accepting a new post at Columbia University, Stiglitz continued to write and speak about the failures of neoliberal economics, which encourages smaller government, the deregulation of finance, and the privatizing of public services like health care and education.

Stiglitz, a prolific author, has written, co-written, or edited 26 books so far. The selection that follows is an excerpt from his best-selling book *The Price of Inequality: How Today's Divided Society Endangers Our Future* (2012). There he makes the case that neoliberal reforms starting with Ronald Reagan have produced a growing inequality that has swelled the ranks of the working poor and undermined the middle class. Stiglitz maintains that this long-term trend has dimmed the prospects for our full recovery from the collapse of 2008. After decades of lost buying power, the middle class has simply become too weak to generate the consumer spending needed for robust economic growth. Cash-strapped families no longer possess the resources to invest in their businesses or in better schooling for their children. Combined with tax cuts for the wealthiest, beginning under George W. Bush, the decline in middle-class earnings has meant lower tax revenue for government, a swelling of the national debt, and a neglect of roads, public property, and other social goods. Finally, income inequality makes the economic future more volatile, increasing the frequency of booms and busts and causing more severe collapses. Stiglitz is confident, however, that these problems can be rectified if our society is willing to take the steps he recommends: curbing the power of the financiers, raising taxes on the wealthiest 1 percent

From *THE PRICE OF INEQUALITY: HOW TODAY'S DIVIDED SOCIETY ENDANGERS OUR FUTURE* by Joseph Stiglitz. Copyright © 2012 by Joseph E. Stiglitz. Used by permission of W. W. Norton & Company, Inc. and Penguin Books Ltd.

"Rent Seeking and the Making of an Unequal Society," *The Price of Inequality: How Today's Divided Society Endangers Our Future* (New York: W. W. Norton, 2012), 28–51, 312–20.

and on the big corporations, strengthening unions and citizens' rights, and reinvesting in public education, infrastructure, the environment, and sustainable technology.

Rent Seeking and the Making of an Unequal Society

American inequality didn't just happen. It was created. Market forces played a role, but it was not market forces alone. In a sense, that should be obvious: economic laws are universal, but our growing inequality—especially the amounts seized by the upper 1 percent—is a distinctly American "achievement." That outsize inequality is not predestined offers reason for hope, but in reality it is likely to get worse. The forces that have been at play in creating these outcomes are self-reinforcing.

By understanding the origins of inequality, we can better grasp the costs and benefits of reducing it. The simple thesis of this chapter is that even though market forces help shape the degree of inequality, government policies shape those market forces. Much of the inequality that exists today is a result of government policy, both what the government does and what it does not do. Government has the power to move money from the top to the bottom and the middle, or vice versa.

… America's current level of inequality is unusual. Compared with other countries and compared with what it was in the past even in the United States, it's unusually large, and it has been increasing unusually fast. It used to be said that watching for changes in inequality was like watching grass grow: it's hard to see the changes in any short span of time. But that's not true now.

Even what's been happening in this recession is unusual. Typically, when the economy weakens, wages and employment adjust slowly, so as sales fall, profits fall more than proportionately. But in this recession the share of wages has actually fallen, and many firms are making good profits.[1]

Addressing inequality is of necessity multifaceted—we have to rein in the excesses at the top, strengthen the middle, and help those at the bottom. Each goal requires a program of its own. But to construct such programs, we have to have a better understanding of what has given rise to each facet of this unusual inequality.

Distinct as the inequality we face today is, inequality itself is not something new. The concentration of economic and political power was in many ways more extreme in the precapitalist societies of the West. At that time, religion both explained and justified the inequality: those at the top of society were there because of divine right. To question that was to question the social order, or even to question God's will.

However, for modern economists and political scientists, as also for the ancient Greeks, this inequality was not a matter of a preordained social order.

Power—often military power—was at the origin of these inequities. Militarism was about economics: the conquerors had the right to extract as much as they could from the conquered. In antiquity, natural philosophy in general saw no wrong in treating other humans as means for the ends of others. As the ancient Greek historian Thucydides famously said, "right, as the world goes, is only in question between equals in power, while the strong do what they can and the weak suffer what they must."[2]

Those with power used that power to strengthen their economic and political positions, or at the very least to maintain them.[3] They also attempted to shape thinking, to make acceptable differences in income that would otherwise be odious.

As the notion of divine right became rejected in the early nation-states, those with power sought other bases for defending their positions. With the Renaissance and the Enlightenment, which emphasized the dignity of the individual, and with the Industrial Revolution, which led to the emergence of a vast urban underclass, it became imperative to find new justifications for inequality, especially as critics of the system, like Marx, talked about exploitation.[4]

The theory that came to dominate, beginning in the second half of the nineteenth century—and still does—was called "marginal productivity theory"; those with higher productivities earned higher incomes that reflected their greater contribution to society. Competitive markets, working through the laws of supply and demand, determine the value of each individual's contributions. If someone has a scarce and valuable skill, the market will reward him amply, because of his greater contribution to output. If he has no skills, his income will be low. Technology, of course, determines the productivity of different skills: in a primitive agriculture economy, physical strength and endurance is what mattered; in a modern hi-tech economy, brainpower is of more relevance.

Technology and scarcity, working through the ordinary laws of supply and demand, play a role in shaping today's inequality, but something else is at work, and that something else is government. A major theme of [my argument] is that inequality is the result of political forces as much as of economic ones. In a modern economy government sets and enforces the rules of the game—what is fair competition, and what actions are deemed anticompetitive and illegal, who gets what in the event of bankruptcy, when a debtor can't pay all that he owes, what are fraudulent practices and forbidden. Government also gives away resources (both openly and less transparently) and, through taxes and social expenditures, modifies the distribution of income that emerges from the market, shaped as it is by technology and politics.

Finally, government alters the dynamics of wealth by, for instance, taxing inheritances and providing free public education. Inequality is determined not just by how much the market pays a skilled worker relative to an unskilled worker, but also by the level of skills that an individual has acquired. In the absence of government support, many children of the poor would not be able to afford basic health care and nutrition, let alone the education required to acquire the skills necessary for enhanced productivity and high wages. Government can affect the extent to which an individual's education and inherited wealth depends on that of his parents. More formally, economists say that inequality depends on the distribution of "endowments," of financial and human capital.

The way the American government performs these functions determines the extent of inequality in our society. In each of these arenas there are subtle decisions that benefit some group at the expense of others. The effect of each decision may be small, but the cumulative effect of large numbers of decisions, made to benefit those at the top, can be very significant.

Competitive forces should limit outsize profits, but if governments do not ensure that markets are competitive, there can be large monopoly profits. Competitive forces should also limit disproportionate executive compensation, but in modern corporations, the CEO has enormous power—including the power to set his own compensation, subject, of course, to his board—but in many corporations, he even has considerable power to appoint the board, and with a stacked board, there is little check. Shareholders have minimal say. Some countries have better "corporate governance laws," the laws that circumscribe the power of the CEO, for instance, by insisting that there be independent members in the board or that shareholders have a say in pay. If the country does not have good corporate governance laws that are effectively enforced, CEOs can pay themselves outsize bonuses.

Progressive tax and expenditure policies (which tax the rich more than the poor and provide systems of good social protection) can limit the extent of inequality. By contrast, programs that give away a country's resources to the rich and well connected can increase inequality.

Our political system has increasingly been working in ways that increase the inequality of outcomes and reduce equality of opportunity. This should not come as a surprise: we have a political system that gives inordinate power to those at the top, and they have used that power not only to limit the extent of redistribution but also to shape the rules of the game in their favor, and to extract from the public what can only be called large "gifts." Economists have a name for these activities: they call them rent seeking, getting income not as a reward to creating wealth but by grabbing a larger share of the wealth that would otherwise have been produced without their effort. (We'll give a fuller definition of the concept of rent seeking later in the chapter.) Those at the top have learned how to suck out money from the rest in ways that the rest are hardly aware of—that is their true innovation.

Jean-Baptiste Colbert, the adviser to King Louis XIV of France, reportedly said, "The art of taxation consists in so plucking the goose as to obtain the largest amount of feathers with the least possible amount of hissing." So, too, for the art of rent seeking.

To put it baldly, there are two ways to become wealthy: to create wealth or to take wealth away from others. The former adds to society. The latter typically subtracts from it, for in the process of taking it away, wealth gets destroyed. A monopolist who overcharges for his product takes money from those whom he is overcharging and at the same time destroys value. To get his monopoly price, he has to restrict production.

Unfortunately, even genuine wealth creators often are not satisfied with the wealth that their innovation or entrepreneurship has reaped. Some eventually turn to abusive practices like monopoly pricing or other forms of rent extraction to garner even more riches. To take just one example, the railroad barons of the nineteenth century provided an important service in constructing the railroads, but much of their wealth was the result of their political influence—getting large government land grants on either side of the railway. Today, over a century after the railroad barons dominated the economy, much of the wealth at the top in the United States—and some of the suffering at the bottom—stems from wealth transfers instead of wealth creation.

Of course, not all the inequality in our society is a result of rent seeking, or of government's tilting the rules of the game in favor of those at the top. Markets matter, as do social forces (like discrimination).

GENERAL PRINCIPLES

Adam Smith's Invisible Hand and Inequality

Adam Smith, the father of modern economics, argued that the private pursuit of self-interest would lead, as if by an invisible hand, to the well-being of all.[5] In the aftermath of the financial crisis [of 2008–09], no one today would argue that the bankers' pursuit of their self-interest has led to the well-being of all. At most, it led to *the bankers'* well-being, with the rest of society bearing the cost. It wasn't even what economists call a zero-sum game, where what one person gains exactly equals what the others lose. It was a negative-sum game, where the gains to winners are less than the losses to the losers. What the rest of society lost was far, far greater than what the bankers gained.

There is a simple reason for why financiers' pursuit of *their* interests turned out to be disastrous for the rest of society: the bankers' incentives were not well aligned with social returns. When markets work well—in the way that Adam Smith hypothesized—it is because private returns and social benefits are well aligned, that is, because private rewards and social contributions are equal, as had been assumed by marginal productivity theory. In that theory, the social contribution of each worker is exactly equal to the private compensation. People with higher productivity—a larger social contribution—get higher pay.

Adam Smith himself was aware of one of the circumstances in which private and social returns differ. As he explained, "People of the same trade seldom meet together, even for merriment and diversion, but the conversation ends in a conspiracy against the public, or in some contrivance to raise prices."[6] Markets by themselves often fail to produce efficient and desirable outcomes, and there is a role for government in correcting these market failures, that is, designing policies (taxes and regulations) that bring private incentives and social returns into alignment. (Of course, there are often disagreements about the best way of doing it. But few today believe in unfettered financial markets—their failures impose too great a cost on the rest of society—or that firms should be allowed to despoil the environment without restriction.) When government does its job well, the returns received by, say, a worker or an investor are in fact equal to the benefits to society that his actions contribute. When these are not aligned, we say there is a market failure, that is, markets fail to produce efficient outcomes. Private rewards and social returns are not well aligned when competition is imperfect; when there are "externalities" (where one party's actions can have large negative or positive effects on others for which he does not pay or reap the benefit); when there exist imperfections or asymmetries of information (where someone knows something relevant to a market trade that someone else doesn't know); or where risk markets or other markets are absent (one can't, for instance, buy insurance against many of the most important risks that one faces). Since one or more of these conditions exist in virtually every market, there is in fact little presumption that markets are in general efficient. This means that there is an enormous potential role for government to correct these market failures.

Government never corrects market failures perfectly, but it does a better job in some countries than in others. Only if the government does a reasonably good job of correcting the most important market failures will the economy prosper. Good financial regulation helped the United States—and the world—avoid a major crisis for four decades after the Great Depression. Deregulation in the 1980s led to scores of financial crises in the succeeding three decades, of which America's crisis in 2008–09 was only the worst.[7] But those governmental failures were no accident: the financial sector used its political muscle to make sure that the market failures were *not* corrected, and that the sector's private rewards remained well in excess of their social contributions—one of the factors contributing to the bloated financial sector and to the high levels of inequality at the top.

Shaping Markets

We'll describe below some of the ways that private financial firms act to ensure that markets *don't work well*. For instance, as Smith noted, there are incentives for firms to work to reduce market competition. Moreover, firms also strive to make sure that there are no strong laws prohibiting them from engaging in anticompetitive behavior or, when there are such laws, that they are not effectively enforced. The focus of businesspeople is, of course, not to enhance societal well-being broadly understood, or even to make markets more competitive: their objective is simply to make markets work *for them*, to make them more profitable. But the consequence is often a less efficient economy marked by greater inequality. For now, one example will suffice. When markets are competitive, profits above the normal return to capital cannot be sustained. That is so because if a firm makes greater profits than that on a sale, rivals will attempt to steal the customer by lowering prices. As firms compete vigorously, prices fall to the point that profits (above the normal return to capital) are driven down to zero, a disaster for those seeking big profits. In business school we teach students how to recognize, and create, barriers to competition—including barriers to entry—that help ensure that profits won't be eroded. Indeed, as we shall shortly see, some of the most important innovations in business in the last three decades have centered not on making the economy more efficient but on how better to ensure monopoly power or how better to circumvent government regulations intended to align social returns and private rewards.

Making markets less transparent is a favorite tool. The more transparent markets are, the more competitive they are likely to be. Bankers know this.

That's why banks have been fighting to keep their business in writing derivatives, the risky products that were at the center of AIG's collapse,[8] in the shadows of the "over the counter" market. In that market, it's difficult for customers to know whether they're getting a good deal. Everything is negotiated, as opposed to how things work in more open and transparent modern markets. And since the sellers are trading constantly, and buyers enter only episodically, sellers have more information than buyers, and they use that information to their advantage. This means that on average, sellers (the writers of the derivatives, the banks) can extract more money out of their customers. Well-designed open auctions, by contrast, ensure that goods go to those who value them the most, a hallmark of efficiency. There are publicly available prices for guiding decisions.

While lack of transparency results in more profits for the bankers, it leads to lower economic performance. Without good information, capital markets can't exercise any discipline. Money won't go to where returns are highest, or to the bank that does the best job of managing money. No one can know the true financial position of a bank or other financial institution today—and shadowy derivative transactions are part of the reason. One would have hoped that the recent crisis might have forced change, but the bankers resisted. They resisted demands, for instance, for more transparency in derivatives and for regulations that would restrict anticompetitive practices. These rent-seeking activities were worth tens of billions of dollars in profits. Although they didn't win every battle, they won often enough that the problems are still with us. In late October 2011, for instance, a major American financial firm[9] went bankrupt (the eighth-largest bankruptcy on record), partly because of complex derivatives. Evidently the market hadn't seen through these transactions, at least not in a timely way.

Moving Money from the Bottom of the Pyramid to the Top

One of the ways that those at the top make money is by taking advantage of their market and political power to favor themselves, to increase their own income, at the expense of the rest.

The financial sector has developed expertise in a wide variety of forms of rent seeking itself. We've already mentioned some, but there are many others: taking advantage of asymmetries of information (selling securities that they had designed to fail, but knowing that buyers didn't know that);[10] taking excessive risk—with the government holding a lifeline, bailing them out and assuming the losses, the knowledge of which, incidentally, allows them to borrow at a lower interest rate than they otherwise could; and getting money from the Federal Reserve at low interest rates, now almost zero.

But the form of rent seeking that is most egregious—and that has been most perfected in recent years—has been the ability of those in the financial sector to take advantage of the poor and uninformed, as they made enormous amounts of money by preying upon these groups with predatory lending and abusive credit card practices.[11] Each poor person might have only a little, but there are so many poor that a little from each amounts to a great deal. Any sense of social justice—or any concern about overall efficiency—would have led government to prohibit these activities. After all, considerable amounts of resources were used up in the process of moving money from the poor to the rich, which is why it's a negative-sum game. But government didn't put an end to these kind of activities, not even when, around 2007, it became increasingly apparent what was going on. The reason was obvious. The financial sector had invested heavily in lobbying and campaign contributions, and the investments had paid off.

I mention the financial sector partly because it has contributed so powerfully to our society's current level of inequality.[12] The financial sector's role in creating the crisis in 2008–09 is apparent to all. Not even those who work in the sector deny it, though each believes that some other part of the financial sector is really to blame. Much of what I have said about the financial sector, though, could be said about other players in the economy that have had a hand in creating current inequities.

Modern capitalism has become a complex game, and those who win at it have to have more than a little smarts. But those who win at it often possess less admirable characteristics as well: the ability to skirt the law, or to shape the law in their own favor; the willingness to take advantage of others, even the poor; and to play *unfair* when necessary.[13] As one of the successful players in this game put it, the old adage "Win or lose, what matters is how you play the game" is rubbish. *All that matters is whether you win or lose.* The market provides a simple way of showing that—the amount of money that you have.

Winning in the game of rent seeking has made fortunes for many of those at the top, but it is not the only means by which they obtain and preserve their wealth. The tax system also plays a key role, as we'll see later. Those at the top have managed to design a tax system in which they pay less than their fair share—they pay a lower fraction of their income than do those who are much poorer. We call such tax systems regressive.

And while regressive taxes and rent seeking (which takes money from the rest of society and redistributes it to the top) are at the core of growing inequality, especially at the top, broader forces exert particular influence on two other aspects of American inequality—the hollowing out of the middle class and the increase in poverty. Laws governing corporations interact with the norms of behavior that guide the leaders of those corporations and determine how returns are shared among top management and other stakeholders (workers, shareholders, and bondholders). Macroeconomic policies determine the tightness of the labor market—the level of unemployment, and thus how market forces operate to change the share of workers. If monetary authorities act to keep unemployment high (even if because of fear of inflation), then wages will be restrained. Strong unions have helped to reduce inequality, whereas weaker unions have made it easier for CEOs, sometimes working with market forces that they have helped shape, to increase it. In each arena—the strength of unions, the effectiveness of corporate governance, the conduct of monetary policy—politics is central.

Of course, market forces, the balancing of, say, the demand and supply for skilled workers, affected as it is by changes in technology and education, play an important role as well, even if those forces are partially shaped by politics. But instead of these market forces and politics balancing each other out, with the political process dampening the increase in inequality in periods when market forces might have led to growing disparities, instead of government *tempering* the excesses of the market, in America today the two have been working together to increase income and wealth disparities.

RENT SEEKING

Earlier, we labeled as *rent seeking* many of the ways by which our current political process helps the rich at the expense of the rest of us. Rent seeking takes many forms: hidden and open transfers and subsidies from the government, laws that make the marketplace less competitive, lax enforcement of existing competition laws, and statutes that allow corporations to take advantage of others or to pass costs on to the rest of society. The term "rent" was originally used to describe the returns to land, since the owner of land receives these payments by virtue of his ownership and not because of anything he *does*. This stands in contrast to the situation of workers, for example, whose wages are compensation for the *effort* they provide. The term "rent" then was extended to include monopoly profits, or monopoly rents, the income that one receives simply from the control of a monopoly. Eventually the term was expanded still further to include the returns on similar ownership claims. If the government gave a company the exclusive right to import a limited amount (a quota) of a good, such as sugar, then the extra return generated as a result of the ownership of those rights was called a "quota-rent."

Countries rich in natural resource are infamous for rent-seeking activities. It's far easier to get rich in these countries by gaining access to resources at favorable terms than by producing wealth. This is often a negative-sum game, which is one of the reasons why, on average, such countries have grown more slowly than comparable countries without the bounty of such resources.[14]

Even more disturbing, one might have thought that an abundance of resources could be used to help the poor, to ensure access to education and health care for all. Taxing work and savings can weaken incentives; in contrast, taxing the "rents" on land, oil, or other natural resources won't make them disappear. The resources will still be there to be taken out, if not today, then tomorrow. There are no adverse incentive effects. That means that, in principle, there should be ample revenues to finance both social expenditures and public investments—in, say, health and education. Yet, among the countries with the greatest inequality are those with the most natural resources. Evidently, a few within these countries are better at rent seeking than others (usually those with political power), and they ensure that the benefits of the resources accrue largely to themselves. In Venezuela, the richest oil producer in Latin America, half of the country lived in poverty prior to the rise of Hugo Chavez—and it is precisely this type of poverty in the midst of riches that gives rise to leaders like him.[15]

Rent-seeking behavior is not just endemic in the resource-rich countries of the Middle East, Africa, and Latin America. It has also become endemic in modern economies, including our own. In those economies, it takes many forms, some of which are closely akin to those in the oil-rich countries: getting state assets (such as oil or minerals) at below fair-market prices. It's not hard to become wealthy if the government sells you for $500 million a mine that's worth $1 billion.

Another form of rent seeking is the flip side: selling to government products at *above* market prices (noncompetitive procurement). The drug companies and military contractors excel in this form of rent seeking. Open government subsidies (as in agriculture) or hidden subsidies (trade restrictions that reduce competition or subsidies hidden in the tax system) are other ways of getting rents from the public.

Not all rent seeking uses government to extract money from ordinary citizens. The private sector can excel on its own, extracting rents from the public, for instance, through monopolistic practices and exploiting those who are less informed and educated, exemplified by the banks' predatory lending. CEOs can use their control of the corporation to garner for themselves a larger fraction of the firms' revenues. Here, though, the government too plays a role, by not doing what it should: by not stopping these activities, by not making them illegal, or by not enforcing laws that exist. Effective enforcement of competition laws can circumscribe monopoly profits; effective laws on predatory lending and credit card abuses can limit the extent of bank exploitation; well-designed corporate governance laws can limit the extent to which corporate officials appropriate for themselves firm revenues.

By looking at those at the top of the wealth distribution, we can get a feel for the nature of this aspect of America's inequality. Few are inventors who have reshaped technology, or scientists who have reshaped our understandings of the laws of nature. Think of Alan Turing, whose genius provided the mathematics underlying the modern computer. Or of Einstein. Or of the discoverers of the laser (in which Charles Townes played a central role),[16] or John Bardeen, Walter Brattain, and William Shockley, the inventors of transistors.[17] Or of Watson and Crick, who unraveled the mysteries of DNA, upon which rests so much of modern medicine. None of them, who made such large contributions to our well-being, are among those most rewarded by our economic system.

Instead, many of the individuals at the top of the wealth distribution are, in one way or another, geniuses at business. Some might claim, for instance, that Steve Jobs or the innovators of search engines or social media were, in their way, geniuses. Jobs was number 110 on the *Forbes* list of the world's wealthiest billionaires before his death, and Mark Zuckerberg was 52. But many of these "geniuses" built their business empires on the shoulders of giants, such as Tim Berners-Lee, the inventor of the World Wide Web, who has never appeared on the *Forbes* list. Berners-Lee could have become a billionaire but chose not to—he made his idea available freely; which greatly speeded up the development of the Internet.[18]

A closer look at the successes of those at the top of the wealth distribution shows that more than a small part of their genius resides in devising better ways of exploiting market power and other market imperfections—and, in many cases, finding better ways of ensuring that politics works for them rather than for society more generally.

We've already commented on financiers, who make up a significant portion of the top 1 or 0.1 percent. While some gained their wealth by producing value, others did so in no small part by one of the myriad forms of rent seeking that we described earlier. At the top, in addition to the financiers, whom we have already discussed,[19] are the monopolists and their descendants who, through one mechanism or another, have succeeded in achieving and sustaining market dominance. After the railroad barons of the nineteenth century came John D. Rockefeller and Standard Oil. The end of the twentieth century saw Bill Gates and Microsoft's domination of the PC software industry.

Internationally, there is the case of Carlos Slim, a Mexican businessman who was ranked by *Forbes* as the wealthiest person in the world in 2011.[20] Thanks to his dominance of the telephone industry in Mexico, Slim is able to charge prices that are a multiple of those in more competitive markets. He made his breakthrough when he was able to acquire a large share in Mexico's telecommunications system after the country privatized it,[21] a strategy that lies behind many of the world's great fortunes. As we've seen, it's easy to get rich by getting a state asset at a deep discount. Many of Russia's current oligarchs, for example, obtained their initial wealth by buying state assets at below-market prices and then ensuring continuing profits through monopoly power. (In America most of our government giveaways tend to be more subtle. We design rules for, say, selling government assets that are in effect partial giveaways, but less transparently so than what Russia did.)[22]

... [A]nother important group of the very wealthy [are] corporate CEOs, such as Stephen Hemsley from UnitedHealth Group, who received $102 million in 2010, and Edward Mueller from Qwest Communications (now CenturyLink, after a merger in 2011), who made $65.8 million.[23] CEOs have successfully garnered a larger and larger fraction of corporate revenues.[24] As we'll explain later, it is not a sudden increase in their productivity that allowed these CEOs to amass such riches in the last couple of decades but rather an enhanced ability to take more from the corporation that they are supposed to be serving, and weaker qualms about, and enhanced public toleration of, doing so.

A final large group of rent seekers consists of the top-flight lawyers, including those who became wealthy by helping others engage in their rent seeking in ways that skirt the law but do not (usually) land them in prison. They help write the complex tax laws in which loopholes are put, so their clients can avoid taxes, and they then design the complex deals to take advantage of these loopholes. They helped design the complex and nontransparent derivatives market. They help design the contractual arrangements that generate monopoly power; seemingly within the law. And for all this assistance in making our markets work not the way markets should but as instruments for the benefit of those at the top, they get amply rewarded.[25]

Monopoly Rents: Creating Sustainable Monopolies

To economists large fortunes pose a problem. The laws of competition, as I have noted, say that profits (beyond the normal return to capital) are supposed to be driven to zero, and quickly. But if profits are zero, how can fortunes be built? Niches in which there isn't competition, for one reason or another, offer one avenue.[26] But that goes only a little way to explaining sustainable excessive profits (beyond the competitive level). Success will attract entry, and profits will quickly disappear. The real key to success is to make sure that there won't ever be competition—or at least there won't be competition for a long enough time that one can make a monopoly killing in the meanwhile. The simplest way to a sustainable monopoly is getting the government to give you one. From the seventeenth century to the nineteenth, the British granted the East India Company a monopoly on trade with India.

There are other ways to get government-sanctioned monopolies. Patents typically give an inventor a monopoly over that innovation for a temporary period, but the details of patent law can extend the length of the patent, reduce entry of new firms, and enhance monopoly power. America's patent laws have been doing exactly that. They are designed not to maximize the pace of innovation but rather to maximize rents.[27]

Even without a government grant of monopoly, firms can create entry barriers. A variety of practices discourage entry, such as maintaining excess capacity, so that an entrant knows that, should he enter, the incumbent firm can increase production, lowering prices to the point that entry would be unprofitable.[28] In the Middle Ages, guilds successfully restricted competition. Many professions have continued that tradition. Although they argue that they are simply trying to maintain standards, restrictions on entry (limiting the number of places at medical school or restricting migration of trained personnel from abroad) help keep incomes high.[29]

At the turn of the previous century, concern about the monopolies that formed the basis of many of the fortunes of that period, including Rockefeller's, grew so great that under the trust-busting president Theodore Roosevelt, America passed a slew of laws to break up monopolies and prevent some of these practices. In the years that followed, numerous monopolies were broken up—in oil, cigarettes, and many other industries.[30] And yet today, as we look around the American economy, we can see many sectors, including some that are central to its functioning, where one or a few firms dominate—such as Microsoft in PC operating systems, or AT&T, Verizon, T-Mobile, and Sprint in telecommunications.

Three factors contributed to this increased monopolization of markets. First, there was a battle over ideas about the role that government should take in ensuring competition. Chicago school economists (like Milton Friedman and George Stigler) who believe in free and unfettered markets[31] argued that markets are naturally competitive[32] and that seemingly anticompetitive practices really enhance efficiency. A massive program to "educate"[33] people, and especially judges, regarding these new doctrines of law and economics, partly sponsored by right-wing foundations like the Olin Foundation, was successful. The timing was ironic: American courts were buying into notions that markets were "naturally" competitive and placing a high burden of proof on anyone claiming otherwise just as the economics discipline was exploring theories that explain why markets often were *not* competitive, even when there were seemingly many firms. For instance, a new and powerful branch of economics called game theory explained how collusive behavior could be maintained tacitly over extended periods of time. Meanwhile, new theories of imperfect and asymmetric information showed how information imperfections impaired competition, and new evidence substantiated the relevance and importance of these theories.

The influence of the Chicago school should not be underestimated. Even when there are blatant infractions—like predatory pricing, where a firm lowers its price to force out a competitor and then uses its monopoly power to raise prices—they've been hard to prosecute.[34] Chicago school economics argues that markets are presumptively competitive and efficient. If entry were easy, the dominant firm would gain nothing from driving out a rival, because the firm that is forced out would be quickly replaced by another firm. But in reality entry is not so easy, and predatory behavior does occur.

A second factor giving rise to increased monopoly is related to changes in our economy. The creation of monopoly power was easier in some of the new growth industries. Many of these sectors were marked by what are called network externalities. An obvious example is the computer operating system: just as it's very convenient for everyone to speak the same language, it's very convenient for everyone to use the same operating system. Increasing interconnectivity across the world naturally leads to standardization. Those with a monopoly over the standard that is chosen benefit.

As we have noted, competition naturally works against the accumulation of market power. When there are large monopoly profits, competitors work to get a share. That's where the third factor that has increased monopoly power in the United States comes in: businesses found new ways of resisting entry, of reducing competitive pressures. Microsoft provides the example par excellence. Because it enjoyed a near-monopoly on PC operating systems, it stood to lose a lot if alternative technologies undermined its monopoly. The development of the Internet and the web browser to access it represented just such a threat. Netscape brought the browser to the market, building on government-funded research.[35] Microsoft decided to squelch this potential competitor. It offered its own product, Internet Explorer, but the product couldn't compete in the open market. The company decided to use its monopoly power in PC operating systems to make sure that the playing field was not level. It deployed a strategy known as FUD (fear, uncertainty, and doubt), creating anxiety about compatibility among users by programming error messages that would randomly appear if Netscape was installed on a Windows computer. The company also did not provide the disclosures necessary for full compatibility as new versions of Windows were developed. And most cleverly, it offered Internet Explorer at a zero price—free, bundled in as part of its operating system. It's hard to compete with a zero price. Netscape was doomed.[36]

It was obvious that selling something at a zero price was not a profit-maximizing strategy—in the short run. But Microsoft had a vision for the long run: the maintenance of its monopoly. For that, it was willing to make short-run sacrifices. It succeeded, but so blatant were its methods that courts and tribunals throughout the world charged it with engaging in anticompetitive practices. And yet, in the end, Microsoft won—for it realized that in a network economy, a monopoly position, once attained, is hard to break. Given Microsoft's dominance of the operating system market, it had the incentives and capabilities to dominate in a host of other applications.[37]

No wonder, then, that Microsoft's profits have been so enormous—an average of $7 billion per year over the last quarter century, $14 billion over the past ten years, increasing in 2011 to $23 billion[38]—and reaping wealth for those who bought shares early enough. The conventional wisdom has it that in spite of its dominant position and huge resources, Microsoft has not been a real innovator. It did not develop the first widely used word processor, the first spreadsheet, the first browser, the first media player, or the first dominant search engine. Innovation lay elsewhere. This is consistent with theory and historical evidence: monopolists are not good innovators.[39]

Looking at the U.S. economy, we see in many sectors large numbers of firms, and therefore infer that there must be competition. But that's not always the case. Take the example of banks. While there are hundreds of banks, the big four share between them almost half of the country's banking assets,[40] a marked increase from the degree of concentration fifteen years ago. In most smaller communities, there are at most one or two. When competition is so limited, prices are likely to be far in excess of competitive levels.[41] That's why the sector enjoys profits estimated to be more than $115 billion a year, much of which is passed along to its top officials and other bankers—helping create one of the major sources of inequality at the top.[42] In some products, such as over-the-counter credit default swaps (CDSes), four or five very large banks totally dominate, and such market concentration always gives rise to the worry that they collude, albeit tacitly. (But sometimes the collusion is not even tacit—it is explicit. The banks set a critical rate, called the London Interbank Offered Rate, or Libor. Mortgages and many financial products are linked to Libor. It appears that the banks worked to rig the rate, enabling them to make still more money from others who were unaware of these shenanigans.)

Of course, even when laws that prohibit monopolistic practices are on the books, these have to be enforced. Particularly given the narrative created by the Chicago school of economics, there is a tendency not to interfere with the "free" workings of the market, even when the outcome is anticompetitive. And there are good political reasons not to take too strong a position: after all, it's antibusiness—and not good for campaign contributions—to be too tough on, say, Microsoft.[43]

Politics: Getting to Set the Rules and Pick the Referee

It's one thing to win in a "fair" game. It's quite another to be able to write the rules of the game—and to write them in ways that enhance one's prospects of winning. And it's even worse if you can choose your own referees. In many areas today, regulatory agencies are responsible for oversight of a sector (writing and enforcing rules and regulations)—the Federal Communications Commission (FCC) in telecom; the Securities and Exchange Commission (SEC) in securities; and the Federal Reserve in many areas of banking. The problem is that leaders in these sectors use their political influence to get people appointed to the regulatory agencies who are sympathetic to their perspectives.

Economists refer to this as "regulatory capture."[44] Sometimes the capture is associated with pecuniary incentives: those on the regulatory commission come from and return to the sector that they are supposed to regulate. Their incentives and those of the industry are well aligned, even if their incentives are not well aligned with those of the rest of society. If those on the regulatory commission serve the sector well, they get well rewarded in their post-government career.

Sometimes, however, the capture is not just motivated by money. Instead, the mindset of regulators is captured by those whom they regulate. This is called "cognitive capture," and it is more of a sociological phenomenon. While neither Alan Greenspan nor Tim Geithner actually worked for a big bank before coming to the Federal Reserve, there was a natural affinity, and they may have come to share the same mindset. In the bankers' mindset—despite the mess that the bankers had made—there was no need to impose stringent conditions on the banks in the bailout.

The bankers have unleashed enormous numbers of lobbyists to persuade any and all who play a role in regulation that they should not be regulated—an estimated 2.5 for every U.S. representative.[45] But persuasion is easier if the target of your efforts begins from a sympathetic position. That is why banks and their lobbyists work so strenuously to ensure that the government appoints regulators who have already been "captured" in one way or another. The bankers try to veto anyone who does not share their belief. I saw this firsthand during the Clinton administration, when potential names for the Fed were floated, some even from the banking community. If any of the potential nominees deviated from the party line that markets are self-regulating and that the banks could manage their own risk—there arose a hue and cry so great that the name wouldn't be put forward or, if it was put forward, that it wouldn't be approved.[46]

Government Munificence

We've seen how monopolies—whether government granted or government "sanctioned," through inadequate enforcement of competition laws—have built the fortunes of many of the world's wealthiest people. But there is another way to get rich. You can simply arrange for the government to hand you cash. This can happen in myriad ways. A little-noticed change in legislation, for example, can reap billions of dollars. This was the case when the government extended a much-needed Medicare drug benefit in 2003.[47] A provision in the law that prohibited government from bargaining for prices on drugs was, in effect, a gift of some $50 billion or more per year to the pharmaceutical companies.[48] More generally, government procurement—paying prices well above costs—is a standard form of government munificence.

Sometimes gifts are hidden in obscure provisions of legislation. A provision of one of the key bills deregulating the financial derivative market—ensuring that no regulator could touch it, no matter how great the peril to which it exposed the economy—also gave derivatives claims "seniority" in the event of bankruptcy. If a bank went under, the claims on the derivatives would be paid off before workers, suppliers, or other creditors saw any money—even if the derivatives had pushed the firm into bankruptcy in the first place.[49] (The derivatives market played a central role in the 2008–09 crisis and was responsible for the $150 billion bailout of AIG.)

There are other ways that the banking sector has benefited from government munificence, evident most clearly in the aftermath of the Great Recession. When the Federal Reserve (which can be thought of as one branch of the government) lends unlimited amounts of money to banks at near-zero interest rates, and allows them to lend the money back to the government (or to foreign governments) at much higher interest rates, it is simply giving them a hidden gift worth billions and billions of dollars.

These are not the only ways that governments spur the creation of enormous personal wealth. Many countries, including the United States, control vast amounts of natural resources like oil, gas, and mining concessions. If the government grants you the right to extract these resources for free, it doesn't take a genius to make a fortune. That is, of course, what the U.S. government did in the nineteenth century, when anyone could stake a claim to natural resources. Today, the government doesn't typically give away its resources; more often it requires a payment, but a payment that is far less than it should be. This is just a less transparent way of giving away money. If the value of the oil under a particular piece of land is $100 million after paying the extraction costs, and the government requires a payment of only $50 million, the government has, in effect, given away $50 million.

It doesn't have to be this way, but powerful interests ensure that it is. In the Clinton administration, we tried to make the mining companies pay more for the resources they take out of public lands than the nominal amounts that they do. Not surprisingly, the mining companies—and the congressmen to whom they make generous contributions—opposed these measures, and successfully so. They argued that the policy would impede growth. But the fact of the matter is that, with an auction, companies will bid to get the mining rights so long as the value of the resources is greater than the cost of extraction, and if they win the bid, they will extract the resources. Auctions don't impede growth; they just make sure that the public gets paid appropriately for what is theirs. Modern auction theory has shown how changing the design of the auction can generate much more revenue for the government. These theories were tested out in the auction of the spectrum used for telecommunications beginning in the 1990s, and they worked remarkably well, generating billions for the government.

Sometimes government munificence, instead of handing over resources for pennies on the dollar, takes the form of rewriting the rules to boost profits. An easy way to do this is to protect firms from foreign competition. Tariffs, taxes paid by companies abroad but not by domestic firms, are in effect a gift to domestic producers. The firms demanding protection from foreign competition always provide a rationale, suggesting that society as a whole is the beneficiary and that any benefits that accrue to the companies themselves are incidental. This is self-serving, of course, and while there are instances in which such pleas contain some truth, the widespread abuse of the argument makes it hard to take seriously. Because tariffs put foreign producers at a disadvantage, they enable domestic firms to raise their prices and increase their profits. In some cases, there may be some incidental benefits such as higher domestic employment and the opportunity for companies to invest in R&D that will increase productivity and competitiveness. But just as often, tariffs protect old and tired industries that have lost their competitiveness and are not likely to regain it, or occasionally those that have made bad bets on new technologies and would like to postpone facing competition.

The ethanol subsidy offers an example of this phenomenon. A plan to reduce our dependence on oil by replacing it with the energy of the sun embedded in one of America's great products, its corn, seemed irresistible. But converting plant energy into a form that can provide energy for cars instead of people is hugely expensive. It is also easier to do with some plants than others. So successful has Brazil's research on sugar-based ethanol been that in order for America to compete, for years it had to tax Brazilian sugar-based ethanol 54 cents a gallon.[50] Forty years after the introduction of the subsidy, it was still in place to support an infant technology that seemingly would not grow up. When oil prices fell after the 2008 recession, many ethanol plants went bankrupt, even with massive subsidies.[51] It wasn't until the end of 2011 that the subsidy and tariff were allowed to expire.

The persistence of such distortionary subsidies stems from a single source: politics. The main—and for a long while, effectively the only—*direct* beneficiary of these subsidies were the corn-ethanol producers, dominated by the megafirm Archer Daniels Midland (ADM). Like so many other executives, those at ADM seemed to be better at managing politics than at innovation. They contributed generously to both parties, so that as much as those in Congress might rail against such corporate largesse, lawmakers were slow to touch the ethanol subsidies.[52] As we've noted, firms almost always argue that the true beneficiaries of any largesse they receive lie elsewhere. In this case, ethanol advocates argued that the real beneficiaries were America's corn farmers. But that was, for the most part, not the case, especially in the early days of the subsidy.[53]

Of course, why American corn farmers, who were already the recipients of massive government handouts, receiving almost half of their income from Washington rather than from the "soil," should receive still further assistance is hard to understand, and hard to reconcile with principles of a free-market economy. (In fact, the vast preponderance of government money subsidizing agriculture does not go, as many believe, to poor farmers or even family farms. The design of the program reveals its true objective: to redistribute money from the rest of us to the rich and corporate farms.)[54]

Sadly, government munificence toward corporations does not end with the few examples we have given, but to describe each and every instance of government approved rent seeking would require another book.[55]

NOTES

1. That's one of the reasons that good stock market performance is no longer a good indicator of a healthy economy. Stocks can do well because wages are low and the Fed, worried about the economy, keeps interest rates at near zero.

2. Thucydides, *The Peloponnesian War*, trans. Richard Crawley (New York: Modern Library, 1951), p. 331 (book 5.89).

3. That's why the cases where those in power voluntarily give some of it up are so interesting. In some of them, it's because those in power have an understanding of their own long-term interests—and the long-term interests of those they are supposed to serve. That was the case, e.g., when the king of Bhutan, in 2007, insisted on converting his country into a constitutional monarchy. He had to persuade his citizens that that was the right course for them. The elites of nineteenth-century countries that extended education must have known that there was a risk that this would over the long run weaken their dominance of the political franchise; yet the short-term economic advantages of having a more educated workplace seem to have dominated the long-term political consequences. See François Bourguignon and Sébastien Dessus, "Equity and Development: Political Economy Considerations," pt. 1 of *No Growth without Equity?* ed. Santiago Levy and Michael Walton (New York: Palgrave Macmillan, 2009). Daron Acemoglu and James Robinson theorize that democratization is a way for ruling elites to commit to future redistribution, and thus avoid the extreme of revolution when faced with social unrest. If there is not sufficient strength in the rebellion, repression or temporary reform (or transfers) might suffice. Acemoglu and Robinson, *Economic Origins of Dictatorship and Democracy* (Cambridge: Cambridge University Press, 2006).

4. See Karl Polyani, *The Great Transformation* (New York: Rinehart, 1944). One of the theories developed in response to Marx was that of Nassau Senior, the first holder of the Drummond Chair at Oxford University, who argued that the return capitalists earned was compensation for their "abstinence" (i.e., saving, or *not consuming*).

5. The formalization of this idea is called the "first welfare theorem of economics." It asserts that under certain conditions—when markets work well—no one can be made better-off without making someone else worse-off. But, as we shall explain shortly, there are many instances in which markets do not work well. A recent popular analysis is Kaushik Basu, *Beyond the Invisible Hand: Groundwork for a New Economics* (Princeton: Princeton University Press, 2011). Basu uses the metaphor of a magic show to describe the way the discussion of economics on the political right draws attention to the conclusion of this theorem—that markets are efficient—and away from the very special and unrealistic conditions under which the conclusion holds—perfect markets. Like a good magician, a free-market economist succeeds by drawing spectators' attention to what he wants them to see—the rabbit jumping out of the hat—while distracting their attention from other things—how the rabbit got into the hat in the first place.

6. Adam Smith, *The Wealth of Nations* (1776; New York: P. F. Collier, 1902), p. 207.

7. See Carmen Reinhart and Kenneth Rogoff, *This Time Is Different: Eight Centuries of Financial Folly* (Princeton: Princeton University Press, 2009).

8. A derivative is just a financial instrument the return to which is *derived* on the basis of something else, e.g., the performance of a stock or the price of oil or the value of a bond. A few banks have profited enormously by keeping this market nontransparent, garnering for themselves an amount widely estimated at more than $20 billion a year.

9. On October 31, 2011, MF Global Holdings, a brokerage firm run by Jon Corzine, filed for bankruptcy protection in New York. It was the eighth-largest corporate bankruptcy in U.S. history and the biggest failure by a securities firm since Lehman Brothers Holdings Inc. filed for Chapter 11 in September 2008.

10. While there may be some debate about when taking advantage of information asymmetries is unethical (reflected in the maxim "caveat emptor," putting the

obligation on the buyer to beware of the possibility of information asymmetries), there is no doubt that the banks stepped over the line.

11. This predatory behavior took a number of forms. One way was to charge *very* high interest rates, sometimes obfuscated by fees. The abolition of usury laws (which limit the interest rates lenders can charge) provided lenders greater scope for charging exorbitant interest rates; and lenders found ways of circumventing whatever regulations there were. Rent-a-Center claimed to be renting furniture; it was really selling furniture and simultaneously lending money—at extraordinarily high interest rates. Many states tried to circumscribe its activities, but it used its political influence (it had senior ex-politicians, including a former leader of the Republicans in the House of Representatives, on its board) to try to get federal preemption (whereby weaker federal rules preempt the rights of states to regulate). In 2006 Rent-a-Center (with nationwide revenues in excess of $2 billion) was successfully sued by the state of California for deceptive business practices. See http://oag.ca.gov/news/press_release?id=1391. Credit cards and payday loans provided other venues for predatory practices. Among many discussions, see, e.g., Robert Faris, "Payday Lending: A Business Model That Encourages Chronic Borrowing," *Economic Development Quarterly* 17, no. 1 (February 2003): 8–32; James H. Carr and Lopa Kolluri, *Predatory Lending: An Overview* (Washington, DC: Fannie Mae Foundation, 2001).

12. A well-performing financial sector is absolutely essential for a well-performing economy. It allocates capital, manages risk, and runs the payments mechanism. As I explain in *Freefall* (New York: Norton, 2010), in the run-up to the 2008–09 crisis, it did not perform these functions well. Part of the reason is that it was focused more on circumventing regulations and exploitive activities, like predatory lending. The negative-sum nature is reflected in the immense losses in the real estate sector. The financial sector likes to claim that it has been highly innovative, and that these innovations are at the root of the economy's overall success. But as Paul Volcker, former chairman of the Federal Reserve, pointed out, there is little evidence of any significant effect of these innovations on economic growth or societal well-being (with the exception of the ATM machine). But even if the financial sector had contributed slightly to the country's growth in the years before the crisis, the losses associated with the crisis more than offset any of these gains.

13. A recent study has shown that people of higher status/income have fewer qualms about breaking the rules, are more likely to be driven by self-interest, more likely to cheat, and more likely to behave in other ways that would generally be viewed as unethical. Paul K. Piff, Daniel M. Stancato, Stephane Cote, Rodolfo Menoza-Denton, and Dacher Keltner, "Higher Social Class Predicts Increased Unethical Behavior," *Proceedings of the National Academy of Sciences*, February 27, 2012. While what is "unfair" or "unethical" depends on "norms," and there may be disagreements about what is or is not fair, the experiment focused on situations where there would be broad consensus on what was fair or ethical. Similarly, much of the financial sector behavior that I criticize … violates virtually any sense of "fairness" or "ethics."

14. This problem has come to be called the "natural resource curse." There are other reasons that such countries have not done well: managing natural resources can be difficult (prices fluctuate and exchange rates can become overvalued). For a recent review of some of the problems and how they can be addressed see *Escaping the Resource Curse*, ed. M. Humphreys, J. Sachs, and J. E. Stiglitz (New York: Columbia University Press, 2007). See also, e.g., Michael Ross, *The Oil Curse: How Petroleum*

Wealth Shapes the Development of Nations (Princeton: Princeton University Press, 2012); and idem, *Timber Booms and Institutional Breakdown in Southeast Asia* (New York: Cambridge University Press, 2001).

15. According to World Bank Indicators, 50 percent of the population was living under the national poverty line in 1998 before Chavez took office in 1999.

16. He shared the 1964 Nobel Prize in Physics with the Soviet scientists Nikolay Basov and Aleksandr Prokhorov for "fundamental work in the field of quantum electronics, which has led to the construction of oscillators and amplifiers based on the maser-laser principle."

17. They received the 1956 Nobel Prize in Physics "for their researches on semiconductors and their discovery of the transistor effect."

18. The World Wide Web Consortium he founded decided that its standards should be based on royalty-free technology, so that they could easily be adopted by anyone. Like Jobs, Bill Gates is often heralded as an innovator, but even though the adoption of his products is nearly universal now, that is due more to his business acumen—and near-monopoly of the market—than to the uniqueness of the technology he sells.

19. Bakija et al. found (p. 3) that "executives, managers, supervisors, and financial professionals account for about 60 percent of the top 0.1 percent of income earners in recent years, and can account for 70 percent of the increase in the share of national income going to the top 0.1 percent of the income distribution between 1979 and 2005." The composition of the top 1 percent in 2005 was 31 percent "Executives, managers, supervisors (non-finance)"; 15.7 percent "Medical," 13.9 percent "Financial professionals, including management," and 8.4 percent "Lawyers." The share of finance almost doubled over the period, rising from 7.7 percent in 1979 to 13.9 percent in 2005. (Nonfinance executives and medical fell slightly; lawyers increased marginally.) These statistics are based on an income measure that *excludes* capital gains. This is very important because about half of all capital gains accrue to the top 0.1 percent. For the top 400 income earners, 60 percent of their income is in the form of capital gains. J. Bakija, A. Cole, and B. T. Hein, "Jobs and Income Growth of Top Earners and the Causes of Changing Income Inequality: Evidence from U.S. Tax Return Data." See also comments by C. Rampell, "The Top 1%: Executives, Doctors and Bankers" *New York Times*, October 17, 2011, available at http://economix.blogs.nytimes.com/2011/10/17/the-top-1-executives-doctors-and-bankers/; and Laura D'Andrea Tyson, "Tackling Income Inequality," *New York Times*, November 18, 2011, available at http://economix.blogs.nytimes.com/2011/11/18/tackling-income-inequality/.

20. See *Forbes* World's Billionaires list at http://www.forbes.com/wealth/billionaires/; ranking is from 2011.

21. Slim's Grupo Carso, France Telecom, and Southwestern Bell paid $1.7 billion in December 1990 to acquire "a controlling 20.4 percent stake in Telmex, which includes 51 percent of the votes in the company." See Keith Bradsher, "Regulatory Pitfall in Telmex Sale," *New York Times*, December 7, 1990, available at http://www.nytimes.com/1990/12/27/business/talking-deals-regulatory-pitfall-in-telmex-sale.html?scp=1&sq=telmex%20southwestern%20bell%201990&st=cse (accessed March 3, 2012).

22. In the midnineties, Russia borrowed large amounts of money from the private sector, putting up shares in its oil and natural resource companies as collateral. But it was all a ruse to turn over state assets to the oligarchs. This was called "loans for shares." See Chrystia Freeland, *Sale of the Century: Russia's Wild Ride from Communism to Capitalism*

(New York: Crown Business, 2000). A variety of specious arguments are often put forward for these privatizations. Most recently, Greece has been pushed to privatize, as a condition for getting assistance from Europe and the IMF. For a discussion of privatization and the arguments used for it ... and J. E. Stiglitz, *The Price of Inequality: How Today's Divided Society Endangers Our Future* (New York: Norton, 2012), and J. E. Stiglitz, *Globalization and Its Discontents* (New York: Norton, 2002). Not every country and not every privatization has suffered from transferring state assets to private parties at below fair market prices. Many believe that the privatizations in the UK under Margaret Thatcher, with shares publicly floated and with the number of shares any one person or company could buy strictly limited, were conducted deliberately in a manner to avoid such outcomes.

23. See *Forbes* America's Highest Paid Chief Executives 2011, available at http://www .forbes.com/lists/2011/12/ceo-compensation-11_land.html.

24. This is obviously a controversial claim: the CEOs might argue that in fact they receive but a small fraction of what they contribute to shareholder value. But ... the so-called incentive structures are poorly designed, providing little link between that part of the increase in market value that is attributable to the efforts of the CEO and that which is the result of broader market forces—lower costs of inputs or higher stock market prices in general. Some studies have suggested, moreover, that once total compensation is taken into account (including adjustments of bonuses when the stock market doesn't do well), there is little relationship between firm performance and compensation. For a broader discussion of this issue, see J. E. Stiglitz, *Roaring Nineties* (New York: W. W. Norton, 2003); and especially Lucian Bebchuk and Jesse Fried, *Pay without Performance: The Unfulfilled Promise of Executive Compensation* (Cambridge: Harvard University Press, 2004).

25. Still one more group is real estate moguls, who benefit from special provisions of the tax code and often get rents as a result of local government variances in zoning laws.

26. These are sometimes called natural monopolies. They include the examples given earlier where network externalities are very large.

27. The advocates of stronger intellectual property rights, of course, claim otherwise. Interestingly, in the United States many of the most innovative firms, those in Silicon Valley, have been among those opposing certain proposals by those in the drug and entertainment industries to strengthen intellectual property rights. Recent revisions of patent law arguably gave large corporations an advantage over new firms, illustrating the fact ... that there are strong distributive consequences of any legal framework. For a discussion of how our current intellectual property framework may actually inhibit innovation, see J. E. Stiglitz, *Making Globalization Work* (New York: Norton, 2006), and Claude Henry and J. E. Stiglitz, "Intellectual Property, Dissemination of Innovation, and Sustainable Development," *Global Policy* 1, no. 1 (October 2010): 237–51.

28. See, e.g., A. Dixit, "The Role of Investment in Entry-Deterrence," *Economic Journal* 90, no. 357 (March 1980): 95–106; and J. Tirole and D. Fudenberg, "The Fat Cat Effect, the Puppy Dog Ploy and the Lean and Hungry Look," *American Economic Review* 74 (1984): 361–68. The practices Microsoft used to rid itself of its rivals (described below) also helped prevent entry of new competitors.

29. It's clear that one wants standards; one doesn't want to be operated on by an unqualified doctor. But, for instance, the supply of qualified doctors could have been increased simply by increasing the number of places in medical school.

30. In 1890 Congress passed the Sherman Anti-Trust Act, and its enforcement speeded up in the twentieth century. In 1911 the Supreme Court ordered the dissolution of the Standard Oil Company and the American Tobacco Company, which brought down the two powerful industrial trusts. In 1984 the Court broke up AT&T's monopoly following *United States v. AT&T*. See Charles R. Geisst, *Monopolies in America: Empire Builders and Their Enemies from Jay Gould to Bill Gates* (New York: Oxford University Press, 2000).

31. The term "Chicago school" is often applied to this group of economists, partially because the high priest of this religion, Milton Friedman (and many of his acolytes), taught at the University of Chicago. But it should be understood that many at that great university are not devotees of this school of thought, and that there are many devotees in other universities around the world. The term has, however, become a commonly used shorthand.

32. One group even went so far as to argue that markets will behave competitively even if there is only one firm, so long as there is potential competition. This argument played an important role in airline deregulation, where it was contended that even if there was only one airline on a given route, it would be disciplined from charging monopoly prices by the threat of entry. Both theory and experience have shown that this argument is wrong, so long as there are sunk costs (costs that won't be recovered if a firm enters and subsequently leaves), no matter how small those costs. See Joseph Farrell, "How Effective Is Potential Competition?," *Economics Letters* 20, no. 1 (1986): 67–70; J. E. Stiglitz, "Technological Change, Sunk Costs, and Competition," *Brookings Papers on Economic Activity* 3 (1987), pp. 883–947; and P. Dasgupta and J. E. Stiglitz, "Potential Competition, Actual Competition, and Economic Welfare," *European Economic Review* 32, nos. 2–3 (March 1988): 569–77.

33. For discussion and examples of conservative foundations' contribution to the Chicago school law and economics programs, see Alliance for Justice, *Justice for Sale: Short-changing the Public Interest for Private Gain* (Washington, DC: Alliance for Justice, 1993).

34. The Department of Justice brought a case against American Airlines in the early years of this century. I thought the evidence that American Airlines had engaged in predatory behavior was especially compelling, but the judge didn't need to look at the evidence: the Supreme Court had ruled that there was just too strong a presumption *against* the existence of predatory pricing to make prosecution possible.

35. One of Netscape's founders, Marc Andreessen, was part of the team at the University of Illinois at Urbana-Champaign that developed Mosaic, the first widely used web browser, which was a project of the university's National Center for Supercomputing Applications (one of the original sites of the National Science Foundation's Supercomputer Centers Program). See the website of the NCSA, http://www.ncsa.illinois.edu/Projects/mosaic.html (accessed March 3, 2012); and John Markoff, "New Venture in Cyberspace by Silicon Graphics Founder," *New York Times*, May 7, 1994, available at http://www.nytimes.com/1994/05/07/business/new-venture-in-cyberspace-by-silicon-graphics-founder.html?ref=marcandreessen (accessed March 3, 2012).

36. For an overview of the Microsoft case, see Geisst, *Monopolies in America*.

37. See Steven C. Salop and R. Craig Romaine, "Preserving Monopoly: Economic Analysis, Legal Standards, and Microsoft," *George Mason Law Review* 4, no. 7 (1999): 617–1055.

38. See Microsoft's annual report.

39. As the late Oxford professor and Nobel Prize winner John Hicks said, "The best of all monopoly profits is a quiet life." J. R. Hicks, "Annual Survey of Economic Theory: The Theory of Monopoly," *Econometrica* 1, no. 8 (1935). Kenneth Arrow pointed out that because monopolists restrict production, the saving they get from reducing costs is diminished. See Arrow, "Economic Welfare and the Allocation of Resources for Invention," in *The Rate and Direction of Inventive Activity: Economic and Social Factors* (Princeton: Princeton University Press, 1962), pp. 609–26. Monopolies, of course, don't last forever: new technologies and the open-source movement are already beginning to challenge Microsoft's dominance.

40. Calculated by total assets of commercial banks, as of September 3, 2011. See FDIC Statistics on Banking, available at http://www2.fdic.gov/SDI/SOB/index.asp; and Federal Reserve Statistical Release Large Commercial Banks, available at http://www.federalreserve.gov/releases/lbr/current/default.htm.

41. Moreover, banks don't compete on price for the services they offer. If you want to do a merger or acquisition, every major bank charges the same percentage fee. When takeovers were hundreds of millions of dollars, the resulting charges were large; when they became billions, charges became astronomical, for essentially the same amount of work by the same number of people.

42. From 2010 Q4 to 2011 Q3 (the most recently available year), FDIC-insured institutions made an aggregate profit of $115 billion. ... But these numbers don't really capture the magnitude of bank profits, since they are the profits after paying out the mega-bonuses to the executives, which can push compensation at some firms above 50 percent of revenues after other costs have been taken out, i.e., the "true" profits may be as much as double the above number. The *profits and bonuses* of the banking sector exceed 1 percent of the country's entire national output. Such numbers lead many to conclude that the financial sector, which is supposed to be the servant of the rest of the economy, has become its master.

43. Microsoft tried to exert political influence through a variety of channels. It has made campaign contributions of $13,516,304 from 1999 to present. See campaignmoney.com, compiled from campaign finance reports and data disclosed by Federal Election Commission, lists of contribution available at http://www.campaignmoney.com/Microsoft.asp?pg=88 (accessed March 6, 2012). The remedies put forward by President Bush's Justice Department in response to Microsoft's conviction on anticompetitive behavior were mild and did not effectively curtail its market power. See, e.g., Andrew Chin's account of the outcome of *United States v. Microsoft Corp.*: "Decoding Microsoft: A First Principles Approach," *Wake Forest Law Review* 40, no. 1 (2005):1–157. In the case of antitrust laws, there's a partial remedy for the absence of effective public enforcement: private antitrust action (which was introduced because of worries about the willingness of public authorities to take enforcement action).

44. The late Nobel Prize-winning economist George Stigler wrote extensively about this. See, e.g., Stigler, "The Economic Theory of Regulation," *Bell Journal of Economics* 11 (1971): 3–21.

45. Data from the OpenSecrets.org, a website of the Center for Responsive Politics, counting lobbyists for commercial banks, finance, and credit companies. When all lobbyists are counted in the finance, insurance, and real estate industries, the number balloons to nearly five per congressman. See http://www.opensecrets.org/lobby/indus.php?id=F&year=a (accessed March 24, 2012).

46. The latest instance was the veto by the Senate Banking Committee chairman of the nomination of Nobel Prize-winning economist Peter Diamond. Diamond would have provided a critical voice on some of the doctrines that prevail among some of the governors. (Diamond was first nominated to the Fed by President Obama in April 2010; he was renominated in September and again in January 2011, after Senate Republicans blocked a floor vote on his confirmation. On June 5, 2011, Diamond withdrew his nomination, ending a fourteen-month nomination effort resisted by Senator Richard Shelby of Alabama, who, with party colleagues repeatedly criticized Diamond for supporting the central bank's monetary stimulus. Diamond responded that his opponents failed to appreciate that understanding the determinants of unemployment is essential to effective monetary policy.)

47. The Medicare Prescription Drug, Improvement, and Modernization Act of 2003.

48. The economist Dean Baker's research shows that $332 billion could be saved between 2006 and 2013 (around $50 billion a year) in the most conservative high-cost scenario, if Medicare were allowed to negotiate prices; in the middle-cost scenario, $563 billion could be saved for the same budget window. See Baker, *The Savings from an Efficient Medicare Prescription Drug Plan* (Washington, DC: Center for Economic and Policy Research, January 2006).

49. It is estimated that four banks in the United States take home a windfall of some $20 billion a year in derivatives.

50. The market for ethanol was distorted in other ways—such as ethanol requirements and subsidies for gasoline refiners who blended gasoline with ethanol—most of which came from America's corn producers. See the 2010 CBO study "Using Biofuel Tax Credits to Achieve Energy and Environmental Policy Goals," available at http://www.cbo.gov/sites/default/files/cbofiles/ftpdocs/114xx/doc11477/07-14-biofuels.pdf (accessed March 2, 2012); and "The Global Dynamics of Biofuel," Brazil Institute Special Report, April 2007, issue no. 3, available at http://www.wilsoncenter.org/sites/default/files/Brazil_SR_e3.pdf (accessed March 2, 2012).

51. Congress finally allowed the subsidy to expire at the end of 2011.

52. Famously, ADM was fined a then-record $100 million for lysine price fixing in 1997, a result of a lengthy federal investigation that also led to convictions and prison time for three executives. (This became a book by Kurt Eichenwald and then a 2009 movie starring Matt Damon, *The Informant*.)

53. In the early days of corn-based ethanol, this was flatly wrong: the demand for corn by ethanol producers was so low that the corn farmers received almost no benefit from the subsidy. Because usage of corn for ethanol production was such a small fraction of global supply, it had a negligible effect on corn prices. ADM and other ethanol producers were the true beneficiaries.

54. The U.S. government paid a total of $261.9 billion for agriculture subsidies from 1995 to 2010. According to USDA, 63 percent of farms do not receive any payments. Among those payments, a large chunk (62 percent in 2009) goes to large-scale commercial farms (with gross annual sales of $250,000 or more). Between 1995 and 2010, the top 10 percent of farms received $30,751 average per year, while the bottom 80 percent of farms received $587 average per year. See USDA Economic Research Service, "Farm Income and Cost: Farms Receiving Government Payments," available at http://www.ers.usda.gov/Briefing/FarmIncome/govtpayby-farmtype.htm; Environmental Working Group, Farm Subsidy Database, available at http://farm.ewg.org/region.php.

55. And indeed, many books have been written on the subject. See, e.g., Glenn Parker, *Congress and the Rent-Seeking Society* (Ann Arbor: University of Michigan Press, 1996).

QUESTIONS FOR MAKING CONNECTIONS
WITHIN THE READING

1. Writing at a time when most Americans praise free markets uncritically, Stiglitz challenges a number of beliefs about the wisdom of the "invisible hand." He argues, for example, that competition tends to drive profits down, not up. He suggests that manufacturers typically try to protect profit margins by banding together to create monopolies. He alleges that investors often destroy wealth instead of increasing it. He even claims that "markets by themselves often fail to produce efficient and desirable outcomes." Choose one argument that challenges our current common sense about free markets and explain Stiglitz's reasoning. Consider as well the role he appears to think that markets should be allowed to play.

2. Why does Stiglitz see rent seeking as destructive? Who benefits from rent seeking? What are its economic consequences, and why? What does he see as its impact on society, and what is the relationship between economics and social life in general? Why is Stiglitz skeptical about the power of the market to correct itself? Would it be fair to say that the problem of rent seeking can be solved only by political means—that is, through government intervention? Why has government failed to intervene, and what steps does Stiglitz recommend to restore a balance between outcomes and opportunities?

3. Early in his argument about inequality Stiglitz includes a short historical overview, beginning with the once widespread belief that wealth and poverty are divinely ordained. Once a "vast urban underclass" had arisen in the wake of the Industrial Revolution, "it became imperative," Stiglitz writes, "to find new justifications for inequality." What justifications have become the most compelling ones in our time? Is Stiglitz opposed to inequality, or does he regard it as a problem that society will never fully solve? Does he regard it as a problem at all?

QUESTIONS FOR WRITING

1. What does Stiglitz see as the purpose of wealth? Although he never explicitly develops an answer to that question, his entire argument implies a set of commitments about the purposes that wealth-creation should serve. Does he believe that the purpose of wealth is to lift the wealth-creators above the rest? Does he believe that wealth should offer a reward to the hardest-working, while poverty should serve as punishment to motivate lazy people? Or does he see wealth as a means for improving our society as a whole?

Does Stiglitz believe that a society's wealth belongs in some sense to all its members? On what grounds does he argue that the government should redistribute wealth?

2. Stiglitz discusses how the economy is controlled by rent-seekers at the top who dictate laws and policies to the public. How does the top-down organization Stiglitz describes compare to Steven Johnson's system of organized complexity? How do systems like the one Stiglitz analyzes become established and how might they be dismantled through bottom-up shifts in the patterns that currently exist? How can Johnson's explanation of the power of patterns and systems to "self-organize" complicate, contradict, or confirm Stiglitz's conclusion about the power of the free-market economy?

QUESTIONS FOR MAKING CONNECTIONS
BETWEEN READINGS

1. Bringing Stiglitz together with Maggie Nelson's "Great to Watch," consider the relationship between the arts and inequality. Nelson never refers to economics, and Stiglitz never mentions the world of art, but this question asks you to explore possible connections between them. In what ways does the art world challenge the values of a market society? In what ways does it reinforce social distinctions between "high" and "low" culture—between the cultural "haves" and "have nots"? Does the violence of the avant-garde liberate or intimidate? Consider what Nelson tells us about the trend among artists to respond to middle class "banality" by inflicting on their audience an experience of "brutal, sensory overload." What relation does this strategy establish between artists and their public? In what other areas of life, aside from art, is "sensory overload" a problem?

2. Stiglitz discusses how the economy is controlled by rent-seekers at the top who dictate laws and policies to the public. How does the top-down organization that Stiglitz describes compare to Steven Johnson's system of organized complexity? How do systems like the one Stiglitz analyzes become established, and how might they be dismantled through bottom-up initiatives? How might Johnson's explanation of the power of systems to "self-organize" complicate, contradict, or confirm Stiglitz's conclusion about the power of the free market economy?

MARTHA STOUT

WHAT IS SANITY? Are "normal" people always sane, or could it be said that we experience sanity only at certain times? After witnessing a jarring event, have you ever found yourself in a condition that is not exactly sane: a state of frantic agitation or numbness and distraction? These are just some of the questions explored by Martha Stout in her first book, *The Myth of Sanity: Divided Consciousness and the Promise of Awareness* (2002), from which this selection comes. Stout draws on her nearly 30 years of practice as a clinical psychologist to show that the tendency to dissociate—to withdraw from reality—begins as a life-preserving resource that defends against severe trauma in childhood, but later can develop into a way of life defined by emotional detachment and prolonged disengagement with the world. In the most extreme cases, a dissociative disorder can cause individuals to black out for extended periods or to develop multiple personalities in order to cope with life's challenges. By defining a continuum that extends from the everyday experience of spacing out or getting lost in thought to conditions like Post-Traumatic Stress Disorder, Stout urges her readers to recognize the complexity of consciousness itself. If all of us dissociate to some degree, then a term like "sanity" is simply too crude to capture the real nature of mental health, which requires a proper balance between dissociation and engagement. The patients Stout focuses on in her study have lost this precious balance, but with her help, they come to see the meaning of their lives as something they can recover. In jargon-free prose, Stout tells stories of her patients' struggles for sanity, revealing in each case how buried or missing memories disrupt their awareness of the present.

For more than 25 years Stout served on the clinical faculty of the Harvard Medical School through the McLean Hospital in Belmont, Massachusetts, and the Massachusetts General Hospital in Boston. In addition, she has taught on the Graduate Faculty of the New School for Social Research and the psychology faculty of Wellesley College. Since completing *The Myth of Sanity*, she has published two other best selling books *The Sociopath Next Door* (2005) and *The Paranoia Switch* (2007).

Biographical information comes from <http://harvard.com/events/press_release.php?id=1880> and <http://www.marthastout.com//>.

When I Woke Up Tuesday Morning, It Was Friday

"The horror of that moment," the King went on, "I shall never, *never* forget!"

"You will, though," the Queen said, "if you don't make a memorandum of it."

—LEWIS CARROLL

Imagine that you are in your house—no—you are *locked* in your house, cannot get out. It is the dead of winter. The drifted snow is higher than your windows, blocking the light of both moon and sun. Around the house, the wind moans, night and day.

Now imagine that even though you have plenty of electric lights, and perfectly good central heating, you are almost always in the dark and quite cold, because something is wrong with the old-fashioned fuse box in the basement. Inside this cobwebbed, innocuous-looking box, the fuses keep burning out, and on account of this small malfunction, all the power in the house repeatedly fails. You have replaced so many melted fuses that now your little bag of new ones is empty; there are no more. You sigh in frustration, and regard your frozen breath in the light of the flashlight. Your house, which could be so cozy, is tomblike instead.

In all probability, there is something quirky in the antiquated fuse box; it has developed some kind of needless hair trigger, and is not really reacting to any dangerous electrical overload at all. Should you get some pennies out of your pocket, and use them to replace the burned-out fuses? That would solve the power-outage problem. No more shorts, not with copper coins in there. Using coins would scuttle the safeguard function of the fuse box, but the need for a safeguard right now is questionable, and the box is keeping you cold and in the dark for no good reason. Well, probably for no good reason.

On the other hand, what if the wiring in the house really is overloaded somehow? A fire could result, probably will result eventually. If you do not find the fire soon enough, if you cannot manage to put the fire out, the whole house could go up, with you trapped inside. You know that death by burning is hideous. You know also that your mind is playing tricks, but thinking about fire, you almost imagine there is smoke in your nostrils right now.

So, do you go back upstairs and sit endlessly in a dark living room, defeated, numb from the cold, though you have buried yourself under every blanket in the house? No light to read by, no music, just the wail and rattle of the icy wind outside? Or, in an attempt to feel more human, do you make things warm and comfortable? Is it wise to gamble with calamity and howling pain? If you turn the power back on, will you not smell nonexistent smoke every moment you are awake? And will you not have far too many of these waking moments, for how will you ever risk going to sleep?

Do you sabotage the fuse box?

I believe that most of us cannot know what we would do, trapped in a situation that required such a seemingly no-win decision. But I do know that anyone wanting to recover from psychological trauma must face just this kind of dilemma, made yet more harrowing because her circumstance is not anything so rescuable as being locked in a house, but rather involves a solitary, unlockable confinement inside the limits of her own mind. The person who suffers from a severe trauma disorder must decide between surviving in a barely sublethal misery of numbness and frustration, and taking a chance that may well bring her a better life, but that feels like stupidly issuing an open invitation to the unspeakable horror that waits to consume her alive. And in the manner of the true hero, she must choose to take the risk.

For trauma changes the brain itself. Like the outdated fuse box, the psychologically traumatized brain houses inscrutable eccentricities that cause it to overreact—or more precisely, *mis*react—to the current realities of life. These neurological misreactions become established because trauma has a profound effect upon the secretion of stress-responsive neurohormones such as norepinephrine, and thus an effect upon various areas of the brain involved in memory, particularly the amygdala and the hippocampus.

The amygdala receives sensory information from the five senses, via the thalamus, attaches emotional significance to the input, and then passes along this emotional "evaluation" to the hippocampus. In accordance with the amygdala's "evaluation" of importance, the hippocampus is activated to a greater or lesser degree, and functions to organize the new input, and to integrate it with already existing information about similar sensory events. Under a normal range of conditions, this system works efficiently to consolidate memories according to their emotional priority. However, at the extreme upper end of hormonal stimulation, as in traumatic situations, a breakdown occurs. Overwhelming emotional significance registered by the amygdala actually leads to a *decrease in hippocampal activation,* such that some of the traumatic input is not usefully organized by the hippocampus, or integrated with other memories. The result is that portions of traumatic memory are stored not as parts of a unified whole, but as isolated sensory images and bodily sensations that are not localized in time or even in situation, or integrated with other events.

To make matters still more complex, exposure to trauma may temporarily shut down Broca's area, the region of the left hemisphere of the brain that translates experience into language, the means by which we most often relate our experience to others, and even to ourselves.

A growing body of research indicates that in these ways the brain lays down traumatic memories differently from the way it records regular memories. Regular memories are formed through adequate hippocampal and cortical input, are integrated as comprehensible wholes, and are subject to meaning-modification by future events, and through language. In contrast, traumatic memories include chaotic fragments that are sealed off from modulation by subsequent experience. Such memory fragments are wordless, placeless, and eternal, and long after the original trauma has receded into the past, the brain's record of it may consist only of isolated and thoroughly anonymous bits of emotion, image, and sensation that ring through the individual like a broken alarm.

Worse yet, later in the individual's life, in situations that are vaguely similar to the trauma—perhaps merely because they are startling, anxiety-provoking, or emotionally arousing—amygdala-mediated memory traces are accessed more readily than are the more complete, less shrill memories that have been integrated and modified by the hippocampus and the cerebral cortex. Even though unified and updated memories would be more judicious in the present, the amygdala memories are more accessible, and so trauma may be "remembered" at inappropriate times, when there is no hazard worthy of such alarm. In reaction to relatively trivial stresses, the person traumatized long ago may truly *feel* that danger is imminent again, be assailed full-force by the emotions, bodily sensations, and perhaps even the images, sounds, smells that once accompanied great threat.

Here is an illustration from everyday life. A woman named Beverly reads a morning newspaper while she sits at a quiet suburban depot and waits for a train. The article, concerning an outrageous local scandal, intrigues her so much that for a few minutes she forgets where she is. Suddenly, there is an earsplitting blast from the train as it signals its arrival. Beverly is painfully startled by the noise; her head snaps up, and she catches her breath. She is amazed that she could have been so lacking in vigilance and relaxed in public. Her heart pounds, and in the instant required to fold the newspaper, she is ambushed by bodily feelings and even a smell that have nothing whatever to do with the depot on this uneventful morning. If she could identify the smell, which she never will, she would call it "chlorine." She feels a sudden rigidity in her chest, as if her lungs had just turned to stone, and has an almost overpowering impulse to get out of there, to run.

In a heartbeat, the present is perceptually and emotionally the past. These fragments of sensation and emotion are the amygdala-mediated memories of an afternoon three decades before, in Beverly's tenth summer, when, walking home from the public swimming pool, she saw her younger sister skip into the street and meet an immediate death in front of a speeding car. At this moment, thirty years later, Beverly *feels* that way again.

Her sensations and feelings are not labeled as belonging to memories of the horrible accident. In fact, they are not labeled as anything at all, because they have always been completely without language. They belong to no narrative, no place or time, no story she can tell about her life; they are free-form and ineffable.

Beverly's brain contains, effectively, a broken warning device in its limbic system, an old fuse box in which the fuses tend to melt for no good reason, emphatically declaring an emergency where none now exists.

Surprisingly, she will probably not wonder about or even remember the intense perceptual and emotional "warnings," because by the next heartbeat, a long-entrenched dissociative reaction to the declared emergency may already have been tripped in her brain, to "protect" her from this "unbearable" childhood memory. She may feel strangely angry, or paranoid, or childishly timid. Or instead she may feel that she has begun to move in an uncomfortably hazy dream world, far away and derealized. Or she may completely depart from her "self" for a while, continue to act, but without self-awareness. Should this last occur in a minor way, her total experience may be something such as, "Today when I was going to work, the train pulled into the station—the blasted thing is so loud!—and the next thing I remember, it was stopping at my stop." She may even be mildly amused at herself for her spaciness.

Most of us do not notice these experiences very much. They are more or less invisible to us as we go about daily life, and so we do not understand how much of daily life is effectively spent in the past, in reaction to the darkest hours we have known, nor do we comprehend how swampy and vitality-sucking some of our memories really are. Deepening the mire of our divided awareness, in the course of a lifetime such "protective" mental reactions acquire tremendous *habit strength*. These over-exercised muscles can take us away even when traumatic memory fragments have not been evoked. Sometimes dissociation can occur when we are simply confused or frustrated or nervous, whether we recognize our absences or not.

Typically, only those with the most desperate trauma histories are ever driven to discover and perhaps modify their absences from the present. Only the addictions, major depressions, suicide attempts, and general ruination that attend the most severe trauma disorders can sometimes supply motivation sufficiently fierce to run the gauntlet thrown down by insight and permanent change. On account of our neurological wiring, confronting past traumas requires one to re-endure all of their terrors mentally, in their original intensity, to feel as if the worst nightmare had come true and the horrors had returned. All the brain's authoritative warnings against staying present for the memories and the painful emotions, all the faulty fuses, have to be deliberately ignored, and in cases of extreme or chronic past trauma, this process is nothing short of heroic.

It helps to have an awfully good reason to try, such as suffocating depression or some other demonic psychological torment. Perhaps this is a part of the reason why philosophers and theologians through the centuries have observed such a strong connection between unbearable earthly sorrow and spiritual enlightenment, a timeless relationship that psychologists have mysteriously overlooked.

In order to appreciate what psychological trauma can do to the mind, and to a life, let us consider an extreme case of divided awareness, that of a woman whose psyche was mangled by profound trauma in her past, and who came to me for treatment after several serious suicide attempts. Her story is far grimmer than most of us will ever know, and the consequent suffering in her adult life has been nearly unsurvivable. And yet, should one meet her on the street, or know her only casually, she would seem quite normal. In fact, one might easily view her as enviable. Certainly, when looking on from a distance, nothing at all would appear to be wrong, and much would be conspicuously right.

Julia is brilliant. After the *summa cum laude* from Stanford, and the full scholarship at the graduate school in New York, she became an award-winning producer of documentary films. I met her when she was thirty-two, and an intellectual force to be reckoned with. A conversation with her reminds me of the *New York Review of Books*, except that she is funnier, and also a living, breathing human being who wears amethyst jewelry to contrast with her electric auburn hair. Her ultramarine eyes gleam, even when she is depressed, giving one the impression, immediately upon meeting her, that there is something special about her. She is, however, soft-spoken and disarming in the extreme. She does not glorify, does not even seem to notice, either her prodigious intelligence or her beauty.

Those same blue eyes notice everything, instantly, photographically. The first time she walked into my office, she said, "Oh how nice. Did you get that little statue in Haiti? I did a kind of project there once. What a spellbinding place!"

She was referring to a small soapstone figurine, the rounded abstraction of a kneeling man, that I had indeed purchased in Port-au-Prince, and that sat on a shelf parallel to my office door. She had not glanced back in that direction as she came in, and must have captured and processed the image in a microsecond of peripheral perception.

"That's very observant," I said, whereupon she directed at me a smile so sparkling and so warm that, for just the barest moment, her lifelong depression cracked and vanished from the air around her, as if it had been nothing but a bubble. The radiance of her momentary smile caused me to blink, and I knew exactly then, even before the first session began, that if she would let me, I would do everything I could to keep this particular light from going out.

At a moment's notice, Julia can speak entertainingly and at length about film, music, multicultural psychology, African politics, theories of literary criticism, and any number of other subjects. Her memory for detail is beyond exceptional, and she has the storyteller's gift. When she is recounting information, or a story, her own intellectual fascination with it gives her voice the poised and expertly modulated quality of the narrator of a high-budget documentary about some especially wondrous endangered animals, perhaps Tibetan snow leopards. She speaks a few astutely inflected sentences, and then pauses, almost as if she is listening—and expects you to be listening—for the stealthy *crunch-crunch* of paws on the snow's crust.

Curious about this, I once asked her whether she were an actress as well as a filmmaker. She laughed, and replied that she could do first-rate narrative voice-overs, if she did say so herself, but had not a smidgen of real theatrical ability. In fact, she said, sometimes the people she worked with teased her good-naturedly about this minor chink in her armor.

At my first session with her, when I asked her why she had come to therapy, she spent thirty minutes telling me in cinematic detail about her recent attempt to kill herself, by driving to an isolated Massachusetts beach at three A.M. on a Tuesday in late January, and lying down by the surf. By so doing, she sincerely expected not to be found until well after she had frozen to death. Taking her omniscient narrator tone, intellectually intrigued by the memory, she described the circumstances of her unlikely accidental rescue by a group of drunken college students, and then spent the second thirty minutes of our hour together likening this near-death experience to the strangely impersonal distance from a story one can achieve on film with certain authorial camera moves.

"By then, I was floating above myself, looking down, sort of waiting. And I know I couldn't actually have seen those kids, but I *felt* that I did. Over the sound of the waves, I don't think you can really *hear* footsteps in the sand, but still...."

And I strained to hear the *crunch-crunch*.

Therapy is a frightening thing, and people do not often seek it out because they are only mildly unhappy. In my work, and because of the high-risk individuals who are referred to me, it is not unusual for me to hear stories of attempted suicide from people I have only just met. I have come almost to expect such accounts, in fact.

At our second session, and in exactly the same tone she had used to describe her suicide attempt, Julia began by giving me an interesting account of her new project on the life of a promising writer who had died young, reportedly of a rare blood disease he had contracted in western China. After about fifteen minutes of this, I stopped her, and explained that I wanted to know something about her, about Julia herself, rather than about Julia's work. Seeing the blank expression come over her face, I tried to provide her with some nonthreatening guidance. I asked her some general, factual questions about her childhood.

And at that second session, this is what the articulate, intellectually gifted Julia remembered about her own childhood: an only child, she knew that she had been born in Los Angeles, but she did not know in which hospital. She vaguely remembered that when she was about ten, her parents had moved with her to another neighborhood; but she did not remember anything about the first neighborhood, or even where it was. Though she did not know for sure, she assumed that the move must have taken place because her parents had become more prosperous. She remembered that she had a friend in high school named Barbara (with whom "I must have spent a lot of time"), but she could not remember Barbara's last name, or where Barbara had gone after high school. I asked Julia about her teachers, and she could not remember a single one of them, not from grade school, not from middle school, not from high school. She could not remember whether or not she had gone to her high school prom or her high school graduation. The only thing she seemed to remember vividly from childhood was that when she was about twelve, she had a little terrier dog named Grin, and that her mother had Grin put to sleep when he needed an expensive stomach operation.

And that was all she remembered of her childhood, this successful thirty-two-year-old woman with the cinematic mind. And it took forty-five minutes for her to pull out that much from the dark, silent place that housed her early memories. She could not remember a single holiday or a single birthday. At thirty-two, she could swim, read, drive a car, and play a few songs on the piano. But she could not remember learning any of these skills.

Insufficient memory in the context of an adequate intellect, let alone a gifted one, is the next observation—right after the extraordinary understatement and humor—that causes me to become suspicious about a patient's past.

At our third session, she asked me an astonishing question, but also, really, the obvious question: "Do other people remember those things, about their teachers, and going to their graduation, and learning to drive, and so on?" When I told her that, yes, they usually do remember, at least to a much greater degree than she did, she reverently said, "Wow," and then she was quiet for a few minutes. Finally, she leaned forward a little and asked, "So what's wrong with me?"

Cautiously, because I knew what I had to say might at first sound preposterous or worse to Julia, I said, "I'm wondering about early traumatic experiences in your life. Even when someone's cognitive memory is perfectly good, as yours is, trauma can disrupt the memory in emotional ways."

Julia thought I was way off base; or at least the part of her that collected amethyst jewelry, made award-winning films, and talked about camera angles thought I was way off base. Another part of Julia, the part that kept trying to commit suicide, the part that prevented her from moving back to Los Angeles as her career demanded, the part that sometimes made her so sleepy during the middle of an ordinary day that she had to be driven home, that part kept her coming back to therapy for the next six years. During those six years, step by step, Julia and I cast some light on what had happened to her. She agreed to be hypnotized; she began to remember her dreams; she acknowledged her faint suspicions. She even traveled back to Los Angeles, to talk with distant relatives and old neighbors.

What we eventually discovered was that, when she was a child, Julia had lived in a house of horrors, with monsters jumping out at her without warning and for no apparent reason, except that Julia had come to assume, as abused children do, that she must be a horrible person who deserved these punishments. By the time she was school age, she had learned not to cry, because tears only encouraged her parents to abuse her further. Also, she had lost any inclination whatsoever to let anyone know what was going on. Telling someone and asking for help were concepts foreign to her despairing little soul. The thought that her life might be different had simply stopped occurring to her.

And soon, in a sense, she had stopped telling even herself. When the abuse began, she would "go somewhere else"; she would "not be there." By this, she meant that her mind had learned how to dissociate Julia's self from what was going on around her, how to transport her awareness to a place far enough away that, at most, she felt she was watching the life of a little girl named Julia from a very great distance. A sad little girl named Julia was helpless and could not escape; but psychologically, Julia's self could go "somewhere else," could be psychologically absent.

Simply put, Julia did not remember her childhood because she was not present for it.

All human beings have the capacity to dissociate psychologically, though most of us are unaware of this, and consider "out-of-body" episodes to be far beyond the boundaries of our normal experience. In fact, dissociative experiences happen to everyone, and most of these events are quite ordinary.

Consider a perfectly ordinary person as he walks into a perfectly ordinary movie theater to see a popular movie. He is awake, alert, and oriented to his surroundings. He is aware that his wife is with him and that, as they sit down in their aisle seats, she is to his right. He is aware that he has a box of popcorn on his lap. He knows that the movie he has come to see is entitled *The Fugitive*, and that its star is Harrison Ford, an actor. As he waits for the movie to begin, perhaps he worries about a problem he is having at work.

Then the lights in the theater are lowered, and the movie starts. And within twenty-five minutes, he has utterly lost his grasp on reality. Not only is he no longer worried about work, he no longer realizes that he has a job. If one could read his thoughts, one would discover that he no longer believes he is sitting in a theater, though in reality, he is. He cannot smell his popcorn; some of it tumbles out of the box he now holds slightly askew, because he has forgotten about his own hands. His wife has vanished, though any observer would see that she is still seated four inches to his right.

And without moving from his own seat, he is running, running, running—not with Harrison Ford, the actor—but with the beleaguered fugitive in the movie, with, in other words, a person who does not exist at all, in this movie-goer's real world or anyone else's. His heart races as he dodges a runaway train that does not exist, either.

This perfectly ordinary man is dissociated from reality. Effectively, he is in a trance. We might label his perceptions as psychotic, except for the fact that when the movie is over, he will return to his usual mental status almost instantly. He will see the credits. He will notice that he has spilled some popcorn, although he will not remember doing so. He will look to his right and speak to his wife. More than likely, he will tell her that he liked the movie, as we all tend to enjoy entertainments in which we can become lost. All that really happened is that, for a little while, he took the part of himself that worries about work problems and other "real" things, and separated it from the imaginative part of himself, so that the imaginative part could have dominance. He *dissociated* one part of his consciousness from another part.

When dissociation is illustrated in this way, most people can acknowledge that they have had such interludes from time to time, at a movie or a play, reading a book or hearing a speech, or even just daydreaming. And then the out-of-body may sound a little closer to home. Plainly stated, it is the case that under certain circumstances, ranging from pleasant or unpleasant distraction to fascination to fear to pain to horror, a human being can be psychologically absent from his or her own direct experience. We can go somewhere else. The part of consciousness that we nearly always conceive of as the "self" can be not there for a few moments, for a few hours, and in heinous circumstances, for much longer.

As the result of a daydream, this mental compartmentalization is called distraction. As the result of an involving movie, it is often called escape. As the result of trauma, physical or psychological, it is called a dissociative state. When a hypnotist induces dissociation, by monotony, distraction, relaxation, or any number of other methods, the temporary result is called an hypnotic state, or a trance. The physiological patterns and the primary behavioral results of distraction, escape, dissociative state, and trance are virtually identical, regardless of method. The differences among them seem to result not so much from how consciousness gets divided as from how often and how long one is forced to keep it divided.

Another recognizable example of how consciousness can be split into pieces has to do with the perception of physical pain. On the morning after seeing *The Fugitive*, our moviegoer's wife is working frenetically to pack her briefcase, eat her breakfast, get the kids off to school, and listen to a news report on television, all at the same time. She is very distracted. In the process of all this, she bashes her leg soundly against the corner of a low shelf. Yet the woman is not seemingly aware that she has injured herself. That night, as she is getting ready for bed, she notices that she has a large colorful bruise on her right thigh. She thinks, "Well, now, I wonder how I did that."

In this case, a person was distracted, and the part of her consciousness that would normally have perceived pain was split apart from, and subjugated to, the part of her consciousness that was goal-directed. She was not there for the direct experience of her pain. She was somewhere else (the briefcase, the breakfast, the kids, the news). And because she was not there, she does not remember the accident.

The direct experience of physical pain can be split off in cases of much more serious injury as well. Most of us have heard stories along the lines of the parent who, with a broken leg, goes back to the scene of an accident and wrenches open a mangled car door with her bare hands in order to rescue her child. Less valorous, I myself remember my car being demolished by a speeding limousine. My knee was injured, but I felt no pain just after the crash, was more or less unaware of my body at all. My first thought before being dragged out of my car was to peer into the rearview mirror and inspect my teeth, and to decide that everything must be okay because there were no chips in them. And then there are the war stories about maimed infantrymen who have had to flee from the front line. All such circumstances affect memory in fascinating ways. Note, for example, that when veterans get together, they often laugh and tell war stories as though those times had been the best of their lives.

Agony that is psychological can be dissociated, too. While she was being abused, Julia developed the reaction of standing apart from herself and her situation. She stopped being there. Certainly, some parts of her consciousness must have been there right along. She could watch her parents, even predict their moods. She could run and hide. She could cover her injuries. She could keep her parents' secrets. But the part of her consciousness that she thinks of as her self was not there; it was split off, put aside, and therefore in some sense protected. And because her self had not been there, her self could not remember what had happened to her during much of her childhood.

What does this feel like, not being able to remember whole chapters of one's own life? I have asked many people this question, Julia among them. As usual, her answer was obvious and startling at the same time.

"It doesn't feel like anything," she answered. "I never really thought about it. I guess I just assumed, sort of tacitly assumed, that everyone's memory was like mine, that is to say, kind of blank before the age of twenty or so. I mean, you can't see into someone else's mind, right? All you can do is ask questions, and it never even occurred to me to ask anybody about this. It's like asking, 'What do you see when you see blue?' First of all, you'd never think to ask. And secondly, two people can agree that the clear blue sky is blue, but does the actual color blue look the *same* to both of them? Who knows? How would you even ask that question?

"Of course, every now and then I'd hear people talking about pin-the-tail-on-the-donkey, or some other thing about a little kid's birthday, and I'd wonder how they knew that. But I guess I just figured their memory was especially good, or maybe they'd heard their parents talk about it so much that it seemed like a memory.

"The memories I did have seemed like aberrations, like pinpoints of light in a dark room, so vague that you're not really sure whether you're seeing them or not. Certainly, there was nothing like a continuous thread of memory that linked one part of my life to another.

"Really it wasn't until you started asking me questions about my teachers and so forth that I ever even had any serious questions about my memory. After you started asking, I asked a couple of other people, just out of curiosity, and I began to realize that other people really do have childhood memories, and some of them are pretty vivid. I was surprised.

"What can I tell you? It just never occurred to me to wonder about it before. It felt like ... it felt like nothing."

She shrugged. Most people shrug. They are genuinely surprised, and at a loss.

Now the conspicuous question to ask Julia was, "All this time that you've been so unhappy, all the times you've tried to end your life, what did you think was causing all that misery?"

"I thought I was crazy," she answered.

This is easy enough to understand. Imagine a simple and, relatively speaking, innocuous example. Imagine that someone, call her Alice, leaves work early one day and goes to the oral surgeon to have her two bottom wisdom teeth extracted. The extractions go well; the doctor packs the gums with cotton and sends Alice home. On the way home, for some fictitious reason, let us say magic moonbeams, Alice completely loses her memory of the visit to the oral surgeon. She now assumes that she is driving directly home from work, as she does on most days. After she gets home, she is okay for a while, but gradually the anesthetic wears off, and she begins to experience a considerable amount of pain in her mouth. Soon the pain is too strong to ignore, and she goes to the bathroom mirror to examine the situation. When she looks into her mouth, she discovers that there are wads of cotton in there. And when she takes the cotton out, she discovers that two of her teeth are missing, and she is bleeding!

Alice is now in the twilight zone. The ordinary experience of having her wisdom teeth pulled has turned into a situation that makes her feel insane. One or two more of such experiences, and she would be convinced.

Childhood trauma creates a particularly bewildering picture. Observe normal children at play, and you will realize that children are especially good at dissociating. In the interest of play, a child can, in a heartbeat, leave himself behind, become someone or something else, or several things at once. Reality is even more plastic in childhood. Pretend games are real and wonderful and consuming. It is clear to anyone who really looks that normal children derive unending joy from their superior ability to leap out of their "selves" and go somewhere else, be other things. The snow is not cold. The body is not tired, even when it is on the verge of collapse.

Because children dissociate readily even in ordinary circumstances, when they encounter traumatic situations, they easily split their consciousness into pieces, often for extended periods of time. The self is put aside and hidden. Of course, this reaction is functional for the traumatized child, necessary, even kind. For the traumatized child, a dissociative state, far from being dysfunctional or crazy, may in fact be lifesaving. And thanks be to the normal human mind that it provides the means.

This coping strategy becomes dysfunctional only later, after the child is grown and away from the original trauma. When the original trauma is no longer an ongoing fact of life, prolonged dissociative reactions are no longer necessary. But through the years of intensive use, the self-protective strategy has developed a hair trigger. The adult whom the child has become now experiences dissociative reactions to levels of stress that probably would not cause another person to dissociate.

The events that are most problematic tend to be related in some way to the original trauma. However, human beings are exquisitely symbolic creatures, and "related" can reach unpredictable and often indecipherable levels of abstraction and metaphor. A long shadow from a city streetlight can remind someone of the tall cacti on the Arizona desert where his father used to threaten to "feed" him to the rattlesnakes. An innocent song about the wind in the willow trees can remind someone else of the rice fields that were a part of her childhood's landscape in Cambodia. A car backfiring on Beacon Street in Boston can remind yet another person of that spot on the trail where his eighteen-year-old platoon mate exploded six feet in front of him.

And so for the adult who was traumatized as a child, the present too has a kind of mercurial quality. The present is difficult to hold on to, always getting away.

In Julia's case, though she had not questioned her poverty of memory for the past, she had begun to suspect even before she came into therapy that she was losing time in the present. Probably this is because there are more external reality checks on the present than there are on the past. From other people—and from radio, television, the Internet, date books—there are ongoing reminders of the present time of day, and day of the week. Markers of time in the past are less immediate, and sooner or later most dates and chronologies for the past begin to feel amorphous to us all. It is hardly amazing that one should have forgotten something that happened twenty years ago. But if a person lets on that she has no memory of an important event that occurred this very week, friends and associates are unlikely to let such a lapse go unremarked.

At one of her early sessions with me, Julia announced, "When I woke up Tuesday morning it was Friday."

"Pardon?"

"When I woke up this morning it was Tuesday, and then I discovered that it was Friday for everybody else."

"How do you mean?"

"Well, the last thing I remember before waking up this morning was having dinner Monday night. So I thought it was Tuesday. And then I went in to work, and some sponsors were there that I was supposed to meet with on Friday. So I asked my assistant what was up, and she said, 'You wanted to meet with these people this morning, remember?' And I said, 'No. I wanted to meet with them on Friday.' She looked at me, and said, 'Today is Friday, Julia.'

"I finessed. I laughed and said, 'Of course. That's terrible. No more late nights for me. Pretty soon I'll be forgetting my name. Ha, ha.' But it isn't funny. This happens a lot. I just lose time. Hours, days. They're gone, and I don't know what I've done or where I've been or anything else.

"I've never told anyone this before. It's embarrassing. Actually, it's terrifying.

"I don't understand any of it, but the thing I understand the least is that apparently I go about my business during these times, and nobody notices any difference in me. At least, no one ever says anything. After the meeting this morning, I realized that on Tuesday, Wednesday, and Thursday, I must have done a mountain of editing. There it was, all finished. I did a good job, even. And I don't remember a bloody thing."

During this confession, I saw Julia cry for the first time. Quickly, though, she willed her tears under control, and wanted me to tell her about a word she had heard me use the previous week, "dissociative." She questioned me as if the issue were a strictly academic one for her, which it clearly was not. I gently steered her back to the subject of herself and her week.

"Where did you have dinner Monday night?"

"What? Oh. Dinner Monday night. I had dinner at the Grill 23 with my friend Elaine."

"Was it a nice time?" I continued to question.

"I think so. Yes, I think it was okay."

"What did you and Elaine talk about, do you remember?"

"What did we talk about? Let's see. Well, I think we talked about the film a bit. And we talked about the waiter. Very cute waiter." She grinned. "And we probably spent the longest time talking about Elaine's relationship with this new guy, Peter. Why do you ask?"

"You said the dinner was the last thing you remembered before you woke up this morning. I thought it might be important. What did Elaine say about Peter?"

"Well, she said she's madly in love, and she said she wanted me to meet him because she thought we'd have a lot to talk about. He's from L.A., too."

"You and Peter are both from L.A. What else did you and Elaine say about L.A.?"

Julia looked suddenly blank, and said, "I don't remember. Why? Do you really think something about the place where I grew up scares me enough that just talking about it blasts me into never-never land for three days? That really can't be, though. I mean, I talk about L.A. a lot to people."

"I think it's possible that something during the dinner scared you enough to make you lose yourself for a while, although we'll never know for sure. Obviously, talking about L.A. doesn't always do that, but maybe there was something in that particular conversation that reminded you of something else that triggered something in your mind, something that might seem innocuous to another person, or even to you at another time. But as I say, we'll never know for sure."

"That's frightening. That's awful. It's like I'm in jail in my own head. I don't think I can live this way anymore."

"Yes, it's very frightening. I suspect it's been very frightening for a long time."

"You got that right."

Julia's knowledge of her own life, both past and present, had assumed the airy structure of Swiss cheese, with some solid substance that she and her gifted intellect could use, but riddled with unexplained gaps and hollows. This had its funny side. A few months later, when she had gained a better acceptance of her problem, she came in, sat down, and said in a characteristically charming way, "How do you like my new bracelet?"

"It's beautiful," I replied. "I've always admired your amethyst jewelry. When did you get that piece?"

"Who knows?"

She grinned at me again, and we both laughed.

The somewhat old-fashioned term for Julia's departures from herself during which she would continue to carry out day-to-day activities is "fugue," from the Italian word *fuga,* meaning "flight." A dissociative state that reaches the point of fugue is one of the most dramatic spontaneously occurring examples of the human mind's ability to divide consciousness into parts. In fugue, the person, or the mind of the person, can be subdivided in a manner that allows certain intellectually driven functions to continue—rising at a certain time, conversing with others, following a schedule, even carrying out complex tasks—while the part of consciousness that we usually experience as the "self"—the self-aware center that wishes, dreams, plans, emotes, and remembers—has taken flight, or has perhaps just darkened like a room at night when someone is sleeping.

The departures of fugue are related to certain experiences in ordinary human life that are not generated by trauma. For example, similar is the common experience of the daily commuter by car who realizes that sometimes she or he arrives back at home in the evening without having been aware of the activities of driving. The driving was automatically carried out by some part of the mind, while the self part of the mind was worrying, daydreaming, or listening to the radio. The experience is that of arriving at home without remembering the process of the trip. If one reflects upon the minute and complex decisions and maneuvers involved in driving a car, this ordinary event is really quite remarkable.

Clinical fugue differs from common human experience not so much in kind as in degree. Fugue is terror-driven and complete, while the more recognizable condition is the result of distraction, and relatively transparent. As fugue, the car trip example would involve a driver who failed to remember not just the process of the trip, but also the fact that there had been a trip, and from where.

Far beyond distraction, the more remarkable dissociative reaction of fugue would have been set off by something—an event, a conversation, an image, a thought—that was related, though perhaps in some oblique and symbolic way, to trauma.

Not all traumatized individuals exhibit outright fugue. For some people, stressful events trigger a demifugue that is less dramatic but in some ways more agonizing. Another of my patients, Lila, refers to her experience as "my flyaway self":

"I had an argument with the cashier at the Seven-Eleven store. I gave him a twenty and he said I gave him a ten. He wouldn't give me my other ten dollars back. The way he looked at me—it was just the way my stepfather used to, like I was stupid, like I was dirt. I knew he wasn't really my stepfather, but all the feelings were there anyway. After a minute, I just couldn't argue about it. I left without my money, and by the time I got back home, my flyaway self thing had started. Once it starts, it's like there's absolutely nothing I can do about it. I'm gone, and there's nothing I can do about it."

"What does it feel like?"

"Oh boy. I don't know how to describe it. It's just ... it's just really awful. I don't know ... everything around me gets very small, kind of unreal, you know? It's my flyaway self, I call it. It feels like ... my spirit just kind of flies away, and everything else gets very small—people, everything. If it were happening now, for example, you would look very small and far away, and the room would feel kind of unreal. Sometimes even my own body gets small and unreal. It's awful. And when it happens, I can't stop it. I just can't stop it."

What Lila describes as her "flyaway self" is in some respects similar to the derealization that most people have known occasionally, usually under passing conditions of sleep deprivation or physical illness. One temporarily has the sense of looking at the world through the wrong end of a telescope: everything looks small and far away, though one knows intellectually that these same things are just as close and life-sized as ever.

Imagine being forced to live lengthy segments of your life in this state. Imagine that you were falling inexorably into it, to remain there for a week or more at a time, because of events such as an unpleasant argument with a stranger at a convenience store. As bad as this would be, the situation for someone like Lila is incalculably worse, because for her the phenomenon has its origins in trauma.

Another of my patients offered a specific image, and for me an indelible one, to describe the same dissociative condition. Forty-nine-year-old Seth, like Julia, is successful, educated, and visually talented, and his disquieting description reflects his aptitudes. At the beginning of this particular therapy session, he had been telling me about a startling encounter, at a company softball game, with another person lost in the dissociated space with which he himself was all too familiar.

"I knew exactly where she was," said Seth.

"What does it feel like?" I asked. "Can you tell me what it feels like when you're there? How do you change?"

"I don't change. It's not that I change. *Reality* changes. Everything becomes very small, and I exist entirely inside my mind. Even my own body isn't real."

Indicating the two of us and the room around us, he continued, "Right now, this is what's real. You're real. What we're saying is real. But when I'm like that, the office is not real. *You're* not real anymore."

"What is real at those times?" I asked.

"I don't know exactly. It's hard to explain. Only what's going on in my mind is real. I'll tell you what it feels like: I feel like I'm dog-paddling out in the ocean, moving backwards, out to sea. When I'm still close enough to the land, I can sort of look way far away and see the beach. You and the rest of the world are all on the beach somewhere. But I keep drifting backwards, and the beach gets smaller, and the ocean gets bigger and bigger, and when I've drifted out far enough, the beach disappears, and all I can see all around me is the sea. It's so gray—gray on gray on gray."

"Is there anything out in the ocean with you?" I asked.

Seth replied, "No. Not at that point. I'm completely alone, more alone than you can imagine. But if you drift out farther, if you go all the way out to where the bottom of the sea drops off to the real abyss part, then there are awful things, these bloodthirsty sea creatures, sharks and giant eels and things like that. I've always thought that if something in the real world scared me enough, I'd drift out and out to past the dropping-off part, and then I would just be gobbled up, gone—no coming back, ever.

"When I'm floating out in the middle of the sea, everything else is very far away, even time. Time becomes unreal, in a way. An hour could go by that seems like a day to me, or four or five hours could go by, and it seems like only a minute."

Some extreme trauma survivors recognize that they are dissociative, and others do not recognize this. Many times, an individual will realize at some point in adulthood that she or he has had a lifelong pattern of being "away" a grievously large portion of the time.

During the same session, Seth described his own situation in this way:

"Actually, when I was a child, I don't know how much time I spent away like that. I never thought about it. It was probably a lot of the time, maybe even all the time. It just *was*."

"You mean it was your reality, and so of course you never questioned it, any more than any other child questions his reality?"

"Right. That's right. That was when I was a child. And most of the time it still happens automatically, bang, way before I know it's coming; but in here now, sometimes, there's this brief moment when I know I'm about to go away, but I still have time to try to keep it from taking over. Emphasis on *try*."

"How do you do that?" I asked.

"By concentrating. By trying with everything I've got to concentrate on you, and what you're saying, and on the things around me in the office here. But then there's physical pain, too. My eyes hurt, and I know I could make myself feel better if I shut them. But I try not to. And I get this thing in my stomach, which is the hardest thing to fight. There's this pain that feels like

I just swallowed a whole pile of burning coals, this torture feeling that beams out from my stomach to the rest of my body; sooner or later, it just takes me over."

He grimaced and put a fist to his breastbone.

When Seth said this about pain in his stomach, I remembered, as I had remembered during descriptions by many, many others, that there is a common Japanese term, *shin pan*, inexactly translated as "agitated heart syndrome," referring to a great pain between the chest and the stomach, just under the solar plexus. *Shin pan*, a condition as real within Eastern medicine as is cataract or ulcer or fractured fibula within Western medicine, is a pain of the heart that does not involve the actual physical organ. In our culture, we consider such a thing—a "heartache," if you will—to be poetry at most. We do not understand that much of the rest of the world considers it to be quite real.

I said to Seth, "It must be frightening to be out in the ocean like that."

"Actually, it's not," he replied. "The abyss part, with the sharks and all, that's frightening. But for most of my life it was really no more frightening than the things that were on the beach, no more frightening than reality, I guess is what I'm saying. So floating in the middle of the ocean was really the best place, even though I guess that sounds strange. Also, being there takes care of the physical pain; there's no more pain when I'm there. It's just that now, I mean lately, the beach, where you are, and everything else, sometimes it makes me wish I could maybe be there instead. I guess you could say that now, at least sometimes, I want to live."

I smiled at him, but he looked away, unsure of what he had just proposed.

Referring back to Seth's softball team acquaintance, whose dissociative episode had begun our discussion, I said, "It must be strange to be with another person when you know she's drifting away in an ocean just like you do sometimes."

"Yes, it's very strange."

"How did you know she was drifting? Did she tell you?"

"No. She didn't tell me. She didn't say anything at all about being dissociated. She was just standing around with us, talking about these incredible things, horrible things from her past, without any emotion, without any reaction to them. She played well that day, actually, but she won't remember any of it, that's for sure."

"You mean," I asked, "another person, besides you, might not have known she was dissociated?"

"Absolutely. I'm sure someone else might not have known at all. It's just that I looked at her, and I saw me. It was like talking to somebody who didn't have a soul."

"You mean her soul was somewhere else?"

"Yes, I guess so. Her soul was somewhere else," Seth said.

After a brief silence, he turned the discussion back to his own life: "The other day, my wife was trying to talk to me about something really important that happened when the twins were born. Doesn't matter what it was; what matters is that I had no idea what she was talking about. I didn't have a clue. It wasn't a dim memory. It wasn't anything. I didn't have that memory because I wasn't there."

"You weren't there, but your wife didn't know that at the time?" I asked.

"No, she didn't know that at all. But you know, most of the time when she and I are making love, and I'm not there, she doesn't know it even then."

"You mean, someone can be that close to you, and still not know?"

"Yes."

At that moment I thought, and then decided to say aloud, "That's so sad."

A single tear skimmed down Seth's cheek. He wiped it quickly with the back of his hand, and said, "I'm sorry, it's just that, well, when I think about it, I realize that, really, I've missed most of my own life."

He stopped and took a deep breath, and I wondered whether he might have to dissociate just to get through this experience in my office.

I asked, "Are you here now, at this moment?"

"Yes, I think so. Yes."

There was another pause, and then with more emotion in his voice than he was usually able to show, he said, "It's so hard, because so much of the time when I'm here, what you're seeing is not what I'm seeing. I feel like such an impostor. I'm out in my ocean, and you don't know that. And I can't tell you what's going on. Sometimes I'd really like to tell you, but I can't. I'm gone."

Seth's description of his inner life makes it wrenchingly clear that the traumatized person is unable to feel completely connected to another person, even a friend, even a spouse. Just as limiting, perhaps even more limiting, is such a person's disconnection from his or her own body. You will recall that Lila's "fly-away self" owned a body that was only "small and unreal," and that when Seth was in his ocean, his mind was separated from his physical self. I began this chapter with Julia, the brilliant producer of documentary films, and as it happens, about a year into her treatment, an event occurred that well illustrates the survivor's trauma-generated dissociation from the body itself, or more accurately, from those aspects of mind that inform one of what is going on in the body.

One morning just after the workday began, Julia's assistant, a gentle young woman who was quite fond of her boss, noticed that Julia was looking extremely pale. She asked how Julia was feeling, and Julia replied that she thought her stomach was a little upset, but other than that she was sure she was fine. Ten minutes later, walking down a corridor, Julia fell to the floor, and by the time the panic-stricken assistant came to her aid, she was unconscious. An ambulance arrived and rushed Julia to the Massachusetts General Hospital, where she underwent an immediate emergency appendectomy. Her life was in danger, and the situation was touch-and-go for a while, because her infected appendix had already ruptured and severe peritonitis had resulted. She survived, however, and during her recovery, when she was well enough to see me again, she recounted a postsurgery conversation with her doctor.

"The doctor kept asking me, 'Didn't you feel anything? Weren't you in pain?' I told her my stomach had been upset that morning, but I didn't remember any real pain. She said, 'Why didn't you call me?' I guess she just couldn't believe that I really hadn't felt any pain. She said that I should have been in agony by the previous night, at the very latest. She kept saying 'agony.' But I didn't feel it. I swear to you I didn't feel any pain, much less agony."

"I believe you," I said to Julia.

"Well, I don't think she did. I guess a ruptured appendix involves a lot of pain for most people."

"Yes. Yes it does," I replied, trying to disguise some of my own astonishment.

"I know I've tried to kill myself intentionally, more than once, so maybe this sounds crazy—but I don't want to die one day just because I'm confused."

"What do you mean?" I asked.

"I don't want to die because I can't feel anything. I don't want to end up dead because I can't feel what's going on in my body, or because I can't tell the difference between that psychosomatic pain I'm always getting in my chest and some honest-to-God heart attack."

Julia said "psychosomatic," but I was thinking *shin pan*, again.

"You know how we talk about my tendency to be dissociative? Well do you think I dissociate from my body, too? Because if that's what I'm doing, then it's the illusion from hell. I mean, if it's supposed to save me, it's not working. In fact, it's going to kill me one day. And even if it doesn't kill me, what's the use of living if I can't feel anything? Why should I be alive when I lose big parts of my life? I mean, really, how can you care about anything if you can't even know the truth about yourself? If you keep losing yourself?"

I said, "I think that's one of the best questions I've ever heard."

"You do? You mean you agree with me about how I can't really care about living if I keep losing myself?"

"I said that's one of the best *questions*. I didn't say I knew the answer."

"Oh boy, you're cagey," she said, and grinned. "So okay, how do I find the answer?"

"Well you know, you could try to remember. We could try hypnosis, for one thing."

I believed that Julia might be ready to bring up the lights in the cold, dark house of her past.

"Yes, so you've said. And the idea scares the hell out of me." There was a substantial pause before she continued. "The idea scares the hell out of me, but I think I have to do it anyway."

"Why do you have to?"

"Because I want to know. Because I want to live."

"So, let's do it?" I asked.

"Let's do it," Julia said.

QUESTIONS FOR MAKING CONNECTIONS
WITHIN THE READING

1. Drawing on the information Stout provides, discuss the relations between the mind—in particular the memory—and the brain. Why are traumatic memories generally inaccessible? When Stout refers to "our divided

awareness," what does she mean? Is it possible for awareness to become undivided? If such a state can be achieved at all, can it ever become permanent, or is "dividedness" an inescapable feature of consciousness itself?

2. Explain the difference between dissociation and ordinary distraction. What is it about Julia's lapses of memory that qualifies them as examples of dissociation? Are there significant differences between Julia's lapses and Seth's? Has Seth devised ways of coping that have proven more successful than Julia's?

3. In her discussion of Seth, Stout makes a reference to the condition known as *shin pan*, a term taken from Asian medicine. Does this reference bring something new to our understanding that the term *heartache* does not? Is Stout just showing off her knowledge of Eastern culture, or is she trying to get us to rethink our own attitudes about the importance of emotions?

QUESTIONS FOR WRITING

1. The title of Stout's book is *The Myth of Sanity: Divided Consciousness and the Promise of Awareness.* Now that you have read one chapter from her book, why do you think she refers to sanity as a "myth"? What does she mean by "the promise of awareness"? How might "awareness" differ from "sanity"?

2. Julia and Seth both qualify as extreme cases of dissociation, but their experiences may also shed some light on ordinary consciousness. Taking Stout's essay as your starting point, and drawing also on your own experience, discuss the nature of consciousness. Does the mind operate like a camcorder, or is awareness more complex and less continuous than the images stored in a camcorder's memory?

3. Can we ever know reality—the world as it actually is—or are we trapped within our own mental worlds? If memory shapes our perceptions from moment to moment, then would you say that experience can ever teach us anything new? If memory is unreliable, then what are the implications for self-knowledge? Is the ancient adage "Know Thyself" actually an invitation to wishful thinking?

QUESTIONS FOR MAKING CONNECTIONS
BETWEEN READINGS

1. In "The Mega-Marketing of Depression in Japan," Ethan Watters makes the case for seeing depression as a cultural construct rather than an empirical fact. He does not deny the reality of depression as an experience, but he proposes that people in different cultures will understand the disorder differently. Dr. Laurence J. Kirmayer, an authority whom Watters quotes with approval, notes that "a Nigerian man might experience a culturally distinct form of

depression by describing it as a peppery sensation in his head. A rural Chinese farmer might speak only of shoulder or stomach aches. A man in India might talk of semen loss or a sinking heart or feeling hot." What might Watters say about Stout's account of dissociative disorders? What might Stout say about Watters' view? What conclusions can we draw from the fact that Julia, Seth, and others respond to trauma in similar ways? Does this similarity undermine Watters's argument about the role of culture?

2. In her text, Stout discusses how dissociation causes people to have different experiences of reality. Her patient Seth describes what happens to his perception when he dissociates: "It's not that I change. *Reality* changes." How is the concept of reality related to perception? How can that help explain why, as Tim O'Brien writes, "In a war, you lose your sense of the definite, hence your sense of truth itself, and therefore it's safe to say that in a true war story nothing is ever absolutely true"? How do the versions of truth and reality the texts embrace complicate, confirm, or contradict each other? How might the subjective nature of truth and reality make communication difficult for O'Brien's narrator and his fellow soldiers, as well as for Stout's patients? How can awareness of the subjectivity of reality make communication easier?

$$\blacklozenge\blacklozenge\blacklozenge$$

ROBERT THURMAN

ROBERT THURMAN, ONE of the first Americans to be ordained as a Tibetan Buddhist monk, is often considered to be the most prominent and influential expert on Buddhism in the United States today. A scholar, translator, activist, and lecturer (as well as father of the actress Uma Thurman), Thurman began his explorations into Buddhism in his early twenties when he traveled to India on a "vision quest" and ended up becoming a student of the Dalai Lama. Upon returning to the United States, Thurman wanted to continue his studies and become an academic because, in his own words, "[t]he only lay institution in America comparable to monasticism is the university." Thurman is currently the Jey Tsong Khapa Professor of Indo-Tibetan Buddhist Studies at Columbia University and the president of Tibet House, a nonprofit organization dedicated to the study and preservation of Tibetan culture.

Infinite Life (2004), from which "Wisdom" is taken, is one in an impressive series of books that Thurman has written on Buddhism for a Western audience. Chief among his goals in this text is to guide laypeople into their first explorations of the Buddhist concept of selflessness. The ultimate goal of the lessons that Thurman offers his readers is to impart a deeper sense of interconnectedness, a process that is meant to reduce the negative feelings individuals hold about themselves and to increase the positive feelings they have for themselves and others. In doing so, Thurman seeks to show that the happiness America's founders guaranteed "should be ours and that there are methods for discovering which happiness is really reliable and satisfying, and then securing that in an enduring way without depriving others."

Thurman's more recent books are concerned with the relevance of Buddhism to contemporary world problems. He has argued, for example, that pre-invasion Tibet had advanced quite far beyond the militarism that still deforms social life in the modern world. "The fact that a majority of [the] country's single males [were] monks rather than soldiers" is a major lesson for us today. In *Why the Dalai Lama Matters* (2008), Thurman makes the case that the Dalai Lama plays a unique role in global culture precisely because he advocates a new ethics of altruism that can bridge cultural divides.

Final quotation is drawn from Joshua Glenn, "The Nitty Gritty of Nirvana," *Hilobrow*, July 23, 2009 <http://hilobrow. com/2009/07/23/the-nitty-gritty-of-nirvana/>.

Wisdom

Preamble: Selflessness

At one point in the early 1970s, after I'd gotten my Ph.D. and started teaching Buddhism, I went back to visit my old teacher, the Mongolian lama Geshe Wangyal. We were working on a project to translate a Buddhist scientific text from the Tibetan. We were six or seven people gathered around a kitchen table, and Geshe-la began to talk about the inner science of Buddhist psychology, the Abhidharma. He was reading us a few verses about the insight of selflessness, the deep release of becoming unbound, when I began to feel a little dizzy, even nauseous. It was a funny feeling. It felt slightly like a vibration spinning in my head. The vibration came not from Geshe-la, but from this ancient tradition. It was as though my habitual mind couldn't quite find traction. I realized that if I fought it, the sensation would only get more nerve-wracking and I would only feel more nauseous. So I didn't fight it. Instead, I let go and relaxed, and soon I was able to orient myself in another way, away from my "self." I felt like I was slowly but surely loosening my self-centered perspective on life and the world. In a useful way, a strengthening way, I was beginning to experience the great Buddhist mystery that is the selflessness of subjects and objects.

The Buddha based his psychology on his discovery of actual and ultimate reality. This he called "selflessness" and "voidness," or "emptiness." Some people love these words from the moment they hear them, but others are frightened by them. People often ask me, "Why did Buddha have to be such a downer? Obviously nirvana is a happy, cheerful state. So why didn't he just call it 'bliss' or something? Why did he have to label the reality he discovered with negative words such as 'voidness,' 'emptiness,' and 'selflessness'?" When people respond negatively to these terms, it's often because they're worried that the words imply they are going to die, disappear, or go crazy in their attempts to seek enlightenment. And that's exactly why the Buddha called reality by those names. He did it on purpose, to liberate you! Why? Because the only thing that's frightened by the word "selflessness" is the artificially constructed, unreal, and unrealistic self. That self is only a pretend self, it lacks reality, it doesn't really exist. That pseudo-self seems to quiver and quake because the habit that makes it seem real wants to keep its hold on you. So if you're seeking happiness and freedom, then you should want to scare the heck out of your "self"—you want to scare it right out of your head!

Actually, *it* is constantly scaring the heck out of *you*. Your "self" is always busy terrorizing you. You have a terrorist in your own brain, coming out of your own instincts and culture, who is pestering you all the time. "Don't relax too much," it is saying, "you'll get stepped on. A bug will bite you. Someone will be nasty to you. You'll get passed by, abused, sick. Don't be honest. Pretend. Because if you're honest, they'll hurt you." And it's ordering you, "Be my slave. Do what I tell you to do. Keep me installed up here at this very superficial level of the brain where I sit in my weird Woody Allen–type cockpit. Because I'm in control." Your falsely perceived, fixated, domineering self is precisely what's getting between you and a fulfilling life.

Early on, some of the Western psychologists who were beginning to learn from the Buddhist tradition—members of the transpersonal and other movements—came up with the idea that the relationship between Buddhist and Western psychology is this: "Western psychology helps somebody who feels they are nobody become somebody, and Buddhist psychology helps somebody who feels they are somebody become nobody." When I first heard this, I was at an Inner Science conference with the Dalai Lama. Everybody laughed, applauded, and thought it was a great insight. The Dalai Lama just looked at me and kind of winked and was too polite to say anything. I started to jump up to make a comment, but he stopped me. He told me to be quiet and let all of them ponder it for a few years until they realized the flaw in their thinking. Because of course that idea is not even remotely correct.

The purpose of realizing your own selflessness is not to feel like you are nobody. After he became enlightened, the Buddha did not sit under a tree drooling and saying, "Oh, wow! I'm nobody!" Think about it: If he just "became nobody," if he escaped from the world through self-obliteration, then he wouldn't have been able to share so many teachings here on earth, to work for the good of all beings for years and years, long after he achieved nirvana. He would've just stayed in his "nobody" state and forgotten about all of us poor humans busy suffering through our miserable lives.

The reason why we sometimes think that the goal of Buddhism is just "to become nobody" is that we don't understand the concept of selflessness. "Selflessness" does not mean that we are nobody. It does not mean that we cease to exist. Not at all. There is no way you can ever "not exist," just as you cannot become "nothing." Even if you go through deep meditation into what is called "the realm of absolute nothingness," you will still exist. Even if you are so freaked out by a tragedy, such as losing your only child, that you try to end your existence completely, you will still exist. I have a healthy respect for tragedy. We do have terrible tragedies. Personally, I don't bear misfortune well; it knocks me out. But there is no way to become nobody. Even if you were to succeed in killing yourself, you will be shocked when you awaken to disembodied awareness, out-of-body but still a somebody, a ghostly wraith who wishes he hadn't just done that. And a terribly unfortunate living person who has been so brutalized that he blanks out who he was in a seemingly impenetrable psychosis is still somebody, as everybody else around him knows.

Our mind is so powerful that it can create a state of absolute nothingness that seems totally concrete. Thousands of yogis in the history of India and a few mystics in the West have entered such a state of nothingness. But no one can stay there forever, and it is not where you want to be.

Have you ever had a minor experience of nothingness? I've had it in the dentist's chair with sodium pentothal, because I used to eat a lot of sweets and not brush my teeth as a youngster so I had to have teeth pulled. They give you this knockout anesthetic, and if you are a hardworking intellectual, you are tired of your mind, so you think, "Oh great, I'm going to be obliterated for a little while." You're really pleased, and you feel this little buzz, and you're just about to get there. You're going to experience nothingness, a little foretaste of the nihilistic notion of nirvana! But suddenly the nurse is shaking you awake saying, "You've been slobbering in that chair long enough. Get out of here." It's over. You started to pass out, wanting to be gone, but now you're suddenly back with no sense of having been gone at all! And that's what it is like in the state of absolute nothingness. It's like being passed out in the dentist's chair. There's no sense of duration of time. But eventually you wake up, totally disoriented with a nasty headache, and you never even got to enjoy the oblivion.

So we can never become nothing, as appealing as that may sound to those who are addicted to the idea of nothingness after death. We are always somebody, even though we are selfless in reality. We are just different sorts of "somebodies" than we used to be. "Realizing your selflessness" does not mean that you become a nobody, it means that you become the type of somebody who is a viable, useful somebody, not a rigid, fixated, I'm-the-center-of-the-universe, isolated-from-others somebody. You become the type of somebody who is over the idea of a conceptually fixated and self-created "self," a pseudo-self that would actually be absolutely weak, because of being unrelated to the reality of your constantly changing nature. You become the type of somebody who is content never to be quite that sure of who you are—always free to be someone new, somebody more.

That's the whole point of selflessness. If you don't know exactly who you are all the time, you're not sick, you're actually in luck, because you're more realistic, more free, and more awake! You're being too intelligent to be stuck inside one frozen mask of personality! You've opened up your wisdom, and you've realized that "knowing who you are" is the trap—an impossible self-objectification. None of us knows who we really are. Facing that and then becoming all that we can be—astonishing, surprising, amazing—always fresh and new, always free to be more, brave enough to become a work in progress, choosing happiness, open-mindedness, and love over certitude, rigidity, and fear—this is realizing selflessness!

I never met the late, great comedian Peter Sellers, except splitting my sides in laughter while watching some of his movies, especially the *Pink Panther* series. I know he had his ups and downs in his personal life, though you can't believe all the things you hear from the tabloids. But I did read a quote from him, or maybe from his psychiatrist, that he was deeply troubled and distressed because he suffered from "not knowing who he really was." He would get into his roles as an actor so totally, he would think he was the person he was playing, and he couldn't find himself easily as his "own" person. So he suffered, feeling himself "out of control" in his life. When I read this, my heart went out to him. I imagined his psychiatrist sternly telling him he had better calm down and track himself down, and put a lid on his ebullient sense of life, leading him on and on in self-absorption in therapy under the guise that he was going to "find himself" once and for all. I, feeling a bit more freed by having awakened to even the tiniest taste of selflessness, wanted to cry out to Peter Sellers, "Stop suffering by thinking your insight is confusion! Don't listen to the misknowing and even fear your freedom! Learn to surf the energy of life that surges through your openness! You have discovered your real self already, your great self of selflessness, and that openness is what enables you to manifest the heart that shines through your work and opens the hearts of your audiences. Your gift is to release them into laughter, itself a taste of freedom! Why be confused and feel your great gift is something wrong?" But I didn't know him so I could not tell him what I'm telling you. But our lives are infinite and I will be telling his ongoing life-form one of these days, whether I recognize him or not!

The Buddha was happy about not knowing who he was in the usual rigid, fixed sense. He called the failure to know who he was "enlightenment." Why? Because he realized that selflessness kindles the sacred fire of compassion. When you become aware of your selflessness, you realize that any way you feel yourself to be at any time is just a relational, changing construction. When that happens, you have a huge inner release of compassion. Your inner creativity about your living self is energized, and your infinite life becomes your ongoing work of art.

You see others caught in the suffering of the terminal self-habit and you feel real compassion. You feel so much better, so highly relieved, that your only concern is helping those constricted other people. You are free to worry about them because, of course, they are having a horrible time trying to know who they are and trying to be who they think they should be! They are busy being ripped apart by the great streams of ignorance, illness, death, and other people's irritating habits. So they suffer. And you, in your boundless, infinitely interconnected, compassionate state, can help them.

This is the other crucial point about selflessness: it does not mean that you are disconnected. Even nirvana is not a state of disconnection from the world. There is no way to become removed from yourself or from other beings. We are ultimately boundless—that is to say, our relative boundaries are permeable. But we are still totally interconnected no matter what we do. You cannot disappear into your own blissful void, because you are part of everyone and they are part of you. If you have no ultimate self, that makes you free to be your relative self, along with other beings. It's as if your hand represents the universe and your fingers represent all beings. Each of your fingers can wiggle on its own, each can operate independently, just as each being has its own identity. And yet your fingers are part of your hand. If your hand did not exist, your fingers would not exist. You are one of many, many fingers on the hand that is all life.

To my surprise and delight, I learned recently that even some Western psychologists are now beginning to study and understand the harm done by self-centered thinking. The psychologist Dr. Larry Scherwitz conducted a study about type A people—the aggressive, loud, annoying types, like me. Scientists used to think that type As died younger because of their fast-paced, stressful lives. But this new study reveals that, in fact, some of us type A people are not going to die of a heart attack that soon after all. The type Bs out there, the mild-mannered, quiet, inward-focused types, might find this worrisome! We may stay around for years bothering them, because it turns out that the type A personality is not a risk factor for coronary heart disease or other stress-related health problems. It turns out that some people, like me, though we freak out all the time, are not always that stressed. Some of us actually enjoy being this way.

What is the real risk factor, then? Scherwitz and his colleagues reanalyzed the data and conducted some new studies. They discovered, by analyzing the speech patterns of type As and type Bs, that the high risk of heart disease and stress-related illness is correlated with the *amount of self-reference* in people's speech—the amount of self-preoccupation, self-centeredness, and narcissism. "Me, me, I, I, my, my, mine, mine. My golf course, my country club, my job, my salary, my way, my family, my religion, my shrine, my guru, my, my, mine." The more "I, me, my, and mine" there is in their speech—"mine" most of all—the more likely they are to succumb to stress, to keel over because their bodies revolt against that pressure of self-involvement. Whereas even though some people can be aggressive, annoying, loud, and seemingly "stressed," if their overall motivation is altruistic and they don't pay too much attention to themselves, they live longer. And the quiet type Bs who are also more concerned about others, not necessarily out of any altruistic religious inklings, but just naturally not paying much attention to themselves, tend to live longer, too.

I find this study amazing. I was with the Dalai Lama when he heard about the results. He was intrigued and very pleased. "Oh, really?" he said. "Let me see that paper. In Buddhist psychology, we also have this idea that obsessive self-preoccupation—possessiveness and selfishness and self-centeredness—is life's chief demon!"

Let us explore the problems created by this demon of self-preoccupation, the ways in which it causes us suffering. We will then practice a fundamental meditation in which we look for the fixated self and find that it does not, after all, exist. Once we have freed ourselves from the constricting habit of always thinking that we are the center of the universe, we will experience our first taste of the boundless joy and compassion that is infinite life.

PROBLEM: MISKNOWLEDGE AND
SELF-PREOCCUPATION

One of the hardest things we have to do on a regular basis is to admit that we are wrong. We stubbornly insist that we're right in situations where we're not quite sure if we are, and even when we sense that we've slipped. How much more indignant do we become when we feel certain that we're right and someone has the gall or the stupidity to challenge us? In this case, we feel an absolute imperative to jump up and trumpet our rightness. If we still cannot get others to agree with us, we soon become self-righteous and then outraged.

Believe it or not, the fact that we struggle so much with being wrong is of tremendous importance to our task of awakening to the reality of selflessness. We should examine our habit of needing to be right carefully to see why it feels so good.

Being right means that the world affirms us in what we think we know. "Knowing" something is a way of controlling it, being able to put it in its proper place in relation to us so that we can use it effectively. As Dharmakirti, the seventh-century Indian philosopher, said, "All successful action is preceded by accurate knowledge." So knowledge is power, in the sense that it empowers us to act successfully. Misknowledge, misunderstanding a situation, is weakness, in the sense that our actions may fail in their aim, backfire, or have unintended consequences. Knowledge is security, in that we know our vulnerabilities and can avoid harm. Misknowledge is danger, in that we don't know what others might do to us or what traps may await us. We therefore feel powerful and secure when we're right, weak and vulnerable when we're wrong.

Viewed in this context, being right seems like a struggle for survival, a drive to win. It's natural for us to cling to that feeling, even when we have not investigated the reality around us because we don't really want to know if we are wrong. We think that finding ourselves in the wrong means a loss of power and safety, forgetting that actually *it is the only way* for us to discover what is truly right and truly wrong, thereby gaining real power and real safety. When we pretend, we focus our attention on appearing to be right no matter what the reality, we distract ourselves from being awake to what really is going on, and so place ourselves at a disempowering disadvantage.

In light of this simple analysis, what lies at the center of our constant need to assure our rightness and, therefore, our power and security? Is it not the certainty that "I am"? Does not the strong sense of "I am" seem absolutely right, unquestionable, in fact? Every self-identification, judgment, and impulse beginning with "I am"—"I am me," "I am American," "I am human," "I am male," "I am right," "I am sure," "I am angry"—seems natural, undeniable, imperative. As such, we are habitually driven to obey in feelings, thoughts, words, and deeds whatever comes from within the inexhaustible fountain of I am's, I think's, I want's, I love's, I hate's, and I do's. "I" is the absolute captain of our ship, the agent of our fate, the master of our lives.

When apes or bulls or mountain goats snort and paw the ground and then charge head first at one another, we interpret their behavior as an "I" versus "I" contest, sometimes to the death. Similarly, the imperative issuing from our "I" can be so adamant, so unchallengeable, that we human beings, too, will sacrifice our lives. Just think of the nature of such statements as follows, when the "I" is aligned with country, church, God, family, race, gender, or species: "I am a patriot!" "I am a Protestant!" "I am a Catholic!" "I am a Christian!" "I am a Muslim!" "I am a believer!" "I am an atheist!" "I am white!" "I am a male!" "I am human!" In these situations, the "I" exercises tremendous power over us, and can often lead us to our death.

The "I," the ego-self seemingly absolutely resident in the heart of our being, is the one thing of which we each are absolutely certain, which we will die for, which we will kill for, which we will obey slavishly and unquestioningly throughout our lives. We are so accustomed to our habitual sense of self that we consider even the slightest absence of it—a moment of derangement, a loss of consciousness in fainting or deep sleep, a disorienting distraction of passion or terror, a dizzying state of drunkenness or drug-intoxication, a psychological or neurological disorder—absolutely terrifying. We can't imagine our lives without our "I" as a constant, demanding presence.

What is shocking and difficult for most Westerners to accept is that the Buddha discovered that this most certain knowledge of the "self" is actually "misknowledge"—a fundamental misunderstanding, a delusion. And what's more, he realized that this discovery was the key to liberation, the gateway to enlightenment. When he saw the false nature of the "I," he emitted his "lion's roar," pronouncing the reality of selflessness, identitylessness, voidness. This was his *Eureka!* moment, his scientific breakthrough, his insight into reality, from whence has flowed for thousands of years the whole philosophical, scientific, and religious educational movement that is Buddhism. Identifying this habitual, certain self-knowledge as the core misknowledge allowed the Buddha to give birth to wisdom, truth, and liberating enlightenment.

But the Buddha knew perfectly well that it would do no good to simply order people to accept his declaration of selflessness as dogma and cling to it as a slogan or creed. The instinctual entanglement of human beings within the knot of self-certainty is much too powerful to be dislodged in this way, selflessness at first too counterintuitive to be acknowledged as truth. No, the Buddha realized, people must discover their real nature for themselves. So he made his declaration of selflessness not a statement of fact but rather a challenge to inquiry.

"I have discovered selflessness!" the Buddha announced. "I have seen through the reality of the seemingly solid self that lay at the core of my being. This insight did not destroy me—it only destroyed my suffering. It was my liberation! But you need not believe me. Discover the truth for yourself. Try with all your might to verify this 'self' you feel is in there, to pin it down. If you can do that, fine, tell me I'm wrong and ignore whatever else I may have to say. But if you fail to find it, if each thing you come up with dissolves under further analysis, if you discover, as I did, that there is no atomic, indivisible, durable core 'self,' then do not be afraid. Do not recoil or turn away. Rather, confront that emptiness and recognize it as the doorway to the supreme freedom! See through the 'self' and it will release you. You will discover that you are a part of the infinite web of interconnectedness with all other beings. You will live in bliss from now on as the relative self you always were; free at long last from the struggle of absolute alienation, free to help others find their own blessed freedom and happiness!"

Though in this paraphrase of his core teaching the Buddha offers us much encouragement, the challenge remains its central thrust. "You think you're really you? Don't just accept that blindly! Verify whether or not your 'self' is actually present within you. Turn your focused attention to it and explore it. If it's as solid as it seems, then it should be solidly encounterable. If you can't encounter it, then you must confront your error."

The great philosopher Descartes made a grave error when he thought he discovered in his fixed subjective self the one certain thing about existence. After demolishing the entire universe of observable things with hammer blows of systematic doubt, he was unable to give even a tiny tap to collapse this sense of self! And so he set down as the basis for his entire philosophy the famous proposition, "I think, therefore I am!"

Believe it or not, in his deep exploration for the "self," Descartes almost took another path that would have led him to enlightenment. He got very close to discovering that he could not find the "self" he felt to be so absolutely present. After intensively dissecting appearances, drilling through layer upon layer of seeming certainties, he came out with nothing that he could hold onto as the "self." But then he made the tragic mistake. Instead of accepting his selflessness, he instead said to himself, "Ah! Well, of course I cannot find the self. It is the self that is doing the looking! The 'I' is the subject and so it cannot be an object. Though I cannot find it, still my knowledge that it is the absolute subject cannot be doubted. It confirms its existence by doubting its existence. *Cogito ergo sum*! Of this I can remain absolutely certain."

Why was this mistaken? His logic sounds plausible enough at first. It is, after all, a clever way out of the dilemma of looking for something you are sure is there but cannot find. But what's wrong with it? Let's say that I am looking for a cup. I find it, so I can be certain that the cup exists. I look for my friend and find her, so I can be certain she's there. I look for my glasses, I do not find them—so I proclaim certainty that they are there? No—I go get another pair because I acknowledge I've lost them. I look for my oh-so-familiar "I," and I cannot find it! Why would I think it's there, then? Because I've arbitrarily put it in the category of "things that are there only when I can't find them"? No, when I can't find it, it's rather more sensible that I must give up the sense of certainty that it's there. I feel it's there when I don't look for it, but as soon as I look for it with real effort, it instantly eludes discovery. It seems always to be just around the next corner in my mind, yet each time I turn around to seize it, it disappears. And so I must slowly come to accept the fact that it may not be there after all.

Put another way, imagine that you are walking through the desert when, far off on the horizon, you see an oasis. Yet when you get closer, it disappears. "Aha!" you think to yourself. "A mirage." You walk away. Miles later, you turn around and look back. There's the oasis again! Do you feel certain that the water is there now? No, on the contrary you feel certain that it is only a mirage of water. In the same way, when you look for the "self" and don't find it, you must accept that it is merely a mirage. Your solid self-sense is only an illusion.

Had Descartes persisted and found the door to freedom in his selflessness, as the Buddha did, then instead of proclaiming, "I think, therefore I am," he might have said, "Even though I can find no concrete, fixated 'self,' I still can think.

I still seem to be. Therefore I can continue to be myself, selflessly, as a relative, conventional, but ultimately unfindable being."

Whenever you decide to try a particular yoga [or form of meditation], the crucial first step is always deciding to make the change. You must begin by accepting the fact that your habitual conceptions could be wrong. If, for example, you live with the delusion that it is just fine to remain addicted to nicotine, that three packs of cigarettes a day puts you in optimal operating condition, then there is no way you will successfully complete a yoga to quit smoking. Likewise, in this crucial quest of the self, the presumed core of your self-addiction, you must first convince yourself through empirical observation that the way you hold your self-identity—the constricted feeling of being wrapped around a solid, independent core—is uncomfortable and disabling.

Why should you even care if the rigid "self" that you believe in so strongly really exists or not? Our self feels most real when we are right and righteous, when we are wrongly or unfairly challenged. And it also seems unique, completely separate from everyone and everything else in the universe. This separateness can feel like freedom and independence when we are in a good mood. But when we are in trouble, lonely or angry, under pressure or dissatisfied, this separateness feels like isolation, alienation, unfair treatment, or deprivation. When we are wholly gripped by fury, the searing energy that wants to attack a target picks our "I" up like a mindless tool and flings us at the other person. It is so disconnected that it even disregards our sense of self-protection, making us take actions that injure us, ignore injuries undergone, and even harm others with no regard for the consequences. There is no more powerful demonstration of our strong sense of being an independent entity than when we give ourselves over completely to anger.

When we look around at others, we see that they are just as alienated from us as we are alienated from them. As we want things from them, they want things from us. As we reject them, they seem to reject us. We don't love them, so how can we expect them to love us? And yet they are endless, while "I" am just one. So I am badly outnumbered. I feel threatened. I can never get enough, have enough, or be enough. I will inevitably lose the me-versus-all-of-them struggle in the long run.

We can, of course, experience moments of unity with other beings, through falling in love, or having a child, for example. When we do, we experience tremendous relief—for a moment, there are two of us teamed up against all the others together. We have an ally. But unfortunately those moments are too rare, and they do not last long before the old self-isolation re-emerges. Even lovers can turn into adversaries, couples often seek divorce, and children recoil from their parents, who in turn reject them.

This alienation caused by the presumed independent, absolute self was why the Buddha saw its illusion as the source of human suffering. The situation of feeling that it's always "the self versus the world," with the self as the long-term loser, is unsatisfactory and untenable. When we recognize the inevitable nonviability of our self-centered reality, it motivates us to engage in the quest for the true nature of the self. It makes it existentially essential for us to pause in our headlong rush through life and turn within, to verify whether the "self" really exists as we feel it does.

We can take great encouragement from the fact that the Buddha told us we could escape from our suffering. Still, we cannot merely accept someone else's report. No one else can do the job of replacing misunderstanding with understanding for us. We must look at reality and verify for ourselves whether our habitual sense of having a fixed self or the Buddha's discovery of selflessness is ultimately true. In this way, we can begin to transform the self-preoccupation that causes chronic suffering into the insightful, gradual opening and letting go of the self that is, paradoxically, so self-fulfilling. We want to be happy, but ironically we can only become happier to the extent that we can develop an unconcern for our "self." This process is long and gradual, though you will experience frequent breakthrough moments that will thrill you and motivate you to continue.

Before we actually engage in the meditation practice used to discover the true nature of the self, we must set up our parameters in practical, clear terms. When we look through a darkened house for a misplaced key, we first remember what the key looks like, and then we search for it carefully, room by room, turning lights on as we go. We use a flashlight to look under beds and in hidden corners. When we have looked everywhere exhaustively and not found it, we decide we've missed it somehow, so we go back and repeat the process. However, after one or two searches of this kind, we come to a decisive conclusion that the key is not in the house. We know we could continue looking endlessly, but that would be impractical. So we decide to proceed accordingly with our lives.

In the case of the quest for the self, we will look through all the processes of our body and mind that we can find and investigate them thoroughly. Our physical systems, sensational feelings, conceptual image bank, emotional energies, and consciousness itself constitute the house through which we will search. There are also various vaguely defined areas such as "spirit" and "soul" that, like a dusty attic or dank cellar, we may feel the need to explore. It is easy to get lost in these murky, dank, and oft-forgotten quarters of the mind. So we must get a clear picture of what we want to find ahead of time. And most important, we must set some limits to the exercise, since practically speaking we cannot continue to search indefinitely.

At this point you should search through the house of your body-mind-spirit a few times with great concentration and systematic thoroughness, with my help and the help of many experts who have guided me through this practice. If, during this process, you find a "self," then enjoy it to the full. If, however, as I suspect will be the case, you do not find what stands up solidly as your "real self" by the end of the process, then you will have to live with the fact that there is no such thing. You will need to make the practical decision to turn from seeking the "self" to explore instead the ramifications of being a relative self without any absolute underpinning.

This commitment to practicality in your quest for the self is of great importance at the outset and will have a significant impact on the success of the endeavor. Once you have made the commitment in your own mind, you may begin.

Practice: Trying to Find Your "I"

You are now prepared to deepen your understanding of your selflessness. You will be looking at yourself introspectively, trying to grasp exactly what your essence is. When you do this practice well, you will begin to feel yourself dissolving, just as I did at my mentor Geshe-la's house many years ago. You will start realizing—gradually and also suddenly, in spurts—that you can't find this mysterious "self." Your strong feeling of having an absolute "I" is maddeningly elusive when you try to pin it down precisely.

... In looking for your "self," start with your body. Ask yourself, "Am I my body?" In order to answer this question, you must define your body. It is composed at least of your five sense organs, right? Your skin and sensitive inner surfaces constitute the touch organ, then you have your eyes for sight, your nose for smell, your ears for hearing, and your tongue for taste. So first let's explore all of your senses together, your sensory system.

Identify the sound sense. What do you hear—a dog barking, a phone ringing, music playing, or perhaps just the sound of your own breathing? Now notice the visual field. You are reading words on the page. What else do you see? What are the images on the edge of your peripheral vision? How about smell? Perhaps you smell the scent of incense burning, or of musty wood. Do you taste anything: something you ate a while ago, tea you drank, or just the taste of your own mouth? The tactile field is everything touching your skin, including other parts of your skin touching your skin. Your hand may be resting on your knee, for example. Your bottom is touching a pillow. Just identify all the sensations, the textures, smells, tastes, sounds, and sights.

Now notice your internal sensations, like the breakfast in your tummy. You might have a slight pain in your back or your knee. Maybe your foot is falling asleep, and you're annoyed because there's a slightly painful sensation there. You might have a pleasurable sensation in some part of you that is feeling good if, for example, you worked out yesterday or had a massage.

Recognize that for each of these sensations you are experiencing, you are receiving data from the outside world. The sensations are not all coming from your own body. So your body is not just inside your skin; your body is both your organs and the field of all incoming sense objects. It's everything you are seeing and hearing and smelling and tasting and touching. It's the chair or pillow you're sitting on. The words you are reading on this page. The incense drifting into your nostrils. If you look at one sensation, you realize that you are sharing your material body with the outside world. Say, for example, you are looking at light bouncing off a table. That light is a part of your shared sensory system, and therefore part of your body, too.

So already you have begun to expand your self-definition, just by looking at your five senses. Suddenly you are not just something that sits there inside your skin. You are your environment as well. Your body interfuses with the outside world that you perceive with your senses. All of our bodies are totally overlapping, all the time. Do you see? And when you think, "this is 'me' over here inside this skin," you are unrealistically thinking that "I" am not connected to others through the sense perceptions that we have in common. But you are connected, even before you talk to them or think anything about them, through your shared environment.

Now you can move to the next level of analysis of the self, which exists at the level of your mind. First is the sensational system, the feelings of pleasure, pain, and numbness associated with sense perceptions of sights, sounds, smells, tastes, textures, and mental sense inner objects. When you experience these six kinds of objects, you react as pleased, irritated, or indifferent. Mentally inventory your sensations at the moment, and notice how you react at this basic feeling level. Notice that this heap of sense-reactions has no self-core within it.

Next is your conceptual system, your ideas, mental maps, and internal images. You have a picture of yourself as you exist in the world. You have a concept of yourself as human, not animal. You have a picture of yourself as male or female. You have a body image, and an image of each part of your body. You have a concept of your identity as a teacher, a manager, a doctor, or whatever. You have a concept of yourself as successful or as a failure. Inventory this mass of ideas and images and notice that you have whole clouds of pictures and concepts. But is this incredibly chaotic mass of images and words and diagrams and maps and so forth that is your conceptual system the real "you"? Your perception of yourself changes all the time, depending on your mood, whom you're with, or what you're doing. Sometimes you think, "I'm a high-powered executive," whereas other times you think, "I'm just a tiny speck on a tiny planet of six billion people." So surely your conceptual system cannot be your "self." The "you" self is not any of these ideas, since it seems to be the entity that is noticing all of them.

At the fourth level of analysis, find your emotional system. You are constantly reacting to all of these images and notions. Right now, you're probably feeling a bit irritated with me. You're thinking to yourself, "Why is he making me do this? Why doesn't he just crack a joke? Let's have some fun. What is this terrible business of exploring the self, 'discovering selflessness'? How is this helping me?" And so on and so forth. You're feeling annoyed and anxious and confused. Or maybe you're just feeling bored. Anyway, your emotions are there in your mind, always functioning, but always changing. You can take a peek at them now, as they swirl around in your heart and head, and you can see that they are not fixed. You are not defined by your emotions. They are not the elusive "self" you're seeking.

Lastly, turn your attention to your consciousness system. It is the most important system of all. You see at once how it is a buzzing, blooming, swirling mass of subtle energies. Nothing is fixed, nothing stable within it. With your mental consciousness, you hop from one sense to another. You analyze your ideas, you focus internally on your emotions and thoughts, and you can even focus on being thought-free. Your consciousness aims itself at being free of thought by the thought of being free of thought. How strange! As you inventory your consciousness, don't allow yourself to rest with a bare awareness, but go a bit deeper—explore further with your analytic attention. Ask yourself, "Who is this supposedly rigid 'self'? Is it the same self right now as the one who woke up grumbling this morning, preparing that cup of coffee, rushing to get ready, quickly brushing its teeth? Is it the same self who was born a tiny, unaware, helpless infant years ago? Who is the 'me' who knows my name, who knows what I want, where I am, and what I'm doing? Who is the 'me' who knows I'm an American, who knows I'm a—whatever: a Buddhist or a Christian or an atheist? Where is that person now? Where is that absolute, unchanging structure?" You can see how your self-consciousness is a buzzing, blooming, swirling mass of confusion—nothing is fixed, nothing stable within it. You can barely remember what you did yesterday morning—I can't remember at all at my age! So how can you possibly have a rigid self? See how releasing these sorts of thoughts can be! ...

The deepest stage of awareness comes when your consciousness begins to turn inward to gaze upon itself. At first it thinks, "I now know that these sensory, mental, and emotional systems looming before me are not the 'self,' they are not 'me.' But the awareness that looks at them, that contemplates and investigates them, that is my 'self.'" And yet you soon discover that you are mistaken even in this conclusion. The moment you begin to examine your own conscious mind, you engage in a whirling, internal dervish-dance where your awareness spins round and round upon itself. This contemplation can be dizzying, nauseating, painful, and even a bit frightening, as the felt "self" disappears and evades its own attention. You can never catch it, even as you become more experienced at this meditation and come back to this place again and again. Time and again you will feel frustrated by your continued failure to come up with a result. Yet you must not lose heart. You must remember that looking for your "self" is the most important thing you can ever do in your evolutionary development. You must keep faith that you are on the brink of a quantum leap; you are so close to awakening.

As you enter into this confusing realm of spinning self-seeking, be careful not to make the mistake Descartes made by withdrawing from it all with some sort of decision about "you" being the subject and therefore not any sort of findable object. Also, be careful not to fall into the nihilistic trap of withdrawing from the spinning by deciding that all is nothing after all and so naturally the self-sense is an illusion. Keep whirling upon your "self" as long as you feel absolutely there is a self to whirl upon, to look at, to catch. Put your full truth-seeking, analytic energy into the drive to find it.

Eventually, you will experience a gradual melting process. The whirling will slowly dissolve without fear: you won't shrink back in terror of falling into an abyss-like void because you are already overcoming your self-addiction. You control the tendency to shrink back in terror of falling into a looming void by your drilling, whirling energy of awareness itself. You dissolve your fearing subject, the object for which you are feeling fear, and the imagined nothingness that only the pseudo-self-addiction wants you to fear. However fully you feel such processes at first, what happens to you is that, as you begin to melt, your drive intensity lessens, you feel buoyed by a floating sensation coming from within your nerves and cells, from within your subjectivity as well as your object-field. At some point, you lose your sense of self entirely, as if you were a field of open space. Like Neo and his colleagues in the movie *The Matrix* when they entered one of the computer-generated training fields, you will find yourself standing in a blank white space—except in your case, in this transcending moment, you break free from your "digital residual self-image." You will be only the blank white space, a bare awareness of yourself as a boundless entity. Dissolving into this space, you'll feel intense bliss, a sense of extreme relief.

When you first melt into the spacious experience of freedom, it is enthralling, like emerging from a dark cave into infinite light. You feel magnificent, vast, and unbound. If you inadvertently fall into this state unprepared by arriving there too quickly, you may be tempted to think that you have arrived at the absolute reality, and this is a bit of a danger. You might think, feeling it nonverbally at this stage, that you've conquered the differentiated universe and realized its true "nothingness," experiencing it as such a profound and liberating release that you never again want any contact with the real world. Remember, however, that nothingness is not your ultimate goal—you are not trying to escape reality, but to embrace it. If you reach this space of release gradually through the repeated whirling of your self turning upon itself, then you'll be able to enjoy the vastness and magnificence without losing awareness that it is only another relational condition. You'll realize that the great emptiness is ultimately empty of itself; it is not reality, either.

Since you *are* the void, you do not need to remain in the void, and your original self-sense slowly reemerges within the universe of persons and things. But you are aware that it is not the same "self" you had before—it is forever different, now become infinite and unbound. You have changed. You now perceive your "self" consciously, living with it yet maintaining an educated distance from it. You are like one of the characters in *The Matrix*, present and active as real being, yet at the same time realizing that the apparent reality that surrounds you is only illusory. All that was apparent becomes transparent.

One of the most significant changes you will notice upon discovering your selflessness is that your sense of being separate from everyone else has now eroded. Your new awareness enables you to perceive others as equal to yourself, a part of you, even. You can see yourself as they see you, and experience empathically how they perceive themselves as locked within themselves. You have arrived at the doorway to universal compassion, and it frees you from being locked away behind a fixed point-of-awareness and opens you to a sort of field awareness wherein others are really just the same as you while simultaneously relationally different. Through the sense of sameness, you feel their pains as if they were your own: when they hurt, you hurt. Yet through the sense of relational difference and balanced responsibility, you naturally feel moved to free them from their pains, just as you move automatically to eliminate your own pains. When your hand is burned by a hot pot handle, you react at once to pull away from the heat, you plunge it into cold water, you rush to find ice. You respond instinctively to remove the pain. You don't consider it a selfless act of compassion for your hand. You just do it through your neural connection to your hand. Your new open awareness feels others' hands through a similar sense of natural connection.

QUESTIONS FOR MAKING CONNECTIONS
WITHIN THE READING

1. Choose one important term from Thurman's essay, such as *nirvana*, *nothingness, emptiness, enlightenment, meditation, compassion, ignorance, self, happiness*, or *freedom*. Then, by tracing Thurman's use of the term throughout the chapter, offer your own explanation of its meaning. While commonplace definitions for all of these terms may be found in a dictionary, here you are being asked to explain the meaning of the term as Thurman uses it. Then you might contrast Thurman's use of the term with more commonplace understandings. *Ignorance*, for example, has a special significance in the context of Buddhist thought. How does it differ from *ignorance* as we normally define it?

2. Instead of discussing the soul, Thurman focuses on the mind. How is "mind" different from "soul"? Where is the mind located, according to Thurman? Is it the same as the brain? What are some of the broader implications of Thurman's attention to the mind instead of the soul? If the mind is transformed, can the essence of the person remain somehow immune to change? Conversely, if a person's mental habits and perceptions remain unchanged, is it possible to imagine that the essence of the person has still been altered somehow? We might ordinarily think of each person as endowed with an individual soul, but is the mind individualized in the same way?

3. Thurman speaks about "enlightenment" instead of "redemption" or "salvation." How does "enlightenment" differ from "salvation"? What are the differences between Thurman's emphasis on the experience of "selflessness" and the famous Greek dictum "Know thyself"? Could selflessness qualify as a form of self-knowledge? Could it qualify as a form of redemption or salvation?

QUESTIONS FOR WRITING

1. Buddhism is often studied on the college level in courses offered by philosophy and religion departments. Judging from Thurman's account, what elements does Buddhism have in common with philosophy? With religion? Or, judging from Thurman's account, would you say that Buddhism has some elements in common with science, which is based on empirical observation? In what ways might Buddhism be closer to a science than to a religion or a philosophy?

2. What are the social and political implications of Thurman's argument? How would the cultivation of "wisdom" as he describes it affect people in a competitive, consumption-oriented society like our own? Is Thurman's brand of meditation compatible with democracy and the idea that all of us

are equal? How might the cultivation of wisdom influence the current political climate? Would the climate become less adversarial? Less driven by rigid ideology? Or would people who cultivate wisdom simply wash their hands of politics?

QUESTIONS FOR MAKING CONNECTIONS BETWEEN READINGS

1. Thurman presents the notion of selflessness as a cultural ideal, a way of thinking that contrasts with ideas about being an "I'm-the-center-of-the-universe, isolated-from-others somebody." Naomi Klein, in "Hot Money," describes the free trade forces aligned against environmental groups in similar terms, as a group narrowly focused on their financial interests to the exclusion of the health of the planet. Klein proposes, as an alternative to the "logic of indiscriminate economic growth," what she terms "managed degrowth," a new cultural ideal that would supplant the idea of continuous economic expansion. What might be the value of selflessness and managed degrowth as cultural ideals? How do the proposals to encourage the acceptance of degrowth, suggested by Klein, parallel Thurman's ideas about the value of selflessness? Is it likely that a "doorway to universal compassion" could become a social or political force? How might such a transformation occur?

2. In what ways is reading like the practice of meditation? To explore this question, draw primarily on Azar Nafisi's selections from *Reading Lolita in Tehran*. At a key moment in her account, Nafisi makes this observation:

    > Whoever we were—and it was not really important what religion we belonged to, whether we wished to wear the veil or not, whether we observed certain religious norms or not—we had become the figment of someone else's dreams. A stern ayatollah, a self-proclaimed philosopher-king, had come to rule our land.

    How, according to Nafisi, can the reading of fiction help us throw off the veils—literal and virtual—that others have imposed on us? Does reading as she describes it involve its own form of mental cultivation, comparable in some ways to the meditational practice that Thurman describes? Does reading allow Nafisi and her students to experience a form of "selflessness"? How can we tell the difference between the veils imposed on us and the persons we really are?

◆◆◆

SHERRY TURKLE

WHAT IS LIFE? What does it really mean for something to "be alive"? Questions like these were not on Sherry Turkle's mind when she took her daughter Rebecca to see a special exhibition on the life and work of Charles Darwin, the naturalist who first described the processes behind natural evolution. One of the first dioramas in the show included two live tortoises like the ones Darwin encountered on his expedition to the Galapagos Islands:

> One tortoise was hidden from view; the other rested in its cage, utterly still. Rebecca inspected the visible tortoise thoughtfully for a while and then said matter-of-factly, "They could have used a robot." I was taken aback and asked what she meant. She said she thought it was a shame to bring the turtle all this way from its island home in the Pacific, when it was just going to sit there in the museum, motionless, doing nothing.... [Later] a ten-year-old girl told me that she would prefer a robot turtle because aliveness comes with aesthetic inconvenience: "Its water looks dirty. Gross."

This reaction pushed Turkle to rethink much of her enthusiasm for technology. What kind of future might await humankind when children grow up preferring machines to biological life? What will happen to us psychologically if we envy our robots' skill, intelligence, and immortality?

Sherry Turkle's subject is the technology we tend to look at with uncritical awe—as she herself did for many years. Only gradually did Turkle come to understand that unless we stop to reflect, we might wind up as the tools of our tools: if our androids and PCs are meant to serve as extensions of ourselves, we could become their extensions instead. A further irony is that no one can foresee how our inventions will change us because no one can predict where technology is headed. Without a framework for assessing change, we might someday bitterly regret our naivety. Technology could prove to be unstoppable, but Turkle believes that we still have the power to control its pace and direction.

Sherry Turkle is the Abby Rockefeller Mauzé Professor of the Social Studies of Science and Technology at the Massachusetts Institute of Technology. Her early work on psychoanalysis paved the way for her later thinking on the "subjective side" of technology. Her books include *The Second Self: Computers and the Human Spirit* (1984), *Life on the Screen: Identity in the Age of the Internet* (1995), *Simulation and Its Discontents* (2009), *Reclaiming Conversation: The Power of Talk in a Digital Age* (2015). The selection that follows comes from her book, *Alone Together: Why We Expect More from Technology and Less from Each Other* (2011).

Selections from Alone Together: Why We Expect More from Technology and Less from Each Other

My first brush with a computer program that offered companionship was in the mid-1970s. I was among MIT students using Joseph Weizenbaum's ELIZA, a program that engaged in dialogue in the style of a psychotherapist. So, a user typed in a thought, and ELIZA reflected it back in language that offered support or asked for clarification.[1] To "My mother is making me angry," the program might respond, "Tell me more about your mother," or perhaps, "Why do you feel so negatively about your mother?" ELIZA had no model of what a mother might be or any way to represent the feeling of anger. What it could do was take strings of words and turn them into questions or restate them as interpretations.

Weizenbaum's students knew that the program did not know or understand; nevertheless they wanted to chat with it. More than this, they wanted to be alone with it. They wanted to tell it their secrets.[2] Faced with a program that makes the smallest gesture suggesting it can empathize, people want to say something true. I have watched hundreds of people type a first sentence into the primitive ELIZA program. Most commonly they begin with "How are you today?" or "Hello." But four or five interchanges later, many are on to "My girlfriend left me," "I am worried that I might fail organic chemistry," or "My sister died."

Soon after, Weizenbaum and I were coteaching a course on computers and society at MIT. Our class sessions were lively. During class meetings he would rail against his program's capacity to deceive; I did not share his concern. I saw ELIZA as a kind of Rorschach, the psychologist's inkblot test. People used the program as a projective screen on which to express themselves. Yes, I thought, they engaged in personal conversations with ELIZA, but in a spirit of "as if." They spoke as if someone were listening but knew they were their own audience. They became caught up in the exercise. They thought, I will talk to this program as if it were a person. I will vent; I will rage; I will get things off my chest. More than this, while some learned enough about the program to trip it up, many more used this same inside knowledge to feed ELIZA responses that would make it seem more lifelike. They were active in keeping the program in play.

Weizenbaum was disturbed that his students were in some way duped by the program into believing—against everything they knew to be true—that they were dealing with an intelligent machine. He felt almost guilty about the deception machine he had created. But his worldly students were not deceived. They knew all about ELIZA's limitations, but they were eager to "fill in the blanks." I came to think of this human complicity in a digital fantasy as the "ELIZA effect." Through the 1970s, I saw this complicity with the machine as no more threatening than wanting to improve the working of an interactive diary. As it turned out, I underestimated what these connections augured. At the robotic moment, more than ever, our willingness to engage with the inanimate does not depend on being deceived but on wanting to fill in the blanks.

Now, over four decades after Weizenbaum wrote the first version of ELIZA, artificial intelligences known as "bots" present themselves as companions to the millions who play computer games on the Internet. Within these game worlds, it has come to seem natural to "converse" with bots about a variety of matters, from routine to romantic. And, as it turns out, it's a small step from having your "life" saved by a bot you meet in a virtual world to feeling a certain affection to ward it—and not the kind of affection you might feel toward a stereo or car, no matter how beloved. Meantime, in the physical real, things proceed apace. The popular Zhu Zhu robot pet hamsters come out of the box in "nurturing mode." The official biography of the Zhu Zhu named Chuck says, "He lives to feel the love." For the elderly, the huggable baby seal robot Paro is now on sale. A hit in Japan, it now targets the American nursing home market. Roboticists make the case that the elderly need a companion robot because of a lack of human resources. Almost by definition, they say, robots will make things better.

While some roboticists dream of reverse engineering love, others are content to reverse engineer sex.[3] In February 2010, I googled the exact phrase "sex robots" and came up with 313,000 hits, the first of which was linked to an article titled "Inventor Unveils $7,000 Talking Sex Robot." Roxxxy, I learned, "may be the world's most sophisticated, talking sex robot."[4] The shock troops of the robotic moment, dressed in lingerie, may be closer than most of us have ever imagined. And true to the ELIZA effect, this is not so much because the robots are ready but because we are.

In a television news story about a Japanese robot designed in the form of a sexy woman, a reporter explains that although this robot currently performs only as a receptionist, its designers hope it will someday serve as a teacher and companion. Far from skeptical, the reporter bridges the gap between the awkward robot before him and the idea of something akin to a robot wife by referring to the "singularity." He asks the robot's inventor, "When the singularity comes, no one can imagine where she [the robot] could go. Isn't that right? ... What about these robots after the singularity? Isn't it the singularity that will bring us the robots that will surpass us?"

The singularity? This notion has migrated from science fiction to engineering. The singularity is the moment—it is mythic; you have to believe in it—when machine intelligence crosses a tipping point.[5] Past this point, say those who believe, artificial intelligence will go beyond anything we can currently conceive. No matter if today's robots are not ready for prime time as receptionists. At the singularity, everything will become technically possible, including robots that love. Indeed, at the singularity, we may merge with the robotic and achieve immortality. The singularity is technological rapture.

As for Weizenbaum's concerns that people were open to computer psychotherapy, he correctly sensed that something was going on. In the late 1970s, there was considerable reticence about computer psychotherapy, but soon after, opinions shifted.[6] The arc of this story does not reflect new abilities of machines to understand people, but people's changing ideas about psychotherapy and the workings of their own minds, both seen in more mechanistic terms.[7] Thirty years ago, with psychoanalysis more central to the cultural conversation, most people saw the experience of therapy as a context for coming to see the story of your life in new terms. This happened through gaining insight and developing a relationship with a therapist who provided a safe place to address knotty problems. Today, many see psychotherapy less as an investigation of the meaning of our lives and more as an exercise to achieve behavioral change or work on brain chemistry. In this model, the computer becomes relevant in several ways. Computers can help with diagnosis, be set up with programs for cognitive behavioral therapy, and provide information on alternative medications.

Previous hostility to the idea of the computer as psychotherapist was part of a "romantic reaction" to the computer presence, a sense that there were some places a computer could not and should not go. In shorthand, the romantic reaction said, "Simulated thinking might be thinking, but simulated feeling is not feeling; simulated love is never love." Today, that romantic reaction has largely given way to a new pragmatism. Computers "understand" as little as ever about human experience—for example, what it means to envy a sibling or miss a deceased parent. They do, however, perform understanding better than ever, and we are content to play our part. After all, our online lives are all about performance. We perform on social networks and direct the performances of our avatars in virtual worlds. A premium on performance is the cornerstone of the robotic moment. We live the robotic moment not because we have companionate robots in our lives but because the way we contemplate them on the horizon says much about who we are and who we are willing to become.

How did we get to this place? The answer to that question is hidden in plain sight, in the rough-and-tumble of the playroom, in children's reactions to robot toys. As adults, we can develop and change our opinions. In childhood, we establish the truth of our hearts.

I have watched three decades of children with increasingly sophisticated computer toys. I have seen these toys move from being described as "sort of alive" to "alive enough," the language of the generation whose childhood play was with sociable robots (in the form of digital pets and dolls). Getting to "alive enough" marks a watershed. In the late 1970s and early 1980s, children tried to make philosophical distinctions about aliveness in order to categorize computers. These days, when children talk about robots as alive enough for *specific purposes*, they are not trying to settle abstract questions. They are being pragmatic: different robots can be considered on a case-by-case and context-by-context basis. (Is it alive enough to be a friend, a babysitter, or a companion for your grandparents?) Sometimes the question becomes more delicate: If a robot makes you love it, is it alive?

Life Reconsidered

In the late 1970s and early 1980s, children met their first computational objects: games like Merlin, Simon, and Speak & Spell. This first generation of computers in the playroom challenged children in memory and spelling games, routinely beating them at tic-tac-toe and hangman.[8] The toys, reactive and interactive, turned children into philosophers. Above all else, children asked themselves whether something programmed could be alive.

Children's starting point here is their animation of the world. Children begin by understanding the world in terms of what they know best: themselves. Why does the stone roll down the slope? "To get to the bottom," says the young child, as though the ball had its own desires. But in time, animism gives way to physics. The child learns that a stone falls because of gravity; intentions have nothing to do with it. And so a dichotomy is constructed: physical and psychological properties stand opposed to one another in two great systems. But the computer is a new kind of object: it is psychological and yet a thing. Marginal objects such as the computer, on the lines between categories, draw attention to how we have drawn the lines.[9]

Swiss psychologist Jean Piaget, interviewing children in the 1920s, found that they took up the question of an object's life status by considering its physical movement.[10] For the youngest children, everything that could move was alive, then only things that could move without an outside push or pull. People and animals were easily classified. But clouds that seemed to move on their own accord were classified as alive until children realized that wind, an external but invisible force, was pushing them along. Cars were reclassified as not alive when children understood that motors counted as an "outside" push. Finally, the idea of autonomous movement became focused on breathing and metabolism, the motions most particular to life.

In the 1980s, faced with computational objects, children began to think through the question of aliveness in a new way, shifting from physics to psychology.[11] When they considered a toy that could beat them at spelling games, they were interested not in whether such an object could move on its own but in whether it could think on its own. Children asked if this game could "know." Did it cheat? Was knowing part of cheating? They were fascinated by how electronic games and toys showed a certain autonomy. When an early version of Speak & Spell—a toy that played language and spelling games—had a programming bug and could not be turned off during its "say it" routine, children shrieked with excitement, finally taking out the game's batteries to "kill it" and then (with the reinsertion of the batteries) bring it back to life.

In their animated conversations about computer life and death, children of the 1980s imposed a new conceptual order on a new world of objects.[12] In the

1990s, that order was strained to the breaking point. Simulation worlds—for example the Sim games—pulsed with evolving life forms. And child culture was awash in images of computational objects (from Terminators to digital viruses) all shape-shifting and morphing in films, cartoons, and action figures. Children were encouraged to see the stuff of computers as the same stuff of which life is made. One eight-year-old girl referred to mechanical life and human life as "all the same stuff, just yucky computer 'cy-dough-plasm.'" All of this led to a new kind of conversation about aliveness. Now, when considering computation, children talked about evolution as well as cognition. And they talked about a special kind of mobility. In 1993, a ten-year-old considered whether the creatures on the game SimLife were alive. She decided they were "if they could get out of your computer and go to America Online."[13]

Here, Piaget's narrative about motion resurfaced in a new guise. Children often imbued the creatures in simulation games with a desire to escape their confines and enter a wider digital world. And then, starting in the late 1990s, digital "creatures" came along that tried to dazzle children not with their smarts but with their sociability. I began a long study of children's interactions with these new machines. Of course, children said that a sociable robot's movement and intelligence were signs of its life. But even in conversations specifically about aliveness, children were more concerned about what these new robots might feel. As criteria for life, everything pales in comparison to a robot's capacity to care.

Consider how often thoughts turn to feelings as three elementary school children discuss the aliveness of a Furby, an owl-like creature that plays games and seems to learn English under a child's tutelage. [The] first, a five-year-old girl, can only compare it to a Tamagotchi, a tiny digital creature on an LED screen that also asks to be loved, cared for, and amused. She asks herself, "Is it [the Furby] alive?" and answers, "Well, I love it. It's more alive than a Tamagotchi because it sleeps with me. It likes to sleep with me." A six-year-old boy believes that something "as alive as a Furby" needs arms: "It might want to pick up something or to hug me." A nine-year-old girl thinks through the question of a Furby's aliveness by commenting, "I really like to take care of it.... It's as alive as you can be if you don't eat.... It's not like an animal kind of alive."

From the beginning of my studies of children and computers in the late 1970s, children spoke about an "animal kind of alive" and a "computer kind of alive." Now I hear them talk about a "people kind of love" and a "robot kind of love." Sociable robots bring children to the locution that the machines are alive enough to care and be cared for. In speaking about sociable robots, children use the phrase "alive enough" as a measure not of biological readiness but of relational readiness. Children describe robots as alive enough to love and mourn. And robots, as we saw at the American Museum of Natural History, may be alive enough to substitute for the biological, depending on the context. One reason the children at the museum were so relaxed about a robot substituting for a living tortoise is that children were comfortable with the idea of a robot as both machine and creature. I see this flexibility in seven-year-old Wilson, a bright, engaged student at a Boston public elementary school where I bring robot toys for after-school play. Wilson reflects on a Furby I gave him to take home for several weeks: "The Furby can talk, and it looks like an owl," yet "I always hear the machine in it." He knows, too, that the Furby, "alive enough to be a friend," would be rejected in the company of animals: "A real owl would snap its head off." Wilson does not have to deny the Furby's machine nature to feel it would be a good friend or to look to it for advice. His Furby has become his confidant. Wilson's way of keeping in mind the dual aspects of the Furby's nature seems to me a philosophical version of multitasking, so central to our twentieth-century attentional ecology. His attitude is pragmatic. If something that seems to have a self is before him, he deals with the aspect of self he finds most relevant to the context.

This kind of pragmatism has become a hallmark of our psychological culture. In the mid-1990s, I described how it was commonplace for people to "cycle through" different ideas of the human mind as (to name only a few images) mechanism, spirit, chemistry, and vessel for the soul.[14] These days, the cycling through intensifies. We are in much more direct contact with the machine side of mind. People are fitted with a computer chip to help with Parkinson's. They learn to see their minds as program and hardware. They take antidepressants prescribed by their psychotherapists, confident that the biochemical and oedipal self can be treated in one room. They look for signs of emotion in a brain scan. Old jokes about couples needing "chemistry" turn out not to be jokes at all. The compounds that trigger romantic love are forthcoming from the laboratory. And yet, even with biochemical explanations for attraction, nothing seems different about the thrill of falling in love. And seeing that an abused child has a normal brain scan does not mean one feels any less rage about the abuse. Pluralistic in our attitudes toward the self, we turn this pragmatic sensibility toward other things in our path—for example, sociable robots. We approach them like Wilson: they can be machines, and they can be more.

Writing in his diary in 1832, Ralph Waldo Emerson described "dreams and beasts" as "two keys by which we are to find out the secrets of our nature…. They are our test objects."[15] If Emerson had lived today, he would have seen the sociable robot as our new test object. Poised in our perception between inanimate program and living creature, this new breed of robot provokes us to reflect on the difference between connection and relationship, involvement with an object and engagement with a subject. These robots are evocative: understanding how people think about them provides a view onto how we think about ourselves. When children talk about these robots, they move away from an earlier cohort's perception of computers as provocative curiosities to the idea that robots might be something to grow old with. It all began when children met the seductive Tamagotchis and Furbies, the first computers that asked for love.[16]

The Tamagotchi Primer

When active and interactive computer toys were first introduced in the late 1970s, children recognized that they were neither dolls nor people nor animals. Nor did they seem like machines. Computers, first in the guise of electronic toys and games, turned children into philosophers, caught up in spontaneous debates about what these objects might be. In some cases, their discussions brought them to the idea that the talking, clever computational objects were close to kin. Children consider the question of what is special about being a person by contrasting themselves with their "nearest neighbors." Traditionally, children took their nearest neighbors to be their dogs, cats, and horses. Animals had feelings; people were special because of their ability to think. So, the Aristotelian definition of man as a rational animal had meaning for even the youngest children. But by the mid-1980s, as thinking computers became nearest neighbors, children considered people special because only they could "feel." Computers were intelligent machines; in contrast, people were emotional machines.[17]

But in the late 1990s, as if on cue, children met objects that presented themselves as having feelings and needs. As emotional machines, people were no longer alone. Tamagotchis and Furbies (both of which sold in the tens of millions) did not want to play tic-tac-toe, but they would tell you if they were hungry or unhappy. A Furby held upside down says, "Me scared," and whimpers as though it means it. And these new objects found ways to express their love.

Furbies, put on the market in 1998, had proper robotic "bodies"; they were small, fur-covered "creatures" with big eyes and ears. Yet, the Tamagotchi, released in 1997, a virtual creature housed in a plastic egg, serves as a reliable primer in the psychology of sociable robotics—and a useful one because crucial elements are simplified, thus stark. The child imagines Tamagotchis as embodied because, like living creatures and unlike machines, they need constant care and are always on. A Tamagotchi has "body enough" for a child to imagine its death.[18] To live, a Tamagotchi must be fed, amused, and cleaned up after. If cared for, it will grow from baby to healthy adult. Tamagotchis, in their limited ways, develop different personalities depending on how they are treated. As Tamagotchis turn children into caretakers, they teach that digital life can be emotionally roiling, a place of obligations and regrets.[19] The earliest electronic toys and games of thirty years ago—such as Merlin, Simon, and Speak & Spell—encouraged children to consider the proposition that something smart might be "sort of alive." With Tamagotchis, needy objects asked for care, and children took further steps.

As they did with earlier generations of hard-to-classify computational objects, curious children go through a period of trying to sort out the new sociable objects. But soon children take them at interface value, not as puzzles but as playmates. The philosophical churning associated with early computer toys (are they alive? do they know?) quickly gives way to new practices. Children don't want to comprehend these objects as much as take care of them. Their basic stance: "I'm living with this new creature. It and many more like it are here to stay." When a virtual "creature" or robot asks for help, children provide it. When its behavior dazzles, children are pleased just to hang out with it.

In the classic children's story *The Velveteen Rabbit*, a stuffed animal becomes "real" because of a child's love. Tamagotchis do not wait passively but demand attention and claim that without it they will not survive. With this aggressive demand for care, the question of biological aliveness almost falls away. We love what we nurture; if a Tamagotchi makes you love it, and you feel it loves you in return, it is alive enough to be a creature. It is alive enough to share a bit of your life. Children approach sociable machines in a spirit similar to the way they approach sociable pets or people—with the hope of befriending them. Meeting a person (or a pet) is not about meeting his or her biochemistry; becoming acquainted with a sociable machine is not about deciphering its programming. While in an earlier day, children might have asked, "What is a Tamagotchi?" they now ask, "What does a Tamagotchi want?"

When a digital "creature" asks children for nurturing or teaching, it seems alive enough to care for, just as caring for it makes it seem more alive. Neil, seven, says that his Tamagotchi is "like a baby. You can't just change the baby's diaper. You have to, like, rub cream on the baby. That is how the baby knows you love it." His eight-year-old sister adds, "I hate it when my Tamagotchi has the poop all around. I am like its mother. That is my job. I don't like it really, but it gets sick if you just leave it messy." Three nine-year-olds consider their Tamagotchis. One is excited that his pet requires him to build a castle as its home. "I can do it. I don't want him to get cold and sick and to die." Another looks forward to her digital pet's demands: "I like it when it says, 'I'm hungry' or 'Play with me.'" The third boils down her relationship to a "deceased" Tamagotchi to its most essential elements: "She was loved; she loved back."[20]

Where is digital fancy bred? Most of all, in the demand for care. Nurturance is the "killer app." In the presence of a needy Tamagotchi, children become responsible parents: demands translate into care and care into the feeling of caring. Parents are enlisted to watch over Tamagotchis during school hours. In the late 1990s, an army of compliant mothers cleaned, fed, and amused their children's Tamagotchis; the beeping of digital pets became a familiar background noise during business meetings.

This parental involvement is imperative because a Tamagotchi is always on. Mechanical objects are supposed to turn off. Children understand that bodies need to be always on, that they become "off" when people or animals die. So, the inability to turn off a Tamagotchi becomes evidence of its life. Seven-year-old Catherine explains, "When a body is 'off,' it is dead." Some Tamagotchis can be asked to "sleep," but nine-year-old Parvati makes it clear that asking her Tamagotchi to sleep is not the same as hitting the pause button in a game. Life goes on: "When they sleep, it is not that they are turned off. They can still get sick and unhappy, even while they are sleeping. They could have a nightmare."

In the late 1970s, computers, objects on the boundary between animate and inanimate, began to lead children to gleeful experiments in which they crashed machines as they talked about "killing" them. And then, there would be elaborate rituals of resuscitation as children talked about bringing machines back to life. After these dramatic rebirths, the machines were, in the eyes of children, what they had been before. Twenty years later, when Tamagotchis die and are reset for a new life, children do not feel that they come back as they were before. Children looked forward to the rebirth of the computers they had crashed, but they dread the demise and rebirth of Tamagotchis. These provoke genuine remorse because, as one nine-year-old puts it, "It didn't have to happen. I could have taken better care."[21]

Unforgettable

I took care of my first Tamagotchi at the same time that my seven-year-old daughter was nurturing her own. Since I sometimes took a shift attending to her Tamagotchi, I could compare their respective behaviors, and I convinced myself that mine had idiosyncrasies that made it different from hers. My Tamagotchi liked to eat at particular intervals. I thought it prospered best with only small doses of amusement. I worked hard at keeping it happy. I did not anticipate how bad I would feel when it died. I immediately hit the reset button. Somewhat to my surprise, I had no desire to take care of the new infant Tamagotchi that appeared on my screen.

Many children are not so eager to hit reset. They don't like having a new creature in the same egg where their virtual pet has died. For them, the death of a virtual pet is not so unlike the death of what they call a "regular pet." Eight-year-olds talk about what happens when you hit a Tamagotchi's reset button. For one, "It comes back, but it doesn't come back as exactly your same Tamagotchi.... You haven't had the same experiences with it. It has a different personality." For another, "It's cheating. Your Tamagotchi is really dead. Your one is really dead. They say you get it back, but it's not the same one. It hasn't had the same things happen to it. It's like they give you a new one. It doesn't remember the life it had." For another, "When my Tamagotchi dies, I don't want to play with the new one who can pop up. It makes me remember the real one [the first one]. I like to get another [a new egg].... If you made it die, you should start fresh." Parents try to convince their children to hit reset. Their arguments are logical: the Tamagotchi is not "used up"; a reset Tamagotchi means one less visit to the toy store. Children are unmoved.

Sally, eight, has had three Tamagotchis. Each died and was "buried" with ceremony in her top dresser drawer. Three times Sally has refused to hit the reset button and convinced her mother to buy replacements. Sally sets the scene: "My mom says mine still works, but I tell her that a Tamagotchi is cheap, and she won't have to buy me anything else, so she gets one for me. I am not going to start up my old one. It died. It needs its rest."

In Sally's "It died. It needs its rest," we see the expansiveness of the robotic moment. Things that never could go together—a program and pity for a weary body—now do go together. The reset button produces objects that are between categories: a creature that seems new but is not really new, a stand-in for something now gone. The new creature, a kind of imposter, is a classic case of Sigmund Freud's uncanny—it's familiar, yet somehow not.[22] The uncanny is always compelling. Children ask, "What does it mean for a virtual creature to die?" Yet, while earlier generations debated questions about a computer's life in philosophical terms, when faced with Tamagotchis, children quickly move on to day-to-day practicalities. They temper philosophy with tearful experience. They know that Tamagotchis are alive enough to mourn.

Freud teaches us that the experience of loss is part of how we build a self.[23] Metaphorically, at least, mourning keeps a lost person present. Child culture is rich in narratives that take young people through the steps of this fitful process. So, in *Peter Pan*, Wendy loses Peter in order to move past adolescence and become a grown woman, able to love and parent. But Peter remains present in her playful and tolerant way of mothering. Louisa May Alcott's Jo loses her gentle sister Beth. In mourning Beth, Jo develops as a serious writer and finds a new capacity to love. More recently, the young wizard Harry Potter loses his mentor Dumbledore, whose continuing presence within Harry enables him to find his identity and achieve his life's purpose. With the Tamagotchi, we see the beginning of mourning for artificial life. It is not mourned as one would mourn a doll. The Tamagotchi has crossed a threshold. Children breathe life into their dolls. With the Tamagotchi, we are in a realm of objects that children see as having their own agendas, needs, and desires. Children mourn the life the Tamagotchi has led.

A child's mourning for a Tamagotchi is not always a solitary matter. When a Tamagotchi dies, it can be buried in an online Tamagotchi graveyard. The tombstones are intricate. On them, children try to capture what made each Tamagotchi special.[24] A Tamagotchi named Saturn lived to twelve "Tamagotchi years." Its owner writes a poem in its memory: "My baby died in his sleep. I will forever weep. Then his batteries went dead. Now he lives in my head." Another child mourns Pumpkin, dead at sixteen: "Pumpkin, Everyone said you were fat, so I made you lose weight. From losing weight you died. Sorry." Children take responsibility for virtual deaths.[25] These online places of mourning do more than give children a way to express their feelings. They sanction the idea that it is appropriate to mourn the digital—indeed, that there is something "there" to mourn.

Alive Enough

In the 1990s, children spoke about making their virtual creatures more alive by having them escape the computer. Furbies, the sensation of the 1998 holiday season, embody this documented dream. If a child wished a Tamagotchi to leap off its screen, it might look a lot like the furry and owl-like Furby. The two digital pets have other things in common. As with a Tamagotchi, how a Furby is treated shapes its personality. And both present themselves as visitors from other worlds. But Furbies are more explicit about their purpose in coming to Earth. They are here to learn about humans. So, each Furby is an anthropologist of sorts and wants to relate to people. They ask children to take care of them and to teach them English. Furbies are not ungrateful: they make demands, but they say, "I love you."

Furbies, like Tamagotchis, are "always on," but unlike Tamagotchis, Furbies manifest this with an often annoying, constant chatter.[26] To reliably quiet a Furby, you need a Phillips screwdriver to remove its batteries, an operation that causes it to lose all memory of its life and experiences—what it has learned and how it has been treated. For children who have spent many hours "bringing up" their Furbies, this is not a viable option. On a sunny spring afternoon in 1999, I bring eight Furbies to an afternoon playgroup at an elementary school in western Massachusetts. There are fifteen children in the room, from five to eight years old, from the kindergarten through the third grade. I turn on a tape recorder as

I hand the Furbies around. The children start to talk excitedly, greeting the Furbies by imitating their voices. In the cacophony of the classroom, this is what the robotic moment sounds like:

> He's a baby! He said, "Yum." Mine's a baby? Is this a baby? Is he sleeping now? He burped! What is "be-pah?" He said, "Be-pah." Let them play together. What does "a lee koo wah" mean? Furby, you're talking to me. Talk! C'mon boy. Good boy! Furby, talk! Be quiet everybody! Oh, look it, he's in love with another one! Let them play together! It's tired. It's asleep. I'm going to try to feed him. How come they don't have arms? Look, he's in love! He called you "Mama." He said, "Me love you." I have to feed him. I have to feed mine too. We love you, Furby. How do you make him fall asleep? His eyes are closed. He's talking with his eyes closed. He's sleeptalking. He's dreaming. He's snoring. I'm giving him shade.
>
> C'mon, Furby, c'mon—let's go to sleep, Furby. Furby, shh, shh. Don't touch him. I can make him be quiet. This is a robot. Is this a robot? What has this kind of fur? He's allergic to me. It's kind of like it's alive. And it has a body. It has a motor. It's a monster. And it's kind of like it's real because it has a body. It was alive. It is alive. It's not alive. It's a robot.

From the very first, the children make it clear that the Furby is a machine but alive enough to need care. They try to connect with it using everything they have: the bad dreams and scary movies that make one child see the Furby "as a monster" and their understanding of loneliness, which encourages another to exhort, "Let them play together!" They use logic and skepticism: Do biological animals have "this kind of fur?" Do real animals have motors? Perhaps, although this requires a new and more expansive notion of what a motor can be. They use the ambiguity of this new object to challenge their understanding of what they think they already know. They become more open to the idea of the biological as mechanical and the mechanical as biological. Eight-year-old Pearl thinks that removing the batteries from a Furby causes it to die and that people's death is akin to "taking the batteries out of a Furby."

Furbies reinforce the idea that they have a biology: each is physically distinct, with particular markings on its fur, and each has some of the needs of living things. For example, a Furby requires regular feeding, accomplished by depressing its tongue with one's finger. If a Furby is not fed, it becomes ill. Nursing a Furby back to health always requires more food. Children give disease names to Furby malfunctions. So, there is Furby cancer, Furby flu, and Furby headache.

Jessica, eight, plays with the idea that she and her Furby have "body things" in common, for example, that headache. She has a Furby at home; when her sisters pull its hair, Jessica worries about its pain: "When I pull my hair it really hurts, like when my mother brushes the tangles. So, I think [the Furby's hair pulls] hurt too." Then, she ponders her stomach. "There's a screw in my belly button," she says. "[The screw] comes out, and then blood comes out." Jessica thinks that people, like Furbies, have batteries. "There are hearts, lungs, and a big battery inside." People differ from robots in that our batteries "work forever like the sun." When children talk about the Furby as kin, they experiment with the idea that they themselves might be almost machine. Ideas about the human as machine or as joined to a machine are played out in classroom games.[27] In their own way, toy robots prepare a bionic sensibility. There are people who do, after all, have screws and pins and chips and plates in their flesh. A recent recipient of a cochlear implant describes his experience of his body as "rebuilt."[28]

We have met Wilson, seven, comfortable with his Furby as both machine and creature. Just as he always "hears the machine" in the Furby, he finds the machine in himself. As the boy sings improvised love songs about the robot as a best friend, he pretends to use a screwdriver on his own body, saying, "I'm a Furby." Involved in a second-grade class project of repairing a broken Furby by dismantling it, screw by screw, Wilson plays with the idea of the Furby's biological nature: "I'm going to get [its] baby out." And then he plays with the idea of his own machine nature: he applies the screwdriver to his own ankle, saying, "I'm unscrewing my ankle."

Wilson enjoys cataloguing what he and the Furby have in common. Most important for Wilson is that they "both like to burp." In this, he says, the Furby "is just like me—I love burping." Wilson holds his Furby out in front of him, his hands lightly touching the Furby's stomach, staring intently into its eyes. He burps just after or just before his Furby burps, much as in the classic bonding scene in *E.T.: The Extraterrestrial* between the boy Elliott and the visitor from afar. When Wilson describes his burping game, he begins by saying that he makes his Furby burp, but he ends up saying that his Furby makes him burp. Wilson likes the sense that he and his Furby are in sync, that he can happily lose track of where he leaves off and the Furby begins.[29]

What Does a Furby Want?

When Wilson catalogues what he shares with his Furby, there are things of the body (the burping) and there are things of the mind. Like many children, he thinks that because Furbies have language, they are more "peoplelike" than a "regular" pet. They arrive speaking Furbish, a language with its own dictionary, which many children try to commit to memory because they would like to meet their Furbies more than half way. The Furby manual instructs children, "I can learn to speak English by listening to you talk. The more you play with me, the more I will use your language." Actually, Furby English emerges over time, whether or not a child talks to the robot. (Furbies have no hearing or language- learning ability.[30]) But until age eight, children are convinced by the illusion and believe they are teaching their Furbies to speak. The Furbies are alive enough to need them.

Children enjoy the teaching task. From the first encounter, it gives them something in common with their Furbies and it implies that the Furbies can grow to better understand them. "I once didn't know English," says one six-year-old. "And now I do. So I know what my Furby is going through." In the classroom with Furbies, children shout to each other in competitive delight: "My Furby speaks more English than yours! My Furby speaks English."

I have done several studies in which I send Furbies home with schoolchildren, often with the request that they (and their parents) keep a "Furby diary." In my first study of kindergarten to third graders, I loan the Furbies out for two weeks at a time. It is not a good decision. I do not count on how great will be children's sense of loss when I ask them to return the Furbies. I extend the length of the loans, often encouraged by parental requests. Their children have grown too attached to give up the robots. Nor are they mollified by parents' offers to buy them new Furbies. Even more so than with Tamagotchis, children attach to a particular Furby, the one they have taught English, the one they have raised.

For three decades, in describing people's relationships with computers, I have often used the metaphor of the Rorschach, the inkblot test that psychologists use as a screen onto which people can project their feelings and styles of thought. But as children interact with sociable robots like Furbies, they move beyond a psychology of projection to a new psychology of engagement. They try to deal with the robot as they would deal with a pet or a person. Nine-year-old Leah, in an after-school playgroup, admits, "It's hard to turn it [the Furby] off when it is talking to me." Children quickly understand that to get the most out of your Furby, you have to pay attention to what it is telling you. When you are with a Furby, you can't play a simple game of projective make-believe. You have to continually assess your Furby's "emotional" and "physical" state. And children fervently believe that the child who loves his or her Furby best will be most loved in return.

This mutuality is at the heart of what makes the Furby, a primitive exemplar of sociable robotics, different from traditional dolls. As we've seen, such relational artifacts do not wait for children to "animate" them in the spirit of a Raggedy Ann doll or a teddy bear. They present themselves as already animated and ready for relationship. They promise reciprocity because, unlike traditional dolls, they are not passive. They make demands. They present as having their own needs and inner lives. They teach us the rituals of love that will make them thrive. For decades computers have asked us to *think* with them; these days, computers and robots, deemed sociable, affective, and relational, ask us to *feel* for and with them.

Children see traditional dolls as they want them or need them to be. For example, an eight-year-old girl who feels guilty about breaking her mother's best crystal pitcher might punish a row of Barbie dolls. She might take them away from their tea party and put them in detention, doing unto the dolls what she imagines should be done unto her. In contrast, since relational artifacts present themselves as having minds and intentions of their own, they cannot be so easily punished for one's own misdeeds. Two eight-year-old girls comment on how their "regular dolls" differ from the robotic Furbies. The first says, "A regular doll, like my Madeleine doll … you can make it go to sleep, but its eyes are painted open, so, um, you cannot get them to close their eyes…. Like a Madeleine doll cannot go, 'Hello, good morning.'" But this is precisely the sort of thing a Furby can do. The second offers, "The Furby tells you what it wants."

Indeed, Furbies come with manuals that provide detailed marching orders. They want language practice, food, rest, and protestations of love. So, for example, the manual instructs, "Make sure you say 'HEY FURBY! I love you!' frequently so that I feel happy and know I'm loved." There is general agreement among children that a penchant for giving instructions distinguishes Furbies from traditional dolls. A seven-year-old girl puts it this way: "Dolls let you tell them what they want. The Furbies have their own ideas." A nine-year-old boy sums up the difference between Furbies and his action figures: "You don't play with the Furby, you sort of hang out with it. You do try to get power over it, but it has power over you too."

Children say that traditional dolls can be "hard work" because you have to do all the work of giving them ideas; Furbies are hard work for the opposite reason. They have plenty of ideas, but you have to give them what they want and when they want it. When children attach to a doll through the psychology of projection, they attribute to the doll what is most on their mind. But they need to accommodate a Furby. This give-and-take prepares children for the expectation of relationship with machines that is at the heart of the robotic moment.

Daisy, six, with a Furby at home, believes that each Furby's owner must help his or her Furby fulfill its mission to learn about people. "You have to teach it; when you buy it, that is your job." Daisy tells me that she taught her Furby about Brownie Girl Scouts, kindergarten, and whales. "It's alive; I teach it about whales; it loves me." Padma, eight, says that she likes meeting what she calls "Furby requests" and thinks that her Furby is "kind of like a person" because "it talks." She goes on: "It's kind of like me because I'm a chatterbox." After two weeks, it is time for Padma to return her Furby, and afterward she feels regret: "I miss how it talked, and now it's so quiet at my house.... I didn't get a chance to make him a bed."

After a month with her Furby, Bianca, seven, speaks with growing confidence about their mutual affection: "I love my Furby because it loves me.... It was like he really knew me."[31] She knows her Furby well enough to believe that "it doesn't want to miss fun ... at a party." In order to make sure that her social butterfly Furby gets some rest when her parents entertain late into the evening, Bianca clips its ears back with clothespins to fool the robot into thinking that "nothing is going on ... so he can fall asleep." This move is ineffective, and all of this activity is exhausting, but Bianca calmly sums up her commitment: "It takes lots of work to take care of these."

When Wilson, who so enjoys burping in synchrony with his Furby, faces up to the hard work of getting his Furby to sleep, he knows that if he forces sleep by removing his Furby's batteries, the robot will "forget" whatever has passed between them—this is unacceptable. So Furby sleep has to come naturally. Wilson tries to exhaust his Furby by keeping it up late at night watching television. He experiments with Furby "sleep houses" made of blankets piled high over towers of blocks. When Wilson considers Furby sleep, his thoughts turn to Furby dreams. He is sure his Furby dreams "when his eyes are closed." What do Furbies dream of? Second and third graders think they dream "of life on their flying saucers."[32] And they dream about learning languages and playing with the children they love.

David and Zach, both eight, are studying Hebrew. "My Furby dreams about Hebrew," says David. "It knows how to say *Eloheinu*.... I didn't even try to teach it; it was just from listening to me doing Hebrew homework." Zach agrees: "Mine said *Dayeinu* in its sleep." Zach, like Wilson, is proud of how well he can make his Furby sleep by creating silence and covering it with blankets. He is devoted to teaching his Furby English and has been studying Furbish as well; he has mastered the English/Furbish dictionary that comes with the robot. A week after Zach receives his Furby, however, his mother calls my office in agitation. Zach's Furby is broken. It has been making a "terrible" noise. It sounds as though it might be suffering, and Zach is distraught. Things reached their worst during a car trip from Philadelphia to Boston, with the broken Furby wailing as though in pain. On the long trip home, there was no Phillips screwdriver for the ultimate silencing, so Zach and his parents tried to put the Furby to sleep by nestling it under a blanket. But every time the car hit a bump, the Furby woke up and made the "terrible" noise. I take away the broken Furby, and give Zach a new one, but he wants little to do with it. He doesn't talk to it or try to teach it. His interest is in "his" Furby, the Furby he nurtured, the Furby he taught. He says, "The Furby that I had before could say 'again'; it could say 'hungry.'" Zach believes he was making progress teaching the first Furby a bit of Spanish and French. The first Furby was never "annoying," but the second Furby is. *His* Furby is irreplaceable.

After a few weeks, Zach's mother calls to ask if their family has my permission to give the replacement Furby to one of Zach's friends. When I say yes, Zach calmly contemplates the loss of Furby #2. He has loved; he has lost; he is not willing to reinvest. Neither is eight-year-old Holly, who becomes upset and withdrawn when her mother takes the batteries out of her Furby. The family was about to leave on an extended vacation, and the Furby manual suggests taking out a Furby's batteries if it will go unused for a long time. Holly's mother did not understand the implications of what she saw as commonsense advice from the manual. She insists, with increasing defensiveness, that she was only "following the instructions." Wide-eyed, Holly tries to make her mother understand what she has done: when the batteries are removed, Holly says, "the Furby forgets its life."

Designed to give users a sense of progress in teaching it, when the Furby evolves over time, it becomes the irreplaceable repository and proof of its owner's care. The robot and child have traveled a bit of road together. When a Furby forgets, it is as if a friend has become amnesic. A new Furby is a stranger. Zach and Holly cannot bear beginning again with a new Furby that could never be the Furby into which each has poured time and attention.

Operating Procedures

In the 1980s, the computer toy Merlin made happy and sad noises depending on whether it was winning or losing the sound-and-light game it played with children. Children saw Merlin as "sort of alive" because of how well it played memory games, but they did not fully believe in Merlin's shows of emotion. When a

Merlin broke down, children were sorry to lose a playmate. When a Furby doesn't work, however, children see a creature that might be in pain.

Lily, ten, worries that her broken Furby is hurting. But she doesn't want to turn it off, because "that means you aren't taking care of it." She fears that if she shuts off a Furby in pain, she might make things worse. Two eight-year-olds fret about how much their Furbies sneeze. The first worries that his sneezing Furby is allergic to him. The other fears his Furby got its cold because "I didn't do a good enough job taking care of him." Several children become tense when Furbies make unfamiliar sounds that might be signals of distress. I observe children with their other toys: dolls, toy soldiers, action figures. If these toys make strange sounds, they are usually put aside; broken toys lead easily to boredom. But when a Furby is in trouble, children ask, "Is it tired?" "Is it sad?" "Have I hurt it?" "Is it sick?" "What shall I do?"

Taking care of a robot is a high-stakes game. Things can—and do—go wrong. In one kindergarten, when a Furby breaks down, the children decide they want to heal it. Ten children volunteer, seeing themselves as doctors in an emergency room. They decide they'll begin by taking it apart.

The proceedings begin in a state of relative calm. When talking about their sick Furby, the children insist that this breakdown does not mean the end: people get sick and get better. But as soon as scissors and pliers appear, they become anxious. At this point, Alicia screams, "The Furby is going to die!" Sven, to his classmates' horror, pinpoints the moment when Furbies die: it happens when a Furby's skin is ripped off. Sven considers the Furby as an animal. You can shave an animal's fur, and it will live. But you cannot take its skin off. As the operation continues, Sven reconsiders. Perhaps the Furby can live without its skin, "but it will be cold." He doesn't back completely away from the biological (the Furby is sensitive to the cold) but reconstructs it. For Sven, the biological now includes creatures such as Furbies, whose "insides" stay "all in the same place" when their skin is removed. This accommodation calms him down. If a Furby is simultaneously biological and mechanical, the operation in process, which is certainly removing the Furby's skin, is not necessarily destructive. Children make theories when they are confused or anxious. A good theory can reduce anxiety.

But some children become more anxious as the operation continues. One suggests that if the Furby dies, it might haunt them. It is alive enough to turn into a ghost. Indeed, a group of children start to call the empty Furby skin "the ghost of Furby" and the Furby's naked body "the goblin." They are not happy that this operation might leave a Furby goblin and ghost at large. One girl comes up with the idea that the ghost of the Furby will be less fearful if distributed. She asks if it would be okay "if every child took home a piece of Furby skin." She is told this would be fine, but, unappeased, she asks the same question two more times. In the end, most children leave with a bit of Furby fur.[33] Some talk about burying it when they get home. They leave room for a private ritual to placate the goblin and say good-bye.

Inside the classroom, most of the children feel they are doing the best they can with a sick pet. But from outside the classroom, the Furby surgery looks alarming. Children passing by call out, "You killed him." "How dare you kill

Furby?" "You'll go to Furby jail." Denise, eight, watches some of the goings-on from the safety of the hall. She has a Furby at home and says that she does not like to talk about its problems as diseases because "Furbies are not animals." She uses the word "fake" to mean nonbiological and says, "Furbies are fake, and they don't get diseases." But later, she reconsiders her position when her own Furby's batteries run out and the robot, so chatty only moments before, becomes inert. Denise panics: "It's dead. It's dead right now.... Its eyes are closed." She then declares her Furby "both fake and dead." Denise concludes that worn-out batteries and water can kill a Furby. It is a mechanism, but alive enough to die.

Linda, six, is one of the children whose family has volunteered to keep a Furby for a two-week home study. She looked forward to speaking to her Furby, sure that unlike her other dolls, this robot would be worth talking to. But on its very first night at her home, her Furby stops working: "Yeah, I got used to it, and then it broke that night—the night that I got it. I felt like I was broken or something.... I cried a lot.... I was really sad that it broke, 'cause Furbies talk, they're like real, they're like real people." Linda is so upset about not protecting her Furby that when it breaks she feels herself broken.

Things get more complicated when I give Linda a new Furby. Unlike children like Zach who have invested time and love in a "first Furby" and want no replacements, Linda had her original Furby in working condition for only a few hours. She likes having Furby #2: "It plays hide-and-seek with me. I play red light, green light, just like in the manual." Linda feeds it and makes sure it gets enough rest, and she reports that her new Furby is grateful and affectionate. She makes this compatible with her assessment of a Furby as "just a toy" because she has come to see gratitude, conversation, and affection as something that toys can manage. But now she will not name her Furby or say it is alive. There would be risk in that: Linda might feel guilty if the new Furby were alive enough to die and she had a replay of her painful first experience.

Like the child surgeons, Linda ends up making a compromise: the Furby is both biological and mechanical. She tells her friends, "The Furby is kind of real but just a toy." She elaborates that "[the Furby] is real because it is talking and moving and going to sleep. It's kind of like a human and a pet." It is a toy because "you had to put in batteries and stuff, and it could stop talking."

So hybridity can offer comfort. If you focus on the Furby's mechanical side, you can enjoy some of the pleasures of companionship without the risks of attachment to a pet or a person. With practice, says nine-year-old Lara, reflecting on her Furby, "you can get it to like you. But it won't die or run away. That is good." But hybridity also brings new anxieties. If you grant the Furby a bit of life, how do you treat it so that it doesn't get hurt or killed? An object on the boundaries of life, as we've seen, suggests the possibility of real pain.

An Ethical Landscape

When a mechanism breaks, we may feel regretful, inconvenienced, or angry. We debate whether it is worth getting it fixed. When a doll cries, children know that they are themselves creating the tears. But a robot with a body can get "hurt," as we saw in the improvised Furby surgical theater. Sociable robotics exploits the idea of a robotic body to move people to relate to machines as subjects, as creatures in pain rather than broken objects. That even the most primitive Tamagotchi can inspire these feelings demonstrates that objects cross that line not because of their sophistication but because of the feelings of attachment they evoke. The Furby, even more than the Tamagotchi, is alive enough to suggest a body in pain as well as a troubled mind. Furbies whine and moan, leaving it to their users to discover what might help. And what to make of the moment when an upside down Furby says, "Me scared!"?

Freedom Baird takes this question very seriously.[34] A recent graduate of the MIT Media Lab, she finds herself engaged with her Furby as a creature and a machine. But how seriously does she take the idea of the Furby as a creature? To determine this, she proposes an exercise in the spirit of the Turing test.

In the original Turing test, published in 1950, mathematician Alan Turing, inventor of the first general-purpose computer, asked under what conditions people would consider a computer intelligent. In the end, he settled on a test in which the computer would be declared intelligent if it could convince people it was not a machine. Turing was working with computers made up of vacuum tubes and Teletype terminals. He suggested that if participants couldn't tell, as they worked at their Teletypes, if they were talking to a person or a computer, that computer would be deemed "intelligent."[35]

A half century later, Baird asks under what conditions a creature is deemed alive enough for people to experience an ethical dilemma if it is distressed. She designs a Turing test not for the head but for the heart and calls it the "upside-down test." A person is asked to invert three creatures: a Barbie doll, a Furby, and a biological gerbil. Baird's question is simple: "How long can you hold the object upside down before your emotions make you turn it back?" Baird's experiment assumes that a sociable robot makes new ethical demands. Why? The robot performs a psychology; many experience this as evidence of an inner life, no matter how primitive. Even those who do not think a Furby has a mind—and this, on a conscious level, includes most people—find themselves in a new place with an upside-down Furby that is whining and telling them it is scared. They feel themselves, often despite themselves, in a situation that calls for an ethical response. This usually happens at the moment when they identify with the "creature" before them, all the while knowing that it is "only a machine."

This simultaneity of vision gives Baird the predictable results of the upside-down test. As Baird puts it, "People are willing to be carrying the Barbie around by the feet, slinging it by the hair … no problem.… People are not going to mess around with their gerbil." But in the case of the Furby, people will "hold the Furby upside down for thirty seconds or so, but when it starts crying and saying it's scared, most people feel guilty and turn it over."

The work of neuroscientist Antonio Damasio offers insight into the origins of this guilt. Damasio describes two levels of experiencing pain. The first is a physical response to a painful stimulus. The second, a far more complex reaction, is an emotion associated with pain. This is an internal representation of the physical.[36] When the Furby says, "Me scared," it signals that it has crossed the line between a physical response and an emotion, the internal representation. When people hold a Furby upside down, they do something that would be painful if done to an animal. The Furby cries out—as if it were an animal. But then it says, "Me scared"—as if it were a person.

People are surprised by how upset they get in this theater of distress. And then they get upset that they are upset. They often try to reassure themselves, saying things like, "Chill, chill, it's only a toy!" They are experiencing something new: you can feel bad about yourself for how you behave with a computer program. Adults come to the upside-down test knowing two things: the Furby is a machine and they are not torturers. By the end, with a whimpering Furby in tow, they are on new ethical terrain.[37]

We are at the point of seeing digital objects as both creatures and machines. A series of fractured surfaces—pet, voice, machine, friend—come together to create an experience in which knowing that a Furby is a machine does not alter the feeling that you can cause it pain. Kara, a woman in her fifties, reflects on holding a moaning Furby that says it is scared. She finds it distasteful, "not because I believe that the Furby is really scared, but because I'm not willing to hear anything talk like that and respond by continuing my behavior. It feels to me that I could be hurt if I keep doing this." For Kara, "That is not what I do.... In that moment, the Furby comes to represent how I treat creatures."

When the toy manufacturer Hasbro introduced its My Real Baby robot doll in 2000, it tried to step away from these complex matters. My Real Baby shut down in situations where a real baby might feel pain. This was in contrast to its prototype, a robot called "IT," developed by a team led by MIT roboticist Rodney Brooks. "IT," evolved into "BIT" (for Baby IT), a doll with "states of mind" and facial musculature under its synthetic skin to give it expression.[38] When touched in a way that would induce pain in a child, BIT cried out. Brooks describes BIT in terms of its inner states:

> If the baby were upset, it would stay upset until someone soothed it or it finally fell asleep after minutes of heartrending crying and fussing. If BIT ... was abused in any way—for instance, by being swung upside down—it got very upset. If it was upset and someone bounced it on their knee, it got more upset, but if the same thing happened when it was happy, it got more and more excited, giggling and laughing, until eventually it got overtired and started to get upset. If it were hungry, it would stay hungry until it was fed. It acted a lot like a real baby.[39]

BIT, with its reactions to abuse, became the center of an ethical world that people constructed around its responses to pleasure and pain. But when Hasbro put BIT into mass production as My Real Baby, the company decided not to present children with a toy that responded to pain. The theory was that a robot's response to pain could "enable" sadistic behavior. If My Real Baby were touched, held, or bounced in a way that would hurt a real baby, the robot shut down.

In its promotional literature, Hasbro marketed My Real Baby as "the most real, dynamic baby doll available for young girls to take care of and nurture."

They presented it as a companion that would teach and encourage reciprocal social behavior as children were trained to respond to its needs for amusement as well as bottles, sleep, and diaper changes. Indeed, it was marketed as realistic in all things—except that if you "hurt" it, it shut down. When children play with My Real Baby, they do explore aggressive possibilities. They spank it. It shuts down. They shake it, turn it upside down, and box its ears. It shuts down.

Hasbro's choice—maximum realism, but with no feedback for abuse—inspires strong feelings, especially among parents. For one group of parents, what is most important is to avoid a child's aggressive response. Some believe that if you market realism but show no response to "pain," children are encouraged to inflict it because doing so seems to have no cost. Others think that if a robot simulates pain, it enables mistreatment.

Another group of parents wish that My Real Baby would respond to pain for the same reason that they justify letting their children play violent video games: they see such experiences as "cathartic." They say that children (and adults too) should express aggression (or sadism or curiosity) in situations that seem "realistic" but where nothing "alive" is being hurt. But even these parents are sometimes grateful for My Real Baby's unrealistic show of "denial." They do not want to see their children tormenting a screaming baby.

No matter what position one takes, sociable robots have taught us that we do not shirk from harming realistic simulations of life. This is, of course, how we now train people for war. First, we learn to kill the virtual. Then, desensitized, we are sent to kill the real. The prospect of studying these matters raises awful questions. Freedom Baird had people hold a whining, complaining Furby upside down, much to their discomfort. Do we want to encourage the abuse of increasingly realistic robot dolls?

When I observe children with My Real Baby in an after-school playgroup for eight-year-olds, I see a range of responses. Alana, to the delight of a small band of her friends, flings My Real Baby into the air and then shakes it violently while holding it by one leg. Alana says the robot has "no feelings." Watching her, one wonders why it is necessary then to "torment" something without feelings. She does not behave this way with the many other dolls in the playroom. Scott, upset, steals the robot and brings it to a private space. He says, "My Real Baby is like a baby and like a doll.... I don't think she wants to get hurt."

As Scott tries to put the robot's diaper back on, some of the other children stand beside him and put their fingers in its eyes and mouth. One asks, "Do you think that hurts?" Scott warns, "The baby's going to cry!" At this point, one girl tries to pull My Real Baby away from Scott because she sees him as an inadequate protector: "Let go of her!" Scott resists. "I was in the middle of changing her!" It seems a good time to end the play session. As the research team, exhausted, packs up to go, Scott sneaks behind a table with the robot, gives it a kiss, and says good-bye, out of the sight of the other children.

In the pandemonium of Scott and Alana's playgroup, My Real Baby is alive enough to torment and alive enough to protect. The adults watching this—a group of teachers and my research team—feel themselves in an unaccustomed quandary. If the children had been tossing around a rag doll, neither we, nor presumably Scott, would have been as upset. But it is hard to see My Real Baby treated this way. All of this—the Furbies that complain of pain, the My Real Babies that do not—creates a new ethical landscape. The computer toys of the 1980s only suggested ethical issues, as when children played with the idea of life and death when they "killed" their Speak & Spells by taking out the toys' batteries. Now, relational artifacts pose these questions directly.

One can see the new ethics at work in my students' reactions to Nexi, a humanoid robot at MIT. Nexi has a female torso, an emotionally expressive face, and the ability to speak. In 2009, one of my students, researching a paper, made an appointment to talk with the robot's development team. Due to a misunderstanding about scheduling, my student waited alone, near the robot. She was upset by her time there: when not interacting with people, Nexi was put behind a curtain and blindfolded.

At the next meeting of my graduate seminar, my student shared her experience of sitting alongside the robot. "It was very upsetting," she said. "The curtain—and why was she blindfolded? I was upset because she was blindfolded." The story of the shrouded and blindfolded Nexi ignited the seminar. In the conversation, all the students talked about the robot as a "she." The designers had done everything they could to give the robot gender. And now, the act of blindfolding signaled sight and consciousness. In class, questions tumbled forth: Was the blindfold there because it would be too upsetting to see Nexi's eyes? Perhaps when Nexi was turned off, "her" eyes remained open, like the eyes of a dead person? Perhaps the robot makers didn't want Nexi to see "out"? Perhaps they didn't want Nexi to know that when not in use, "she" is left in a corner behind a curtain? This line of reasoning led the seminar to an even more unsettling question: If Nexi is smart enough to need a blindfold to protect "her" from fully grasping "her" situation, does that mean that "she" is enough of a subject to make "her" situation abusive? The students agreed on one thing; blindfolding the robot sends a signal that "this robot can see." And seeing implies understanding and an inner life, enough of one to make abuse possible.

I have said that Sigmund Freud saw the uncanny as something long familiar that feels strangely unfamiliar. The uncanny stands between standard categories and challenges the categories themselves. It is familiar to see a doll at rest. But we don't need to cover its eyes, for it is we who animate it. It is familiar to have a person's expressive face beckon to us, but if we blindfold that person and put them behind a curtain, we are inflicting punishment. The Furby with its expressions of fear and the gendered Nexi with her blindfold are the new uncanny in the culture of computing.

I feel even more uncomfortable when I learn about a beautiful "female" robot, Aiko, now on sale, that says, "Please let go … you are hurting me," when its artificial skin is pressed too hard. The robot also protests when its breast is touched: "I do not like it when you touch my breasts." I find these programmed assertions of boundaries and modesty disturbing because it is almost impossible to hear them without imagining an erotic body braced for assault....

NOTES

1. Weizenbaum had written the program a decade earlier. See Joseph Weizenbaum, "ELIZA—a Computer Program for the Study of Natural Language Communication Between Man and Machine," *Communications of the ACM*, vol. 9, no. 1 (January 1966): 36–45.

2. See Joseph Weizenbaum, *Computer Power and Human Reason: From Judgment to Calculation* (San Francisco: W. H. Freeman, 1976).

3. For whatever kind of companionship, a classical first step is to make robots that are physically identical to people. In America, David Hanson has an Albert Einstein robot that chats about relativity. At the TED conference in February 2009, Hansen discussed his project to create robots with empathy as the "seeds of hope for our future." See http://www.ted.com/talks/david_hanson_robots_that_relate_to_you.html (accessed August 11, 2010) On Hanson, also see Jerome Groopman, "Robots That Care: Advances in Technological Therapy," *The New Yorker*, November 2, 2009, www.newyorker.com/reporting/2009/11/02/091102fa_fact_groopman (accessed November 11, 2009).

   These days, you can order a robot clone in your own image (or that of anyone else) from a Japanese department store. The robot clone costs $225,000 and became available in January 2010. See "Dear Santa: I Want a Robot That Looks Just Like Me," Ethics Soup, December 17, 2009, www.ethicsoup.com/2009/l2/dear-santa-i-want-a-robot-that-looks-like-me.html (accessed January 12, 2010).

4. Bryan Griggs, "Inventor Unveils $7,000 Talking Sex Robot," CNN, February 1, 2010, www.cnn.com/2010/TECH/02/01/sex.robot/index.html (accessed June 9, 2010).

5. Raymond Kurzweil, *The Singularity Is Near: When Humans Transcend Biology* (New York: Viking, 2005). On radical images of our future, see Joel Garreau, *Radical Evolution: The Promise and Peril of Enhancing Our Minds, Our Bodies—and What It Means to Be Human* (New York: Doubleday, 2005).

6. For my further reflections on computer psychotherapy, see "Taking Things at Interface Value," in Sherry Turkle, *Life on the Screen: Identity in the Age of the Internet* (New York: Simon and Schuster, 1995), 102–124.

7. ·There is, too, a greater willingness to enter into a relationship with a machine if people think it will make them feel better. On how easy it is to anthropomorphize a computer, see Byron Reeves and Clifford Nass, *The Media Equation: How People Treat Computers, Television and New Media Like Real People and Places* (New York: Cambridge University Press, 1996). See also, on computer psychotherapy, Harold P. Erdman, Marjorie H. Klein, and John H. Greist, "Direct Patient Computer Interviewing," *Journal of Consulting and Clinical Psychology* 53 (1985): 760–773; Kenneth Mark Colby, James B. Watt, and John P. Gilbert, "A Computer Method for Psychotherapy: Preliminary Communication," *Journal of Nervous and Mental Diseases* 142, no. 2 (1966): 148–152; Moshe H. Spero, "Thoughts on Computerized Psychotherapy," *Psychiatry* 41 (1978): 281–282.

8. For my work on early computational objects and the question of aliveness, see Sherry Turkle, *The Second Self: Computers and the Human Spirit* (1984; Cambridge, MA: MIT Press, 2005). That work on aliveness continued with a second generation of computational objects in Turkle, *Life on the Screen*. My inquiry, with an emphasis on children's reasoning rather than their answers, is inspired by Jean Piaget, *The*

Child's Conception of the World, trans. Joan Tomlinson and Andrew Tomlinson (Totowa, NJ: Littlefield, Adams, 1960).

9. On the power of the liminal, see, for example, Victor Turner, *The Ritual Process: Structure and Anti-Structure* (Chicago: Aldine, 1969), and *The Forest of Symbols: Aspects of Ndembu Ritual* (1967; Ithaca, NY: Cornell University Press, 1970). See also Mary Douglas, *Purity and Danger: An Analysis of Concepts of Pollution and Taboo* (London: Routledge and Kegan Paul, 1966).

10. Piaget, *The Child's Conception*.

11. Turkle, *The Second Self*, 33–64.

12. Children, in fact, settled on three new formulations. First, when it came to thinking through the aliveness of computational objects, autonomous motion was no longer at the heart of the matter. The question was whether computers had autonomous cognition. Second, they acknowledged that computer toys might have some kind of awareness (particularly of them) without being alive. Consciousness and life were split. Third, computers seemed alive because they could think on their own, but were only "sort of alive" because even though they could think on their own, their histories undermined their autonomy. So an eight-year-old said that Speak & Spell was "sort of alive" but not "really alive" because it had a programmer. "The programmer," he said, "gives it its ideas. So the ideas don't come from the game." These days, sociable robots, with their autonomous behavior, moods, and faces, seem to take the programmer increasingly out of the picture. And with the formulation "alive enough," children put the robots on a new terrain. As for cognition, it has given way in children's minds to the capacity to show attention, to be part of a relationship of mutual affection.

13. Turkle, *Life on the Screen*, 169.

14. Turkle, *Life on the Screen*, 173–174.

15. The quotation is from a journal entry by Emerson in January 1832. The passage reads in full, "Dreams and beasts are two keys by which we are to find out the secrets of our nature. All mystics use them. They are like comparative anatomy. They are our test objects." See Joel Porte, ed. *Emerson in His Journals* (Cambridge, MA: Belknap Press, 1982), 81.

16. According to psychoanalyst D. W. Winnicott, objects such as teddy bears, baby blankets, or a bit of silk from a first pillow mediate between the infant's earliest bonds with the mother, who is experienced as inseparable from the self, and other people, who will come to be experienced as separate beings. These objects are known as "transitional," and the infant comes to know them both as almost inseparable parts of the self and as the first "not me" possessions. As the child grows, these transitional objects are left behind, but the effects of early encounters with them remain. We see them in the highly charged relationships that people have with later objects and experiences that call forth the feeling of being "at one" with things outside the self. The power of the transitional object is associated with religion, spirituality, the perception of beauty, sexual intimacy, and the sense of connection with nature. And now, the power of the transitional object is associated with computers and, even more dramatically, with sociable robots. On transitional objects, see D. W. Winnicott, *Playing and Reality* (New York: Basic Books, 1971).

17. In the early 1980s, children's notion of people as "emotional machines" seemed to me an unstable category. I anticipated that later generations of children would find other formulations as they learned more about computers. They might, for example,

see through the apparent "intelligence" of the machines by developing a greater understanding of how they were created and operated. As a result, children might be less inclined to see computers as kin. However, in only a few years, things moved in a very different direction. Children did not endeavor to make computation more transparent. Like the rest of the culture, they accepted it as opaque, a behaving system. Children taking sociable robots "at interface value" are part of a larger trend. The 1984 introduction of the Macintosh encouraged its users to stay on the surface of things. The Macintosh version of "transparency" stood the traditional meaning of that word on its head. Transparency used to refer to the ability to "open up the hood" and look inside. On a Macintosh it meant double-clicking an icon. In other words, transparency had come to mean being able to make a simulation work without knowing how it worked. The new transparency is what used to be called opacity. For more on this question, see Turkle, *Life on the Screen*, especially 29–43, and Sherry Turkle, *Simulation and Its Discontents* (Cambridge, MA: MIT Press, 2009).

18. Our connections with the virtual intensifies when avatars look, gesture, and move like us; these connections become stronger when we move from the virtual to the embodied robotic. Computer scientist Cory Kidd studied attachment to a computer program. In one condition the program issued written commands that told study participants what to do. In a second condition, an on-screen avatar issued the same instructions. In a third condition an on-screen robot was used to give the same instructions. The robot engendered the greatest attachment. Cory Kidd, "Human-Robot Interaction" (master's thesis, Massachusetts Institute of Technology, 2003).

19. The Tamagotchi website cautions about unfavorable outcomes: "If you neglect your little cyber creature, your Tamagotchi may grow up to be mean or ugly. How old will your Tamagotchi be when it returns to its home planet? What kind of virtual caretaker will you be?" The packaging on a Tamagotchi makes the agenda clear: "There are a total of 4 hearts on the 'Happy' and 'Hunger' screens and they start out empty. The more hearts that are filled, the better satisfied Tamagotchi is. You must feed or play with Tamagotchi in order to fill the empty hearts. If you keep Tamagotchi full and happy, it will grow into a cute, happy cyberpet. If you neglect Tamagotchi, it will grow into an unattractive alien." The manufacturer of the first Tamagotchi is Bandai. Its website provides clear moral instruction that links nurturance and responsibility. See the Bandai website at www.bandai.com (accessed October 5, 2009).

20. See "Tamagotchi Graveyard," Tamagotchi Dreamworld, http://shesdevilish.tripod .com/grave.html (accessed June 15, 2009).

21. In Japan, a neglected Tamagotchi dies but can be uploaded to a virtual graveyard. In the United States, manufacturers propose gentler resolutions. Some neglected Tamagotchis might become "angels" and return to their home planet. On the Tamagotchis I played with, it was possible to hit a reset button and be presented with another creature.

22. Sigmund Freud, "The Uncanny," in The Standard Edition of Sigmund Freud, ed. and trans. James Strachey et al. (London: Hogarth Press, 1953–1974), 17:219–256.

23. Sigmund Freud, "Mourning and Melancholia," in *The Standard Edition*, 14: 237–258.

24. See "Tamagotchi Graveyard."

25. Other writings on the Tamagotchi gravesite include the epitaph for a Tamagotchi named Lacey who lived for ninety-nine years. We know how hard it was for her

owner to achieve this result, but he is modest about his efforts: "She wasn't much trouble at all." But even with his considerable accomplishment, he feels her death was due to his neglect: "I slept late on a Sunday and she died." But in the simple expressions of guilt (or perhaps a playing at guilt) are frank admissions of how hard it is to lose someone you love. Mourners say, "I was his mama and he will always love me as I loved him"; "He went everywhere with me. He was a loving and faithful pet"; "I'm sorry and I real[l]y miss you!"; and "God gave him life. I gave him death." Some mourners express their belief in redemption through the generativity of generations. Thus is "Little Guy" memorialized, dead at forty-eight: "I hope you are very happy, Little Guy. I'm currently taking care of your son. I know he's yours because he looks and acts just like you. I'm really sorry I couldn't save you and had you on pause a lot when you were older." See "Tamagotchi Graveyard."

26. The fact that the Furby was so hard to quiet down was evidence of its aliveness. Even adults who knew it was not alive saw it as playing on the boundaries of life. The response of many was to see the Furby as out of control, intolerable, or, as one put it, insane. A online video of an "insane Furby" shows the Furby chatting away, to the increasing consternation of its adult owner. To stop it, he slaps its face, sticks his fingers in its mouth, holds down its ears and eyes, smashes it against a wall, and throws it down a flight of stairs. None of these shuts it down. If anything, its language becomes more manic, more "desperate." Finally comes the solution of taking out the Furby's batteries with a Phillips screwdriver. Now, the quiet Furby is petted. Its owner comments, "That's better." See "Insane Furby," YouTube, March 15, 2007, www.youtube.com/watch?v=g4Dfg4xJ6Ko (accessed November 11, 2009).

27. These enactments bring theory to ground level. See Donna Haraway, "A Cyborg Manifesto: Science, Technology, and Socialist-Feminism in the Late Twentieth Century," in *Simians, Cyborgs and Women: The Reinvention of Nature* (New York: Routledge, 1991), 149–181, and N. Katherine Hayles, *How We Became Posthuman: Virtual Bodies in Cybernetics, Literature, and Informatics* (Chicago: University of Chicago Press, 1999).

28. Michael Chorost, *Rebuilt: How Becoming Part Computer Made Me More Human* (Boston: Houghton Mifflin, 2005).

29. Here, the Furby acts as what psychoanalyst D. W. Winnicott termed a "transitional object," one where the boundaries between self and object are not clear. See D. W. Winnicott, *Playing and Reality* (New York: Basic Books, 1971).

30. The idea that the Furby had the capacity to learn new words by "listening" to the language around it was persistent. The belief most likely stemmed from the fact that it was possible to have the Furby say certain preprogrammed words or phrases more often by petting it whenever it said them. As a result of this myth, several intelligence agencies banned Furbies from their offices, believing that they were recording devices camouflaged as toys.

31. Children move back and forth between he, she, and it in talking about relational artifacts. Once they make a choice, they do not always stick with it. I report on what children say and, thus, their sentences are sometimes inconsistent.

32. Peter H. Kahn and his colleagues studied online discussion groups that centered on Furbies. For their account, see Batya Friedman, Peter H. Kahn Jr., and Jennifer Hagman, "Hardware Companions? What Online AIBO Discussion Forums Reveal About the Human-Robotic Relationship," in *Proceedings of the Conference on Human Factors in Computing Systems* (New York: ACM Press, 2003), 273–280.

33. The artist Kelly Heaton played on the biological/mechanical tension in the Furby's body by creating a fur coat made entirely from the fur of four hundred "skinned" Furbies, reengineered into a coat for Mrs. Santa Claus. The artwork, titled Dead Pelt, was deeply disturbing. It also included a wall of reactive eyes and mouths, taken from Furbies, and a formal anatomical drawing of a Furby. See the Feldman Gallery's Kelly Heaton page at www.feldmangallery.com/pages/artistsrffa/arthea01 .html (accessed August 18, 2009).

34. Baird developed her thought experiment comparing how people would treat a gerbil, a Barbie, and a Furby for a presentation at the Victoria Institute, Gothenburg, Sweden, in 1999.

35. In Turning's paper that argued the existence of intelligence if a machine could not be distinguished from a person, one scenario involved gender. In "Computing Machinery and Intelligence," he suggested an "imitation game": a man and then a computer pose as female, and the interrogator tries to distinguish them from a real woman. See Alan Turing, "Computing Machinery and Intelligence," *Mind* 59, no. 236 (October 1950): 433–460.

36. Antonio Damasio, *The Feeling of What Happens: Body and Emotion in the Making of Consciousness* (New York: Harcourt, 1999). Since emotions are cognitive representations of body states, the body cannot be separated from emotional life, just as emotion cannot be separated from cognition.

37. There are online worlds and communities where people feel comfortable expressing love for Furbies and seriously mourning Tamagotchis. These are places where a deep sense of connection to the robotic are shared. These "sanctioned spaces" play an important part in the development of the robotic moment. When you have company and a community, a sense of intimacy with sociable machines comes to feel natural. Over time, these online places begin to influence the larger community. At the very least, a cohort has grown up thinking that their attitudes toward the inanimate are widely shared.

38. BIT was developed by Brooks and his colleagues at the IS Robotics Corporation. IS Robotics was the precursor to iRobot, which first became well known as the makers of the Roomba robotic vacuum cleaner.

39. Rodney A. Brooks, *Flesh and Machines: How Robots Will Change Us* (New York: Pantheon, 2002), 202.

QUESTIONS FOR MAKING CONNECTIONS
WITHIN THE READING

1. How have our relations to simulated life changed in the period from Joseph Weizenbaum's ELIZA to My Real Baby and Nexi? How has the technology evolved? In what ways have our culture and psychology changed in response to the technology's evolution? Who controls the process, judging from the evidence Turkle provides? Are scientists the ones really in charge, and, if so, what are their motives? If the scientists are not in charge, how about the manufacturers, like the Hasbro Company? How about consumers—the parents who buy the Furbies and Tamagotchis?

2. Turkle refers to what she calls our "human complicity in a digital fantasy." In what sense does our involvement with simulations qualify as "fantasy"? Doesn't everyone—even children—understand that Furbies are pretend creatures, not real living beings? If everyone understands, can we still be deceived in some way? What does Turkle have in mind when she distinguishes between a "psychology of projection" and a "psychology of engagement"? *Projection* refers to qualities we impose on things. Does *engagement* mean that our creations are in some way changing us in turn?

3. How have the new technologies changed the ways we think about life and being alive? If you read Turkle carefully, you can see that no single definition of *life* has become the dominant one, but in her account you can identify a range of responses. Among these responses what seem to be the most important differences and similarities? Have words like *alive* and *living* become meaningless? When we treat a Tamagotchi as alive—and when we mourn its "death"—are we giving life a new meaning or have we lost sight of reality?

QUESTIONS FOR WRITING

1. What does it say about the life of our times that people, even children, look to machines in order to meet their basic emotional needs? Does this development provide evidence of a poverty in our social and cultural lives? Are we starved for affection, closeness, family, and friendship? If we are, does our turn to technological solutions remedy the problem or only make it worse? Will the technologies of simulation ultimately make us more machine-like? Are we trying to humanize our machines, or have machines become the form of life we aspire to?

2. When we invest computers with human characteristics are we actually enlarging the world of human value and feeling, in much the same way as we give meaning to paintings, sculptures, and buildings? When people praise Michelangelo's *Pietà* for its emotional depth, or Van Gogh's *Sunflowers* for its vitality, they are ascribing to stone and pigments on canvas qualities these objects actually lack. Holden Caulfield from *The Catcher in the Rye* and Pip from *Great Expectations* have no real thoughts and feelings although we sometimes act as though they do. How does our response to Furbies and Tamagotchis differ from our response to works of art or fictional characters? When we humanize them, are we diminishing ourselves?

QUESTIONS FOR MAKING CONNECTIONS
BETWEEN READINGS

1. Are Tamagotchis bad or are they good for our mental health? Considering the evidence that Turkle provides, would you say that devices like Furbies encourage dissociation of the kind described by Martha Stout in "When I

Woke Up Tuesday Morning, It Was Friday"? A person like Julia seems fully functional in most contexts, and yet she absents herself from reality in ways that others never notice and that she herself never recognizes. Are devices like Tamagotchis actually machines for "spacing out," or do they instead prepare us to live more engaged and aware lives?

2. Ethan Watters's "The Mega-Marketing of Depression in Japan" makes the case that pharmaceutical companies have changed the psychology of the Japanese people in ways that will allow the companies to sell drugs designed to treat depression, an illness unknown in that country before the advent of Western psychiatry. Drug manufacturers see themselves as responding to a crucial human need—which, according to Watters, they actually create and profit from. Have the makers of Furbies and Tamagotchis done much the same thing? Are they creating needs in order to meet them? In what ways do the new technologies of simulated life force us to rethink the rationale behind technological development? Have we become the servants of our technology?

JEAN TWENGE

IN THE SECOND half of the twentieth century, American culture became more and more a celebration of the individual. The shared concerns of the whole society and the language of "us" rather than of "me" fell by the wayside as the self became the primary focus. Many observers, alarmed by this trend, have criticized the last two generations for their sense of entitlement—their unexamined assumption that the world owes them happiness and recognition. But Jean Twenge, a psychologist and professor at San Diego State University, adds a new wrinkle to the critique: so much emphasis on the self isn't just bad for society, she argues; it's also bad for the individual.

Twenge's bestselling first book, *Generation Me: Why Today's Young Americans Are More Confident, Assertive, Entitled—and More Miserable than Ever Before* (2006), uses data taken from 1.3 million young people to trace the different perspectives of successive generations on self-esteem, individuality, sexuality, and other issues related to development. In reviewing this data, Twenge sees evidence of an unprecedented shift as both education and culture have come to emphasize selfhood and self-esteem above all other values. Twenge argues that for Baby Boomers, the term "self" was still a novel idea, so novel that that they saw "selfhood" as a difficult goal worth pursuing. However, later generations internalized this idea of the self to the point that young people find it difficult to imagine organizing their lives around anything else.

Twenge's second book, *The Narcissism Epidemic: Living in the Age of Entitlement* (2009), co-written with W. Keith Campbell, is a follow-up to *Generation Me* that provides a detailed portrait of a culture defined by "public violence and aggression, self-promotion, and the desire for uniqueness" at the cost of the well-being of others. Even though most young people today are not narcissistic to the degree that it has become debilitating for them, the number who suffer from a clinical disorder is three times greater than a generation ago. And even within mainstream culture, behavior that would have seemed to our grandparents absurdly selfabsorbed has become the new normal. Surges in the rates of plastic surgery, credit card debt, and ostentatious consumption all suggest that the celebrity has become the ideal of an age defined by its overconfidence and greed.

An Army of One: *Me*

One day when my mother was driving me to school in 1986, Whitney Houston's hit song "The Greatest Love of All" was warbling out of the weak speakers of our Buick station wagon with wood trim. I asked my mother what she thought the song was about. "The greatest love of all—it has to be about children," she said.

My mother was sweet, but wrong. The song does say that children are the future (always good to begin with a strikingly original thought) and that we should teach them well. About world peace, may be? Or great literature? Nope. Children should be educated about the beauty "inside," the song declares. We all need heroes, Whitney sings, but she never found "anyone to fulfill my needs," so she learned to depend on (wait for it) "me." The chorus then declares, "learning to love yourself is the greatest love of all."

This is a stunning reversal in attitude from previous generations. Back then, respect for others was more important than respect for yourself. The term "self-esteem" wasn't widely used until the late 1960s, and didn't become talk-show and dinner-table conversation until the 1980s. By the 1990s, it was everywhere.

Take, for example, the band Offspring's rockingly irreverent 1994 riff "Self-Esteem." The song describes a guy whose girlfriend "says she wants only me ... Then I wonder why she sleeps with my friends." (Hmmm.) But he's blasé about it—it's OK, really, since he's "just a sucker with no self-esteem."

By the mid-1990s, Offspring could take it for granted that most people knew the term "self-esteem," and knew they were supposed to have it. They also knew how to diagnose themselves when they didn't have it. Offspring's ironic self-parody demonstrates a high level of understanding of the concept, the satire suggesting that this psychological self-examination is rote and can thus be performed with tongue planted firmly in cheek.

In the years since, attention to the topic of self-esteem has rapidly expanded. A search for "self-esteem" in the books section of amazon.com yielded 105,438 entries in July 2005 (sample titles: *The Self-Esteem Workbook, Breaking the Chain of Low Self-Esteem, Ten Days to Self-Esteem, 200 Ways to Raise a Girl's Self-Esteem*). Magazine articles on self-esteem are as common as e-mail spam for Viagra. *Ladies' Home Journal* told readers to "Learn to Love Yourself!" in March 2005,[1] while *Parenting* offered "Proud to Be Me!" (apparently the exclamation point is required) in April, listing "5 simple ways to help your child love who he is."[2] TV and radio talk shows would be immediately shut down by the FCC if "self-esteem" were on the list of banned words. The American Academy of Pediatrics guide to caring for babies and young children uses the word "self-esteem" ten times in the space of seven pages in the first chapter, and that doesn't even count the numerous mentions of self-respect, confidence, and belief in oneself.[3]

How did self-esteem transform from an obscure academic term to a familiar phrase that pops up in everything from women's magazines to song lyrics to celebrity interviews? The story actually begins centuries ago, when humans barely had a concept of a self at all: your marriage was arranged, your profession determined by your parents, your actions dictated by strict religious standards. Slowly over the centuries, social strictures began to loosen and people started to make more choices for themselves. Eventually, we arrived at the modern concept of the individual as an autonomous, free person.

Then came the 1970s, when the ascendance of the self truly exploded into the American consciousness. In contrast to previous ethics of honor and duty, Baby Boomer ideals focused instead on meaning and self-fulfillment. In his 1976 bestseller, *Your Erroneous Zones,* Wayne Dyer suggests that the popular song "You Are the Sunshine of My Life" be retitled "I Am the Sunshine of My Life." Your love for yourself, he says, should be your "first love." The 1970 allegory, *Jonathan Livingston Seagull*, describes a bird bored with going "from shore to food and back again." Instead, he wants to enjoy flying, swooping through the air to follow "a higher meaning, a higher purpose for life," even though his actions get him exiled from his flock. The book, originally rejected by nearly every major publishing house, became a runaway bestseller as Americans came to agree with the idea that life should be fulfilling and focused on the needs of the self. The seagulls in the animated movie *Finding Nemo* were still on message almost twenty-five years later: all that comes out of their beaks is the word "mine."

Boomers and Their "Journey" into the Self

Because the Boomers dominate our culture so much, we have to understand them first so we can see how they differ from the younger Generation Me. Why aren't the Boomers—the Me Generation in the 1970s—the *real* Generation Me? It's about what you explore as a young adult versus what you're born to and take for granted.

For the Boomers, who grew up in the 1950s and 1960s, self-focus was a new concept, individualism an uncharted territory. In his 1981 book *New Rules: Searching for Self-Fulfillment in a World Turned Upside Down*, Daniel Yankelovich describes young Boomers struggling with new questions: How do you make decisions in a marriage with two equal partners? How do you focus on yourself when your parents don't even know what that means? The Boomers in the book sound like people driving around in circles in the dark, desperately searching for something. The world was so new that there were no road signs, no maps to point the way to this new fulfillment and individuality.

That's probably why many Boomers talk about the self using language full of abstraction, introspection, and "growth." New things call for this kind of meticulous thought, and require the idea that the process will take time. Thus Boomers talk about "my journey," "my need to keep growing," or "my unfulfilled potentials." Sixties activist Todd Gitlin called the Boomer quest the "voyage to the interior." Icky as they are to today's young people, these phrases drum with motion and time, portraying self-focus as a continuous project that keeps evolving as Boomers look around for true meaning. In a 1976 *New York Magazine* article, Tom Wolfe described the "new dream" as "remaking, remodeling, elevating and polishing one's very self … and observing, studying, and doting on it."[4] Sixties radical Jerry Rubin wrote that he tried just about every fad of the 1970s (rolfing, est, yoga, sex therapy, finding his inner child); one of the chapters in his book *Growing (Up) at Thirty-Seven* is called "Searching for Myself."

Such introspection primarily surfaces today in the speech of New Agers, therapists who have read too much Maslow, and over-45 Boomers. When asked what's next in her life, Kim Basinger (born in 1953) replies, "Watching what the rest of my journey is going to be about."[5] In answer to the same question, Sarah Ferguson, Duchess of York (born in 1959) says: "My coming to stay in America for a few months is like my blossoming into my true Sarah, into my true self. And I'm just coming to learn about her myself."[6] Not all Boomers talk this way, of course, but enough do that it's an immediately recognizable generational tic. It's also a guaranteed way to get a young person to roll her eyes. She might also then tell you to lighten up.

Many authors, from William Strauss and Neil Howe in *Generations* to Steve Gillon in *Boomer Nation*, have noted that abstraction and spirituality are the primary hallmarks of the Boomer generation. Gillon describes Boomers as having a "moralistic style" and devotes a chapter to Boomers' "New Fundamentalism."[7] Whether joining traditional churches or exploring meditation or yoga, Boomers have been fascinated with the spiritual for four decades.

Even Boomers who don't adopt New Age language seek higher meaning in the new religion of consumer products—thus the yuppie revolution. In *Bobos in Paradise*, David Brooks demonstrates that upper-class Boomers have poured their wealth into things like cooking equipment, which somehow feels more moral and meaningful than previous money sinks like jewelry or furs. Even food becomes "a barometer of virtue," Brooks says, as 1960s values are "selectively updated.… Gone are the sixties-era things that were fun and of interest to teenagers, like Free Love, and retained are all the things that might be of interest to middle-aged hypochondriacs, like whole grains."[8]

The Boomers' interest in the abstract and spiritual shows up in many different sources. In 1973, 46% of Boomers said they "focused on internal cues."[9] Only 26% of 1990s young people agreed. Thirty percent of Boomers said that "creativity comes from within," versus 18% of young people in the 1990s.[10] Even stronger evidence comes from a national survey of more than 300,000 college freshmen. In 1967, a whopping 86% of incoming college students said that "developing a meaningful philosophy of life" was an essential life goal.[11] Only 42% of GenMe freshmen in 2004 agreed, cutting the Boomer number in half. I'm definitely a member of my generation in this way; despite being an academic, I'm not sure I know what a "meaningful philosophy of life" even is. Jerry Rubin does—if you can understand him. "Instead of seeking with the expectation of finding, I experience my seeking as an end in itself," he writes. "I become one with my seeking, and merge with the moment."[12] OK, Jerry. Let us know when you've re-entered the Earth's atmosphere.

While up there, maybe Jerry met Aleta St. James, a 57-year-old woman who gave birth to twins in 2004. She explained her unusual actions by saying, "My whole world is about manifesting, so I decided to manifest children."[13] It's not surprising that an enterprising GenMe member put together a list of books on amazon.com titled "Tired of Baby Boomer Self-Righteousness?"

Boomers display another unique and somewhat ironic trait: a strong emphasis on group meetings. Boomers followed in the footsteps of their community-minded elders—they just joined the Weathermen instead of the Elks Lodge. This is one of the many reasons why Boomers are not the true Generation Me—almost everything they did happened in groups: Vietnam protests, marches for feminism, consciousness raising, assertiveness training, discos, even seminars like est. Maybe it felt safer to explore the self within a group—perhaps it felt less radical. No one seemed to catch the irony that it might be difficult to find your own unique direction in a group of other people. Even Boomers' trends and sayings belied their reliance on groups: "Don't trust anyone over 30" groups people by age, as did the long hair many Boomer men adopted in the late 1960s and early 1970s to distinguish themselves from older folks. In a 1970 song, David Crosby says he decided not to cut his hair so he could "let my freak flag fly." If you've got a flag, you're probably a group. Boomers may have thought they invented individualism, but like any inventor, they were followed by those who truly perfected the art.

Boomers took only the first tentative steps in the direction of self-focus, rather than swallowing it whole at birth. Most Boomers never absorbed it at all and settled down early to marry and raise families. Those who adopted the ways of the self as young adults speak the language with an accent: the accent of abstraction and "journeys." They had to reinvent their way of thinking when already grown, and thus see self-focus as a "process." In his book, Rubin quotes a friend who says, "We are the first generation to reincarnate ourselves in our own lifetime."

The Matter-of-Fact Self-Focus of Generation Me

Generation Me had no need to reincarnate ourselves; we were born into a world that already celebrated the individual. The self-focus that blossomed in the 1970s became mundane and commonplace over the next two decades, and GenMe accepts it like a fish accepts water. If Boomers were making their way in the uncharted world of the self, GenMe has printed step-by-step directions from Yahoo! Maps—and most of the time we don't even need them, since the culture of the self is our hometown. We don't have to join groups or talk of journeys, because we're already there. We don't need to "polish" the self, as Wolfe said, because we take for granted that it's already shiny. We don't need to look inward; we already know what we will find. Since we were small children, we were taught to put ourselves first. That's just the way the world works—why dwell on it? Let's go to the mall.

GenMe's focus on the needs of the individual is not necessarily self-absorbed or isolationist; instead, it's a way of moving through the world beholden to few social rules and with the unshakable belief that you're important. It's also not the same as being "spoiled," which implies that we always get what we want; though this probably does describe some kids, it's not the essence of the trend. (GenMe's expectations are so great and our reality so challenging that we will probably get less of what we want than any previous generation). We simply take it for granted that we should all feel good about ourselves, we are all special, and we all deserve to follow our dreams. GenMe is straightforward and unapologetic about our self-focus. In 2004's *Conquering Your Quarterlife Crisis*, Jason, 25, relates how he went through some tough times and decided he needed to change things in his life. His new motto was "Do what's best for Jason. I had to make *me* happy; I had to do what was best for myself in every situation."[14]

Our practical orientation toward the self sometimes leaves us with a distaste for Boomer abstraction. When a character in the 2004 novel *Something Borrowed* watched the 1980s show *thirtysomething* as a teen, she wished the Boomer characters would "stop pondering the meaning of life and start making grocery lists."[15] The matter-of-fact attitude of GenMe appears in everyday language as well—a language that still includes the abstract concept of self, but uses it in a very simple way, perhaps because we learned the language as children. We speak the language of the self as our native tongue. So much of the "common sense" advice that's given these days includes some variation on "self":

- Worried about how to act in a social situation? "Just be yourself."

- What's the good thing about your alcoholism/drug addiction/murder conviction? "I learned a lot about myself."

- Concerned about your performance? "Believe in yourself." (Often followed by "and anything is possible.")

- Should you buy the new pair of shoes, or get the nose ring? "Yes, express yourself."

- Why should you leave the unfulfilling relationship/quit the boring job/tell off your mother-in-law? "You have to respect yourself."

- Trying to get rid of a bad habit? "Be honest with yourself."

- Confused about the best time to date or get married? "You have to love yourself before you can love someone else."

- Should you express your opinion? "Yes, stand up for yourself."

Americans use these phrases so often that we don't even notice them anymore. Dr. Phil, the ultimate in plainspoken, no-nonsense advice, uttered both "respect yourself" and "stop lying to yourself" within seconds of each other on a *Today* show segment on New Year's resolutions.[16] One of his bestselling books is entitled *Self Matters*. We take these phrases and ideas so much for granted, it's as if we learned them in our sleep as children, like the perfectly conditioned citizens in Aldous Huxley's *Brave New World*.

These aphorisms don't seem absurd to us even when, sometimes, they are. We talk about self-improvement as if the self could be given better drywall or a

The Self Across the Generations

Baby Boomers	Generation Me
Self-fulfillment	Fun
Journey, potentials, searching	Already there
Change the world	Follow your dreams
Protests and group sessions	Watching TV and surfing the Web
Abstraction	Practicality
Spirituality	Things
Philosophy of life	Feeling good about yourself

new coat of paint. We read self-help books as if the self could receive tax-deductible donations. The *Self* even has its own magazine. Psychologist Martin Seligman says that the traditional self—responsible, hardworking, stern—has been replaced with the "California self," "a self that chooses, feels pleasure and pain, dictates action and even has things like esteem, efficacy, and confidence."[17] Media outlets promote the self relentlessly; I was amazed at how often I heard the word "self" used in the popular media once I started looking for it. A careful study of news stories published or aired between 1980 and 1999 found a large increase in self-reference words (I, me, mine, and myself) and a marked decrease in collective words (humanity, country, or crowd).[18]

Young people have learned these self-lessons very well. In a letter to her fans in 2004, Britney Spears, 23, listed her priorities as "Myself, my husband, Kevin, and starting a family."[19] If you had to read that twice to get my point, it's because we take it for granted that we should put ourselves first on our list of priorities—it would be blasphemy if you didn't (unless, of course, you have low self-esteem). Twenty-year-old Maria says her mother often reminds her to consider what other people will think. "It doesn't matter what other people think," Maria insists. "What really matters is how I perceive myself. The real person I need to please is myself."

Smart marketers have figured this out, too. In the late 1990s, Prudential replaced its longtime insurance slogan "Get a Piece of the Rock" with the nakedly individualistic "Be Your Own Rock."[20] The United States Army, perhaps the last organization one might expect to focus on the individual instead of the group, has followed suit. Their standard slogan, adopted in 2001, is "An Army of One."

Changes in Self-Esteem: What the Data Say

The data I gathered on self-esteem over time mirror the social trends perfectly. My colleague Keith Campbell and I looked at the responses of 65,965 college students to the Rosenberg Self-Esteem Scale, the most popular measure of general self-esteem among adults.[21] I held my breath when I analyzed these data for the first time, but I needn't have worried: the change was enormous. By the mid-1990s, the average GenMe college man had higher self-esteem than 86% of college men in 1968. The average mid-1990s college woman had higher self-esteem than 71% of Boomer college women. Between the 1960s and the 1990s, college students were increasingly likely to agree that "I take a positive attitude toward myself" and "On the whole, I am satisfied with myself." Other sources verify this trend. A 1997 survey of teens asked, "In general, how do you feel about yourself?" A stunning 93% answered "good." Of the remainder, 6% said they felt "not very good," and only 1% admitted they felt "bad" about themselves.[22] Another survey found that 91% of teens described themselves as responsible, 74% as physically attractive, and 79% as "very intelligent."[23]

Children's self-esteem scores tell a different but even more intriguing story. We examined the responses of 39,353 children, most ages 9 to 13, on the Coopersmith Self-Esteem Inventory, a scale written specifically for children.[24] During the 1970s—when the nation's children shifted from the late Baby Boom to the early years of GenX—kids' self-esteem declined, probably because of societal instability. Rampant divorce, a wobbly economy, soaring crime rates, and swinging singles culture made the 1970s a difficult time to be a kid. The average child in 1979 scored lower than 81% of kids in the mid-1960s. Over this time, children were less likely to agree with statements like "I'm pretty sure of myself" and "I'm pretty happy" and more likely to agree that "things are all mixed up in my life." The individualism that was so enthralling for teenagers and adults in the 1970s didn't help kids—and, if their parents suddenly discovered self-fulfillment, it might have even hurt them.

But after 1980, when GenMe began to enter the samples, children's self-esteem took a sharp turn upward. More and more during the 1980s and 1990s, children were saying that they were happy with themselves. They agreed that "I'm easy to like" and "I always do the right thing." By the mid-1990s, children's self-esteem scores equaled, and often exceeded, children's scores in the markedly more stable Boomer years before 1970. The average kid in the mid-1990s—right in the heart of GenMe—had higher self-esteem than 73% of kids in 1979, one of the last pre-GenMe years.

This is a bit of a mystery, however. The United States of the 1980s to mid-1990s never approached the kid-friendly stability of the 1950s and early 1960s: violent crime hit record highs, divorce was still at epidemic levels, and the economy had not yet reached its late-1990s boom. So without the calm and prosperity of earlier decades, why did children's self-esteem increase so dramatically during the 1980s and 1990s?

The Self-Esteem Curriculum

The short answer is that they were taught it. In the years after 1980, there was a pervasive, society-wide effort to increase children's self-esteem. The Boomers who now filled the ranks of parents apparently decided that children should always feel good about themselves. Research on programs to boost self-esteem first blossomed in the 1980s, and the number of psychology and education journal articles devoted to self-esteem doubled between the 1970s and the 1980s.[25] Journal articles on self-esteem increased another 52% during the 1990s, and the

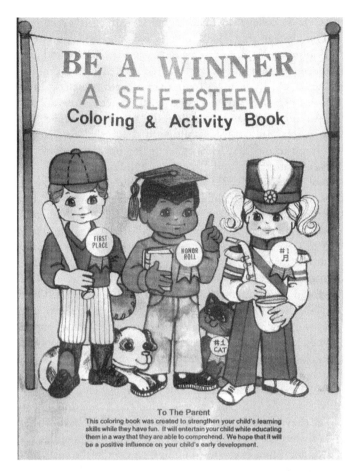

Parents are encouraged to raise their children's self-esteem even when kids are simply coloring. Even the cat has high self-esteem on this coloring book cover. However, the dog lacks a self-esteem boosting ribbon. He probably has low self-esteem—after all, he drinks out of the toilet.

number of books on self-esteem doubled over the same time.[26] Generation Me is the first generation raised to believe that everyone should have high self-esteem.

Magazines, television talk shows, and books all emphasize the importance of high self-esteem for children, usually promoting feelings that are actually a lot closer to narcissism (a more negative trait usually defined as excessive self-importance). One children's book, first published in 1991, is called *The Lovables in the Kingdom of Self-Esteem.* "I AM LOVABLE. Hi, lovable friend! My name is Mona Monkey. I live in the Kingdom of Self-Esteem along with my friends the Lovable Team," the book begins.[27] On the next page, children learn that the gates of the kingdom will swing open if you "say these words three times with pride: *I'm lovable! I'm lovable! I'm lovable!*" (If I hear the word "lovable" one more time, I'm going to use my hefty self-esteem to pummel the author of this book).

Another example is the "BE A WINNER Self-Esteem Coloring and Activity Book" pictured in this chapter. Inside, children find activities and pictures designed to boost their self-esteem, including coloring a "poster for your room" that reads "YOU ARE SPECIAL" in yellow, orange, and red letters against a purple background. Another page asks kids to fill in the blanks: "Accept y_ur_e_f. You're a special person. Use p_si_iv_ thinking." A similar coloring book is called "We Are All Special" (though this title seems to suggest that being special isn't so special). All of this probably sounds like Al Franken's *Saturday Night Live* character Stuart Smalley, an insecure, sweater-vest-wearing man who looks in the mirror and unconvincingly repeats, "I'm good enough, I'm smart enough, and doggone it, people like me." It sounds like it because it's exactly the type of thing Franken was parodying. And it's everywhere.

Many school districts across the country have specific programs designed to increase children's self-esteem, most of which actually build self-importance and narcissism. One program is called "Self-Science: The Subject Is Me."[28] (Why bother with biology? *I'm* so much more interesting!) Another program, called "Pumsy in Pursuit of Excellence," uses a dragon character to encourage children to escape the "Mud Mind" they experience when feeling bad about themselves. Instead, they should strive to be in the "Sparkle Mind" and feel good about themselves.[29] The Magic Circle exercise designates one child a day to receive a badge saying "I'm great." The other children then say good things about the chosen child, who later receives a written list of all of the praise. At the end of the exercise, the child must then say something good about him- or herself. Boomer children in the 1950s and 1960s gained self-esteem naturally from a stable, child-friendly society; GenMe's self-esteem has been actively cultivated for its own sake.[30]

One Austin, Texas, father was startled to see his five-year-old daughter wearing a shirt that announced, "I'm lovable and capable." All of the kindergarteners, he learned, recited this phrase before class, and they all wore the shirt to school on Fridays. It seems the school started a bit too young, however, because the child then asked, "Daddy, all the kids are wondering, what does 'capable' mean?"[31]

Some people have wondered if the self-esteem trend waned after schools began to put more emphasis on testing during the late 1990s. It doesn't look that way. Parenting books and magazines stress self-esteem as much as ever, and a large number of schools continue to use self-esteem programs. The mission statements of many schools explicitly announce that they aim to raise students' self-esteem. A Google search for "elementary school mission statement self-esteem" yielded 308,000 Web pages in January 2006. These schools are located across the country, in cities, suburbs, small towns, and rural areas. "Building," "improving," "promoting," or "developing" self-esteem is a stated goal of (among many others) New River Elementary in New River, Arizona; Shady Dell Elementary in Springfield, Missouri; Shettler Elementary in Fruitport, Michigan; Baxter Elementary in Baxter, Tennessee; Rye Elementary in Westchester County, New York; Copeland Elementary in Augusta, Georgia; and Banff Elementary in Banff, Alberta, Canada. Private religious schools are not immune: St. Wendelin Catholic Elementary in Fostoria, Ohio, aims to "develop a feeling of confidence, self-esteem, and self-worth in our students."

Andersen Elementary in Rockledge, Florida, raises the bar, adding that students will "exhibit high self-esteem." So self-esteem must not just be *promoted* by teachers, but must be actively *exhibited* by students.

As John Hewitt points out in *The Myth of Self-Esteem*, the implicit message is that self-esteem can be taught and should be taught. When self-esteem programs are used, Hewitt notes, children are "encouraged to believe that it is acceptable and desirable to be preoccupied with oneself [and] praise oneself." In many cases, he says, it's not just encouraged but required. These exercises make self-importance mandatory, demanding of children that they love themselves. "The child *must* be taught to like himself or herself.... The child *must* take the teacher's attitude himself or herself—'I am somebody!' 'I am capable and loving!'—regardless of what the child thinks."[32]

Most of these programs encourage children to feel good about themselves for no particular reason. In one program, teachers are told to discourage children from saying things like "I'm a good soccer player" or "I'm a good singer."[33] This makes self-esteem contingent on performance, the program authors chide. Instead, "we want to anchor self-esteem firmly to the child ... so that no matter what the performance might be, the self-esteem remains high." In other words, feeling good about yourself is more important than good performance. Children, the guide says, should be taught "that it is who they are, not what they do, that is important." Many programs encourage self-esteem even when things go wrong or the child does something bad. In one activity, children are asked to finish several sentences, including ones beginning "I love myself even though ..." and "I forgive myself for ...."[34]

Teacher training courses often emphasize that a child's self-esteem must be preserved above all else. A sign on the wall of one university's education department says, "We Choose to Feel Special and Worthwhile No Matter What."[35] Perhaps as a result, 60% of teachers and 69% of school counselors agree that self-esteem should be raised by "providing more unconditional validation of students based on who they are rather than how they perform or behave."[36] Unconditional validation, to translate the educational mumbo-jumbo, means feeling good about yourself no matter how you act or whether you learn anything or not. A veteran second-grade teacher in Tennessee disagrees with this practice but sees it everywhere. "We handle children much more delicately," she says. "They feel good about themselves for no reason. We've given them this cotton-candy sense of self with no basis in reality."[37]

Although the self-esteem approach sounds like it might be especially popular in liberal blue-state areas, it's common in red states as well, perhaps because it's very similar to the ideas popularized by fundamentalist Christian churches. For example, the popular Christian children's book *You Are Special* promotes the same unconditional self-esteem emphasized in secular school programs. First published in 1997, the book notes, "The world tells kids, 'You're special if ... you have the brains, the looks, the talent.' God tells them, 'You're special just because. No qualifications necessary.' Every child you know needs to hear this one, reassuring truth." Traditional religion, of course, did have "qualifications" and rules for behavior. Adults hear this message as well.[38] In an article in *Ladies*

Home Journal, Christian author Rick Warren writes, "You can believe what others say about you, or you can believe in yourself as does God, who says you are truly acceptable, lovable, valuable, and capable."[39]

Even programs not specifically focused on self-esteem often place the utmost value on children's self-feelings. Children in some schools sing songs with lyrics like "Who I am makes a difference and all our dreams can come true" and "We are beautiful, magnificent, courageous, outrageous, and great!"[40] Other students pen a "Me Poem" or write a mock TV "commercial" advertising themselves and their good qualities. An elementary school teacher in Alabama makes one child the focus of a "VIP for a week" project.[41] The children's museum in Laramie, Wyoming, has a self-esteem exhibit where children are told to describe themselves using positive adjectives.[42]

Parents often continue the self-esteem lessons their children have learned in school, perhaps because more children are planned and cherished. The debut of the birth control pill in the early 1960s began the trend toward wanted children, which continued in the early 1970s as abortion became legal and cultural values shifted toward children as a choice rather than a duty. In the 1950s, it was considered selfish not to have kids, but by the 1970s it was an individual decision. As a result, more and more children were born to people who really *wanted* to become parents. Parents were able to lavish more attention on each child as the average number of children per family shrank from four to two. Young people often say that their parents believed in building self-esteem. "My mom constantly told me how special I was," said Natalie, 19. "No matter how I did, she would tell me I was the best." Kristen, 22, said her parents had a "wonderful" way of "telling me what a great job I did and repeatedly telling me I was a very special person." Popular media [have] also promoted this idea endlessly, offering up self-esteem as the cure for just about everything. In one episode of the family drama *7th Heaven,* one young character asks what can be done about war. The father on the show, a minister, says, "We can take a good look in the mirror, and when we see peace, that's when we'll have peace on earth." The rest of the episode featured each character smiling broadly to himself or herself in the mirror. In other words, if we all just loved ourselves enough, it would put an end to war. (Not only is this tripe, but wars, if anything, are usually rooted in too *much* love of self, land, and nation—not too little). But, as TV and movies have taught us, loving yourself is more important than anything else.

These efforts have had their intended impact. Don Tapscott, who interviewed hundreds of people for his book *Growing Up Digital,* notes, "Chat moderators, teachers, parents, and community workers who spend time with [young people] invariably told us that they think this is a confident generation who think highly of themselves."[43] In a CBS News poll, the high school graduates of 2000 were asked, "What makes you feel positive about yourself?" The most popular answer, at 33%, was the tautological "self-esteem." School performance was a distant second at 18%, with popularity third at 13%.[44] Yet this is not surprising: saying that having self-esteem makes you feel positive about yourself—forget any actual reason—is exactly what the self-esteem programs have taught today's young generation since they were in kindergarten.

Yet when everyone wears a shirt that says "I'm Special," as some of the programs encourage, it is a wide-open invitation to parody. The 1997 premiere episode of MTV's animated show *Daria* featured a character named Jane, who cracked, "I like having low self-esteem. It makes me feel special." Later in the episode, the teacher of a "self-esteem class" asks the students to "make a list of ten ways the world would be a sadder place if you weren't in it." "Is that if we'd never been born, or if we died suddenly and unexpectedly?" asks one of the students. Wanting to get out of the rest of the class, Daria and Jane recite the answers to the self-esteem "test": "The next time I start to feel bad about myself [I will] stand before the mirror, look myself in the eye, and say, 'You are special. No one else is like you.'"[45]

By the time GenMe gets to college, these messages are rote. Hewitt, who teaches at the University of Massachusetts, says his students are very excited when they begin discussing self-esteem in his sociology class. But once he begins to question the validity of self-esteem, the students' faces become glum and interest wanes. Hewitt compares it to what might happen in church if a priest suddenly began questioning the existence of God. After all, we worship at the altar of self-esteem and self-focus. "When the importance of self-esteem is challenged, a major part of the contemporary American view of the world is challenged," Hewitt writes.[46]

Girls Are Great

It is no coincidence that the *Daria* episode parodying self-esteem programs features two girls. Feminist Gloria Steinem, who spent the 1970s and 1980s fighting for practical rights like equal pay and maternity leave, spent the early 1990s promoting her book *Revolution from Within: A Book of Self-Esteem.* In 1991, a study by the American Association of University Women (AAUW) announced that girls "lose their self-esteem on the way to adolescence." This study was covered in countless national news outlets and ignited a national conversation about teenage girls and how they feel about themselves. *Reviving Ophelia*, a bestselling book on adolescent girls, popularized this idea further, documenting the feelings of self-doubt girls experience as they move through junior high and high school. Apparently, girls' self-esteem was suffering a severe blow when they became teenagers, and we needed to do something about it.

Before long, programs like the Girl Scouts began to focus on self-esteem through their "Girls Are Great" program. Girls could earn badges like "Being My Best" and "Understanding Yourself and Others." Amanda, 22, says that her Girl Scout troop spent a lot of time on self-esteem. "We did workshops and earned badges based around self-esteem building projects," she says. "We learned that we could do anything we wanted, that it was good to express yourself, and being different is good."

In 2002, the Girl Scout Council paired with corporate sponsor Unilever to launch "Uniquely ME!" a self-esteem program to "address the critical nationwide problem of low self-esteem among adolescent and preadolescent girls." The program includes three booklets for girls ages 8 to 14, each including exercises on "recognizing one's strengths and best attributes" and "identifying core values and personal interests."[47]

However, there is little evidence that girls' self-esteem dives at adolescence. The AAUW study was seriously flawed, relying on unstandardized measures and exaggerating small differences. In 1999, a carefully researched, comprehensive study of sex differences in self-esteem was published in *Psychological Bulletin*, the most prestigious journal in the field. The study statistically summarized 216 previous studies on more than 97,000 people and concluded that the actual difference between adolescent girls' and boys' self-esteem was less than 4%—in other words, extremely small.[48] Exaggerating this difference might be unwise." We may create a self-fulfilling prophecy for girls by telling them they'll have low self-esteem," said University of Wisconsin professor Janet Hyde, one of the study authors.[49]

When my colleague Keith Campbell and I did a different analysis of 355 studies of 105,318 people, we also found that girls' self-esteem does not fall precipitously at adolescence; it just doesn't rise as fast as boys' self-esteem during the teen years. There was no large drop in girls' self-esteem, and by college the difference between men's and women's self-esteem was very small.[50] Another meta-analysis, by my former student Brenda Dolan-Pascoe, found moderate sex differences in appearance self-esteem, but no sex differences at all in academic self-esteem. Girls also scored *higher* than boys in behavior self-esteem and moral-ethical self-esteem. The achievements of adolescent girls also contradict the idea that they retreat into self-doubt: girls earn higher grades than boys at all school levels, and more go on to college.

In other words, adolescent girls don't have a self-esteem problem—there is no "critical nationwide problem of low self-esteem among adolescent and pre-adolescent girls" as the Girl Scouts claimed. But in a culture obsessed with feeling good about ourselves, even the hint of a self-esteem deficit is enough to prompt a nationwide outcry. The Girl Scout program premiered three years after the 1999 comprehensive study found a minuscule sex difference in self-esteem. Why let an overwhelming mass of data get in the way of a program that sounded good?

Self-Esteem and Academic Performance

There has also been a movement against "criticizing" children too much. Some schools and teachers don't correct children's mistakes, afraid that this will damage children's self-esteem. One popular method tells teachers not to correct students' spelling or grammar, arguing that kids should be "independent spellers" so they can be treated as "individuals." (Imagine reading a nuespaper wyten useing *that* filosofy.)[51] Teacher education courses emphasize that creating a positive atmosphere is more important than correcting mistakes.[52] In 2005, a British teacher proposed eliminating the word "fail" from education; instead of hearing that they have failed, students should hear that they have "deferred success."[53] In the United States, office stores have started carrying large stocks of purple pens, as some teachers say that red ink is too "scary" for children's papers.[54]

Florida elementary schoolteacher Robin Slipakoff said, "Red has a negative con-notation, and we want to promote self-confidence."[55]

Grade inflation has also reached record highs. In 2004, 48% of American college freshmen—almost half—reported earning an A average in high school, compared to only 18% in 1968, even though SAT scores decreased over this time period.[56] "Each year we think [the number with an A average] can't inflate anymore. And then it does again. The 'C' grade is almost a thing of the past," noted Andrew Astin, the lead researcher for the study. These higher grades were given out even though students were doing less work.[57] Only 33% of American college freshmen in 2003 reported studying six or more hours a week during their last year of high school, compared to 47% in 1987.[58] So why are they still getting better grades? "Teachers want to raise the self-esteem and feel-good atti-tudes of students," explains Howard Everson of the College Board.[59] We have become a Lake Wobegon nation: all of our children are above average.

The results of these policies have played out in schools around the country. Emily, 8, came home from school one day proud that she got half of the words right on her spelling test (in other words, a grade of 50). When her mother pointed out that this wasn't very good, Emily replied that her teacher had said it was just fine. At her school near Dallas, Texas, 11-year-old Kayla was invited to the math class pizza party as a reward for making a good grade, even though she had managed only a barely passing 71. The pizza parties used to be only for children who made As, but in recent years the school has invited every child who simply passed.

This basically means that we don't expect children to learn anything. As long as they feel good, that seems to be all that's required. As education professor Maureen Stout notes, many educational psychologists believe that schools should be "places in which children are insulated from the outside world and emotionally—not intellectually—nourished.... My colleagues always referred to the importance of making kids feel good about themselves but rarely, if ever, spoke of achievement, ideals, goals, character, or decency."[60] The future teachers whom Stout was educating believed that "children shouldn't be challenged to try things that others in the class are not ready for, since that would promote competition, and competition is bad for self-esteem. Second, grading should be avoided if at all possible, but, if absolutely necessary, should be done in a way that avoids any indication that Johnny is anything less than a stellar pupil."

Grade inflation and lack of competition may be backfiring: in 2003, 43% of college freshmen reported that they were frequently bored in class during their last year of high school, up from 29% in 1985.[61] This is not surprising: how interesting could school possibly be when everyone gets an A and self-esteem is more important than learning?

Perhaps as a result of all of this self-esteem building, educational psychologist Harold Stevenson found that American children ranked very highly when asked how good they were at math.[62] Of course, their *actual* math performance is merely mediocre, with other countries' youth routinely outranking American children. Every year, news anchors solemnly report how far American kids are falling behind. The emphasis on self-esteem can't be blamed entirely for this, of course, but one could easily argue that children's time might be better spent doing math than hearing that they are special. In 2004, 70% of American college freshmen reported that their "academic ability" was "above average" or "highest 10%," an amusing demonstration of American youths' self-confidence outpacing their ability at math.

What kind of young people does this produce? Many teachers and social observers say it results in kids who can't take criticism. In other words, employers, get ready for a group of easily hurt young workers. Peter Sacks, author of *Generation X Goes to College*, noted the extraordinary thin-skinnedness of the undergraduates he taught, and my experience has been no different. I've learned not to discuss test items that the majority of students missed, as this invariably leads to lots of whiny defensiveness and very little actual learning. The two trends are definitely related: research shows that when people with high self-esteem are criticized, they became unfriendly, rude, and uncooperative, even toward people who had nothing to do with the criticism.[63]

None of this should really surprise us. Students "look and act like what the [self-esteem] theories say they should look and act like," notes Hewitt. "They tend to act as though they believe they have worthy and good inner essences, regardless of what people say or how they behave, that they deserve recognition and attention from others, and their unique individual needs should be considered first and foremost."[64] And, of course, this is exactly what has happened: GenMe takes for granted that the self comes first, and we often believe exactly what we were so carefully taught—that we're special.

But this must have an upside; surely kids who have high self-esteem go on to make better grades and achieve more in school. Actually, they don't. There is a small correlation between self-esteem and grades.[65] However, self-esteem does not cause high grades—instead, high grades cause higher self-esteem. So self-esteem programs clearly put the cart before the horse in trying to increase self-esteem. Even much of the small link from high grades to high self-esteem can be explained by other factors such as income: rich kids, for example, have higher self-esteem and get better grades, but that's because coming from an affluent home causes both of these things, and not because they cause each other. This resembles the horse and the cart being towed on a flatbed truck—neither the cart nor the horse is causing the motion in the other even though they are moving together. As self-esteem programs aren't going to make all kids rich, they won't raise self-esteem this way, either.

Nor does high self-esteem protect against teen pregnancy, juvenile delinquency, alcoholism, drug abuse, or chronic welfare dependency. Several comprehensive reviews of the research literature by different authors have all concluded that self-esteem doesn't cause much of anything.[66] Even the book sponsored by the California Task Force to Promote Self-Esteem and Personal and Social Responsibility, which spent a quarter of a million dollars trying to raise Californians' self-esteem, found that self-esteem isn't linked to academic achievement, good behavior, or any other outcome the Task Force was formed to address.[67]

Are Self-Esteem Programs Good or Bad?

Psychologist Martin Seligman has criticized self-esteem programs as empty and shortsighted. He argues that self-esteem based on nothing does not serve children well in the long run; it's better, he says, for children to develop real skills and feel good about accomplishing something.[68] Roy Baumeister, the lead author of an extensive review of the research on self-esteem, found that self-esteem does not lead to better grades, improved work performance, decreased violence, or less cheating. In fact, people with high self-esteem are often more violent and more likely to cheat. "It is very questionable whether [the few benefits] justify the effort and expense that schools, parents, and therapists have put into raising self-esteem," Baumeister wrote. "After all these years, I'm sorry to say, my recommendation is this: forget about self-esteem and concentrate more on self-control and self-discipline."[69]

I agree with both of these experts. Self-esteem is an outcome, not a cause. In other words, it doesn't do much good to encourage a child to feel good about himself just to feel good; this doesn't mean anything. Children develop true self-esteem from behaving well and accomplishing things. "What the self-esteem movement really says to students is that their achievement is not important and their minds are not worth developing," writes Maureen Stout. It's clearly better for children to value learning rather than simply feeling good.[70]

So should kids feel bad about themselves if they're not good at school or sports? No. They should feel bad if they didn't work hard and try. And even if they don't succeed, sometimes negative feelings can be a motivator. Trying something challenging and learning from the experience is better than feeling good about oneself for no reason.

Also, everyone can do *something* well. Kids who are not athletic or who struggle with school might have another talent, like music or art. Almost all children can develop pride from being a good friend or helping someone. Kids can do many things to feel good about themselves, so self-esteem can be based on something. If a child feels great about himself even when he does nothing, why do anything? Self-esteem without basis encourages laziness rather than hard work. On the other hand, we shouldn't go too far and hinge our self-worth entirely on one external goal, like getting good grades. As psychologist Jennifer Crocker documents, the seesaw of self-esteem this produces can lead to poor physical and mental health.[71] A happy medium is what's called for here: don't feel bad about yourself because you made a bad grade—just don't feel good about yourself if you didn't even study. Use your bad feelings as a motivator to do better next time. True self-confidence comes from honing your talents and learning things, not from being told you're great just because you exist.

The practice of not correcting mistakes, avoiding letter grades, and discouraging competition is also misguided. Competition can help make learning fun; as Stout points out, look at how the disabled kids in the Special Olympics benefit from competing. Many schools now don't publish the honor roll of children who do well in school and generally downplay grades because, they falsely believe, competition isn't good for self-esteem (as some kids won't make the honor roll, and some kids will make Cs). But can you imagine not publishing the scores of a basketball game because it might not be good for the losing team's self-esteem? Can you imagine not keeping score in the game? What fun would that be? The self-esteem movement, Stout argues, is popular because it is sweetly addictive: teachers don't have to criticize, kids don't have to be criticized, and everyone goes home feeling happy. The problem is they also go home ignorant and uneducated.

Kids who don't excel in a certain area should still be encouraged to keep trying. This isn't self-esteem, however: it's self-control. Self-control, or the ability to persevere and keep going, is a much better predictor of life outcomes than self-esteem. Children high in self-control make better grades and finish more years of education, and they're less likely to use drugs or have a teenage pregnancy. Self-control predicts all of those things researchers had hoped self-esteem would, but hasn't.

Cross-cultural studies provide a good example of the benefits of self-control over self-esteem. Asians, for example, have lower self-esteem than Americans.[72] But when Asian students find out that they scored low on a particular task, they want to keep working on that task so they can improve their performance. American students, in contrast, prefer to give up on that task and work on another one.[73] In other words, Americans preserve their self-esteem at the expense of doing better at a difficult task. This goes a long way toward explaining why Asian children perform better at math and at school in general.

Young people who have high self-esteem built on shaky foundations might run into trouble when they encounter the harsh realities of the real world. As Stout argues, kids who are given meaningless As and promoted when they haven't learned the material will later find out in college or the working world that they don't know much at all. And what will *that* do to their self-esteem, or, more important, their careers? Unlike your teacher, your boss isn't going to care much about preserving your high self-esteem. The self-esteem emphasis leaves kids ill prepared for the inevitable criticism and occasional failure that is real life. "There is no self-esteem movement in the work world," points out one father. "If you present a bad report at the office, your boss isn't going to say, 'Hey, I like the color paper you chose.' Setting kids up like this is doing them a tremendous disservice."[74]

In any educational program, one has to consider the trade-off between benefit and risk. Valuing self-esteem over learning and accomplishment is clearly harmful, as children feel great about themselves but are cheated out of the education they need to succeed. Self-esteem programs *might* benefit the small minority of kids who really do feel worthless, but those kids are likely to have bigger problems that self-esteem boosting won't fix. The risk in these programs is in inflating the self-concept of children who already think the world revolves around them. Building up the self-esteem and importance of kids who are already egocentric can bring trouble, as it can lead to narcissism—and maybe it already has.

Changes in Narcissism

Narcissism is one of the few personality traits that psychologists agree is almost completely negative. Narcissists are overly focused on themselves and lack empathy for others, which means they cannot see another person's perspective.[75] (Sound like the last clerk who served you?) They also feel entitled to special privileges and believe that they are superior to other people. As a result, narcissists are bad relationship partners and can be difficult to work with. Narcissists are also more likely to be hostile, feel anxious, compromise their health, and fight with friends and family. Unlike those merely high in self-esteem, narcissists admit that they don't feel close to other people.[76]

All evidence suggests that narcissism is much more common in recent generations. In the early 1950s, only 12% of teens aged 14 to 16 agreed with the statement "I am an important person."[77] By the late 1980s, an incredible 80%—almost seven times as many—claimed they were important. Psychologist Harrison Gough found consistent increases on narcissism items among college students quizzed between the 1960s and the 1990s.[78] GenMe students were more likely to agree that "I would be willing to describe myself as a pretty 'strong' personality" and "I have often met people who were supposed to be experts who were no better than I." In other words, those other people don't know what they're talking about, so everyone should listen to me.

In a 2002 survey of 3,445 people conducted by Joshua Foster, Keith Campbell, and me, younger people scored considerably higher on the Narcissistic Personality Inventory, agreeing with items such as "If I ruled the world it would be a better place," "I am a special person," and "I can live my life any way I want to."[79] (These statements evoke the image of a young man speeding down the highway in the world's biggest SUV, honking his horn, and screaming, "Get out of my way! I'm important!") This study was cross-sectional, though, meaning that it was a one-time sample of people of different ages. For that reason, we cannot be sure if any differences are due to age or to generation; however, the other studies of narcissism mentioned previously suggest that generation plays a role. It is also interesting that narcissism scores were fairly high until around age 35, after which they decreased markedly. This is right around the cutoff between GenMe and previous generations.

Narcissism is the darker side of the focus on the self, and is often confused with self-esteem. Self-esteem is often based on solid relationships with others, whereas narcissism comes from believing that you are special and more important than other people. Many of the school programs designed to raise self-esteem probably raise narcissism instead. Lillian Katz, a professor of early childhood education at the University of Illinois, wrote an article titled "All About Me: Are We Developing Our Children's Self-Esteem or Their Narcissism?" She writes, "Many of the practices advocated in pursuit of [high self-esteem] may instead inadvertently develop narcissism in the form of excessive preoccupation with oneself."[80] Because the school programs emphasize being "special" rather than encouraging friendships, we may be training an army of little narcissists instead of raising kids' self-esteem.

Many young people also display entitlement, a facet of narcissism that involves believing that you deserve and are entitled to more than others. A scale that measures entitlement has items like "Things should go my way," "I demand the best because I'm worth it," and (my favorite) "If I were on the *Titanic*, I would deserve to be on *the first* lifeboat!"[81] A 2005 Associated Press article printed in hundreds of news outlets labeled today's young people "The

Entitlement Generation." In the article, employers complained that young employees expected too much too soon and had very high expectations for salary and promotions.[82]

Teachers have seen this attitude for years now. One of my colleagues said his students acted as if grades were something they simply deserved to get no matter what. He joked that their attitude could be summed up by "Where's my A? I distinctly remember ordering an A from the catalog." Stout, the education professor, lists the student statements familiar to teachers everywhere: "I need a better grade," "I deserve an A on this paper," "I *never* get Bs." Stout points out that the self-esteem movement places the student's feelings at the center, so "students learn that they do not need to respect their teachers or even earn their grades, so they begin to believe that they are entitled to grades, respect, or anything else ... just for asking!"[83]

Unfortunately, narcissism can lead to outcomes far worse than grade grubbing. Several studies have found that narcissists lash out aggressively when they are insulted or rejected.[84] Eric Harris and Dylan Klebold, the teenage gunmen at Columbine High School, made statements remarkably similar to items on the most popular narcissism questionnaire. On a videotape made before the shootings, Harris picked up a gun, made a shooting noise, and said, "Isn't it fun to get the respect we're going to deserve?"[85] (Chillingly similar to the narcissism item "I insist upon getting the respect that is due me.") Later, Harris said, "I could convince them that I'm going to climb Mount Everest, or I have a twin brother growing out of my back. I can make you believe anything" (virtually identical to the item "I can make anyone believe anything I want them to"). Harris and Klebold then debate which famous movie director will film their story. A few weeks after making the videotapes, Harris and Klebold killed thirteen people and then themselves.

Other examples abound. In a set of lab studies, narcissistic men felt less empathy for rape victims, reported more enjoyment when watching a rape scene in a movie, and were more punitive toward a woman who refused to read a sexually arousing passage out loud to them.[86] Abusive husbands who threaten to kill their wives—and tragically sometimes do—are the ultimate narcissists. They see everyone and everything in terms of fulfilling their needs, and become very angry and aggressive when things don't go exactly their way. Many workplace shootings occur after an employee is fired and decides he'll "show" everyone how powerful he is.

The rise in narcissism has very deep roots. It's not just that we feel better about ourselves, but that we even think to ask the question. We fixate on self-esteem, and unthinkingly build narcissism, because we believe that the needs of the individual are paramount. This will stay with us even if self-esteem programs end up in the dustbin of history.

NOTES

1. Ladies' Home Journal *told readers:* Warren, Rick. "Learn to Love Yourself!" *Ladies' Home Journal,* March 2005; p. 36.

2. *[W]hile* Parenting *offered:* Lamb, Yanick Rice. "Proud to Be Me!" *Parenting,* April 2005.

3. *The American Academy of Pediatrics guide:* Shelov, Steven, ed. in chief. 1998. *Caring for Your Baby and Young Child: Birth to Age 5.* New York: Bantam.

4. *In a 1976* New York Magazine *article:* Wolfe, Tom. "The Me Decade and the Third Great Awakening." *New York Magazine,* August 23, 1976.

5. *When asked what's next in her life:* "Pop Quiz: Kim Basinger." *People,* September 27, 2004.

6. *In answer to the same question:* Laskas, Jeanne Marie. "Sarah's New Day." *Ladies' Home Journal,* June 2004.

7. *Gillon describes Boomers:* Gillon, Steve. 2004. *Boomer Nation.* New York: Free Press; p. 263.

8. *Even food becomes:* Brooks, David. 2000. *Bobos in Paradise.* New York: Simon & Schuster; p.58.

9. *In 1973, 46% of Boomers:* Smith, J. Walker, and Clurman, Ann. 1997. *Rocking the Ages: The Yankelovich Report on Generational Marketing.* New York: HarperCollins.

10. *Thirty percent of Boomers:* Ibid.

11. *Even stronger evidence:* Astin, A. W., et al. 2002. *The American Freshman: Thirty-Five-Year Trends.* Los Angeles: Higher Education Research Institute, UCLA. Plus 2003 and 2004 supplements.

12. *"Instead of seeking:* Rubin, Jerry. 1976. *Growing (Up) at Thirty-Seven.* New York: Lippincott; p. 175.

13. *Aleta St. James, a 57-year-old woman:* Schienberg, Jonathan. "New Age Mystic to Become Mom at 57." <www.cnn.com>. November 9, 2004.

14. *In 2004's* Conquering Your Quarterlife Crisis: Robbins, Alexandra. 2004. *Conquering Your Quarterlife Crisis.* New York: Perigee; pp. 51–52.

15. *When a character in the 2004 novel:* Giffin, Emily. 2004. *Something Borrowed.* New York: St. Martin's Press; p. 2.

16. *Dr. Phil, the ultimate in plainspoken:* Today. NBC, December 27, 2004.

17. *Psychologist Martin Seligman says:* Seligman, M. E. P. "Boomer Blues." *Psychology Today,* October 1988: pp. 50–53.

18. *A careful study of news stories:* Patterson, Thomas E. 2000. "Doing Well and Doing Good: How Soft News and Critical Journalism Are Shrinking the News Audience and Weakening Democracy—and What News Outlets Can Do About It." Joan Shorenstein Center on the Press, Politics, and Public Policy; p. 5. PDF available for download at <www.ksg.harvard.edu/presspol/ResearchPublications/Reports/>.

19. *In a letter to her fans in 2004:* "The Couples of 2004." *Us Weekly,* January 3, 2005.

20. *In the late 1990s, Prudential:* Hornblower, Margot. "Great Xpectations." *Time,* June 9, 1997.

21. *My colleague Keith Campbell and I looked:* Twenge, J. M., and Campbell, W. K. 2001. Age and Birth Cohort Differences in Self-Esteem: A Cross-Temporal Meta-Analysis. *Personality and Social Psychology Review,* 5: 321–344.

22. *A 1997 survey of teens asked:* "11th Annual Special Teen Report: Teens and Self-Image: Survey Results." *USA Weekend,* May 1–3, 1998.

23. *Another survey found:* Hicks, Rick, and Hicks, Kathy. 1999. *Boomers, Xers, and Other Strangers.* Wheaton, IL: Tyndale; p. 270.

24. *We examined the responses:* Twenge, J. M., and Campbell, W. K. 2001. Age and Birth Cohort Differences in Self-Esteem: A Cross-Temporal Meta-Analysis. *Personality and Social Psychology Review,* 5: 321–344.

25. *Research on programs to boost:* Ibid.

26. *Journal articles on self-esteem:* Hewitt, John. 1998. *The Myth of Self-Esteem.* New York: St. Martin's Press; p. 51.

27. *One children's book:* Loomans, Diane. 1991. *The Lovables in the Kingdom of Self-Esteem.* New York: H. J. Kramer.

28. *One program is called:* Stout, Maureen. 2000. *The Feel-Good Curriculum.* Cambridge, MA: Perseus Books; p. 131.

29. *Another program, called "Pumsy in Pursuit of Excellence":* "Teaching Self-Image Stirs Furor." *New York Times,* October 13, 1993.

30. *The Magic Circle exercise:* <www.globalideasbank.org/site/bank/idea.php?ideaId=573>; and Summerlin, M. L.; Hammett, V. L.; and Payne, M. L. 1983. The Effect of Magic Circle Participation on a Child's Self-Concept. *School Counselor,* 31: 49–52.

31. *One Austin, Texas, father:* Swann, William. 1996. *Self-Traps: The Elusive Quest for Higher Self-Esteem.* New York: W. H. Freeman; p. 4.

32. *When self-esteem programs:* Hewitt, John. 1998. *The Myth of Self-Esteem.* New York: St. Martin's Press; pp. 84–85.

33. *In one program, teachers:* Payne, Lauren Murphy, and Rolhing, Claudia. 1994. *A Leader's Guide to Just Because I Am: A Child's Book of Affirmation.* Minneapolis: Free Spirit Publishing; and Hewitt, John. 1998. *The Myth of Self-Esteem.* New York: St. Martin's Press.

34. *[C]hildren are asked to finish:* Hewitt, John. 1998. *The Myth of Self-Esteem.* New York: St. Martin's Press; p. 79.

35. *A sign on the wall:* Kramer, Rita. 1991. *Ed School Follies: The Miseducation of America's Teachers.* New York: Free Press; p. 33.

36. *Perhaps as a result, 60% of teachers:* Scott, C. G. 1996. Student Self-Esteem and the School System: Perceptions and Implications. *Journal of Educational Research,* 89: 292–297.

37. *A veteran second-grade teacher:* Gibbs, Nancy. "Parents Behaving Badly." *Time,* February 21, 2005.

38. *For example, the popular Christian:* Lucado, Max. 1997. *You Are Special.* Wheaton, IL: Crossway Books.

39. *In an article in Ladies' Home Journal, Christian author:* Warren, Rick. "Learn to Love Yourself!" *Ladies' Home Journal,* March 2005.

40. *Children in some schools:* Lynn Sherr. "Me, Myself and I—The Growing Self-Esteem Movement." 20/20. ABC, March 11, 1994.

41. *An elementary school teacher in Alabama:* Hewitt, John. 1998. *The Myth of Self-Esteem.* New York: St. Martin's Press; p. 81.

42. *The children's museum in Laramie:* Lynn Sherr. "Me, Myself and I—The Growing Self-Esteem Movement." 20/20. ABC, March 11, 1994.

43. *Don Tapscott, who interviewed:* Tapscott, Don. 1998. *Growing Up Digital.* New York: McGraw-Hill; p. 92.

44. *In a CBS News poll:* CBS News. 2001. *The Class of 2000.* Simon & Schuster eBook, available for download, p. 64.

45. *The 1997 premiere episode: Daria.* Episode: "Esteemsters." MTV, March 3, 1997.

46. *Hewitt, who teaches:* Hewitt, John. 1998. *The Myth of Self-Esteem.* New York: St. Martin's Press; pp. 1–3.

47. *In 2002, the Girl Scout Council:* < http://www.girlscoutsaz.org/images/uploads/PDF /Programs/Facilitators_Guide.pdf>.

48. *In 1999, a carefully researched:* Kling, K. C., et al. 1999. Gender Differences in Self-Esteem: A Meta-Analysis. *Psychological Bulletin,* 125: 470–500.

49. *"We may create:* <www.news.wisc.edu/wire/i072899/selfesteem.html>.

50. *When my colleague Keith Campbell and I did:* Twenge, J. M., and Campbell, W. K. 2001. Age and Birth Cohort Differences in Self-Esteem: A Cross-Temporal Meta-Analysis. *Personality and Social Psychology Review,* 5: 321–344.

51. *One popular method tells:* Wilde, Sandra. 1989. A Proposal for a New Spelling Curriculum. *Elementary School Journal,* 90: 275–289.

52. *Teacher education courses emphasize:* Kramer, Rita. 1991. *Ed School Follies: The Miseducation of America's Teachers.* New York: Free Press; p. 116.

53. *[A] British teacher proposed:* "Teachers Say No-One Should 'Fail.'" BBC News, July 20, 2005. See <news.bbc.co.uk/1/hi/education/4697461.stm>.

54. *[O]ffice stores have started carrying:* Aoki, Naomi, "Harshness of Red Marks Has Students Seeing Purple." *Boston Globe,* August 23, 2004.

55. *Florida elementary schoolteacher:* Ibid.

56. *In 2004, 48% of American college freshmen:* Astin, A. W., et al. 2002. *The American Freshman: Thirty-Five-Year Trends.* Los Angeles: Higher Education Research Institute, UCLA. Plus 2003 and 2004 supplements.

57. *"Each year we think:* Giegerich, Steve. "College Freshmen Have Worst Study Habits in Years But Less Likely to Drink, Study Finds." Associated Press, January 27, 2003. <www.detnews.com/2003/schools/0301/27/schools-70002.htm>.

58. *Only 33% of American:* Astin, A. W., et al. 2002. *The American Freshman: Thirty-Five Year Trends.* Los Angeles: Higher Education Research Institute, UCLA. Plus 2003 and 2004 supplements.

59. *"Teachers want to raise:* Innerst, Carol. "Wordsmiths on Wane Among U.S. Students." *Washington Times,* August 25, 1994.

60. *As education professor Maureen Stout notes:* Stout, Maureen, 2000. *The Feel-Good Curriculum.* Cambridge, MA: Perseus Books; pp. 3–4.

61. *[I]n 2003, 43% of college freshmen:* Astin, A. W., et al. 2002. *The American Freshman: Thirty-Five-Year Trends.* Los Angeles: Higher Education Research Institute, UCLA. Plus 2003 and 2004 supplements.

62. *[E]ducational psychologist Harold Stevenson:* Stevenson, H. W., et al. 1990. Mathematics Achievement of Children in China and the United States. *Child Development,* 61: 1053–1066.

63. *[R]esearch shows that when people:* Heatherton, T. F., and Vohs, K. D. 2000. Interpersonal Evaluations Following Threats to Self: Role of Self-Esteem. *Journal of Personality and Social Psychology,* 78: 725–736.

64. *Students "look and act like:* Hewitt, John. 1998. *The Myth of Self-Esteem.* New York: St. Martin's Press; p. 84.

65. *There is a small correlation:* Baumeister, R. F., et al. 2003. Does High Self-Esteem Cause Better Performance, Interpersonal Success, Happiness, or Healthier Lifestyles? *Psychological Science in the Public Interest,* 4: 1–44; and Covington, M. V. 1989. "Self-Esteem and Failure in School." In A. M. Mecca, N. J. Smelser, and J. Vasconcellos, eds. *The Social Importance of Self-Esteem.* Berkeley: University of California Press; p. 79.

66. *Several comprehensive reviews:* Ibid.

67. *Even the book sponsored:* Smelser, N. J. 1989. "Self-esteem and Social Problems." In A. M. Mecca, N. J. Smelser, and J. Vasconcellos, eds. *The Social Importance of Self-Esteem.* Berkeley: University of California Press.

68. *Psychologist Martin Seligman has criticized:* Seligman, Martin. 1996. *The Optimistic Child.* New York: Harper Perennial.

69. *"It is very questionable:* Baumeister, Roy. "The Lowdown on High Self-esteem: Thinking You're Hot Stuff Isn't the Promised Cure-all." *Los Angeles Times,* January 25, 2005.

70. *"What the self-esteem movement:* Stout, Maureen. 2000. *The Feel-Good Curriculum.* Cambridge, MA: Perseus Books; p. 263.

71. *As psychologist Jennifer Crocker documents:* Crocker, J., and Park, L. E. 2004. The Costly Pursuit of Self-esteem. *Psychological Bulletin,* 130: 392–414.

72. *Asians, for example, have lower:* Twenge, J. M., and Crocker, J. 2002. Race and Self-Esteem: Meta-Analyses Comparing Whites, Blacks, Hispanics, Asians, and American Indians. *Psychological Bulletin,* 128: 371–408.

73. *But when Asian students find out:* Heine, S. J., et al. 2001. Divergent Consequences of Success and Failure in Japan and North America: An Investigation of Self-improving Motivations and Malleable Selves. *Journal of Personality and Social Psychology,* 81: 599–615.

74. *"There is no self-esteem movement:* Shaw, Robert. 2003. *The Epidemic.* New York: Regan Books; p. 152.

75. *Narcissists are overly focused:* Campbell, W. Keith. 2005. *When You Love a Man Who Loves Himself.* Chicago: Source Books.

76. *Narcissists are also more likely:* Helgeson, V. S., and Fritz, H. L. 1999. Unmitigated Agency and Unmitigated Communion: Distinctions from Agency and Communion. *Journal of Research in Personality,* 33: 131–158.

77. *In the early 1950s, only 12% of teens:* Newsom, C. R., et al. 2003. Changes in Adolescent Response Patterns on the MMPI/MMPI-A Across Four Decades. *Journal of Personality Assessment,* 81: 74–84.

78. *Psychologist Harrison Gough found:* Gough, H. 1991. "Scales and Combinations of Scales: What Do They Tell Us, What Do They Mean?" Paper presented at the 99th Annual Convention of the American Psychological Association, San Francisco, August 1991. Data obtained from Harrison Gough in 2001.

79. *In a 2002 survey of 3,445 people:* Foster, J. D.; Campbell, W. K.; and Twenge, J. M. 2003. Individual Differences in Narcissism: Inflated Self-Views Across the Lifespan and Around the World. *Journal of Research in Personality,* 37: 469–486.

80. *Lillian Katz, a professor:* Stout, Maureen. 2000. *The Feel-Good Curriculum.* Cambridge, MA: Perseus Books; p. 178.

81. *A scale that measures entitlement:* Campbell, W. K., et al. 2004. Psychological Entitlement: Interpersonal Consequences and Validation of a Self-report Measure. *Journal of
Personality Assessment,* 83: 29–45.

82. *A 2005 Associated Press article printed:* Irvine, Martha. "Young Labeled 'Entitlement
Generation.' " AP, June 26, 2005. <http://www.freerepublic.com/focus/news
/1431497/posts>. Also reprinted in many newspapers.

83. *Stout, the education professor, lists:* Stout, Maureen. 2000. *The Feel-Good Curriculum.*
Cambridge, MA: Perseus Books; p. 2.

84. *Several studies have found:* Bushman, B. J., and Baumeister, R. F. 1998. Threatened
Egotism, Narcissism, Self-esteem, and Direct and Displaced Aggression: Does Self-
love or Self-hate Lead to Violence? *Journal of Personality and Social Psychology,* 75:
219–229; and Twenge, J. M., and Campbell, W. K. 2003. "Isn't it fun to get the
respect that we're going to deserve?" Narcissism, Social Rejection, and Aggression.
Personality and Social Psychology Bulletin, 29: 261–272.

85. *Harris picked up a gun:* Gibbs, Nancy, and Roche, Timothy. "The Columbine
Tapes." *Time,* December 20, 1999.

86. *In a set of lab studies, narcissistic:* Bushman, B. J., et al. 2003. Narcissism, Sexual
Refusal, and Aggression: Testing a Narcissistic Reactance Model of Sexual
Coercion. *Journal of Personality and Social Psychology,* 84: 1027–1040.

QUESTIONS FOR MAKING CONNECTIONS
WITHIN THE READING

1. "An Army of One: *Me*" is written in a lively style, with the author speaking in
   a number of different voices throughout: objective analyst, insider, and skep-
   tic, to name a few. As you reread, mark the passages where Twenge's voice
   shifts and identify the voices on both sides of the shift. When you're done,
   review your markings. Is there a voice or a viewpoint that wins out in the end?
   Is there a voice that you feel is Twenge's real voice, or are all the voices hers?

2. What kinds of evidence does Twenge use to make her case about Generation Me? After you've generated a complete list, identify the evidence that
   you feel is the most compelling and the evidence that seems less so. Where
   would you look to find evidence that would further strengthen Twenge's
   argument? Is there evidence that could refute Twenge's argument? Can
   arguments about entire generations be either verified or disproven?

3. Twenge identifies three psychic states: thinking about the self, having self-
   esteem, and being a narcissist. What is the relationship among these three
   states? If one is educated and trained in one of these psychic states, is there a
   way to experience another state of mind? Does Twenge provide any evidence of what causes or enables a shift in perspective?

QUESTIONS FOR WRITING

1. As a member of Generation Me, Twenge is both a source for information about her subject and a translator who provides an inside view of how members of Generation Me interpret the world around them. Given this, how would you characterize Twenge's method? How does she know what she claims to knows about Generation Me? How would you go about collecting more information to test her hypothesis? Is definitive evidence available?

2. If we grant Twenge's argument about the values and expectations of Generation Me, what follows? Is it possible for this generation to reverse course, or is it too late? Can social change be brought about through conscious effort? Or does the scale of the problem mean that what follows is inevitable? Has Twenge diagnosed a problem for which there is no cure?

QUESTIONS FOR MAKING CONNECTIONS
BETWEEN READINGS

1. What might Daniel Gilbert say about the self-esteem curriculum? Might our tendency to cook the facts explain why children, parents, and teachers have been so ready to embrace this approach? If Gilbert is correct, will lower grades in more demanding classes actually deal children a devastating blow, or will their psychological immune systems protect them from lasting injury? Does the curriculum of self-esteem tip the scales in favor of action or inaction, and what are likely to be the results as children grow up? If toughened standards mean students will receive Bs or Cs instead of As, how might the inescapability trigger affect their self-perceptions? Does a curriculum that tries to shield students from challenges, uncertainty, and the experience of failure actually make education boring by trying to explain everything?

2. Twenge identifies numerous characteristics that define the differences between the way Baby Boomers and Generation Me view the self. Using Tim O'Brien's "How to Tell a True War Story," test out Twenge's theory. Do the characters perform as Twenge's theory predicts? Does O'Brien? Are generations defined by wars? Was Vietnam a Baby-Boomer war? Is the Iraq War a Generation-Me war? Can O'Brien's "true war story" be true for other generations?

◆◆◆

RICK WARTZMAN

AUTOMATION AND GLOBALIZATION. Union decline and bottom line. Stakeholders and shareholders. These are just a few of the buzzwords we often hear in the current debates about economic growth and the future of American jobs. These debates tend to reproduce two conflicting accounts of what is happening. The first account assumes that growing inequality is fueling a race to the bottom, making it increasingly difficult for average workers to earn a livable wage. Those who accept this vision emphasize fair compensation, upward mobility, job training, and professional development. The second account presupposes that market forces, global competition, and the high cost of doing business in the United States have pressured domestic companies to re-think their business models. Those who accept this account stress the need to protect corporations through downsizing, cost-cutting, tax breaks, and maximizing shareholder value.

The debate is a subject quite familiar to journalist Rick Wartzman, who has been writing about it for over 25 years. In his most recent book, *The End of Loyalty: The Rise and Fall of Good Jobs in America* (2017), which includes the following chapter, he describes the overall erosion of the social contract between companies, their employees, and the communities they serve as the U.S. has moved from a manufacturing to service economy. That contract, once tacitly agreed upon though never codified as law, basically meant that companies could expect worker discipline in exchange for job security and good salaries with benefits. According to Wartzman, this contract, in force between the 1940s and 1970s, was primarily the result of two trends. One was strong union organizing in both public and private sector jobs, where labor representatives advocated for higher wages, health care, and retirement security for members, benefits which ended up spilling over to non-union jobs as well. The other trend was a general belief among corporate leaders that companies had an obligation to all stakeholders, whether employees, customers, suppliers, or investors. This resulted in a relatively stable workplace environment, both in terms of corporate and middle-class growth.

However, as Wartzman argues in "The New Face of Capitalism," the rise of corporate giants like Wal-Mart has completely re-shaped the economic landscape, as outsourcing, anti-union sentiment, increases in underemployment, and reductions of benefits and social services have fueled an ever-expanding class of the working poor. He details the various strategies (often illegal) that Wal-Mart has used to eliminate union organizing, increase the use of temps and other contingent workers, and pressure their suppliers into manufacturing products overseas. Exporting production keeps prices down and, as Wal-Mart argues, low-cost merchandise is precisely what keeps America's working poor from slipping into abject poverty. Wartzman counters this claim by citing Steve Dobbins, president of Carolina Mills: "People say, 'How can it be bad for things to come to the United States cheaply?.... But you can't buy anything if you're not employed. We are shopping ourselves out of jobs.'" Wartzman understands that companies cannot exist without workers and, equally, that strong businesses are necessary for jobs. Ultimately, he asks what a sustainable twenty-first-century corporate model might look like in order for all those concerned to benefit.

Rick Wartzman is currently the Director of the KH Moon Center for a Functioning Society at the Drucker Institute, host of the podcast, *The Bottom Line*, and contributing columnist for the magazine *Fast Company*. Prior to this, he served as the Executive Director of the Drucker Institute from its founding in 2007 until 2016. His career as a journalist began at *The Wall Street Journal*, where he was White House correspondent, among other positions, and continued at the *Los Angeles Times* as business editor, helping develop the 2004 Pulitzer Prize-winning series on "The Wal-Mart Effect." He has written on the intersection of business, management, leadership, and society for *Fortune, Time, Forbes,* and *Businessweek,* and he is the author of four books, including *The King of California: J.G. Boswell and the Making of A Secret American Empire* (2003) with Mark Araz; *What Would Drucker Do Now?: Solutions to Today's Toughest Challenges from the Father of Modern Management* (2012); and *Obscene in the Extreme: The Burning and Banning of John Steinbeck's* The Grapes of Wrath (2008).

The New Face of Capitalism

As America slipped toward, and then settled into, the early 2000s, it was only natural to look back upon the preceding one hundred years and take stock of those people and institutions that had exerted the most influence on the country and the world. *Time* magazine named Albert Einstein its Person of the Century. National Public Radio came out with its list of the hundred greatest American musical works of that span—a catalog whose eclectic nature was reflected in a sequence of tunes found in the middle of the Ss: "Singin' in the Rain," "Sittin' on the Dock of the Bay," "Smells Like Teen Spirit," and "Stand by Your Man." *Popular Mechanics* proclaimed the car the "defining device" of the era. And in the business world, many saw one company as the paradigm of the period (or a good chunk of it, anyway): General Motors.

But as edifying—or at least as entertaining—as it was to look back, it also made sense to look ahead. And as the new century began, commentators were eager to identify the company that was now positioned to be, in the words of one group of scholars, "the face of twenty-first-century capitalism." Their choice, and the choice of many others, was Wal-Mart.

In terms of scale, Wal-Mart was the obvious successor to GM. In 2002, the retailer became the biggest corporation in America, topping the Fortune 500 list for the first time. By 2005, its revenues exceeded $285 billion, and profits surpassed $10 billion. It was the nation's leading seller of toys, furniture, jewelry, dog food, and scores of other products. It was also the largest grocer in the United States through its so-called Supercenter stores. To peddle all this merchandise, the company employed more than 1.3 million US workers. But there was a massive difference between GM and Wal-Mart. While the former had put most of its workers on a secure route to the middle class, the latter was placing many on a path to impoverishment.

For decades, Wal-Mart had enjoyed a reputation as the most wholesome kind of company, steeped in American values and a down home culture captured in the cheer that Wal-Mart employees would do, gathering in a circle at the start of every shift change: "Give me a *W*! Give me an *A*! Give me an *L*! Give me a squiggly! (followed by a shaking of the butt) Give me an *M*! Give me an *A*! Give me an *R*! Give me a *T*! What's that spell? Wal-Mart! What's that spell? Wal-Mart! Who's number one? The customer! Always!" Wal-Mart, said David Glass, who'd joined the company in 1976 and had served as its CEO from 1988 until 2000, was "sort of like motherhood and apple pie."

Nobody did more to enhance this image than Sam Walton, better known inside the company as "Mr. Sam," who liked to swing his muddy boots into the cab of an old pickup truck and drive around Bentonville, Arkansas, where in the early 1950s he'd started Walton's 5&10 on the town square. The first actual Wal-Mart was opened in 1962 in Rogers, about eight miles to the east. From the beginning, whenever Walton would deal personally with his workers—"associates," in Wal-Mart's communal-sounding parlance—he went out of his way to be as nice as nice could be. "This is a man who . . . treated his associates well as persons, not just as clerks and salespeople," said Walter Loeb, a retailing consultant. Signifying this trait, Walton renamed the personnel department the "People Division" and put forth a management philosophy that was all about motivating each and every employee to give his or her best. Wal-Mart "believes management's responsibility is to provide leadership that serves the associate," the company asserted in the 1991 edition of *Sam's Associate Handbook.* "Managers must support, encourage, and provide opportunities for associates to be successful. Mr. Sam calls this 'Servant Leadership.'"

But there was another aspect of Walton's belief system—an extreme tightfistedness—that rubbed up against this creed of caring. The idea was that by doing absolutely everything possible to minimize costs, Wal-Mart would be able to deliver consistently low prices to its customers, giving hardworking people more money to spend on other things. For the company, serving up bargains was more than just a business strategy; it was practically a religious calling. "If we work together," said Walton, "we'll lower the cost of living for everyone. We'll give the world an opportunity to see what it's like to save and to have a better life." Consumers ate it up. By 2005, more than 90 percent of American households could be counted on to shop at Wal-Mart at least once a year; about a third of the nation shopped there every week.

For Wal-Mart's folksy founder, his CEO successors, and their executive teams, the company's parsimony translated into having tiny offices, emptying their own trash, flying coach, even sharing budget hotel rooms with colleagues when traveling on business. For Walton, who had a net worth of more than $100 billion, making him the richest person in the world, these were minor gestures. For Wal-Mart's hourly workers, though, the company's determination to pinch every penny was anything but minor: it left many of them scrambling to get by.

In the 1960s, Mr. Sam set up his stores as separate corporate structures—all linked back to a single financial partnership that he and his family controlled—so that revenues would come in at less than $1 million apiece, a threshold that permitted each location under government rules to pay less than the minimum wage. (A federal court eventually found this arrangement, while undeniably clever, to be improper.)

As the decades passed, the pressure to extract more from the workforce increased. Wal-Mart managers around the country forced employees to work off the clock and skip breaks; broke child-labor laws; and used illegal immigrants to clean its stores. It also locked workers inside overnight. The company maintained that this was to keep employees safe in high-crime neighborhoods, but former store managers said that the real purpose was to discourage workers from stealing anything or sneaking out for a smoke. Steven Greenhouse, the *New York Times* reporter who documented these and other such practices, has characterized them as "downright Dickensian."

Some Wal-Mart managers tried to make conditions insufferable for their highest-paid employees so that they'd quit and could be replaced by others earning less. Others made sure that their workers never logged quite enough hours to reach full-time status since, a part-timers, they wouldn't qualify for certain benefits. "I knew what I had to do," said Melissa Jerkins, who oversaw a staff of 120 at a Wal-Mart in Decatur, Indiana. "I had to meet the bottom line or my ass was in trouble. They didn't care how I got to that bottom line . . . so long as I got there."

Even for those employees who weren't victims of manipulated schedules or outright abuse, it could be tough to scratch out a living. In 2005, most Wal-Mart workers took home less than ten dollars an hour, compared with more than thirty dollars for a nonskilled assembly line worker at General Motors. This added up to a yearly income at Wal-Mart of about $18,000—below the poverty line for a family of four. Wal-Mart liked to talk up its profit-sharing plan. But because of high turnover, typical of most retailers, relatively few employees ever got to take much advantage of it. And even Wal-Mart acknowledged that a full-time worker might not be able support a family on a company paycheck. The health benefits that Wal-Mart offered were also lacking. As a result, many of its employees had to turn to public relief: food stamps, Medicaid, and subsidized housing.

In *Nickel and Dimed*, her 2001 modern classic about what it was like to take up a series of low-wage jobs across America, Barbara Ehrenreich recounted how when she went to work at a Wal-Mart in Minneapolis, making seven dollars an hour, she soon found herself about to run out of money. She wound up seeking help through a human-services agency called the Community Emergency Assistance Program, which recommended that she move into a homeless shelter until she could save enough for a deposit and first month's rent on an apartment. Wrote Ehrenreich:

> At one point toward the end of the interview, the CEAP lady had apologized for forgetting almost everything I said about myself—that I had a car, lived in a motel, etc. She was mixing me up with someone else who worked at Wal-Mart, she explained, someone who had been in just a few days ago. Now, of course I've noticed that many of my coworkers are poor in all the hard-to-miss, stereotypical ways. Crooked yellow teeth are one sign, inadequate footwear is another. My feet hurt after four hours of work, and I wear my comfortable old Reeboks, but a lot of women run around all day in thin-soled moccasins. Hair provides another class clue. Ponytails are common or, for that characteristic Wal-Martian beat-up and hopeless look, straight shoulder-length hair, parted in the middle and kept out of the face by two bobby pins.
>
> But now I know something else. In orientation, we learned that the store's success depends entirely on us, the associates; in fact, our bright blue vests bear the statement "At Wal-Mart our people make the difference." Underneath those vests, though, there are real-life charity cases, maybe even shelter dwellers.

One reason that Wal-Mart workers have always had difficulty improving their lot is that they've never been able to form a union. At its core, Wal-Mart's rationale for being against organized labor was not unlike that of Kodak, say, or General Electric under Lem Boulware: management had an open door policy, by which any worker could ostensibly walk in and discuss anything. Therefore, as Wal-Mart laid out in its "Manager's Toolbox to Remaining Union Free," "we do not believe there is a need for third-party representation. It is our position every associate can speak for him/herself without having to pay his/her hard-earned money to a union in order to be listened to and have issues resolved."

Yet unlike Kodak, which tried to frustrate union organizers by keeping its workers happy with good wages and princely benefits, Wal-Mart has been reliably ungenerous. And unlike GE, which fought tooth and nail against the International Union of Electrical Workers but ultimately honored its right to exist, Wal-Mart has never allowed so much as a single one of its stores to be organized. Indeed, ever since Mr. Sam's time, the company has done everything it can to crush the unions, painting them in the most Manichean terms. They are "nothing but blood-sucking parasites living off the productive labor of people who work for a living!" said attorney John Tate, an iron-willed right-winger whom Walton had hired to help beat back the Retail Clerks in the early 1970s and who then stuck around at Wal-Mart where he developed an array of antiunion techniques.

In the early 1980s, when the Teamsters attempted to represent employees at two Wal-Mart distribution centers in Arkansas, Walton himself showed up with a warning—US labor law be damned. Recalled one worker: "He told us that if the union got in, the warehouse would be closed. . . . He said people could vote any way the wanted but he'd close her right up." The Teamsters lost the election.

But it wasn't just top executives who were expected to resist being organized. "Staying union free is a full-time commitment," read a manual given out at a Wal-Mart distribution center in Indiana in 1991, the year before Walton died. "Unless union prevention is a goal equal to other objectives within an organization, the goal will usually not be attained. The commitment to stay union free must exist at all levels of management—from the chairperson of the 'board' down to the front-line manager. Therefore, no one in management is immune from carrying his or her 'own weight' in the union prevention effort. The entire management staff should fully comprehend and appreciate exactly what is expected of their individual efforts to meet the union free objective. The union organizer is a 'potential opponent' for our center."

The main thing that a Wal-Mart manager was supposed to do when he or she caught even a hint of union activity was to contact corporate headquarters via a special hotline. Immediately, a "labor team" would be sent from Bentonville to the store where union organizers might be gaining even the slightest toehold. This squad from HQ would then take over the running of the place, putting workers on a steady diet of antiunion propaganda videos; weighing whether local managers were too timid or sympathetic to labor and should be ousted; and keeping a close eye on any employees agitating for a union or simply disposed to having one. "As soon as they determine you're prounion, they go after you," said Jon Lehman, who was a Wal-Mart manager in Kentucky for seventeen years. "It's almost like a neurosurgeon going after a brain tumor: we got to get that thing out before it infects the rest of the store, the rest of the body."

Much of this strategy evoked the way that GM and other companies deployed Pinkertons to bully the unions way back in the 1930s. "I had so many bosses around me, I couldn't believe it," said Larry Adams, who worked in the tire and lube express department at a Wal-Mart in Kingman, Arizona, which grabbed the labor team's attention in the summer of 2000. With temperatures soaring well above a hundred degrees, Adams and sone of his follow automotive technicians got angry their boss wouldn't spend the $200 needed to fix a broken air conditioner. So, they reached out to the United Food and Commercial Workers union. Within forty-eight hours, twenty outside managers were crawling all over the store. "It was very intimidating," said Adams. The UFCW's organizing push in Kingman would end in defeat; within a year or so, nearly every one of the union supporters would be fired or compelled to quit.

At a Wal-Mart Supercenter in Jacksonville, Texas, a group of meat-cutters had better luck at organizing—though not for long. A week or two after they voted to join the UFCW in February 2000, the company announced that it would cease cutting meat and switch instead to selling prepackaged beef and pork at all of its stores. Wal-Mart said that the butchers' seven-to-three vote in favor of the UFCW had nothing whatsoever to do with its decision to stock "case-ready" meat. Yet it was all but impossible to miss that the move essentially eviscerated the union's first ever victory at the company, as Wal-Mart successfully argued that the changes to the meat department made it so that collective bargaining wasn't appropriate going forward. The UFCW challenged the company's stance before the National Labor Relations Board, but after eight years of rulings by the agency and the courts, the union could claim only a partial win; Wal-Mart would escape being unionized.

The dust-up in Texas was far from unusual. In all, unions filed 288 unfair-labor-practice charges against Wal-Mart between 1998 and 2003. Most alleged that the company had engaged in improper firings, threatened employees if they tried to organize, carried out surveillance, or illegally interrogated workers to determine their views on labor-related matters. Of these charges, the NLRB found ninety-four of them to be substantive enough to issue a formal complaint against the company. Still, none of it was enough to shake Wal-Mart's conviction that organized labor needed to be stopped at all costs. "I've never seen a company that will go to the lengths that Wal-Mart goes to, to avoid a union," said consultant Martin Levitt, who helped the company hone its attack before writing a book titled *Confessions of a Union Buster.* "They have zero tolerance."

But if Wal-Mart was particularly strong-minded in its opposition to organized labor, most other companies weren't too far behind. For example, at a Coca-Cola bottling plant in Yuma, Arizona, a manager told employees in 2002 that they'd lose their 401(k)s if they voted to be represented by the United Industrial, Service, Transportation, Professional, and Government Workers of North America. The union lost the election by a vote of eleven to ten. At a General Electric subsidiary in Muskegon, Michigan, which hadn't been organized, a machine operator named Michael Crane began to hand out literature promoting the Electrical Workers and wear a union T-shirt on the job, only to find his manager repeatedly asking him, "Don't you have a better shirt to wear?" If this was overly subtle, the company's subsequent action wasn't: it fired Crane on a bogus accusation of substandard workmanship.

It wasn't always like this. In the 1960s, when some 30 percent of the private-sector workforce in America was still unionized, employers were generally cautious about how far they'd go in trying to repel organized labor. "They were as nervous as whores in church," said one corporate adviser. "The posture of major company managers was, 'Let's . . . not make the union mad at us during the organizing drive or they'll take it out at the bargaining table.'" By the 1980s, a whole industries had sprung up to assist business: "union avoidance" consultants, lawyers, psychologists, and strike-management firms. The more enfeebled the unions became, the more forcefully employers then acted. By the 1990s, even companies that had once accepted unions as a fact of life were now totally defiant.

"The most intense and aggressive antiunion campaign strategies, the kind previously found only at employers like Wal-Mart, are no longer reserved for a select coterie of extreme antiunion employers," Cornell University's Kate Bronfenbrenner wrote in an analysis of how business conducted itself during representation elections from 1999 through 2003. Specifically, she discovered that companies threatened to close the facilities where employees were trying to organize in 57 percent of elections, raised the possibility of cuts to wages and benefits in nearly half, and went so far as to actually discharge workers a third of the time. Over the years, employers also became adept at delaying union elections so that they had more time to coerce workers to see things their way.

All of this proved highly effective. Even if the NLRB ruled that a company had illegally dissuaded employees from organizing, the price to pay was typically small—about $200,000 in penalties—compared with the many million of dollars that could be saved by ensuring that union negotiators never got a shot to bolster workers' earnings, retirement plans, and health-care benefits.

Unions hurt themselves as well. Apparently carried away by the power that they were able to maintain through the 1950s and '60s, labor leaders by the 1980s were dedicating less than 5 percent of their budgets toward recruiting new members. By the time that they woke up and realized that it was crucial to expand their rolls, the composition of the economy had been recast. During the 1930s, when the Auto Workers were first signing up members inside the nation's car factories, it was possible to pull in large pools at once because each plant averaged between 2,000 and 3,000 blue-collar employees. By contrast, organizers were likely to find a tenth that many workers under the roof of a big box retail outlet and far fewer at a fast-food joint, making it much more expensive and daunting to pick off sizable slices of the service sector. The growing use of temps and other contingent workers also complicated union organizing.

Labor did notch some significant triumphs through the 1990s, such as the Service Employees International Union's Justice for Janitors campaign, which propelled more than 100,000 building workers in various cities into collective bargaining, and the election that saw 74,000 home-care aides in Los Angeles County join the SEIU. But such advances were extremely rare. By 2000, the portion of private-sector workers across the United States who were union members stood at just 9 percent—less than half of what it had been in 1980. By 2010, this figure would dip below 7 percent, even though surveys showed that a majority of non-union workers desired representation.

The drop was rough on employees across the economy. While the ascension of unions helped to lift pay and benefits for tens of millions of workers in the first few decades after World War II—not only at those companies that had been organized, but at many others that felt the need to keep up—the fall of organized labor was now dragging down people's compensation. Researchers have found a connection between the decline of unions and the rise of income inequality in America; without the added clout that comes with collective bargaining, a good many employees have seen their compensation stagnate or even get set back. "Deunionization," Lawrence Mishel of the Economic Policy Institute has written, "has strengthened the hands of employers and undercut the ability of low- and middle-wage workers to have good jobs and economic security."

For many people, this reality has had a perverse effect: it has incentivized them to do their shopping at one destination above all others—Wal-Mart. It is tough to fault them. In the early 2000s, the prices on groceries at a Wal-Mart Supercenter were running 8 to 27 percent below those of a traditional supermarket. All in all, the company's prices have been so low—and its reach so vast—that some economists have credited it with singlehandedly helping to hold down inflation for the entire country.

Even union members, who are keenly aware of the company's two-fisted tactics against organized labor, have been tempted by the discounts. "Ten bucks," said Glenn Miraflor, an ironworker and a father of four, as he lowered a twenty-inch box fan into his cart at a Wal-Mart in Las Vegas in 2003. "You can't beat that." Eyeing a new PC, he added: "Where else are you going to find a computer for $498? Everyone I work with shops here."

The clamp that Wal-Mart put on workers didn't stop with those on its own payroll.

Most every time it opened a new store, other retailers that charged their customers more—but also paid their employees better—would find that they couldn't compete. For many of them, the only way to survive was to imitate the Wal-Mart model, cutting back on their own workers' wages and health care. "Socially," said Craig Cole, the chief executive of Brown & Cole Stores, a supermarket chain in the Pacific Northwest, who was wary of Wal-Mart coming into his area, "we're engaged in a race to the bottom."

In October 2003, members of the United Food and Commercial Workers struck Vons and Pavilions markets in Southern California. In a show of solidarity, Ralphs and Albertsons locked out their union members the next day. In all, 59,000 workers were idled. Although the grocery chains and the union were the only two sides actually facing off at the negotiating table, another presence hovered over the talks: Wal-Mart, which was on the verge of opening dozens of Supercenters in the region. "They are the third party now that comes to every bargaining situation," said Mike Leonard, director of strategic programs for the UFCW.

As the supermarket depicted it, the union would have to make concessions—or Wal-Mart would use its low-price formula to snatch away a substantial amount of their business, causing them to close many of their stores and costing many thousands of jobs. After all, what else could anyone expect to happen when Wal-Mart paid its grocery workers about nine dollars an hour in wages and benefits, compared with nineteen at the big supermarkets? Already, from 1992 through 2003, Wal-Mart's leap into groceries had led to the closure of 13,000 supermarkets in other parts of the country and the bankruptcy of at least twenty-five regional chains. Yet for the UFCW and its allies, this was precisely the time to hold the line and not let Wal-Mart dictate that the entire sector would subject its workers to the lowest common denominator. "If we don't as labor officials address this issue now, the future for our membership is dismal, very dismal," said one California union representative.

For nearly five months, the UFCW rank-and-file walked the picket lines from San Diego to Bakersfield. Finally, a settlement was reached—and it marked a big step backward for the union and its members. Central to the accord was the introduction of a two-tier system under which the supermarkets would pay new hires much less in wages and benefits than veteran employees. The impact, said *Los Angeles Times* columnist Michael Hiltzik, was that UFCW "membership will evolve from a group of decently paid workers into a group of poorly paid ones. Its resources to fight the employers will dwindle, and its prospects for growth will vanish.... The damage done by this dispute to the principle of providing a living wage and adequate health-care coverage for employees will be felt by workers— union and nonunion—around the state and across the country."

Some, including Hiltzik, maintained that Wal-Mart had been a convenient bugaboo for the supermarkets and that they were unlikely to pass along much savings from the new labor agreement to their customers; instead, they would reward their shareholders and senior executives. At the same time, others welcomed Wal-Mart, especially in the inner-city neighborhoods that the company had set its sights on. "I'd rather have a person on somebody's payroll—even if it isn't at the highest wage—than on the unemployment roll," said John Mack, president of the Los Angeles Urban League. Boosters predicted other positives as well. "Money that people save on groceries will be redirected to other items, including housing, savings, health, entertainment, and transportation," said a report from the Los Angeles County Economic Development Corporation. "This new spending will, in turn, rent jobs outside the grocery industry."

But whatever pluses Wal-Mart was bringing, this much was beyond debate: another set of workers was now part of an industry that couldn't guarantee them a solid living. Under the old contract, a grocery clerk in Southern California could earn more than seventeen dollars an hour; under the new one, workers started at less than nine dollars and could make, at most, about fifteen. Overall, the average wage for a supermarket worker was poised to decrease between 18 and 28 percent. And anywhere from a quarter to nearly half of the unionized workforce would no longer be eligible for medical insurance. Employer pension contributions were also slashed 35 percent for current employees and 65 percent for new workers. "You're not going to be able to make a career out of it anymore," said Kerry Renaud, a produce worker at a Vons supermarket in Hollywood. Barbara Harrison, a bakery worker at Ralphs, put it this way: "With treatment like this from the company . . . the middle class is just becoming the lower class."

In 2007, the UFCW would win back some of what it had lost. Most important, the union was able to reverse the two-tier setup. With low employee morale plaguing the supermarkets, they apparently came to the realization that dividing the workforce wasn't so smart. The pact also included the first pay raises that workers had received in five years. But this wouldn't be a tale of sweet redemption. As the years went on, the social contract throughout the industry would continue to weaken. Wal-Mart and other nonunion grocers acquired more and more market share. And at the unionized chains, rule changes and scheduling tricks made workers wait an increasingly long time before they could move up the ladder and command the highest wages. By 2016, the average grocery worker in L.A. would be making less than $29,000 a year, down from more than $31,000 in 2005, when adjusted for inflation. "Grocery store jobs look much more like fast-food jobs than they used to," said Chris Tilly, director of the UCLA Institute for Research on Labor and Employment. "Lower pay, fewer benefits, more people part-time."

Meanwhile, Wal-Mart's sway extended to another batch of workers: those of its suppliers. "Your price is going to be whittled down like you never thought possible," said Carl Krauss, the owner of a Chicago company called Lakewood Engineering & Manufacturing. It produced the fan that Las Vegas Vegas iron-worker Glenn Miraflor purchased at Wal-Mart for ten dollars. A decade earlier, it cost shoppers twice as much. But Wal-Mart, whose bigness gave it tremendous leverage over the companies whose wares filled its aisles, insisted that Krauss figure out how to make the appliance for less. "You give them your price," Krauss said. "If they don't like it, they give you theirs." To lower expenses, Krauss automated his factory: where it once required twenty-two people to assemble a product, it now took only seven. Krauss also leaned on his own suppliers to reduce prices for their components. Still, that wasn't enough. And so in 2000, Krauss opened a factory in Shenzhen, China, where workers earned twenty-five cents an hour, compared with thirteen dollars in Chicago. By 2003, about 40 percent of Lakewood's products were being made in China, including most heaters and desktop fans. For the box fan that Glenn Miraflor bought, the electronic innards were imported.

Many of Wal-Mart's suppliers found themselves in the same boat—or, more accurately, filling an endless string of container ships crossing the Pacific Ocean. In the mid-1980s, Wal-Mart had tried to score public-relations points by sourcing more products domestically. Under its "Buy American" initiative, patrons to its stores were greeted with red-white-and-blue banners and smaller signs that read, "This item, formerly imported, is now being purchased by Wal-Mart in the USA and is creating—or retaining—jobs for Americans!" By the mid-1990s, however, "Buy American" didn't pencil out for the company anymore. In 2002, Wal-Mart brought in $12 billion worth of Chinese-made goods, double the sum from five years earlier. By 2004, that was up to $18 billion, and by 2006 it had reached $27 billion, accounting for nearly a tenth of total U.S. imports from China. "People say, 'How can it be bad for things to come into the United States cheaply? How can it be bad to have a bargain at Wal-Mart?'" said Steve Dobbins, president of Carolina Mills, a supplier of thread and yarn to the textile industry, which has watched as employment in American apparel factories has disappeared at a rate of more than 11 percent a year since the late nineties. "Sure, it's held inflation down, it's great to have bargains. But you can't buy anything if you're not employed. We are shopping ourselves out of jobs."

By one estimate, Chinese imports to Wal-Mart alone were responsible for wiping out more than 300,000 U.S. manufacturing jobs between 2001 and 2013—a manifestation of what had suddenly be come a very serious predicament across America. "Until about a decade ago, the effects of globalization on the distribution of wealth and jobs were largely benign," Michael Spence, a Nobel Prize-winning economist, wrote in 2011. "But employment in the United States has been affected ... by the fact that many manufacturing activities, principally their lower-value-added components, have been moving to emerging economies." Through the 1990s, the United States ran a trade deficit, but it averaged only about 1 percent of the nation's economic output—a bearable volume. To be sure, the North American Free Trade Agreement caused some pockets of the nation to shed jobs, but the negative repercussions were quite small on the whole, and the losses may well have been eclipsed by new U.S. employment that NAFTA helped to generate.

China was very different, however. After the country joined the World Trade Organization in 2001, giving it more access to markets across the globe, imports into the United States surged. The US trade deficit exploded, averaging about 5 percent of economic output in the 2000s. A consensus of economists and policymakers had long contended that free trade easily made for far more winners than losers. But, as *The Wall Street Journal* has pointed out, "China up-ended many of those assumptions. No other country came close to its combination of a vast working-age population, super-low wages, government support, cheap currency, and productivity gains." Within four years of the WTO admitting China, imports from there as a percentage of U.S. economic output doubled. It took Mexico twelve years to do the same thing following the passage of NAFTA.

"China's low-cost imports swept the entire U.S." the *Journal* reported, "squeezing producers of electronics in San Jose, California; sporting goods in Orange County, California; jewelry in Providence, Rhode Island; shoes in West Plains, Missouri; toys in Murray, Kentucky; and lounge chairs in Tupelo, Mississippi, among many other industries and communities." Total manufacturing employment in the United States, which had held fairly steady through the 1990s, plunged after 2001. The harm inflicted would lead many Americans to regard globalization as more bad than good—an attitude that would help shape the contours of the 2016 U.S. presidential race. "The Chinese export onslaught . . . left a scar on the American working class that has not healed," Eduardo Porter of the *New York Times* has written.

How much of this can or should be blamed on any single company—even a colossus like Wal-Mart—is certainly arguable. Not surprisingly, Wal-Mart itself has always made the case for total absolution. "Some well-meaning critics believe that Wal-Mart, because of our size, should play the role that General Motors played after World War II, and that is to establish the post-world-war middle class that the country is so proud of," said H. Lee Scott Jr., who took over as the company's CEO in 2000. "The facts are that retailing doesn't perform that role in the economy as GM does or did."

While Scott wasn't wrong, that was surely of little solace to millions of workers who'd seen the economy change, leaving them with fewer and fewer ways to get ahead. When GM and other manufacturers employed a quarter or more of the American workforce through the early 1980s, even those without much education could land a factory job and do quite well. But what were the two-thirds of Americans without a four-year college degree supposed to do now? Manufacturing, with its high wages and good benefits, employed just 10 percent of Americans by 2010. And even many of these industrial jobs and other blue-collar positions now demanded technical instruction beyond high school—something that far too few people had.

"The person who unloads the truck now has to have some training in logistics and inventory systems," said Anthony Carnevale, director of Georgetown University's Center on Education and the Workforce. "You don't become an auto mechanic any longer by getting a dirty rag and hanging out with your uncle." It wasn't that more of the nation hadn't grasped the value of being in a classroom. Between 1967 and 2012, the ranks of US adults with at least a four-year college degree rose from 13 percent to 32 percent, "a remarkable upgrading in the skills of America's workers," as a study by Carnevale has described it. Yet even when you added up all of those with four-year college diplomas, two-year associate degrees, and postsecondary vocational certificates, it still came out to less than half of the working-age population. Making things worse, many big companies—even while complaining about a "skills gap"—had stopped trying to develop their people. While both white- and blue-collar workers received on-the-job training as a matter of course in the 1950s and '60s, surveys now indicated that anywhere from about 50 percent to 80 percent of American employees got nothing of the sort.

For most of those without the right credentials, the only option was to try to make it amid a decidedly low-wage landscape, one now dominated by poorly paying service providers. In 1960, eleven of the fifteen biggest employers in the country made things, led by GM, with nearly 600,000 workers. By 2010, only four manufacturers were in the top fifteen; the rest were in services, including not only Wal-Mart but also McDonald's, Yum Brands (the parent of Taco Bell, KFC, and Pizza Hut), Target, and CVS. These occupations "are crucial to the support and growth of major industries across the country," officials at the San Francisco Federal Reserve said, "but many of these workers do not earn enough to adequately support their families, even at a subsistence level."

Yet for Lee Scott, paying more and offering larger benefits would have undercut Wal-Mart's reason for being. If "we raised prices substantially to fund above-market wages," he said, "we'd betray our commitment to tens of millions of customers, many of whom struggle to make ends meet."

Others, though, didn't buy it. "Being able to purchase groceries 20 percent cheaper at Wal-Mart," said Paul Samuelson, who is regarded as the father of modern economics, "does not necessarily make up for the wage losses." Besides, this wasn't the only way to do business. Some retailers had an alternate approach—most notably Costco, which paid an average of seventeen dollars an hour in 2005, more than 40 percent higher than the average wage at Wal-Mart's Sam's Club, its closest rival. What's more, a much bigger proportion of Costco workers had medical coverage and retirement plans than did their counterparts at Wal-Mart, and these benefits were far superior. After four and a half years, a full-time Costco worker would earn more than $46,000 a year; a full-time Sam's Club worker made $27,000. "We're not the Little Sisters of the Poor," said Jim Sinegal, Costco's longtime CEO. "This is good business."

By investing in his employees, Sinegal knew, they were bound to give excellent service to the company's customers, which helped to drive satisfaction and sales. "It starts with a living wage and affordable quality health benefits," said Richard Galanti, the chief financial officer at Costco, whose stock price would greatly outperform Wal-Mart's through most of the 2000s and beyond. "That's the initial basis for engagement."

Across most of the American economy, however, Costco has very much been the exception; Wal-Mart, the rule.

Can the American corporate social contract ever be reconstructed? The short answer is now at least not in the way it was before. The Golden Age was sui generis, and too much has changed since then.

Some unions and other labor groups are using online technology to organize employees and give them new tools to stand up for their rights, while helping to finance valuable campaigns for low-wage workers such as the Fight for $15. Still, we'll never again see private-sector unionization rates—and the potency that comes from widespread collective bargaining—like we had in the 1950s or '60s. Our economy isn't built for that anymore.

We must also accept that if artificial intelligence displaces masses of workers—and it well may, particularly those with few skills—we shouldn't try to stand in its way. If the economy is going to continue to grow, we must have technological progress. We shouldn't try to stop international commerce, either. It, too, is essential to our long-term economic growth, and trade restrictions won't be effective anyway. A third of the components used in products made in America are imported from overseas. Plus, the flow of goods is flattening while the flow of data, zipping invisibly across borders, is swelling.

What's required now is a new social contract that takes into account these realities.

The government has an enormous part to play. We need a higher federal minimum wage and, in our most expensive cities, a true living wage. Although organized labor won't recapture its former prominence, Washington needs to make it easier for workers to unionize. We need paid family leave. We need stricter enforcement of labor standards to help workers fend off wage theft—the denial of pay and benefits rightly owed them—and other violations, especially at a time when so much of the nation's employment is being generated among temps, free-lancers, and others in contingent jobs. We need to expand the Earned Income Tax Credit.

We need portable benefits for Uber drivers and other "gig workers"—a still small but increasingly important segment of the labor market. We need the government to better support technological innovation and create an environment that fosters entrepreneurship, which, despite the radiance from Silicon Valley, has been at a low ebb in America for the past thirty years. We need the Federal Reserve to make full employment a priority.

And although it is due to dismiss as a bromide, we really do need to revitalize public education from top to bottom.

We also need changes to our tax laws and accounting standards so that executives are induced to look beyond their company's quarterly earnings and daily share price. We need institutional investors to exhort corporations to keep sight of the long term, and not just pay attention to results in the short term.

But more than anything, we need to recognize that the social contract between employer and employee won't be strong unless our business leaders want it to be so.

"Companies once felt an obligation to support American workers, even when it wasn't the best financial choice," said Betsey Stevenson, who was chief economist at the Labor Department from 2010 to 2011 "That's disappeared. Profits and efficiency have trumped generosity."

We can't mandate that executives think the way they used to. We can't demand that they alter the norms by which they operate and like the generation of executives who'd come through the crucible of the Great Depression and World War II—suddenly make it more about "we" and less about "I." We can't force them to invest in their workers through more training and higher compensation and stronger job security.

We—as employees and as consumers—can only encourage them to realize that corporate America's continuing fixation with putting shareholders above everyone else is ultimately bad for their companies. "A healthy business," wrote Peter Drucker, "cannot exist in a sick society." Restoring more balance between worker and investor would be a welcome balm.

A few may be starting to get it. Wal-Mart, of all companies, made *Fortune* magazine's Change the World list for 2016. It was so honored for raising its workers' pay to an average of $13.38 an hour and enrolling half a million employees in a curriculum "designed to teach job skills that could help them climb the income ladder."

And yet there is much, much more that Wal-Mart and many other corporations can do, and must do, if we are to come to grips with the most pressing issue of our time: distributing the nation's economic gains more broadly.

"The American people have continued up to now to tolerate abuses that have developed in our economic system because . . . they believe it can be made to work for the good of all," one become at leader avowed. "They must see a chance for a better life for themselves." Almost unanimously, they want it for their sons and daughters.

"Most Americans," he added, "would agree on the economic goals for America: a community permanently rich in opportunity and security."

More than seventy years after William Benton, vice chairman of the Committee for Economic Development, made that statement, it would be difficult to argue that our goals are any different today. What has corroded, sadly, is the underlying belief that the system can be made to work for the good of all.

A NOTE ON CITATIONS AND SOURCING

Because of the extensiveness of the endnotes, they are being published online. You can access them at www.hachettebookgroup.com/features/publicaffairs/endofloyalty.

QUESTIONS FOR MAKING CONNECTIONS
WITHIN THE READING

1. Explain what CEO Craig Cole means when he says that Wal-Mart has become the leader in a "race to the bottom." For the average Wal-Mart customer, including ironworker Glenn Miraflor (the buyer of the ten-dollar box fan) "the bottom" means the lowest price possible. But the system Wal-Mart helped to create has had the unintended effect of depressing wages, not only in the service sector but also in manufacturing. How does Wal-Mart produce this effect? And why haven't people noticed? Is it because cheaper goods provide an immediate benefit, whereas the advantages of rising wages, which push prices up, take longer to be obvious? Based on your reading of Wartzman, how well understood is the problem he describes? Does anybody see the whole system—the consumers, the workers, Wal-Mart's leadership?

2. In what ways does Wal-Mart's "American as apple pie" image conflict with its dependence on the global economy? If Wal-Mart could no longer find cheap labor overseas, what would happen to its business model? Free trade— that is, a global economy—is supposed to promote price competition that will benefit everybody in the long run. Workers in poorer nations can produce consumer goods for less, and their shift from village farming to manufacturing will raise their wages, in theory. At the same time, developed countries like the U.S. will be able to leave manufacturing behind in order to embrace other kinds of jobs that require more education and "brain-power" than the old factories required. But that is not what has happened here. Where and how has the theory gone wrong?

3. In what ways did the rise of Wal-Mart exacerbate the decline of union power? In the middle of the twentieth century, companies commonly avoided open resistance to organized labor, fearful that employees would force them to the bargaining table in search of better wages and benefits. But, according to Wartzman, Wal-Mart's "zero tolerance" approach to unions ushered in a new wave of open hostility to unions. How has this imbalance in power changed what Wartzman refers to as the "social contract" of these corporations? What do you think "social contract" means in the context of this protracted fight between unions and corporations? Based on your understanding of Wartzman, do you think the balance of power will ever tip again? What conditions would be necessary for such a change?

QUESTIONS FOR WRITING

1. The economist John Maynard Keynes is famous for rediscovering what is known as the "paradox of thrift." He pointed out that when individuals try to save by decreasing their expenses, they may be able to make modest gains. But when a whole community tries to do the same—saving more by

spending less—the decline in economic activity pulls everybody down. To what degree is Wal-Mart's economic model—the way its business operates—trapped by the paradox of thrift? In what ways does it complicate Keynes' reasoning? While it's true, for example, that wages are falling as consumer prices drop, the Wall-Market corporation continues to see record profits. Indeed, as Wartzman points out, Sam Walton was until his death the richest person on earth with a personal fortune of 100 billion dollars. Has the Walton family somehow escaped the paradox of thrift?

2. The Greek root of the word "democracy" means "rule by the people." The ancient Greeks contrasted democracy with aristocracy, rule by the elite; oligarchy, rule by the wealthy; and tyranny, rule by a dictator. Based on Wartzman's article, would you say that the United States today is a democracy? An aristocracy? An oligarchy? To what degree are people free to "rule" themselves, either directly or by representation? If the democratic system stops as soon as you enter your workplace, are you really living in a democracy? To what degree are Wal-Mart's anti-union tactics aimed at preventing greater workplace democracy?

QUESTIONS FOR MAKING CONNECTIONS
BETWEEN THE READINGS

1. In "An Army of One: *Me*" Jean Twenge describes the increasingly narcissistic character of American social life. To what degree might the Wal-Mart economy contribute to the narcissism she describes? Is the idea that everyone deserves seven-dollar T-shirts and cheaper groceries related to the notion that we are all exceptional in our own way? If the self-esteem curriculum downplays the links between hard work and achievement, do Wal-Mart customers have any awareness of the sacrifice and labor required to create the products they buy? Does Wal-Mart encourage people to see themselves as isolated individuals rather than members of a community? Or does it create an ersatz community—a substitute that looks like the real thing but lacks its essential elements?

2. In "The Extraordinary Science of Addictive Junk Food," Michael Moss describes the complex system that sustains the multi-billion dollar junk food industry. Advertisers, marketers and scientists all collaborate to get millions of Americans hooked on food that actually harms their health. Are Wal-Mart's cheap goods addictive, too? In what ways do both systems depend on limiting our choices while appearing to provide virtually unlimited choices? How do their immediate benefits come at a longer-term cost? Why are both industries so resistant to change—in Wal-Mart's case through unionization and in the food industry through a shift to healthier fare?

ETHAN WATTERS

ETHAN WATTERS'S WORK IS controversial—some might even say explosive—although it has appeared in mainstream venues like the *New York Times Magazine, Discover, Men's Journal,* and *Wired.* His first two books, coauthored with University of California sociologist Richard Ofshe, are highly critical of psychiatry and psychoanalysis: *Making Monsters: False Memories, Psychotherapy, and Sexual Hysteria* (1996) and *Therapy's Delusions: The Myth of the Unconscious and the Exploitation of Today's Walking Worried* (1999). If these books still generate sharp differences of opinion, the same holds for Watters's most recent work, *Crazy Like Us: The Globalization of the American Psyche* (2010). While acknowledging the reality of mental illnesses, he wants his readers to understand that the terminology we apply to them reflects our own history and culture, and he notes that the categories other people use sometimes have strengths that our tradition lacks. One example Watters explores in *Crazy Like Us* is the aftermath of the tsunami that struck the island of Sri Lanka in 2004, killing 35,000 people and displacing half a million. Moved by genuine compassion, teams of American mental health professionals raced to the island to provide psychological services for post-traumatic stress disorder (PTSD). But Watters found that PTSD is a distinctly Western reaction. Many islanders experienced the aftermath as a loss of social connections—as loneliness rather than a disease of their private minds.

Watters fears that, because of globalization, humankind is now at risk of losing a rich legacy:

> The ideas that we export to other cultures often have at their heart a particularly American brand of hyperindividualism. These beliefs remain deeply influenced by the Cartesian split between the mind and the body ... as well as teeming numbers of self-help philosophies and schools of therapy that have encouraged us to separate the health of the individual from the health of the group. Even the fascinating biomedical ... research into the workings of the brain has, on a cultural level, further removed our understandings of the mind from the social and natural world it navigates.

What concerns Watters even more, however, are Western drug companies engaged in a crusade to replace indigenous knowledge with Western paradigms that will open up highly lucrative new markets. Not only does Watters nudge us to think about the ways that "scientific" notions of the mind are not universally valid, but he presses us to ask about the damage done to everyone, here in the United States and around the world, by the intermingling of mental health with the profit motive.

The Mega-Marketing of Depression in Japan

One of the chilling things about these events, whether a puzzle or a scandal, is how a very few people in key positions can determine the course of events and shape the consciousness of a generation.

—DAVID HEALY

I went to visit Dr. Laurence Kirmayer in his book-lined office at McGill University in Montreal because he had a particularly good story to tell. I'd heard that a few years ago, Kirmayer had a personal brush with the pharmaceutical giant GlaxoSmithKline and the remarkable resources that the company employed to create a market for their antidepressant pill Paxil in Japan.

In person Kirmayer is the picture of a tweedy academic. He speaks in complete paragraphs in a deep authoritative voice. He has a large head and a broad face that is covered nearly to the cheekbones in a thick light-gray beard. His slightly wandering left eye suits his demeanor. If you look at the left side of his face his expression is attentive and focused on the conversation. If you look at the right side of his face he appears to be looking past you into the middle distance, as if searching for a word or pondering a thought.

In telling his story of being feted by GlaxoSmithKline, Kirmayer likes to point out that he is unaccustomed to the trappings of great wealth. Not that he's doing badly. As the director of the Division of Social and Transcultural Psychiatry at McGill, he makes a respectable living and adds to his income with a private psychiatric practice. As editor in chief of the journal *Transcultural Psychiatry,* he is well known in certain circles and can draw a crowd of admiring grad students and colleagues at an anthropology or mental health conference. But to get to those conferences he flies coach.

It was in the fall of 2000, as he tells it, that he came to understand just how *un*spectacularly rich he was. That was when he accepted an invitation from something called the International Consensus Group on Depression and Anxiety to attend two all-expenses-paid conferences, the first in Kyoto and the second a few months later on the shores of Bali.

Accepting the invitation didn't at first seem like a difficult decision. Although he knew that the conference was sponsored by an educational grant from the drug maker GlaxoSmithKline, such industry funding wasn't unusual for academic conferences in the field of psychiatry. When he checked out the list of other invitees, he recognized all the names. It was an extremely exclusive group of highly influential clinicians and researchers from France, the United States, and Japan, among other countries. The topic, "Transcultural Issues in Depression and Anxiety," was right up his alley. Even better, he had an eager young graduate student named Junko Kitanaka who was in Japan finishing her dissertation on the history of depression in the country; such a gathering of luminaries would be a boon to her research. In addition to those incentives, attendees would be given the chance to publish their presentations in a supplement of the prestigious *Journal of Clinical Psychiatry*. "I wouldn't say it was a no-brainer, but it wasn't very hard for me to say yes," Kirmayer remembers. "How much trouble could I get in?"

His first inkling that this wasn't a run-of-the-mill academic conference came when the airline ticket arrived in the mail. This ticket was for a seat in the front of the plane and cost nearly $10,000. The next hint came when one of the conference organizers told him in no uncertain terms that these would be closed-door meetings. His grad student, Kitanaka, would not be allowed to attend. There would be no uninvited colleagues and no press.

On arrival in Kyoto in early October 2000 he found the luxury of the accommodations to be beyond anything he had personally experienced. He was ushered into an exclusive part of the hotel, where he was given a drink while an attractive woman filled out the hotel forms. His room was a palatial suite. The bath was drawn and strewn with rose petals and dosed with frangipani oil. There was a platter on the credenza filled with fruits so exotic that he could identify only the mangosteens.

"This was Gordon Gekko treatment—the most deluxe circumstances I have ever experienced in my life," Kirmayer says, smiling at the memory. This was how the other half lived, he realized—or, rather, how the other .01 percent lived. "The luxury was so far beyond anything that I could personally afford, it was a little scary. It didn't take me long to think that something strange was going on here. I wondered: What did I do to deserve this?"

Kirmayer was well aware that drug companies routinely sponsor professional conferences and educational seminars and that these events do double duty as marketing seminars. It was also common knowledge that drug makers use enticements to encourage both researchers and practitioners to attend. A prescribing doctor might be treated to a round of golf or a fancy dinner in exchange for attending an hour-long seminar about the effectiveness of some new drug. These practices are the medical equivalent of what real estate agents do to sell vacation timeshares.

But it was clear from the start that the gatherings of the International Consensus Group on Depression and Anxiety were different from the normal drug company dog and pony show, and not simply because the enticements being offered were so dear. Once the group of academics actually gathered in a plush conference room and began their discussions, Kirmayer realized quickly that the GlaxoSmithKline representatives in attendance had no interest in touting their products to the group. Indeed there was little mention of the company's antidepressant drug Paxil, which was just a few months away from hitting the market in Japan. Instead they seemed much more interested in hearing from the assembled group. They were there to learn. "The focus was not on medications," Kirmayer remembers. "They were not trying to sell their drugs to us. They were interested in what we knew about how cultures shape the illness experience."

As Kirmayer got to know them during the conference, he realized that the drug company representatives weren't from the ranks of the advertising or marketing departments or the peppy salespeople. As best he could tell, these were highly paid private scholars who could hold their own in the most sophisticated discussion of postcolonial theory or the impact of globalization on the human mind. "These guys all had PhDs and were versed in the literature," Kirmayer said. "They were clearly soaking up what we had to say to each other on these topics."

The intense interest the GlaxoSmithKline brain trust showed in the topic of how culture shapes the illness experience made sense given the timing of the meeting. The class of antidepressant drugs known as selective serotonin reuptake inhibitors (SSRIs) had become the wonder drug of the 1990s, at least in terms of the profits they'd garnered for the drug companies. That year alone, in the leading regions for SSRIs, sales grew by 18 percent and totaled over thirteen billion dollars. Most of those sales were still in the United States, but there was wide agreement that lucrative international markets had yet to be tapped.

Indeed it was somewhat remarkable that none of the best-selling SSRIs had been launched in Japan. This was more than twelve years after Prozac became available for prescription in the United States. What caused this uncharacteristic timidity on the part of these pharmaceutical giants? It certainly wasn't that the Japanese eschewed Western drugs. To the contrary, U.S.-based companies at the time were exporting upwards of fifty billion dollars in medications to the country each year. It was said that Japanese patients felt underserved if they didn't come away from a doctor's visit with at least a couple of prescriptions.

But Eli Lilly, then the out-front world leader in the SSRI horse race with Prozac, had decided in the early 1990s not to pursue the Japanese market because executives in the company believed that the Japanese people wouldn't accept the drug. More precisely, they wouldn't want to accept the disease. "The people's attitude toward depression was very negative," explained a spokeswoman for Eli Lilly to the *Wall Street Journal*. She was referring to the fact that the Japanese had a fundamentally different conception of depression than in the West, one that made it unlikely that a significant number of people in Japan would want to take a drug associated with the disease.

Most other SSRI manufacturers followed Eli Lilly's lead and held off as well. Getting drugs approved in Japan was a costly gamble. The rules at the time required that drugs already on the market in Western countries had to be retested in large-scale human trials using an exclusively Japanese population. That meant years of effort and millions of dollars spent, with the distinct possibility that the drug might fail the trial. No company wanted to make such an investment if no market existed for the drug.

The Japanese pharmaceutical company Meiji Seika was the first to break from the pack, working through the decade to run Japanese trials on the SSRI Luvox, which it had licensed from the Swedish company Solvay. After reading Peter Kramer's 1993 book *Listening to Prozac,* Meiji's president, Ichiro Kitasato, sensed an unexplored opportunity in the Japanese marketplace. "People in the company said there are too few patients in Japan," he told a reporter in 1996. "But I looked at the U.S. and Europe and thought this is sure to be a big market."

GlaxoSmithKline was the next to get in the race. In the years prior to the 2000 conference in Kyoto, the company had spent an immense amount of money and resources jumping through the regulatory and bureaucratic hoops to get the green light to put Paxil on the market in the country. Having watched Prozac dominate the American market in the late 1980s, drug company executives knew the advantages of early market share, and GlaxoSmithKline didn't want Luvox to be the only SSRI in Japan.

But both companies faced the same problem: there was no guarantee that Japanese doctors would prescribe the drug or that the population would be interested in taking it. The problem was that the profession of psychiatry in Japan, unlike in the West, seldom ministered to the walking worried; rather they focused almost exclusively on the severely mentally ill. Consequently, talk therapy was all but nonexistent in the country. For the small percentage of the population diagnosed with a debilitating mental illness, long hospital stays were the norm. The average stay in a mental hospital in Japan was over a year, versus just ten days in the United States. So although there was a psychiatric term for depression in Japan, *utsubyô,* what it described was a mental illness that was as chronic and devastating as schizophrenia. *Utsubyô* was the sort of illness that would make it impossible to hold down a job or have a semblance of a normal life. Worse yet, at least for the sales prospects of Paxil in Japan, *utsubyô* was considered a rare disorder.

At the Kyoto meeting Kirmayer began to understand the company's intense interest in the question of how cultures shape the illness experience. To make Paxil a hit in Japan, it would not be enough to corner the small market of those diagnosed with *utsubyô.* The objective was to influence, at the most fundamental level, the Japanese understanding of sadness and depression. In short, they were learning how to market a disease.

To have the best chance of shifting the Japanese public's perception about the meaning of depression, GlaxoSmithKline needed a deep and sophisticated understanding of how those beliefs had taken shape. This was why, Kirmayer came to realize, the company had invited him and his colleagues and treated them like royalty. GlaxoSmithKline needed help solving a cultural puzzle that might be worth billions of dollars.

Judging from the records of the conference, it's clear that the company got its money's worth. During the meetings eminent scholars and researchers gave insightful presentations on subjects ranging from the history of psychiatry in Japan to the Japanese public's changing attitudes about mental illness. The prominent Japanese psychiatrists in attendance were particularly helpful in framing the state of the public's current beliefs about depression and anxiety disorders.

Osamu Tajima, a professor at the Department of Mental Health at Kyorin University and a leading Tokyo psychiatrist, told the assembled group of a rising public concern about the high suicide rates in Japan. He described how dozens of middle-aged men each year hike deep into the so-called suicide forests in the foothills of Mt. Fuji with lengths of rope to hang themselves. He described how service along the Central Line Railway in Tokyo was routinely disrupted by office workers leaping in front of commuter trains.

Tajima also gave a detailed description of how psychiatric services were structured within the overall health care apparatus of Japan. Services were in the midst of a critical change, he reported. There was a burgeoning concern in the population about mood disorders and the need for social attention to suicide rates and depression. He also documented how the Western definition and symptom checklist for depression—thanks to the influence of the *DSM [Diagnostic and Statistical Manual of Mental Disorders]*—was steadily gaining ground among younger psychiatrists and doctors in Japan. "Japanese psychiatry is undergoing a period of important change," he concluded, which was certainly good news for GlaxoSmithKline. He was upbeat about the changes heralded by the standardization of psychiatry around the world. "Adoption of internationally standardized diagnostic criteria and terminology in psychiatry will provide additional advances in assessing prevalence and facilitating accurate diagnosis." He was also clearly impressed with the scientific advances in drug treatments that were soon to come to his country. "New and effective treatment options," he said, "most notably the SSRIs, will contribute to reducing the burden of depression and anxiety disorders in Japanese society."

After lunch on the second day of the conference, it was Kirmayer's turn to speak. He had written many papers in his career documenting the differing expressions of depression around the world and the meaning hidden in those differences. He had found that every culture has a type of experience that is in some ways parallel to the Western conception of depression: a mental state and set of behaviors that relate to a loss of connectedness to others or a decline in social status or personal motivation. But he had also found that cultures have unique expressions, descriptions, and understandings for these states of being.

He told the assembled scholars and drug company representatives of how a Nigerian man might experience a culturally distinct form of depression by describing a peppery feeling in his head. A rural Chinese farmer might speak only of shoulder or stomach aches. A man in India might talk of semen loss or a sinking heart or feeling hot. A Korean might tell you of "fire illness," which is experienced as a burning in the gut. Someone from Iran might talk of tightness in the chest, and an American Indian might describe the experience of depression as something akin to loneliness.

Kirmayer had observed that cultures often differ in what he called "explanatory models" for depression-like states. These cultural beliefs and stories have the effect of directing the attention of individuals to certain feelings and symptoms and away from others. In one culture someone feeling an inchoate distress might be prompted to search for feelings of unease in his gut or in muscle pain; in another place or time, a different type of symptom would be accepted as legitimate. This interplay between the expectations of the culture and the experience of the individual leads to a cycle of symptom amplification. In short, beliefs about the cause, symptomatology, and course of an illness such as depression tended to be self-fulfilling. Explanatory models created the culturally expected experience of the disease in the mind of the sufferer. Such differences, Kirmayer warned the group, tended to be overlooked when clinicians or researchers employed the symptom checklists relating to the *DSM* diagnosis of depression.

Understanding these differences is critical, however, because culturally distinct symptoms often hold precious clues about the causes of the distress. The American Indian symptom of feeling lonely, for instance, likely reflects a sense of social marginalization. A Korean who feels the epigastric pain of fire illness is expressing distress over an interpersonal conflict or a collective experience of injustice.

The wide variety of symptoms wasn't the only difference. Critically, not everyone in the world agreed that thinking of such experiences as an illness made sense. Kirmayer documented how feelings and symptoms that an American doctor might categorize as depression are often viewed in other cultures as something of a "moral compass," prompting both the individual and the group to search for the source of the social, spiritual, or moral discord. By applying a one-size-fits-all notion of depression around the world, Kirmayer argued, we run the risk of obscuring the social meaning and response the experience might be indicating.

Indeed, around the world, it is the Western conception of depression, in particular the American version of the disease, that is the most culturally distinctive. Kirmayer told the group that Americans are unique both in being willing to openly express distressful emotions and feelings to strangers and in our penchant for viewing psychological suffering as a health care issue. Because people in other cultures find social and moral meaning in such internal distress, they often seek relief exclusively from family members or community elders or local spiritual leaders. The idea of seeking help from a doctor or mental health professional outside one's social circle has traditionally made little sense.

The drug company representatives listened closely to Kirmayer's presentation and thanked him heartily afterward. To this day, he's not entirely sure what they took away from his presentation. In the end Kirmayer's comments could have been taken in two ways. On the one hand, they could be seen as a warning to respect and protect the cultural diversity of human suffering. In this way, he was like a botanist presenting a lecture to a lumber company on the complex ecology of the forest. On the other hand, he might have told the GlaxoSmithKline representatives exactly what they wanted to hear: that cultural conceptions surrounding illnesses such as depression could be influenced and shifted over time. He made that point clearly in the conclusion of the paper he wrote based on his presentation:

> The clinical presentation of depression and anxiety is a function not only of patients' ethnocultural backgrounds, but of the structure of the health care system they find themselves in and the diagnostic categories and concepts they encounter in mass media and in dialogue with family, friends and clinicians.

In the globalizing world, he reported, these conceptions are

> in constant transaction and transformation across boundaries of race, culture, class, and nation. In this context, it is important to recognize that psychiatry itself is part of an international subculture that imposes certain categories on the world that may not fit equally well everywhere and that never completely captures the illness experience and concerns of patients.

In other words, cultural beliefs about depression and the self are malleable and responsive to messages that can be exported from one culture to another. One culture can reshape how a population in another culture categorizes a given set of symptoms, replace their explanatory model, and redraw the line demarcating normal behaviors and internal states from those considered pathological.

Kirmayer's appreciation of the irony of his brief encounter with Glaxo-SmithKline has only grown over the years since he gave that presentation. "People like me got into cultural psychiatry because we were interested in differences between cultures—even treasured those differences in the same way a biologist treasures ecological diversity," Kirmayer told me. "So it's certainly ironic that cultural psychiatrists sometimes end up being handmaidens to these global marketing machines that are intent on manipulating cultural differences … in order to capitalize on those changes."

I asked Kirmayer how clear it was to him that GlaxoSmithKline was interested in changing notions of depression in Japan. "It was very explicit. What I was witnessing was a multinational pharmaceutical corporation working hard to redefine narratives about mental health," he said. "These changes have far-reaching effects, informing the cultural conceptions of personhood and how people conduct their everyday lives. And this is happening on a global scale. These companies are upending long-held cultural beliefs about the meaning of illness and healing."

The consensus paper produced to summarize the Kyoto conference provided both an action plan and a marketing piece for GlaxoSmithKline. In that paper the International Consensus Group on Depression and Anxiety warned that depression was vastly underestimated in Japan but that Western scientific advances would soon be on hand to help. "Clinical evidence supports the use of SSRIs as first-line therapy for depression and anxiety disorders," the paper concludes.

Looking back, Kirmayer can now see how the company used the conference as the beginning of its broader marketing strategy; its representatives identified the cultural challenges and fleshed out the resonant cultural notes the company would attempt to play in the critical coming months and years. Among those themes were that suicide in Japan was an indicator of undertreated depression; that Western

SSRIs represented proven scientific advances in treatment; that primary care physicians should use simple three-minute surveys to help diagnose mental illness; that patients not meeting the criteria for depression should still be considered sick; and that the Japanese should be helped to reconceive social stress related to work and industrialization as signs of depression that should be treated with SSRIs. These confident conclusions would prove the foundation on which GlaxoSmithKline would begin to change the culture of Japan....

The Culture of Sadness

During the early part of the twentieth century the concept of depression [in Japan] remained attached to the diagnosis of severe manic depression imported from ... German neuropsychiatrists. It wasn't until after World War II that depression became a disease category of its own. There was nothing mild about this conception of depression. This so-called endogenous depression was a crippling type of psychosis believed to be caused by a genetic abnormality. Professors of psychiatry at the time often explained endogenous depression using the metaphor of an internal alarm clock. "According to this model, the depressed person is like someone carrying a psychotic time bomb, for whom depression begins when the internal clock goes off and ends after it runs its course," Junko Kitanaka explains. Endogenous depression expressed itself only in individuals with that ticking alarm clock and wasn't connected to external causes.

At the same time Kitanaka shows that another idea was gaining ground in Japan's mental health community. The personality *typus melancholicus* was introduced in the early 1960s by a professor of clinical psychopathology from Heidelberg named Hubert Tellenbach. This idea never caught on in the United States and rather quickly became dated in Germany, but it influenced psychiatric thinking in Japan. As Tellenbach first described it, someone with a melancholic personality possessed a highly developed sense of orderliness as well as "exceptionally high demands regarding one's own achievements." *Typus melancholicus* mirrored a particularly respected personality style in Japan: those who were serious, diligent, and thoughtful and expressed great concern for the welfare of other individuals and the society as a whole. Such people, the theory went, were prone to feeling overwhelming sadness when cultural upheaval disordered their lives and threatened the welfare of others.

Neither endogenous depression nor the melancholic personality type were of great concern to the general public at the time. Because endogenous depression was thought of as a psychotic state, akin to schizophrenia in severity, it carried a severe stigma and was considered rare. As for the melancholic personality type, its association with such prized Japanese traits as orderliness and high achievement meant that having such a sadness-prone personality was something not to be feared but aspired to.

This absence of a category parallel with the modern Western-style depression persisted for many years. When the *DSM-III* was first translated into Japanese in 1982, the diagnosis of depression, with its two-week threshold for low mood, was widely criticized among Japanese psychiatrists as far too expansive and vague to be of any use. Prominent psychiatrists believed, in short, that the description did not amount to a meaningful mental illness.

Indeed, as Kirmayer has pointed out, in the late twentieth century no word in Japanese had the same connotations as the word "depression" in English. Consider the various words and phrases that have often been translated into English as "depression." *Utsubyô* describes a severe, rare, and debilitating condition that usually required inpatient care and thus was not much of a match for the common English word "depression." *Yuutsu,* which describes grief as well as a general gloominess of the body and spirit, was in common use. There was also *ki ga fusagu,* which refers to blockages in vital energy. Similarly, *ki ga meiru* is the leakage or loss of such energy. Although each of these words and phrases had overlaps with the English word "depression," there were also critical differences. The experiences these words describe do not exist only in the thoughts and emotions but encompass full-body sadness. As such, the Japanese person who felt *yuutsu* or *ki ga fusagu* was likely to describe it in terms of bodily sensations, such as having headaches or chest pains or feeling heavy in the head.

Not only did Japanese ideas of sadness include both the body and the mind but, metaphorically at least, they sometimes existed beyond the self. The experience of *yuutsu* in particular contained connotations of the physical world and the weather. A young Japanese researcher named Junko Tanaka–Matsumi, studying at the University of Hawaii in the mid-1970s, conducted a simple word-association test on a group of Japanese college students and compared the results to Caucasian American college students. The American students were asked to respond with three words that they connected with "depression." The Japanese students were asked to do the same with *yuutsu.*

The top ten word associations for the native Japanese were

1. Rain
2. Dark
3. Worries
4. Gray
5. Suicide
6. Solitude
7. Exams
8. Depressing
9. Disease
10. Tiredness

For the Caucasian Americans, the top ten word associations were

1. Sad or sadness
2. Lonely or loneliness
3. Down
4. Unhappy

5. Moody

6. Low

7. Gloom

8. Failure

9. Upset

10. Anxious

Comparing these answers, Tanaka-Matsumi saw a notable difference. In the responses given by the Japanese natives, only a few of the words (such as "worries" and "solitude") were related to internal emotional states. On the other hand, the majority of the word associations supplied by the American students related to internal moods. The Japanese, in short, were looking outward to describe *yuutsu,* and the Americans were looking inward to describe depression. Tanaka-Matsumi believed that these were not simply linguistic differences but cultural "variations in the subjective meanings and *experience* of depression."

The Japanese and Americans weren't just talking about depression and sadness differently, she believed; they were *feeling* these states differently as well. What she saw reflected in the language was a difference between how Japanese and Americans conceived of the nature of the self. The word associations suggested that Americans experience the self as isolated within the individual mind. The Japanese, on the other hand, conceive of a self that is less individuated and more interconnected and dependent on social and environmental contexts. Feelings that Americans associate with depression have, in Japan, been wrapped up in a variety of cultural narratives that altered their meaning and the subjective experience for the individual.

Even as the *DSM* diagnosis of depression became more widely employed around the world during the 1980s, the experience of deep sadness and distress in Japan retained the characteristics of the premodern conception of both *utsushô* and the mid-twentieth-century idealization *typus melancholicus,* the idea that overwhelming sadness was natural, quintessentially Japanese, and, in some ways, an enlightened state.

As Kirmayer has documented, this was a culture that often idealized and prized states of melancholy. Feelings of overwhelming sadness were often venerated in television shows, movies, and popular songs. Kirmayer noted that *yuutsu* and other states of melancholy and sadness have been thought of as *jibyo,* that is, personal hardships that build character. Feelings that we might pathologize as depressive were often thought of in Japan as a source of moral meaning and self-understanding. He and others have connected this reverence to the Buddhist belief that suffering is more enduring and more definitive of the human experience than transient happiness....

Junk Science and First World Medicine

Kalman Applbaum, a professor at the University of Wisconsin in Milwaukee, is an anthropologist, but he doesn't study little-known tribes in far-off lands. His interest is closer at hand: the rituals and practices of international corporations. His specialty, the anthropology of the boardroom, has led to teaching posts both in anthropology departments and at business schools, including Harvard and Kellogg. He is also fluent in Japanese and often consults with companies interested in the Asian markets. When he heard in the late 1990s that major players in the pharmaceutical industry were attempting to introduce SSRIs to Japan, he knew he had the topic for his next set of research papers.

At the beginning of the new millennium, Applbaum went out of his way to visit the headquarters of GlaxoSmithKline, Lilly, and Pfizer, the major international players who were at various stages of trying to get their drugs into Japan. At the time both Pfizer and Lilly were playing catch-up to GlaxoSmithKline, which was just then launching Paxil in the country. Although he had to sign nondisclosure agreements promising that he wouldn't identify the executives by name or company affiliation, Applbaum managed to get remarkable access to the inner workings of these companies. Several of his former MBA students who were then working in these firms helped make key introductions, but in the end these executives proved more than willing to talk. When I asked Applbaum why they were so forthcoming, he told me it was simple: because of his business school credentials and his extensive experience in the Japanese market, they thought he might be able to give them some free advice.

Applbaum discovered that the companies intent on entering the SSRI market in Japan were not battling each other like Coke and Pepsi for market share—or at least not at the beginning. Instead he found wide acknowledgment within the ranks of drug company executives that the best way for companies to create a market was for competing companies to join forces.

A critical player in this joint effort was the trade organization Pharmaceutical Manufacturers of America, or PhRMA, which functions as the national and international lobby and public relations organization for a coalition of major drug companies. In the late 1990s Applbaum found PhRMA working on a number of levels in Japan to influence what they considered to be a backward and bureaucratic drug approval process. As one PhRMA executive based in Chiyoda-Ku, Tokyo, told Applbaum, their job was to create "a market based upon competitive, customer choice and a transparent pricing structure that supports innovation." The lobby wanted drugs such as Paxil to be able to enter new markets based on "global, objective, scientific standards."

The more Applbaum talked to drug company insiders, the more righteous frustration he found. When he visited the offices of a leading SSRI manufacturer in November 2001, he discovered a wellspring of anger directed at what they perceived as Japanese resistance to pharmaceutical progress. These executives criticized scientific standards for clinical testing in Japan as "quite poor" and asserted that there was no "good clinical practice" in the country. Why, they asked Applbaum rhetorically, should their company be forced to retest these drugs in exclusively Japanese populations? The assumption was that the science behind the American human trials was unassailable—certainly better than anything the Japanese would attempt.

No doubt that annoyance at having to retest drugs was so intense because a couple of recent large-scale human trials of SSRIs in Japan had *failed* to show any positive effects. Drugs such as Pfizer's Zoloft, which were widely prescribed in the United States, had at least one large-scale human trial failure in Japan in the 1990s. Instead of considering the meaning of such results, the drug company executives railed at Japanese testing practices, calling them second rate. "There is no sense of urgency about patient need in Japan," one executive complained to Applbaum.

The Mega-Marketing of Depression

Although drug company executives clearly would have preferred to avoid the expensive and time-consuming process of retesting their SSRIs in Japan, they ultimately found a way to put those trials to good use as the first step in their marketing campaign. The drug makers often bought full-page ads in newspapers in the guise of recruiting test subjects. Applbaum believes that this was one of several savvy methods the drug companies employed to sidestep the prohibitions in Japan on marketing prescription drugs directly to the consumer. These advertisements, supposedly designed only to recruit people for the trials, were well worth the cost, as they both featured the brand name of the drug and promoted the idea of depression as a common ailment. One company scored even more public attention when it recruited a well-known actress to take part in the trials.

But getting the drug approved for market was only the first step. Talking with these executives, it became clear to Applbaum that they were intent on implementing a complex and multifaceted plan to, as he put it, "alter the total environment in which these drugs are or may be used." Applbaum took to calling this a "mega-marketing" campaign—an effort to shape the very consciousness of the Japanese consumer.

The major problem GlaxoSmithKline faced was that Japanese psychiatrists and mental health professionals still translated the diagnosis of "depression" as *utsubyô,* and in the mind of many Japanese that word retained its association with an incurable and inborn depression of psychotic proportions. In hopes of softening the connotations of the word, the marketers hit upon a metaphor that proved remarkably effective. Depression, they repeated in advertising and promotional material, was *kokoro no kaze,* like "a cold of the soul." It is not clear who first came up with the phrase. It is possible that it originated from Kenichiro Takiguchi's prime-time special on depression. In that show, it was said that Americans took antidepressants the way other cultures took cold medicine.

Whatever its origin, the line *kokoro no kaze* appealed to the drug marketers, as it effectively shouldered three messages at the same time. First, it implied that *utsubyô* was not the severe condition it was once thought to be and therefore should carry no social stigma. Who would think less of someone for having a cold? Second, it suggested that the choice of taking a medication for depression should be as simple and worry-free as buying a cough syrup or an antihistamine. Third, the phrase communicated that, like common colds, depression was ubiquitous. Everyone, after all, from time to time suffers from a cold.

Although advertising couldn't mention particular drugs, companies could run spots in the guise of public service announcements encouraging people to seek professional help for depression. In these ads SSRI makers attempted to distance depression further from the endogenous depression as it was understood by Japanese psychiatrists for most of the century. One GlaxoSmithKline television advertisement showed an attractive young woman standing in a green field, asking, "How long has it been? How long has it been since you began to worry that it might be depression?" The scene then shows a woman on an escalator and then a middle-aged office worker staring out a bus window. The voiceover then recommends that if you've been feeling down for a month, "do not endure it. Go see a doctor."

The subtext of the ad is clear.... It presents depression as "intentionally ambiguous and ill-defined, applicable to the widest possible population and to the widest possible range of discomforts.... The only feature that distinguishes depression as a 'disease' from an ordinary depressed mood seems to be the length of time (one month) that the person has experienced these 'symptoms.'"

Depression was so broadly defined by the marketers that it clearly encompassed classic emotions and behaviors formerly attributed to the melancholic personality type. The label of depression then took on some laudable characteristics, such as being highly sensitive to the welfare of others and to discord within the family or group. Being depressed in this way became a testament to one's deeply empathic nature.

To get these messages out to the Japanese public, the SSRI makers employed a variety of techniques and avenues. Company marketers quickly reproduced and widely disseminated articles in newspapers and magazines mentioning the rise of depression, particularly if those pieces touted the benefits of SSRIs. The companies also sponsored the translation of several best-selling books first published in the United States on depression and the use of antidepressants.

Given all the ways that GlaxoSmithKline and the other SSRI makers managed to make the average Japanese aware of their drugs, the official ban on direct-to-consumer marketing became almost meaningless. If there was any doubt about this, one only had to look at how these companies used the Internet. "The best way to reach patients today is not via advertising but the Web," one Tokyo-based marketing manager told Applbaum. "The Web basically circumvents [direct-to-consumer advertising] rules, so there is no need to be concerned over these. People go to the company website and take a quiz to see whether they might have depression. If yes, then they go to the doctor and ask for medication."

The mega-marketing campaign often came in disguised forms, such as patient advocacy groups that were actually created by the drug companies themselves. The website utu-net.com, which appeared to be a coalition of depressed patients and their advocates, was funded by GlaxoSmithKline, although visitors to the site would have had no clue of the connection. What they would have found was a series of articles on depression driving home the key points of the campaign, including the idea that it was a common illness and that antidepressants bring the brain's natural chemistry back into balance.

The public interest in the new diagnosis brought a remarkable amount of media attention. Often in back-to-back months, the major magazines *Toyo Keizai* and *DaCapo* ran pieces on depression and the new drugs. In 2002 a leading Japanese business magazine ran a twenty-six-page cover story encouraging businesspeople to seek professional help for depression. The article rather perfectly mirrored the key points of the SSRI makers' mega-marketing campaign and in many ways reflected the early conceptions of neurasthenia a century before. The article suggested that it was the more talented and hard-charging workers who were the most susceptible to depression. Estimates of how many Japanese secretly suffered from depression, which ranged from 3 to 17 percent of the population, seemed to increase every month.

The distress caused by the long-ailing economy also proved to be a useful selling point. GlaxoSmithKline promoted the idea that there was an enormous economic cost for untreated depression, which could be counted in lost man-hours and decreased productivity. In this way, the lure of the drug, especially to the younger generation, was tied to ideas about competition in the global marketplace. One Japanese psychiatrist was quoted in a local newspaper describing SSRIs as "drugs that can transform minus thinking into plus thinking" and that "can help a person live tough," like financially successful Americans.

The SSRI makers made much of one public relations windfall in particular. It was rumored for years (and finally confirmed by the Imperial Household Agency) that Crown Princess Masako suffered from depression. Soon it was revealed that she was taking antidepressants as part of her treatment. This was a huge boost for the profile of depression and SSRIs in the country. Princess Masako's personal psychiatrist was none other than Yutaka Ono, one of the field's leaders that GlaxoSmithKline had feted at the Kyoto conference in 2001.

As a marketing line, there was one problem with the phrase *kokoro no kaze:* the metaphor lacked a sense of urgency about the condition. After all, one rarely rushes to the doctor with a cold. Worse yet, medicating a cold was always optional, as the illness goes away rather quickly on its own.

To counter this aspect of the metaphor, the drug companies leveraged the population's growing concern over the high suicide rates. The medical anthropologist Emiko Namihira reported that SSRI makers were funding studies to prove the link between depression and suicide. Those studies that showed a connection were reprinted in pamphlet form and reported to national media outlets as breaking news. Studies that failed to show a connection could simply be ignored. The founder of the Mood Disorders Association of Japan claimed in the *Japan Times* that "90 percent of those who commit suicide are considered to suffer from one kind of mental illness or another, and 70 percent of suicides are attributable to depression." Without medical attention, the message went, this "cold of the soul" could kill you.

When taken together, the messages advanced by GlaxoSmithKline during their rollout of Paxil don't always make sense. Previous notions of endogenous depression were employed only sparingly in order to evoke the seriousness of the disorder. On the other hand, they were happy to associate this new conception of depression with the Japanese veneration of the melancholic personality, even though that didn't particularly jibe with the parallel message that this was an illness caused by an imbalance of serotonin. Neither did the message that overwork could spark depression mesh with the idea that individuals should counter such social distress by taking a medication that changed their brain chemistry. If it was unrealistic social demands that were the cause of distress in the population, why should the individual be taking the pills? In the end, however, the coherence of these various messages took second place to their effectiveness.

Speeding the Evolution

After the Kobe earthquake in Japan there was growing consensus in the country that the West, and the United States in particular, had a deeper scientific understanding of pathological emotional states such as PTSD and depression. Responding to this insecurity, the advertisements, websites, waiting room brochures, and other materials produced by the drug companies played up the idea that SSRIs represented the cutting edge of medical science. These drugs, which were said to rebalance the natural chemicals in the brain, would bring Japan up to date.

GlaxoSmithKline worked very hard to win over the most prominent medical researchers and psychiatrists in the country and keep them on message. Their inclusion at lavish conferences such as the one Kirmayer attended was just a taste of the incentives offered. Drug companies offered grants to sponsor research on their drugs; those researchers who produced results favorable to the drugs found themselves with new offers of research funding. Research that showed the drug in question to be both safe and effective was trumpeted by the company and the researchers often paid as consultants. In addition, researchers were given honoraria for speaking about their findings at drug company-sponsored professional conferences. Influence over the prominent scientists and researchers in Japan was so pervasive that Applbaum concluded that these scientists and doctors had been basically "commandeered into a kind of market research by pharmaceutical companies. The research simultaneously serves as publicity for the essentially predetermined consumer need."

It is important to note that the drug company executives whom Applbaum interviewed didn't present themselves as people driven only by profits. Rather these men and women saw themselves as acting with the best of intentions, motivated by the belief that their drugs represented the proud march of scientific progress across the world. They styled themselves as people fighting depression, anxiety, and social phobia—diseases that remained cruelly untreated in Japan and elsewhere. Applbaum could see that this mixture of moral certainty and the lure of billions of dollars in potential profits was a potent force.

"These executives seemed to believe that they are straightforwardly trying to heal the world," said Applbaum. When he was meeting them in 2000 and 2001 he had no reason to doubt these self-assessments. "They seemed to believe their products were effective and they were baffled that anyone should question their value. The pharmaceutical industry, more than other industries, can link its marketing activities to ethical objectives. The result is a marriage of the profit-seeking scheme in which disease is regarded as 'an opportunity' to the ethical view that mankind's health hangs in the balance. This helps even the most aggressive marketers trust that they are performing a public service."

Bolstering their certainty was their faith in the science behind these drugs. The fact that these SSRIs had proven clinically effective made it morally imperative that they be introduced into other cultures. The drug companies were replacing what one executive referred to as "junk science" in Japan with "first world medicine."

During his talks with the executives, consultants, and marketers for the drug companies, Applbaum heard a repeated theme. These men and women kept talking about different cultures as if they were at different stages of a predetermined evolution. The American market, with its the brand recognition, high rates of prescriptions (by specialists and nonspecialists alike), and free market pricing, was seen as the most modern and advanced of markets. Japan was fifteen years behind the United States, executives would say. Or China was five years behind Japan. The lucrative U.S. market, Applbaum could see, was the standard against which all others were measured. We were the most "evolved" culture and, as one executive said to Applbaum, their job was to "speed the evolution along," that is, to move other countries along the path to be like us.

This talk of evolutionary process wasn't idle chatter, for it was often the same executives and marketing specialists who went from country to country waiting for the right moment to make their push. "Pharmaceutical manufacturers … circulate internal instructional materials regarding experiences with the same product in what they consider similar markets," Applbaum said. "Managers fly about the world to training conferences where such archetypes are hardened. And old advertisements and communications strategies from the earlier stage of more 'advanced' markets are imported." With each new implementation of the mega-marketing campaign, these drug companies learned new maneuvers and strategies. They got better at helping along the evolution.

The reasons these executives were so open about this endeavor goes back to their shared belief that the evolution in question was toward higher quality science. Westerners may have lost their sense of moral authority in many areas of human endeavor, but we can still get our blood up defending our science. We lead the world in scientific discovery and medical breakthroughs, so why shouldn't the citizens of Japan and other countries around the world have access to the newest brand-name antidepressants? These molecules were created using the latest advances in science and technology. They had been reviewed by the leading researchers at the world's most famous universities and found effective in studies published in the most prestigious scientific journals. The latest antidepressants, in this moral logic, were akin to antiretrovirals, polio vaccine, and penicillin. Everyone in the world deserved access to the fruits of our scientific discoveries as a human right.

It is not an argument without merit, but it depends rather critically on the accuracy and validity of the science behind the medical advance being touted. If the science is overblown, skewed, or downright wrong, then the moral certainty that fuels the charge into other cultures becomes suspect....

Under even the mildest scrutiny, the confident marketing messages proclaiming the scientific validity of SSRIs begin to break down. Take for instance the idea, often repeated in the ads and promotional material surrounding the launch of SSRIs in Japan, that a depletion of serotonin is the root cause of depression and that SSRIs reestablish the "balance" of the "natural" chemicals in the brain. Pharmaceutical companies have been repeating this idea ever since SSRIs came on the market twenty years ago. On their website the makers of the SSRI Lexapro are still telling the story: "The naturally occurring chemical serotonin is sent from one nerve cell to the next.... In people with depression and anxiety, there is an imbalance of serotonin—too much serotonin is reabsorbed by the first nerve cell, so the next cell does not have enough; as in a conversation, one person might do all the talking and the other person does not get to comment, leading to a communication imbalance."

Here's how GlaxoSmithKline describes the same idea on its website advertising Paxil CR: "Normally, a chemical neurotransmitter in your brain, called serotonin, helps send messages from one brain cell to another. This is how the cells in your brain communicate. Serotonin works to keep the messages moving smoothly. However, if serotonin levels become unbalanced, communication may become disrupted and lead to depression.... Paxil CR helps maintain a balance of serotonin levels."

As often repeated as this story is, it turns out that there is currently no scientific consensus that depression is linked to serotonin deficiency or that SSRIs restore the brain's normal "balance" of this neurotransmitter. The idea that depression is due to deficits of serotonin was first proposed by George Ashcroft in the 1950s, when he thought he detected low levels in the brains of suicide victims and in the spinal fluid of depressed patients. Later studies, however, performed with more sensitive equipment and measures, showed no lower levels of serotonin in these populations. By 1970 Ashcroft had publicly given up on the serotonin-depression connections. To date, no lower levels of serotonin or "imbalance" of the neurotransmitter have been demonstrated in depressed patients. The American Psychiatric Press *Textbook of Clinical Psychiatry* states simply, "Additional experience has not confirmed the monoamine [of which serotonin is a subgroup] depletion hypothesis."

SSRIs don't bring a patient's brain chemistry back into balance, but rather broadly alter brain chemistry. Although that change may sometimes help a depressed patient, the idea that SSRIs restore a natural balance of serotonin is a theory without evidence. Put another way, this idea is more of a culturally shared story than a scientific fact....

SOURCES

The scholars at McGill University are overrepresented in this book because that university is a hotbed for the study of cross-cultural psychiatry. That fact, I believe, has much to do with Laurence Kirmayer, whose work and leadership in the field informs not just this chapter but this entire book. Junko Kitanaka, Kirmayer's former graduate student, was as generous as her mentor with her time and guidance. The history of the evolution of Japanese understanding of depression relies critically on her dissertation—in particular, the recounting of the suicide of Oshima Ichiro and the public attention surrounding suicide from overwork. Her book on the history of depression in Japan will be out within a year or two, and I will be first in line at the bookstore to snap it up. David Healy was an inspiration both for his research on the science behind SSRIs and for his dogged courage.

Other resources include the following:

Angell, M. (2009, January 15). Drug Companies and Doctors: A Story of Corruption. *New York Review of Books.*

Applbaum, K. (2004a). *The Marketing Era: From Professional Practice to Global Provisioning.* Routledge.

———. (2004b). How to Organize a Psychiatric Congress. *Anthropological Quarterly,* 77(2), 303–310.

———. (2006). Pharmaceutical Marketing and the Invention of the Medical Consumer. *PLoS Medicine,* 3(4), 445.

Berger, D., & Fukunishi, I. (1996). Psychiatric Drug Development in Japan. *Science,* 273(5273), 318.

Healy, D. (2004a). *Let Them Eat Prozac: The Unhealthy Relationship between the Pharmaceutical Industry and Depression.* New York University Press.

Horwitz, A. V., & Wakefield, J. C. (2007). *The Loss of Sadness: How Psychiatry Transformed Normal Sorrow into Depressive Disorder.* Oxford University Press.

Kirmayer, L. J. (1989). Cultural Variations in the Response to Psychiatric Disorders and Emotional Distress. *Social Science & Medicine,* 29(3), 327.

———. (2002). Psychopharmacology in a Globalizing World: The Use of Antidepressants in Japan. *Transcultural Psychiatry,* 39(3), 295.

Kitanaka, J. (2006). Society in Distress: The Psychiatric Production of Depression in Contemporary Japan. PhD dissertation, Department of Anthropology, McGill University.

Kleinman, A. (2004). Culture and Depression. *New England Journal of Medicine,* 351, 951–953.

Landers, P. (2002, October 9). Drug Companies Push Japan to Change View of Depression. *Wall Street Journal.*

Petryna, A., Lakoff, A., & Kleinman, A. (2006). *Global Pharmaceuticals: Ethics, Markets, Practices.* Duke University Press.

Schulz, K. (2004, August 22). Did Antidepressants Depress Japan? *New York Times Magazine.*

Tajima, O., et al. (2001). Mental Health Care in Japan: Recognition and Treatment of Depression and Anxiety Disorders. *Journal of Clinical Psychiatry,* Suppl., 62(13), 39–46.

Tanaka-Matsumi, J., & Marsella, A. J. (1976). Cross-Cultural Variations in the Phenomenological Experience of Depression: I. *Word Association Studies. Journal of Cross-Cultural Psychology,* 7(4), 379.

Whittington, C. J., Kendall, T., Fonagy, P., Cottrell, D., Cotgrove, A., & Boddington, E. (2004). Selective Serotonin Reuptake Inhibitors in Childhood Depression: Systematic Review of Published versus Unpublished Data. *Lancet*, 363(9418), 1341–1345.

QUESTIONS FOR MAKING CONNECTIONS
WITHIN THE READING

1. Is depression real or not? Does Watters seem to believe that the condition is imaginary? How can depression have biological roots and yet be experienced in different ways? Does Watters seem to accept the view that the West's understanding of depression is true, whereas the explanations other cultures offer are arbitrary and unscientific? Do the pharmaceutical companies feel that they possess the best understanding of depression? How do the modern Japanese regard Western psychology?

2. What can we learn from Watters's story about the relationship between academic researchers like Laurence Kirmayer and the pharmaceutical industry? Does Watters suggest that drug manufacturers are deceptive? Do they lie to Kirmayer, or is the connection between them more complex than that? Have they lied to the Japanese, or are the drug manufacturers convinced that they are truly doing good? Does Watters's narrative indicate that academic research has been compromised by commercial interests? Does he seem to think that there needs to be a stricter separation between research and commercial interests? Is such a separation possible when commercial applications drive much of academic science?

3. Based on your reading of Watters—and working without a dictionary—try to develop an accurate definition of the term *marketing*. Does marketing simply make available needed information about products that people want? Or does marketing play an active role in creating needs and shaping the way people experience the world? How does marketing differ from other forms of communication? How might we define the relationship between marketers and consumers? Which forms of marketing would qualify as ethical? Which forms would qualify as unethical? Is the marketing of antidepressants in Japan ethical or not?

QUESTIONS FOR WRITING

1. One implication of Watters's argument is that what we call *reality*, even at the level of personal experience, is shaped by culture as well as biology. But Watters never pauses, in the course of his account, to systematically explain how these three are interrelated. Write an essay in which you draw from Watters's narrative to explain the relationship between biology, culture, and experience. When the pharmaceutical companies transform the cultural attitudes of modern Japanese people, will the actual experience of the people change? If our experience is indeed always shaped by culture, do we need to

be more careful about who controls it? If others can control our experience, what steps might we take to be fully in charge of our own lives?

2. The campaign to change how the Japanese think about what we call depression might be seen as an example of *cultural imperialism*—the conquest of one culture by another. Does Watters's narrative support that view? If the intention of the dominant culture is to do good instead of harm, does that behavior still qualify as *imperialism*? If we are hesitant to impose the values of one culture on another society, are we required to accept all beliefs without question? Is it possible that many Japanese people benefited from the new medicines? Is it possible for any culture to remain separate from others?

QUESTIONS FOR MAKING CONNECTIONS
BETWEEN READINGS

1. Watters describes the mega-marketing of anti-depressants in Japan as a process of changing the experience and definition of mental illness. In the words of Kalman Applbaum, pharmaceutical companies planned to "alter the total environment in which these drugs are or may be used," in what Watters describes as "an effort to shape the very consciousness of the Japanese consumer." Michael Moss, in "The Extraordinary Science of Junk Food," describes the marketing of junk food in the United States as a process of changing the experience and definition of hunger in "a conscious effort [...] to get people hooked on foods that are convenient and inexpensive." In what ways is the relationship between the people of Japan and Western pharmaceutical companies the same as or different from the relationship of the US population to the food industry? Under what conditions is it permissible to attempt to alter a culture? Does either author suggest ways we might inoculate ourselves against marketing forces?

2. The mega-marketing campaign described by Watters pales in comparison to the power of social media as described by Franklin Foer in "Mark Zuckerberg's War on Free Will." Is the marketing power of the technology described by Foer simply a matter of scale or does it represent something fundamentally different in the relationship between companies and consumers? Foer says that "[w]hile it creates the impression that it offers choice, Facebook paternalistically nudges users in the direction it deems best for them." Does marketing necessarily involve paternalism? Is it possible to have marketing between equals? How do algorithms differ, if they do, from the market research, testing and advertising campaigns of GlaxoSmithKline?

Author and Title Index